Computer Confluence
IT Edition

Exploring Tomorrow's Technology

Fifth Edition

Computer Confluence
IT Edition

Exploring Tomorrow's Technology

George Beekman
Oregon State University

Eugene J. Rathswohl
University of San Diego

Prentice Hall
Upper Saddle River, New Jersey 07458

Acquistions Editor: Melissa Whitaker-Oliver
VP/Publisher: Natalie Anderson
Senior Development Editor: Lena Buonanno
Assistant Editor: Melissa Edwards
Media Project Manager: Cathleen Profitko
Senior Marketing Manager: Sharon Turkovich
Marketing Assistant: Scott Patterson
Associate Director, Manufacturing: Vincent Scelta
Production Manager: Gail Steier de Acevedo
Project Manager: Lynne Breitfeller
Manufacturing Buyer: Lynne Breitfeller
Full-Service Composition: Pre-Press Company
Design Manager: Pat Smythe
Interior and Cover Design: Jill Little
Printer: Von Hoffman Press

Photo, screen capture, and text credits appear on pages 545–548.

Library of Congress Cataloging-in-Publication Data

Computer confluence
    p. cm.
  ISBN 0-13-066185-6 (alk. paper)
    1. Computer science. 2. Information technology.

QA76 .C5628 2002
004—dc21

2002021431

Pearson Education Limited (UK)
Pearson Education Australia Pty Ltd
Prentice Hall Canada Ltd
Pearson Educación de Mexico, S.A. de C.V.
Pearson Education Japan KK
Pearson Education China Ltd
Pearson Education Asia Pte Ltd

10 9 8 7 6 5 4 3 2 1
ISBN 0-13-066185-6

To

Rosie Beekman (1924-2002)

my first—and most important—teacher.

—G.E.B.

To

Polly

—E.J.R

Brief Contents

Contents

Chapter 4   Software Basics: The Ghost in the Machine   100

PART 2   Using Computers
Essential Applications   129

Chapter 5   Revolution in Writing: From Word Processing to Paperless Publishing   130

Chapter 8   Database Applications and Implications 210

PART 3   Exploring with Computers
Networks and Gateways   241

Chapter 9   Networking and Telecommunication 242

Chapter 10 Inside the Internet and the Web 264

Chapter 11 From Internet to Information Infrastructure 288

Chapter 12   Computer Security and Risks   308

PART 4   Managing Computers
Information Systems at Work   338

Chapter 13   Systems and Organizations in the Information Age   339

Chapter 14   Information Technology in Management   366

Chapter 15   Electronic Commerce and E-Business   404

Chapter 16   Systems Design and Development 426

PART 5   Living with Computers
Information Age Implications   469

Chapter 17   Computers at Work, School, and Home   470

Chapter 18   Inventing the Future   490

About this Book

> **Confluence**
> 1: a **coming or flowing together**, meeting, or gathering
>   at one point (a happy confluence of weather and scenery);
> 2a: the flowing together of **two or more streams**;
>   b: the **place of meeting** of two streams;
>   c: the **combined stream** formed by conjunction
>
> —*Merriam Webster's Collegiate Dictionary, Electronic Edition*

When powerful forces come together, change is inevitable. As we enter the 21st century, we're standing at the confluence of three powerful technological forces: computers, telecommunications, and electronic entertainment. The computer's digital technology is showing up in everything from telephones to televisions, and the lines that separate these machines are eroding. This digital convergence is rapidly—and radically—altering the world's economic landscape. Start-up companies and industries are emerging to ride the waves of change. Some thrive; others dive into oblivion. Meanwhile, older organizations reorganize, regroup, and redefine themselves to keep from being washed away.

Smaller computers, faster processors, smarter software, larger networks, new communication media—in the world of information technology, it seems like change is the only constant. In less than a human lifetime, this technological cascade has transformed virtually every facet of our society—and the transformation is just beginning. As old technologies merge and new information technologies emerge, far-fetched predictions routinely come true. This headlong rush into the high-tech future poses a challenge for all of us: How can we extract the knowledge we need from the deluge of information? What must we understand about information technology to successfully navigate the waters of change that carry us into the future? *Computer Confluence: Exploring Tomorrow's Technology* is designed to aid travelers on their journey into that future.

What Is Computer Confluence?

Computer Confluence presents computers and information technology on three levels:

▶ Explanations: *Computer Confluence* clearly explains what a computer is and what it can (and can't) do; it clearly explains the basics of information technology, from multimedia PCs to the Internet and beyond.
▶ Applications: *Computer Confluence* illustrates how computers and networks are used as practical tools by individuals and organizations to solve a wide variety of problems.
▶ Implications: *Computer Confluence* puts computers in a human context, illustrating how information technology affects our lives, our world, and our future.

The book consists of 19 chapters, numbered 0 through 18 in the grand tradition of computer science. Chapter 0, *ReadMe*, new to this edition, provides an introduction for students who have little or no experience with PCs and the Internet. The chapter also includes an orientation to the *Computer Confluence* book, CD-ROM, and Web site.

The remaining chapters are organized into five broad sections:

1. Approaching Computers: Hardware and Software Fundamentals
2. Using Computers: Essential Applications
3. Exploring with Computers: Networks and Gateways
4. Managing Computers: Information Systems at Work
5. Living with Computers: Information Age Implications

Throughout the five parts, the book's focus flows from the concrete to the controversial and from the present to the future. Individual chapters have a similarly expanding focus. After a brief introduction, each chapter flows from basic concepts toward abstract, future-oriented questions and ideas.

About the Authors

George Beekman is a Senior Instructor in the Department of Computer Science at Oregon State University. An innovative computer literacy course he created more than a decade ago served as the inspiration for *Computer Confluence*. He has since designed several classes in interactive multimedia and the social and ethical issues surrounding information technology. He coordinates multimedia components of OSU's New Media program, which focuses on the digital convergence of multimedia, telemedia, and print media.

He has taught workshops in computer literacy and multimedia for students, educators, and economically disadvantaged families from the Atlantic to Alaska. He has written more than 20 books on computers, information technology, and multimedia, as well as more than 100 articles and reviews for *Macworld* and other popular publications. In his spare time he runs with his dog in the woods and plays music with his band, Oyaya.

Eugene Rathswohl is Professor of Information Management in the School of Business Administration at the University of San Diego. He teaches a variety of information technology courses including Information Systems, Management Information Systems, and Website Design. He has developed many teaching innovations for his IT courses, especially community service-learning to emphasize the ethical use of information technologies. His research interests include the international issues of information systems and the human factors aspects of information technology, particularly how people search the Internet for information and how to design effective Web sites. Over the years he has consulted with several organizations and has published widely, including several computer applications textbooks. He enjoys international travel, studying French and German, and backpacking in the Sierra Nevada.

About this Edition

The pace of change threatens to make even the most successful introductory computer classes irrelevant. *Computer Confluence, IT Edition*, helps students and instructors deal with rapid changes by emphasizing big ideas, broad trends, and the human aspects of technology—critical concepts that tend to

> Even if you're on the right track, **you'll get run over** if you just sit on it.
> —Pat Koppman

remain constant even while hardware and software change. Every edition of *Computer Confluence* is rewritten to reflect changes in the technological landscape. This edition places new emphasis on the latest Web technologies, electronic commerce and e-business, multimedia trends, and emerging software platforms such as Windows XP, Linux, and Mac OS-X, and Palm OS. Here's a list of highlights new to this edition:

Chapter 0, "ReadMe," is brand new. It addresses the most commonly reported problem of introductory computer concepts classes—the diverse backgrounds of students in those classes. Many instructors report that the majority of their new students have some PC and Internet experience. These students don't need to be told about keyboarding, using a CD-ROM, or navigating a Web site. But if these topics aren't covered, the inexperienced students are at a distinct disadvantage. The ReadMe Chapter is designed for those beginners, so they can fill in the gaps in their knowledge before launching into the rest of the book, the CD-ROM, and the Web site. The chapter also includes an orientation to all three components of *Computer Confluence* that includes time-saving tips for everyone.

Chapter 1, "Computer Currents: From Calculation to Connection," has been streamlined and updated; some of the most basic material has been moved to Chapter 0.

Chapter 2, "Hardware Basics: Inside the Box," and Chapter 3, "Hardware Basics: Peripherals," have been updated with coverage of state-of-the-market hardware. There's a more practical emphasis on equipment that students will encounter in their day-to-day computing experience. An expanded section on disk technology helps students make sense of the ever-growing list of storage options, from rewritable CDs to DVD-R. This edition also includes updated coverage of USB and FireWire (IEEE 1394), modern I/O standards that are taking center stage in new machines. Chapter 3 now includes Computer Consumer Concepts, a Rules of Thumb box that illuminates the concepts *behind* PC buyer's guides.

Chapter 4, "Software Basics: The Ghost in the Machine," has been updated and streamlined. User's View boxes covering Windows XP and Mac OS X are now in Chapter 0. Chapter 4 includes examples and explanations of Linux, UNIX, and other operating systems to provide a broader perspective for students familiar with PCs. The chapter includes an updated Rules of Thumb box, Green Computing, containing tips for minimizing our technological impact on the environment.

Chapter 5, "Revolution in Writing: from Word Processing to Paperless Publishing," reflects its new title with expanded coverage of publishing for the Web, electronic books, and speech input for word processors. The basic word processing material has been condensed.

Chapter 7, "Graphics, Hypermedia, and Multimedia," includes new desktop video material, with coverage of nonlinear video editing and desktop DVD authoring. The image editing User's View box has been completely reworked using the latest version of Photoshop. The material on multimedia Web publishing has been updated and expanded.

Chapter 9, "Networking and Telecommunication," has been reorganized and updated to reflect changes in this dynamic industry. A new section on wireless communication introduces several important wireless technologies.

Chapter 10, "Inside the Internet and the Web," and Chapter 11, "From Internet to Information Infrastructure," replace the previous edition's Chapter 11. The new Chapter 10 includes clear explanations of basic Internet technology, including protocols, addresses, and connections. There's expanded coverage of DSL, cable modems, and wireless Internet connections. There's also more on dynamic Web tools, multimedia Web technology, and database-driven Web sites. The chapter includes a new Rules of Thumb box, Weaving Winning Web Sites. Chapter 11 opens with a new profile of Web visionary Tim Berners-Lee. The chapter focuses on the ways people put the Internet to work, including expanded coverage of search engines, portals, email, newsgroups, teleconferencing, peer-to-peer computing, grid computing, and electronic commerce.

Chapter 12, "Computer Security and Risks," has been updated with the latest data on computer crime and security. The chapter now includes discussions of *fair use*, the potential for abuse of intellectual property laws, and several controversial cases involving the Digital Millennium Copyright Act. There's more of an ethical emphasis in the expanded and updated section called "Security, Privacy, Freedom, and Ethics: The Delicate Balance."

Chapter 13, "Systems and Organizations in the Information Age," has been reorganized slightly to improve readability. For example, the section "Social Responsibility in the Information Age" discusses ethical issues directly related to transaction-oriented information systems. The chapter-ending real-world cases have been updated.

Chapter 14, "Information Technology in Management," includes new examples illustrating how managers in organizations use information technology, such as decision support systems and expert systems, to communicate and make decisions effectively. Several new examples show how organizations use technology strategically in the global marketplace. Two new chapter-ending cases have been added that illustrate the use of wireless technology and corporate intranets.

Chapter 15, "Electronic Commerce and E-Business," has been reorganized slightly to differentiate more clearly between e-commerce models, such as business-to-business, business-to-employee, business-to-consumer, and consumer-to-consumer. Two new chapter-ending cases illustrate the competitive use of e-commerce and how extranets are used to support business alliances. Additional text and examples emphasizing e-business ethics have been added.

Chapter 16, "Systems Design and Development," includes a new Rules of Thumb box, Avoiding Information Technology Project Failures. Two new chapter-ending cases illustrate the systems development process.

Chapter 17, "Computers at Work, School, and Home" include several more current examples.

Chapter 18, "Inventing the Future," is downsized and updated. Since the short-term future of technology is explored throughout the book, this chapter looks further down the road, with discussions of optical computing, sensory computing, ubiquitous computing, microtechnology, nanotechnology, biotechnology, and artificial life. As in previous editions, the chapter ends by giving this futuristic technology a human context; the final pages raise difficult questions and pose ethical challenges for all of us.

Crosscurrents articles that close each chapter are, with a few exceptions, new to this edition. They include some of the best short essays on our relationship to technology that have been published in the past year. Topics include the role of information technology in terrorism, the erosion of personal privacy, the abuse of intellectual property laws, software reliability, machine intelligence, pros and cons of websites, and our future as borgs.

The CD-ROM has been updated with new multimedia material and interactive explorations.

The Web site (**www.prenhall.com/beekman**) is continually updated to reflect changes in the Web and the subject matter. New to this edition is Prentice Hall Web support material, including a syllabus manager, student chat rooms, and self-assessment quizzes.

For the Student

If you're like most students, you aren't taking this course to read about computers—you want to use them. That's sensible. You can't really understand computers without some hands-on experience, and you'll be able to apply your computer skills to a wide variety of future projects. But it's a mistake to think that you're computer savvy just because you can use a PC to write term papers and surf the Internet. It's important to understand how people and organizations use and abuse computer technology, because that technology has a powerful and growing impact on your personal life and career. (If you can't imagine how your life would be different without computers, read the vignette called "Living without Computers" in Chapter 1.) Even if you have lots of computer experience, future trends are almost certain to make much of that experience obsolete—probably sooner than you think. In the next few years, computers are likely to take on entirely new forms and roles because of breakthroughs in artificial intelligence, voice recognition, virtual reality, interactive multimedia, networking, and cross-breeding with telephone and home entertainment technologies. If your knowledge of computers stops with a handful of PC and Internet applications, you may be standing still while the world changes around you.

When you're cascading through white water, you need to be able to use a paddle, but it's also important to know how to read a map, a compass, and the river. *Computer Confluence, IT Edition* is designed to serve as a map, compass, and book of river lore to help you ride the information currents into the future.

Computer Confluence will help you understand the important trends that will change the way you work with computers and the way computers work for you. This book discusses the promise and the problems of computer technology without overwhelming you with technobabble.

Computer Confluence is intentionally nontechnical and down to earth. Occasional ministories bring concepts and speculations to life. Illustrations and photos make abstract concepts concrete. Quotes add thought-provoking and humorous seasoning.

Whether you're a hard-core hacker or a confirmed computerphobe, there's something for you in *Computer Confluence*. Dive in and enjoy!

George Beekman
Eugene Rathswohl

For the Instructor

Instructor Resources

Instructor's Resource CD-ROM

The **Instructor's Resource CD-ROM** that is available with *Computer Confluence* contains:

▶ Instructor's Manual in Word and PDF.
▶ Solutions to all questions and exercises from the book and web site
▶ PowerPoint lectures with PresMan software
▶ A Windows-based test manager and the associated test bank in Word format with over 1500 new questions

Tools for Online Learning

www.prenhall.com/beekman

This text is accompanied by a companion Web site at **www.prenhall.com/beekman**. This site brings you and your students a richer, more interactive Web experience. Features of this site include the ability for you to customize your homepage with real-time news headlines, current events, exercises, an interactive study guide, and downloadable supplements.

ONLINE Courseware for Blackboard, WebCT and Course Compass
Now you have the freedom to personalize your own online course materials!

Prentice Hall provides the content and support you need to create and manage your own online course in WebCT, Blackboard, or Prentice Hall's own Course Compass. Content includes lecture material, interactive exercises, e-commerce case videos, additional testing questions and projects.

CourseCompass www.coursecompass.com

CourseCompass is a dynamic, interactive online course-management tool powered exclusively for Pearson Education by Blackboard. This exciting product allows you to teach market-leading Pearson Education content in an easy-to-use, customizable format.

BlackBoard www.prenhall.com/blackboard

Prentice Hall's abundant online content, combined with Blackboard's popular tools and interface, result in robust Web-based courses that are easy to implement, manage, and use—taking your courses to new heights in student interaction and learning.

WebCT www.prenhall.com/webct

Course-management tools within WebCT include page tracking, progress tracking, class and student management, gradebook, communication, calendar, reporting tools, and more. GOLD LEVEL CUSTOMER SUPPORT, available exclusively to adopters of Prentice Hall courses, is provided free-of-charge upon adoption and provides you with priority assistance, training discounts, and dedicated technical support.

Train & Assess IT: www.prenhall.com/phit

Prentice Hall offers Performance Based Training and Assessment in one product, Train&Assess IT. The Training component offers computer-based training that a student can use to preview, learn, and review Microsoft Office applications and computer literacy skills. Web- or CD-ROM delivered, the training component offers interactive, multimedia, computer-based training to augment classroom learning. Built-in prescriptive testing suggests a study path based not only on student test results but also on the specific textbook chosen for the course.

The assessment component offers computer-based testing that shares the same user interface and is used to evaluate a student's knowledge about specific topics in Word, Excel, Access, PowerPoint, Windows, Outlook, and the Internet. It does this in a task-oriented environment to demonstrate proficiency as well as comprehension of the topics by the students.

EXPLORE IT: www.prenhall.com/phit

Prentice Hall offers computer based training just for computer literacy. Designed to cover some of the most difficult concepts, as well as some current topical areas—EXPLORE IT is a web and CD-ROM based product designed to compliment a course. Available for free with any Prentice Hall title, our new lab coverage includes: Troubleshooting, Programming Logic, Mouse and Keyboard Basics, Databases, Building a Web Page, Hardware, Software, Operating Systems, Building a Network and more!

Throughout **Computer Confluence,** special focus boxes compliment the text:

Human Connection

Human Connection boxes at the beginning of all chapters feature stories of personalities who made an impact on the world of computing, and in some cases, people whose lives were transformed by computers and information technology.

How It Works

How It Works boxes are designed to provide additional technical material for courses and students who need it. How does the CPU execute a program? Why does a color image look different on the screen than on a printout? How does compression make files smaller? How can messeges be encrypted? Students will find answers to these kinds of questions in the How It Works boxes. For classes where this kind of technical detail isn't necessary, students can safely skip these boxes without missing any critical information. How It Works boxes are numbered to make it easy for instructors to create customized reading assignments by specifying which are required and which are optional.

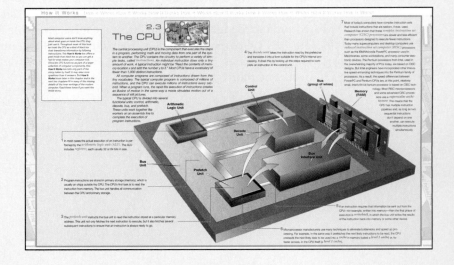

User's View

User's View boxes show the reader, through screens and text, what it's like to work with computer applications without getting bogged down in the details of button pushing. Featured applications are the latest versions of applications used by professionals, including Microsoft Office, Quark XPress, and Adobe Photoshop. These applications are available in similar versions on both Windows and Macintosh platforms.

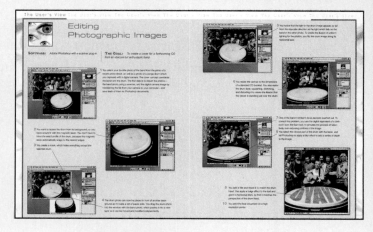

Crosscurrents

Crosscurrents boxes at the end of each chapter provide thought-provoking, timely, and sometimes controversial essays and articles by respected writers, analysts, and industry insiders. How is this technology changing our lives? What have we given up in return for a high-tech future? Who stands to gain the most, and who stands to lose the most, as we move into an information-based economy? How will future generations experience you digital works of art and literature? Is personal privacy history? Does our high-tech infrastructure make us more or less vulnerable to terrorists? Are digital implants in our medical future? These and other questions are raised—and wrestled with—in Crosscurrents

Rules of Thumb

Rules of Thumb boxes provide practical, nontechnical tips for avoiding the pitfalls and problems created by computer technology. How can you use graphics effectively and tastefully in a computer document? How can you minimize the health hazards of extended computer use? How can you protect your data from viruses and other software risks? What's the best way to communicate effectively with electronic mail? These are the types of questions that are answered in Rules of Thumb boxes.

Case Studies

Illustrate how today's information technology relates to real-world businesses and organizations. The cases cover the Internet, extranets, decision support systems, and the people responsible for using these technology in their day-to-day lives.

ACM Guidelines

Appendix. The ACM Code of Ethics is the most widely known code of conduct specifically for computer professionals. This appendix reprints the code, along with detailed annotations that link specific tenants to related ethics material throughout the text.

Concise Computer Consumer Guide

Concise Computer Consumer's Guide. For those students who are ready to buy a computer system, this guide provides up-to-date guidance on how to narrow down the myriad of options and make good decisions.

Companion Website at
www.prenhall.com/beekman

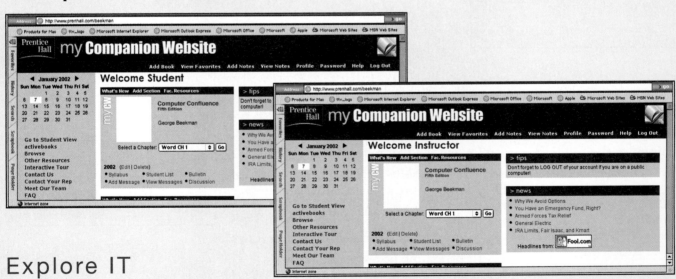

Explore IT

Acknowledgments

We're deeply grateful to all of the people who've come together to make *Computer Confluence* a success. Their names may not be on the cover, but their high-quality work shows in every detail of this project.

We're fortunate to be working with many of the same Prentice Hall people who helped with the fourth edition. Melissa Whitaker-Oliver, the Managing Editor for the Fourth Edition, took on the role of Acquisitions Editor for this new edition. In spite of the shortened publication schedule and the trauma that followed the terrorist tragedy of September 11, 2001, Melissa kept the project on track.

We're especially indebted to Developmental Editor Lena Buonanno, who worked closely with us on the development of this edition. Lena's skill, professionalism, patience, and attention to detail helped us to stay the course during the most trying of times. The book is much better thanks to her.

Many others brought their considerable talents to *Computer Confluence*. Patricia Smythe, design director, and Jill Little, designer, are the people most responsible for the design of the book. Lynne Breitfeller and Gail Steier de Acevedo worked on all aspects of production, helping ensure that the project could make all those nearly impossible deadlines. Editorial Assistant Mary Ann Broadnax played a central role at every step of this complex project. Abby Reip's patient and persistent research uncovered most of the excellent photos in these pages. The staff at Pre-Press produced the final book from all of the raw materials supplied by the others listed here. The details of the CD-ROM and the Web site were coordinated by Cathleen Profitko, media product manager. Content for the Web site is provided by Paul Berk.

I owe special thanks to members of my family who temporarily set aside many of their own personal and professional goals to help me with this project. My daughter, Johanna Beekman, helped organize the massive amounts of paper resources I've accumulated since the last edition.

It's not so easy to list the contributions of my wife Susan Grace Beekman. She was there to help in all kinds of ways, from research and organization to communication and collaboration. Just as importantly, she selflessly maintained the infrastructure of our home, our family, and our business, making it possible for me to meet the difficult deadlines of this project.

But the biggest contributions came from my son Ben Beekman, who served as my assistant throughout the project. As a college student, Ben is an ideal partner—he knows our readership from the inside. But Ben also knows the business of writing and the business of multimedia, and he's applied his expertise to every phase of this massive project—writing, research, information organization, screen shots, fact checking, graphic design, Web-page construction and editing, CD-ROM work, and more. I simply couldn't have completed this edition of *Computer Confluence* without his help.

All of this effort would be wasted if *Computer Confluence* didn't reach its intended audience. Thankfully, Sharon Turkovich, senior marketing manager, and her team have a strong track record for getting the good word out to the right people.

There are others who contributed to *Computer Confluence* in all kinds of ways, including critiquing chapters, answering technical questions, tracking down obscure references, guiding me through difficult decisions, and being there with support. There's no room here to detail their contributions, but we want to thank the people who gave time, energy, talent, and support during the years that this book was under development, including Scobel

Wiggins, Jim Folts, Jan Dymond, Mike Quinn, Michelle Artery, Nicole Mahan, Mark Dinsmore, Dave Trenkel, Paul Thurrott, Gary Brent, Robert Rose, Marion Rose, Anthony Debons, Maureen Allaire, Michelle Baxter, Natalie Anderson, Sherry Clark, Mike Johnson, Walter Rudd, Cherie Pancake, Bruce D'Ambrosio, Bernie Feyerham, Rajeev Pandey, Dave Stuve, Clay Cowgill, Keith Vertanen, Megan Slothover, Claudette Hastie-Baehrs, Shjoobedebop, Sujita, Isaiah Jones, Inner Strength, Oyaya, Breitenbush, Oregon Public Broadcasting, KLCC, and all of the editors and others who helped with previous editions of *Computer Confluence*. Thanks also to all the hardware and software companies whose cooperation made our work easier. George—And most of all, thanks to my family, whose patience, support, love, and sacrifice inspired me every day through all these years. Gene—Thanks Sheila, Diana, and Erin for being patient with Dad, again.

Computer Confluence Academic Advisors

A special thanks to the *Computer Confluence* Academic Advisors, a group of dedicated professors from all areas of the United States and Canada who were committed to providing valuable feedback and suggestions for all parts of this text. *Computer Confluence IT Edition*, Fourth Edition, benefited tremendously from your honest and insightful analyses. Their comments are also reflected in the new Fifth Edition.

Warren Boe, University of Iowa; David Bozak, SUNY Oswego; Nancy Cosgrove, University of Central Florida; Allen Dooley, Pasadena City College; Dwight Graham, Prairie State College; Margaret Guertin, Boston University; Lynne Hanrahan, Salem State College; Edward Kaplan, Bentley College; Linda Kieffer, Eastern Washington University; Larry Lagerstrom, University of California, Berkeley; Doug MacDormand, Red Deer College; Virginia Phillips, Youngstown State University; Paul Ryburn, University of Memphis; Susan Switzer, Central Michigan University; Dale Underwood, Lexington Community College.

Academic Reviewers

Thanks to all of the dedicated educators who reviewed the manuscript at various stages of development; *Computer Confluence* and its accompanying CD-ROM are significantly more valuable educational tools as a result of your ideas, suggestions, and constructive criticism.

William Allen, University of Central Florida; Dennis Anderson, Pace University; Linda J. Behrens, University of Central Oklahoma; Revis L. Bell, St. Philips College; William Boroski, Trident Technical College; Frederick Bounds, DeKalb College; Gary Brent, Scottsdale Community College; Judy Cameron, Spokane Community College; Mark Ciampa, Volunteer State Community College; Daniel Combellick, Scottsdale Community College; Elaine Cousins, University of Michigan at Ann Arbor; H. E. Dunsmore, Purdue University; Joseph Fahs, Elmira College; Pat Fenton, West Valley College; David Fickbohm, Golden Gate University; Blaine Garfolo, San Francisco State University; Tom Gerace, Tulane University; Wade Graves, Grayson County College; Ananda Gunawardena, University of Houston-Downtown; Dale Gust, Central Michigan University; Michael Hansen, Midlands Technical College; Sally Ann Hanson, Mercer County Community College; Shelly Hawkins, Duquesne University; Rachel E. Hinton, Broome Community College and Binghamton University; Edward Hom, Nassau Community College; Monte J. Johnson, St. Cloud State University; Trevor Jones, Duquesne University; Fred Klappenberger, Anne Arundel City College; Robert Kuhn, Muskingum Area Technical College; Larry Lagerstrom, University of California, Berkeley; Edward L. Lamie, California State University at Stanislaus; Deborah Ludford, Glendale Community College; Valerie A. Martin, Immaculata College; Brenda Mathews, University College of the Cariboo; Pat Mattsen, St. Cloud University; Maribeth L. McAnally, Texas A&M University-Commerce; Vicki McCullough, Palomar College; J. Michael McGrew,

Ball State University; Doris McPherson, Schoolcraft College; Linda Wise Miller, University of Idaho; William Moates, Indiana State University; Namdar Mogharreban, Southern Illinois University; Angela Peace, NorthWest Arkansas Community College; Sally Peterson, University of Wisconsin at Madison; Gerhard Plenert, Brigham Young University; Loreto Porte, Hostos City College; John Rezac, Johnson County Community College; Mike Quinn, Oregon State University; Jennifer Sedelmeyer, Broome City College; Margaret Sklar, Northern Michigan University; Raoul Smith, Northeastern University; Jayne Stasser, Miami University; Randy Stolze, Marist College; Tim Sylvester, Maricopa City College; John Telford, Salem State College; Dwight Watt, Athens Area Technical Institute; Patricia Wermers, North Shore City College; Alan Whitehurst, Brigham Young University; Tom Wiggen, University of North Dakota; Melissa Wiggins, Mississippi College; Floyd Jay Winters, Manatee City College; Rich Yankosky, Frederick City College.

Computer Confluence
IT Edition

Exploring Tomorrow's Technology

ReadMe

When you purchase computer software, the software commonly comes with a file or document called "ReadMe" or "ReadMe First." The ReadMe file typically tells you things you should know before you use the software: a broad overview or orientation, tips for getting started and making the most of the product, and background information for bringing beginners up to speed before using the product. This short ReadMe chapter is like a ReadMe file. In the introduction you'll find instructions that will help you determine how to make the most efficient use of this chapter—and of the complete Computer Confluence package—based on your background, interests, and needs.

After you read this chapter you should be able to:

Describe the basic parts of a PC and how they work together

Explain the relationship between hardware and software

Describe how the Internet extends the functionality of a PC

Use a Windows PC or Macintosh to explore the *Computer Confluence* CD-ROM

Use a Windows PC or Macintosh to explore the *Computer Confluence* Web site

▼ In this chapter:

A basic introduction to computers and the Internet

Instructions for launching the *Computer Confluence* CD-ROM and opening the *Computer Confluence* Web site

. . . *and more.*

▼ On the CD-ROM:

An interactive tour of the CD's most useful tools

A self-test of PC and Internet basics

. . . *and more.*

▼ On the Web:

www.prenhall.com/beekman

A tour of the most important features of the Web site

A self-test of PC and Internet basics

. . . *and more.*

Human Dreams and Dream Machines

The obvious choices **aren't the only choices**.

Steve Roberts

Steve Roberts with BEHEMOTH

In 1983 Steve Roberts realized he wasn't happy chained to his desk and his debts. He decided to build a new lifestyle that combined his passions—writing, adventure, computers, bicycling, learning, and networking. Six months later he hit the road on Winnebiko, a recumbent bike equipped with a laptop and solar panel. He connected each day to the CompuServe network through pay phones, transmitting magazine articles and book chapters.

Years later Roberts was exploring America on BEHEMOTH (Big Electronic Human-Energized Machine . . . Only Too Heavy), a million-dollar bike with seven networked computers and wireless communication capability. Roberts pedaled 17,000 miles before pursuing a new dream: "life with no hills." His latest project is Microship, a high-tech craft that will allow him to extend his technomadic lifestyle to the ocean. "There's a *lot* of world to explore out there. Having had a taste of it, how could I spend my life in one place?" ◗

Vaughn Rogers in his own art work

Vaughn Rogers "wasn't into computers." Computers, he thought, were useful for typing papers, but they weren't exciting. *Art* was exciting to Rogers, who had been drawing all his life.

In 1995 he went with a friend to the Computer Clubhouse, a nonprofit educational center at the Science Museum in Cambridge, Massachusetts. He saw other teens using computers to create art, edit video, and mix music. Before long, Vaughn was doing his art at the Computer Clubhouse after school.

Today 21-year-old Rogers studies visual communication and animation at Catherine Gibbs College. His goal is to work in computer animation and video, using his drawing talent enhanced with computer technology. He now works as an assistant manager at the Computer Clubhouse, helping others learn to use computers to pursue their passions. ◗

When Patricia Walsh lost her sight at 14, she almost lost sight of her dreams. She had already completed the advanced mathematics and science classes at her high school, and she wanted to go further. She learned to read and write Braille, but Braille couldn't help with the equations and formulas she needed to study. Her PC could talk using text-to-speech software, but it had nothing to say about scientific graphs and charts.

Fortunately, Walsh met John Gardner, a blind physics professor at Oregon State University. Gardner was developing tools to make math and science accessible to visually impaired people. His Tiger Tactile Graphics

Patricia Walsh

and Braille Embosser printed equations, formulas, and graphs as raised patterns that could be read by touch. Using this technology, Walsh could read class notes emailed by her professors. Once again she could "see" the figures that were critical to her studies.

Walsh started helping Gardner develop accessibility tools. She became a spokesperson for adaptive technology, telling others about tools that can open doors for people with disabilities. Walsh is now a junior at Winona University in Minnesota, where she uses the tools that she helped develop to pursue her dream. "Computers have allowed me to get in the mainstream. Now I can do what I used to love before I became blind. I've even become a CS major." ◗

Steve Roberts, Vaughn Rogers, and Patricia Walsh would be living very different lives today if they hadn't connected with computers. Their stories are interesting and inspiring, but they aren't unique. Every day computer technology changes people's lives all around the world.

Sometimes it seems like everybody uses computers. In fact, the great majority of people on our planet have never touched a computer!

Most of the people who *do* use computers have fairly limited experience and ability—typically the basics of word processing, electronic mail, and finding information on the World Wide Web. The percentage of people who can go beyond the basics and harness the power of a modern PC is relatively small.

If you're a member of this tiny community of **power users,** the next few pages aren't for you. But before you move on to Chapter 1, take a look at the *Computer Confluence* Quick Start and Navigating *Computer Confluence* starting on page xxx. You'll find tips for getting the most out of this book and the companion CD and Web site. This chapter closes with a CrossCurrents article that will give you something to think about.

If you're a **casual computer user,** comfortable with the basic operation of a PC, a CD-ROM drive, and a Web browser, you may want to look through this chapter quickly and spend more time with the Quick Start, Navigating *Computer Confluence*, and CrossCurrents sections before moving on to Chapter 1, where the real story begins. (If you're not sure about your knowledge level, check out the questions at the end of the chapter. If you have trouble answering them, spend a little more time looking over this chapter before you move on.)

If you're a **beginner,** your experience is limited or out of date, you're uncomfortable with PC technology, or you just want to be thorough, this chapter is for you. Here you'll find the basic knowledge you'll need to bring you up to speed, so you're not struggling to catch up as you explore the rest of the book. You'll also learn what you need to know to take full advantage of the *Computer Confluence* CD-ROM and Web site. Along with this book, these resources can provide you with a rich multimedia introduction to the world of computers and information technology.

Whichever path you choose, don't wait until you're sitting in front of a computer to read *Computer Confluence*. Hands-on computer experience is important, but you won't need the computer to take advantage of this book. Wherever you are, just dive in.

Key terms in this chapter, and throughout the book, are highlighted in blue boldface. Secondary terms are highlighted in blue italics. In this chapter, the key terms are the ones that are critical for getting started with the Computer Confluence book, CD-ROM, and Web site; secondary terms are terms that are introduced briefly here and covered in more detail later.

PC Basics

The beginning is the
most important part of the work.

—Plato

Computers come in all kinds of packages, from massive supercomputers to tiny computers embedded in cell phones, credit cards, and even microscopic machines and "smart" pills. But in this chapter, we'll focus on the typical desktop computer—the **personal computer**, or **PC**. We'll start with a look at the physical parts of a PC—the PC's **hardware**. This whirlwind tour will offer a quick, practical overview; you'll learn more in later chapters.

PC Hardware Basics

Hardware: the parts of a computer
that **can be kicked**.

—Jeff Pesis

Modern desktop PCs don't all look alike, but under the skin, they're more alike than different. Every PC is built around a tiny *microprocessor* that controls the workings of the system. This **central processing unit**, or **CPU**, is usually housed in a box, called the *system unit* (or, more often, just "the computer" or "the PC") that serves as command central for the entire computer system. The CPU is the real computer—it controls the operation of all the other computer components. Some of these components are housed in the system unit with the *CPU*; others are *peripheral devices*—or simply *peripherals*—external devices connected via cables to the system unit.

The system unit includes built-in **memory** and a **hard disk** for storage and retrieval of information. The CPU uses memory for instant access to information while it's working. The built-in hard disk serves as a longer-term storage device for large quantities of information.

The PC's main hard disk is a permanent fixture in the system unit. Other types of disk drives work with *removable media*—disks that can be separated from their drives, just as an audio CD can be removed from a stereo system. A typical PC system unit includes a diskette drive and a CD-ROM drive (or some other kind of optical drive). A *diskette drive* (also known as a *floppy disk drive*) enables you to store small amounts of information on pocket-sized plastic-covered magnetic **diskettes**. A **CD-ROM drive** enables the computer to read and use information stored on 5-1/4-inch optical disks, including audio CDs and CD-ROMs (such as the one packaged with this book). Disk drives that are included in the system unit are called *internal drives*. (*External drives* can be attached to the system unit via cables. For example, a PC system might include an external hard disk for additional storage, a Zip drive for accessing removable Zip disks, and a CD-RW drive for reading and writing CDs.)

Other system unit components, including the video display card, the sound card, the network interface card, and the modem, communicate with external devices, with other computers, and with networks.

CD-ROM drive

diskette drive

keyboard

monitor

mouse

But the PC's main purpose isn't to communicate with other machines—it's there to communicate with you. Four common *peripherals* aid this human-computer interaction:

▌ A **keyboard** enables you to type text and numerical data into the computer's memory.
▌ A **mouse** enables you to point to text, graphical objects, menu commands, and other items on the screen.
▌ A **monitor** displays text, numbers, and pictures from the computer's memory.
▌ A **printer** generates printed letters, papers, transparencies, labels, and other hard copies. (The printer might be directly connected to the computer, or it might be shared by several computers on a network.)

The next two pages illustrate the fundamentals of as basic PC keyboard and mouse. Chapter 3 explores peripherals in more detail.

A standard desktop PC is made up of several components, including a system unit, a monitor, a keyboard, and a mouse. The system unit typically includes an internal hard drive, a CD-ROM drive, and a diskette drive.

Using a Keyboard

Typing letters, numbers, and special characters with a computer keyboard is similar to typing on a standard typewriter keyboard. But unlike a typewriter, the computer responds by displaying the typed characters on the monitor screen at the position of the line or rectangle called the cursor. Some keys on the computer keyboard—*cursor (arrow) keys*, the *Delete key*, the *Enter key*, *function keys (f-keys)*, and others— send special commands to the computer. These keys may have different names or meanings on different computer systems. This figure shows a typical keyboard on a Windows-compatible PC. Keyboards for Macintoshes and other types of systems have a few differences but operate on the same principles.

Function keys (f-keys), labeled F1, F2, and so on, send signals to the computer that have no inherent meaning. The function of these keys depends on the software being used. F1 might mean "Save file" to one program and "Delete file" to another. In other words function keys are programmable.

Backspace on a PC tells the computer to delete the character just typed (or the one to the left of the cursor on the screen, or the currently selected data).

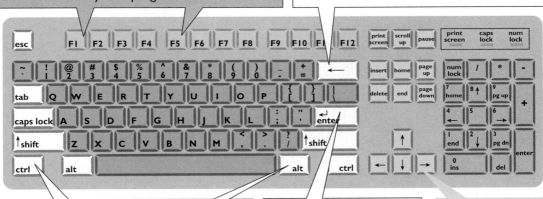

Control and *Alt* are modifier keys that cause nothing to happen by themselves but change the meaning of other keys. When you hold down a modifier key while pressing another key, the combination makes that other key behave differently. For example, typing S while holding down the Control key might send a command to save the current document.

Enter sends a signal telling the computer or terminal to move the cursor to the beginning of the next line on the screen. For many applications this key also "enters" the line just typed, telling the computer to process it.

Cursor (arrow) keys are used to move the cursor up, down, left, or right.

Using a Mouse

The mouse enables you to perform many tasks quickly that might be tedious or confusing with a keyboard. As you slide the mouse across your desktop, a pointer echoes your movements on the screen. You can click *the mouse—press*

the button while the mouse is stationary—or drag *it—move it while holding the button down. On a two-button mouse, the left button is usually used for clicking and dragging. You can use these two techniques to perform a variety of operations.*

Clicking the Mouse

If the pointer points to an onscreen **button**, clicking the mouse presses the button.

If the pointer points to a picture of a tool or object on the screen, clicking the mouse *selects* the tool or object; for example, clicking the pencil tool enables you to draw with the mouse.

If the pointer points to a part of a text document, it turns from an arrow into an *I-beam*; clicking repositions the flashing cursor.

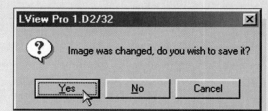

Dragging the Mouse

If you hold the button down while you drag the mouse with a selected graphic tool (like a paintbrush), you can draw by remote control.

If you drag the mouse from one point in a text document to another, you select all the text between those two points so you can modify or move it. For example, you might select this movie title so you could italicize it.

You can drag the mouse to select a command from a **menu** of choices. For example, this command enables you to locate specific documents that are stored on your computer.

Other Mouse Operations

If you **double-click** the mouse—click twice in rapid succession—while pointing to an onscreen object, the computer will probably **open** the object so you can see inside it. For example, double-clicking this *icon* representing a letter causes the letter to open.

If you *right-click*—click the right mouse button—while pointing to an object, the computer will probably display a menu of choices of things you can do to the object. For example, if you right-click the letter icon, a menu appears at the pointer.

PC Software Basics

Computers can figure out **all kinds of problems**, except the things in the world that **just don't add up**.

—James Magary

All of this hardware is controlled, directly or indirectly, by the tiny CPU in the system unit. And the CPU is controlled by **software**—instructions that tell it what to do. *System software*, including the **operating system (OS)**, continuously takes care of the behind-the-scenes details and (usually) keeps things running smoothly. The operating system also determines what your screen display looks like as you work and how you tell the computer what you want it to do. Most PCs today use some version of the *Microsoft Windows* operating system; Macintosh computers use some version of Apple's *Mac OS*.

Application programs, also called simply **applications**, are the software tools that enable you to use a computer for specific purposes. Some applications are designed to accomplish well-defined short-term goals. For example, the *Computer Confluence* CD-ROM includes an application that supplements and expands on the material in this book using interactive quizzes, animated demos, video presentations, and other multimedia material. Other applications programs are more general and open-ended in their goals. For example, you can use a word processing program, such as Microsoft Word, to create memos, letters, term papers, novels, textbooks, or World Wide Web pages—just about any kind of text-based document. (In the PC world, a **document** is something created by an application, regardless of whether it has actually been printed. If you write a letter with the Microsoft Word application and save it as a disk file, the saved file is a Microsoft Word document.)

The User's View boxes on the following pages show examples of software at work. In these two simple examples, we'll use a word processing application to edit and print a term paper we created in an earlier session and stored as a document on the hard disk. In the first example, we'll use Microsoft Word on a PC with the Microsoft Windows XP operating system. In the second example we'll do the same thing using Microsoft Word on a Macintosh with Mac OS X. In both examples, we'll perform the following steps:

1. Locate the document on the hard disk.
2. **Open** the application—copy it from the computer's hard disk into memory so we can use it—and open the document.
3. Type some additional text at the end of the document.
4. Print the document.
5. Close the application.
6. Delete the document file from the hard disk.

Before we begin, a reminder and a disclaimer:

The reminder: The *User's View* examples are designed to give you a feel for the software, not to provide how-to instructions. You can learn how to use the software using lab manuals or other books on the subject, some of which are listed in *Sources and Resources* at the end of chapters in this book.

The disclaimer: These examples are intended to compare different types of interfaces—not to establish a favorite. The brand of software in a particular User's View box isn't as important as the general concepts built into that software. One of the best things about computers is that they offer lots of different ways to do things. These examples, and others throughout the book, are designed to expose you to possibilities. Even if you have no plans to use the operating systems or applications in the examples—*especially* if you have no plans to use them—you can learn something by looking at them as a curious observer.

Software makes it possible for PCs to be put to work in homes, schools, offices, factories, and farms.

The User's View The User's View The User's View The Use

Using
Microsoft Word with
Microsoft Windows

SOFTWARE: *Microsoft Windows XP and Microsoft Word.* **THE GOAL:** *To edit, print, and delete a term paper file.*

1 After the PC completes its startup process, you see a Login screen with a list of users. You click your user name from the list, so Windows will use your personal settings.

2 The Windows *desktop* appears—a screen that includes icons representing objects used in your work.

3 You click Start in the lower-left corner of the screen. The *Start menu* appears, enabling you to select. from the applications and documents you use most frequently.

4 You select Microsoft Word, and click to open the program.

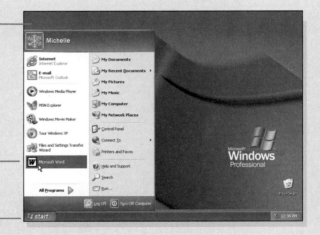

5 The Microsoft Word application opens, and you are presented with a blank document and a *task bar* containing buttons that represent frequently used commands and files.

6 You use the task bar to open your paper.

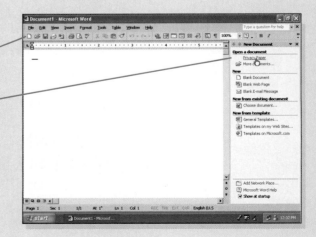

7 When you open the term paper document, Microsoft Word displays the term paper in a window.

8 You use the mouse to move the pointer to the end of the text; you click the mouse button. A flashing **cursor** (sometimes called an **insertion point**) indicates your location in the document.

9 You type additional text to be added at that point. As you type, the cursor moves to the right, leaving a trail of text in its wake. At the same time, those characters are stored in the computer's memory. If you mistype a character or string of characters, you can press Delete or Backspace to eliminate the typos.

10 As you type, the top-most lines **scroll** out of view to make room on the screen for the new ones. The text you've entered is still in memory, even though you can't see it on the screen. You can retrieve it anytime by scrolling backward through the text. In this respect a word processor document is like a modern version of ancient paper scrolls.

11 Every few minutes you select the Save command to save your document in a disk file containing your work so far. This provides insurance against accidental erasure of the text you've entered.

12 You choose the Print command to print the paper.

13 You select Print from the *dialog box* that appears.

14 You close the application by clicking the red Close button in the upper right corner of the window.

15 You return to the desktop. To locate your document in Windows Explorer, you open your Documents folder using the Start menu.

16 After you open the School Work folder which contains your paper, you can delete the printed file by dragging its icon over the Recycle Bin icon.

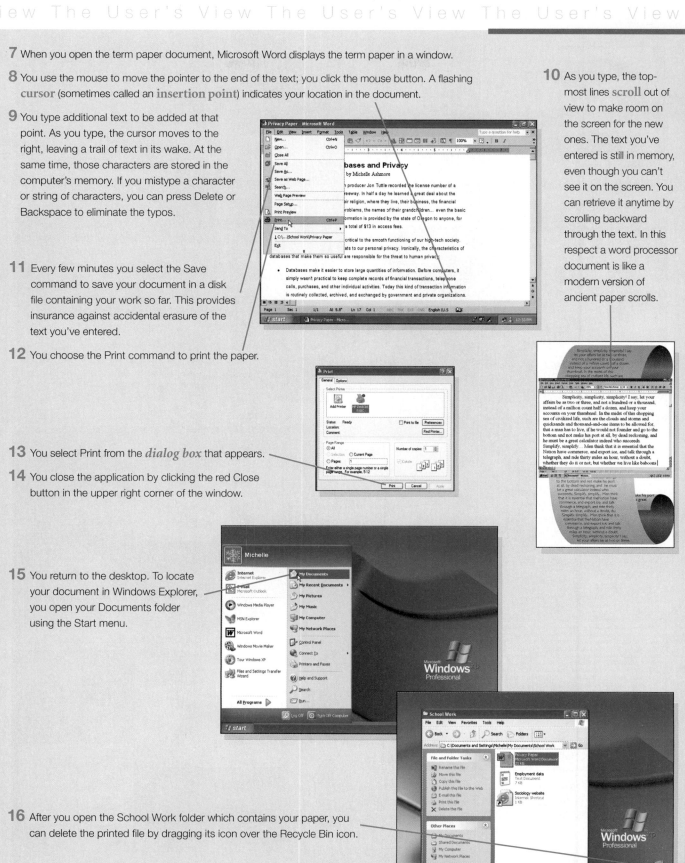

Using Microsoft Word with Mac OS

SOFTWARE: *Mac OS X and Microsoft Word*

THE GOAL: *To edit, print, and delete a term paper file*

1 The Macintosh Login screen asks you to type in your name and **password** — a string of letters and numbers known only by you and the computer—to verify your identity. As you type your password, only asterisks appear on the screen, so there's no risk of anyone reading it over your shoulder.

2 Like the Windows desktop, the Macintosh desktop includes icons representing objects used in your work. The Macintosh menu bar spans the top of the screen.

3 An open window shows the contents of the hard disk called Macintosh HD. At the bottom of the screen is the *Dock*, which is a holding place for frequently used programs, documents, and folders. Folders, like their real-world counterparts, enable you to group related documents.

4 You click and hold the mouse button down on the School Work folder in the Dock. A pop-up menu enables you to select the term paper to open it.

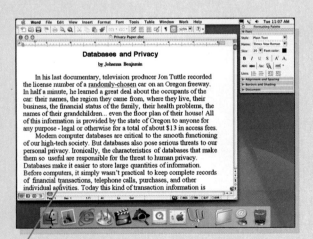

5 You edit and print the document; the process is similar for the Macintosh and Windows versions of Word.

6 When you close the application (using the Quit command from the File menu), you return to the desktop. You can delete the printed file by dragging its icon over the Trash icon in the Dock. (Until you choose the Empty Trash command, you can change your mind and retrieve the file.)

PC Network Basics

> Networks aren't made of printed circuits, but of **people**. . . . **My terminal is a door** to countless, intricate pathways, leading to **untold numbers of neighbors**.
> —Cliff Stoll, in *The Cuckoo's Egg*

Today's PCs are powerful tools that can perform a variety of tasks that go far beyond the basic word processing examples illustrated here. In later chapters we'll explore many of these applications, from money management to multimedia. But a PC becomes even more powerful when it's connected to other computers through a network.

A computer may have a *direct connection* to a network—for example, cables might connect it to other computers, printers, and other devices in an office or student lab. These networked machines can easily and quickly share information with each other. When a computer isn't physically close to the other machines in the network, it can still communicate with those machines through a *remote access* connection. Using a *modem*, the remote computer can connect to the network through an ordinary phone line.

An entire computer network can be connected to other networks through cables, wireless radio transmissions, or other means. The Internet is an elaborate network of interconnected networks—a network that is dramatically changing the way people work, play, and communicate.

Networked computers in this lab allow students to share files, send messages, and connect to the Internet.

Internet Basics

> What interests me about it . . . is that it's a form of communication **unlike any other** and yet **the second you start doing it** you understand it.
> —Nora Ephron, Director of *You've Got Mail*

There was a time, not too many years ago, when word processing was the most popular computer activity among students. For most students, the computer was little more than a high-powered typewriter. Today a PC can be a window into the global system of interconnected networks known as the Internet, or just the *Net*.

The Internet is used by mom-and-pop businesses and multinational corporations that want to communicate with their customers, sell products, and track economic conditions; by kindergarteners and college students doing research and exploration; by consumers and commuters who need access to timely information, goods, and services; and by families and friends who just want to stay in touch. Most people connect to the Internet because it gives them the power to do things that they couldn't easily do otherwise.

Using the Internet you can

- Study material designed to supplement this book, including late-breaking news, interactive study aids, and multimedia simulations that can't be printed on paper.
- Send a message to 1 or 1,001 people, around town or around the world, and receive replies almost as quickly as the recipients can read the message and type a response.
- Explore vast libraries of research material, ranging from classic scholarly works to contemporary reference works.
- Find instant answers to time-sensitive questions such as "What's the weather like in Boston right now?" or "What software do I need to make my new computer work with my new printer?" or "Who won this morning's Olympic high-diving competition?" or "What did the United Nations secretary general say on National Public Radio's *All Things Considered* last night?" or "Where in the world is the Federal Express package I sent yesterday?"
- Get medical, legal, or technical advice from a wide variety of experts.
- Listen to live radio broadcasts from around the world.
- Participate in discussions or play games with people all over the globe who share your interests; with the right equipment, you can set aside your keyboard and communicate through live audio-video links.

In Seattle, WA, (left) a mother checks on her four-year-old daughter from work using Internet-linked video cameras. In Philadelphia, PA, (right) the press corps at the Republican National Convention used the Internet to conduct and transmit live telecasts.

▶ Shop for obscure items such as out-of-print books and CDs that you can't find elsewhere.

▶ Download free software or music clips from servers all over the world onto your computer.

▶ Order a custom-built computer, car, or condominium.

▶ Track hourly changes in the stock markets and buy and sell stocks based on those changes.

▶ Take a course for college credit from a school thousands of miles away.

▶ Publish your own writings, drawings, photos, and multimedia works so Internet users all over the world can view them.

▶ Start your own business and have a worldwide clientele.

Every revolution has a dark side, and the Internet explosion is no exception. The Internet has plenty of worthless information, scams, and questionable activities. People who make the most of the Internet know how to separate the best of the Net from the rest of the Net. Every chapter of this book contains information that will help you to understand and use the Internet wisely. In this chapter we'll focus on the basics of the two most popular Internet applications: communicating with electronic mail and finding information on the World Wide Web.

Electronic mail (also called **email** or *e-mail*) is the application that lures many people to the Internet for the first time. Email programs make it possible for even casual computer users to easily send messages to family, friends, and colleagues. Because an email message can be written, addressed, sent, delivered, and answered in a matter of minutes—even if the correspondents are on opposite sides of the globe—email has replaced air mail for rapid, routine communication in many organizations. Closer to home, email makes it possible to replace time-consuming phone calls and meetings with more efficient online exchanges.

Email Basics

> Each person on the **"Internet"** has a unique email **"address"** created by **having a squirrel run** across a computer keyboard. . . .
>
> —Dave Barry, humorist

Details vary, but the basic concepts of email are the same for almost all systems. When you sign up for an email account—through your school, your company, or a private *Internet service provider (ISP)*—you receive a **user name** (sometimes called a *login name* or *alias*) and a storage area for messages (sometimes called a *mailbox*). Any user can send a mail message to anyone else, regardless of whether the recipient is currently *logged in*—connected to the network. The message will be waiting in the recipient's *inbox* the next time he launches his email program and logs in. An email message can be addressed to one person or hundreds of people. Most email messages are plain text, without the kinds of formatting and graphic images found in printed documents. Messages can carry documents, pictures, multimedia files, and other computer files as *attachments*.

You can send messages to anyone on your local system or ISP by simply addressing the message to that person's user name. You can also send messages to anyone with access to Internet email, provided you know that person's Internet address. An Internet email address is

Communicating with Electronic Mail

SOFTWARE: *America Online*

THE GOAL: *To catch up on your email. Using a PC, a modem, and America Online software, you're about to connect to America Online, an information service that serves as your electronic post office.*

1 When you double-click the America Online (AOL) icon, the application asks you to identify yourself with your user name and password.

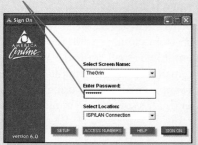

2 When you click the Sign On button, the software passes the necessary commands to the modem along with the network phone number and other information. You hear the dial tone, the touch-tone dialing signals, a high whistle, and a hiss as the modem dials and establishes the connection.

3 When a connection is made, AOL locates your screen name in its billing database and checks your password. If you typed the password correctly, you're greeted by an AOL headline screen and a digitized voice telling you that you have mail. You're now online—connected to the computer system and ready to communicate. You click the You've Got Mail icon to get your mail.

4 The New Mail window lists one new message; you click on the message title to read it.

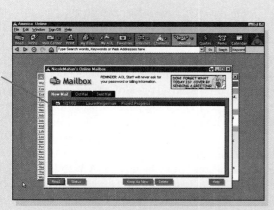

5 After reading the message, you click on the Reply icon.

6 The software automatically fills in the address and subject.

7 You type a message in the message box.

8 Then you click on Send to send the letter. Your message should be in Laurel Reigelman's mailbox waiting until Laurel Reigelman logs in. Your job is done so you can now explore other areas in America Online until you're ready to log off.

made up of two parts separated by an at sign (@): the person's user name and the *host name*—the name of the host computer, network, or ISP address where the user receives mail. Here's the basic form:

```
username@hostname
```

```
Here are a few examples of typical email addresses:
```

```
realgeorge999@aol.com
jandumont@engr.ucla.edu
enathab@pop3.ispchannel.com
```

Some organizations use standardized email addresses so it's easy to guess member addresses. For example, every employee at ABCXYZ Company might have an email address of the form *firstname_lastname@abcxyzco.com*. (The underscore character is sometimes used as a substitute for a space because spaces can't be embedded in email addresses).

It's important to address email messages with care—they can't be delivered if even a single character is mistyped. Fortunately, most email programs include address books, so users can look up email addresses by name and automatically address messages. Many World Wide Web sites, including Yahoo!, Excite, and search.com, offer free email search services and directories.

Many commercial Web sites offer free email accounts. Sometimes these free email services are subsidized by advertisers; sometimes they're provided to attract Web site visitors. Free email services are popular with users of public computers (for example, in libraries), people who don't receive email from their ISPs, people who want multiple email addresses not associated with their workplace, and travelers who want to check email on the road without lugging a laptop.

The example in the User's View box shows a simple email session using America Online—one of the most popular Internet Service Providers. AOL's software is unique, but the concepts illustrated in the example apply to all email programs.

World Wide Web Basics

Email may be the most popular Internet application, but the World Wide Web (WWW) opens up all kinds of other possible Internet activities. The *Web* is a huge portion of the Internet that includes a wealth of multimedia content accessible through simple point-and-click programs called Web browsers. Web browsers on PCs and other devices serve as windows into the Web's richly diverse information space.

The World Wide Web is made up of millions of interlinked documents called Web pages. A Web page is typically made up of text and images, like a page in a book. A collection of related pages stored on the same computer is called a Web site; a typical Web site is organized around a home page that serves as an entry page and a stepping off point for other pages in the site. Each Web page has a unique address, technically referred to as a URL (uniform resource locator). For example, the URL for this book's home page is **http://www.prenhall.com/beekman**. You can visit the site by typing the exact URL into the address box of your Web browser.

At the heart of the Web is the concept of *hypertext*. A Web browser enables you to jump from one Web page to another by clicking hyperlinks (often called just *links*)—words, pictures, or menu items that act as buttons. For example, at the *Computer Confluence* Web site you can select chapter number to jump to pages related to that chapter. Within the chapter, you can click Multiple Choice to jump to a page containing practice quiz questions. Or you can click Chapter Connections to jump to a page full of hyperlinks that can take you to pages on other Web sites. These off-site pages contain articles, illustrations, audio clips, video segments, and other resources created by others. They reside on computers owned by of corporations, universities, libraries, institutions, and individuals around the world.

Text links are typically, but not always, underlined and displayed in a different color than standard text on the page. In the example shown here, the offsite chapter connection hyperlinks are underlined in blue; the Chapter Connection hyperlink is part of a white-on-black menu on the left side of the screen, and the original Chapter link is part of a pop-up menu.

You can explore an amazing variety of Web pages by clicking links. But this kind of random jumping isn't without frustrations. Some links lead to cobwebs—Web pages that haven't been kept up to date by their owners—and dead-ends—pages that have been removed or moved.

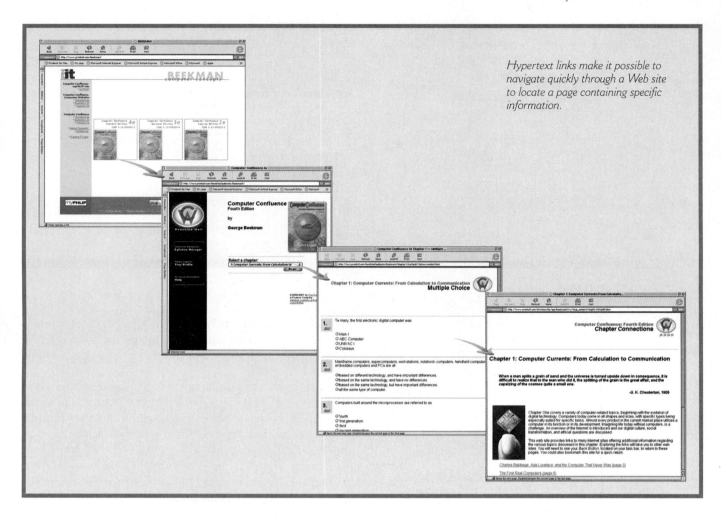

Hypertext links make it possible to navigate quickly through a Web site to locate a page containing specific information.

Even if a link is current, it may not be reputable or accurate; since anybody can create Web pages, they don't all have the editorial integrity of trusted print media.

It can also be frustrating to try to find your way back to pages you've seen on the Web. That's why browsers have *Back* and *Forward buttons*; you can retrace your steps and re-retrace your steps as often as you like. These buttons won't help, though, if you're trying to find an important page from an earlier session. Most browsers include tools for keeping personal lists of memorable sites, called *bookmarks* or *favorites*. When you run across a page worth revisiting, you can mark it with a Bookmark or Add to Favorites command. Then you can revisit that site anytime by selecting it from the list.

Web Search Basics

The ability to **ask the right question** is more than half the battle of finding the answer.
—Thomas J. Watson, founder of IBM

The World Wide Web is like a giant, loosely woven, constantly changing document created by thousands of unrelated authors and scattered about in computers all over the world. The biggest challenge for many Web users is extracting the useful information from the rest. If you're looking for a specific information resource, but you don't know where it is located on the Web, you might be able to find it using a search engine.

A search engine is built around a database that catalogs Web locations based on content. (Databases are covered later in the book; for now, you can just think of it as an indexed collection of information stored in a computer.) For some search engines, researchers organize and evaluate Web sites. Other search engines use software to search the Web and catalog information automatically. The usefulness of a search engine depends in part on the information in its database. But it also depends on how easy it is for people to find what they're looking for in the database.

A search for the phrase "global warming" yields hundreds of hits on the Google search engine.

Yahoo's subject tree enables you to narrow your search by clicking categories within a subject.

To find information with a typical search engine, you type a keyword or keywords into a search field, click a button, and wait a few seconds for your Web browser to display a list of *hits*— pages that contain requested keywords. A search engine can easily produce a list of hundreds or thousands of hits. Most search engines attempt to list pages in order from best to worst, but these automatic rankings aren't always reliable.

Another popular way to use a search engine is to repeatedly narrow the search using a *directory* or *subject tree*—a hierarchical catalog of Web sites compiled by researchers. The search engine at Yahoo! is probably the best-known example. A screen presents you with a menu of subject choices. When you click a subject—say, Government—you narrow your search to that subject, and you're presented with a menu of subcategories within that subject—Military, Politics, Law, Taxes, and so on. You can continue to narrow your search by proceeding through subject menus until you reach a list of selected Web sites related to the final subject. The sites are usually rank-ordered based on estimated value. The list of Web sites on a given index page is not exhaustive—there may be hundreds of pages related to the subject that aren't included in any directory. It's simply not possible to keep a complete index of all the pages on the ever-changing Web.

Popular search engines are located on Excite, Yahoo, and other Internet *portals*—Web sites designed as first-stop gateways for Internet explorers. The Windows and Macintosh operating systems include search engines. Internet Explorer, Netscape Communicator, and other Web browsers include Search buttons that connect to popular search engines. And many large Web sites include search engines that enable you to search for site-specific information.

Applying the Basics

> It is good to have **an end** to journey toward,
> but it is **the journey** that matters in the end.
>
> Ursula K. LeGuin, author of *The Dispossessed*

In a few pages, you've learned the bare-bones basic concepts behind the PC and the Internet. Now it's time to apply what you've learned in a practical, hands-on way. The next few pages guide you, step-by-step, through an opening session with the *Computer Confluence* CD-ROM and Web Site. They're followed by a few helpful rules of thumb for navigating through the remaining chapters of this book. Once you've completed this quick tour, you'll be ready to dive into the heart of *Computer Confluence*, starting with Chapter 1. So what are you waiting for?

Navigating Computer Confluence

Here are a few pointers for exploring *Computer Confluence*. Take a minute to read these and you'll probably save hours later.

▶ **Know your boxes.** Text chapters include several types of boxes, each of which is designed to be read in a particular way.

The **User's View** boxes show you what it's like to be in the driver's seat with some of today's most popular software. Even if you have experience with the software, take a little time to look over these boxes. Some key concepts are introduced here. These boxes can be especially helpful if they cover applications you aren't learning first-hand. A User's View box in the main text means "This is a good time to look over The User's View box." The *Computer Confluence* CD-ROM includes multimedia versions of many of these boxes.

Rules of Thumb boxes (similar to this one) provide practical tips on everything from designing a publication to protecting your privacy. They bring concepts down to earth with useful suggestions that can save you time, money, and peace of mind.

How It Works boxes are for those readers who want—or need—to know more about what's going on under the hood. These boxes use words and pictures to take you deeper into the inner workings without getting bogged down in technical detail. The *Computer Confluence* CD-ROM includes multimedia versions of many of these boxes as well as bonus How It Works features that aren't in the text. If your course objectives or personal curiosity doesn't motivate you to learn how it works, that's okay; you can skip every How It Works box and still understand the rest of *Computer Confluence*.

CrossCurrents boxes showcase diverse, timely, and often controversial points of view on the technology and its impact on our lives. These short essays, which close each chapter, offer perspectives from some of the most important writers and thinkers on information technology.

▶ **Read it and read it again.** If possible, read each chapter twice: once for the big ideas and the second time for more detailed understanding. You may also find it helpful to survey each chapter's outline in the table of contents before reading the chapter for the first time.

▶ **Don't try to memorize every term the first time through.** Throughout the text, key terms are introduced in **boldface blue**, and secondary terms are *italicized in blue*. Use the Key Terms list at the end of each chapter to review and the glossary to recall any forgotten terms. The CD-ROM contains an interactive cross-referenced version of the glossary to find any term quickly.

▶ **Don't overanalyze examples.** *Computer Confluence* is designed to help you understand concepts, not memorize keystrokes. You can learn the nuts and bolts of working with computers in labs or at home. The examples in this text may not match the applications in your lab, but the concepts are similar.

▶ **Don't get stuck.** If a concept seems unclear on the first reading, make a note and move on. Sometimes ideas make more sense after you've seen the bigger picture. If you still don't understand the concept the second time through, check the CD-ROM and the Web site for further clarification. When in doubt, ask questions.

▶ **Remember that there's more than one way to learn.** Some of us learn best by reading, others learn best by exploring interactive examples, and still others learn best by discussing ideas with others, online or in person. *Computer Confluence* offers you the opportunity to learn in all of these ways. Use the learning tools that work best for you.

▶ **Get your hands dirty.** Try the applications while you're reading about them. Your reading and lab work will reinforce each other and help solidify your newfound knowledge.

▶ **Study together.** There's plenty to discuss here, and discussion is a great way to learn.

In a hurry? Turn the page. The next page will give you a quick start—just enough information so you can start using the CD-ROM, the Web site, and related computer applications right away.

Computer Confluence Quick Start

The first few chapters of this book provide you with a broad orientation to computers, CD-ROMs, the Internet, and related technology. In the meantime, this Quick Start provides the basics—without detailed explanations—so you can get started with the *Computer Confluence* CD-ROM and Web site right away.

Details vary from computer to computer, but the basics are generally the same. If you're working in a computer lab, you'll probably need a few additional lab instructions to supplement the steps in this Quick Start.

Launching the *Computer Confluence* CD-ROM

1. Turn on the computer. After a minute or so the screen will show icons that represent disks and other computer resources. It may also show open windows that reveal the contents of these resources. A row of menus appears at the top of each window (or, if you're using a Macintosh, at the top of the screen).

2. As you move the mouse around, the pointer on the screen moves in the same motion. (If you run out of space on the mouse pad or desk, you can lift the mouse and reposition it.) Point to an icon and click it by pressing the mouse button. (If there are two or more buttons, use the left button.) You'll click this way to select objects, press onscreen buttons, and navigate around the Web site and CD-ROM.

3. Insert the *Computer Confluence* CD-ROM in the CD-ROM drive. Press the drive's button to make the CD tray slide open. Place the CD, label side up, on the tray, being careful not to handle the other side. Close the CD tray by pressing the button again. (Some CD-ROM drives automatically close.) The *Computer Confluence* CD-ROM application may launch automatically, filling your screen with a Welcome screen. If it does, skip to Step 5.

4. The next step depends on your operating system software. If you're not sure, ask.

Windows

a. Point to the icon called "My Computer" and double-click it (click twice in rapid succession with the left mouse button).

b. Double-click the CD-ROM icon in the My Computer window.

c. Double-click the CCWin.EXE icon.

Macintosh

a. Point to the CCCD icon and double-click it (click twice in rapid succession).

b. Double-click the CCMac icon in the CCCD window.

5. The application takes a few seconds to load into the computer's memory. When it does, a new window will open on your screen. On-screen instructions will guide you through the CD's contents.

Exploring the *Computer Confluence* Web Site

To explore the *Computer Confluence* Web site, you'll need a Web browser and an Internet connection. Your computer probably includes one or more of these browsers: Internet Explorer, Netscape Navigator, Netscape Communicator, or America Online's Web browser.

1. Locate the browser and double-click its icon. If you're using a modem to connect to the Internet, this will probably cause the modem to dial the appropriate number.

2. Point to the long rectangle at the top of the browser window. If the text in that window is black on a white background, double-click it to highlight it. Then type **www.prenhall.com/beekman** to replace the highlighted text. (Depending on your browser, you may be able to get the same results by simply typing **computerconfluence**.) Press Return or Enter.

3. If an error message appears, click the OK button, check your typing carefully, correct any errors, and press Return or Enter again. When you type it correctly, you'll be taken to the *Computer Confluence* opening screen.

4. If you're using your own computer, you can mark this page so you can return by selecting it from a menu rather than retyping its name. If you're using Internet Explorer, select Add to Favorites from the Favorites menu. If you're using Netscape Navigator or Communicator, select Add Bookmark from the Bookmark menu.

5. At the *Computer Confluence* site you can click on on-screen images and menus to select the edition of the book you're using, select a chapter, and then select activities within that chapter.

CrossCurrentsCrossCurrentsCrossCurrents **CrossCurrents**

Brain Gain

Nick Montfort

Every chapter of this book ends with an article that explores issues related to computer technology and its impact on our lives. Many of these articles present controversial points of view; all of them raise interesting, important questions. In this article, first published in the November, 2000 issue of Smart Business for the New Economy, *writer Nick Montfort discusses changes higher education will face as computers, the Internet, and related technologies evolve. Montfort presents visions of a future in which textbooks and classrooms might be replaced by virtual reality simulations and microscopic robots. Since you don't have a robot tutor, take some of your own time to read this thought-provoking article.*

At last, the intersection of education and technology is about to jump beyond the film-strip projector. Already, almost all U.S. public schools and just more than half of all public school classrooms have Internet access. In the next 10 years, concepts like virtual reality and distance learning will have a broad impact.

Students at high schools and universities already use the Internet as a reference tool. The more adventurous are now taking distance education courses using the Web. Jack Wilson, a professor at Rensselaer Polytechnic Institute in Troy, New York, says that traditional students, corporate trainees, and other learners will benefit in coming years from Internet classes and from meeting with far-away students in real time. While "18- to 21-year-old college students will probably still want to have the university experience," he says, live online classes will allow those students to learn and collaborate with others in different countries and take advantage of resources not available on campus. "Live online learning lets students in Hong Kong work with those in the United States on a routine basis," he says. As chairman of software developer LearnLinc (www.learnlinc.com, now part of a company called Mentergy), Wilson is putting his ideas into practice and helping others use live Internet learning.

Virtual environments have become the norm in networked entertainment, but they haven't found widespread use in education. Ray Kurzweil, author of *The Age of Spiritual Machines* (Viking, 1999), says that will change in the next 10 years. He says virtual environments will be ubiquitous by 2010, being used in many contexts, including secondary schools. Says Bruce Campbell of the University of Washington's Human Interface Technology Laboratory, "I think it might be another 15 years or so," noting that while the technology may be ready much sooner, it may not be accepted by educators.

Certain disciplines will benefit from virtual environments sooner than others will. Campbell says that fields such as chemistry, astronomy, physics, and meteorology "are the natural ones" for teaching through virtual environments. "They let you interact with

things at a scale you can't easily interact with in the real world," he says.

John Sutherland of the University of Abertay in Dundee, Scotland, says other fields are appropriate for this technology as well. "Surgery is already a strong virtual learning environment," he says, "but primarily for very high-end operations that are rare, costly, and risky." Sutherland says virtual environments will probably not aid the teaching of abstract topics, such as computer programming.

Though virtual reality has yet to live up to the expectations that arose out of the cyberpunk fiction of the 1980s and '90s, an even more outlandish notion advanced by cyberpunks—downloading knowledge directly into the brain—is increasingly discussed with a straight face.

"In order to download knowledge, we will need the ability to directly access and augment the neural networks in which memory and knowledge are stored," Kurzweil says. To do this, he says we would use "massively distributed nanobot-based neural implants," tiny networked robots that will meld directly to our neurons to offer enhanced senses and improved cognitive capabilities. The implants could also provide a truly immersive virtual environment experience, or allow us to experience our usual senses. While Kurzweil asserts that the technology is about three decades away, he points out that 5mm-wide robots, called "smart dust," are already being developed at the University of California at Berkeley.

2004	2-D and 3-D simulations become standard tools in teaching some subjects.
2012	The average U.S. high schooler studies in at least one immersive virtual environment.
2020	Artificial intelligence teachers become better than the real thing.
2032	Nanobot neural implants enhance the brain directly.

DISCUSSION QUESTIONS

1. Which of the future visions presented here seem most realistic to you? Explain your answer.
2. Which of the future visions presented here seem most appealing to you? Explain your answer.

Summary

PCs come in a variety of shapes and sizes, but they're all made up of two things—the physical parts of the computer, called hardware, and the software instructions that tell the hardware what to do. The PC's system unit contains the CPU, which controls the other components, including memory, disk drives, and monitor screens. The keyboard and mouse enable a person to communicate with the computer, which sends information back to the person through displays on the monitor.

The computer's operating system software takes care of details of the computer's operation. Application software provides specific tools for computer users.

PCs can be networked to other computers using cables, radio waves, or other means. A computer can also connect to a network through standard phone lines using a modem.

The Internet is a global network of computer networks used for education, commerce, and communication. Electronic mail is the most popular Internet application. Email enables almost instant communication among Internet users.

A Web browser is a PC application that provides easy access to the World Wide Web — a wide-ranging array of multimedia information on the Internet. Web pages are interconnected by hyperlinks that make it easy to follow information trails. Search engines serve as indices for the Web, locating pages with subject matter that matches keywords.

The *Computer Confluence* CD-ROM and Companion Web site use PC multimedia and Internet technology to enhance and expand the information and ideas presented in this book.

Chapter Review

▼ Key Terms

(Terms introduced in this chapter will be revisited in later chapters.)

application program (p. 8)
button (p. 7)
CD-Rom drive (p. 5)
click (p. 7)
CPU (p. 4)
desktop (p. 10)
diskette (p. 5)
document (p. 8)
double-click (p. 7)
drag (the mouse) (p. 7)
electronic mail (email, e-mail) (p. 14)
hard disk (p. 5)

hardware (p. 4)
hyperlink (p. 16)
Internet (p. 13)
keyboard (p. 5)
memory (p. 5)
menu (p. 7)
monitor (p. 5)
mouse (p. 5)
open (p. 7)
operating system (OS) (p. 8)
password (p. 12)
personal computer (PC) (p. 4)

printer (p. 5)
save (p. 6)
search engine (p. 17)
software (p. 8)
user name (p. 14)
URL (uniform resource locator) (p. 16)
Web browser (p. 16)
Web page (p. 16)
Web site (p. 16)
World Wide Web (WWW) (p. 16)

▼ Interactive Quiz Questions

1. The *Computer Confluence* CD-ROM contains self-test quiz questions related to this chapter, including multiple choice, true or false, and matching questions.
2. The *Computer Confluence* Web site, **www.prenhall.com/beekman**, contains self-test exercises related to this chapter. Follow the instructions for taking a quiz. After you've completed your quiz, you can email the results to your instructor.

The Web site also contains open-ended discussion questions called Internet Explorations. Discuss one or more of the Internet Exploration questions at the section for this chapter.

▼ Review Questions

1. Briefly define or describe each of the key terms listed in the "Key Terms" section.
2. How are hardware and software related?
3. Which computer component is the most critical to the computer's functioning, and why?
4. Which two computer components are most often used by people for getting information into PCs?
5. What is the difference between operating system software and application software?
6. List some ways that a computer might be connected to a network.
7. Give examples of ways email can change the way you communicate with other people.
8. How can you use hyperlinks to explore the World Wide Web? Give an example.
9. How can you find a site on the Web if you don't know the URL?

▼ Discussion Questions

1. Spend some time exploring the *Computer Confluence* CD-ROM. What features of the software do you think will be most helpful to you? Why?
2. Spend some time exploring the *Computer Confluence* Web Site, **www.prenhall.com/beekman**. What features of the site do you think will be most helpful to you? Why?

▼ Project

1. Keep a log of your progress as you use the *Computer Confluence* book, CD-ROM, and Web site. Make notes on which features are most helpful and which are least helpful. When you finish the book and related material, you may want to send a summary of your log to the author c/o Prentice Hall. Your notes will help make future editions of *Computer Confluence* more useful for others.

 # Sources and Resources

At the end of every chapter of *Computer Confluence*, you'll find an annotated list of valuable resources for learning more about the subjects covered in the chapter. Some of these resources are magazines, journals, and other periodicals that with particularly good coverage of computers, the Internet, and the impact of technology on our lives. Some of the resources are books, both fiction and nonfiction, that provide insights into the world of information technology. Some are films and videos that vividly portray concepts and issues related to the technology. And, of course, some are Web sites that can take you far beyond the basic ideas covered in this book. If you want to learn more, start with these sources and resources.

Part I
Approaching Computers
Hardware and Software Fundamentals

1

Computer Currents:
From Calculation to Connection

After you read this chapter you should be able to:

Characterize what a computer is and what it does

Describe several ways computers play a critical role in modern life

Discuss the circumstances and ideas that led to the development of the modern computer

Describe several trends in the evolution of modern computers

Comment on the fundamental difference between computers and other machines

Explain the relationship between hardware and software

Outline the four major types of computers in use today and describe their principal uses

Describe how the explosive growth of the Internet is changing the way people use computers and information technology

Discuss the social and ethical impact of information technology on our society

▼ **In this chapter:**

The evolution of digital technology

The many faces and forms of computers

How the Internet changed everything

Our digital culture: social transformation and ethical questions

Self-study questions and projects

Minireviews of helpful resources for further study

…and more.

▼ **On the CD-ROM:**

Video lab highlighting a cutting edge internet company

An activity on a new security technology

Instant access to glossary and key word references

Interactive self-study quizzes

…and more.

▼ **On the Web:**

www.prenhall.com/beekman

Important documents tracing the history of computers, the Internet, and digital technology

Links to Web sites of the most important computer companies

A quick tour of some of the most popular and innovative sites on the Web

Self-study exercises

…and more.

Charles Babbage, Lady Lovelace, and the Mother of All Computers

The Analytical Engine has no **pretensions whatever** to originate anything. It can do **whatever** we know how **to order it** to perform.

—Augusta Ada King, Countess of Lovelace

The Analytical Engine Lady Lovelace referred to was the mother of all computers, conceived by Charles Babbage, a 19th-century mathematics professor at Cambridge University. Babbage was an eccentric genius known by the public for his war with street musicians. He calculated that they sapped him of 25 percent of his working power, and he strove to have them outlawed. But Babbage was more than a crank; his many inventions included the skeleton key, the speedometer, and… the computer.

Babbage's computer vision grew out of frustration with the tedious and error-prone process of creating mathematical tables. In 1823, he received a grant from the British government to develop a "difference engine"—a mechanical device for performing repeated additions. Two decades earlier, Joseph-Marie Charles Jacquard, a French textile maker, had developed a loom that could automatically reproduce woven patterns by reading information encoded in patterns of holes punched in stiff paper cards. After learning of

Charles Babbage (1791–1871)

Jacquard's programmable loom, Babbage abandoned the difference engine for a more ambitious enterprise: an **Analytical Engine** that could be programmed with punched cards to carry out any calculation to 20 digits of accuracy. Babbage's design included the four basic components found in every modern computer: components for performing the basic functions of input, output, processing, and storage.

Augusta Ada King, Countess of Lovelace (sometimes erroneously called "Ada Lovelace"), the daughter of poet Lord Byron, visited Babbage and the Analytical Engine. Ada corresponded regularly with him. She is often called the first computer

Analytical Engine

programmer, because she wrote a plan for using the Analytical Engine to calculate sequences of Bernoulli numbers. But programmer is probably the wrong term to describe her actual contribution. She was more of an interpreter and promoter of Babbage's visionary work.

Babbage was obsessed with completing the Analytical Engine. Eventually the government withdrew financial support; there simply wasn't enough public demand to justify the ever-increasing cost. The technology of the time was not sufficient to turn their ideas into reality. The world wasn't ready for computers, and it wouldn't be for another 100 years. ❱

Augusta Ada King, Countess of Lovelace (1815–1852)

Computers are so much a part of modern life that we hardly notice them. But computers are everywhere, and we'd certainly notice them if they suddenly stopped working. Imagine…

Computer screens and television screens populate today's television control rooms.

Living without Computers

You wake up with the sun well above the horizon and realize your alarm clock hasn't gone off. You wonder if you've overslept. You have a big research project to finish today. The face of your digital wristwatch stares back at you blankly. The TV and radio are no help; you can't find a station on either one. You can't even get the time by telephone, because the telephone doesn't work either.

The morning newspaper is missing from your doorstep. You'll have to guess the weather forecast by looking out the window. No music to dress by this morning—your CD player refuses your requests. How about some breakfast? Your automatic coffeemaker refuses to be programmed; your microwave oven is on strike too.

Computers are used to coordinate thousands of Union Pacific trains in this high-tech Omaha control room.

You decide to go out for breakfast. Your car won't start. In fact, the only cars moving are at least 15 years old. The lines at the subway are unbelievable. People chatter nervously about the failure of the subway's computer-controlled scheduling device.

You duck into a coffee shop and find long lines of people waiting while cashiers handle transactions by hand. While you're waiting, you join the conversation that's going on around you. People seem more interested in talking to each other since all the usual tools of mass communication have failed.

You're down to a couple of dollars in cash, so you stop after breakfast at an automated teller machine. Why bother?

You return home to wait for the book you ordered online. You soon realize that you're in for a long wait; planes aren't flying because air traffic control facilities aren't working. You head for the local library to see if the book is in stock. Of course, it's going to be tough to find since the book catalog is computerized.

As you walk home, you speculate on the implications of a worldwide computer failure. How will people function in high-tech, high-rise office buildings that depend on computer systems to control everything from elevators to humidity? Will electric power plants be able to function without computer control? What will happen to patients in computerized medical facilities? What about satellites that are kept in orbit by computer-run control systems? Will the financial infrastructure collapse without computers to process and communicate transactions? Will the world be a safer place if all computer-controlled weapons are grounded?

This cart's built-in computer helps golfers navigate the course.

Our story could go on, but the message should be clear enough by now. Computers are everywhere, and our lives are affected in all kinds of ways by their operation—and nonoperation. It's truly amazing that computers have infiltrated our lives so thoroughly in such a short time.

Computers in Perspective: An Evolving Idea

> Consider the past and you shall **know the future**.
> —Chinese Proverb

While the computer has been with us for only about half a century, its roots go back to a time long before Charles Babbage conceived of the Analytical Engine in 1823. This extraordinary machine is built on centuries of insight and intellectual effort.

Before Computers

Computers grew out of a human need to quantify. Early humans were content to count with fingers or rocks. As cultures became more complex, so did their counting tools. The abacus (a type of counting tool and calculator used by the Babylonians, the Chinese, and others for thousands of years) and the Hindu-Arabic number system are examples of early calculating tools that had an immediate and profound effect on society. (Imagine trying to conduct business without a number system that allows for easy addition and subtraction.)

The Analytical Engine had little impact until a century after its invention, when it served as a blueprint for the first real programmable computer. Virtually every computer in use today follows the basic plan laid out by Babbage and Lady Lovelace.

The Information-Processing Machine

Like the Analytical Engine, the computer is a machine that changes information from one form to another. All computers take in information (**input**) and give out information (**output**) as shown here.

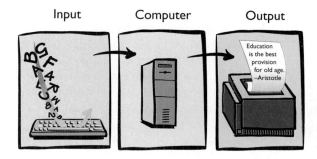

Because information can take many forms, the computer is an incredibly versatile tool, capable of everything from computing federal income taxes to guiding the missiles those taxes buy. For calculating taxes, the input to the computer might be numbers representing wages, other income, deductions, exemptions, and tax tables, and the output might be the number representing the taxes owed. If the computer is deploying a missile, the input might be radio and radar signals for locating the missile and the target, and the output might be electrical signals to control the flight path of the missile. Amazingly enough, the same computer could be used to accomplish both of these tasks.

How can a machine be so versatile? The computer's flexibility isn't hidden in **hardware**—the physical parts of the computer system. The secret of its functionality is in its **software**, or **programs**—the instructions that tell the hardware how to transform the input **data** (information in a form it can read) into the necessary output.

Whether a computer is performing a simple calculation or producing a complex animation, a program controls the process from beginning to end. In effect, changing programs can turn the computer into a different tool. Because it can be programmed to perform various tasks, the typical modern computer is a general-purpose tool.

The First Real Computers

Although Lady Lovelace predicted that the Analytical Engine might someday compose music, the scientists and mathematicians who designed and built the first working computers a century later had a more modest goal: to create machines capable of doing repetitive mathematical calculations. Here are some landmark examples:

> First we shape our tools, thereafter **they shape us**.
>
> —Marshall McLuhan

▶ In 1939 a young German engineer named Konrad Zuse completed the first programmable, general-purpose digital computer—a machine he built from electric relays to automate the process of doing engineering calculations. "I was too lazy to calculate and so I invented the computer," Zuse recalls. In 1941, Zuse and a friend asked the German government for funds to build a faster electronic computer to help crack enemy codes. The Nazi military establishment turned him down, confident that their aircraft could quickly win the war without the aid of sophisticated calculating devices.

▶ At about the same time, the British government was assembling a top-secret team of mathematicians and engineers to crack Nazi military codes. In 1943 the team, led by mathematician Alan Turing and others, completed Colossus, considered by many to be the first electronic digital computer. This special-purpose computer successfully broke codes, allowing British military intelligence to eavesdrop on even the most secret German messages throughout most of the war.

▶ In 1939, Iowa State University professor John Atanasoff, seeking a tool to help his graduate students solve long, complex differential equations, developed what could have been the first electronic digital computer, the Atanasoff-Berry Computer (ABC). His university neglected to patent Atanasoff's ground-breaking machine, and Atanasoff never managed to turn it into a fully operational product. The International Business Machines Corporation responded to his queries by telling him "IBM will never be interested in an electronic computing machine."

▶ Harvard professor Howard Aiken was more successful in financing the automatic general-purpose calculator he was developing. In 1944, with a million dollars from IBM, he completed the Mark I. This 51-foot-long, 8-foot-tall monster used noisy electromechanical relays to calculate five or six times faster than a person could, but it was far slower than a modern $5 pocket calculator.

▶ After consulting with Atanasoff and studying the ABC, John Mauchly teamed up with J. Presper Eckert to help the U.S. effort in World War II by constructing a machine to calculate trajectory tables for new guns. The machine was the ENIAC (Electronic Numerical Integrator and Computer), a 30-ton behemoth with 18,000 vacuum tubes that failed at an average of once every seven minutes. When it was running, it could calculate 500 times faster than the existing electromechanical calculators—about as fast as a modern pocket calculator. Nevertheless, it failed in its first mission: It wasn't completed until two months after the end of the war. Still, it convinced its creators that large-scale computers were commercially feasible. After the war, Mauchly and Eckert started a private company called Sperry and created UNIVAC I, the first general-purpose commercial computer. UNIVAC I went to work for the U.S. Census Bureau in 1951.

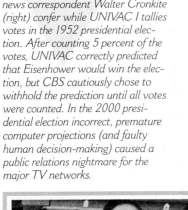

J. Presper Eckert (middle) and CBS news correspondent Walter Cronkite (right) confer while UNIVAC I tallies votes in the 1952 presidential election. After counting 5 percent of the votes, UNIVAC correctly predicted that Eisenhower would win the election, but CBS cautiously chose to withhold the prediction until all votes were counted. In the 2000 presidential election incorrect, premature computer projections (and faulty human decision-making) caused a public relations nightmare for the major TV networks.

Evolution and Acceleration

> Invention breeds
> **invention**.
> —Ralph Waldo Emerson

Computer hardware evolved rapidly from those early days, with new technologies replacing old every few years. Historians marked major hardware changes in the first decades of the computer age by defining four generations of computers. UNIVAC I and other computers in the early 1950s were, according to this common classification scheme, first-generation computers. This was the era of machines built around vacuum tubes—light-bulb-sized glass tubes that housed switching circuitry. First-generation machines were big, expensive, and finicky. Only a big institution like a major bank or the U.S. government could afford a computer, not to mention the climate-controlled computer center needed to house it and the staff of technicians needed to program it and keep it running. But with all their faults, first-generation computers quickly became indispensable tools for scientists, engineers, and other professionals.

The transistor, invented in 1948, could perform the same function as a vacuum tube by transferring electricity across a tiny resistor. Transistors were first used in a computer in 1956, an event generally viewed as the beginning of the computer's second generation. Computers that used transistors were radically smaller, more reliable, and less expensive than tube-based computers. Because of improvements in software at about the same time, these machines were also much easier and faster to program and use. As a result, computers became more widely used in business as well as in science and engineering.

But America's fledgling space program, determined to surpass the Soviet satellite successes of the 1950s, needed computers that were even smaller and more powerful than the second-generation machines, so researchers developed technology that enabled them to pack hundreds of transistors into a single **integrated circuit** on a tiny **silicon chip**. By the mid-1960s, transistor-based computers were replaced by smaller, more powerful third-generation machines built around the new integrated circuits.

Integrated circuits rapidly replaced early transistors for the same reasons that transistors superseded vacuum tubes:

These three devices define the first three computer generations. The vacuum tube (left) housed a few switches in a space about the size of a light bulb. The transistor (middle) allowed engineers to pack the same circuitry in a semiconductor package that was smaller, cooler, and much more reliable. The first silicon chips packed several transistors' worth of circuitry into a speck much smaller than a single transistor.

▶ *Reliability.* Machines built with integrated circuits were less prone to failure than their predecessors, because the chips could be rigorously tested before installation.

▶ *Size.* Single chips could replace entire circuit boards containing hundreds or thousands of transistors, making it possible to build much smaller machines.

▶ *Speed.* Because electricity had shorter distances to travel, the smaller machines were markedly faster than their predecessors.

▶ *Efficiency.* Since chips were so small, they used less electrical power. As a result, they created less heat.

▶ *Cost.* Mass production techniques made it easy to manufacture inexpensive chips.

Just about every breakthrough in computer technology since the dawn of the computer age has presented similar advantages over the technology it replaced.

The relentless progress of the computer industry is illustrated by **Moore's Law**. In 1965 Gordon Moore, the chairman of Intel, predicted half-seriously that the power of a silicon chip of the same price would double about every 18 months for at least two decades. So far Moore's prediction has been uncannily accurate!

The Microcomputer Revolution

Computer cost-effectiveness has risen **100 millionfold** since the late 1950s— a 100,000-fold rise in **power** times a thousandfold drop in **cost**.

—George Gilder

The inventions of the vacuum tube, the transistor, and the silicon chip had tremendous impact on our society, which is why they're used as computer-generational boundaries by many historians. But none of these had a more profound effect than the invention in 1971 of the first **microprocessor**—the critical components of a complete computer housed on a tiny silicon chip. The development of the microprocessor by Intel engineers marked the beginning of the fourth generation of computers and the end of an era when it made sense to count computer generations. The microprocessor's invention caused immediate and radical changes in the appearance, capability, and availability of computers.

The research and development costs for the first microprocessor were awesome. But once the assembly lines were in place, silicon computer chips could be mass produced cheaply. The raw materials were certainly cheap enough; silicon, the main ingredient in beach sand, is the second most common element (behind oxygen) in the Earth's crust.

U.S. companies soon flooded the marketplace with watches and pocket calculators built around inexpensive microprocessors. The economic effect was immediate: Mechanical calculators and slide rules became obsolete overnight; electronic hobbyists became wealthy entrepreneurs, and California's San Jose area gained the nickname Silicon Valley when dozens of microprocessor manufacturing companies sprouted and grew there.

The **microcomputer revolution** began in the late 1970s when companies like Apple, Tandy, and Commodore introduced low-cost, typewriter-sized computers as powerful as many of the room-sized computers that had come before. **Personal computers**, or **PCs**, as microcomputers

Today a single chip the size of your fingernail can contain the equivalent of millions of transistors.

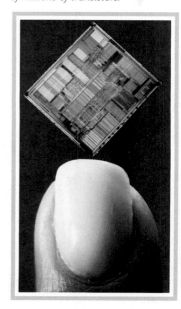

The microcomputer revolution didn't just increase the number of computers in offices; it opened up entirely new possibilities for computer habitats. This police officer uses a computer to record case notes and track crime information. David Solove uses a portable computer, a digital camera, and a scanner to produce an online diary of circus life for his family and friends. The marine biologist uses a laptop computer to record research notes and analyze data in the field.

have come to be known, are now common in offices, factories, homes, schools, and just about everywhere else. Because chip manufacturers have been so successful at obeying Moore's Law, microcomputers have steadily increased in speed and power during the last two decades. At the same time, personal computers have taken over many tasks formerly performed by large computers, and every year people find new, innovative ways to harness these tiny workhorses.

The 1950s and 1960s represented an era of *institutional computing*. Corporations and government institutions used the large, expensive computers of the time to transform and streamline their operations, and the world changed as a result. Small computers had an even greater impact on society during the decades that followed—the *personal computer era*. Still, desktop computers haven't completely replaced big computers, which have also evolved. Today's world is populated with a variety of computers, each particularly well suited to specific tasks.

Computers Today: A Brief Taxonomy

An IBM electronic calculator speeds through **thousands of intricate computations** so quickly that on many complex problems, it's just like having **150 extra engineers...**
—IBM ad showing dozens of slide-rule-toting engineers in *National Geographic*, February, 1952

People today work with mainframe computers, supercomputers, workstations, notebook computers, handheld computers, embedded computers, and, of course, PCs. Even though they're based on the same technology, these machines have important differences.

Mainframes and Supercomputers

Computer-driven display systems are important fixtures in meeting rooms.

Before the microcomputer revolution, most information processing was done on **mainframe computers**—room-sized machines with price tags to match. Today large organizations, such as banks and airlines, still use mainframes for big computing jobs. Today's mainframes are smaller and cheaper than their ancestors; a typical mainframe today might be the size of a refrigerator and cost around a million U.S. dollars. These industrial-strength computers are largely invisible to the general public, because they're hidden away in climate-controlled rooms.

But the fact that you can't see them doesn't mean you don't use them. When you make an airline reservation or deposit money in your bank account, a mainframe computer is involved in the transaction. Your travel agent and your bank teller communicate with a mainframe using a computer **terminal**—a combination keyboard and screen that transfers information to and from the computer. The computer might be in another room or another country.

A mainframe computer can communicate with several users simultaneously through a technique called **timesharing**. For example, a timesharing system allows travel agents all over the country to make reservations using the same computer and the same information at the same time.

Timesharing also makes it possible for users with diverse computing needs to share expensive computing equipment. Many research scientists and engineers, for example, need more mathematical computing power than they can get from personal computers. Their computing needs might require a powerful mainframe computer. A timesharing machine can simultaneously serve the needs of scientists and engineers in different departments working on a variety of projects.

Terminals like the one in the photo on the right make it possible for ticket agents all over the world to send information to a single mainframe computer like the one shown on the left.

Many researchers can't get the computing power they need from a mainframe computer; traditional "big iron" simply isn't fast enough for their calculation-intensive work such as weather forecasting, telephone network design, simulated car crash testing, oil exploration, computer animation, and medical imaging. These power users need to have access to the fastest, most powerful computers made. Super fast, super powerful computers are called **supercomputers** or **high-performance computers**.

Until a few years ago people commonly referred to another class of multiuser machine called the *minicomputer*. According to traditional definitions minicomputers were smaller and less expensive than mainframes but larger and more powerful than personal computers. But most of today's mainframes are no bigger than yesterday's minicomputers, and most desktop computers are more powerful than those early minis. By most accounts, the minicomputer is history.

The Blue Mountain supercomputer at the U.S. Department of Energy's Los Alamos National Laboratory can perform 1.6 trillion operations per second. The machine is used to simulate nuclear tests and perform intensive calculations for other research projects.

Workstations and PCs

For many applications the minicomputer has been replaced by a **server**—a computer designed to provide software and other resources to other computers over a network. Just about any computer can be used as a server, but some computers are specifically designed with this purpose in mind. (Networks and servers are discussed later in this chapter and in later chapters.)

For other applications, such as large-scale scientific data analysis, the minicomputer has been replaced by the workstation—a high-end desktop computer with massive computing power at a fraction of the cost. **Workstations** are widely used by scientists, engineers, financial analysts, designers, and animators whose work involves intensive computations. Although many workstations are capable of supporting multiple users simultaneously, in practice they're typically used by only one person at a time.

Of course, like many computer terms, *workstation* means different things to different people. Some people refer to all desktop computers and terminals as workstations. Those who reserve the term for the most powerful desktop machines admit that the line separating workstations and high-end personal computers is fading. As workstations become less expensive and personal computers become more powerful, the line becomes as much a marketing distinction as a technical one.

This engineer uses a workstation to analyze the temperature distribution in electronic telecommunications equipment.

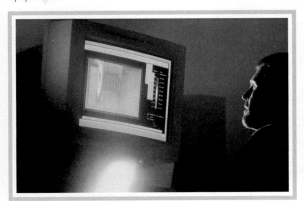

Most computer users don't need the power of a scientific workstation to do their day-to-day business. A modern **personal computer (PC)** has plenty of computing power for word processing, accounting, and other common applications. No surprise there—today's personal computers are far more powerful than the mainframes that dominated the world of computing a human generation ago. A personal computer, as the name implies, is almost always dedicated to serving a single user.

A word about terminology: The terms *personal computer* and *PC* occasionally generate confusion because in 1981 IBM named its desktop computer the IBM Personal Computer. That's why the terms *personal computer* and *PC* often are used to describe only IBM computers or machines compatible with IBM hardware. ("The office has a network of Macs and PCs.") But in another context, PC might describe any general-purpose single-user computer. ("Every student needs a PC to connect to the Internet.")

Portable Computers

Two decades ago the terms *personal computer* and *desktop computer* were interchangeable; virtually all PCs were desktop computers. Today, however, one of the fastest growing segments of the PC market involves machines that aren't tied to the desktop—**portable computers**.

Of course, portability is a relative term. The first "portable" computers were 20-pound suitcases with fold-out keyboards and small TV-like screens. Today those "luggable" computers have been replaced by flat-screen, battery-powered **laptop computers** that are so light you can rest one on your lap while you work or carry it in a briefcase when it's closed.

Today's laptop, commonly called a **notebook computer**, weighs between 3 and 8 pounds. Many laptops compare favorably with powerful desktop PCs. Extra-light, stripped down notebooks are sometimes called **subnotebooks**. To keep size and weight down, manufacturers often leave out some components that would be standard equipment on desktop machines. For example, some laptops don't have built-in CD-ROM or diskette drives. Some have expansion bays that allow these devices to be inserted one at a time. Most have ports that allow external drives to be attached with cables. A few models can be expanded with **docking stations**. A docking station enables a user to connect the laptop to an external monitor, keyboard, mouse, and disk drives. Many mobile workers use docking stations to turn their laptops into full-featured desktop PCs when they return to their offices. Even without docking stations, a laptop can be easily connected to peripherals and networks when it's deskbound.

Handheld computers, which are small enough to tuck into a jacket pocket, serve the needs of users who value mobility over a full-sized keyboard and screen. Docking **cradles** for handheld computers enable them to share information with desktop and laptop PCs.

Personal computers today come in a variety of forms. Apple's iMac includes the CPU, monitor, and storage devices in an all-in-one device; only the keyboard and mouse are separate. IBM's NetVista PC is a more traditional design, with monitor separate from the system unit containing the CPU and storage.

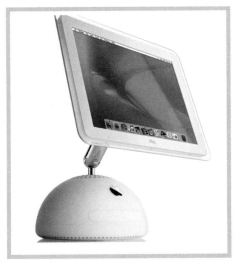

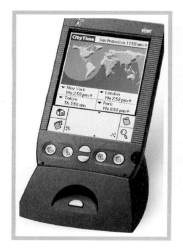

Handheld computers are sometimes called **personal digital assistants (PDAs)** or **palmtop computers**.

Size notwithstanding, most portable computers in all their variations are general-purpose computers built around microprocessors similar to those that drive desktop models. But portability comes at a price—portable computers generally cost more than comparable desktop machines. They're also more difficult to upgrade when newer hardware components become available.

Embedded Computers and Special-Purpose Computers

Not all computers are general-purpose machines. Many are **special-purpose (dedicated) computers** that perform specific tasks, ranging from controlling the temperature and humidity in a high-rise office building to monitoring your heart rate while you work out. **Embedded computers** enhance all kinds of consumer goods: wristwatches, toys, game machines, stereos, video cassette recorders, and ovens. In fact, more than 90 percent of the world's microprocessors are hidden inside common household and electronic devices! Because of embedded computers, a typical new car probably has more computing power than the salesperson's PC! Embedded computers are also used in industry, the military, and science for controlling a variety of hardware devices, including robots. Ninety percent of all microprocessors are embedded in some kind of consumer or electronic device other than a PC.

Most special-purpose computers are, at their core, similar to general-purpose personal computers. But unlike their desktop cousins, these special-purpose machines typically have their programs etched in silicon so they can't be altered. When a program is immortalized on a silicon chip, it becomes **firmware**—a hybrid of hardware and software.

The portable computers shown here represent just a small sample of sizes and types available today. Apple's Titanium Powerbook G4 (above left) is a full-featured multimedia computer in a slim, sleek package. The IBM ThinkPad (above right) can be converted from a laptop to a desktop PC using the docking station shown here. The Handspring Visor Prism is a handheld computer designed to accept input from a stylus; it's shown here in a cradle that provides a communication link to a PC. The RIM Blackberry is a handheld computer designed for email communication using a tiny keyboard. The Compaq iPac Pocket PC uses a version of the Windows operating system designed for handheld computers.

Computer Connections: The Internet Revolution

Embedded computers are so common in today's world that they're all but invisible. This experimental children's doll is a robot in disguise. The Independence™ 3000 IBOT Transporter™ is an intelligent wheelchair that allows disabled people to climb and descend stairs, "stand up" on two wheels, and even stroll on the beach. The dashboard computer in this car provides maps and navigation information for the driver.

All persons are caught in an **inescapable network of mutuality**, tied in a single garment of destiny. Whatever affects **one** directly, affects **all** indirectly. . . .
—Martin Luther King, Jr.

We've seen how breakthroughs in switching, storage, and processor technology have produced new types of computers. Each of these technological advances had an impact on our society as people found new ways to put computers to work. Most historians stopped counting computer generations after the microcomputer became commonplace; it was hard to imagine another breakthrough having as much impact as the tiny microprocessor. But while the world was still reeling from the impact of the microcomputer revolution, another information technology revolution was quietly building up steam: a network revolution. If current trends continue, we may look back on the 1990s as the beginning of the era of *interpersonal computing*.

The Emergence of Networks

The first computers were large, expensive, self-contained machines that could process only one job at a time. As demand for computing power grew, computer scientists searched for ways to make scarce computer resources more accessible. The invention of timesharing in the 1960s allowed multiple users to connect to a single mainframe computer through individual terminals. When personal computers started replacing terminals, many users found they had all the computing power they needed on their desktops. Still, there were advantages to linking some of these computers in local-area networks (LANs). When clusters of computers were networked, they could share scarce, expensive resources. For example, a single high-speed printer could meet the needs of an entire office if it was connected to a network. As a bonus, people could use computers to send and receive messages electronically through the networks.

The advantages of electronic communication and resource sharing were multiplied when smaller networks were joined to larger networks. Emerg-ing telecommunication technology eventually allowed wide-area networks (WANs) to span continents and oceans. A remote computer could connect to a network through standard telephone lines by using a modem—an electronic device that could translate computer data into signals compatible with the telephone system. Banks, government agencies, and other large, geographically distributed institutions gradually built information-processing systems to take advantage of long-distance networking technology. But for most computer users outside of these organizations, networking was not the norm. People saw computers as tools for doing calculations, storing data, and producing paper documents—not as communication tools.

There were exceptions: A group of visionary computer scientists and engineers, with financial backing from the U.S. government, built an experimental network called ARPANET in 1969. This groundbreaking network would become the Internet—the global collection of networks that radically transformed the way the world uses computers.

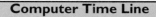

Computer Time Line

These *Time* covers symbolize changes in the way people saw and used computers as they evolved through the last half of this century. Notice that the beginning of each new "era" doesn't mean the end of the old ways of computing; today we live in a world of institutional, personal, and interpersonal computing.

1950   1975   1995

Institutional Computing Era (Starting approximately 1950)	Personal Computing Era (Starting approximately 1975)	Interpersonal Computing Era (Starting approximately 1995)

Characterized by a few large, expensive mainframe computers in climate-controlled rooms; controlled by experts and specialists; used mainly for data storage and calculation.	Characterized by millions of small, inexpensive micro-computers on desktops in offices, schools, homes, factories, and almost everywhere else; controlled mostly by independent users; used mostly for document creation, data storage, and calculation.	Characterized by networks of interconnected computers in offices, homes, schools, vehicles, and almost everywhere else; controlled by users (clients) and network operators; used mostly for communication, document creation, data storage, and calculation.

The Internet Explosion

> It is **not proper** to think of networks as connecting computers. Rather they connect people using computers to **mediate**. The **great success of the Internet** is not technical, but **its human impact**.
>
> —Dave Clark, Internet pioneer, now a senior research scientist at MIT

In its early years, the Internet was the domain of researchers, academics, and government officials. It wasn't designed for casual visitors; users had to know cryptic commands and codes that only a programmer could love. In the 1990s, Internet software took giant leaps forward in usability.

In the early 1950s, the first computers were changing the military, and a few government agencies and big businesses. By 1980, the microcomputer revolution was transforming offices, schools, and some homes. In the early 21st century, the network revolution is likely to have an even bigger impact on our society.

Electronic mail (email) programs first attracted nontechnical people to the Internet. Email software made it easy to send messages across the office or around the world without learning complex codes.

But the biggest changes came in the early 1990s with the development of the World Wide Web (WWW), a vast tract of the Internet accessible to just about anyone who could point to buttons on a computer screen. The Web, as it's often called, led the Internet's transformation from a text-only environment into a multimedia landscape incorporating pictures, animation, sounds, and video. Millions of people connect to the Web each day through Web browsers—programs that, in effect, serve as navigable windows into the Web. Hypertext links loosely tie together millions of Web pages created by diverse authors, making the Web into a massive, ever-changing global information storehouse.

Widespread email and Web use have led to astounding Internet growth in the last decade. In 1994, three million people were connected; seven years later more than 400 million people had connections. More than half of all American households are

This computer-generated 3-D map represents major Internet connections in the United States.

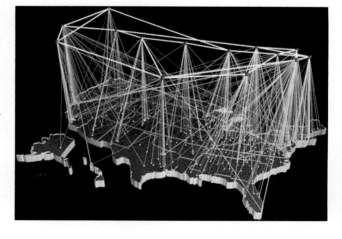

connected to the Internet; before the first decade of the 21st century is over, 90 percent of U.S. households will likely be connected, making the Internet almost as universal as the television and the telephone. The United States leads the world in Internet activity, but the rest of the world is catching up. About one-fifth of all Europeans were online in 2001, and their numbers are rising quickly.

A passenger in a Sao Paulo, Brazil, cab accesses the Internet through a wireless connection.

Internet users tend to be younger, better educated, and wealthier than the rest of the population. But as the Internet's population grows, it looks more like the population at large. According to the U.S. Internet Council, the percentage of African Americans and Hispanics who use the Internet is rising rapidly. More than half of all active Internet users are now female. And while there are still some areas, even in the United States, with no Internet access, those are becoming harder to find. In just about any city on Earth, you can rent time on a PC to check your email or explore the Web.

The Internet is growing faster than television, radio, or any other communication technology that came before it. This growth is largely fueled by the rapid expansion of commerce on the Web. The U.S. Internet economy generates hundreds of billions of dollars in revenues and millions of jobs each year.

The Internet has become so pervasive that many organizations have rebuilt their entire information-processing systems around Internet technology. A growing number of companies are replacing their aging mainframe-and-PC-based systems with **intranets**—private intraorganizational networks based on Internet technology. Intranets mimic the Internet in the ways in which they enable people to transmit, share, and store information within an organization.

Many people believe we'll soon use computers mostly as gateways to intranets and the Internet. In fact, several companies, including IBM, Sun, and Hewlett Packard, are developing and marketing stripped-down computers designed to function mainly as network terminals. These companies don't all agree on exactly what these boxes should include, how much they should be able to do without the aid of a server, or even what they should be called. You might hear people referring to **network computers**, *NCs*, *thin clients*, *net PCs*, or *Windows terminals* when they talk about network-centric machines.

The Wyse Winterm thin client is designed to function only as part of a network, providing network access without the high maintenance costs of traditional PCs.

In spite of their different names and designs, all these machines share two common characteristics: They cost less than typical PCs, because they contain less hardware, and they are easier to maintain, because much of the software can be stored on a central server. Like a TV, a network computer is designed to receive information from elsewhere. But unlike a TV, an NC allows you to send and receive information; it's a two-way connection to the wired world.

Network computers make economic sense in many workplaces, but most of them are not designed for use in homes. But some manufacturers now sell **information appliances** (or *Internet appliances*) that enable home and office users to connect to the Internet without a full-blown PC. (Some people use the terms *Internet appliance* and *information appliance* to refer to network computers in offices and homes; the terminology is, at this point, as fluid as the technology.) For example, Internet telephones have screens and keyboards to enable easy access to email and the Web. **Set-top boxes**, including some game consoles, provide Internet access through television sets. Some handheld computers provide wireless access to the Internet. Even a few cellular phones can display Internet data on tiny screens. Who knows? Future homes and businesses may have dozens of devices—computers, telephones, televisions, stereos, security systems, and even kitchen appliances—continually connected to the Internet, monitoring all kinds of data that can have an impact on our lives and our livelihoods. Whatever happens, it's clear that the Internet is going to play an increasing role in our future.

Millions of homes may soon be connecting to the Internet using televisions through set-top boxes like this one.

Living with Computers

> Just as Michelangelo's contemporaries couldn't have foreseen **abstract expressionism**, we **can't foresee** how people will use the computing medium in the future.
>
> —Clement Mok, in *Designing Business*

In less than a human lifetime, computers have evolved from massive, expensive, error-prone calculators like the Mark I and ENIAC into (mostly) dependable, versatile machines that have worked their way into just about every nook and cranny of modern society. The pioneers who created and marketed the first computers did not foresee these spectacular advances in computer technology.

Thomas Watson, Sr., the founding father of IBM, declared in 1953 that the world would not need more than five computers! And the early pioneers certainly couldn't have predicted the extraordinary social changes that resulted from the computer's rapid evolution. In the time of UNIVAC, who could have imagined Sun workstations, Sony PlayStations, handheld Palms, smart bombs, or dot-coms?

Technological breakthroughs encourage further technological change, so we can expect the rate of change to continue to increase in coming decades. In other words, the technological and social transformations of the past five decades may be dwarfed by the changes that occur over the next half century! It's just a matter of time, and not very much time, before today's state-of-the-art PCs and Palms look as primitive as ENIAC looks to us today. Similarly, today's high-tech society just hints at a future world that we haven't begun to imagine.

What do you really need to know about computers today? The remaining chapters of this book, along with the accompanying CD-ROM and Web site, provide answers to that question by looking at the technology on three levels: explanations, applications, and implications.

Explanations: Clarifying Technology

You don't need to be a computer scientist to coexist with computers. But your encounters with technology will make more sense if you understand a few basic computer concepts. Computers are evolving at an incredible pace; many hardware and software details change every few years. And the Internet is evolving even faster; some suggest that one normal year is equal to several "Internet years." But most of the underlying concepts remain constant as computers and networks evolve. If you understand the basics, you'll find that it's a lot easier to keep up with the changes.

Applications: Computers in Action

Many people define *computer literacy* as the ability to use computers. But because computers are so versatile, you can learn no single set of skills to become computer literate in every situation. **Application programs**, also known simply as **applications**, are the software tools that enable you to use a computer for specific purposes. Many computer applications in science, government, business, and the arts are far too specialized and technical to be of use or of interest to people outside the field. On the other hand, some applications are so flexible that nearly anyone can use them.

Regardless of your background or aspirations, you can almost certainly benefit from knowing a little about the following applications:

▶ *Word processing and desktop publishing.* Word processing is a critical skill for anyone who communicates in writing—on paper or on the Web. Desktop-publishing software can transform written words into polished, visually exciting publications.

▶ *Spreadsheets and other number-crunching applications.* In business, the electronic spreadsheet is the personal computer application that pays the rent—or at least calculates it. If you work with numbers of any kind, spreadsheets and statistical software can help you turn those numbers into insights.

▶ *Databases.* Word processors may be the most popular standalone-PC applications, but databases reign supreme in the world of mainframes. Of course, databases are widely used on PCs, too. Even if you don't have database software on a PC, you can apply database-searching skills to find books in your library—or just about anything on the Internet.

11th century movable type, decimal number system, musical notation

12th century modern abacus

15th century Gutenberg's printing press

16th century algebraic symbols, lead pencil

17th century calculus, Pascal's calculator, probability, binary arithmetic, newspapers, mailboxes

18th century typewriter, three-color printing, industrial revolution

19th century automated loom, Analytical Engine, telegraph, vacuum tube, cathode ray tube, telephone, color photograph, Hollerith's data-processing machine, radio, sound recordings

Early 20th century assembly-line automated production, analog computer, television, motion pictures

1939 Atanasoff creates the first digital computer

1939 Zuse completes first programmable, general-purpose computer

1945 Von Neumann proposes storing programs as data

1946 Mauchly and Eckert design ENIAC

1954 IBM makes first mass-produced computer

1955 Sony introduces portable transistor radio

1956 Bell Labs build first transistorized computer

1962 DEC introduces minicomputer

1962 first timesharing operating system

1963 Doug Engelbart patents mouse

1969 first person on moon

1969 First microprocessor

1970 ROM developed

1975 Cray-1 supercomputer is introduced

1977 Xerox pioneers graphical user interface

1984 Apple introduces the Macintosh

1984 Volkswagen loses hundreds of millions to computer fraud

1988 First fiber-optic trans-Atlantic cable

1990 Microsoft introduces Windows 3.0 for IBM-compatible computers

1992 several pen-based computers and hand-held communications devices introduced

1993 computer companies, phone companies, and cable TV companies form alliances to create new interactive media

1996 PCs outsell TVs in the U.S. for the first time

1996 Palm handheld computer introduces as "Pilot" by US Robotics

1996 WebTV ships boxes that allow Internet access via TVs

1998 Sharp introduces wristwatch PC

1998 Apple's iMac starts trend toward stylish designer computers

1999 Yugoslav hackers attack one of NATO's computer servers

1999 Internet stock explosion pushes Dow past 10,000

2000 Hackers form a corporation to advise corporations on security

2000 Arizona holds first Internet primary election

2000 Love Bug email virus infiltrates millions of computers worldwide within hours of release

2001 Napster music-sharing Web site loses legal battle over copyrighted music

2001 Peer-to-peer computing take off in spite of Napster's legal proble

The floodgates are open, and information technology ideas are flowing faster all the time.

1943 Turing's Colossus computer breaks Nazi codes

1944 Aiken completes the Mark I

1947 Shockley, Brittain, and Ardeen invent the transistor

1949 Orwell writes 1984, a novel about totalitarianism and computers

1951 computerized banking begins

1957 U.S..S.R. launches Sputnik; U.S. responds by forming ARPA

1959 Jack Kilby and Robert Noyce develop the integrated circuit

1960 laser invented

1964 first prosecuted computer crime

1967 software first sold separately

1969 first nationwide network (ARPANET)

1969 Bell Labs develops UNIX

1972 first home computer game; first email message sent

1974 first microcomputer

1974 first computer-controlled industrial robot

1977 Apple introduces the Apple II

1978 first spreadsheet program

1979 Pac Man appears

1981 IBM introduces its first personal computer

1986 desktop publishing takes off

1986 Connection Machine massively parallel computer introduced

1988 Internet worm cripples 6,000 computers for two days

1990 Hewlett-Packard and others introduce pocket computers

1991 many PC makers launch multimedia products

1991 World Wide Web introduced

1994 Apple introduces Power Macintosh using CPU developed by IBM

1994 White House announces its World Wide Web page

1994 Intel replaces thousands of Pentium processors because of bugs

1995 Microsoft introduces Windows 95 with $200 million marketing campaign

1997 Several companies introduce network computers for Internet access

1997 U.S. Supreme Court defends Internet free speech by striking down Communications Decency Act

1998 U.S. Justice Department sues Microsoft and Intel for separate antitrust violations

1999 free PCs offered to lure Internet subscribers for the first time

1999 Internet email outpaces the post office

1999 Y2K millennium bug captures public attention, costs businesses billions

2000 Denial of service attacks cripple many of the largest commercial Web sites

2000 Microsoft is found guilty of illegal monopolistic practices

2000 AOL buys Time Warner, creating the world's largest media company

2000 Internet economy takes a nose-dive when hundreds of dot-com businesses declare bankruptcy

2001 U.S. government settles Microsoft antitrust suit

2001 Terrorist attacks fuel explosion of interest in security

▶ *Computer graphics*. Computers make it possible to produce and manipulate all kinds of graphics, including charts, drawings, digital photographs—even realistic 3-D animation. As graphics tools become more accessible, visual communication skills become more important for all of us.

▶ *Multimedia*. Modern desktop computers make it easy to edit and manipulate audio and video, opening up creative possibilities for all kinds of potential artists. Multimedia software can combine audio and video with traditional text and graphics, adding new dimensions to computer communication. Interactive multimedia documents, including many Web sites, enable users to explore a variety of paths through media-rich information sources.

▶ *Telecommunication and networking*. A network connection is a door into a world of email, online discussion groups, Web-publishing ventures, and database sharing. If current trends continue, telecommunication—long-distance communication—may soon be the single most important function of computers.

▶ *Artificial intelligence*. Artificial intelligence is the branch of computer science that explores the use of computers in tasks that require intelligence, imagination, and insight—tasks that have traditionally been performed by people rather than machines. Until recently, artificial intelligence was mostly an academic discipline—a field of study reserved for researchers and philosophers. But that research is paying off today with commercial applications that exhibit intelligence, from basic speech recognition to sophisticated expert systems.

▶ *General problem solving*. People use computers to solve problems. Most people use software applications written by professional programmers. But some kinds of problems can't easily be solved with off-the-shelf applications; they require at least some custom programming. Programming languages aren't applications; they're tools that enable you to build and customize applications. Many computer users find their machines become more versatile and valuable when they learn a little about programming.

Implications: Social and Ethical Issues

> True **computer literacy** is not just **knowing how** to make use of computers and **computational ideas**. It is knowing **when it is appropriate** to do so.
>
> —Seymour Papert, in *Mindstorms*

Computers and networks are transforming the world rapidly and irreversibly. Jobs that existed for hundreds of years are eliminated by automation while new careers are built on emerging technology. Start-up businesses create multiple millionaires overnight, while older companies struggle to keep pace with "Internet time." Instant worldwide communication changes the way businesses work and challenges the role of governments. Computers routinely save lives in hospitals, keep space flights on course, and predict the weekend weather.

More than any other recent technology, the computer is responsible for profound changes in our society; we just need to imagine a world without computers to recognize their impact. Of course, computer scientists and computer engineers are not responsible for all the technological turbulence. Developments in fields as diverse as telecommunications, genetic engineering, medicine, and atomic physics contribute to the ever-increasing rate of social change. But researchers in all these fields depend on computers to produce their work.

The future is rushing toward you, and computer technology is a big part of it. It's exciting to consider the opportunities arising from advances in artificial intelligence, multimedia, robotics, and other cutting-edge technologies of the electronic revolution—opportunities in the workplace, the school, and the home. But it's just as important to pay attention to the potential risks. Here's a sampling of the kinds of issues we'll confront in this book:

▶ *The threat to personal privacy posed by large databases and computer networks*. When you use a credit card, buy an airline ticket, place a phone call, visit your doctor, send an email message, or explore the World Wide Web, you are leaving a trail of personal information in one or more computers. Who owns that information? Is it okay for the business or organization that collected the information to share it with others or make it public? Do you have the right to check its accuracy and change it if it's wrong? Do laws protecting individual privacy rights place undue burdens on businesses and governments?

▶ *The hazards of high-tech crime and the difficulty of keeping data secure*. Even if you trust the institutions and businesses that collect data about you, you can't be sure that data will remain secure in their computer systems. Computer crime is at an all-time high, and law enforcement officials are having a difficult time keeping it under control. How can society protect itself from information thieves and high-tech vandals? How can lawmakers write laws about technology that they are just beginning to understand? What kinds of personal risk do you face as a result of computer crime?

▶ *The difficulty of defining and protecting intellectual property in an all-digital age.* Software programs, musical recordings, videos, and books can be difficult and expensive to create. But in our digital age, all of these can easily be copied. What rights do the creators of intellectual property have? Is a teenager who copies music files from the Web a computer criminal? What about a shopkeeper who sells pirated copies of Microsoft Office for $10? Or a student who posts a clip from *Star Wars* on his Web site? Or a musician who uses a two-second sample from a Beatles song in an electronic composition?

▶ *The risks of failure of computer systems.* Computer software is difficult to write, because it is incredibly complex. As a result, no computer system is completely fail-safe. Computer failures routinely cause communication problems, billing errors, lost data, and other inconveniences. But they also occasionally result in power blackouts, telephone system meltdowns, weapons failure, and other potentially deadly problems. Who is responsible for loss of income—or loss of life—caused by software errors? What rights do we have when buying and using software? How can we, as a society, protect ourselves from software disasters?

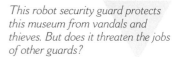

This robot security guard protects this museum from vandals and thieves. But does it threaten the jobs of other guards?

▶ *The threat of automation and the dehumanization of work.* Computers and the Internet fueled unprecedented economic growth in the last decade of the 20th century, producing plenty of new jobs for workers with the right skills. But the new information-based economy has cost many workers— especially older workers—their jobs and their dignity. And many workers today find that their jobs involve little more than tending to machines—and being monitored by bosses with high-tech surveillance devices. As machines replace people in the workplace, what rights do the displaced workers have? Does a worker's right to privacy outweigh an employer's right to read employee email or monitor worker actions? What is the government's role in the protection of worker rights in the high-tech workplace?

▶ *The abuse of information as a tool of political and economic power.* The computer age has produced an explosion of information, and most of that information is concentrated in corporate and government computers. The emergence of low-cost personal computers and the Internet makes it possible for more people to access information and the power that comes with that information. But the majority of the people on the planet have never made a phone call, let alone used a computer. Will the information revolution leave them behind? Do information-rich people and countries have a responsibility to share technology and information with the information-poor?

▶ *The dangers of dependence on complex technology.* One of the biggest news stories of 1999 was the impending threat of massive problems caused by the Y2K bug—the failure of some computer programs on January 1, 2000, because those systems represented the year with only two digits. People stockpiled food and fuel, hid cash and jewels, and prepared for the possibility that the power grid would fail, leaving much of the world's population helpless and hungry. Businesses and governments spent billions of dollars repairing and replacing computer systems, and the Y2K crisis never materialized. But the Y2K scare reminded us how much we have come to depend on this far-from-foolproof technology. Are we, as a society, addicted to computer technology? Should we question new technological innovations before we embrace them? Can we build a future in which technology never takes precedence over humanity?

Today's technology raises fascinating and difficult questions. But these questions pale in comparison to the ones we'll have to deal with as the technology evolves in the coming years:

▶ *The death of privacy.* Governments and private companies alike are installing extensive video surveillance networks to monitor security and track lawbreakers. Computer databases are accumulating more information about you all the time, and networks are making it easier to transmit, share, and merge that information. Will these converging technologies destroy the last of our personal privacy, as some experts have suggested? Is there anything we can do about it?

What impact will computer technology have on traditional cultures that have evolved for thousands of years without computers?

▶ *The blurring of reality.* Virtual reality (VR) is widely used by scientific researchers and computer gamers alike. But if VR doesn't live up to its name, it does suggest a future technology in which artificial environments look and feel real. Rapid developments in Internet technology are likely to lead us to shared virtual environments ranging from shopping malls to gaming centers. Already some people are suffering from computer and Internet addictions. Will these diseases become epidemics when VR feels like real life, only better? Will VR technology be abused by unscrupulous con artists? Should governments limit what's legal when just about anything is possible?

▶ *The evolution of intelligence.* Artificial intelligence research is responsible for many products, including software that can read books to the blind, understand spoken words, and play world-class chess. But tomorrow's machine intelligence will make today's smartest machines look stupid. What rights will human workers have when software can do their jobs better, faster, and smarter? What rights will smart machines have in a world run by humans? Will there come a time when humans aren't smart enough to maintain control of their creations?

▶ *The emergence of bio-digital technology.* Today thousands of people walk around with computer chips embedded in their bodies, helping them to overcome disabilities and lead normal lives. At the same time, researchers are attempting to develop computers that use biology, rather than electronics, as their underlying technology. As the line between organism and machine blurs, what happens to our vision of ourselves? What are the limits of our creative powers, and what are our responsibilities in using those powers?

For better and for worse, we will be coexisting with computers until death do us part. As with any relationship, a little understanding can go a long way. The remaining chapters of this book will help you gain the understanding you need to survive and prosper in a world of computers.

Tech's Double-Edged Sword

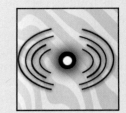

Steven Levy

Is technology good, evil, both, or neither? Writer Steven Levy wrote this powerful essay in the wake of the terrorist attack on the World Trade Center and the Pentagon. The article, first published in the September 24, 2001, issue of Newsweek, *outlines the role technology played in that monumental tragedy. It raises some difficult questions about our relationship to technology in an uncertain future.*

From American Flight 77, en route to death and the Pentagon, lawyer Barbara Olson cell-phoned her husband, the U.S. solicitor general, and told him of the hijacking. On United Flight 93, both Jeremy Glick and Thomas Burnett Jr. called their wives and confided their (apparently successful) intentions to counterattack the hijackers. Others on the stolen planes, as well as dozens trapped in the World Trade Center towers, pulled out their cells to speak one more time to a wife or parent and say "I love you."

The recipients of those calls, while justifiably inconsolable, are undoubtedly grateful for the final opportunity to hear those voices. But before we celebrate another irreplaceable use of wireless communications, consider this: according to government officials, within hours of the explosions, mobile phones of suspected terrorists linked to Osama bin Laden were buzzing with congratulations for the murderous acts. *They use them, too.*

The contrast dramatizes a long-recognized truism: modern technologies that add efficiency, power and wonder to our lives inevitably deliver the same benefits to evildoers. The Internet is no exception. On Sept. 11 the Net seemed like a godsend. Email worked when phones didn't, allowing countless New Yorkers to assure worried friends and families around the world that they were still alive. Web sites were quickly home-brewed to carry lists of companies affected and family members missing. But there is also every likelihood that the terrorists had exploited the Internet as well, using easily available and virtually untraceable accounts on Yahoo or Hotmail, and meeting in ad hoc chat rooms.

Perhaps the terrorists cloaked their planning with cryptography, once an exotic technology, now a commonplace computer utility. Communications could also be shrouded with steganography (hiding messages between pixels of a graphic—a reputed bin Laden technique) or anonymizers (which make email untraceable). Such tools are lionized by freedom-loving "cypherpunks," who have shrugged off potential dark-side usage as a reasonable trade-off for the protection that crypto can provide just plain citizens; as with cars and telephones, the benefits way overwhelm the abuses.

So goes the attitude that has taken us to where we are today, in the best sense and now the worst sense. Technology drives civilization; it augments and amplifies human effort. Our own age is marked by computers and software, which have democratized formerly specialized pursuits. With the right software and the Web, anyone can be a publisher, a music distributor, a photo refinisher… the list is endless.

But the sophistication of our technology also leverages the efforts of those who would destroy. And the very structure of our society—a dense thicket of connections, where skyscrapers hold thousands of workers, "just in time" factories rely on next-day deliveries and air-traffic controllers manage hundreds of planes at once—allows a single act of terror to generate torrents of disruption and pain.

Thus a barely armed band of 19 can slam our nation with the force of many armies. The implements they used were strictly off the shelf. We don't know if they practiced their aeronautical skills by flying into virtual Twin Towers on Microsoft Flight Simulator (which was quickly taken off the shelves). But they did apparently train by renting time on computer-powered flight simulators that democratize the experience of flying a 767. Then, by way of the dime-store technology of small sharpened blades, they were able to take charge of sophisticated commercial airlines. Suddenly those benign carriers were powerful, targetable bombs.

It was a nightmarish fulfillment of science-fiction writer William Gibson's proclamation that the street finds its own uses for technology. The more powerful our tools are, the more dangerous they are when turned against us. For centuries we've accepted that. It's simply the downside of tech.

Sun Microsystems chief scientist Bill Joy has been pondering this downside while writing a book tentatively called "Why the Future Doesn't Need Us." Coincidentally, Joy was in lower Manhattan in the early part of last week. As bad as it was, Joy believes, the tragedy was nothing like what might be possible with biological weaponry. The coming age of biotech will undoubtedly make programmable bacteria and viruses more accessible—to doctors, business and bio-terrorists. "The things I'm worried about haven't happened yet," says Joy.

Virtually no one dares ask whether the balance of technology might tilt too far toward empowering the evil. Who would have a clue of how to address that situation? Human beings have a track record of pursuing what they see as progress and asking questions later. While refusing to think the Unthinkable, we create the circumstances that allow it to occur.

Should we be giving the Unthinkable more consideration as we drive technology ever further? The answer seems obvious. Yet it almost goes without saying that any safeguards we institute won't be perfect. What assurance do we have that future terrorists will not feast on the contents of Pandora's box? "Knowledge itself is dangerous," says Joy. "Scientific information we pursue in an unfettered way is a weapon. And we're not ready to deal with that." Maybe after last week, we are closer.

DISCUSSION QUESTIONS

1. Do you think it's possible to keep technology out of the hands of terrorists and other "evil" people? Explain your answer.
2. Do you think we should be "giving the Unthinkable more consideration" as we develop new technologies? Explain your answer.

Summary

While the basic idea behind a computer goes back to Charles Babbage's 19th-century plan for an Analytical Engine, the first real computers were developed during the 1940s. Computers have evolved at an incredible pace since those early years, becoming consistently smaller, faster, more efficient, more reliable, and less expensive. At the same time, people have devised all kinds of interesting and useful ways to put computers to work to solve problems.

Computers today, like their ancestors, are information-processing machines designed to transform information from one form to another. When a computer operates, the hardware accepts input data from some outside source, transforms the data by following instructions called software, and produces output that can be read by a human or by another machine.

Computers today come in all shapes and sizes, with specific types being well suited for particular jobs. Mainframe computers and supercomputers provide more power and speed than smaller desktop machines, but they are expensive to purchase and operate. Timesharing makes it possible for many users to work simultaneously at terminals connected to these large computers. At the other end of the spectrum, workstations, personal computers, and a variety of portable devices provide computing power for those of us who don't need a mainframe's capabilities. Microprocessors aren't just used in general-purpose computers; they're embedded in appliances, automobiles, and a rapidly growing list of other products.

Connecting to a network enhances the value and power of a computer—it can share resources with other computers and facilitate electronic communication with other computer users. Some networks are local to a particular building or business; others connect users at remote geographic locations. The Internet is a collection of networks that connects the computers of businesses, public institutions, and individuals around the globe. Email provides hundreds of millions of people with instant world-wide communication capabilities. With Web browsing software, those same Internet users have access to millions of Web pages on the World Wide Web. The Web is a distributed network of interlinked multimedia documents. Although it started out as a tool for researchers and scholars, the Web has quickly become a vital center for entertainment and commerce.

Computers and information technology have changed the world rapidly and irreversibly. We can easily list dozens of ways in which computers make our lives easier and more productive. Personal computer applications, such as word processing, spreadsheets, graphics, multimedia, and databases, continue to grow in popularity. Emerging technologies, such as artificial intelligence, offer promise for future applications. At the same time, computers threaten our privacy, our security, and perhaps our way of life. As we rush into the information age, our future depends on computers and on our ability to understand and use them in productive, positive ways.

Chapter Review

▼ Key Terms

analytical engine (p. 27)

application program (application) (p. 39)

data (p. 29)

embedded computer (p. 35)

firmware (p. 35)

handheld computer (p. 34)

hardware (p. 29)

high-performance computer (p. 33)

input (p. 29)

information appliance (p. 38)

integrated circuit (p. 31)

intranet (p. 38)

laptop computer (p. 34)

mainframe computer (p. 32)

microcomputer revolution (p. 31)

microprocessor (p. 31)

Moore's Law (p. 31)

network computer (NC) (p. 38)

notebook computer (p. 34)

output (p. 29)

personal computer (PC) (p. 31)

personal digital assistant (PDA) (p. 35)

program (p. 29)

server (p. 33)

set-top box (p. 38)

silicon chip (p. 31)

software (p. 29)

special-purpose (dedicated) computer (p. 35)

supercomputer (p. 33)

terminal (p. 32)

timesharing (p. 33)

transistor (p. 30)

Web browser (p. 37)

workstation (p. 33)

World Wide Web (WWW (p. 37))

▼ Interactive Quiz Questions

1. The *Computer Confluence* CD-ROM contains self-test quiz questions related to this chapter, including multiple choice, true or false, and matching questions.
2. The *Computer Confluence* Web site, **www.prenhall.com/beekman**, contains self-test exercises related to this chapter. Follow the instructions for taking a quiz. After you've completed your quiz, you can email the results to your instructor.

    The Web site also contains open-ended discussion questions called Internet Explorations. Discuss one or more of the Internet exploration questions at the section for this chapter.

▼ Review Questions

1. Provide a working definition of each of the key terms listed in the "Key Terms" section. Check your answers in the glossary.
2. List several ways you interact with computers in your daily life.
3. Why was the Analytical Engine never completed during Charles Babbage's lifetime?
4. Outline the evolution of the computer from World War II to the present.
5. How are hardware and software related?
6. What is the most important difference between a computer and a calculator?
7. What is the difference between a mainframe and a microcomputer? What are the advantages and disadvantages of each?
8. What kinds of computer applications require the speed and power of a supercomputer? Give some examples.
9. What types of computers typically employ timesharing?
10. List several common personal computer applications.
11. Why is it important for people to know about and understand computers?
12. Describe some of the benefits and drawbacks of the computer revolution.

▼ Discussion Questions

1. What do people mean when they talk about the computer revolution? What is revolutionary about it?
2. How do you feel about computers? Examine your positive and negative feelings.
3. What major events before the 20th century influenced the development of the computer?
4. Suppose Charles Babbage and Lady Lovelace had been able to construct a working Analytical Engine and develop a factory for mass producing it. How do you think the world would have reacted? How would the history of the 20th century have been different as a result?
5. How would the world be different today if a wrinkle in time transported a modern desktop computer system, complete with software and manuals, onto the desk of Herbert Hoover? Adolf Hitler? Albert Einstein?
6. The automobile and the television set are two examples of technological inventions that changed our society drastically in ways that were not anticipated by their inventors. Outline several positive and negative effects of each of these two inventions. Do you think, on balance, that we are better off as a result of these machines? Why or why not? Now repeat this exercise for the computer.
7. Should all students be required to take at least one computer course? Why or why not? If so, what should that course cover?
8. Computerphobia—fear or anxiety related to computers—is a common malady among people today. What do you think causes it? What, if anything, should be done about it?
9. In your opinion what computer applications offer the most promise for making the world a better place? Which computer applications pose the most significant threats to our future well-being?

▼ Projects

1. Start a collection of news articles, cartoons, or television segments that deal with computers. Does your collection say anything about popular attitudes toward computers?
2. Trace computer-related articles through several years in the same magazine. Do you see any changes or trends?
3. Develop a questionnaire to try to determine people's attitudes about computers. Once you have people's answers to your questions, summarize your results.
4. Take an inventory of all the computers you encounter in a single day. Be sure to include embedded computers such as those in cars, appliances, entertainment equipment, and other machines.

Sources and Resources

Books

Dictionary of Computer and Internet Words: An A to Z Guide to Hardware, Software, and Cyberspace, edited by American Heritage Dictionaries (New York: Houghton Mifflin, 2001). It sometimes seems like the computer industry makes three things: hardware, software, and jargon. Many computer terms are too new, too obscure, or too technical to appear in standard dictionaries. Fortunately, several good dictionaries specialize in computer terminology. This is one of the most comprehensive and up to date. It covers PC, Macintosh, and Internet terms.

The Difference Engine: Charles Babbage and the Quest to Build the First Computer, by Doron Swade and Charles Babbage (New York: Viking Press, 2001). This book tells the story of the design of Babbage's visionary computing machine. It also reveals the problems Babbage faced getting funding for the ill-fated project. Swade led a team that built a working model of a Difference Engine for the 1991 Babbage bicentenary.

ENIAC: The Triumphs and Tragedies of the World's First Computer, by Scott McCartney (Walker and Co., 1999). This engaging book tells the human story of two pioneers and their struggles to be recognized for their monumental achievements in those early days of computing.

Crystal Fire: The Birth of the Information Age, by Michael Riordan and Lillian Hoddeson (New York: Norton, 1997). One of the defining moments of the information age occurred in 1947 when William Shockley and his colleagues invented the transistor. Crystal Fire tells the story of that earthshaking invention, clearly describing the technical and human dimensions of the story.

A History of Modern Computing, by Paul E. Ceruzzi (Cambridge, MA: MIT Press, 2000). This book traces the first fifty years of computer history, from ENIAC to internetworked PCs. The social context of the technology is clear throughout the book.

Fire in the Valley: The Making of the Personal Computer, Second Edition, 1999, by Paul Freiberger and Michael Swaine (Berkeley, CA: Osborne/McGraw-Hill, 1999). This book chronicles the early years of the personal computer revolution. The text occasionally gets bogged down in details, but the photos and quotes from the early days are fascinating. The 1999 film *Pirates of Silicon Valley* is based loosely on this book.

Accidental Empires: How the Boys of Silicon Valley Make Their Millions, Battle Foreign Competition, and Still Can't Get a Date, Revised Edition, by Robert X. Cringely (New York: Harper Business, 1996). Robert X. Cringely is the pen name for *InfoWorld's* computer-industry gossip columnist. In this opinionated, irreverent, and highly entertaining book Cringely discusses the past, present, and future of the volatile personal computer industry. When you read the humorous, colorful characterizations of the people who run this industry, you'll understand why Cringely didn't use his real name. *Triumph of the Nerds,* a 1996

PBS TV show and video based loosely on this book, lacks much of the humor and insight of the book, but includes some fascinating footage of the pioneers reminiscing about the early days.

Faster—The Acceleration of Just About Everything, by James Gleick (New York: Pantheon Books, 1999). The title says it all. In this age of ever-faster computers, electronic organizers, and Internet time, we're setting speed records at just about everything—but at what cost? Well worth reading if you have time.

The Difference Engine, by William Gibson and Bruce Sterling (New York: Spectra, 1992). How would the world of the 19th century be different if Charles and Ada had succeeded in constructing the Analytical Engine 150 years ago? This imaginative mystery novel takes place in a world where the computer revolution arrived a century early. Like other books by these two pioneers of the "cyberpunk" school of science fiction, *The Difference Engine* is dark, dense, detailed, and thought-provoking.

Dave Barry in Cyberspace, by Dave Barry (New York: Fawcett Columnbine, 1996). Dave Barry, the irreverent humor columnist, turns his wit loose on the information revolution in this hilarious little book. Here's a typical chapter title: "A Brief History of Computing from Cave Walls to Windows 95—Not That This Is Necessarily Progress." Whether you think computers are frustrating or funny, you'll probably find a few good laughs here.

Periodicals

Wired (www.wired.com). This high-style monthly started out as "the first consumer magazine for the digital generation to track technology's impact on all facets of the human condition." Today *Wired* devotes more pages to the business of technology and less to the impact of technology, but it's still a thought-provoking, influential magazine.

Computerworld (www.computerworld.com). This venerable newsweekly has provided up-to-the-week news on computers for decades.

InfoWorld (www.infoworld.com). *Computerworld's* younger sibling covers business computing, including applications for mainframes, servers, and other behind-the-scenes machines that aren't covered in PC publications.

E-Week. In 2000 this newsweekly changed its name from *PC Week* to *E-Week* to reflect its expanded coverage of the electronic digital business world.

PC World (www.pcworld.com). Because the world of personal computers changes so rapidly, computer users depend on magazines to keep them up to date on hardware and software developments. This periodical is one of the most popular sources for keeping up with developments in the PC world. The companion Web site offers up-to-the-minute information along with archives from past issues.

PC Magazine (www.pcmag.com). *PC Magazine* is another popular PC periodical, containing news, reviews, and feature articles for a variety of interests.

Macworld (www.macworld.com). This is the premiere periodical for Mac users, covering hardware, software, and Internet issues with clear, dependable articles and reviews.

MacAddict (www.macaddict.com). This magazine for Macintosh true-believers tends to be slightly more technical—and more partisan—than *Macworld*.

Mobile Computing & Communication (www.mobilecomputing.com). This is a good source of news and information on portable computing devices, from laptops to palmtops, as well as mobile phones and other traveling companions.

Pen Computing (www.pencomputing.com). This magazine covers pen-based computers, from tiny Palm devices to full-sized pen PCs.

Web Pages

Some of the best sources and resources on computers and information technology are on the Internet's World Wide Web. But the Web is changing quickly, and new sites are appearing every day. The *Computer Confluence* Web pages include up-to-date links to many of the best computer-related resources on the Web. To find them, open your Web browsing software, enter the address **www.prenhall.com/beekman**, follow the on-screen buttons to the table of contents, select a chapter, and click the links that interest you.

2 | Hardware Basics: Inside the Box

After you read this chapter you should be able to:

Explain in general terms how computers store and manipulate information

Describe the basic structure and organization of a computer

Discuss the functions and interactions of a computer system's principal internal components

Explain why a computer typically has different types of memory and storage devices

▼ In this chapter:

Bits and bytes: the nature of digital information

Inside the box: the computer's "brain" and memory

How it works: visual explanations of the computer's inner workings

Self-study questions and projects

Mini-reviews of helpful resources for further study

…and more.

▼ On the CD-ROM:

Activities highlighing how memory works

Animated tutorials explaining how CPU and memory work

Instant access to glossary and key word references

Interactive self-study quizzes

…and more.

▼ On the Web:

www.prenhall.com/beekman

Documents describing and illustrating CPU and memory technology

Links to binary number counting games

Articles on the evolution of the CPU and memory technology

Self-study exercises

…and more.

Thomas J. Watson, Sr., and the Emperor's New Machines

There is no invention—**only discovery**.

—Thomas J. Watson, Sr.

Thomas J. Watson, Sr. (1874–1956)

As president or, as he has been called, the "emperor" of IBM, Thomas J. Watson, Sr., created a corporate culture that fostered both invention and discovery. In 1914 he joined the ailing Computing-Tabulating-Recording Company as a salesperson. The company specialized in counting devices that used punched cards to read and store information. Ten years later Watson took it over, renamed it International Business Machines, and turned it into the dominant force in the information industry.

Thomas Watson has been called autocratic. He demanded unquestioning allegiance from his employees and enforced a legendary dress code that forbade even a hint of color in a shirt. But in many ways Watson ran his company like a family, rewarding loyal employees with uncommon favors. During the Depression he refused to lay off workers, choosing instead to stockpile surplus machines. As if to prove that good deeds don't go unrewarded, the director of the newly formed Social Security Administration bought Watson's excess stock.

Watson's first involvement with computers was providing financial backing for Howard Aiken's Mark I, the pioneering electromechanical computer developed in the early 1940s at Harvard. But Watson stubbornly refused to develop a commercial computer, even as UNIVAC I achieved fame and commercial contracts for the fledgling Sperry company.

Shortly after Watson retired from the helm of IBM in 1949, his son, Thomas Watson, Jr., took over. When Watson Senior died of a heart attack in 1956 at the age of 82, he still held the title of chairman of IBM. The younger Watson led IBM into the computing field with a vengeance, eventually building a computing empire that dwarfed all competitors for decades to come.

The conservative giant was slow to adjust to the rapid-fire changes of the '80s and '90s, making it possible for smaller, more nimble companies such as Compaq, Dell, Sun, and Microsoft to seize emerging markets. Massive revenue losses forced IBM to reorganize, replace many of its leaders, and abandon the company's longstanding no-layoffs policy. (IBM also abandoned the legendary dress code, opting for a more casual image.) Today, in spite of stiff competition (or perhaps *because* of it), IBM is a major source of innovation in the industry, with major research projects in everything from massive supercomputers to microscopic storage devices. Thomas Watson is long gone, but invention and discovery are alive and well at IBM.

Computers schedule airline flights, predict the weather, play music, control space stations, and keep the world's economic wheels spinning. How can one kind of machine do so many things?

To understand what really makes computers tick, you would need to devote considerable time and effort to studying computer science and computer engineering. Most of us don't need to understand every detail of a computer's inner workings, any more than a parent needs to explain wave and particle physics when a child asks why the sky is blue. We can be satisfied with simpler answers, even if those answers are only approximations of the technical truth. We'll spend the next three chapters exploring answers to the question, "How do computers do what they do?"

The main text of each of these chapters provides simple, nontechnical answers and basic information. How It Works boxes use text and graphics to dig deeper into the inner workings of the computer. Depending on your course, learning style, and level of curiosity, you may read these boxes as they appear in the text, read them after you've completed the basic material in the chapter, or (if you don't need the technical details) bypass some or all of them. You'll find interactive multimedia versions of many of these How It Works boxes on the *Computer Confluence* CD-ROM. Use the Sources and Resources section at each chapter's end for further explorations.

PCs are assembled in factories like this one at Dell Computer, Inc. In the next two chapters, we'll examine the components that make up the modern computer.

What Computers Do

> Stripped of its interfaces, **a bare computer** boils down to little more than a pocket calculator that can **push its own buttons** and **remember** what it has done.
> —Arnold Penzias, in *Ideas and Information*

The simple truth is that computers perform only four basic functions:

▶ *Receive input.* Computers accept information from the outside world.
▶ *Process information.* Computers perform arithmetic or logical (decision-making) operations on information.
▶ *Produce output.* Computers communicate information to the outside world.
▶ *Store information.* Computers move and store information in memory.

Every computer system contains hardware components—physical parts—that specialize in each of these four functions:

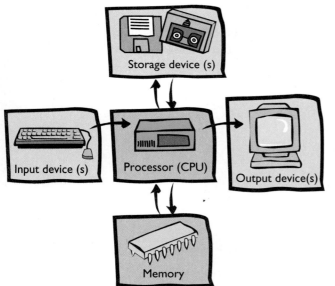

The basic components of every computer system include the central components (the CPU and memory), and peripherals (input, output, and storage devices).

▶ **Input devices** accept input from the outside world. The most common input devices, of course, are keyboards and pointing devices such as mice.
▶ **Output devices** send information to the outside world. Most computers use a TV-like video monitor as their main output device and a printer to produce paper printouts.
▶ A **processor**, or **central processing unit (CPU)**, is, in effect, the computer's "brain." The CPU processes information, performing arithmetic calculations and making basic decisions by comparing information values.
▶ **Memory** and **storage devices** both store information, but they serve different purposes. The computer's **memory** (sometimes called *primary storage*) is used to store programs and data that need to be instantly accessible to the CPU. Storage devices (sometimes called *secondary storage*), including disk and tape drives, serve as long-term repositories for data. You can think of a storage device, such as a disk drive, as a combination input and output device because the computer sends information to the storage device (output) and later retrieves that information from it (input).

These four types of components, when combined, make up the hardware part of a computer system. Of course, the system isn't complete without software—the instructions that tell the hardware what to do. But for now we concentrate on hardware. In this chapter, we focus on the central processing unit and the computer's memory; these components are at the center of all computing operations. In the next chapter, we look at the input, output, and storage devices—that is, the peripherals of the computer system. Because every computer hardware component is designed either to transport or to transform information, we start with a little bit of information about information.

A Bit About Bits

The term information is difficult to define because it has many meanings. According to one popular definition, information is communication that has value because it *informs*. This distinction can be helpful for dealing with data from televisions, magazines, computers, and other sources. But it's not always clear and it's not absolute. As Richard Saul Wurman points out, "Everyone needs a personal measure with which to define information. What constitutes information to one person may be data to another. If it doesn't make sense to you, it doesn't qualify."

> The great Information Age is really **an explosion of non-information**; it is an explosion of data. To deal with the increasing **onslaught of data**, it is **imperative** to distinguish between the two; information is **that which leads to understanding**.
> —Richard Saul Wurman, in *Information Anxiety 2*

At the opposite extreme, one communication theory defines information as anything that can be communicated, whether it has value or not. By this definition, information comes in many forms. The words, numbers, and pictures on these pages are symbols representing information. If you underline this sentence, you're adding new information to the page. Even the sounds and pictures that emanate from a television commercial are packed with information.

Some people attempt to strictly apply the first definition to computers, claiming that computers turn raw data, which has no value in its current form, into information, which is valuable. This approach emphasizes the computer's role as a business data-processing machine. But in our modern interconnected world, one computer's output is often another's input. If a computer receives a message from another computer, is the message worthless data or valuable information? And whose personal measure of value applies?

For our purposes, describing the mechanics of computers in these chapters, we lean toward the second, more subjective, approach and use the terms data and information more-or-less interchangeably. In later chapters we present plenty of evidence to suggest that not all computer output has value. In the end, it is up to you to decide what the real information is.

Bit Basics

Whatever you call it, in the world of computers information is digital: It's made up of discrete, countable units, so it can be subdivided. In many situations, people need to reduce information to simpler units to use it effectively. For example, a child trying to pronounce an unfamiliar word can sound out each letter individually before tackling the whole word.

A computer doesn't understand words, numbers, pictures, musical notes, or even letters of the alphabet. Like a young reader, a computer can't process information without dividing it into smaller units. In fact, computers can only digest information that has been broken into bits. A bit (binary digit) is the smallest unit of information. A bit can have one of two values. You can also think of these two values as yes and no, zero and one, on and off, black and white, or high and low.

If you think of the innards of a computer as a collection of microscopic on/off switches, it's easy to understand why computers process information bit by bit. Each switch stores a tiny amount of information: a signal to turn on a light, for example, or the answer to a yes/no question. (In modern integrated circuits, high and low electrical charges represent bits, but these circuits work the same as if they were really made up of tiny switches.)

Remember Paul Revere's famous midnight ride? His co-conspirators used a pair of lanterns to convey a choice between two messages, "One if by land, two if by sea"—a binary

2.1
Binary Numbers

*This is the first of many **How It Works** boxes you'll find in this book. **How It Works** boxes provide more technical detail than you'll find in the main text. Nothing in the **How It Works** boxes is essential for understanding the matter in the rest of the book.*

In a computer, all information—program instructions, pictures, text, sounds, or mathematical values—is represented by patterns of microscopic switches. In most cases these groups of switches represent numbers or numerical codes.

The easiest kind of switch to manufacture is an on/off toggle switch: It has just two settings, on and off, like an ordinary light switch. That's the kind of switch that's used in every modern computer.

Binary arithmetic follows the same rules as ordinary decimal arithmetic. But with only two digits available for each position, you have to borrow and carry (manipulate digits in other positions) more often. Even adding 1 and 1 results in a two-digit number. Multiplication, division, negative numbers, and fractions can also be represented in binary, but most people find them messy and complicated compared with decimal arithmetic.

The MITS Altair, the first personal computer, came with no keyboard or monitor. It could only be programmed by using a bank of binary switches for input; binary patterns of lights provided the output.

1 In our decimal number system the position of a digit is important: In the number 7357, the 7 on the left stands for seven thousands, the other 7 for seven ones. The use of switches to represent numbers would be easy to understand if the switches each had 10 settings (0 through 9). The decimal number 67 might look like this:

choice. It's theoretically possible to send a message like this with just one lantern. But "One if by land, zero if by sea" wouldn't have worked very well unless there was some way to know exactly when the message was being sent. With two lanterns, the first lantern could say "Here is the message" when it was turned on. The second lantern communicated the critical bit's worth of information: land or sea. If the revolutionaries had wanted to send a more complex message, they could have used more lanterns. ("Three if by subway!")

In much the same way, a computer can process larger chunks of information by treating groups of bits as units. For example, a collection of 8 bits, called a **byte**, can represent 256 different messages ($256 = 2^8$). If you think of each bit as a light that can be either on or off, you can make different combinations of lights represent different messages. (Computer scientists usually speak in terms of 0 and 1 instead of on and off, but the concept is the same either way.) The computer has an advantage over Paul Revere in that it sees not just the number of lights turned on but also their order, so 01 (off–on) is different from 10 (on–off).

orks How It Works How It Works How It Works How It Works How It Works

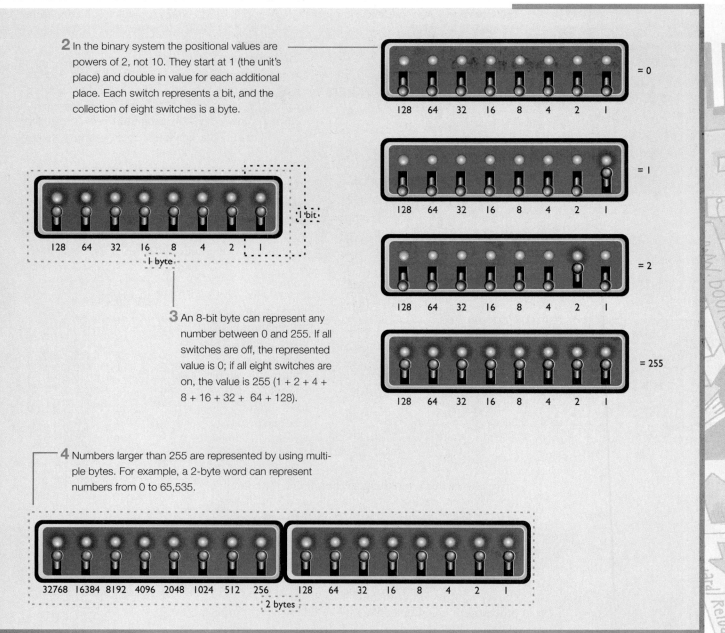

2 In the binary system the positional values are powers of 2, not 10. They start at 1 (the unit's place) and double in value for each additional place. Each switch represents a bit, and the collection of eight switches is a byte.

128 64 32 16 8 4 2 1 = 0

128 64 32 16 8 4 2 1 = 1

128 64 32 16 8 4 2 1 = 2

128 64 32 16 8 4 2 1 = 255

1 bit

128 64 32 16 8 4 2 1

1 byte

3 An 8-bit byte can represent any number between 0 and 255. If all switches are off, the represented value is 0; if all eight switches are on, the value is 255 (1 + 2 + 4 + 8 + 16 + 32 + 64 + 128).

4 Numbers larger than 255 are represented by using multiple bytes. For example, a 2-byte word can represent numbers from 0 to 65,535.

32768 16384 8192 4096 2048 1024 512 256 128 64 32 16 8 4 2 1

2 bytes

Building with Bits

There's a **runaway market** for bits.
—Russell Schweickart, astronaut

What does a bit combination like 01100110 mean to the computer? There's no single answer to that question; it depends on context and convention. A string of bits can be interpreted as a number, a letter of the alphabet, or almost anything else.

Bits as Numbers

Because computers are built from switching devices that reduce all information to 0s and 1s, they represent numbers using the *binary number system*—a system that denotes all numbers with combinations of two digits. Like the 10-digit decimal system you use every day, the binary system has clear, consistent rules for every arithmetic operation.

The people who worked with early computers had to use binary arithmetic. But today's computers include software that converts decimal numbers into binary numbers automatically, and vice versa. As a result, the computer's binary number processing is completely hidden from the user.

In the binary number system, every number is represented by a unique string of 0s and 1s.

Decimal representation	Binary representation
0	0
1	1
2	10
3	11
4	100
5	101
6	110
7	111
8	1000
9	1001
10	1010
11	1011
12	1100
13	1101
14	1110
15	1111

Bits as Codes

Today's computers work as much with text as with numbers. To make words, sentences, and paragraphs fit into the computer's binary-only circuitry, programmers have devised codes that represent each letter, digit, and special character as a unique string of bits.

The most widely used code, ASCII (an abbreviation of American Standard Code for Information Interchange, pronounced "as-kee"), represents each character as a unique 8-bit code. Out of a string of 8 bits, 256 unique ordered patterns can be made—enough to make unique codes for 26 letters (upper- and lowercase), 10 digits, and a variety of special characters.

As the world shrinks and our information needs grow, ASCII's 256 unique characters simply aren't enough. ASCII is too limited to accommodate Greek, Hebrew, Japanese, Chinese, and other lan-

Character	ASCII binary code
A	01000001
B	01000010
C	01000011
D	01000100
E	01000101
F	01000110
G	01000111
H	01001000
I	01001001
J	01001010
K	01001011
L	01001100
M	01001101
N	01001110
O	01001111
P	01010000
Q	01010001
R	01010010
S	01010011
T	01010100
U	01010101
V	01010110
W	01010111
X	01011000
Y	01011001
Z	01011010
0	00110000
1	00110001
2	00110010
3	00110011
4	00110100
5	00110101
6	00110110
7	00110111
8	00111000
9	00111001

guages. To facilitate multilingual computing, the computer industry is embracing Unicode, a coding scheme that supports 65,000 unique characters—more than enough for all major world languages.

Of course, today's computers work with more than characters. A group of bits can also represent colors, sounds, quantitative measurements from the environment, or just about any other kind of information that's likely to be processed by a computer. We explore other types of information in later chapters.

Bits as Instructions in Programs

So far we've dealt with the ways bits represent data—information from some outside source that's processed by the computer. But another kind of information is just as important to the computer: the programs that tell the computer what to do with the data you give it. The computer stores programs as collections of bits, just as it stores data.

Program instructions, like characters, are represented in binary notation through the use of codes. For example, the code 01101010 might tell the computer to add two numbers. Other groups of bits—instructions in the program—contain codes that tell the computer where to find those numbers and where to store the result. You learn more about how these computer instructions work in later chapters.

The capital letters and numeric digits are represented in the ASCII character set by 36 unique patterns of 8 bits. (The remaining 92 ASCII bit patterns represent lowercase letters, punctuation characters, and special characters.)

2.2
Representing the World's Languages

The United States has long been at the center of the computer revolution; that's why the ASCII character set was originally designed to include only English-language characters. ASCII code numbers range from 0 to 127, but this isn't enough to handle all of the characters used in the languages of Western Europe, including accents and other diacritical marks.

The Latin I character set appends 128 additional codes onto the original ASCII 128 to accommodate additional characters.

65 A 66 B 67 C 68 D   97 a 98 b 99 c   252 ü 253 ý 254 þ 255 ÿ

Both the ASCII and the Latin 1 character sets can use 8 bits—1 byte—to represent each character, but there's no room left for the characters used in languages such as Greek, Hebrew, Hindi, and Arabic, each of which has its own 50- to 150-character alphabet or syllabary. East Asian languages such as Chinese, Japanese, and Korean present bigger challenges for computer users. Chinese alone has nearly 50,000 distinct characters, of which about 13,000 are in current use.

A character set that uses two bytes, or 16 bits, per character allows for 256 x 256, or 65,536 distinct codes—more than enough for all modern languages. The emerging international standard double-byte character set called Unicode is designed to facilitate multilingual computing. In Unicode the first 256 codes (0 through 255) are identical to the codes of the Latin I character set. The remaining codes are distributed among the writing systems of the world's other languages.

Most major new software applications and operating systems are designed to be transported to different languages. Making a software application work in different languages involves much more than translating the words. For example, some languages write from right to left or top to bottom. Pronunciation, currency symbols, dialects, and other variations often make it necessary to produce customized software for different regions even when the same language is spoken.

Computer keyboards for East Asian languages don't have one key for each character. Using phonetic input, a user types a pronunciation for a character using a Western-style keyboard and then chooses the character needed from a menu of characters that appears on the screen. The software can make some menu choices automatically based on common language-usage patterns.

Bits, Bytes, and Buzzwords

> Even the most **sophisticated** computer is really only a large, well-organized **volume of bits**.
>
> —David Harel, in *Algorithmics: The Spirit of Computing*

Trying to learn about computers by examining their operation at the bit level is a little like trying to learn about how people look or act by studying individual human cells; there's plenty of information there, but it's not the most efficient way to find out what you need to know. Fortunately, people can use computers without thinking about bits. Some bit-related terminology does come up in day-to-day computer work, though. Most computer users need to have at least a basic understanding of the following terms for quantifying data:

▶ *Byte*: A grouping of 8 bits. If you work mostly with words, you can think of a byte as one character of ASCII-encoded text.

▶ *K (kilobyte or KB)*: About 1,000 bytes of information. For example, about 5K of storage is necessary to hold 5,000 characters of ASCII text. (Technically, 1K is 1,024 bytes because 1,024 is 2^{10}, which makes the arithmetic easier for binary-based computers. For those of us who don't think in binary, 1,000 is close enough.)

▶ *MB (megabyte or meg)*: Approximately 1,000K, or 1 million bytes.

▶ *GB (gigabyte or gig)*: Approximately 1,000MB.

▶ *TB (terabyte)*: Approximately 1 million megabytes. This astronomical unit of measurement applies to the largest storage devices commonly available today.

The abbreviations K, MB or meg, and GB or gig describe the capacity of memory and storage components. You would, for example, describe a computer as having 256MB of memory and a hard disk as having a 40GB storage capacity. The same terms are used to quantify sizes of computer files. A file is an organized collection of information, such as a term paper or a set of names and addresses, stored in a computer-readable form. For example, the text for this chapter is stored in a file that occupies about 70K of space on a disk.

To add to the confusion, people often measure data transfer speed or memory size in *megabits (Mb)* rather than megabytes (MB). A megabit, as you might expect, is approximately 1,000 bits—one-eighth the size of a megabyte. When you're talking in bits and bytes, a little detail like capitalization can make a significant difference.

The Computer's Core: The CPU and Memory

> The **microprocessor** that makes up your personal computer's *central processing unit*, or CPU, is the **ultimate computer brain**, **messenger**, **ringmaster**, and **boss**. All the other components—RAM, disk drives, the monitor— exist only to **bridge the gap** between you and the processor.
>
> —Ron White, in *How Computers Work*

It may seem strange to think of automated teller machines, video game consoles, and supercomputers as bit processors. But whatever it looks like to the user, a digital computer is at its core a collection of on/off switches designed to transform information from one form to another. The user provides the computer with patterns of bits—input—and the computer follows instructions to transform that input into a different pattern of bits—output—to return to the user.

The CPU: The Real Computer

The CPU, often called just the processor, performs the transformations of input into output. Every computer has at least one CPU to interpret and execute the instructions in each program, to do arithmetic and logical data manipulations, and to communicate with all the other parts of the computer system indirectly through memory.

A modern CPU is an extraordinarily complex collection of electronic circuits. When all of those circuits are built into a single silicon chip, as they are in most computers today, that chip is referred to as a *microprocessor*. In a desktop computer, the CPU is housed along with other chips and electronic components on a circuit board. The circuit board that contains a computer's CPU is called the motherboard or *system board*.

Many different kinds of CPUs are in use today; when you choose a computer, the type of CPU in the computer is an important part of the decision. Although there are many variations in design among these chips, only two factors are important to a casual computer user: compatibility and speed.

The motherboard of a typical PC contains the CPU, memory, and several other important chips and components.

Compatibility

Not all software is compatible with every CPU; that is, software written for one processor may not work with another. Every processor has a built-in *instruction set*—a vocabulary of instructions the processor can execute. CPUs in the same family are generally designed so newer processors can process all of the instructions handled by earlier models. For example, Intel's Pentium 4 chip is backward compatible with the Pentium III, Pentium II, Pentium Pro, Pentium, 486, 386, and 286 chips that preceded it, so it can run most software written for those older CPUs. But software written for the PowerPC family of processors used in Macintosh computers won't run on the Intel processors found in most IBM-compatible computers; the Intel processors can't understand programs written for the PowerPC CPUs. Similarly, the Macintosh Power PC processor can't generally run Windows software. (In Chapter 4, "Software Basics: The Ghost in the Machine," you see how emulation software can partially overcome incompatibility problems by translating instructions written for one CPU into instructions that another can execute.)

Speed

There's a tremendous variation in how fast different processors can handle information. Most computer applications, such as word processing, are more convenient to use on a faster machine. Many applications that use graphics or do computations, such as statistical programs, graphic design programs, and many computer games, require faster machines to produce satisfactory results.

This inspector is adding a silicon wafer before it is sliced into many silicon chips.

A computer's speed is determined in part by the speed of its internal *clock*—the timing device that produces electrical pulses to synchronize the computer's operations. A computer's clock speed is measured in units called *megahertz (MHz)*, for millions of clock cycles per second. Ads for new computer systems often emphasize megahertz ratings as a measure of speed. But these numbers can be misleading; judging a computer's speed by its megahertz rating alone is like measuring a car's speed by the engine's RPM (revolutions per minute). A 700-MHz Celeron system isn't necessarily faster than a 600-MHz Pentium II or a 500-MHz PowerPC G4 chip; in fact, for some tasks, it's much slower.

The Intel Pentium 4 chip (left) contains intricate circuitry that looks like geometric colored patterns when magnified (right).

Clock speed by itself doesn't adequately describe how fast a computer can process words, numbers, or pictures. Speed is also limited by the architecture of the processor—the design that determines how individual components of the CPU are put together on the chip. For example, newer chips can manipulate more bits simultaneously than older chips, which makes them more efficient, and therefore faster, at performing most operations. The number of bits a CPU can process at one time—typically 8, 16, 32, or 64—is sometimes

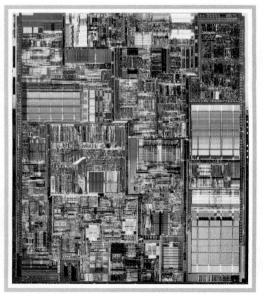

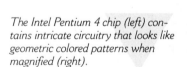

2.3
The CPU

*Most computer users don't know anything about what goes on inside the CPU; they just use it. Throughout most of this book we treat the CPU as a kind of black box that transforms information by following instructions. This **How It Works** box offers a peek inside that black box so you can get a feel for what makes your computer tick. Since the CPU functions as part of a larger collection of computer components, this **How It Works** box tells only part of the story; taken by itself, it may raise more questions than it answers. But **How It Works** boxes later in this chapter and in the next two chapters fill in many of the missing details of the inner workings of the modern computer. Read these boxes if you want the inside story.*

*The central processing unit (CPU) is the component that executes the steps in a program, performing math and moving data from one part of the system to another. The CPU contains the circuitry to perform a variety of simple tasks, called **instructions**. An individual instruction does only a tiny amount of work. A typical instruction might be "Read the contents of memory location x and add the number y to it." Most CPUs have a vocabulary of fewer than 1,000 distinct instructions.*

All computer programs are composed of instructions drawn from this tiny vocabulary. The typical computer program is composed of millions of instructions, and the CPU can execute millions of instructions every second. When a program runs, the rapid-fire execution of instructions creates an illusion of motion in the same way a movie simulates motion out of a sequence of still pictures.

The typical CPU is divided into several functional units: control, arithmetic, decode, bus, and prefetch. These units work together like workers on an assembly line to complete the execution of program instructions.

Arithmetic Logic Unit

Bus Unit

Prefetch Unit

1 In most cases the actual execution of an instruction is performed by the *arithmetic logic unit (ALU)*. The ALU includes *registers*, each usually 32 or 64 bits in size.

2 Program instructions are stored in primary storage (memory), which is usually on chips outside the CPU. The CPU's first task is to read the instruction from memory. The bus unit handles all communication between the CPU and primary storage.

3 The *prefetch unit* instructs the bus unit to read the instruction stored at a particular memory address. This unit not only fetches the next instruction to execute, but it also fetches several subsequent instructions to ensure that an instruction is always ready to go.

orks How It Works How It Works How It Works How It Works

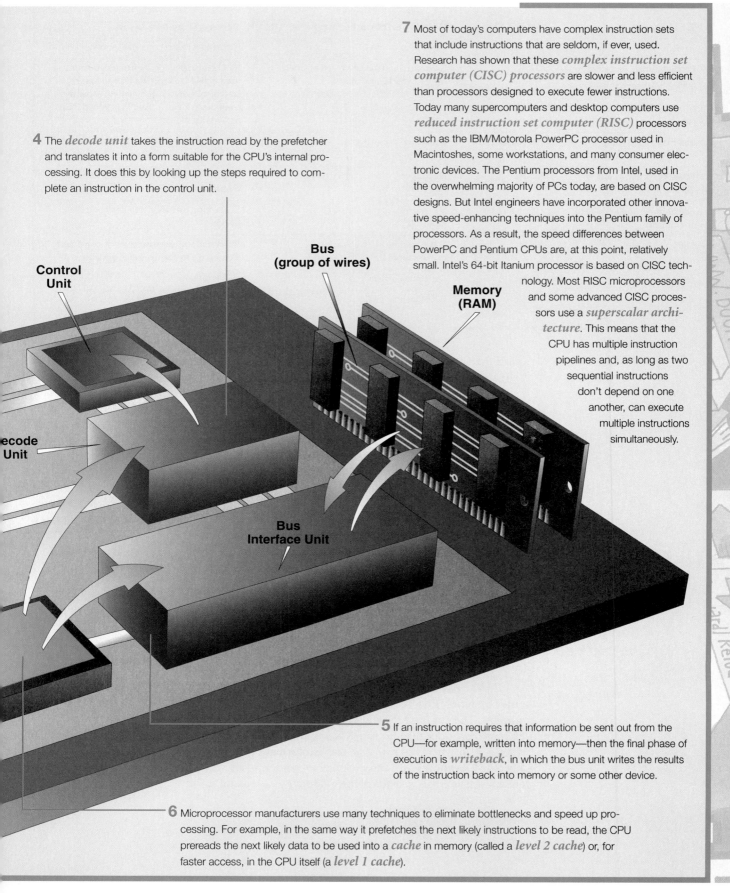

7 Most of today's computers have complex instruction sets that include instructions that are seldom, if ever, used. Research has shown that these *complex instruction set computer (CISC) processors* are slower and less efficient than processors designed to execute fewer instructions. Today many supercomputers and desktop computers use *reduced instruction set computer (RISC)* processors such as the IBM/Motorola PowerPC processor used in Macintoshes, some workstations, and many consumer electronic devices. The Pentium processors from Intel, used in the overwhelming majority of PCs today, are based on CISC designs. But Intel engineers have incorporated other innovative speed-enhancing techniques into the Pentium family of processors. As a result, the speed differences between PowerPC and Pentium CPUs are, at this point, relatively small. Intel's 64-bit Itanium processor is based on CISC technology. Most RISC microprocessors and some advanced CISC processors use a *superscalar architecture*. This means that the CPU has multiple instruction pipelines and, as long as two sequential instructions don't depend on one another, can execute multiple instructions simultaneously.

4 The *decode unit* takes the instruction read by the prefetcher and translates it into a form suitable for the CPU's internal processing. It does this by looking up the steps required to complete an instruction in the control unit.

Control Unit

Bus (group of wires)

Memory (RAM)

ecode Unit

Bus Interface Unit

5 If an instruction requires that information be sent out from the CPU—for example, written into memory—then the final phase of execution is *writeback*, in which the bus unit writes the results of the instruction back into memory or some other device.

6 Microprocessor manufacturers use many techniques to eliminate bottlenecks and speed up processing. For example, in the same way it prefetches the next likely instructions to be read, the CPU prereads the next likely data to be used into a *cache* in memory (called a *level 2 cache*) or, for faster access, in the CPU itself (a *level 1 cache*).

POPULAR CPU FAMILIES AND WHERE TO FIND THEM

CPU Family	Word Size	Developer/Manufacturer	Where They Are Used
Itanium Family	64 bit	Developed by Intel	High-end workstations and servers.
Pentium Family (including Celeron and Xeon)	32 bit	Developed and manufactured by Intel; clones by AMD and others.	IBM-compatible computers. (Pentium is used in mid- to high-end PCs and workstations; Celeron is used in less expensive computers; Xeon is used in high-end PCs and workstations.)
x86 Family (386, 486)	16 and 32 bit	Developed and manufactured by Intel; clones by others.	Older IBM-compatible computers.
PowerPC family, including G3 and G4	32 bit	Developed by IBM, manufactured by IBM and Motorola.	Macintoshes, network computers, special-purpose devices.
680x0 Family (68000, 68020, and others)	16 and 32 bit	Developed and manufactured by Motorola.	Older Macintoshes, computer-controlled devices.
MIPS	64 bit	Developed by Silicon Graphics, manufactured by many companies.	Workstations, servers, network computers, video game machines, other devices.
SPARC	64 bit	Developed by Sun.	Workstations.
ARM	32 bit	Developed by Intel.	Handheld computers, PDAs, special-purpose devices.

called the CPU's *word size*. More often, though, people use the number without a label, as in "The Itanium is Intel's first 64-bit processor." High-end workstations and servers today use 64-bit processors. Most PCs and Macintoshes use 32-bit processors. Some embedded and special-purpose computers still use 8- and 16 bit processors.

Because speed is so important, engineers and computer scientists are constantly developing techniques for speeding up a computer's ability to manipulate and move bits. One common techique for improving a computer's performance is to put more than one processor in the computer. Many personal computers, for example, have specialized subsidiary processors that take care of mathematical calculations or graphics displays. Most supercomputers have multiple processors that can divide jobs into pieces and work in parallel on the pieces. This kind of processing, known as **parallel processing** or **multiprocessing**, is becoming more commonplace throughout the computing world.

The Computer's Memory

"**What's one** and one and one and one and one and one and one and one and one and one?"
"**I don't know**," said Alice. "I lost count."
"**She can't do addition**," said the Red Queen.
—Lewis Carroll, in *Through the Looking Glass*

The CPU's main job is to follow the instructions encoded in programs. But like Alice in *Through the Looking Glass*, the CPU can handle only one instruction and a few pieces of data at a time. The computer needs a place to store the rest of the program and data until the processor is ready for them. That's what RAM is for.

RAM (*random access memory*) is the most common type of primary storage, or computer memory. RAM chips contain circuits that store program instructions and data temporarily. The computer divides each RAM chip into many equal-sized memory locations. Memory locations, like houses, have unique addresses so the computer can tell them apart when it is instructed to save or retrieve information. You can store a piece of information in any RAM location—you can pick one at random—and the computer can, if so instructed, quickly retrieve it. Hence the name random access memory.

The information stored in RAM is nothing more than a pattern of electrical current flowing through microscopic circuits in silicon chips. This means that when the power goes off the computer instantly forgets everything it was remembering in RAM. RAM is called **volatile memory** because information stored there is not held permanently.

This could be a serious problem if the computer didn't have another type of memory to store information that you don't want to lose. This **nonvolatile memory** is called **ROM (read-only memory)** because the computer can only read information from it; it can never write any new information on it. All modern computers include ROM that contains start-up instructions and other critical information. The information in ROM was etched in when the chip was manufactured, so it is available whenever the computer is operating, but it can't be changed except by replacing the ROM chip.

Other types of memory are available; most are seldom used outside of engineering laboratories. There are two notable exceptions:

▶ *CMOS* (complementary metal oxide semiconductor) is a special low-energy kind of RAM that can store small amounts of data for long periods of time on battery power. CMOS RAM stores the date, time, and calendar in a PC. (CMOS RAM is called *parameter RAM* in Macintoshes.)

▶ *Flash memory* chips, like RAM chips, can be written and erased rapidly and repeatedly. But unlike RAM, flash memory is nonvolatile; it can keep its contents without a flow of electricity. Cell phones, pagers, portable computers, handheld PDAs, and other digital devices use flash memory to store data that needs to be changed from time to time. Data flight recorders also use it. Flash memory is still too expensive to replace RAM and other common storage media, but it may in the future replace disk drives as well as memory chips.

It takes time for the processor to retrieve data from memory—but not very much time. The *access time* for most memory is measured in *nanoseconds*—billionths of a second. Compare this to hard disk access time, which is measured in *milliseconds*—thousandths of a second. Memory speed (access time) is another factor that affects the computer's overall speed.

Slots and ports enable the CPU to communicate with the outside world via peripheral devices. Here a circuit board is being inserted into a slot. The panel holding the slot has been temporarily removed from the computer for easier viewing. The gray flat wire is a bus.

Buses, Ports, and Peripherals

In a desktop computer, the CPU and memory chips are attached to circuit boards along with other key components. Information travels between components through groups of wires called **buses**. Buses typically have 8, 16, or 32 wires, or data paths; a bus with 16 wires is called a ***16-bit bus*** because it can transmit 16 bits of information at a time, twice as many as an 8-bit bus. Just as multilane freeways allow masses of automobiles to move faster than they could on single-lane roads, wider buses can transmit information faster than narrower buses. Newer, more powerful computers have wider buses so they can process information faster.

Buses connect to storage devices in **bays**—open areas in the system box for disk drives and other peripheral devices. Buses also connect to **expansion slots** (sometimes called just *slots*) inside the computer's housing. Users can customize their computers by inserting special-purpose circuit boards (called *cards*, or *expansion cards*) into these slots. Buses also connect to external **ports**—sockets on the outside of the computer chassis. The back of a computer typically has a variety of ports to meet a variety of needs. Some of these ports—the keyboard and mouse ports, for example—are connected directly to the system board. Others, such as the monitor port, are generally attached to an expansion card. In fact, many expansion cards do little more than provide convenient ports for attaching particular types of peripherals. Macintosh computers generally have

A portable computer typically has one or more slots to accommodate credit-card-sized PC cards like this one.

2.4
Memory

Memory is the work area of the CPU. Think of memory as millions of tiny storage cells, each of which can contain a single byte of information. A typical personal computer has from 64 to 256 megabytes (million bytes) of memory. The information in memory includes program instructions, numbers for arithmetic, codes representing text characters, digital codes representing pictures, and other kinds of data.

Memory chips are usually grouped on small circuit boards called **SIMMs** *(single in-line memory modules) and* **DIMMs** *(dual in-line memory modules) and are plugged into the motherboard.*

Two SIMMs plugged into a circuit board.

Like mailboxes in a row, bytes of memory have unique addresses that identify them and help the CPU keep track of where things are stored.

fewer expansion boards than their PC counterparts, because their system boards include more components as standard equipment.

In portable computers, where size is critical, most common ports go directly to the system board. Because portable computers don't have room for full-sized cards, many have slots for **PC cards**—credit-card-sized cards that contain memory, miniature peripherals, and additional ports. (When these cards were first released, they were known as *PCMCIA cards*. One writer suggested that this stood for "People Can't Memorize Computer Industry Acronyms." Thankfully, the name was shortened to PC cards.)

orks How It Works How It Works How It Works How It Works

The CPU can only see into and access memory. Memory addresses make up the CPU's entire world, so any program that needs to be executed or data that needs to be modified must make its way into memory.

Most computer systems use ***memory-mapped I/O****, where information for input and output is stored in special areas of memory. For example, information to be displayed on the monitor screen is written into a special range of memory addresses that is continually scanned by the video subsystem.*

1 When you turn on the computer, the CPU automatically begins executing instructions stored in read-only memory (ROM). On most computer systems, ROM also contains parts of the operating system. The firmware programs in ROM are sometimes called the ***BIOS*** (basic input/output system).

2 The executing instructions help the system start up and tell it how to load the operating system—copy it from disk into memory.

3 Once executing instructions are loaded into memory, the CPU is able to execute them.

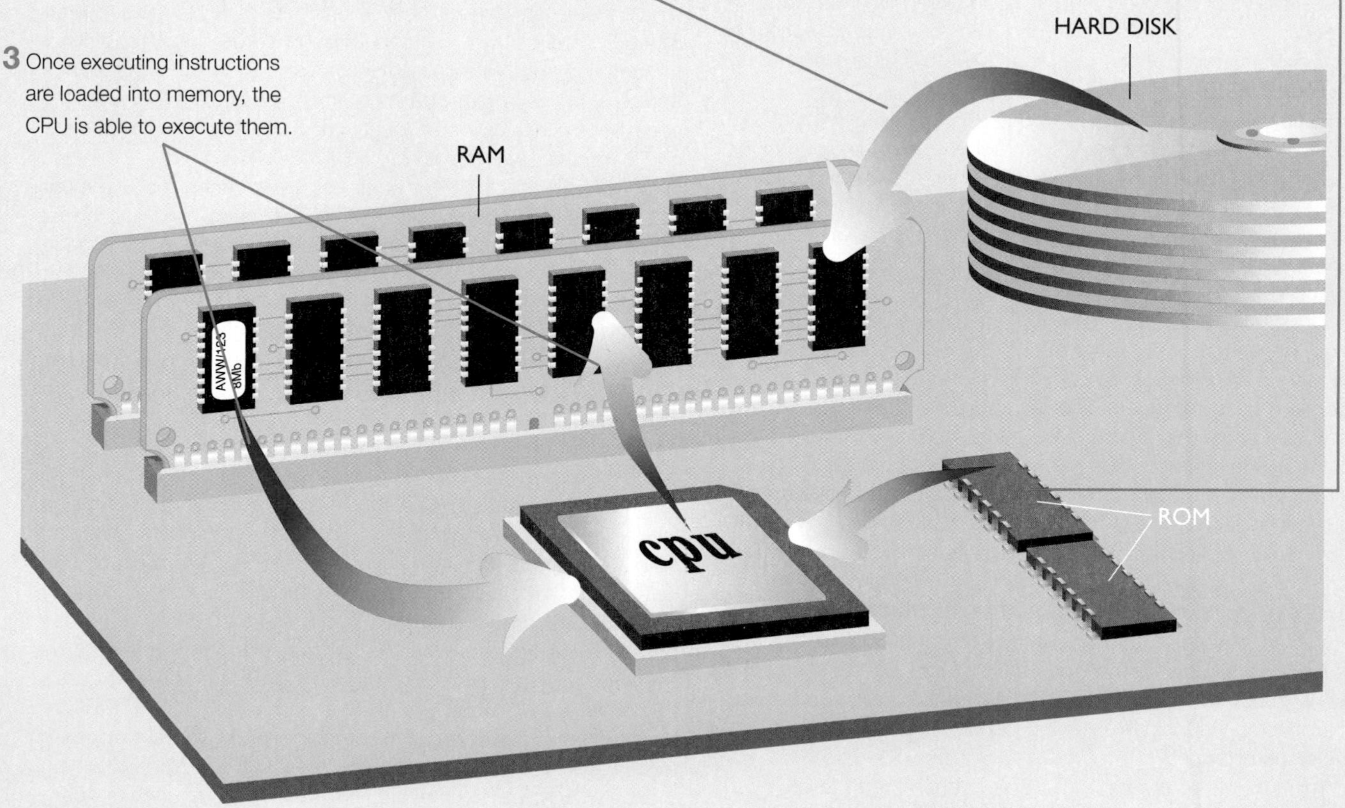

HARD DISK
RAM
AVWW423
8Mb
cpu
ROM

Slots and ports make it easy to add external devices, or ***peripherals***, to the computer system so the CPU can communicate with the outside world and store information for later use. Without peripherals, CPU and memory together are like a brain without a body. Some peripherals such as keyboards and printers serve as communication links between people and computers. Other peripherals link the computer to other machines. Still others provide long-term storage media. In the next chapter, we explore a variety of input, output, and storage peripherals, and then revisit the slots and ports that connect those peripherals to the CPU and memory.

CrossCurrents CrossCurrentsCrossCurrentsCrossCurrents

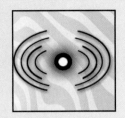

Bit Literacy

Mark Hurst

In Information Anxiety 2, Richard Saul Wurman explores a problem faced by many of us: too much information. In this edited article from that book, Consultant Mark Hurst of Creative Good discusses the problem and a solution: bit literacy.

Information anxiety is more important today than ever, thanks to the arrival of the bit. The tiniest one- or zero-pulse of digital data, the bit will affect our lives as much as the atom. Ten years ago, Americans may have felt some anxiety over the magazines and newspapers piling up at home, but today the anxiety is increasing as bits appear in all areas of our lives. Email, Web sites, e-newsletters, chat rooms, email, instant messages, and more email—all of these streams of bits can interrupt us, and keep us engaged, anywhere and anytime. Devices made to hold these bits are springing up, too: PDAs and cell phones bring us the bits when we're away from our PC.

For those who own a PC or a PDA, there is little escape from the bits. Even when we turn off the device, the bits pile up quietly, ready to flood us with anxiety when we return to the device. If anything, an escape from the bits can be dangerous. Take a week-long vacation without email, and upon return, a bloated inbox welcomes us back to work with seven times more bits.

And this is still *early* in the current explosion of digital information. One research study recently predicted that, within a few years, the number of emails we receive every day will increase to *forty* times its current volume. That's a lot of bits demanding our attention—just from email. It's likely that still other devices and other bitstreams will threaten the typical American with exponentially more information anxiety.

The problem of near-infinite bits, however, does have a solution. The solution is what I call "bit literacy." Bit literacy is an awareness of bits: what bits are, how they affect our lives, and how we can survive in a society permeated by bits. With that awareness, bit literate people are able to *control* the bits, and not be *controlled* by the bits, that are becoming central to our lives and jobs.

All of bit literacy can be distilled into a simple philosophy that allows people to regain their life, free from information anxiety, while still living in the bits. Here is the four-word philosophy:

Let the bits go.

That's right, let the bits go. Don't acquire them. Don't try to acquire them, and don't worry about acquiring them, since the bits will come to you. The bits touch our lives at so many points that it's impossible to escape them, and it's insane to try to acquire *all* of them. Instead, being bit literate means constantly working on *letting go* of as many of the bits as we can. Bit literacy allows us to clear a path of emptiness through the jungle of bits that surround and distract us; the emptiness allows us to see.

Here's a real-life example. Recently I visited a Web site where visitors can sign up to receive email newsletters, published by respected companies, on any number of topics. Internet news, sports commentary, entertainment gossip—all of these were available to me at the click of a button. I could get *all* of this information, delivered to my email inbox weekly . . . for free! And unlike subscriptions to paper magazines, these bits wouldn't clutter my apartment or need recycling. (I didn't sign up; I was there to unsubscribe from a newsletter.) So, one might reasonably ask, what's the problem with getting some potentially valuable or entertaining bits, if they don't clutter my living space, don't weigh me down, and don't cost a penny?

The problem is that the bits are different from paper-based information. Bits are more engaging, more immediate, more personal, and more abundant than other types of information. In the middle of lunch with a friend, we're interrupted by bits—perhaps a stock quote—and we instinctively reach for our PDAs to see what it is. Or we sit down to "read through some email" and blow through two hours like it was twenty minutes. Like the magazines and other anxiety-producing information, the bits call for our attention—but the bits call more loudly, more sweetly, more frequently, and in more areas of our lives.

These radically different qualities of bits mean that we must engage bits in a radically different way. Bit literacy is radical about letting the bits go. We can't let all the bits go—we must engage them first, and inevitably save the few most important bits—but our *default* behavior must be to let the bits go, rather than acquire and save them.

Here are some ways you can let the bits go: Keep your email inbox empty, by deleting your emails after saving the few that you *must* retain for later reference. Restrict the interruptions you allow on your cell phone and PDA, so that the interruptions that do come through are the important ones. And certainly don't open up any new bitstream—a newsletter, a ticker, or any other ongoing feed—unless it's vitally important. Instead, concentrate on letting go of the bits that find their way to you; the few remaining bits will be all the more valuable to you as a result.

I'd like to emphasize that last sentence: When a person becomes bit literate, what remains after all the letting go is *valuable*. I equate that with *meaningful*. Because—and here's the kicker—the bits by themselves aren't meaningful. Bits are just pointers to meaning, just containers of thoughts, just phantom images of the real item. The meaning is what lies behind the bits, what *drives* the bits. In their super-abundant quantities, swarming and overwhelming our consciousness, bits obscure the very meaning that created them. It's only after clearing out a path of emptiness that we can arrive at the meaning *behind* the bits.

DISCUSSION QUESTIONS:

1. Do you think information anxiety is a serious problem for many people? Explain your answer.

2. Do you think "bit literacy," as described by the author, makes sense? Explain your answer.

Summary

Whether it's working with words, numbers, pictures, or sounds, a computer is manipulating patterns of bits—binary digits of information that it can store in switching circuitry and that are represented by two symbols. Groups of bits can be treated as numbers for calculations using the binary number system. Bits can be grouped into coded messages that represent alphabetic characters, pictures, colors, sounds, or just about any other kind of information. Even the instructions computers follow—the software programs that tell the computer what to do—must be reduced to strings of bits before the computer accepts them. Byte, kilobyte, megabyte, and other common units for measuring bit quantities are used in descriptions of memory, storage, and file size.

The central processing unit (CPU) follows software instructions to perform the calculations and logical manipulations that transform input data into output. Not all CPUs are compatible with each other; each is capable of processing a particular set of instructions, so a program written for one family of processors can't be understood by a processor from another family. Engineers are constantly improving the clock speed and architecture of CPUs, making computers capable of processing information faster.

The CPU uses RAM (random access memory) as a temporary storage area—a scratch pad—for instructions and data. Another type of memory, ROM (read-only memory), contains unchangeable information that serves as reference material for the CPU as it executes program instructions.

The CPU and main memory are housed in silicon chips on one or more circuit boards inside the computer. Buses connect to slots and ports that enable the computer to communicate with peripherals.

Chapter Review

▼ Key Terms

architecture (p. 59)
ASCII (p. 56)
backward compatible (p. 59)
bay (p. 63)
binary (p. 53)
bit (p. 53)
bus (p. 61)
byte (p. 54)
central processing unit (CPU) (p. 52)
circuit board (p. 58)
compatible (p. 59)
digital (p. 53)

expansion slot (p. 63)
file (p. 58)
GB (gigabyte) (p. 58)
information (p. 53)
input device (p. 52)
K (kilobyte) (p. 58)
MB (megabyte) (p. 58)
memory (p. 52)
motherboard (p. 58)
multiprocessing (p. 62)
nonvolatile memory (p. 63)
output device (p. 52)

parallel processing (p. 62)
PC card (p. 64)
peripheral (p. 53)
port (p. 63)
processor (p. 52)
RAM (random access memory) (p. 62)
ROM (read-only memory) (p. 63)
storage device (p. 52)
TB (terabyte) (p. 58)
Unicode (p. 56)
volatile memory (p. 63)

▼ Interactive Quiz Questions

1. The *Computer Confluence* CD-ROM contains self-test quiz questions related to this chapter, including multiple choice, true or false, and matching questions.
2. The *Computer Confluence* Web site, **www.prenhall.com/beekman**, contains self-test exercises related to this chapter. Follow the instructions for taking a quiz. After you've completed your quiz, you can email the results to your instructor.

The Web site also contains open-ended discussion questions called Internet Explorations. Discuss one or more of the Internet Exploration questions at the section for this chapter.

▼ Review Questions

1. Provide a working definition of each of the key words listed in the "Key Terms" section. Check your answers in the glossary.
2. Draw a block diagram showing the major components of a computer and their relationship. Briefly describe the function of each component.
3. Think of this as computer input: 123.4. The computer might read this as a number or as a set of ASCII codes. Explain how these concepts differ.
4. Why is information stored in some kind of binary format in computers?
5. Why can't you normally run Macintosh software on a PC with an Intel Pentium II CPU?
6. Clock speed is only one factor in determining a CPU's processing speed. What is another?
7. How does a RISC processor differ from a CISC processor?
8. Explain how parallel processing can increase a computer's speed; use an example or a comparison with the way people work if you like.
9. What is the difference between RAM and ROM? What is the purpose of each?
10. What is the difference between primary and secondary storage?

▼ Discussion Questions

1. Why are computer manufacturers constantly releasing faster computers? How do computer users benefit from the increased speed?
2. How is human memory similar to computer memory? How is it different?

▼ Projects

1. Collect computer advertisements from newspapers, magazines, and other sources. Compare how the ads handle discussions of speed. Evaluate the usefulness of the information in the ads from a consumer's point of view.
2. Interview a salesperson in a computer store. Find out what kinds of questions people ask when buying a computer. Develop profiles for the most common types of computer buyers. What kinds of computers do these customers buy, and why?

 Sources and Resources

Books

Building IBM: Shaping an Industry and Its Technology, by Emerson W. Pugh (Cambridge, MA: MIT Press, 1995). This book traces IBM's history from Herman Hollerith's invention of the punch card machine more than a century ago. This thoroughly researched and clearly written book is a valuable resource for anyone interested in understanding IBM's history.

ThinkPad: A Different Shade of Blue, by Deboarh Dell and J. Gerry Purdy (Indianapolis: Sams, 2000). This is an insider's look at the making of IBM's wildly successful portable. Thomas Watson's philosophy inspired this product—a product that helped revive the company Watson founded.

Information Anxiety 2, by Richard Saul Wurman (Indianapolis: Que, 2001). This is a revised and updated version of Wurman's popular 1989 book. The style and organization are sometimes quirky, but the content is useful and thought-provoking. Wurman discusses the nature and value of information, and offers advice about how to cope with the explosion of non-information—"stuff that doesn't inform."

How Computers Work, Sixth Edition, by Ron White (Indianapolis: Que, 2001). The first edition of *How Computers Work* launched a series and inspired many imitators. Like its predecessor, this revised and expanded edition clearly illustrates with beautiful pictures and accessible prose how each component of a modern personal computer system works. If you're interested in looking under the hood, this is a great place to start. The book was produced on a Macintosh, but the explanations and illustrations are based on Wintel (Windows/Intel) computers. Still, most of the concepts apply to computers in general. A Windows-only CD-ROM includes a multimedia tour of a computer.

How the Mac Works: Millennium Edition, by John Rizzo and K. Daniel Clark (Indianapolis: Que, 2000). This book covers the basics of Macintosh anatomy in the same style as *How Computers Work*.

The Soul of a New Machine, by Tracy Kidder (Back Bay Books, 2000). This Pulitzer Prize winning book provides a journalist's inside look at the making of a new computer in the late

1970s, including lots of insights into what makes computers (and computer people) tick. It's still a good read more than two decades later.

The Essential Guide to Computing: The Story of Information Technology, by E. Garrison Walters (Upper Saddle River, NJ: Prentice Hall, 2001). This is a highly readable and surprisingly broad overview of computer technology, with coverage of hardware, software, and networks. The book provides historical and industry perspectives along with solid technical information that goes beyond the usual introductory books.

Personal Computers for Technology Students, by Charles Raymond (Upper Saddle River, NJ: Prentice Hall, 2001). This is a technical but readable text on the PC, from CPU to peripherals. It includes a useful glossary of acronyms, in case you need to know what SRAM or SVGA stands for.

Computer Sourcebook, by Alfred and Emily Glossbrenner (New York: Random House, 1997). This massive book is an eclectic collection of facts, figures, lists, and anecdotes related to PCs. Reading this book may give you the feeling that these two prolific authors are allowing you to rummage through their file cabinets. Want to learn how to get free computer magazine subscriptions? How to get help when something goes wrong with your PC? How to choose a backup system? You're almost certain to find plenty of useful information here, along with quite a bit that's of little value.

Peter Norton's Inside the PC, Eighth Edition, by Peter Norton and John Goodman (Indianapolis: Sams, 1999). Norton's name is almost a household word among PC enthusiasts, many of whom consider Norton Utilities to be indispensable software. This book offers clear, detailed explanations of the inner workings of the PC, from CPU to peripherals, from hardware to software. You don't need to be a technical wizard to understand and learn from this book.

World Wide Web Pages

Most computer hardware manufacturers have World Wide Web pages on the Internet. Use a Web browser such as Netscape Navigator or Microsoft Internet Explorer to visit some of these sites for information about the latest hardware from these companies. It's not hard to guess the Web addresses of computer companies; most follow the pattern suggested by these examples:

www.ibm.com

www.apple.com

www.dell.com

The *Computer Confluence* Web site, **www.prenhall.com/beekman**, will guide you to these and other hardware pages of interest.

3

Hardware Basics:
Peripherals

After you read this chapter you should be able to:

List several examples of input devices and explain how they can make it easier to get different types of information into the computer

List several examples of output devices and explain how they make computers more useful

Explain why a typical computer has different types of storage devices

Diagram how the components of a computer system fit together

▼ In this chapter:

Why the letters on a keyboard are all mixed up

Pointing, painting, typing, and talking to your computer

Why onscreen pictures look different when you print them

Sound in, sound out

How a PC can hurt your health, and how to protect yourself

Self-study questions and projects

Mini-reviews of helpful resources for further study

… and more.

▼ On the CD-ROM:

Interactive activities on how input devices work

Instant access to glossary and key word references

Interactive self-study quizzes

…and more.

▼ On the Web:

www.prenhall.com/beekman

Documents describing and illustrating a variety of state-of-the-art peripherals

Links to the most important computer peripheral companies

Self-study exercises

… and more.

Steve Wozniak, Steve Jobs, and the
Garage that Grew Apples

It's **not** like we were all smart enough to see a **revolution coming**.
Back then, I thought there might be a revolution in **opening** your garage door,
balancing your checkbook, **keeping** your recipes, that sort of thing.
There are **a million people** who study markets and analyze economic trends,
people who are **more brilliant than I am**, people who worked for
companies like Digital Equipment and IBM and Hewlett-Packard.
None of them foresaw what was going to happen, either.

—Steve Wozniak

What Steve Wozniak ("the Woz") and all those other people failed to foresee was the personal computer revolution—a revolution that he helped start. Wozniak, a brilliant engineer with an eye for detail, worked days as a calculator technician at Hewlett-Packard; he was refused an engineer's job because he lacked a college degree. At night he designed and constructed a scaled-down computer system that would fit the home hobbyist's budget. When he completed it in 1975, he offered it to HP; they turned it down.

Steve Wozniak and Steve Jobs.

Wozniak took his invention to the Homebrew Computer Club in Palo Alto, where it caught the imagination of another college dropout, Steven Jobs. A free-thinking visionary, Jobs persuaded Wozniak to quit his job in 1976 to form a company and market the machine, which they named the Apple I. Jobs raised $1,300 in seed capital by selling his Volkswagen, and Apple Computer, Inc., was born in Jobs's garage.

With the help and financial backing of businessman A.C. Markkula, the two Steves turned Apple into a thriving business. Wozniak created the Apple II, a more refined machine, and invented the first personal computer disk operating system so computers wouldn't be dependent on cassette tapes for storage. Jobs assumed the leadership role in the company. Because it put computing power within everyone's reach, the Apple II became popular in businesses, homes, and especially schools. Apple became the first company in American history to join the Fortune 500 in less than five years. Still in his mid-twenties, Jobs was running a corporate giant. But troubled times were ahead for Apple.

When IBM introduced its PC in 1982, it overshadowed Apple's presence in the business world, where people were accustomed to working with IBM mainframes. Other companies developed PC clones, treating the IBM PC as a standard—a standard that Apple refused to accept. Inspired by a visit to Xerox's Palo Alto Research Center (PARC), Jobs worked with a team of Apple engineers to develop the Macintosh, a futuristic computer he hoped would leapfrog IBM's advantage. When Jobs insisted on focusing most of Apple's resources on the Macintosh, Wozniak resigned to pursue other interests.

Businesses failed to embrace the Mac, and Apple stockholders grew uneasy with Jobs's controversial management style. In 1985, a year and a half after the Macintosh was introduced, Jobs was ousted. He went on to form NeXT, a company that produced workstations and software. He later bought Pixar, the computer animation company that captured the public's attention with *Toy Story*, the first computer-generated full-length motion picture.

After Apple's fortunes declined under a string of CEOs, the company bought NeXT in 1997 and invited an older and wiser Jobs to retake the helm. He agreed to share his time between Pixar and Apple. Under his leadership, Apple has regained its innovative edge, releasing a flurry of successful products that combine high technology with high style. Apple's rising market share is small in a business world dominated by IBM-compatible PCs running Microsoft Windows. Still, Apple retains an almost fanatically loyal customer base focused mainly in homes and creative markets, such as publishing, graphic design, multimedia, and education. While Jobs continues to lead Apple and Pixar, Woz is content to teach computing skills to kids in his community. ❱

The Apple II's phenomenal success wasn't due to a powerful processor or massive memory; the machine had at its core a relatively primitive processor and only 16K of memory. The Apple II was more than a processor and memory; it included a keyboard, a monitor, and disk and tape drives for storage. While other companies sold computer kits to tinkerers, the two Steves delivered complete computer systems to hobbyists, schools, and businesses. They recognized that a computer wasn't complete without peripherals.

In this chapter we'll complete the tour of hardware we started in the last chapter. We've seen the CPU and memory at the heart of the system unit; now we'll explore the peripherals that radiate out from those central components. We'll start with input devices, then move on to output devices, and finish with a look at external storage devices. As usual, the main text provides the basic overview; if you want or need to know more about the inner workings, consult the *How It Works* boxes scattered throughout the chapter.

Input: From Person to Processor

A computer terminal is **not** some **clunky old** television with a typewriter in front of it. It is an **interface** where the **mind** and **body** can **connect** with the **universe** and **move bits** of it about.
—Douglas Adams, author of *The Hitchhiker's Guide to the Galaxy*

The nuts and bolts of information processing are usually hidden from the user, who sees only the input and output, or as the pros say, *I/O*. This wasn't always the case. Users of the first computers communicated one bit at a time by flipping switches on massive consoles or plugging wires into switchboards; they had to be intimately familiar with the inner workings of the machines before they could successfully communicate with them. In contrast, today's users have a choice of hundreds of input devices, which make it easy to enter data and commands into their machines. Of these input devices, the most familiar is the computer **keyboard**.

The Keyboard

A standard computer keyboard has straight rows of keys.

An ergonomic keyboard puts the keys at an angle to allow your wrists to assume a more natural position while you type.

In spite of nearly universal acceptance as an input device, the QWERTY keyboard (named for the first row of letter keys) seems strangely out of place in a modern computer system. The original arrangement of the keys, chosen to reduce the likelihood of jammed keys on early typewriters, stays with us a century later, forcing millions of people to learn an awkward system just so they can enter text into their computers. Alternatives to the QWERTY key arrangements have been shown to be easier to learn and use. For example, on the Dvorak keyboard the most frequently typed letters are located closest to the fingers' resting positions. But technological traditions die hard, and the QWERTY keyboard is still standard equipment on virtually all PCs.

Some modern computer keyboards stray from the traditional typewriter design in other ways. Typing on a standard keyboard, with keys lined up in straight rows, forces you to hold your arms and wrists at unnatural angles. Evidence suggests that long hours of typing this way may lead to medical problems, including **repetitive-stress injuries** such as tendonitus and carpal tunnel syndrome. **Ergonomic keyboards** place the keys at angles that are easier on your arms and hands without changing the ordering of the keys.

Whether it's straight or ergonomic, a typical keyboard sends signals to the computer through a coiled cable. A *wireless keyboard* can send infrared signals (similar to those of a TV remote control) so it isn't tethered to the rest of the system by a cable.

Other variations on keyboard design include folding keyboards for use with palm-sized computers, miniature keyboards built into pocket-sized devices, one-handed keyboards for people who need to (or prefer to) keep one hand free for other work, and keyboards printed on membranes that can be rolled or folded like paper. Innovative ideas are still emerging from that ancient typewriter technology.

This portable keyboard, designed for use with a Handspring Visor PDA, folds so it can easily fit in your pocket.

This half keyboard enables the user to type with one hand so the other hand is free for other tasks, including pointing.

Some pocket computers have QWERTY keyboards even though they're too small for touch typing.

This fabric keyboard can be folded, crumpled, or even washed like a piece of clothing.

Pointing Devices

Computer users today use their keyboards mostly to enter text and numeric data. For other traditional keyboard functions such as sending commands and positioning the cursor, they typically use a **mouse**. The mouse is designed to move a pointer around the screen and point to specific characters or objects. The most common type of mouse has a ball on its underside that allows it to roll around on the desktop. Another type of mouse uses reflected light to detect movement. The mouse has one or more buttons that can be used to send signals to the computer, conveying messages such as "Perform this command," "Activate the selected tool," and "Select all the text between these two points." Many modern PC mice include a scrolling wheel between the two standard buttons.

It's virtually impossible to find a new computer today that doesn't come with a mouse as standard equipment, but there is one exception: The mouse is impractical as a pointing device on portable computers because these machines are often used where there's no room for a mouse to roam across a desktop. Portable computer manufacturers provide a variety of alternatives to the mouse as a general-purpose pointing device:

▶ The **touchpad** (sometimes called *trackpad*) is a small flat panel that's sensitive to light pressure. The user moves the pointer by dragging a finger across the pad.

▶ The **pointing stick** (often called TrackPoint, IBM's brand name for the device) is a tiny handle that sits in the center of the keyboard, responding to finger pressure by moving the pointer in the direction in which it's pushed. It's like a miniature embedded joystick.

▶ The **trackball** is like an upside-down mouse. It remains stationary while the user moves the protruding ball to control the pointer on the screen. (Trackballs are also available as space-saving mouse alternatives for desktop machines.)

The most common type of computer mouse has two buttons. The Microsoft Mouse has multiple buttons and a scroll wheel to streamline the process of scrolling through text or graphical windows; other mice have a similar design. The Apple Mouse has no buttons, but the entire surface of the mouse serves as a button.

Other pointing devices offer advantages for specific types of computer work (and play). Here are some examples:

▶ The **joystick** is a gearshift-like device that's a favorite controller for arcade-style computer games.

▶ The **graphics tablet** is popular with artists and designers. Most touch tablets are pressure sensitive, so they can send different signals depending on how hard the user presses on the tablet with a stylus. The stylus performs the same point-and-click functions as a mouse.

▶ The **touch screen** responds when the user points to or touches different screen regions. Computers with touch screens are frequently used in public libraries, airports, and shopping malls where many users are unfamiliar with computers. Touch screens are also used in many handheld computers and PDAs; a *stylus* can be used for pointing or writing on these tiny screens.

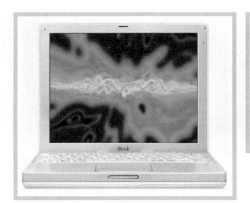

This Apple iBook (top left), like many portable computers, includes a built-in touchpad as a pointing device. The IBM ThinkPad (top center) has a tiny pointing stick (called a TrackPoint) embedded in its keyboard (above the B key) for positioning the cursor on the screen. Many video game machines and some portable and desktop PCs use trackballs (top right) for pointing devices. Joysticks (bottom left) are the chief weapons of the arcade army. Many computer artists find that drawing and painting are easier with a graphics tablet (bottom center) than with a mouse. Touch-screen monitors are ideal for kiosks, ATM machines, and self-serve checkout stands in stores and other public buildings (bottom right).

Reading Tools

In spite of their versatility, pointing devices are woefully inefficient for the input of large quantities of text into computers, which is why the mouse hasn't replaced the keyboard on the standard personal computer. Still, there are alternatives to typing for entering numbers and words into computers. Some types of devices allow computers to rapidly read marks, representing codes, specifically designed for computer input:

▶ **Optical-mark readers** use reflected light to determine the location of pencil marks on standardized test answer sheets and similar forms.

▶ **Magnetic-ink character readers** read those odd-shaped numbers printed with magnetic ink on checks.

▶ **Bar-code readers** use light to read *universal product codes (UPCs)*, inventory codes, and other codes created from patterns of variable-width bars. In many stores, bar-code readers are attached to **point-of-sale (POS) terminals**. These terminals send scanned information to a mainframe computer. The computer determines the item's price, calculates taxes and totals, and records the transaction for future use in inventory, accounting, and other areas.

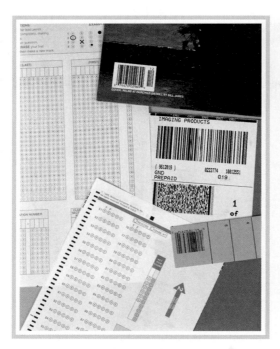

Computers use specialized input devices to read information stored as optical marks, bar codes, and specially designed characters.

This self-service POS terminal uses two input devices for gathering information about a purchase: a touch screen for entering commands and answering questions and a bar-code reader for scanning product information. Before the transaction is completed, another input device reads information encoded in the magnetic strip on the customer's credit card.

Because test forms, magnetic ink characters, and bar codes were designed to be read by computers, the devices that read them are extremely accurate. Reading text from books, magazines, and other printed documents is more challenging because of the great variety of printed text. **Optical character recognition (OCR)** is the technology of recognizing individual characters on a printed page, so they can be stored and edited as text.

Before a computer can recognize handwriting or printed text, it must first create a digital image of the page that it can store in memory. This is usually done with an input device known as a scanner. There are many types of scanners, as you'll see in the next section. A scanner doesn't actually read or recognize letters and numbers on a page—it just makes a digital "picture" of the page available to the computer. The computer can then use OCR software to interpret the black and white scanned patterns as letters and numbers.

Actually, a few special-purpose scanners take care of the OCR work themselves. *Pen scanners* look like highlighters, but they're actually wireless scanners that can perform character recognition on the fly. When you drag a pen scanner across a line of printed text, it creates a text file in its built-in memory, where it's stored until you transfer it into your computer's memory through a cable or infrared beam. A wireless pen scanner actually contains a small computer programmed to recognize printed text. This kind of optical character recognition isn't 100 percent accurate, but it's getting better all the time.

A pen scanner can capture text from a printed document and transfer it to a PC.

Handwriting recognition is far more difficult and error-prone than printed character recognition. But handwriting recognition has many practical applications today, especially in **pen-based computers**. A pen-based computer is a keyboardless machine that accepts input from a stylus applied directly to a flat-panel screen. The computer electronically simulates a pen and pad of paper. **Handwriting recognition software** translates the user's handwritten forms into ASCII characters. Most such systems require users to modify their handwriting so that it's consistent and unambiguous enough for the software to decipher reliably.

Personal digital assistants (PDAs) are pen computers that serve as pocket-sized organizers, notebooks, appointment books, and communication devices. These popular, verasatile devices can also be programmed for specialized work ranging from sports scorekeeping to medical analysis.

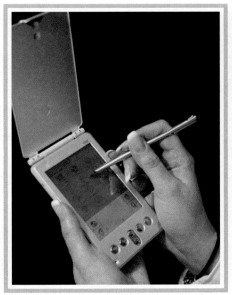

The Palm OS software can recognize hand-drawn characters, but only if they're printed according to the rules of the Graffiti system (above). Pen input is used in handheld computers such as this Handspring Visor (center). The much larger Tablet PC (right) is a prototype of a full-featured Windows computer designed to accept pen input.

A smart whiteboard can send its contents to a PC, simplifying and streamlining the note-taking process for many meetings and classes.

Information workers who spend lots of time filling out forms use special-purpose pen-based systems. You've probably signed for a package or a credit card purchase using a pen-based computer system.

Handwriting recognition software can even be applied to notes scrawled on a whiteboard in a meeting room or classroom. A *smart whiteboard* can serve as an input device for a PC, so each board full of information is stored as a digital image on the computer's disk. If the writing is clear enough, handwriting recognition software can turn the whiteboard notes into a text file that can be emailed to meeting or class participants. (OCR and handwriting recognition are covered in more detail in later chapters.)

Digitizing the Real World

> The . . . **number-one peripheral device** is not a drive. It's not a printer, scanner, hub, or network. It's you, the user.
> —John K. Rizzo and K. Daniel Clark, in *How the Mac Works*

Before a computer can recognize handwriting or printed text, a scanner or other input device must **digitize** the information—convert it into a digital form. Because real-world information comes in so many forms, a variety of input devices have been designed for capturing and digitizing information. In this section we'll examine several of these devices, from common scanners to exotic sensors.

A **scanner** is an input device that can create a digital representation of a printed image. The most common models today are *flatbed scanners*, which look and work like photocopy machines, except that they create computer files instead of paper copies. Inexpensive flatbed scanners are designed for home and small business use. More expensive models used by graphics professionals are capable of producing higher-quality reproductions, and, with attachments, scan photographic negatives and slides. Some scanners, called *slide scanners*, can scan *only* slides and negatives. These special-

A slide scanner can produce high-quality digital reproductions from photographic negatives and slides.

Flatbed scanners capture and digitize images from external paper sources.

ized tools generally produce higher-quality results than flatbed scanners when scanning transparencies. *Drum scanners* are larger and more expensive than flatbeds; they're used in publishing applications where image quality is critical. At the other end of the spectrum, *sheet-fed scanners* are small, portable, and inexpensive. Regardless of its type or capabilities, however, a scanner converts photographs, drawings, charts, and other printed information into bit patterns that can be stored and manipulated in a computer's memory, usually using graphics software.

In the same way, a **digital camera** can capture snapshots of the real world as digital images. Unlike a scanner, a digital camera isn't limited to capturing flat printed images; it can record anything that a normal camera can. A digital camera looks like a normal camera. But instead of capturing images on film, a digital camera stores bit patterns on disks or other digital storage media.

A *video digitizer* is a collection of circuits that can capture input from a video camera, video cassette recorder, television, or other video source and convert it to a digital signal that can be stored in memory and displayed on computer screens. A *digital video camera* can send video signals directly into a computer without a video digitizer, because its video images are digitized when they're captured by the camera. Digital video input makes it possible for professionals and hobbyists to edit videos with a computer. Digital video is also used for multimedia applications such as Web page and CD-ROM development. And a growing number of businesses use video cameras and PCs for desktop *videoconferencing*. With videoconferencing software and hardware, people in diverse locations can see and hear each other while they conduct long-distance meetings; their video images are transmitted through networks. These video applications are discussed in more detail in later chapters.

Audio digitizers contain circuitry to digitize sounds from microphones and other audio devices. Digitized sounds can be stored in a computer's memory and modified with software. Of course, audio digitizers can capture spoken words as well as music and sound effects. But digitizing spoken input isn't the same thing as converting speech into text. Like scanned text input, digitized *voice input* is just data to the computer. *Speech recognition* software, a type of artificial

Consumer cameras like the one shown in the top-left photo sell for a few hundred dollars; professional models like this one in the top-center photo cost much more. A plug-in module turns the Handspring PDA into a digital camera in the top-right photo. Digital video cameras like the one in the bottom-left photo can deliver video data directly to a PC or Macintosh. A PC camera or Web cam like the one in the bottom-right photo can continuously feed still pictures or video directly to an attached PC.

3.1
Digitizing the Real World

We live in an analog world, where we can perceive smooth, continuous changes in color and sound. Modern digital computers store all information as discrete binary numbers. To store analog information, such as an analog sound or image, in a computer we must digitize it—convert it from analog to digital form.

Digitizing involves using an input device, such as a desktop scanner or audio board, to take millions of tiny samples of the original. A sample of an image might be one pinpoint-sized area of the image; each sample from an audio source is like a brief recording of the sound at a particular instant.

The value of a sample can be represented numerically and therefore stored on a computer. A representation of the original image or sound can be reconstructed by assembling all the samples in sequence.

Scanners

A typical desktop scanner contains a camera similar to the kind found in many video camcorders. The scanner camera moves back and forth across an original image, recording for each sample the intensities of red, green, and blue light at that point. (Human eyes have receptors for red, green, and blue light; all colors are perceived as combinations of these three.) A single byte commonly represents the intensity of each color component; a 3-byte (24-bit) code represents the color for each sample. The scanner sends each digital code to the computer, where it can be stored and manipulated.

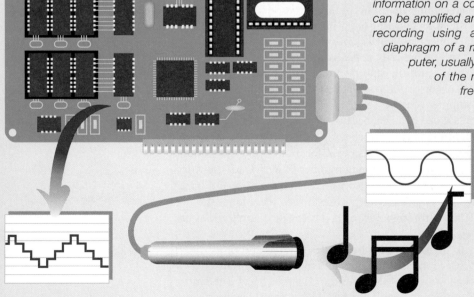

Audio Digitizers

Digital audio is commonplace today; the CD player is really a computer system designed to translate digital information on a compact disc into analog signals that can be amplified and sent to speakers. In digital audio recording using a PC, sound waves vibrate the diaphragm of a microphone connected to the computer, usually through a sound card. The position of the microphone diaphragm is sampled frequently—as much as 44,000 times each second—and its level is stored as a number. The faster the sampling frequency, the better the sound recording. Using more storage to represent finer gradations of the sound level also offers better sound. An 8-bit sample can represent 256 distinct levels; a 16-bit sample can represent 65,536 levels. Whether digitizing sounds or images, attempts to increase fidelity to the original usually increases storage requirements.

intelligence software, can convert voice data into words that can be edited and printed. Speech recognition software has been available for years, but until recently it wasn't reliable enough to be of much practical use. The latest products are still too limited to replace keyboards for most people. They generally must be trained to recognize individual voices; they typically require the speaker to carefully articulate each word, and they often work with only a limited vocabulary. Still, they're invaluable for people with disabilities and others who can't use their hands while they work. The promise and problems of automated speech recognition will be explored in later chapters.

Sensors designed to monitor temperature, humidity, pressure, and other physical quantities provide data used in robotics, environmental climate control, weather forecasting, medical monitoring, biofeedback, scientific research, and hundreds of other applications. Even our sense of smell can be simulated with sensors. Such sensors might soon be used to detect spoiled foods, land mines, chemical spills, or halitosis.

Computers can accept input from a variety of other sources, including manufacturing equipment, telephones, communication networks, and other computers. New input devices are being developed all the time as technologies evolve and human needs change. By stretching the computer's capabilities, these devices stretch our imaginations to develop new ways of using computers. We'll consider some of the more interesting and exotic technologies later; for now we turn our attention to the output end of the process.

Speech recognition software allows this officer to record spoken notes without using a keyboard.

Output: From Pulses to People

As a rule, men **worry** more about **what they can't see** than about what they can.
—Julius Caesar

A computer can do all kinds of things, but none of them is worth anything to us unless we have a way to get the results out of the box. Output devices convert the computer's internal bit patterns into a form that humans can understand. The first computers were limited to flashing lights, teletypewriters, and other primitive communication devices. Most computers today produce output through two main types of devices: monitor screens for immediate visual output and printers for permanent paper output.

Screen Output

The **monitor**, or **video display terminal (VDT)**, serves as a one-way window between the computer user and the machine. Early computer monitors were designed to display characters—text, numbers, and tiny graphic symbols. Today's monitors are as likely to display graphics, photographic images, animation, and video as they are to display text and numbers. Because of the monitor's ever-expanding role as a graphical output device, computer users need to know a bit about the factors that control image size and quality.

Monitor size, like television size, is measured as the length of a diagonal line across the screen; a typical desktop monitor today measures from 15 to 21 inches diagonally, but the actual viewable area is usually smaller. Images on a monitor are composed of tiny dots, called **pixels** (for picture elements). A square inch of an image on a monitor is typically a grid of dots about 72 pixels on each side. Such a monitor has a **resolution** of 72 dots per inch (dpi). The higher the resolution, the closer together the dots and the clearer the image. Another way to describe resolution is to refer to the total number of pixels displayed on the screen. Assuming that two monitors are the same size, the one that places the dots closest together displays more pixels—and creates a sharper, clearer image. When describing resolution in this way, people usually indicate the number of columns and rows of pixels rather than the total number of pixels. For example, a 1,024 × 768 image is composed of 1,024 columns by 768 rows of pixels, for a total of 786,432 pixels.

Resolution isn't the only factor that determines image quality. Computer monitors are limited by *color depth*—the number of different colors they can display at the same time. Color depth is sometimes called *bit depth,* because a wider range of colors per pixel takes up more bits of space in video memory. If each pixel is allotted 8 bits of memory, the resulting image can have up to 256 different colors on screen at a time. (There are 256 unique combinations of 8 bits to use as color codes.) In other words, 8-bit color, common in older PCs, has a color depth of 256. Most graphics professionals use 24-bit color, or *true color*, because it allows more than 16 million color choices

These four images show the same photograph displayed in four different bit depths: 1, 4, 8, and 16 bits.

per pixel—more than enough for photorealistic images. *Monochrome monitors* can display only monochrome images. *Gray-scale monitors* (which can display black, white, and shades of gray but no other colors) and *color monitors* (which can display a range of colors) have greater color depth. A modern PC or Macintosh can display different combinations of resolution and color depth on the same monitor.

The monitor is connected to the computer by way of the *video adapter*, which is a circuit board installed in a slot inside the main system unit. An image on the monitor exists inside the computer in *video memory*, or *VRAM*, a special portion of RAM dedicated to holding video images. The amount of VRAM determines the maximum resolution and color depth that a computer system can display. The more video memory a computer has, the more detail it can present in a picture.

Most monitors fall into one of two classes: television-style **CRT (cathode-ray tube) monitors** and flat-panel **LCD (liquid crystal display) monitors**. Because of their clarity, speedy response time, and low cost, CRTs still dominate desktops. Lighter, more compact LCDs are used primarily in portable computers. But *overhead projection panels* and *video projectors* also use them to project computer screen images for meetings and classes. As LCDs are dropping in price, they are turning up on more and more desktops; many experts predict they'll eventually replace bulky CRTs on most desks.

Paper Output

Output displayed on a monitor is immediate but temporary. A **printer** can produce a hard copy on paper of any static information that can be displayed on the computer's screen. Printers

Most desktop computers use CRT monitors because they're inexpensive and they produce high-quality images. But lightweight, flat-screen LCD monitors are becoming more popular on desktops as their prices come down and their image quality improves (right). LCDs are also used in projectors that allow computer screen images to be projected for large viewing audiences (below).

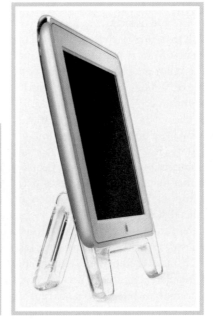

come in several varieties, but they all fit into two basic groups: *impact printers* and *nonimpact printers*.

Impact printers include line printers and dot-matrix printers. Printers of this type share one common characteristic: They form images by physically striking paper, ribbon, and print hammer together, the way a typewriter does. Mainframes use **line printers** to produce massive printouts; these speedy, noisy beasts hammer out thousands of lines of text per minute. You've undoubtedly seen form letters from banks and stores, bills from utility companies, and report cards from schools

3.2
Color Video

The colors in some CRT video images glow because the monitor is a luminous source of light using additive color synthesis—colors are formed by adding different amounts of red, green, and blue light.

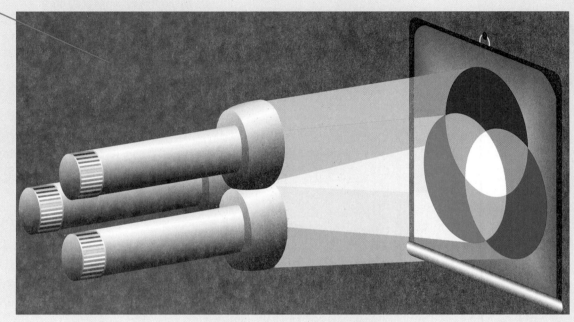

Like television sets, computer monitors refresh or update their images many times per second. If a monitor refreshes its image fewer than 70 times per second (70 hertz), the flicker may be enough to cause eye strain, headaches, and nausea. Many monitors slow down their refresh rates if the resolution is increased, so if you're shopping for a monitor, buy one with a refresh rate of more than 70 hertz at the maximum resolution you expect to be using.

Another factor that should figure into your purchasing decision is the monitor's dot pitch—the measurement of how close the holes in the grid are to each other. The smaller the dot pitch, the closer the holes and the sharper the image.

When viewed from a distance of more than a few inches, the three dots visually merge; the color created by this mixing depends on the strength of each of the color electron beams.

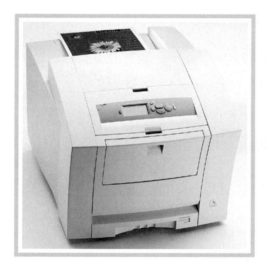

Dot-matrix printer (top left), desktop inkjet printer (top right), portable inkjet printer (bottom left), and laser printer (bottom right). All provide different forms of hard copy output.

that were printed with line printers. Because they're limited to printing characters, line printers are inadequate for applications such as desktop publishing, where graphics are essential.

Dot-matrix printers print text and graphics with equal ease. Instead of printing each character as a solid object, a dot-matrix printer uses pinpoint-sized hammers to transfer ink to the page. The printed page is a matrix of tiny dots, some white and some black (or, for color printers, other colors). It's almost as if the computer were hammering bits directly on the page. The final printout might be a picture, text, or a combination of the two. A typical dot-matrix printer produces printouts with a resolution—relative closeness of dots—of less than 100 dots per inch (dpi). An image displayed on a computer screen looks fine at this resolution, but a 100 dpi printout of a photo or drawing looks rough and ragged. The pixels that make up characters and pictures are obvious to even casual viewers.

Except for those applications, such as billing, where multipart forms need to be printed, **nonimpact printers** have replaced impact printers in most offices. The two main types of nonimpact printers are laser printers and inkjet printers. **Laser printers** can print four to thirty pages per minute of high-quality text and graphical output. Because of their speed, durability, and reliability, they're often shared in office environments. Laser printers use the same technology as photocopy machines: A laser beam creates patterns of electrical charges on a rotating drum; those charged patterns attract black toner and transfer it to paper as the drum rotates. Color laser printers can print multicolor images by mixing different toner shades.

People who work in color tend to use less expensive **inkjet printers**, which spray ink directly onto paper to produce printed text and graphic images. Inkjets generally print fewer pages per minute (one to twelve) than laser printers. But high-quality color inkjet printers cost far less than color laser printers, and many are less expensive than the cheapest black-and-white laser printers. Inkjet printers are also smaller and lighter than laser printers. Portable inkjet printers designed to travel with laptops weigh only a couple of pounds each. Some inkjet printers, called photo printers, are specially optimized to print high-quality photos captured with digital cameras and scanners.

3.3
Color Printing

Printed colors can't be as vivid as video colors because printed images don't produce light like a monitor does; they only reflect light. Most color printers use subtractive synthesis to produce colors: They mix together various amounts of cyan (light blue), magenta (reddish purple), yellow, and black pigments to create a color.

Most printers, like monitors, are raster devices—they form images from little dots. The resolution of raster printers is normally measured in dots per inch (dpi). Printers have resolutions of hundreds—or even thousands—of dpi.

Matching on-screen color with printed color is difficult because monitors use additive color synthesis to obtain the color, whereas printers use subtractive synthesis. Monitors are able to display more colors than printers, though printers can display a few colors that monitors can't. But the range of colors that humans can perceive extends beyond either technology.

You can demonstrate subtractive synthesis by painting overlapping areas of cyan, magenta, and yellow ink. The combination of all three is black; combinations of pairs produce red, green, and blue, which are secondary colors of the subtractive system.

Both laser and inkjet printers produce output with much higher resolution—usually 600 or more dots per inch—than is possible with dot-matrix models. At these resolutions it's hard to tell with the naked eye that characters are, in fact, composed of dots. The best color printers can reproduce photographs with striking accuracy. Because of their ability to print high-resolution text and pictures, nonimpact printers dominate the printer market today.

Multifunction peripherals (**MFP**, also called *all-in-one devices*) take advantage of the fact that different tools can use similar technologies. A multifunction device can combine a scanner, a printer, and a fax modem (described in the Telecommunications and Networking chapter). Such a device can serve as a printer, a scanner, a color photocopy machine, and a fax machine.

A multifunction peripheral combines a printer with a scanner and a modem so it can serve as a printer, a scanner, a photocopy machine, and a fax machine.

For certain scientific and engineering applications, a **plotter** is more appropriate than a printer for producing hard copy. A plotter is an automated drawing tool that can produce large, finely scaled drawings, engineering blueprints, and maps by moving the pen and/or the paper in response to computer commands.

Output You Can Hear

Most modern PCs include sound cards. A **sound card** enables the PC to accept microphone input, play music and other sound through speakers or headphones, and process sound in a variety of ways. (All Macintoshes and some PCs have audio circuitry integrated with the rest of the system so they don't need separate sound cards.) With a sound card, a PC can play digital recordings of all kinds of sounds, from personal recordings made with the PC and a microphone to music downloaded from the Internet.

Most sound cards also include *synthesizers*—specialized circuitry designed to generate sounds electronically. These synthesizers can be used to produce music, noise, or anything in between. A computer also can be connected to a stand-alone music synthesizer, so the computer has complete control of the instrument. Computers can also generate synthesized speech with the right software. Of course, to produce any kind of sound, the computer needs to include or be attached to speakers or headphones.

Controlling Other Machines

In the same way that many input devices convert real-world sights and sounds into digital pulses, many output devices work in the other direction, taking bit patterns and turning them into nondigital movements or measurements. Robot arms, telephone switchboards, transportation devices, automated factory equipment, spacecraft, and a host of other machines and systems accept their orders from computers.

In one example familiar to computer gamers, an enhanced input device delivers output. The force feedback joystick can receive signals from a computer and give tactile feedback—jolts, scrapes, and bumps—that match the visual output of the game or simulation. Many video arcades take the concept further by having the computer shake, rattle, and roll the gamer's chair while displaying onscreen movements that match the action. Output devices that generate synthetic smells are also beginning to appear. If these devices catch on, Web sites might commonly include smells as well as sights and sound. While you're virtually visiting your favorite beach resort you might smell synthetic surf, sand, and sunblock.

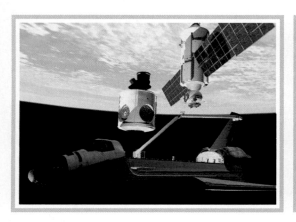

Computers control the movements of spacecrafts and virtual reality arcade games using output devices that operate on similar principles.

Of course, computers can send information directly to other computers, bypassing human interaction altogether. The possibilities for computer output are limited only by the technology and the human imagination, both of which are stretching further all the time.

Storage Devices: Input Meets Output

> A **retentive memory** may be a good thing, but **the ability to forget** is the true token of greatness.
> —Elbert Hubbard

Some computer peripherals are capable of performing both input and output functions. These devices, which include tape and disk drives, are the computer's **storage devices**. They're sometimes referred to as *secondary storage* devices, because the computer's memory is its *primary storage*. Unlike RAM, which forgets everything when the computer is turned off, and ROM, which can't learn anything new, storage devices enable the computer to record information semi-permanently so it can be read later by the same computer or by another computer.

Magnetic Tape

Tape drives are common storage devices on most mainframe computers and some PCs. A tape drive can write data onto, and read data off of, a magnetically coated ribbon of tape. The reason for the widespread use of **magnetic tape** as a storage medium is clear: A magnetic tape can store massive amounts of information in a small space at a relatively low cost. The spinning tape reels that symbolized computers in so many old science fiction movies have for the most part been replaced by tape cartridges based on similar technology.

Ergonomics and Health

Along with the benefits of computer technology comes the potential for unwelcome side effects. For people who work long hours with computers, the side effects include risks to health and safety due to radiation emissions, repetitive-stress injuries, or other computer-related health problems. Inconclusive evidence suggests that low-level radiation emitted by video display terminals (VDTs) and other equipment might cause health problems, including miscarriages in pregnant women and leukemia. The scientific jury is still out, but the mixed research results so far have led many computer users and manufacturers to err on the side of caution.

More concrete evidence relates keyboarding to occurrences of **repetitive-stress injuries** such as *carpal tunnel syndrome*, a painful affliction of the wrist and hand that results from repeating the same movements over long periods. Prolonged computer use also increases the likelihood of headaches, eyestrain, fatigue, and other symptoms of "techno-stress."

Ergonomics (sometimes called human engineering) is the science of designing work environments that enable people and things to interact efficiently and safely. Ergonomic studies suggest preventative measures you can take to protect your health as you work with computers:

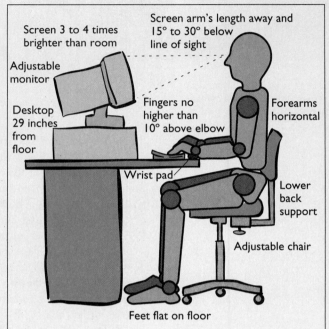

Screen 3 to 4 times brighter than room

Screen arm's length away and 15° to 30° below line of sight

Adjustable monitor

Desktop 29 inches from floor

Fingers no higher than 10° above elbow

Forearms horizontal

Wrist pad

Lower back support

Adjustable chair

Feet flat on floor

▌ ***Choose equipment that's ergonomically designed.*** When you're buying computer equipment, look beyond functionality. Use magazine reviews, manufacturer's information, and personal research to check on health-related factors, such as monitor radiation and glare, disk-drive noise levels, and keyboard layout. A growing number of computer products, such as split, angled ergonomic keyboards, are specifically designed to reduce the risk of equipment-related injuries.

▌ ***Create a healthy workspace.*** Keep the paper copy of your work at close to the same height as your screen. Position your monitor and lights to minimize glare. Sit at arm's length from your monitor to minimize radiation risks.

▌ ***Build flexibility into your work environment.*** Whenever possible work with an adjustable chair, an adjustable table, an adjustable monitor, and a removable keyboard. Change your work position frequently.

▌ ***Rest your eyes.*** Look up from the screen periodically and focus on a far-away object or scene. Blink frequently. Take a 15-minute break from using a VDT every 2 hours.

▌ ***Stretch.*** While you're taking your rest break, do some simple stretches to loosen tight muscles. Occasional stretching of the muscles in your arms, hands, wrists, back, shoulders, and lower body can make hours of computer work more comfortable and less harmful.

▌ ***Listen to your body.*** If you feel uncomfortable, your body is telling you to change something or take a break. Don't ignore it. Ergonomic keyboards like the split, angled keyboard allow computer users to hold their hands and arms in more natural positions while typing to reduce the risk of repetitive-stress injuries.

▌ ***Seek help when you need it.*** If your wrists start hurting when you work, or you have persistent headaches, or you're feeling some other problem that may be related to excessive computer work, talk to a professional. A medical doctor, chiropractor, physical therapist, or naturopath may be able to help you to head off the problem before it becomes chronic.

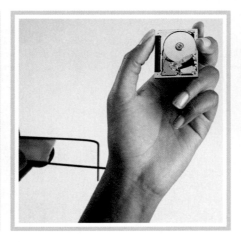

Magnetic tape has one clear limitation: Tape is a **sequential access** medium. Whether a tape holds music or computer data, the computer must zip through information in the order in which it was recorded. Retrieving information from the middle of a tape is far too time-consuming for most modern computer applications, because people expect immediate response to their commands. As a result, magnetic tape is used today primarily for backup of data and a few other operations that aren't time-sensitive.

Standard-sized internal hard drives and microdrives mounted in removable cartridges are, below the surface, based on similar technology.

Magnetic Disks

Like magnetic tape, a **magnetic disk** has a magnetically coated surface that can store encoded information; a *disk drive* writes data onto the disk's surface and reads data from the surface. But unlike a tape drive, a **disk drive** can rapidly retrieve information from any part of a magnetic disk without regard for the order in which the information was recorded, in the same way you can quickly select any track on an audio compact disc. Because of their **random access** capability, disks are the most popular media for everyday storage needs.

Most computer users are familiar with the 3.5-inch **diskette** (also called **floppy disk**, or just *disk*)—a small, magnetically sensitive, flexible plastic wafer housed in a plastic case. The diskette is commonly used for transferring small data files between machines because just about every PC includes a disk drive that can read and write on these inexpensive disks. The most notable exception: Macintoshes no longer include diskette drives as standard equipment, because diskettes are too slow and limited for modern multimedia applications. A typical diskette has a capacity of less than 2MB—enough space to hold the words for half of this book, but not enough for even one large detailed photograph.

Virtually all PCs include hard disks as their main storage devices. A **hard disk** is a rigid, magnetically sensitive disk that spins rapidly and continuously inside the computer chassis or in a separate box connected to the computer housing. This type of hard disk is never removed by the user. Information can be transferred to and from a hard disk much faster than from a diskette. A hard disk might hold several gigabytes (thousands of megabytes) of information—more than enough room for every word and picture in this book.

To fill the gap between low-capacity, slow diskettes and nonremovable, fast hard disks, manufacturers have developed high-capacity transportable storage solutions. There are many choices beyond diskettes in **removable cartridge media**. The most popular are listed here:

Iomega's Zip disks are widely used for storing and transporting data that won't fit on old-fashioned diskettes.

▶ *Zip disks*, developed by Iomega. A Zip disk looks like a thicker version of a standard diskette. The most common Zip disks can hold up to 100 megabytes of data; a newer variety can hold up to 250 MB. Zip drives cannot read or write standard floppy disks, even though they use a similar technology. Zip drives are popular add-ons for PCs and Macintoshes; they're even installed as standard equipment on some models. Their popularity makes Zip disks useful for exchanging large data files between machines.

▶ *SuperDisks*, developed by Imation. A SuperDisk looks similar to a standard diskette, but it is capable of holding 120 megabytes of data—roughly 80 times as much as a typical diskette. The SuperDisk drive can't read or write data as fast as some other removable storage devices, but it has one big advantage: It can also read and write standard diskettes, so it can replace a standard floppy disk drive in a computer system. Sony offers a similar but less widely used device called a HiFD drive.

▶ *Jaz disks*, also developed by Iomega. Jaz disks, unlike Zip and SuperDisks, are based on hard disk technology. As a result, they have a much higher capacity (1 to 2 gigabytes) and faster read/write speeds. Jaz disks are, in effect, removable hard disk cartridges. They're often used for storing and transporting large multimedia files.

▶ *Peerless cartridges*, from Iomega, will likely replace Jaz disks because of their huge 10 to 20 gigabyte capacity and high speed.

▶ *Magneto-optical (MO) disks* use a combination of magnetic disk technology and optical disk technology to store and retrieve information. They're not as fast as hard disks, and they're expensive, but they're extremely reliable and they can hold hundreds of megabytes of data.

Magnetic media aren't the only removable storage options. Today, optical storage technology is widely used for storage and retrieval of information.

Optical Disks

An **optical disk drive** uses laser beams rather than magnets to read and write bits of data on a reflective layer of the disk. A transparent plastic disk surface protects the reflective layer from routine physical damage while letting laser light through. Access speeds are slower for optical disks than for magnetic hard disks. But optical storage is generally highly reliable, especially for long-term storage.

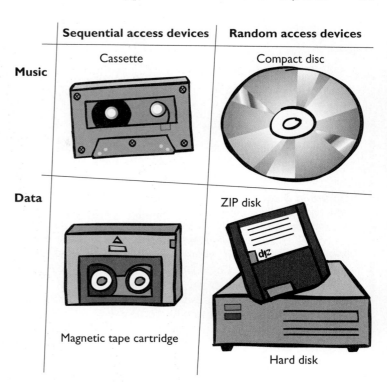

Most stereo systems include sequential access devices—cassette decks—and random access devices—compact disc players. The advantages of random access are the same for stereos as for computers.

From CD-ROM to DVD-R/CD-RW, there's an alphabet soup of choices in optical disk drives for PCs today. The names can be especially confusing because they aren't consistent. Does *R* stand for Read, Recordable, Rewriteable, or Random? It depends on the context. Many of these drive types will undoubtedly go by the wayside as the cost of the expensive all-purpose drives comes down. But until then, it's helpful to know something about these oddly-named devices.

The most common optical drive in computers is the **CD-ROM drive.** A CD-ROM drive can read data from **CD-ROM** (compact disc—read-only memory) disks—data disks that are physically identical to music compact discs. The similarity of audio and data CDs is no accident; it makes it possible for CD-ROM drives to play music CDs under computer control. A CD-ROM can hold up to about 800 megabytes of data—more raw text than you could type in your lifetime. But because CD-ROM drives are read-only devices, they can't be used as storage devices. Instead, they're mostly used to read commercially pressed CD-ROMs containing everything from business applications to multimedia games and reference libraries.

Many PCs include **CD-RW drives** (sometimes refered to as *CD-R/RW drives*) instead of CD-ROM drives. Like a CD-ROM drive, a CD-RW drive can read data from CD-ROMs and play music from audio CDs. But a CD-RW drive can also *burn*, or record, data onto CD-R and CD-RW disks.

CD-R (compact disc-recordable) disks are *WORM* (write-once, read-many) media. That is, a drive can write onto a blank (or partially filled) CD-R disk, but it can't erase the data once it's burned in. CD-Rs are commonly used to make archival copies of large data files, backup copies of software CDs, and personal music CDs. They're also useful for creating master copies of CD-ROMs and audio CDs for professional duplication.

CD-RW (compact disc-rewritable) disks are more expensive than CD-R media, but they have the advantage of being erasable. A drive can write, erase, and rewrite a CD-RW disk repeatedly. Many people use CD-RW disks instead of removable cartridge media for storing, transporting, and backing up large quantities of data.

CD-RW drives are advertised with three different speeds: a speed for burning CD-Rs, a speed for writing CD-RWs, and a much faster speed for reading CD-ROMs. All three *data transfer rates* are expressed as multiples of 150K per second, the speed of the original CD-ROM drives. A typical drive might have maximum speeds specified as 12X/10X/32X. Actual drives speeds don't always measure up to these values. Even the fastest CD-RW drives are pokey compared to a magentic hard drive.

3.4
Disk Storage

Magnetic Disks

Both hard disks and floppy disks are coated with a magnetic oxide similar to the material used to coat cassette tapes and videotapes. The read/write head of a disk drive is similar to the record/play head on a tape recorder; it magnetizes parts of the surface to record information. The difference is that a disk is a digital medium—binary numbers are read and written. The typical hard disk consists of several *platters*, each accessed via a read/write head on a movable *armature*. The magnetic signals on the disk are organized into concentric tracks; the tracks in turn are divided into sectors. This is the traditional scheme used to construct addresses for data on the disk.

Hard disks spin much faster than floppy disks and have a higher storage density (number of bytes per square inch). The **read/write head** of a hard disk glides on a thin cushion of air above the disk and never actually touches the disk.

CD-ROM

A CD-ROM drive contains a small laser that shines on the surface of the disk, "reading" the reflections. Audio CDs and computer CD-ROMs have similar formats; that's why you can play an audio CD with a CD-ROM drive. Information is represented optically—the bottom surface of the CD, under a protective layer of plastic, is coated with a reflective metal film. A laser burns unreflective pits into the film to record data bits. After a pit is burned, it can't be smoothed over and made shiny again; that's why CD-ROMs are read-only.

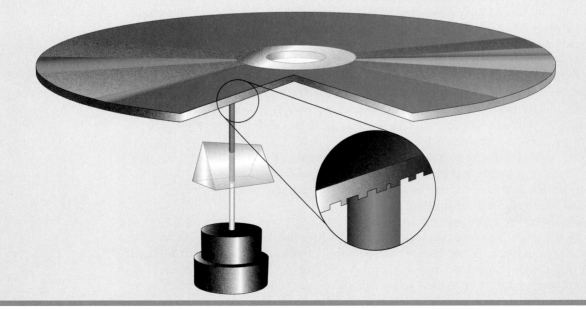

DVD-ROM

A DVD-ROM drive works on the same principle as a CD-ROM drive; the main difference is that the pits are packed much closer together on a DVD, so about seven times as many can fit on the disk surface. (To read these tightly packed bits, the DVD-ROM uses a narrower laser beam.) A DVD can hold even more data—up to 8.5 gigabytes—if it has a second layer of data. On a layered DVD, the top layer is semi-reflective, allow-

ing a second readback laser to penetrate to the layer below. The laser can "see through" the top layer, just as you can see through a picket fence when you look at it from exactly the right angle. For truly massive storage jobs, a DVD can have data on both sides—up to 17 gigabytes. Two-sided DVDs usually have to be turned over for the reader to read both sides; future drives may use additional readback lasers to read the second side without flipping the disk.

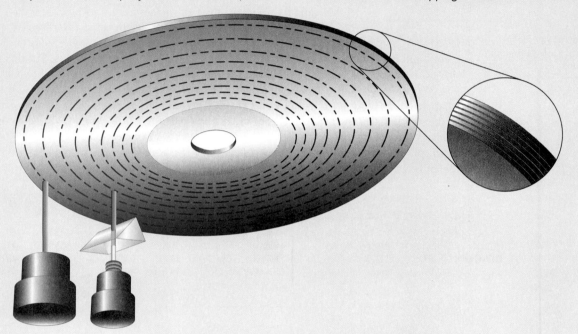

CD-RW Drives

CD-RW drives use laser beams to write data on CD-RW disks. But CD-RW media have layers with chemical structures that react to different temperatures created by different types of lasers. To write data, a high-intensity laser beam produces high temperatures that break down the crystalline structure of the original surface. The result-ing pits dissipate, rather than reflect, low-level lasers during the process of reading recorded data. To erase data, a laser heats the pits to about 400 degrees, causing them to revert to their original reflective crystalline state.

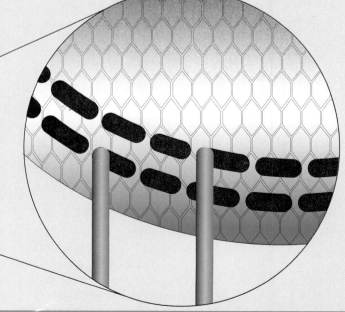

A CD-RW drive can read CD-ROMs, play audio CDs, burn audio CDs, and read and write data onto CD-RW disks.

Several types of DVD drives are also used as replacements for CD-ROM drives in PCs. The **DVD** is the same size as a standard CD-ROM, but can hold between 3.8 and 17 gigabytes of information, depending on how the information is stored. DVD originally stood for *digital video disk*, because the disks were designed to replace VHS tapes in video stores. (Home DVD players *are* extremely popular, but they haven't replaced VHS recorders because they can't be used to record televison programs.) Today many people say DVD stands for *digital versatile disks*, because these high-capacity disks are used to store and distribute all kinds of data.

DVD-ROM drives can play DVD movies, read DVD data disks, read standard CD-ROMs, and play audio CDs. But because they're read-only, they can't record data, music, or movies.

A combination *DVD/CD-RW drive* offers the advantages of a DVD-ROM drive and a CD-RW drive in a single unit that can play DVD movies, play audio CDs, record and erase data on CD-RW disks, and burn audio CDs and CD-ROMs. But this type of drive can't record movies or other large files on blank DVDs; it can only record on CD-R and CD-RW media. *DVD-RAM drives* can read, erase, and write data (but not DVD video) on multi-gigabyte *DVD-R* (but not CD-R or CD-RW) media. The do-it-all *DVD-R/CD-RW drive* can read all the standard CD and DVD disk types and record on CD-R, CD-RW, and **DVD-R** (recordable) media. With the right software, it can be used to create DVD videos that you can play on DVD movie players. Apple refers to the DVD-R/CD-RW drive as the SuperDrive. Hopefully, the rest of the industry will settle on a name for this versatile drive that goes beyond acronyms.

Common Optical Drives: What They Can Do										
Drive type	Read CD-ROM data	Play Audio CDs	Write CD-R data	Record Audio CDs	Write/ rewrite CD-RW data	Read DVD-ROM data	Play DVD Movie	Write DVD data	Write/ rewrite DVD-RAM data	Record DVD Video
CD-ROM	◉	◉								
CD-RW	◉	◉	◉	◉	◉					
DVD-ROM	◉	◉				◉	◉			
DVD/ CD-RW	◉	◉	◉	◉	◉	◉	◉			
DVD-RAM	◉	◉				◉	◉	◉	◉	
DVD-R CD-RW	◉	◉	◉	◉	◉	◉	◉	◉		◉

Solid-State Storage Devices

Until recently, disk drives were the only realistic random-access storage devices for most computer applications. In spite of their popularity, disk drives present problems for today's computer users. The moving parts in disk drives are more likely to fail than other computer components. For airline travelers and others who must depend on battery power for long periods of time, spinning disk drives consume too much energy. Disk drives can be noisy—a problem for musicians and others who use computers for audio applications. And disk drives are bulky when compared with computer memory; they're not practical for palm-sized computers and other applications where space is tight.

Flash memory is a type of erasable memory chip that can serve as a reliable, low-energy, quiet, compact alternative to disk storage. Until recently, flash memory was too expensive for most storage applications. It's still more expensive than disk storage, but flash memory is now practical for many applications. Some flash memory formats are designed for specific applications, such as storing pictures in digital cameras and transferring them to PCs for editing. Sony's *memory stick* is an all-purpose digital storage card about the size of a stick of gum. Most experts believe that flash memory or some other type of **solid state storage** technology—storage with no moving parts—will eventually replace disk and tape storage in computers and other digital devices.

Computer Systems: The Sum of Its Parts

> The computer is by all odds the most **extraordinary** of the **technological clothing** ever devised by man, since it is an **extension** of our **central nervous system**. Beside it **the wheel is a mere hula hoop** . . .
>
> —Marshall McLuhan, in *War and Peace in the Global Village*

The DiskOnKey fits on a key chain, but can store up to 50 megabytes of data when plugged into a computer's USB port (described in the next section).

Most personal computers fall into one of four basic design classes:

▶ *Tower systems*—tall, narrow boxes that generally have more expansion slots and bays than other designs.

▶ Flat "pizza box" systems (sometimes ambiguously referred to as *desktop systems*) designed to sit under the monitor like a platform.

▶ *All-in-one systems* (like the iMac) combine monitor and system unit into a single housing.

▶ *Portable computers* include all the essential components, including keyboard and pointing device, in one compact box.

Sony's Memory Stick is a solid-state storage medium that can be used in cameras, audio devices, video equipment, and computers, making it easy for these devices to share information.

Whatever the design, a PC must allow for attachment of input, output, and storage peripherals. That's where slots, ports, and bays figure in. Now that we've explored the peripherals landscape, we can look again at the ways of hooking those peripherals into the system.

Ports and Slots Revisited

The system board, or motherboard, of a computer system generally includes several ports. The most common ports on system boards have been standard on PCs for years. They include the following:

▶ A *serial port* for attaching a modem or other device that can send and receive messages one bit at a time

▶ A *parallel port* for attaching a printer or other device that communicates by sending or receiving bits in groups, rather than sequentially

▶ *Keyboard/mouse ports* for attaching a keyboard and a mouse

Other ports are typically included on expansion boards rather than the system board:

▶ A *video port* for plugging a color monitor into the video board

▶ *Microphone, speaker, headphone,* and *MIDI* (musical instrument digital interface) ports for attaching sound equipment to the sound card

All of these ports follow **interface standards** agreed on by the industry so that devices made by one manufacturer can be attached to systems made by other companies. The downside of industry standards is that they can sometimes hold back progress. For example, today's fastest modems outpace the classic serial port, and today's color printers are kept waiting by the pokey parallel port.

This wearable Flash memory card carries 16 megabytes of critical medical information—information that might save a life in an emergency.

This rear view of a tower system unit shows several ports, including some (below) that are included in add-on-boards in slots.

Computer manufacturers and owners use expansion cards to get around the limitations of these standard ports. For example, most modern computers include an *internal modem* in an expansion slot; this modem card adds a standard phone jack as a communication port. For faster connection to a local-area network (LAN), many modern PCs include a *network card* that adds a LAN port. For faster communication with external drives, scanners, and other peripherals, a PC might include a *SCSI* (Small Computer Systems Interface, pronounced "scuzzy") card that adds a SCSI port to the back of the system box. (SCSI ports are standard on older Macintoshes.) The SCSI interface design enables users to daisy-chain (string together) several peripherals and attach them to a single port.

Internal and External Drives

Disk drives generally reside in *bays* inside the system unit. A new PC almost always has a floppy disk drive in one bay, a hard drive in another, and some kind of CD or DVD drive in a third bay. Some PCs have extra bays for additional internal hard drives or removable media. Tall tower models generally have more expansion bays than flat systems designed to sit under monitors. But even if there's no room in the system unit for additional internal drives, external drives can be connected to the system through ports like the SCSI port.

Most portable computers are too small to include three drive bays. But some models have bays that enable you to swap drives. For example, you might remove the CD-ROM drive from a laptop and insert a floppy disk drive so you can save a backup copy of your work. Some models enable you to *hot swap* devices—remove and replace them without powering down. Most portables enable you to attach external peripherals through ports. Some portables can be plugged into docking stations that contain, or are attached to, all the necessary peripherals. When docked, a portable can function like a desktop computer, complete with large-screen monitor, full-sized keyboard, mouse, sound system, and a variety of other peripherals.

This tower system has its side panel removed so you can see the storage bays containing disk drives (top right) and the expansion boards inserted into slots (top left).

Expansion Made Easy: Emerging Interfaces

It's clear that the *open architecture* of the PC—the design that enables you to add expansion cards and peripherals—gives it flexibility and longevity that it wouldn't have otherwise. Many hobbyists have been using the same computer system for years; they just swap in new cards, drives, and even CPUs and motherboards to keep their systems up to current standards. But most computer users today prefer to use their computers, not take them apart. Fortunately, new interface standards are emerging that will enable casual computer users to add the latest and greatest devices to their systems without cracking the box.

A **USB**, or **universal serial bus**, can transmit data at approximately 11 megabits—roughly 100 times faster than the PC serial port—and a newer, faster version is in the works. Up to 126 devices, including keyboards, mice, digital cameras, scanners, and storage devices—can be chained together from a single USB port. USB devices can be hot swapped, so the system instantly recognizes the presence of a new device when it is plugged in. And USB, like SCSI, is *platform independent*, so USB devices work on both PCs and Macintoshes. In fact, this paragraph is being typed on a keyboard that's shared by a PC and a Mac through a USB hub. All new PCs and Macintoshes include at least one USB port. In time, computer manufacturers may phase out other ports made unnecessary by USB's presence. Some, including Compaq, have started producing *legacy-free PCs* that cost less because they use USB ports instead of older serial, parallel, keyboard, mouse, and SCSI ports.

Another interface standard that shows promise is **FireWire**, an extremely high-speed connection standard developed by Apple. Most PC makers refer to FireWire by the less friendly designation, *IEEE 1394*, assigned by the Institute of Electrical and Electronics Engineers when they approved it as a standard. (Sony calls their version iLink.) FireWire can move data between devices at 400 or more megabits per second—far faster than most peripheral devices can handle it. This high speed makes it ideal for data-intensive work like digital video. Most modern digital

Computer Consumer Concepts

The **best computer** for your specific needs is the one that will come on the market **immediately after** you actually purchase some other model.

—Dave Barry, humorist

This book's appendix, CD-ROM, and Internet Web site contain specific information about the nuts and bolts of buying hardware and software to make your own computer system. Of course, any brand-specific advice on choosing computer equipment is likely to be outdated within a few months of publication. Still, some general principles remain constant while the technology races forward. Here are nine consumer criteria worth considering, even if you have no intention of buying your own computer:

▶ **Cost.** Buy what you can afford, but be sure to enable for extra memory, extended warranties, peripherals (printer, extra storage devices, modem, cables, speakers, and so on), and software. If you join a user group or connect to an online shareware site, you'll be able to meet some of your software needs at low (or no) cost. But you'll almost certainly need some commercial software, too. Don't be tempted to copy copyrighted software from your friends or public labs; software piracy is theft, prosecutable under federal laws. (Choosing software isn't easy, but many periodicals and Web sites publish regular reviews to help you sort out the best programs.)

▶ **Capability.** Is it the right tool for the job? Buy a computer that's powerful enough to meet your needs. Make sure the processor is fast enough to handle your demands. If you want to take advantage of state-of-the-art multimedia programs, consider only machines that meet the latest standards. If you want to create state-of-the-art multimedia programs, you'll need a powerful computer that can handle audio and video input as well as output—FireWire (IEEE 1394) if you'll be using a digital video camera. Be sure the machine you buy can do the job you need it to do, now and in the foreseeable future.

▶ **Capacity.** If you plan to do graphic design, publishing, or multimedia authoring, make sure your machine has enough memory and disk storage to support the resource-intensive applications you'll need. Consider adding removable media drives for backup and transport of large files.

▶ **Customizability.** Computers are versatile, but they don't all handle all jobs with equal ease. If you'll be using word processors, spreadsheets, and other mainstream software packages, just about any computer will do. If you have off-the-beaten-path needs (video editing, instrument monitoring, and so on), choose a system with enough slots and ports to enable it to be extended for your work.

▶ **Compatibility.** Will the software you plan to use run on the computer you're considering? Most popular computers have a good selection of compatible software, but if you have specific needs, such as being able to take your software home to run on Mom's computer, study the compatibility issue carefully. Total compatibility isn't always possible or necessary. A typical Windows-compatible computer, for example, probably won't run every "Windows-compatible" program, but it will almost certainly run the mainstream applications that most users need. Many people don't care if all their programs will run on another kind of computer; they just need data compatibility—the ability to move documents back and forth between systems on disk or through a network connection. It's common, for example, for Windows users and Macintosh users to share documents over a network.

▶ **Connectivity.** In today's networked world, it's shortsighted to see your computer as a self-contained information appliance. Make sure you include a high-speed modem and/or network connection in your system so you can take full advantage of the communication capabilities of your computer.

▶ **Convenience.** Just about any computer can do most common jobs, but which is the most convenient for you? Do you value portability over having all the peripherals permanently connected? Is it important to you to have a machine that's easy to install and maintain so you can take care of it yourself? Or do you want to choose the same kind of machine as the people around you so you can get help easily when you need it? Which user interface makes the kind of work you'll be doing easiest?

▶ **Company.** If you try to save money by buying an off-brand computer, you may find yourself the owner of an orphan computer. High-tech companies can vanish overnight. Make sure you'll be able to get service and parts down the road.

▶ **Curve.** Most models of personal computers seem to have a useful life span of just a few years—if they survive the first year or two. If you want to minimize financial risk, avoid buying a computer during the first year of a model's life, when it hasn't been tested on the open market. Also avoid buying a computer that's over the hill; you'll know it because most software developers will have abandoned this model for greener CPUs. In the words of 18th century British poet Alexander Pope, "Be not the first by whom the new are tried, nor yet the last to lay the old aside."

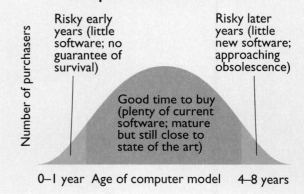

Computer consumer's curve

Risky early years (little software; no guarantee of survival)

Risky later years (little new software; approaching obsolescence)

Good time to buy (plenty of current software; mature but still close to state of the art)

Number of purchasers

0–1 year   Age of computer model   4–8 years

video cameras have FireWire ports, so they can be connected directly to 1394-equipped PCs. Like USB, FireWire allows multiple devices to be connected to the same port and to be hot swapped. FireWire can also supply power to peripherals so they don't need an external power supply. Because of its speed and versatility, FireWire is expected to be standard equipment on all new PCs soon.

Putting It All Together

A typical computer system might have several different input, output, and storage peripherals. From the computer's point of view, it doesn't matter which of these devices is used at any given time. Each input device is just another source of electrical signals; each output device is just another place to send signals; each storage device is one or the other, depending on what the program calls for. Read from here, write to there—the CPU doesn't care; it dutifully follows instructions. Like a stereo receiver, the computer is oblivious to which input and output devices are attached and operational, as long as they're compatible.

A typical desktop computer system includes a computer and several peripheral devices.

Networks: Systems without Boundaries

Unlike a stereo system, which has clearly defined boundaries, a computer system can be part of a network that blurs the boundaries between computers. When computers are connected in a network, one computer can, in effect, serve as an input device for another computer, which serves as an output device for the first computer. Networks can include hundreds of different computers, each of which might have access to all peripherals on the system. Many public and private networks span the globe by taking advantage of satellites, fiber optic cables, and other communication technologies. Using a modem, a computer can connect to a network through an ordinary phone line. The rise in computer networks is making it more difficult to draw lines between individual computer systems. If you're connected to the Internet, your computer is, in effect, just a tiny part of a global system of interconnected networks.

Software: The Missing Piece

In the span of a few pages we've surveyed a mind-boggling array of computer hardware, but, in truth, we've barely scratched the surface. Nonetheless, all this hardware is worthless without software to drive it. In the next chapter we'll take a look at the software that makes a computer system come to life.

Use It or Lose It

Arthur H. Bell, Ph.D.

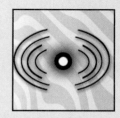

Much has been written about the impact of computer technology on our physical health. Research has raised questions about repetitive-stress injuries, eyestrain, backaches, and other potential hazards of spending too much time in front of a computer. But excessive screen time may also have a negative impact on our social health, too. Arthur H. Bell, Ph.D., is a Professor of Management Communication at the McLaren School of Business, University of San Francisco. In this article, first published in the February, 2000, issue of Adobe *magazine, Bell addresses the problem and suggests ways to keep your communication edge intact.*

I'm worried about a subtle but dangerous occupational hazard. You and I sit in deep communion with our computer monitors for most of our waking hours; our minds may be engaged, but our faces look like out-takes from Night of the Living Dead. (Peek around the office right now. Johnson sits slack-jawed, locked in the tractor beam of his monitor. Williams slumps in her chair, her eyes half-open toward the flitting video images.) What's going on here? A vital component in our repertoire of professional skills is in danger of atrophy—the nonverbal side of our day-to-day communication isn't getting exercise. We're all becoming poster children for the Deadpan Society.

So what? I'm not suggesting that we start smiling and gesturing at our computer monitors. But when we turn way from our CRTS for face-to-face meetings with clients or coworkers, we have increasing trouble jump-starting our nonverbal charms (such as eye contact, facial expressiveness, gestures, and posture). That's bad for business, bad for the team, and bad for individual careers.

Virtually all research on human communication points to the predominant influence of nonverbal cues in interpersonal relations. When nonverbal cues are missing, communication itself breaks down in the workplace. (Results: bad meetings, boring interviews, unproductive contacts with clients, and crossed signals with the boss.)

What you show is as important as what you say in getting your message across. Don't believe it? Put this idea to the test by recalling the last time you returned an article of clothing to a store (or, heaven help you, a software package you've opened). Was it the clerk's words, "Yes, we'll exchange it," or the clerk's expression and tone of voice that communicated the real message and left a lasting impression? We "read" nonverbal signals very accurately. When the dictionary meanings of words conflict with the nonverbal signals that accompany them, we believe the messages sent by the nonverbal signals, not the words.

There's a rueful irony here for specialists in fonts, graphics, and effects. Designers know better than most how important the "look" can be in making an impression and communicating the whole message. Yet they are as prone as anyone to ignore their own nonverbal signals—in effect, their facial graphics—when talking to others in the workplace.

I can't prescribe what your face, eyes, and hands should be doing during nonvirtual communication. But I can share my own short list of reminders when I turn from the monitor to meet with colleagues, students, and clients.

▶ **Maintain comfortable eye contact.** Shifty, nervous eyes send messages that undercut your words.
▶ **Use your hands to emphasize ideas.** "Handling" your words in meaningful ways helps others interpret your message.
▶ **Show obvious interest with your face.** Neutral expressions will be interpreted as signs of disapproval or lack of attention.
▶ **Lean a bit forward to listen.** The laid-back sprawl communicates a lack of concern and energy.
▶ **Touch things you're talking about (within limits, of course).** Holding a proposal, picking up the new software release, or touching your finger to numbers on a chart are all high-involvement communication techniques.

The language of nonverbal cues and signals is a must-have for your professional success. And yes, I'm looking right at you and gesturing as I write this.

DISCUSSION QUESTIONS

1. Can you think of examples of recent interactions you've had with other people that support the main points of this article?
2. Do you think computers are, in fact, interfering with our ability to communicate? Explain your answer.

Summary

A computer with just a CPU and internal memory is of limited value; peripherals allow that computer to communicate with the outside world and store information for later use. Some peripherals are strictly input devices. Others are output devices. Some are external storage devices that accept information from and send information to the CPU.

The most common input devices today are the keyboard and the mouse, but a variety of other input devices can be connected to the computer. Trackballs, touch-sensitive pads, touch screens, and joysticks provide alternatives to the mouse as a pointing device. Bar-code readers, optical-mark readers, and magnetic-ink readers are designed to recognize and translate specially printed patterns and characters. Scanners and digital cameras convert photographs, drawings, and other analog images into digital files that the computer can process. Sound digitizers do the same thing to audio information. All input devices are designed to do one thing: convert information signals from an outside source into a pattern of bits that the computer can process.

Output devices perform the opposite function: They accept strings of bits from the computer and transform them into a form that is useful or meaningful outside the computer. Video monitors, including CRTs and LCDs, are almost universally used to display information continually as the computer functions. A variety of printers are used for producing paper output. Sound output from the computer, including music and synthesized speech, is delivered through audio speakers. Output devices also allow computers to control other machines.

Unlike most input and output peripherals, storage devices such as disk drives and tape drives are capable of two-way communication with the computer. Because of their high-speed random access capability, magnetic disks—high-capacity hard disks, inexpensive diskettes, and a variety of removable media—are the most common forms of storage on modern computers. Sequential access tape devices are generally used only to archive information that doesn't need to be accessed often. Optical disks are used mostly as high-capacity, read-only media, but newer types of optical drives can both read and write data. In the future solid-state storage technology will probably replace disks and tapes for most applications.

The hardware for a complete computer system generally includes at least one processor, memory, storage devices, and several I/O peripherals for communicating with the outside world. Network connections make it possible for computers to communicate with one another directly. Networks blur the boundaries between individual computer systems. With the hardware components in place, a computer system is ready to receive and follow instructions encoded in software.

Chapter Review

▼ Key Terms

bar-code reader (p. 74)
CD-R (p. 87)
CD-ROM (p. 87)
CD-ROM drive (p. 87)
CD-RW (p. 87)
CD-RW drive (p. 87)
CRT (cathode-ray tube) monitor
　(p. 80)
digital camera (p. 77)
digitize (p. 76)
disk drive (p. 86)
diskette (floppy disk) (p. 86)
dot-matrix printer (p. 82)
DVD (p. 90)
DVD-R (p. 90)
DVD-ROM drive (p. 90)
ergonomics (p. 72)
FireWire (IEEE 1394) (p. 91)
flash memory (p. 91)
graphics tablet (p. 74)
handwriting recognition software
　(p. 75)

hard disk (p. 86)
impact printer (p. 80)
inkjet printer (p. 82)
interface standards (p. 91)
joystick (p. 74)
keyboard (p. 72)
laser printer (p. 82)
LCD (liquid crystal display) monitor
　(p. 80)
line printer (p. 80)
magnetic disk (p. 86)
magnetic-ink character reader (p. 74)
magnetic tape (p. 84)
monitor (p. 79)
mouse (p. 73)
multifunction peripheral (MFP)
　(p. 83)
nonimpact printer (p. 82)
optical character recognition (OCR)
　(p. 75)
optical disk drive (p. 87)
optical-mark reader (p. 74)

pen-based computer (p. 75)
pen scanners (p. 75)
pixel (p. 79)
plotter (p. 83)
pointing stick (TrackPoint) (p. 73)
point-of-sale (POS) terminal (p. 74)
printer (p. 80)
random access (p. 86)
removable cartridge media (p. 86)
repetitive-stress injuries (p. 72)
resolution (p. 79)
scanner (p. 76)
sensor (p. 79)
sequential access (p. 86)
sound card (p. 83)
tape drive (p. 84)
touchpad (trackpad) (p. 73)
touch screen (p. 74)
trackball (p. 73)
USB (universal serial bus) (p. 92)
video display terminal (VDT) (p. 79)

▼ Interactive Quiz Questions

1. The *Computer Confluence* CD-ROM contains self-test quiz questions related to this chapter, including multiple choice, true or false, and matching questions.
2. The *Computer Confluence* Web site, **www.prenhall.com/beekman**, contains self-test exercises related to this chapter. Follow the instructions for taking a quiz. After you've completed your quiz, you can email the results to your instructor.

   The Web site also contains open-ended discussion questions called Internet Explorations. Discuss one or more of the Internet Exploration questions at the section for this chapter.

▼ Review Questions

1. Provide a working definition for each of the key terms listed in the "Key Terms" section. Check your answers in the glossary.
2. List five input devices and three output devices that might be attached to a PC. Describe a typical use for each.
3. Name and describe three special-purpose input devices people commonly use in public places, such as stores, banks, and libraries.
4. The mouse is impractical for use as a pointing device on a laptop computer. Describe at least three alternatives that are more appropriate.
5. What are the advantages of CRT monitors over LCDs?
6. Name at least two hardware devices that use LCDs because using a CRT would be impractical.
7. What are the advantages of nonimpact printers such as laser printers over impact printers? Are there any disadvantages?
8. Some commonly used peripherals can be described as both input and output devices. Explain.
9. What is the difference between sequential access and random access storage devices? What are the major uses of each?

▼ Discussion Questions

1. If we think of the human brain as a computer, what are the input devices? What are the output devices? What are the storage devices?
2. What kinds of new input and output devices do you think future computers might have? Why?

▼ Projects

1. The keyboard is the main input device for computers today. If you don't know how to touch-type, you're effectively handicapped in a world of computers. Fortunately, many personal computer software programs are designed to teach keyboarding. If you need to learn to type, try to find one of these programs, and use it regularly until you are a fluent typist.
2. Using the inventory of computers you developed in Project 4 in Chapter 1, determine the major components of each (input devices, output devices, storage, and so on).
3. Visit a bank, store, office, or laboratory. List all the computer peripherals you see, categorizing them as input, output, or storage devices.
4. Using computer advertisements in magazines, newspapers, and catalogs, try to break down the cost of a computer to determine, on the average, what percentage of the cost is for the system unit (including CPU, memory, and disk drives), what percentage is for input and output devices, and what percentage is for software. How do the percentages change as the price of the system goes up?

Sources and Resources

Books

Insanely Great: The Life and Times of Macintosh, the Computer That Changed Everything, Reissue Edition, by Steven Levy (New York: Penguin, 2000). Levy is one of the best writers in the field; his style is lively and inviting, even when he's writing about high-tech subjects. In this book he recounts the first ten years of the Macintosh's history.

Infinite Loop: How the World's Most Insanely Great Computer Company Went Insane, by Michael S. Malone (New York: Doubleday, 1999). Malone's book tells the Apple story from the early days of the Apple I through the roller-coaster years of the Macintosh.

The Second Coming of Steve Jobs, by Alan Deutschman (New York: Broadway Books, 2000). This book focuses on Apple's controversial CEO in the years between his reigns at Apple. Jobs is a complex, private person who has achieved fame that rivals rock stars. His story makes good reading.

How Computers Work: 6th Edition, by Ron White (Indianapolis: Que, 2001). This book, described at the end of Chapter 2, provides clear explanations of the inner workings of most commonly used personal computer peripherals.

The Essential Guide to Computer Data Storage: From Floppy to DVD, by Dr. Andrei Khurshudov (Upper Saddle River, NJ: Prentice Hall, 2001). This book provides in-depth explanations of a variety of PC peripherals and interface standards, including magnetic disks, optical disks, and storage for cameras and MP3 music players.

Upgrading PCs: Visual Quickstart Guide, by Bart G. Farkas and Jeff Govier (Berkeley, CA: Peachpit Press, 1999). There are basically two ways to keep up with the rapid-fire changes in PC technology: buy a new computer system every two or three years, or upgrade individual components regularly. This book is designed for people who'd like to be in the upgrade crowd but don't know much about electronic technology. Like other Visual Quickstart books, it clearly and concisely explains procedures with lots of pictures and a minimum of technobabble. If you're comfortable with a screwdriver, you'll probably be comfortable with this book.

Build Your Own Pentium III PC, by Aubrey Pilgrim (New York: McGraw-Hill, 2000). Building your own PC isn't as hard as it sounds—especially if you have a good guide. This book is designed to guide you step-by-step through the process—even if you're not an engineer. In today's competitive PC market, you may not save a lot of money by building your own, but you'll learn a lot—and hopefully have fun along the way.

Troubleshooting, Maintaining, and Repairing PCs, Millennium Edition, by Stephen J. Bigelow (New York: McGraw-Hill, 2000), and ***Bigelow's Drive and Memory Troubleshooting Pocket Reference,*** by Stephen J. Bigelow (New York: McGraw-Hill, 2000). PCs today are relatively easy to use—as long as nothing goes wrong. When trouble arises, or when it's time to upgrade a component, a PC can be frustrating and bewildering. If you want to—or need to—get inside your PC or its peripherals, Bigelow's hardbound PC reference may help you find your way around. The drive and memory pocket reference has a narrower focus, but a similar style. (In spite of its name, it probably won't fit in your pocket.) Some of the material in these books is highly technical, but that goes with the territory.

Upgrading and Troubleshooting Your Mac, by Gene Steinberg (Berkeley, CA: Osborne/McGraw-Hill, 2000). Macintoshes are generally easier to troubleshoot and repair than other PCs; from the beginning, they've been designed that way. This easy-to-read book is full of answers about making Macs and their peripherals work together.

Mac Answers, Second Edition, by Bob Levitus and Shelly Brisbin (Berkeley, CA: Osborne/McGraw-Hill, 2000). This book offers a wealth of information on Macintoshes and their peripherals in a question-and-answer format. The writing style is clear and friendly.

Real World Scanning and Halftones, by David Blatner and Steve Roth (Berkeley, CA: Peachpit Press, 1998). It's easy to use a scanner, but it isn't always easy to get high-quality scans. This illustrated book covers scanner use from the basics to advanced tips and techniques.

Start with a Digital Camera: A Guide to Using Digital Cameras to Create High-Quality Graphics, by John Odam (Berkeley, CA: Peachpit Press, 1999). This lavishly illustrated book provides an excellent overview of the world of digital photography. Technological issues, aesthetics, and practical shooting tips are all covered.

Desktop Yoga, by Julie T. Lusk (New York: Perigee, 1998). Like any activity, computer work can be hazardous to your health if you don't exercise care and common sense. This book describes stretching and relaxation exercises for desk-bound workers and students. If you spend hours a day in front of a computer screen, these activities can help you to take care of your body and mind.

Disclosure, by Michael Crichton (New York: Ballantine Books, 1977). This book-turned-movie provides an inside look at a fictional Seattle corporation that manufactures computer peripherals. Even though the author has clearly tampered with credibility for the sake of a suspenseful plot, the story provides insights into the roles money and power play in today's high-stakes computer industry.

Periodicals

E-media. This slick trade monthly focuses on storage technologies, including CD-RW and DVD.

Computer Shopper. This massive monthly typically includes a few consumer-oriented articles, but most people read it for the ads—hundreds each month, complete with an index.

World Wide Web Pages

Most computer peripheral manufacturers have World Wide Web pages. The *Computer Confluence* Web site will guide you to many of the most interesting pages.

4 Software Basics: The Ghost in the Machine

Linus Torvalds and the Software Nobody Owns

I had **no idea** what I was doing. I knew I was the
best programmer in the world.
Every 21-year-old programmer knows that.
"How hard can it be,
it's just an **operating system?"**

—Linus Torvalds

When Linus Torvalds bought his first PC in 1991, he never dreamed it would be a critical weapon in a software liberation war. He just wanted to avoid waiting in line to get a terminal to connect to his university's mainframe.

Torvalds, a 21-year-old student at the University of Helsinki in Finland, had avoided buying a PC because he didn't like the standard PC's "crummy architecture with this crummy MS-DOS operating system." The operating system is the basic set of programs that tells the computer what to do; MS-DOS (Microsoft Disk Operating System) was the operating system on most PCs in 1991. But Torvalds had been studying operating systems, and he decided to try to build something on his own.

He based his work on Minix, a scaled-down textbook version of the powerful UNIX operating system. Little by little, he cobbled together pieces of a *kernel*, the part of the system where the real processing and control work is done.

Linus Torvalds

When he mentioned his project on an Internet discussion group, a member offered him space to post it on a university server. Others copied it, tinkered with it, and sent the changes back to Torvalds. The communal work-in-progress became known as **Linux** (usually pronounced "Linn-uks"). Within a couple of years, it was good enough to release as a product.

Instead of copyrighting and selling Linux, Torvalds made it freely available under General Public License (GPL) developed by the Free Software Foundation. According to the GPL, anyone could give away, modify, or even sell Linux, as long as the source code—the program instructions—remain freely available for others to improve. Linux is the best known example of **open source software**; it spearheads the popular open source software movement.

Thousands of programmers around the world have worked on Linux, with Torvalds at the center of the activity. Some do it because they believe there should be alternatives to expensive corporate products; others do it because they can customize the software; still others do it just for fun. As a result of all their efforts, Linux has matured into a powerful, versatile product with millions of satisfied users.

Linux powers Web servers, film and animation workstations, scientific supercomputers, a handful of handheld computers, and even Internet-savvy appliances like refrigerators. Linux is especially popular among people who do heavy-duty computing on a tight budget—particularly in debt-ridden Third World countries.

The success of Linux has inspired Apple, Sun, Hewlett-Packard, and other software companies to release products with open source code. Even the mighty Microsoft is paying attention as this upstart operating system grows in popularity.

Today Torvalds is an Internet folk hero. Web pages pay homage to him, his creation, and the stuffed penguin that has become the Linux mascot. In 1996, he completed his master's degree in computer science and went to work for Transmeta Corp., a chip design company in Silicon Valley. He still spends hours every week online with the Linux legions, improving the operating system that belongs to everybody—and nobody. ❯

Chapters 2 and 3 told only part of the story of how computers do what they do. Here's a synopsis of our story so far:

On one side we have a person—you, me, or somebody else; it hardly matters. We all have problems to solve—problems involving work, communication, transportation, finances, and more. Many of these problems cry out for computer solutions.

The communication gap . . .

On the other side we have a computer—an incredibly sophisticated bundle of hardware capable of performing all kinds of technological wizardry. Unfortunately, the computer *recognizes only zeros and ones.*

A great chasm separates the person who has a collection of vague problems from the stark, rigidly bounded world of the computer. How can humans bridge the gap to communicate with the computer?

That's where software comes in. Software enables people to communicate certain kinds of problems to computers and makes it possible for computers to communicate solutions back to those people.

Modern computer software didn't just materialize out of the atmosphere; it evolved from the plug boards and patch cords and other hardware devices that were used to program early computers like the ENIAC. Mathematician John von Neumann, working with ENIAC's creators, J. Presper Eckert and John Mauchly, wrote a 1945 paper suggesting that program instructions could be stored with the data in memory. Every computer created since has been based on the *stored-program concept* described in that paper. That idea established the software industry and liberated programmers from the tyranny of hardware.

Instead of flipping switches and patching wires, today's programmers write *programs*—sets of computer instructions designed to solve problems—and feed them into the computer's memory through keyboards and other input devices. These programs are the computer's software. Because software is stored in memory, a computer can switch from one task to another and then back to the first without a single hardware modification. For instance, the computer that serves as a word processor for writing this book can, at the click of a mouse, turn into an email terminal, a window into the World Wide Web, a reference library, an accounting spreadsheet, a drawing table, a video-editing workstation, a musical instrument, or a game machine.

What is software, and how can it transform a mass of circuits into an electronic chameleon? This chapter provides some general answers to that question along with details about each of the three major categories of software:

▶ Compilers and other translator programs, which enable programmers to create other software
▶ Software applications, which serve as productivity tools to help computer users solve problems
▶ System software, which coordinates hardware operations and does behind-the-scenes work the computer user seldom sees.

Processing with Programs

Leonardo **da Vinci** called music **"the shaping of the invisible"** and his phrase is even more apt as a description of **software**.
—Alan Kay, developer of the concept of the personal computer

Software is invisible and complex. To make the basic concepts clear, we start our exploration of software with a down-to-earth analogy.

Food for Thought

Think of the hardware in a computer system as the kitchen in a short-order restaurant: It's equipped to produce whatever output a customer (user) requests, but it sits idle until an order (command) is placed. Robert, the computerized chef in our imaginary kitchen, serves as the CPU, waiting for requests from the users/customers. When somebody provides an input command—say, an order for a plate of French toast—Robert responds by following the instructions in the appropriate recipe.

As you may have guessed, the recipe is the software. It provides instructions telling the hardware what to do to produce the output the user desires. If the recipe is correct, clear, and precise, the chef turns the input data—eggs, bread, and other ingredients—into the desired output—French toast. If the instructions are unclear or if the software has **bugs**, or errors, the output may not be what the user wanted.

For example, suppose Robert has this recipe for "Suzanne's French Toast Fantastique."

This seemingly foolproof recipe has several trouble spots. Since step 1 doesn't say otherwise, Robert might include the shells in the "slightly beaten eggs." Step 2 says nothing about separating the six slices of bread before dipping them in the batter; Robert would be within the letter of the instruction if he dipped all six at once. Step 3 has at least two potential bugs. Since it doesn't specify what to fry in butter, Robert might conclude that the mixture, not the bread, should be fried. Even if Robert decides to fry the bread, he may let it overcook waiting for the butter to turn golden brown, or he may wait patiently for the top of the toast to brown while the bottom quietly blackens. Robert, like any good computer, just follows instructions.

> **Suzanne's French Toast Fantastique**
> 1. Combine 2 slightly beaten eggs with 1 teaspoon vanilla extract, ½ teaspoon cinnamon, and ⅔ cup milk.
> 2. Dip 6 slices of bread in mixture.
> 3. Fry in small amount of butter until golden brown.
> 4. Serve bread with maple syrup, sugar, or tart jelly.

Suzanne's French Toast Fantastique: The Recipe

A Fast, Stupid Machine

Our imaginary automated chef may not seem very bright, but he's considerably more intelligent than a typical computer's CPU. Computers are commonly called "smart machines" or "intelligent machines." In truth, a typical computer is incredibly limited, capable of doing only the most basic arithmetic operations (such as $7 + 3$ and $15 - 8$) and a few simple logical comparisons ("Is this number less than that number?" "Are these two values identical?").

> The **most useful word** in any computer language is **"oops."**
> —David Lubar, in *It's Not a Bug, It's a Feature*

Computers *seem* smart because they can perform these arithmetic operations and comparisons quickly and accurately. A typical desktop computer can do thousands of calculations in the time it takes you to pull your pen out of your pocket. A well-crafted program can tell the computer to perform a sequence of simple operations that, when taken as a whole, print a term paper, organize the student records for your school, or simulate a space flight. Amazingly, everything you've ever seen a computer do is the result of a sequence of extremely simple arithmetic and logical operations done very quickly. The challenge for software developers is to devise instructions that put those simple operations together in ways that are useful and appropriate.

Suzanne's French Toast Fantastique: The Algorithm

Suzanne's recipe for French toast isn't a computer program; it's not written in a language that a computer can understand. But it could be considered an **algorithm**—a set of step-by-step procedures for accomplishing a task. A computer program generally starts as an algorithm written in English or some other human language. Like Suzanne's recipe, the initial algorithm is likely to contain generalities, ambiguities, and errors.

The programmer's job is to turn the algorithm into a program by adding details, hammering out rough spots, testing procedures, and **debugging**—correcting errors. For example, if we were turning Suzanne's recipe into a program for our electronic-brained short-order cook, we might start by rewriting it like the recipe shown here.

> **Suzanne's French Toast Fantastique**
> 1. Prepare the batter by following these instructions:
>   - **1a.** Crack 2 eggs so whites and yolks drop in bowl; discard shells.
>   - **1b.** Beat eggs slightly with wire whip, fork, or mixer.
>   - **1c.** Mix in 1 teaspoon vanilla extract, ½ teaspoon cinnamon, and ⅔ cup milk.
> 2. Place small amount of butter in frying pan and place on medium heat.
> 3. For each of 6 pieces of bread, follow these steps:
>   - **3a.** Dip slice of bread in mixture.
>   - **3b.** For each of the two sides of the bread do the following steps:
>   - **3b1.** Place the slice of bread in the frying pan with this (uncooked) side down.
>   - **3b2.** Wait 1 minute and then peek at underside of bread; if lighter than golden brown, repeat this step.
>   - **3c.** Remove bread from fry pan and place on plate.
> 4. Serve bread with maple syrup, sugar, or tart jelly.

4.1
Executing a Program

Most programs are composed of millions of simple machine language instructions. Here we'll observe the execution of a tiny part of a running program: a series of instructions that performs some arithmetic. The machine instructions are similar to those in actual programs, but the details have been omitted. The computer has already loaded (copied) the program from disk into memory so that the CPU can see it.

The CPU automatically fetches and executes instructions in sequence—from a series of consecutive memory addresses—unless it's told to "jump" somewhere else. The CPU is about to read the next instruction from memory location 100. This instruction and the ones that follow (in locations 101, 102, and 103) tell the CPU to read a couple of numbers from memory (locations 2000 and 2001), add them, and store the result back

into memory (location 2002). Translated into English, the instructions look like this:

(100) Get (read) the number at memory address 2000 (not the number 2000, but the number stored in location 2000) and place it in register A.

(101) Get the number at memory address 2001 and place it in register B.

(102) Add the contents of registers A and B, placing the result in register C.

(103) Write (copy) the number in register C to memory address 2002.

For this example, let's suppose that memory location 2000 contains the number 7 and memory location 2001 contains 9.

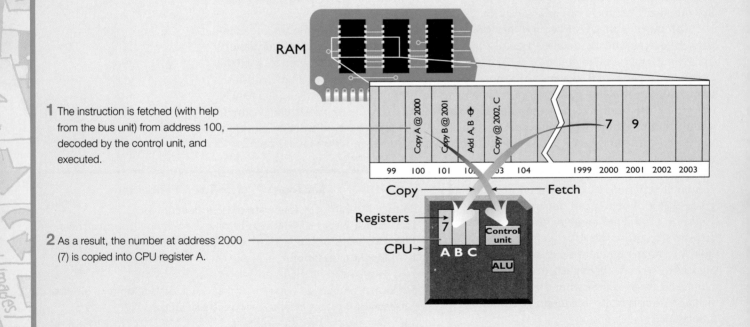

1 The instruction is fetched (with help from the bus unit) from address 100, decoded by the control unit, and executed.

2 As a result, the number at address 2000 (7) is copied into CPU register A.

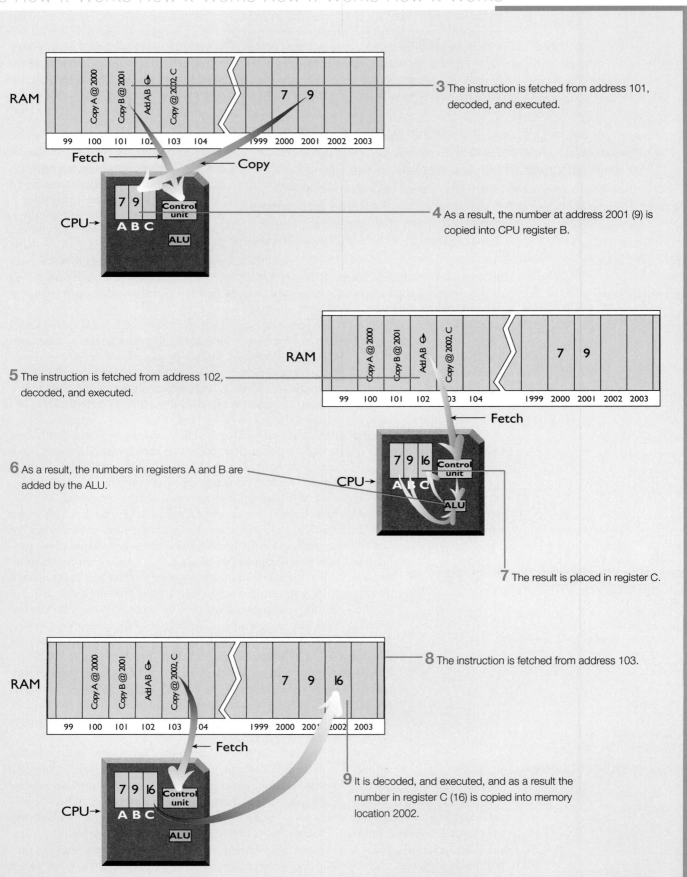

3 The instruction is fetched from address 101, decoded, and executed.

4 As a result, the number at address 2001 (9) is copied into CPU register B.

5 The instruction is fetched from address 102, decoded, and executed.

6 As a result, the numbers in registers A and B are added by the ALU.

7 The result is placed in register C.

8 The instruction is fetched from address 103.

9 It is decoded, and executed, and as a result the number in register C (16) is copied into memory location 2002.

We've eliminated much of the ambiguity from the original recipe. Ambiguity, while tolerable (and sometimes useful) in conversations between humans, is a source of errors for computers. In its current form the recipe contains far more detail than any human chef would want but not nearly enough for a computer. If we were programming a computer (assuming we had one with input hardware capable of recognizing golden brown French toast and output devices capable of flipping the bread), we'd need to go into excruciating detail, translating every step of the process into a series of absolutely unambiguous instructions that could be interpreted and executed by a machine with a vocabulary smaller than that of a 2-year-old child!

The Language of Computers

The programmer, **like the poet**, works only slightly removed from **pure thought-stuff**. He builds **castles in the air**, creating by exertion of the imagination. Yet the program construct, unlike the poet's words, is real in the sense that **it moves and works**, producing visible outputs **separate from the construct itself**.

—Frederick P. Brooks, Jr., in *The Mythical Man Month*

Every computer processes instructions in a native **machine language**. Machine language uses numeric codes to represent the most basic computer operations—adding numbers, subtracting numbers, comparing numbers, moving numbers, repeating instructions, and so on. Early programmers were forced to write every program in a machine language, tediously translating each instruction into binary code. This process was an invitation to insanity; imagine trying to find a single mistyped character in a page full of zeros and ones!

Today most programmers use programming languages such as C++, Java, and Visual BASIC that fall somewhere between natural human languages and precise machine languages. These languages, referred to as **high-level languages**, make it possible for scientists, engineers, and businesspeople to solve problems using familiar terminology and notation rather than cryptic machine instructions. For a computer to understand a program written in one of these languages, it must use a translator program to convert the English-like instructions to the zeros and ones of machine language.

To clarify the translation process, let's go back to the kitchen. Imagine a recipe translator that enables our computer chef to look up phrases like "fry until golden brown." Like a reference book for beginning cooks, this translator fills in all of the details of testing and flipping foods in the frying pan, so Robert understands what to do whenever he encounters "fry until golden brown" in any recipe. As long as our computer cook is equipped with the translator, we don't need to include so many details in each recipe. We can communicate at a higher level. The more sophisticated the translator, the easier the job of the programmer. The most common type of translator program is called a **compiler** because it compiles a complete translation of the program in a high-level computer language (such as C++) before the program runs for the first time. The compiled program can run again and again; it doesn't need to be recompiled unless instructions need to be changed.

Compilers enable programmers to write in high-level languages such as C.

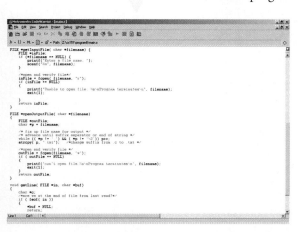

Programming languages have steadily evolved during the last few decades. Each new generation of languages makes the programming process easier by taking on, and hiding from the programmer, more of the detail work. The computer's unrelenting demands for technical details haven't gone away; they're just handled automatically by translation software. As a result, programming is easier and less error prone. As translators become more sophisticated, programmers can communicate in computer languages that more closely resemble **natural languages**—the languages people speak and write every day.

Even with state-of-the-art computer languages, programming requires a considerable investment of time and brain power. Fortunately, many tasks that required programming two decades ago can now be accomplished with spreadsheets, and graphics programs, and other easy-to-use software applications. Programming languages are still used to solve problems that can't be handled with off-the-shelf software, but most computer users manage to do their work without programming. Programming today is done mainly by professional software developers, who use programming languages to create and refine the applications and other programs the rest of us use.

Software Applications: Tools for Users

Software applications enable users to control computers without thinking like programmers. We now turn our attention to applications.

> The computer is only a **fast idiot**, it has no imagination; it **cannot originate** action. It is, and will remain, **only a tool** to man.
> —American Library Association reaction to the UNIVAC computer exhibit at the 1964 New York World's Fair

Consumer Applications

Computer stores, software stores, and mail-order houses sell thousands of software titles: publishing programs, accounting software, personal-information managers, graphics programs, multimedia tools, educational games, and more. The process of buying computer software is similar to the process of buying music software (CDs or cassettes) to play on a stereo system. But there are some important differences; we'll touch on a few here.

Documentation

A computer software package generally includes printed documentation with instructions for installing the software on a computer's hard disk. Some software packages also include tutorial manuals and reference manuals that explain how to use the software. Many software companies have replaced these printed documents with tutorials, reference materials, and *help files* that appear onscreen at the user's request. Most help files are supplemented and updated with *online help* at the company's Web site. Many programs are so easy to use that it's possible to put them to work without reading the documentation. But most programs include advanced features that aren't obvious through trial-and-error experimentation.

Most modern computer software provides some kind of online help on demand. Microsoft Windows provides context-sensitive help—help windows whose contents depend on what else is currently on the screen. Many software companies, including Microsoft, use Web databases to provide online help.

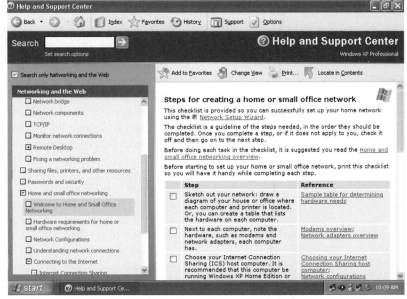

Upgrading

Most software companies continually work to improve their products by removing bugs and adding new features. As a result, new versions of most popular programs are released every year or two. To distinguish between versions, program names are generally followed by version numbers, such as 6.0 in Photoshop 6.0. Most companies use decimals to indicate minor revisions and whole numbers to indicate major revisions. For example, Adobe Premiere 5.1, a video editing program, includes only a few more features than Premiere 5.0, but Premiere 6.0 is significantly different from version 5.1. Not all software follows this logical convention. For example, the last five versions of Microsoft's consumer operating system have been labeled Microsoft Windows 3.1, Windows 95, Windows 98, Windows Millennium Edition (Windows ME), and Windows XP, Home Edition. When you buy a software program, you generally buy the current version. When a new version is released, you can upgrade your program to the new version by paying an upgrade fee to the software manufacturer.

Compatibility

A computer software buyer must be concerned with compatibility. When you buy a music CD you don't need to specify the brand of your CD player, because all manufacturers adhere to common industry standards. But no complete, universal software standards exist in the computer world, so a program written for one type of computer system may not work on another. Software packages contain labels with statements such as "Requires Windows 9x, ME, or XP with 128MB of RAM." (An x in a version specification generally means "substitute any number" so "Windows 9x" means "Windows ninety-*something*.") These demands should not be taken lightly; without compatible hardware and software, most software programs are worthless.

Disclaimers

According to the warranties printed on many software packages, the applications might be worthless even if you have compatible hardware and software. Here's the first paragraph from a typical "limited warranty:"

This program is provided "as is" without warranty of any kind. The entire risk as to the result and performance of the program is assumed by you. Should the program prove defective, you—and not the manufacturer or its dealers—assume the entire cost of all necessary servicing, repair, or correction. Further, the manufacturer does not warranty, guarantee, or make any representations regarding the use of, or the result of the use of, the program in terms of correctness, accuracy, reliability, currentness, or otherwise, and you rely on the program and its results solely at your own risk.

Software companies hide behind disclaimers because nobody's figured out how to write error-free software. Remember our problems providing Robert with a foolproof set of instructions for producing French toast? Programmers who write applications such as word-processing programs must try to anticipate and respond to all combinations of commands and actions performed by users under any conditions. Given the difficulty of this task, most programs work amazingly well—but not perfectly.

Licensing

When you buy a typical computer software package, you're not actually buying the software. Instead, you're buying a software license to use the program on a single machine. While licensing agreements vary from company to company, most include limitations on your right to copy disks, install software on hard drives, and transfer information to other users. Many companies offer *site licenses*—special licenses for entire companies, schools, or government institutions. A few companies now rent software to corporate and government clients.

Virtually all commercially marketed software is copyrighted so it can't be legally duplicated for distribution to others. Some disks (mostly entertainment products) are physically *copy protected* so they can't be copied *at all*. A milder, more common form of copy protection is to require the user to type in his or her name and a product serial number before a newly installed program will work. Because programming is so difficult, software development is expensive. Software developers use copyrights and copy protection to ensure that they sell enough copies of their products to recover their investments and stay in business to write more programs.

Distribution

Software is distributed through direct sales forces to corporations and other institutions. Software is sold to consumers in computer stores, software specialty stores, book and record stores, and other retail outlets. Much software is sold through mail-order catalogs and Web sites. Web distribution makes it possible for some companies to offer software without packaging or disks. For example, you might download (copy) a demo version of a commercial program from a company's Web site or some other source; the demo program is identical to the commercial version, but with some key features disabled. After you try the program and decide you want to buy it, you can contact the company (by phone or through the Web site), pay (by credit card) for the full version of the program, and receive (by email) a code that you can type in to unlock the disabled features of the program.

Not all software is copyrighted and sold through commercial channels. Web sites, user groups, and other sources commonly offer public domain software (free for the taking) and shareware (free for the trying, with a send-payment-if-you-keep-it honor system) along with demonstration versions of commercial programs. Unlike copyrighted commercial software, public domain software, shareware, and demo software can be legally copied and shared freely.

It may seem strange that anyone would pay several hundred dollars for a product that comes with no war-

Word processors are based on the visual metaphor of a typewriter, but a modern word processor makes it easy to add graphics, video, and even Web links to an onscreen document.

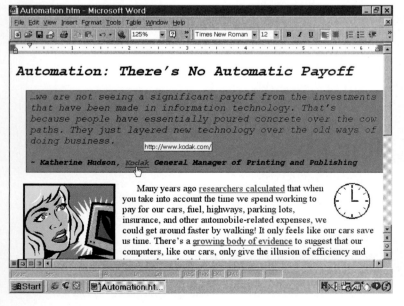

ranty and dozens of legal restrictions about how you can use it. In fact, the rapidly growing software industry has spawned dozens of programs that have sold millions of copies. Why do so many people buy and use these hit programs? Of course, the answer varies from person to person and from product to product. But in general most successful software products share these two important characteristics:

▶ *They are built around visual metaphors of real-world tools.* A drawing program turns the screen into a sheet of drawing paper and a collection of drawing tools. Spreadsheets resemble an accountant's ledger sheets. Video editing software puts familiar VCR controls on the screen. But if these programs merely mimicked their real-world counterparts, people would have no compelling reason to use them.

▶ *They extend human capabilities in some way.* Popular programs enable people to do things that can't be done easily, or at all, with conventional tools. An artist using a graphics program can easily add an eye-catching distortion effect to a drawing and just as easily remove it if it doesn't look right. Spreadsheet programs enable managers to project future revenues based on best guesses and then instantly recalculate the bottom line with a different set of assumptions. And the possibilities opened up by computer video editing are mind-boggling. All kinds of software applications that extend human capabilities are the driving force behind the computer revolution.

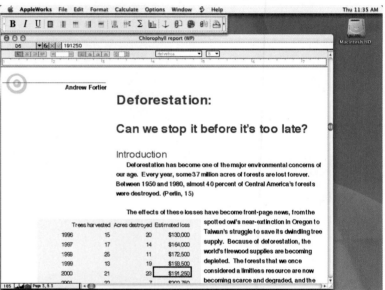

AppleWorks is an integrated application program that combines several popular applications in an easy-to-use package.

Integrated Applications and Suites: Software Bundles

While most software packages specialize in a particular application, such as word processing or photographic editing, low-priced **integrated software** packages include several applications designed to work well together. Popular integrated packages, such as AppleWorks and Microsoft Works, generally include word processing, database, spreadsheet, graphics, telecommunication, and personal information management (PIM) modules.

The parts of an integrated package may not have all the features of their separately packaged counterparts, but integrated packages still offer advantages. They apply a similar look and feel to all of their applications so users don't need to memorize different commands and techniques for doing different tasks. The best integrated programs blur the lines between applications so, for example, you can create a table full of calculations right in the middle of a typed letter without explicitly switching from a word processor to a spreadsheet. *Interapplication communication* enables automatic transfer of data among applications so, for example, changes in a financial spreadsheet are automatically reflected in a graphic table embedded in a word-processed memo.

These advantages aren't unique to integrated packages. Many software companies offer **application suites**—bundles containing several application programs that might also be sold as separate programs. The best-selling suite, Microsoft Office, comes in several different versions designed for different types of users. The core programs of Microsoft Office include Microsoft Word (a word processor), Excel (a spreadsheet program), PowerPoint (a presentation graphics

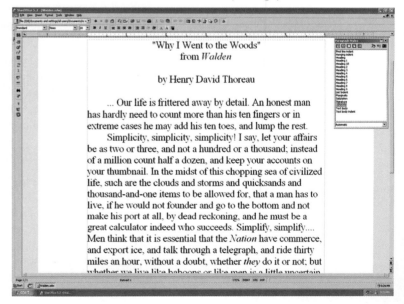

StarOffice is a popular freeware office suite from Sun Microsystems. StarOffice is available for many operating systems.

program), Access (a database program), Outlook (an email/personal-information management program), and Internet Explorer (a Web browser). Microsoft has designed these applications so they have similar command structures and easy interapplication communication. The price of a suite such as Microsoft Office is generally less than the total price of its applications purchased separately, but more than the cost of an integrated package such as Microsoft Works. Suites have more features than integrated programs but also make greater demands on system memory, disk storage, and the CPU. Many older computers simply aren't powerful enough to run a modern application suite. Still, Microsoft Office is the most widely used application package on newer PCs and Macintoshes.

Vertical-Market and Custom Software

Vertical-market software helps this researcher track geographic information.

Because of their flexibility, word processors, spreadsheets, databases, and graphics programs are used in homes, schools, government offices, and all kinds of businesses. But many computer applications are so job specific that they're of little interest or use to anybody outside a given profession. Medical billing software, library cataloging software, legal reference software, restaurant management software, and other applications designed specifically for a particular business or industry are called **vertical-market** or **custom applications**.

Vertical-market applications tend to cost far more than mass-market applications, because companies that develop the software have very few potential customers through which to recover their development costs. In fact, some custom applications are programmed specifically for single clients. For example, the software used to control the space shuttle was developed with a single customer—NASA—in mind.

System Software:
The Hardware-Software Connection

> Originally, **operating systems** were envisioned as a way to handle one of the most **complex** input/output operations: **communicating** with a variety of disk drives. But, the operating system quickly **evolved** into an **all-encompassing bridge** between your PC and the software you run on it.
>
> —Ron White, in *How Computers Work*

When you're typing a paper or writing a program, you don't need to concern yourself with the parts of the computer's memory that hold your document, the segments of the word-processing software currently in the computer's memory, or the output instructions sent by the computer to the printer. **System software**, a class of software that includes the *operating system* and *utility programs,* handles these details, and hundreds of others behind the scenes.

What the Operating System Does

Virtually every general-purpose computer today, whether a timesharing supercomputer or laptop PC, depends on an **operating system (OS)** to keep hardware running efficiently and to make the process of communication with that hardware easier. Operating system software runs continuously whenever the computer is on. The operating system provides an additional layer of insulation between you and the bits-and-bytes world of computer hardware. Because the operating system stands between the software application and the hardware, application compatibility is often defined by the operating system as well as the hardware.

The operating system, as the name implies, is a system of programs that performs a variety of technical operations, from basic communication with peripherals to complex networking and security tasks.

Communicating with Peripherals

Some of the most complex tasks performed by a computer involve communicating with screens, printers, disk drives, and other peripheral devices. A computer's operating system includes programs that transparently communicate with peripherals.

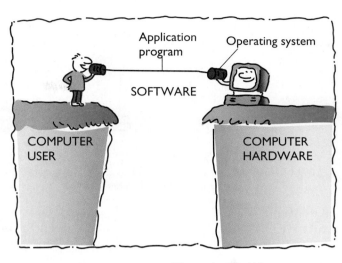

Coordinating Concurrent Processing of Jobs

Large, multiuser computers often work on several jobs at the same time—a technique known as **concurrent processing**. State-of-the-art parallel-processing machines use multiple CPUs to process jobs simultaneously. But a typical computer has only one CPU, so it must work on several projects by rapidly switching back and forth between projects. The computer takes advantage of idle time in one process (for example, waiting for input) by working on another program. (Our computerized chef, Robert, might practice concurrent processing by slicing fruit while he waits for the toast to brown.) A timesharing computer practices concurrent processing whenever multiple users are connected to the system. The computer quickly moves from terminal to terminal, checking for input and processing each user's data in turn. If a PC has **multitasking** capabilities, the user can issue a command that initiates a process (for example, to print this chapter) and continue working with other applications while the computer executes the command.

The user's view: When a person uses an application, whether a game or an accounting program, the person doesn't communicate directly with the computer hardware. Instead, the user interacts with the application, which depends on the operating system to manage and control hardware.

Memory Management

When several jobs are being processed concurrently, the operating system must keep track of how the computer's memory is being used and make sure that no job encroaches on another's territory.

Memory management is accomplished in a variety of ways, from simple routines that subdivide the available memory between jobs to elaborate schemes that temporarily swap information between the computer's memory and external storage devices. One common technique for dealing with memory shortages is to set aside part of a hard disk as **virtual memory**. Thanks to the operating system, this chunk of disk space looks just like internal memory to the CPU, even though access time is slower.

Resource Monitoring, Accounting, and Security

Many multiuser computer systems are designed to charge users for the resources they consume. These systems keep track of each user's time, storage demands, and pages printed so accounting programs can calculate and print accurate bills. Each user generally has a unique identification name and password, so the system can track and bill for individual resource usage. Even in environments where billing isn't an issue, the operating system should monitor resources to ensure the privacy and security of each user's data.

Program and Data Management

In addition to serving as a traffic cop, a security guard, and an accountant, the operating system acts as a librarian, locating and accessing files and programs requested by the user and by other programs.

Coordinating Network Communications

Until recently, network communications weren't handled by the typical operating system; they were coordinated by specialized network operating systems. But many modern operating systems are designed to serve as gateways to networks, from the inner office to the Internet. These network communication functions are described in detail in later chapters.

4.2

The Operating System

Most of what you see onscreen when you use an application program and most of the common tasks you have the pro- *gram perform, such as saving and opening files, are being performed by the operating system at the application's request.*

When a computer is turned off, there's nothing in RAM, and the CPU isn't doing anything. The operating system (OS) programs must be in memory and running on the CPU before the system can function. When you turn on the computer, the CPU automatically begins executing instructions stored in ROM. These instructions help the system boot, and the operating system is loaded from disk into part of the system's memory.

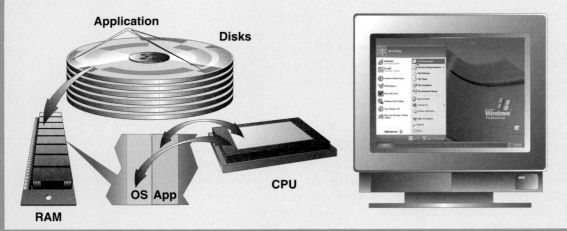

Using the mouse, you "ask" the operating system to load a word processing application program into memory so it can run.

Utility Programs

Even the best operating systems leave some housekeeping tasks to other programs and to the user. **Utility programs** serve as tools for doing system maintenance and repairs that aren't automatically handled by the operating system. Utilities make it easier for users to copy files between storage devices, to repair damaged data files, to translate files so that different programs can read them, to guard against viruses and other potentially harmful programs (as described in the chapter on computer security and risks), to compress files so they take up less disk space, and to perform other important, if unexciting, tasks.

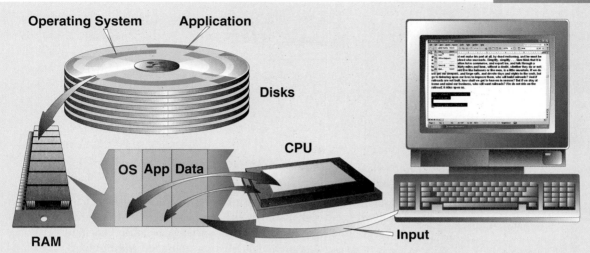

The loaded application occupies a portion of memory, leaving that much less for other programs and data. The OS remains in memory, so it can provide services to the application program, helping it to display onscreen menus, communicate with the printer, and perform other common actions. Because the OS and application are in constant communication, control— the location in memory where the CPU is reading program instructions—jumps all around. If the application calls the OS to help display a menu, the application tells the CPU, "Go follow the menu display instructions at address x in the operating system area; when you're done, return here and pick up where you left off."

To avoid losing your data file when the system is turned off, you save it to the disk—write it into a file on the disk for later use. The OS handles communication between the CPU and the disk drive, ensuring that your file doesn't overwrite other information. (Later, when you reopen the file, the OS locates it on the disk and copies it into memory so the CPU—and therefore any program—can see it and work with it.)

The operating system can directly invoke many utility programs, so they appear to the user to be part of the operating system. For example, *device drivers* are small programs that enable I/O devices—keyboard, mouse, printer, and others—to communicate with the computer. Once a device driver—say, for a new printer—is installed, the printer driver functions as a behind-the-scenes intermediary whenever the user requests that a document be printed on that printer.

Some utility programs are included with the operating system. Others, including many device drivers, are bundled with peripherals. Still others are sold or given away as separate products.

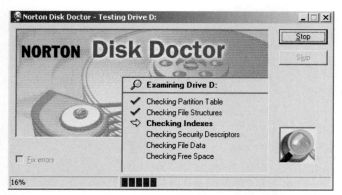

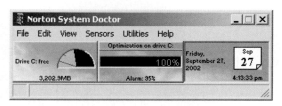

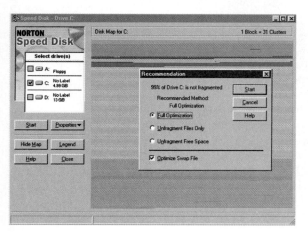

Norton Utilities (from Symantec) is a popular utility package that includes software tools for recovering damaged files, repairing damaged disks, and improving disk performance.

Where the Operating System Lives

Some computers—mostly game machines, handheld computers, and special-purpose computers—store their operating systems permanently in ROM (read-only memory) so they can begin working immediately at start-up time. But since ROM is unchangeable, these machines can't have their operating systems modified or upgraded without hardware transplants. Some computers, including many handheld devices, store their operating system in flash memory so they can be upgraded. But most computers, including all modern PCs, include only part of the operating system in ROM. The remainder of the operating system is loaded into memory in a process called **booting**, which occurs when you turn on the computer. (The term *booting* is used because the computer seems to pull itself up by its own bootstraps.)

Most of the time the operating system works behind the scenes, taking care of business without the knowledge or intervention of the user. But occasionally it's necessary for a user to communicate directly with the operating system. For example, when you boot a PC, the operating system takes over the screen, waiting until you tell it—with the mouse, the keyboard, or some other input device—what to do. If you tell it to open a graphics application, the operating system locates the program, copies it from disk into memory, turns the screen over to the application, and then accepts commands from the application while you draw pictures on the screen.

Interacting with the operating system, like interacting with an application, can be intuitive or challenging. It depends on something called the *user interface*. Because of its profound impact on the computing experience, the user interface is a critically important component of almost every piece of software.

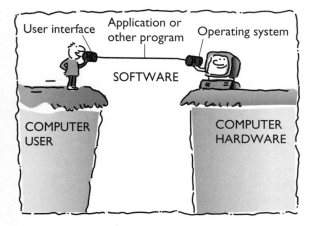

The user's view revisited: The user interface is the part of the computer system that the user sees. A well-designed user interface hides the bothersome details of computing from the user.

The User Interface: The Human–Machine Connection

> The anthropologist Claude Levi-Strauss has called human beings **tool makers** and **symbol makers**. The user interface is potentially the most sophisticated of these constructions, one in which the **distinction between tool and symbol is blurred**.
> —Aaron Marcus and Andries van Dam, user interface experts

Early computer users had to spend tedious hours writing and debugging machine-language instructions. Later users programmed in languages that were easier to understand but still technically challenging. Today users spend much of their time working with preprogrammed applications, such as word processors, that simulate and amplify the capabilities of real-world tools. As software evolves, so does the **user interface**—the look and feel of the computing experience from a human point of view.

Character-Based User Interfaces

The earliest PC operating systems, created for the Apple II, the original IBM PC, and other machines, looked nothing like today's Macintosh and Windows operating systems. When IBM introduced its first personal computer in 1981, a typical computer monitor displayed 24 80-column lines of text, numbers, and/or symbols. The computer sent messages to the monitor telling it which character to display in each location on the screen. To comply with this hardware arrangement, the PC's operating system, MS-DOS, was designed with a **character-based interface**—a user interface based on characters rather than graphics.

Whether typing commands to the OS or selecting options from menus in applications, MS-DOS users work with a character-based interface.

MS-DOS (Microsoft Disk Operating System, sometimes called just DOS), became the standard operating system on IBM-compatible computers—computers functionally identical to an IBM personal computer and therefore capable of running IBM-compatible software. Unlike the Windows desktop, MS-DOS uses a **command-line interface**: The user types commands, and the computer responds. Some MS-DOS-compatible applications have a command-line interface, but it's more common for applications to have a **menu-driven interface** that enables users to choose commands from onscreen lists called **menus**.

Graphical User Interface Operating Systems

In the years since the introduction of the IBM-PC, graphic displays have become the norm. A computer with a graphic display is not limited to displaying rows and columns of characters; it can individually control every dot on the screen. When the Apple Macintosh was introduced in 1984, it was the first low-cost computer whose operating system was designed with a graphic display in mind. The **Mac OS** sports a **graphical user interface**—abbreviated **GUI**, pronounced "gooey."

Instead of reading typed commands and file names from a command line, the Macintosh operating system determines what the user wants by monitoring movements of the mouse. With the mouse the user points to **icons** (pictures) that represent applications, **documents** (files, such as term papers and charts created with applications), **folders** (collections of files), and disks. These pictures are arranged on a metaphorical **desktop**—a virtual workspace designed to resemble in some ways the physical desktops we use in day-to-day work. Documents are displayed in **windows**—framed areas that can be opened, closed, and rearranged with the mouse.

The Mac OS was the first operating system to popularize the graphical user interface. Today's Mac OS X adds several new elements to the traditional windows, icons, and pull-down menus. Shown here are Mac OS 9, the last descendant of the "original" Mac OS, and Mac OS-X, a new operating system released by Apple in 2001.

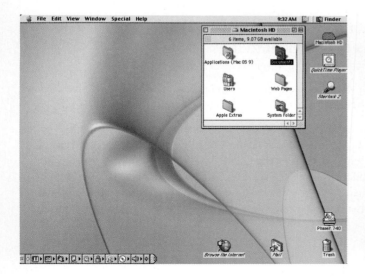

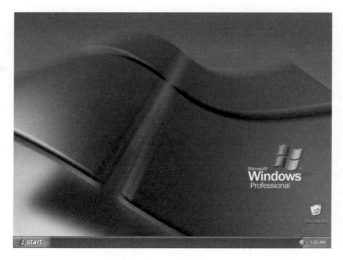

Windows has replaced MS-DOS as the standard operating system on IBM-compatible PCs. Like the Mac OS, Windows has evolved and added many new features over the years.

The user selects commands from **pull-down menus** at the top of the screen. **Dialog boxes** enable users to specify preferences by simply filling in onscreen blanks and clicking check boxes and buttons. (A User's View box in Chapter 0, ReadMe presents a short session with Mac OS.)

Ironically, the Macintosh has been eclipsed in the GUI operating system market by a product from Microsoft, the company that produces MS-DOS. Originally, **Microsoft Windows** (commonly called *Windows*, or just *Win*) was a type of program, known as a **shell**, that put a graphical face on MS-DOS. The Windows shell stood between the user and the operating system, translating mouse movements and other user input into commands that could be recognized by MS-DOS. With the introduction of Windows 95 in 1995, Microsoft completed the transition of Windows from an operating system shell into an operating system that seldom shows its MS-DOS roots. (A User's View box in Chapter 0, ReadMe presents a short session with Windows.)

Windows and Mac OS have evolved over the years, adding new features to their GUIs to make them easier to use. *Task bars* provide instant one-click access to open applications, making it easy to switch back and forth between different tasks. **Hierarchical menus** organize commands into compact, efficient submenus. **Pop-up menus** can appear anywhere on the screen. Many of these menus are **context-sensitive**—the choices they offer depend on the context.

There are many differences between Windows and Mac OS, but the two have user interfaces that are more alike than different—especially when working with cross-platform applications such as Microsoft Office and Adobe Photoshop. Many users effortlessly switch back and forth between the two operating systems every day.

Why WIMP Won

> The first principle of human interface design,
>
> whether for a **doorknob** or a **computer**,
>
> is to keep in mind the **human being** who wants to use it.
>
> **The technology is subservient to that goal**.
>
> —Donald Norman, in *The Art of Human-Computer Interface Design*

Graphical user interfaces with windows, icons, menus, and pointing devices (collectively known as *WIMP*) offer several clear advantages from the user's point of view:

▶ *They're intuitive.* Visual metaphors like trash cans and folders are easier for people to understand and learn than typed commands. Users feel safe learning by trial and error, because it's usually easy to predict the results of each action.

▶ *They're consistent.* GUI applications have the same user interface as their operating systems, so users don't need to learn new ways of doing things whenever they switch applications. Many Macintosh and Windows users have mastered dozens of applications without ever consulting a manual.

▶ *They're forgiving.* Almost every dialog box includes a Cancel button, enabling the user to say, in effect, "Never mind." The **Undo command** can almost always take back the last command, restoring everything the way it was before the current command was issued.

▶ *They're protective.* When you're about to do something that may have unpleasant consequences (such as replacing the revised version of your term paper with an older version), the software opens a dialog box, reminding you to make sure you're doing what you want before you proceed.

▶ *They're flexible.* Users who prefer to keep their hands on the keyboard can use keyboard short-cuts instead of mouse movements to invoke most commands. Most actions can be accomplished in several different ways; each user can, in effect, customize the user interface.

Of course, all of this user-friendliness doesn't come free. GUIs and friendly operating systems require more expensive graphics display systems, more memory, more disk space, faster processors, and more complex software. Character-based operating systems have minimal hardware requirements when compared with just about any GUI operating system or shell. But steadily falling hardware prices have made even the least expensive PCs powerful enough to handle GUIs.

Character-based interfaces aren't dead. They're common in VCRs, cell phones, microwave ovens, stereos, and other consumer devices with limited memory and limited options for users. They're also widely used in applications built on older computer systems and in applications that involve transmitting data through networks. In fact, the Internet explosion has fueled growth in popularity of several versions of UNIX, a character-based operating system that is older than any of the operating systems we've looked at so far.

Many consumer devices today, including VCRs, cell phones, and pagers, use character-based user interfaces.

Multiple User Operating Systems: UNIX and Linux

Because of its historical ties to academic and government research sites, the Internet is heavily populated with computers running the UNIX operating system. UNIX, developed at Bell Labs in the time before PCs, enables a timesharing computer to communicate with several other computers or terminals at one time. UNIX has long been the operating system of choice for workstations and mainframes in research and academic settings. In recent years it has taken root in many business environments. In spite of competition from Microsoft, UNIX is still the most widely available multiuser operating system today. Some form of UNIX is available for personal computers, workstations, servers, mainframes, and supercomputers.

Unlike the other operating systems listed here, UNIX isn't owned and controlled by a single company. Many commercial brands of UNIX are available, including Sun's Solaris, Hewlett Packard's HP-UX, and IBM's AIX. Linux, described at the beginning of this chapter, is widely distributed for free and supported without cost by a devoted, technically savvy group of users.

At its heart, in all its versions, UNIX is a command-line, character-based operating system. The command-line interface is similar to that of MS-DOS, although the commands aren't the same. For most tasks the UNIX command-line interface feels like a single-user system, even when many users are *logged in*—connected to and using the system. Until recently, some knowledge of UNIX commands was necessary for taking advantage of most Internet services. The character-based UNIX interface is still widely used on Internet servers. The User's View box, *Connecting to a Multiuser UNIX System*, shows how you might use a command-line interface to connect to a multiuser mainframe UNIX system from a terminal. Like the other User's View boxes in this book, it's designed to give you a peek at the process, not a tutorial.

Today's UNIX systems don't just work with typed commands. Several companies, including Sun and IBM, market UNIX variations and shells with graphical interfaces. The User's View box, *Using a Linux GUI,* shows a short Linux session with a GUI shell that looks like a cross between Microsoft Windows and Mac OS.

The User's View The User's View The User's View The Us

Connecting to a Multiuser UNIX System

SOFTWARE: *UNIX operating system.*

THE GOAL: *To log into your school's UNIX mainframe from a terminal.*

1 When you press Return, UNIX displays a system message to indicate that it's waiting for you to log in, that is, to provide an ID and password.

2 You type your login name—the one-word name assigned to your computer account (in this example sanchez) and press Enter or Return.

3 The program then prompts you to enter your password so the host computer can verify your identity. When you type your password, it isn't echoed on the screen.

4 After you press Return, UNIX displays a system message to indicate that you've successfully logged in.

5 This UNIX system assumes you're using a VT-100 terminal (or at least a terminal that can emulate, or imitate, a VT-100)— the default type. When you press Return without typing anything else, you're saying that the VT-100 default settings will work with your terminal.

6 On this particular UNIX system you can launch a menu program that enables you to access common commands through menus. But you'll stick with the command-line interface for this example.

```
UNIX(r) System V Release 4.0

login: sanchez
Password:
AFS (R) 3.4 Login
==================================================================
=Welcome to node ai.asu.edu - Sparc 20 1000 running Solaris 2.3=
        =This system is only for use authorized by ASU=
==================================================================

You have mail.
Terminal type is vt100
Erase is Backspace
type 'menu' without quotes and press the enter key for our menu


ai > ls
AppleVolumes        Mail            dead.letter
Backup              Work            mbox
School              Reports         News
booklist            saved.notes     readme
ai > pine
```

7 This UNIX system responds to commands typed after the ai *prompt*. Different systems have different prompts, but they all mean the same thing: the system is waiting for you to type a command.

8 You type LS to list the files in your current directory. If you misspell or mistype the command, the system responds with an *error message* telling you, in effect, that it doesn't recognize the command. But since you typed it correctly, the system responds by displaying a multicolumn list of files.

Using a Linux GUI

SOFTWARE: *KDE, Linux, and Corel® WordPerfect® (part of the Corel® WordPerfect® Suite).*

THE GOAL: *To open and print a term paper, this time with Linux. You'll use KDE, a shell that puts a graphical desktop environment between you and the Linux command-line environment. Then, for the sake of comparison, you'll repeat part of the process with a command-line interface.*

1 KDE has a customizable graphical user interface; here it's configured with familiar features of Windows and the Macintosh OS. You select WordPerfect from the personal pop-up menu that resembles the Windows Start menu.

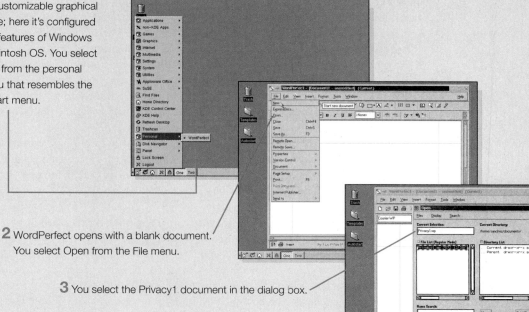

2 WordPerfect opens with a blank document. You select Open from the File menu.

3 You select the Privacy1 document in the dialog box.

4 When the document opens, you select Print from the File menu, respond to the dialog box, close WordPerfect, and wait for your printout. You'd be done now, except . . .

5 You decide to test your Linux literacy by launching the program again, but this time using the operating system's command-line interface. You use a terminal program to connect to a server called Laurel; you type commands to locate the directory and launch WordPerfect.

Hardware and Software Platforms

In most electronic devices the operating system operates invisibly and anonymously. But some operating systems, especially those in PCs, are recognized by name and reputation. The most well-known operating system platforms include:

▶ *Microsoft Windows XP*. This is Microsoft's flagship product introduced in 2001. For years Microsoft has sold two very different versions of Windows: one for home users and one for businesses. With Microsoft XP, the two product lines have merged into one. There are still different versions of Windows, including one especially designed for servers—computer systems that serve data and programs to networked PCs. But all of these products are based on the same core programs.

▶ *Microsoft Windows Millennium Edition (Windows ME)*. This is Microsoft's last "consumer" operating system before XP. Previous versions of this OS include Windows 98, Windows 95, and Windows 3.1; all are still widely used.

▶ *Microsoft Windows 2000* and *Windows NT*. These are the predecessors to Windows XP; they were aimed at networked computers that need features not found in the consumer version of Windows.

▶ *Microsoft Windows CE*. This stripped-down Windows variant is designed mostly for handheld computers—especially the Pocket PC, a Microsoft standard for handheld computers that competes directly with Palm's operating system (see following). Other versions of Win CE have been embedded into car accessories, televisions, and other electronic devices. Several other companies make operating systems for consumer devices and PDAs. But unlike Windows CE, most of these are designed to work on specific devices rather than whole classes of devices.

▶ *Palm OS*. This OS, originally developed for the Palm Pilot, is now used in handheld devices manufactured by many companies, including Palm, Handspring, Sony, and IBM. Its pen-based user interface is intuitive and convenient to use. The Palm OS has communication capabilities that make it easy to transfer data between a handheld device and another computer. Palm OS is now available in phones and other communication devices.

▶ *Mac OS X* (10). OS X is the completely new operating system for the Mac introduced in 2001. On the surface OS X sports a stylish, animated user interface that looks strikingly different than previous Mac operating systems. Underneath its friendly exterior OS X is built on UNIX, the powerful OS known for security and stability rather than simplicity. OS X runs only on Macintosh hardware.

▶ *Mac OS 9*. This is the last in a long line that started with the original Macintosh operating system in 1984. OS 9 and its predecessors run only on Macs.

▶ *Linux, Sun's Solaris, and other UNIX variations*. Some form of UNIX or LINUX can be found on PCs, Macs, workstations, supercomputers, mainframes, and a variety of other devices. Linux is especially popular because it is free—and freely supported by its partisans. Since Linux doesn't offer as many applications programs as Windows, some people use dual-boot PCs that can switch back and forth between Windows and Linux by simply rebooting.

▶ *IBM's OS/2*. Originally designed in partnership with Microsoft, OS/2 has been losing market share since IBM took over sole control of the product. OS/2 is now only being updated for existing corporate customers and is no longer in active development. In the operating system wars, even Big Blue has trouble competing with the marketing power of Microsoft.

Operating systems by themselves aren't very helpful to people. They need application software so they can do useful work. But application software can't exist by itself; it needs to be built on some kind of platform. People often use the term **platform** to describe the combination of hardware and operating system software on which application software is built.

The trends are unmistakable. In the early days of the personal computer revolution, there were dozens of different platforms—machines from Apple, Commodore, Tandy, Texas Instruments, Atari, Coleco, and other companies. All of these products have

Compatibility issues: Hardware platforms and software environments. Most personal computers today are built on what's sometimes called the Wintel platform: Some form of the Windows OS running on an Intel (or compatible) CPU. The Macintosh platform—Mac OS software running on PowerPC processors—makes up a much smaller segment of the market. The Linux OS can run on many hardware platforms, including Intel and PowerPC processors, but different versions of Linux aren't necessarily compatible. Other hardware and software platforms represent smaller shares of the market.

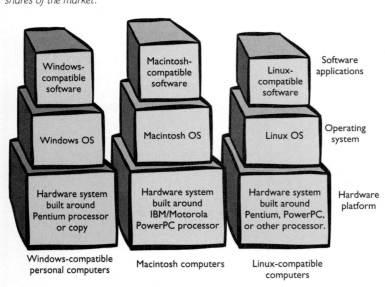

Windows-compatible software	Macintosh-compatible software	Linux-compatible software	Software applications
Windows OS	Macintosh OS	Linux OS	Operating system
Hardware system built around Pentium processor or copy	Hardware system built around IBM/Motorola PowerPC processor	Hardware system built around Pentium, PowerPC, or other processor.	Hardware platform
Windows-compatible personal computers	Macintosh computers	Linux-compatible computers	

vanished from the marketplace, sometimes taking their parent companies with them. Today's market for new PC hardware and software is dominated by three general platforms: Windows in all its variations, the Mac OS, and various versions of UNIX. UNIX isn't often found in desktop PCs; it's mostly used in servers and high-end workstations. While the Mac commands a hefty share of specialized markets like graphic design, publishing, music, multimedia, and education, it runs far behind Windows in the massive corporate desktop market.

To compete in a Windows-dominated world, Apple works with other companies to offer emulation options to make Windows and DOS software run on Macintoshes. One technique involves *software emulation*; a software program creates a *simulated* Windows machine in the Mac, translating all Windows-related instructions into signals the Mac's operating system and CPU can understand. But translation takes time, so software emulation isn't adequate when speed is critical. The other solution, *hardware emulation*, involves adding a circuit board containing an Intel-compatible CPU and additional PC hardware. This board effectively puts a second computer in the Mac's system unit. Emulation technology isn't unique to the Macintosh; there are emulation programs, for example, that enable Windows and Mac programs to run on UNIX-based Sun workstations. Emulation blurs the lines between platforms and enables users to avoid having to choose a single operating system and user interface.

Emulation software enables software written for one computer platform to be used on another. For example, this Macintosh can run Macintosh and Windows programs simultaneously—and transfer data back and forth between them—using Virtual PC from Connectrix.

Tomorrow's User Interfaces

As attractive and popular as today's graphical user interfaces are, they're not likely to reign forever. Future user interfaces will be built around technologies that are still in development today. Here are some likely candidates:

> I **hate** computers. **Telepathy** would be better.
> —John Perry Barlow, writer and cofounder
> of the Electronic Frontier Foundation

- *The end of applications.* As more programs take advantage of interapplication communication, the boundaries between individual applications are likely to blur. Future computer users may not think in terms of word processors, spreadsheets, and such; they'll just use their computers like we use pencils today—as all-purpose tools.

- *Network applications.* With the growing importance of the Internet and other networks, future applications may be more tied to networks than to desktop computer platforms. Computer users are spending less time on their desktops and more time on the Web. Microsoft has responded to that trend with .NET, a strategy that blurs the line between the Web and Microsoft's operating systems and applications. As .NET evolves, more and more software components will be delivered by the network rather than residing on the desktop. Microsoft's .NET strategy is a response to the popularity of Java, a platform-neutral computer language developed by Sun Microsystems for use on multiplatform networks. Programs written in Java can run on computers running Windows, Macintosh, UNIX, and other operating systems, provided those computers have *Java virtual machine* software installed. Java *applets*—miniature application pieces designed to work with other applications or applets—are routinely included in World Wide Web pages today to add animation and interactivity. As this technology matures, it may make it possible for computer users to do their work without knowing—or caring—where in the world their software is.

- *Natural-language interfaces.* It's just a matter of time before we'll be able to communicate with computers in English, Spanish, Russian, Japanese, or some other natural language. Today many computers can reliably read subsets of the English language or can be trained to understand spoken English commands and text. Tomorrow's machines should be able to handle much day-to-day work through a natural-language interface, written or spoken. Natural-language processing is discussed in more depth in later chapters.

- *Agents.* Artificial intelligence research will lead to intelligent *agents* that "live" in our computers and act as digital secretaries, anticipating our requests, filling in details in our work, searching networks for critical information, and adjusting the computerized workspace to fit our needs. Today's software agents only begin to suggest future possibilities. The last chapter of this book

Virtual reality is used for work and for play; here are two examples. This researcher (left) practices virtual surgery using a type of software that may allow surgeons to practice before performing difficult operations. It may also someday allow surgeons to perform operations on patients thousands of miles away. This virtual thrill ride (right) of Monument Valley, Arizona offers low-risk adventure through simulation software.

describes tomorrow's agents and other futuristic user interface technologies, including the technology of virtual reality.

▶ *Virtual realities.* Further into the future, many experts predict that user interfaces will become so sophisticated that we'll be hard-pressed to detect the difference between the real world outside the computer and the **virtual reality** created by the computer, except that the virtual reality will enable us to do things that we can't do on the physical plane. Some computer games today provide surprisingly convincing simulations of the experience of driving a car or flying a plane. These games represent the tip of a gigantic iceberg of research into virtual reality software. More sophisticated virtual reality interfaces can be achieved today with specially designed hardware—for input, a glove or body suit equipped with motion sensors, and for output, a helmet with eye-sized screens whose views change as the helmet moves. This equipment, when coupled with appropriate software, enables the user to explore an artificial world of data as if it were three-dimensional physical space. Today's clumsy virtual reality technology is a long way from living up to its name; virtual reality illusions are interesting, but they're poor substitutes for reality. Still, virtual reality has practical applications: Virtual walk-throughs are used by architects and engineers to preview buildings and mechanical assemblies; virtual reality models are used for education and simulations, and virtual worlds are popping up in amusement parks and arcades.

The best known example of the kind of virtual reality researchers are working toward is the Holodeck on TV's *Star Trek.* The Holodeck can create absolutely convincing simulations of anything from a Sherlock Holmes detective story to a 24th-century antimatter generator. No keyboards or screens are in sight; the user interface is a three-dimensional artificial world full of people, places, and things—real or imaginary—that can be seen, touched, talked to, and controlled by one or more "users." Far-fetched? Absolutely. Possible? Maybe. When? Don't sell your keyboard yet. . . .

Green Computing

When compared with heavy industries such as automobiles and energy, the computer industry is relatively easy on the environment. But the manufacture and use of computer hardware and software does have a significant environmental impact, especially now that so many of us are using the technology. Fortunately, you have some control over the environmental impact of your computing activities. Here are a few tips to help minimize your impact:

▷ *Buy green equipment.* Today's computer equipment uses relatively little energy, but as world energy resources dwindle, less is always better. Many modern computers and peripherals are specifically designed to consume less energy. Look for the Environmental Protection Agency's Energy Star certification on the package.

▷ *Use a laptop.* Portable computers use far less energy than desktop computers. They're engineered to preserve precious battery power. But if you use a laptop, keep it plugged in when you have easy access to an electrical outlet. Batteries wear out from repeated usage, and their disposal can cause environmental problems of a different sort. (If you're the kind of person who always needs to have the latest and greatest technology, a laptop isn't the greenest choice for you, because laptops are difficult or impossible to upgrade.)

▷ *Take advantage of energy-saving features.* Most modern systems can be set up to go to sleep (a sort of suspended animation state that uses just enough power to preserve RAM) and turn off the monitor or printer when idle for more than an hour or so. If your equipment has automatic energy-saving features, use them. You'll save energy and money.

▷ *Turn it off when you're away.* If you're just leaving your computer for an hour or two, you won't save much energy by turning the CPU off. But if you're leaving it for more than a few hours and it's not on duty receiving faxes and email, you'll do the environment a favor by turning it off or putting it to sleep.

▷ *Save energy, not screens.* Your monitor is probably the biggest power guzzler in your system. A screen saver can be fun to watch, but it doesn't save your screen, and it doesn't save energy, either. As long as your monitor is displaying an image, it's consuming power. Use sleep.

▷ *Print only once.* Don't print out a rough draft just to proofread; try to get it clean onscreen. (Most people find this one hard to follow 100% of the time; some errors just don't seem to show up until you print.)

▷ *Recycle your waste products.* When you do have to reprint that 20-page report because of a missing paragraph on page 1, recycle the flawed printout. When your laser printer's toner cartridge runs dry, ship or deliver it to one of the many companies that recycle cartridges. They may even pay you a few dollars for the empty cartridge. When your portable's battery dies, follow the manufacturer's instructions for recycling it. While you're in recycling mode, don't forget all those computer magazines and catalogs.

▷ *Pass it on.* When you outgrow a piece of hardware or software, don't throw it away. Donate it to a school, civic organization, family member, or friend who can put it to good use.

▷ *Send bits, not atoms.* It takes far more resources to send a letter by truck, train, or plane than to send an electronic message through the Internet. Whenever possible, use your modem instead of your printer.

Windows and Macintosh operating systems have energy-saver control panels that can be set to automatically switch the monitor and CPU to low-power sleep modes after specified periods of inactivity.

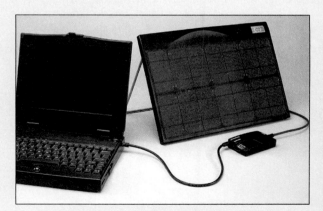

Portable computers consume far less energy than desktop models; this one is powered by the sun using a Neptune Solar Panel.

'Read the Manual!' What Manual?

Stephen Manes

Stephen Manes, PC World *Contributing Editor and cohost of PBS series Digital Duo, has been using computers since the days when computer manuals came packaged with new computer software and hardware. In this column from the June 2001 issue of* PC World *magazine, Manes discusses the disappearance of the manual from the box—and what it means to those of us who use this technology.*

Customer service shouldn't begin when you have a problem. It should start when a product is built, so that you don't have to futz around on the Web or wait on hold to get answers. One form of that service is good product design. Another is a great manual.

A what? As hardware and software grow dizzyingly more complicated, the manual—if any—now amounts to a scrap of tissue. The online help that supposedly replaces it inevitably runs out of information just as you close in on what you need to know.

Back in 1982, my first IBM PC—with 64KB of memory, a 4.77-MHz 8088 processor, and DOS—came with loose-leaf manuals that were boxed in linen and full of useful examples. My new 1-GHz Dell Pentium III came with its own box of documentation, but no linen and not much information—even if you count a grand total of ten pages on Microsoft Office 2000 that tout new features but offer virtually no details on how they actually work.

A Vicious Circle

Documentation is getting worse because companies treat it the way they do customer service—as a cost center. Their miserly policies push expenses out to the users. It's a vicious circle: Companies refuse to spend a nickel more than they have to for documentation; faced with useless help, customers learn not to bother with it; and after discovering from surveys and focus groups that nobody uses the manuals, companies make them even worse.

That merry-go-round sends users to sources that actually explain things. Since Microsoft makes money selling books designed to fill the gaping holes in its abysmal manuals, it's no wonder some ugly adjectives characterize documentation circa 2001:

▶ **Unspecific.** To cut costs, vendors release one-size-fits-all docs to cover 17 similar but not identical models. Before you can use the manual, you need to figure out which facts apply to the product you have—assuming the information is there at all. Want a challenge? Try to get details on the particular CD-RW or DVD drive the computer maker stuck into your machine.

▶ **Immovable.** Several things are wrong with manuals meant to be read on computer screens. How do you proceed when you need information on what to do when your machine won't boot? Since my computer screen doesn't face my printer or scanner, it's not exactly easy to read online documentation while I'm fiddling with peripherals' front panels. The latest affront to common sense comes from Kyocera, which delivers the detailed manual for its nifty new Palm-based Smartphone on CD-ROM. Maybe you're supposed to bring along a laptop whenever you use the phone.

▶ **Incomplete.** You need two basic pieces of information to get a home networking gateway to work: the proper settings for your broadband provider, and those for Windows networking. Unless you have experience with networks, you have little chance of getting the settings right from the meager info the ISPs and Microsoft supply. Yet not one of the gateways I've tried offers any real help in these two essential areas. Listen up, manufacturers: Decent documentation might well reduce the number of returns you get from people who simply can't figure out how to set up your product.

▶ **Unusable.** Professional indexing by a human being has become a quaint concept. At best, you can expect to get full-text searching in an online document, but that's a poor substitute for a real index. More often, though, you get a travesty generated by some half-bright indexing program—or no index at all.

▶ **Unreal.** How many times have you followed step-by-step directions that were flat-out wrong? If you're lucky, the Readme file or an errata sheet will point out some of the howlers. Better idea: Manufacturers should get the documentation right in the first place, particularly when it's in online form.

The need for documentation grows more acute as consumer products go digital and inherit the complexity of PCs. Much of the problem is poor design: You shouldn't have to read a manual just to dope out some simple function of a VCR or coffeemaker.

But you do. Manuals for those devices stink, too, but at least they don't come on CD-ROM—so far.

DISCUSSION QUESTIONS

1. Why do you think computer manuals have become so scarce?
2. Do you think CD-ROM and Web documentation is an adequate substitute for manuals? Why or why not?

Summary

Software provides the communication link between humans and their computers. Because software is soft—stored in memory rather than hard-wired into the circuitry—it can easily be modified to meet the needs of the computer user. By changing software, you can change a computer from one kind of tool into another.

Most software falls into one of three broad categories: compilers and other translator programs, software applications, and system software. A compiler is a software tool that enables programs written in English-like languages such as BASIC and C to be translated into the zeros and ones of the machine language the computer understands. A compiler frees the programmer from the tedium of machine-language programming, making it easier to write quality programs with fewer bugs. But even with the best translators, programming is a little like communicating with an alien species. It's a demanding process that requires more time and mental energy than most people are willing or able to invest.

Fortunately, software applications make it easy for most computer users today to communicate their needs to the computer without learning programming. Applications simulate and extend the properties of familiar real-world tools like typewriters, paintbrushes, and file cabinets, making it possible for people to do things with computers that would be difficult or impossible otherwise. Integrated software packages combine several applications in a single unified package, making it easy to switch between tools. For situations when a general commercial program won't do the job, programmers for businesses and public institutions develop vertical-market and custom packages.

Whether you're writing programs or simply using them, the computer's operating system is functioning behind the scenes, translating your software's instructions into messages that the hardware can understand. An operating system serves as the computer's business manager, taking care of the hundreds of details that need to be handled to keep the computer functioning. A timesharing operating system has the particularly challenging job of serving multiple users concurrently, monitoring the machine's resources, keeping track of each user's account, and protecting the security of the system and each user's data. Many of those system-related problems that the operating system can't solve directly can be handled by utility programs. Popular operating systems today include several versions of Microsoft Windows, the Mac OS, and several versions of UNIX.

Applications, utilities, programming languages, and operating systems all must, to varying degrees, communicate with the user. A program's user interface is a critical factor in that communication. User interfaces have evolved over the years to the point where sophisticated software packages can be operated by people who know little about the inner workings of the computer. A well-designed user interface shields the user from the bits and bytes, creating an onscreen façade or shell that makes sense to the user. Today the computer industry has moved away from the tried-and-true command-line interfaces toward a friendlier graphical user interface that uses windows, icons, mice, and pull-down menus in an intuitive, consistent environment. Tomorrow's user interfaces are likely to depend more on voice, three-dimensional graphics, and animation to create an artificial reality.

Chapter Review

▼ Key Terms

algorithm (p. 103)
application suite (office suite) (p. 109)
booting (p. 114)
bug (p. 103)
character-based interface (p. 115)
command-line interface (p. 115)
compatibility (p. 107)
compiler (p. 106)
concurrent processing (p. 111)
context-sensitive menus (p. 116)
copyrighted software (p. 108)
custom application (p. 110)
debugging (p. 00)
desktop (p. 115)
dialog box (p. 116)
document (p. 115)
documentation (p. 107)
emulation (p. 121)

folder (p. 115)
graphical user interface (GUI) (p. 115)
hierarchical menus (p. 116)
high-level language (p. 106)
icon (p. 115)
integrated software (p. 109)
Java (p. 121)
Linux (p. 101)
machine language (p. 106)
Mac OS (p. 115)
menu (p. 115)
menu-driven interface (p. 115)
Microsoft Windows (p. 116)
MS-DOS (p. 115)
multitasking (p. 111)
natural language (p. 106)
open source software (p. 101)
operating system (OS) (p. 110)

platform (p. 120)
pop-up menus (p. 116)
public domain software (p. 108)
pull-down menu (p. 116)
shareware (p. 108)
shell (p. 116)
software license (p. 108)
system software (p. 110)
Undo command (p. 117)
UNIX (p. 117)
upgrade (p. 107)
user interface (p. 114)
utility program (p. 112)
vertical-market application (p. 110)
virtual memory (p. 111)
virtual reality (p. 122)
window (p. 115)

▼ Interactive Quiz Questions

1. The *Computer Confluence* CD-ROM contains self-test quiz questions related to this chapter, including multiple choice, true or false, and matching questions.
2. The *Computer Confluence* Web site, **www.prenhall.com/beekman**, contains self-test exercises related to this chapter. Follow the instructions for taking a quiz. After you've completed your quiz, you can email the results to your instructor.

The Web site also contains open-ended discussion questions called Internet Explorations. Discuss one or more of the Internet Exploration questions at the section for this chapter.

▼ Review Questions

1. Define or describe each of the key terms listed in the Key Terms section. Check your answers in the glossary.
2. What is the relationship between a program and an algorithm?
3. Most computer software falls into one of three categories: compilers and other translator programs, software applications, and system software. Describe and give examples of each.
4. Which must be loaded first into the computer's memory, the operating system or software applications? Why?
5. Write an algorithm for changing a flat tire. Check your algorithm carefully for errors and ambiguities. Then have a classmate or your instructor check it. How did your results compare?

6. Describe several functions of a single-user operating system. Describe several additional functions of a multiuser operating system.
7. What does it mean when software is called IBM-compatible or Macintosh-compatible? What does this have to do with the operating system?
8. Why is the user interface such an important part of software?
9. What is a graphical user interface? How does it differ from a character-based interface? What are the advantages of each?
10. What are the three main platforms for desktop computers today? Briefly describe each of them.

▼ Discussion Questions

1. In what way is writing instructions for a computer more difficult than writing instructions for a person? In what way is it easier?
2. How would using a computer be different if it had no operating system? How would programming be different?
3. Speculate about the user interface of a typical computer in the year 2010. How would this user interface differ from those used in today's computers?

4. If you had the resources to design a computer with a brand new user interface, what would your priorities be? Make a rank-ordered list of the qualities you'd like to have in your user interface.
5. How do you feel about the open software movement? Would you be willing to volunteer your time to write software or help users for free?

▼ Projects

1. Write a report about available computer applications in your field of study or in your chosen profession.

2. Take an inventory of computer applications available in your computer lab. Describe the major uses for each application.

 Sources and Resources

Books

Just for Fun: The Story of an Accidental Revolutionary, by Linus Torvalds and David Diamond (New York: Harperbusiness, 2001). *Red Herring* Executive Editor convinced Linus Torvalds to tell his story. The result is this book, a quirky collection of tidbits from the life of the creator of Linux.

Rebel Code: Linux and the Open Source Revolution, by Glyn Moody (New York: Perseus, 2001). This book tells the Linux story in a style that's more conventional, and for many readers, more readable, than the Torvalds/Diamond book.

Windows XP for Dummies, by Andy Rothbone (Indianapolis: Hungry Minds, 2001). The *Dummies* series that started with *DOS* *for Dummies* has expanded to cover everything from art to yoga. This approachable reference book is likely to be the flagship book in the series as Windows XP takes over the desktop. But unlike Microsoft, this book isn't a monopoly. There are hundreds of books on Windows for dummies and non-dummies alike.

The Little Mac Book, Seventh Edition, by Robin Williams (Berkeley, CA: Peachpit Press, 2001), and **The Little Mac OS X Book, Seventh Edition,** by Robin Williams (Berkeley, CA: Peachpit Press, 2001). These popular guides succinctly and clearly introduce first-time users to the Mac OS. They're ideal for people who don't want to spend a lot of time reading long manuals.

The Macintosh Bible, Seventh Edition, by Clifford Colby and Marty Cortinas (Berkeley, CA: Peachpit Press, 2001). At the other end of the spectrum from the *Little* books, this massive *Bible* contains enough information to keep you reading and learning for weeks.

Crossing Platforms: A Macintosh/Windows Phrasebook, by Adam Engst and David Pogue (Sebastapol, CA: O'Reilly, 1999). Windows and Macintosh computers are just different enough to be confusing to people who occasionally have to switch platforms. Example: An alias on the Macintosh is roughly speaking, the equivalent of a Windows shortcut, but what are the differences? This book includes two A-to-Z translation guides—one for Mac-to-Win translation, one for Win-to-Mac. The writing is clear, concise, and clever. Highly recommended.

UNIX: Visual QuickStart Guide, by Deborah S. Ray and Eric J. Ray (Berkeley, CA: Peachpit Press, 1998). Many UNIX books assume that you speak fluent techno-jargon and that you want to know all about the operating system and how it works. This book is designed for people who want to (or need to) use UNIX but don't particularly want to read a massive volume of UNIX lore. No book can make mastering UNIX simple, but this one at least makes getting started with UNIX simpler.

The Little Palm Book, by Corbin Collins (Berkeley, CA: Peachpit Press, 1999). This book introduces the Palm OS, using the same non-technical approach as other books in Peachpit's *Little* series.

PalmPilot: The Ultimate Guide, Second Edition, by David Pogue (Sebastapol, CA: O'Reilly, 1999). The Palm OS is far and away the most popular operating system for handheld computers. In this book David Pogue offers a wealth of information for Palm owners and users. Pogue is a great writer and a Palm expert. The accompanying CD enables you to download software from your Windows, Mac, or Linux computer into your handheld machine.

Special Edition: Using StarOffice, by Michael Koch and Sarah Murray, with Werner Roth (Indianapolis: Que, 1999). There are dozens of books on Microsoft Office and other commercial PC applications, but very few on freeware apps. This book can serve as an introduction and a valuable reference for anyone wanting to use the powerful, free StarOffice Suite on Windows or Linux.

The Cathedral and the Bazaar: Musings on Linux and Open Source by an Accidental Revolutionary, by Eric S. Raymond (Sebastapol, CA: O'Reilly, 2000). This widely praised book is an expanded version of the original manifesto for the open-source software movement—the movement that threatens to revolutionize the software industry. Tom Peters calls it "wonderful, witty, and, ultimately, wise."

The Art of Human–Computer Interface Design, edited by Brenda Laurel (Reading, MA: Addison-Wesley, 1990). This entertaining, provocative, and highly informative book is filled with essays by the experts on what makes a user interface work or not work. Chapters cover everything from menus and icons to virtual reality.

Things That Make Us Smart: Defending Human Attributes in the Age of the Machine, by Donald A. Norman (Reading, MA: Addison-Wesley, 1993). Norman left his position as the founding Chair of the Department of Cognitive Science at the University of California, San Diego, to work in the computer industry. His research on the relationship between technology and the human cognitive system is especially relevant in an industry where user interface decisions affect millions of users every day. This book, like Norman's others, is informative, thought provoking, and enjoyable. His argument for a more human-centered technology should be required reading for all software designers.

Designing the User Interface: Strategies for Effective Human–Computer Interaction, Third Edition, by Ben Schneiderman (Reading, MA: Addison-Wesley, 1998). This book thoroughly explores the issues that face anyone designing a user interface, whether it's a simple application program, a complex hypermedia document, or a virtual reality environment. In a style that's both academic and approachable, Schneiderman discusses everything from input and output hardware to the ultimate social impact of the technology.

A Guide to Usability: Human Factors in Computing, edited by Jenny Preece (Reading, MA: Addison-Wesley, 1993). User interface design is part psychology and part technology. This little book clearly and concisely outlines many of the most important issues in this rapidly growing field.

The Inmates Are Running the Asylum: Why High-Tech Products Drive Us Crazy and How to Restore the Sanity, by Alan Cooper (Indianapolis: Sams, 1999). User interface issues aren't just about computers. The same questions apply to all kinds of devices. Cooper clearly lays out the issues in this call-to-arms for friendlier technology.

World Wide Web Pages

Software companies, like hardware companies, have established their presence on the Net. Most of the companies use addresses that follow the formula **http://www.companyname.com**. Examples include **http://www.microsoft.com**, **http://www.apple.com**, and **http://www.corel.com**. Content varies from company to company; you might find technical support, product descriptions, demo software, software updates, and user tips on a typical software home page. For more software information check the home pages of publishers that specialize in computer books. For example, Peachpit Press(**http://www.peachpit.com**), McGraw-Hill (**http://www.books.mcgraw-hill.com**), and other publishers include sample chapters from software books on their Web sites. As usual, **www.prenhall.com/beekman** provides up-to-date links to a variety of valuable Web resources.

Part 2
Using
Computers

Essential Applications

5 | Revolution in Writing: From Word Processing to Paperless Publishing

After you read this chapter you should be able to:

Describe how computers can make the writing process more efficient, more effective, and more fun

Describe how a modern word processor can be used to create, edit, format, and print a document

Explain how to use a computer to proofread your work and how to recognize the limitations of proofreading software

Describe how other kinds of software can help you organize your ideas and improve your writing

Explain how desktop publishing relates to word processing and how it relates to traditional publishing

Discuss the potential impact of desktop publishing and Web publishing on the concept of freedom of the press

Speculate about future developments in word processing and digital publishing

▼ In this chapter:

Professional publishing applications

Tips for producing great-looking documents

How fonts work

The future of digital publishing

Self-study questions and projects

A word processing movie

. . . *and more.*

▼ On the CD-ROM:

An e-book activity

Animated interactive demonstration of font technology

Instant access to glossary and key word references

Interactive self-study quizzes

. . . *and more.*

▼ On the Web:

www.prenhall.com/beekman

Links to valuable resources for writers and desktop publishers

Links to Web sites of the most important word-processing and desktop-publishing companies

Self-study exercises

. . . *and more.*

Mark Twain Goes for Broke

This **newfangled writing machine**
has several virtues.
It piles an **awful stack** of words on one page.
It **don't muss things** or scatter ink blots around.
Of course it **saves paper.**

—Mark Twain

In 1874, Mark Twain bought a Remington Type-Writer for $125. One year later he became the first author in history to submit a typewritten manuscript.

Twain later invested almost $200,000 (the equivalent of $1.5 million today) in the promising new Paige typesetting technology. He wrote, "All the other wonderful inventions of the human brain sink pretty nearly into commonplaces contrasted with this awful mechanical miracle. Telephones, telegraphs, locomotives, cotton gins, sewing machines, Babbage calculators, Jacquard looms, perfecting presses, all mere toys, simplicities! The Paige Compositor marches alone and far in the land of human inventions," and on a more down-to-earth level, "This typesetter does not get drunk."

The Paige might very well have transformed book and magazine publishing, as Twain predicted, had not Ottmar Mergenthaler invented

Mark Twain (1835–1910)

the Linotype casting machine in 1886. The Linotype set and cast type in properly spaced leaden lines. An operator would produce the type by pressing keys on a board similar to the keyboard of a typewriter. The Linotype was adopted by major newspapers around the world. Because of the Linotype, Twain's promising publishing machine was obsolete at its inception, and Twain was forced into bankruptcy.

Linotypes dominated the publishing industry until the 1960s, when electronic typesetting with mainframe computers took over. Now mainframe publishing systems are being displaced by PCs, and digital documents on the Web have displaced many print publications. Technology continues to transform the world of publishing, and there's no end in sight.

Remington Type-writer

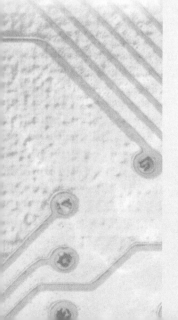

Early computers were no threat to typewriters; they were too unfriendly, inconvenient, inflexible, and expensive to be used by anyone but highly skilled experts. Special-purpose "word-processing machines" used by clerical workers in the 1960s represented a step forward, but they were a far cry from the word processing programs on modern personal computers.

The entire writing process has been transformed by modern word processing software. Instead of suffering through the painful and disjointed process of typing and retyping in pursuit of a "clean" draft, a writer can focus on developing ideas and let the machine take care of the details of laying out the words neatly on the page. Today's word processing technology makes it possible for just about any literate person to communicate effectively in writing. More than any other software application, word processing is a tool for everybody.

In this chapter we take a brief writer's tour of word processing, from the first stages of entering text right on through to printing the final document. We consider software tools for working with words, from outliners to sophisticated reference tools. We look at how desktop-publishing technology has transformed the publishing process and provided more people with the power to communicate in print. Finally, we look at how cutting-edge technologies will soon change writing and publishing in even more profound ways.

The Word Processing Process

> I . . . **cannot imagine** now that I **ever** wrote with a typewriter.
> —Arthur C. Clarke, author and scientist

Working with any word processor (a common way of referring to word processing software) involves several steps:

- Entering text
- Editing text
- Formatting the document
- Proofreading the document
- Saving the document on disk
- Printing the document.

Early word processing systems generally forced users to follow these steps in a strict order. Some systems still in use today—mainly on mainframes and other timesharing systems—segregate these processes into steps that can't easily be mixed. But modern word processing systems provide all the necessary tools in a single, seamless program. Most writers today switch freely between editing and formatting, in some cases doing both at the same time. Still, for our discussion it makes sense to consider these as separate processes.

Entering Text

As you type on the computer keyboard, your text is displayed on the screen and stored in the computer's RAM. Because of a feature called **word wrap**, the word processor automatically transports any words that won't fit on the current line to the next line along with the cursor. The only time you need to press Return or Enter is when you want to force the program to begin a new line—such as at the end of a paragraph.

Since RAM is not a permanent storage medium, it's important to **save your document** regularly—that is, create a disk file containing your work in progress. If the computer fails, or you accidentally erase part of the text, or if you want to take a break, you can restart the machine (if necessary) and **open** the saved version of your document—copy it back from a disk into the computer's memory.

Editing Text

All word processors enable you to **edit text**—to write and refine a document on screen until it's good enough to commit to paper. If you're working with a modern **WYSIWYG** (short for "what you see is what you get" and pronounced "wizzy-wig") word processor, the arrangement of the words on the screen represents a close approximation to the arrangement of the words on the printed page.

With a word processor you can easily:

▶ **Navigate** to different parts of the document by **scrolling** or by using a **Find command** to locate a particular word or phrase

▶ **Insert text** at any point in the document

▶ **Delete text** from any part of the document

▶ **Move text** from one part of the document to another section of the same document or to another document

▶ **Copy text** from one part of a document and duplicate it in another section of the document or in a different document

▶ **Find and replace** selected words or phrases throughout a document (sometimes called *search and replace*).

Most modern word processing programs contain sophisticated variations of these basic editing features. But even with this basic set of features, you can eliminate much of the drudgery that plagued writers in the precomputer era.

Formatting Text

When you're editing text, you only need to concern yourself with the words. But before you print your document, you'll need to consider the *format* of the document—how the words will look on the page. Text **formatting** commands enable you to control the format and style of the document. Most modern word processors enable users to control the formats of individual characters and paragraphs, as well as complete documents.

Formatting Characters

Most modern printers can print text in a variety of point sizes, typefaces, and styles that aren't possible with typewriters. Characters are measured by **point size**, with one point equal to 1/72 inch. Most documents, including this book, use smaller point sizes for text to fit more information on each page and larger point sizes to make titles and headings stand out.

In the language of typesetters, a **font** is a size and style of **typeface**. For example, the Helvetica typeface includes many fonts, one of which is 12-point Helvetica bold. In the PC world, many people use the terms *font* and *typeface* interchangeably.

Whatever you call them, you have hundreds of choices of typefaces for most modern computers. **Serif fonts**, like those in the Times family, are embellished with serifs—fine lines at the ends of the main strokes of each character. **Sans-serif fonts**, like those in the Helvetica family, have plainer, cleaner lines. **Monospaced fonts** that mimic typewriters, like those in the Courier family, produce characters that always take up the same amount of space, no matter how skinny or fat the characters are. In contrast, **proportionally spaced fonts** enable more

These fonts represent just a few of the hundreds of typefaces available for personal computers and printers today. The two symbol fonts given, Symbol and Zapf Dingbats, provide special characters not available with other fonts.

Examples of	12-point size	24-point size
Serif fonts	Times Courier	Times Courier
Sans-serif fonts	Helvetica Avant Garde	Helvetica Avant Garde
Script fonts	Zapf Chancery Kuenstler Script	Zapf Chancery Kuenstler Script
Display fonts	Regular Joe Birch Remedy	Regular Joe Birch Remedy
Symbol fonts (Symbol and Zapf Dingbats)	Συμβολ ✳❀❑❊ ✢✻■	Συμβολ ✳❀❑❊ ✢✻■

5.1
Font Technology

When a computer displays a character on a monitor or prints it on a laser, inkjet, or dot-matrix printer, the character is nothing more than a collection of dots in an invisible grid. Bit-mapped fonts store characters in this way, with each pixel represented as a black or white bit in a matrix. A bit-mapped font usually looks fine on screen in the intended point size but doesn't look smooth when printed on a high-resolution printer or enlarged on screen.

Most computer systems now use scalable outline fonts to represent type in memory until it is displayed or printed. A scalable font represents each character as an outline that can be scaled—increased or decreased in size without distortion. Curves and lines are smooth and don't have stair-stepped, jagged edges when they're resized. The outline is stored inside the computer or printer as a series of mathematical statements about the position of points and the shape of the lines connecting those points.

A bit-mapped font suffers from pixellization when enlarged.

This outline for a lowercase letter "a" retains its original shape at any size or resolution.

Downloadable fonts (soft fonts) are stored in the computer system (not the printer) and downloaded to the printer only when needed. These fonts usually have matching screen fonts and are easily moved to different computer systems. Most importantly, you can use the same downloadable font on many printer models.

Laser printers are really dedicated computer systems that contain their own CPU, RAM, ROM, and specialized operating system. Printer fonts are stored in the printer's ROM and are always available for use with that printer, but you may not be able to achieve WYSIWYG if your computer doesn't have a screen font to match your printer font. And if you move your document to a different computer and printer, the same printer font may not be available on the new system.

Fonts are most commonly available in two scalable outline forms: Adobe PostScript and Apple/Microsoft TrueType. Because Apple and Microsoft supply TrueType downloadable fonts with their operating systems, TrueType fonts are more popular among general computer users. PostScript fonts usually require additional software but are the standard among many graphics professionals. PostScript is actually a complete page description language particularly well suited to the demands of professional publishers.

For the past few years, Adobe and Microsoft have been codeveloping OpenType, a universal font format that combines TrueType and PostScript technology. OpenType enables character shapes to travel with documents in compressed forms so that a document transmitted electronically or displayed on the World Wide Web will look like the original even if the viewer's system doesn't include the original document's fonts.

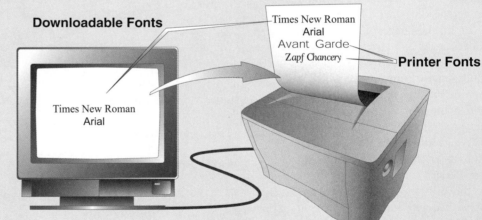

Downloadable Fonts

Times New Roman
Arial

Times New Roman
Arial
Avant Garde
Zapf Chancery

Printer Fonts

room for wide characters like *w*'s than for narrow characters like *i*'s. (See the font table on the previous page for examples.)

Formatting Paragraphs

Many formatting commands apply to paragraphs rather than characters: those commands that control margins, space between lines, indents, tab stops, and justification. **Justification** refers to the alignment of text on a line. Four justification choices are commonly available: left justification (with a smooth left margin and ragged right margin), right justification, full justification (both margins are smooth), and centered justification.

Formatting the Document

Some formatting commands are applied to entire documents. For example, Word's Page Setup command enables you to control the margins that apply throughout the document. Other commands enable you to specify the content, size, and style of **headers** and **footers**—blocks that appear at the top and bottom of every page, displaying repetitive information, such as chapter titles, author names, and automatically calculated page numbers.

The User's View box shows a sample of entering, editing, and formatting text with Microsoft Word, the most popular word processing program in use today. Like most of the applications featured in this book, Microsoft Word is available for both Macintosh and Windows-compatible computers.

Most modern word processing programs provide a great deal of formatting flexibility. Here are some examples of what you can do:

Most word processors provide four different options for justifying text.

This text illustrates centered justification. For centered text both margins are ragged. Centered text is often used for titles.

This text illustrates left justification. For left-justified text the left margin is smooth and the right margin is ragged.

This text illustrates right justification. For right-justified text the right margin is smooth and the left margin is ragged.

This text illustrates full justification. For fully justified text, spaces between words are adjusted to make both m a r g i n s smooth.

- ▶ Define **style sheets** containing custom styles for each of the common elements in a document. (For example, you can define a style called "subhead" as a paragraph that's left-justified in a boldface, 12-point Helvetica font with standard margins and then apply that style to every subhead in the document without reselecting all three of these commands for each new subhead. If you decide later to change the subheads to 14-point Futura, your changes in the subhead style are automatically reflected throughout the document.)
- ▶ Define alternate headers, footers, and margins so that left- and right-facing pages can have different margins, headers, and footers.
- ▶ Create documents with variable-width multiple columns.
- ▶ Create, edit, and format multicolumn tables.
- ▶ Incorporate graphics created with other applications.
- ▶ Use **automatic footnoting** to save you from having to place footnotes and endnotes; the program automatically places them where they belong on the page.
- ▶ Use **automatic hyphenation** to divide long words that fall at the ends of lines.
- ▶ Use **automatic formatting** (**autoformat**) to automatically apply formatting to your text. For example, to automatically number lists (like the exercises at the end of this chapter) and apply proper indentation to those lists.
- ▶ Use **automatic correction** (**autocorrect**) to catch and correct common typing errors. For example, if you type *THe* or *Teh*, the software will automatically change it to *The*.
- ▶ Generate tables of contents and indexes for books and other long works (with human help for making judgments about which words belong in the index and how they should be arranged).
- ▶ Attach hidden comments that can be seen without showing up in the final printed document.
- ▶ Use coaching or help features (sometimes called **wizards**) to walk you through complex document formatting procedures.
- ▶ Convert formatted documents to *HTML* (*hypertext markup language*) so they can be easily published on the Web.

Word Processing

SOFTWARE: *Microsoft Word*

Most applications today enable you to do common tasks using either menu commands or onscreen buttons. This example illustrates both techniques.

THE GOAL: *To enter, edit, format the text of a classic work to be read in an English class presentation.*

1 You hurriedly enter the text, forgetting to include the title and author at the beginning. You decide to add them to the bottom and move them to the top. You **select text** to be edited using the mouse or the keyboard. Selected text appears highlighted on the screen.

2 Choosing the Cut command from the Edit menu, you tell the computer to cut the selected text from the document and place it in the **Clipboard**—a special portion of memory for temporarily holding information for later use.

3 After using the mouse or arrow keys to reposition the cursor at the beginning of the document, you select the Paste command from the Edit menu. The computer places a copy of the Clipboard's contents at the insertion point; the text below the cursor moves down to make room for the inserted text. This type of **cut-and-paste** editing is possible in most application programs; you can also use it to move text from one document to another. To speed up the process, most applications enable **drag-and-drop** editing so you can simply drag (with the mouse) selected text to another part of the document.

4 To italicize the title *Walden*, you select the characters to be changed . . .

5 . . . . choose the Font command from the Format menu . . .

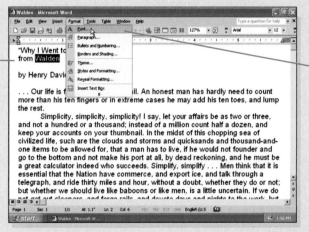

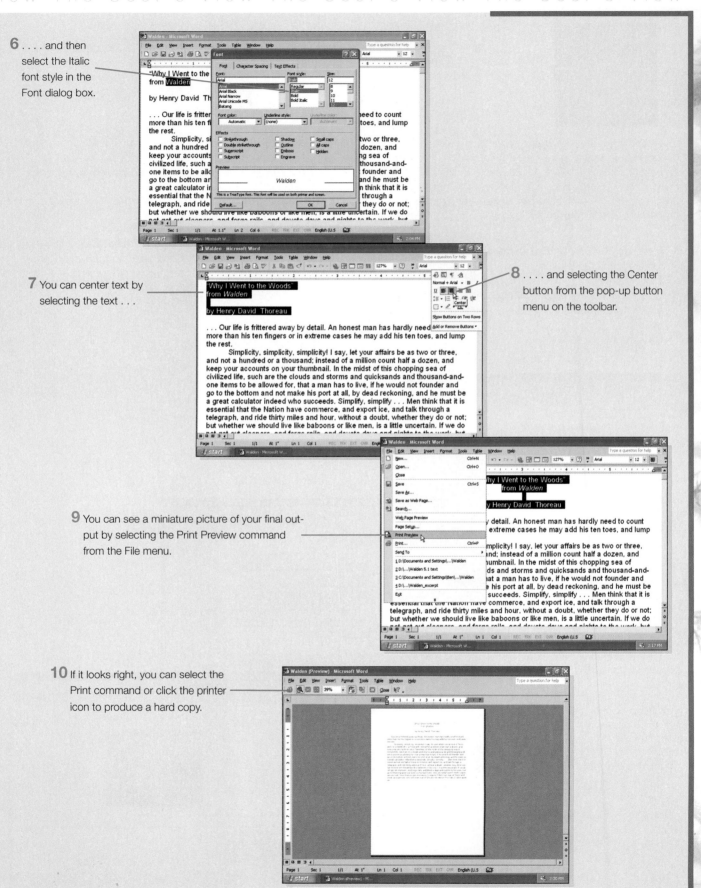

6 . . . . and then select the Italic font style in the Font dialog box.

7 You can center text by selecting the text . . .

8 . . . . and selecting the Center button from the pop-up button menu on the toolbar.

9 You can see a miniature picture of your final output by selecting the Print Preview command from the File menu.

10 If it looks right, you can select the Print command or click the printer icon to produce a hard copy.

Word Processing Is Not Typing

If you're already a touch typist, your typing skills will help you become proficient at word processing quickly. (If you're not a touch typist, see Project 1, Chapter 3, "Hardware Basics: Peripherals.") Unfortunately, a few typing skills are counterproductive on a modern word processor. Here's a short list of new word processing habits that should replace your outmoded typing habits:

▶ **Use the Return or Enter key only when you must.** Let the computer's automatic word wrap handle routine end-of-line business.

▶ **Use tabs and margin guides, not the spacebar, to align columns.** WYSIWYG is a matter of degree, and text that looks perfectly aligned onscreen may not line up on paper if you depend on your eyes and the spacebar.

▶ **Don't underline.** Use italics and boldface for emphasis. Italicize book and journal titles.

▶ **Use only one space after a period.** Most type experts agree that proportionally spaced fonts look better if you avoid double spaces.

▶ **Take advantage of special characters.** Bullets (•), em dashes (—), curly quotes (" "), and other nontypewriter characters make your work look more professional, and they don't cost a thing.

Microsoft Word is one of many word processors that can save documents in HTML format so they can be published on the World Wide Web. The screen shown on the left is a formatted Microsoft Word document. The center screen shows the same document saved in HTML format. Notice how embedded codes have replaced the formatting in the document. The screen on the right shows what the HTML document looks like as a Web page.

The Wordsmith's Toolbox

In addition to basic editing and formatting functions, a typical word processor might include a built-in outliner, spelling checker, and thesaurus. But even word processors that don't include those features can be enhanced with stand-alone programs specifically designed to accomplish the same things. We examine a few of these tools next.

When you had to carve things in **stone**, you got the Ten Commandments. When things had to be written with a **goose quill** and you had to boil blood or whatever to make ink, you got Shakespeare. When you went over to the **steel pen** and manufactured inks, you got Henry James. You get to the **typewriter**, you get Jack Kerouac. When you get down to the **word processor**—you get me. So improvement in **the technology** of writing hasn't improved **writing itself**, as far as I can tell.

—P. J. O'Rourke, Humorist

Outliners and Idea Processors

If any man wishes to write in a **clear style**, let him first **be clear in his thoughts**.

—Johann W. von Goethe

For many of us the hardest part of the writing process is collecting and organizing our thoughts. Traditional English-class techniques, including outlines and 3×5 note cards, involve additional work. But when computer technology is applied to these time-honored techniques, they're transformed into high-powered tools for extending our minds and streamlining the process of turning vague thoughts into solid prose.

Outliners, such as the *Outline View* option built into Microsoft Word are, in effect, idea processors. Outliners are particularly effective at performing three functions:

▶ Arranging information into hierarchies or levels so that each heading can be fleshed out with more detailed subheads, which can then be broken into smaller pieces

▶ Rearranging ideas and levels so that sub-ideas are automatically moved with their parent ideas

▶ Hiding and revealing levels of detail as needed so that you can examine the forest, the trees, or an individual leaf of your project.

For a project that requires research, an outliner can be used as a replacement for note cards. Ideas can be collected, composed, refined, rearranged, and reorganized much more efficiently when they're stored in an outline. When the time comes to turn research into a research paper, the notes don't need to be retyped; they can be polished with standard text-editing techniques. If the outliner is built into the word processor, the line between notes and finished product blurs to the point where it almost disappears.

Microsoft Word's Outline view enables you to examine and restructure the overall organization of the document, while showing each topic in as much detail as you need. When you move headlines, the attached subheads and paragraphs follow automatically.

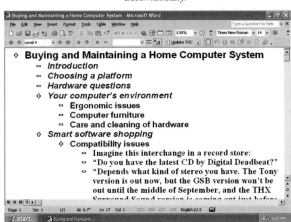

Synonym Finders

The difference between the **right word** and the **almost-right word** is the difference between the **lightning** and the **lightning bug**.

—Mark Twain

The classic synonym finder, or thesaurus, is an invaluable tool for finding just the right word, but it's not particularly user-friendly. A computerized thesaurus is another matter altogether. With a good onscreen thesaurus, it's a simple matter to select a word and issue a command for a synonym search. The computerized thesaurus provides almost instant gratification, displaying all kinds of possible replacements for the word in question. If you find a good substitute in the list, you can indicate your preference with a click or a keystroke; the software even makes the substitution for you.

Microsoft Word's online thesaurus puts synonyms at your fingertips. In this case, the computer is providing synonyms for the word "improve."

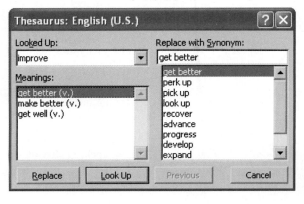

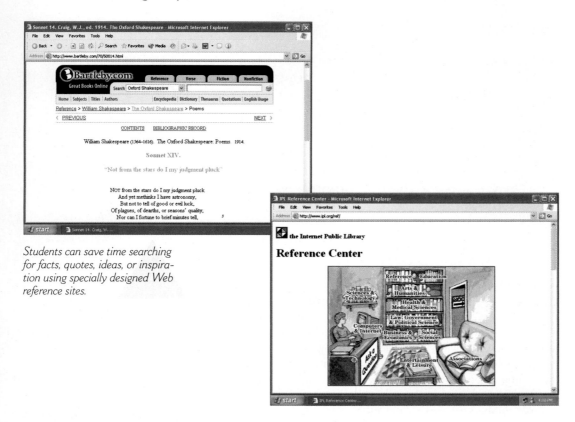

Students can save time searching for facts, quotes, ideas, or inspiration using specially designed Web reference sites.

Digital References

Writers rely on dictionaries, quotation books, encyclopedias, atlases, almanacs, and other references. Just about all of these resources are now available in digital form, both on CD-ROM and on the Web.

The biggest advantage of digital references is speed; searching for subjects or words by computer is usually faster than thumbing through a book. Even Web searches that *seem* to take a long time can produce results in a fraction of the time it would take you to locate sources in a library. Well-designed electronic references make it easy to jump between related topics in search of elusive facts. In addition, copying quotes electronically takes a fraction of the time it takes to retype information from a book. Of course, this kind of quick copying makes plagiarism easier than ever and may tempt more writers to violate copyright laws and ethical standards.

Some references lose meaning or clarity in the translation to electronic form. Because pictures, maps, and drawings take up so much disk space (and Internet transmission time), they're sometimes removed or modified in computerized references. On the other hand, many digital references include sounds, animation, video, and other forms of information that aren't possible to include in books.

Reference materials are everywhere on the Web. Regardless of the topic, you're likely to find multiple sources. Unfortunately, not all of those sources are useful or reliable. Still, the Web offers a combination of currency and cross-referencing that can't be found in any other reference source. We'll revisit Web references in later chapters.

Spelling Checkers

It's a **darn poor mind** that can only think of one way to spell a word.

—Andrew Jackson

While many of us sympathize with Jackson's point of view, the fact remains that correct spelling is an important part of most written communication. That's why most word processors include a built-in spelling checker. A spelling checker compares the words in your document with words in a disk-based dictionary.

Every word that's not in the dictionary is flagged as a suspect word—a potential misspelling. In many cases, the spelling checker suggests the corrected spelling and offers to replace the suspect word. Ultimately, though, it's up to you to decide whether the flagged word is, in fact, spelled incorrectly.

A *batch spelling checker* checks all of the words in your document in a batch when you issue the appropriate command. An *interactive spelling checker* checks each word as it's typed; a typical interactive spelling checker might mark each mistyped word with a distinct underlining. Some spelling checkers, including the one in Microsoft Word, can operate in either batch or interactive mode.

While spelling checkers are wonderful aids, they can't replace careful proofreading by alert human eyes. When you're using a spelling checker, it's important to keep two potential problems in mind:

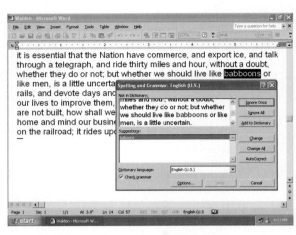

Most spell checkers offer a user several choices for handling words that aren't in the dictionary (Software: Microsoft Word.)

▶ *Dictionary limitations and errors.* No dictionary includes every word, so you have to know what to do with unlisted words—proper names, obscure words, technical terms, foreign terms, colloquialisms, and other oddities. If you add words to your spelling checker's dictionary, you run the risk of adding an incorrectly spelled word, making future occurrences of that misspelling invisible to the spelling checker and to you.

▶ *Errors of context.* The fact that a word appears in a dictionary does not guarantee that it is correctly spelled in the context of the sentence. The following passage, for example, contains eight spelling errors, none of which would be detected by a spelling checker:

I wood never have guest that my spelling checker would super seed my editor as my mane source of feed back. I no longer prophet from the presents of an editor while I right.

Grammar and Style Checkers

The errors in the preceding quote would have slipped by a spelling checker; but many of them would have been detected by a **grammar and style checker**. In addition to checking spelling, grammar-and-style-checking software analyzes each word in context, checking for errors of context ("I wood never have guest"), common grammatical errors ("Ben and me went to Boston"), and stylistic foibles ("Suddenly the door was opened by Bethany"). In addition to pointing out possible errors and suggesting improvements, it can analyze prose complexity using measurements such as sentence length and paragraph length. This kind of analysis is useful for determining whether your writing style is appropriate for your target audience.

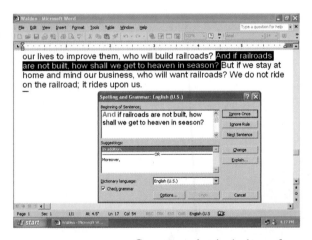

Grammar-and-style-checking software flags possible errors and makes suggestions about how they might be fixed. (Software: Microsoft Word.)

Grammar-and-style-checking software is, at best, imperfect. A typical program misses many true errors, while flagging correct passages. Still, it can be a valuable writing aid, especially for students who are mastering the complexities of a language for the first time. But software is no substitute for practice, revision, editing, and a good English teacher.

Form Letter Generators

> ▍ **Congratulations, Mr. <lastname>.**
> You may already have won!
> —Junk mail greeting

Most word processors today have **mail merge** capabilities for producing personalized form letters. When used with a database containing a list of names and addresses, a word processor can quickly generate individually addressed letters and mailing labels. Many programs can incorporate custom paragraphs based on the recipient's personal data, making each letter look as if it were individually written. This kind of technology was exploited by direct-mail marketing companies for years before it became available in inexpensive PC software.

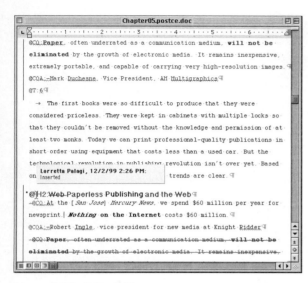

Microsoft Word's Track Changes feature enables several writers and editors to contribute to the same document and see each other's changes.

Collaborative Writing Tools

Writing only leads to **more writing**.
—Colette

Most large writing projects, including this one, involve groups of people working together. Computer networks make it easy for writers and editors to share documents; but it's not always easy for one person to know how a document has been changed by others. Groupware—software designed to be used by a workgroup—can keep track of a document's history as it's passed among group members and make sure that all changes are incorporated into a single master document. Using groupware, each writer can monitor and make suggestions concerning the work of any other writer on the team. Editors can "blue pencil" corrections and attach notes directly to the electronic manuscript. The notes can be read by any or all of the writers—even those who are on the other side of the continent.

This kind of collaborative writing and editing doesn't require specialized software anymore; it can be done with many word-processing and publishing programs. For example, Microsoft Word's Track Changes option can record and display contributions of several writers and editors; it can also compare document versions and highlight differences between versions.

The Desktop Publishing Story

Freedom of the press
belongs to the person who **owns** one.
—A. J. Liebling, the late media critic for *The New Yorker*

Just as word processing changed the writer's craft in the 1970s, the world of publishing was radically transformed in the 1980s when Apple introduced its first LaserWriter printer and a new company named Aldus introduced PageMaker, a Macintosh program that could take advantage of that printer's high-resolution output capabilities. Publishing—traditionally an expensive, time-consuming, error-prone process—instantly became an enterprise that just about anyone with a computer and a little cash could undertake.

What Is Desktop Publishing?

The process of producing a book, magazine, or other publication includes several steps:

1. Writing text
2. Editing text
3. Producing drawings, photographs, and other graphics to accompany the text
4. Designing a basic format for the publication
5. Typesetting text
6. Arranging text and graphics on pages
7. Typesetting and printing pages
8. Binding pages into a finished publication

In traditional publishing, many of these steps required expensive equipment, highly trained specialists to operate the equipment, and lots of time.

With modern **desktop publishing (DTP)** technology, the bulk of the production process can be accomplished with tools that are small, affordable, and easy to use. A desktop publishing system generally includes one or more Macs or PCs, a scanner, a high-resolution printer, and software. It's now possible for a single person with a modest equipment investment to do all the writing, editing, graphic production, design, page-layout, and typesetting for a desktop publication. Of course, few individuals have the skills to handle all of these tasks, so most

A typical desktop publishing system includes a personal computer, a high-resolution printer, a scanner, and a variety of software programs.

publications are still the work of teams that include writers, editors, designers, artists, and supervisors. But even if the titles remain the same, each of these jobs is changing because of desktop publishing technology.

The first steps in the publishing process involve producing **source documents**—articles, chapters, drawings, maps, charts, and photographs that are to appear in the publication. Desktop publishers generally use standard word processors and graphics programs to produce most source documents. Scanners with image editing software are used to transform photographs and hand-drawn images into computer-readable documents. Page-layout software, such as Quark Xpress, PageMaker, or InDesign, is used to combine the various source documents into a coherent, visually appealing publication. Pages are generally laid out one at a time onscreen, although most programs have options for automating multiple-page document layout.

Page-layout software provides graphic designers with control over virtually every element of the design, right down to the spacing between each pair of letters (*kerning*) and the spacing between lines of text (*leading*). Today's word processing programs include basic page-layout capabilities, too; they're sufficient for producing many types of books and periodicals, complete with graphics. For users without background in layout and design, most page-layout and word processing programs include **templates**—professionally designed "empty" documents that can easily be adapted to specific user needs. Even without templates, it's possible for beginners to create professional-quality publications with a modest investment of money and time.

Desktop publishing becomes more complicated when color is introduced. *Spot color*—the use of a single color (or sometimes two) to add interest—is relatively easy. But *full-color* desktop publishing, including color photos, drawings, and paintings, must deal with the inconsistencies of different color output devices. Because printers and monitors use different types of color-mixing technologies (as described in the *How It Works* boxes in Chapter 3, "Hardware Basics: Peripherals"), what you see on the screen isn't always what you get when you print it. It's even difficult to get two monitors (or two printers) to produce images with exactly the same color balance. Still, color desktop publishing is big business, and advances in *color-matching* technology are making it easier all the time.

The User's View box shows how a simple publication is created with page-layout software.

Whether a document is created with a word processor or professional page-layout software, it can be printed on a variety of high-resolution output devices. Most black-and-white desktop publications are printed on laser printers capable of producing output with a resolution of at least 600 dots per inch (dpi). The number of dots per inch influences the resolution and clarity of the image. Output of 600 dpi is sufficiently sharp for most applications, but it's less than the 1,200 dpi that is the traditional minimum for professional typesetting. High-priced devices, called *phototypesetting machines* or *imagesetters*, enable desktop publications to be printed at 1,200 dpi or higher. Many desktop publishers rely on outside **service bureaus** with phototypesetting machines to print their final **camera-ready** pages—pages that are ready to be photographed and printed.

Why Desktop Publishing?

More than any other application, desktop publishing was responsible for the initial acceptance by large corporations of computers with graphical user interfaces. Desktop publishing offers several advantages for businesses. Desktop publishing saves money. Publications that used to cost hundreds or thousands of dollars to produce through outside publishing services can now be

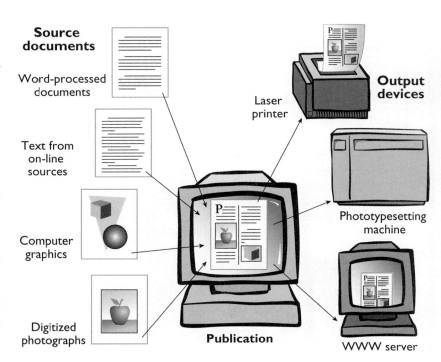

Source documents

Word-processed documents

Text from on-line sources

Computer graphics

Digitized photographs

Publication

Laser printer

Output devices

Phototypesetting machine

WWW server

Source documents are merged in a publication document, which can be printed on a laser or inkjet printer, printed on a high-resolution phototypesetter, or even published on the World Wide Web.

Desktop Publishing

SOFTWARE: *Adobe® Photoshop® with Umax VistaScan plug-in, QuarkXPress page-layout software.*

THE GOAL: *To create a publication that includes a collection of class projects and presentations with graphic illustrations.*

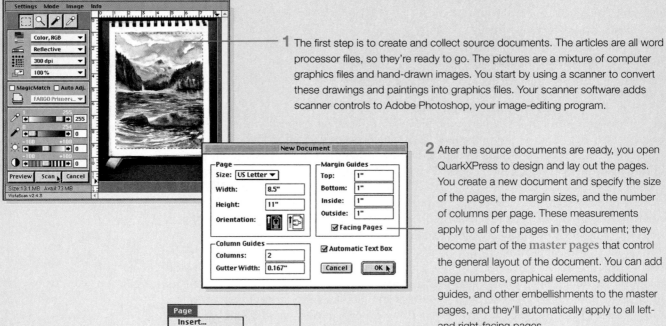

1 The first step is to create and collect source documents. The articles are all word processor files, so they're ready to go. The pictures are a mixture of computer graphics files and hand-drawn images. You start by using a scanner to convert these drawings and paintings into graphics files. Your scanner software adds scanner controls to Adobe Photoshop, your image-editing program.

2 After the source documents are ready, you open QuarkXPress to design and lay out the pages. You create a new document and specify the size of the pages, the margin sizes, and the number of columns per page. These measurements apply to all of the pages in the document; they become part of the **master pages** that control the general layout of the document. You can add page numbers, graphical elements, additional guides, and other embellishments to the master pages, and they'll automatically apply to all left- and right-facing pages.

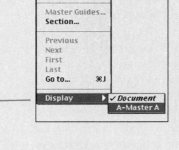

3 You choose View Master Page, and add a horizontal guide so it's easy to see the exact center of each page.

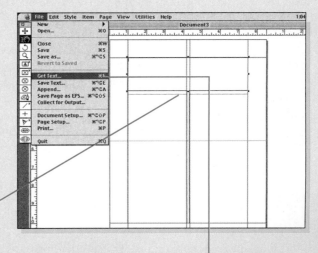

4 On the first page, you use the text box tool to draw boxes to contain text from the Walden document you created earlier. The box for the title spans both columns; the boxes for text fill the remainder of the two columns.

5 You place the cursor in the horizontal text box and choose the Get Text command.

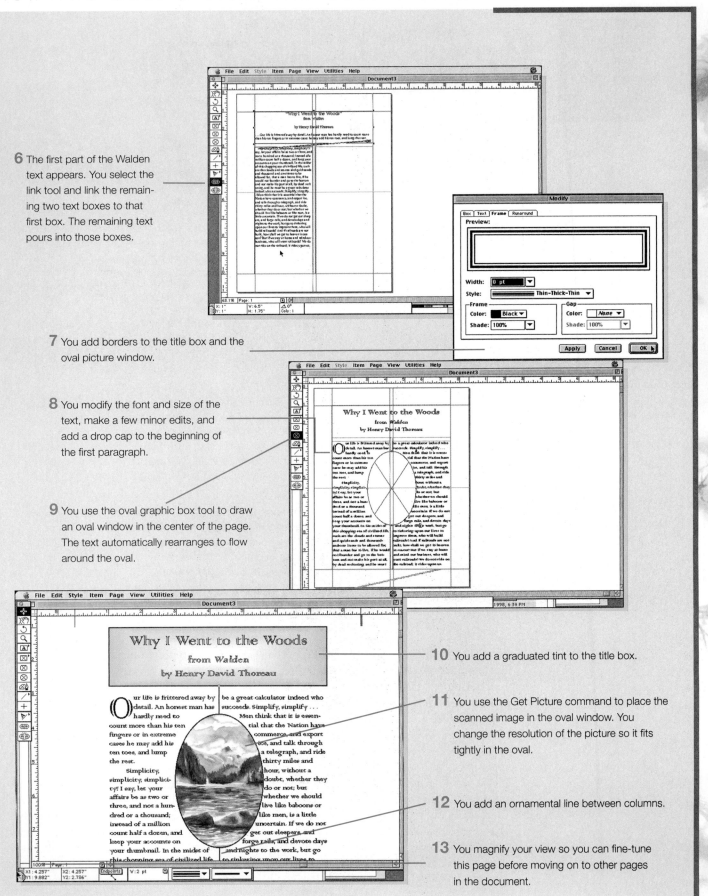

6 The first part of the Walden text appears. You select the link tool and link the remaining two text boxes to that first box. The remaining text pours into those boxes.

7 You add borders to the title box and the oval picture window.

8 You modify the font and size of the text, make a few minor edits, and add a drop cap to the beginning of the first paragraph.

9 You use the oval graphic box tool to draw an oval window in the center of the page. The text automatically rearranges to flow around the oval.

10 You add a graduated tint to the title box.

11 You use the Get Picture command to place the scanned image in the oval window. You change the resolution of the picture so it fits tightly in the oval.

12 You add an ornamental line between columns.

13 You magnify your view so you can fine-tune this page before moving on to other pages in the document.

Beyond DESKTOP TaCkY!

Many first-time users of WYSIWYG word processors and desktop publishing systems become intoxicated with the power at their fingertips. It's easy to get carried away with all those fonts, styles, and sizes and to create a document that makes supermarket tabloids look tasteful. While there's no substitute for a good education in the principles of design, it's easy to avoid tacky-looking documents if you follow a few simple guidelines:

▶ **Plan before you publish.** Design (or select) a simple, visually pleasing format for your document, and use that format throughout the document.

▶ **Use appropriate fonts.** Limit your choices to one or two fonts and sizes per page, and be consistent throughout your document. Serif fonts like the one used in the main text of this book generally are good choices for paragraphs of text; the serifs gently guide the reader's eye from letter to letter. Sans-serif fonts, like the one used in the box you are reading, work well for boxed text, tables, headings, and titles. It's generally better to use only one sans-serif font in a document. Make sure all your chosen fonts work properly with your printer.

▶ **Don't go style-crazy.** Avoid overusing *italics*, **boldface**, ALL CAPS, <u>underlines</u>, and other styles for emphasis. When in doubt, leave it out.

▶ **Look at your document through your readers' eyes.** Make every picture say something. Don't try to cram too much information on a page. Don't be afraid of white space. Use a format that speaks clearly to your readers. Make sure the main points of your document stand out. Whatever you do, do it for the reader.

▶ **Learn from the masters.** Study the designs of successful publications. What makes them work? Use design books, articles, and classes to develop your aesthetic skills along with your technical skills. With or without a computer, publishing is an art.

▶ **Know your limitations.** Desktop publishing technology makes it possible for anyone to produce high-quality documents with a minimal investment of time and money. But your equipment and skills may not be up to the job at hand. For many applications, personal desktop publishing is no match for a professional design artist or typesetter. If you need the best, work with a pro.

▶ **Remember the message.** Fancy fonts, tasteful graphics, and meticulous design can't turn shoddy ideas into words of wisdom, or lies into the truth. The purpose of publishing is communication; don't try to use technology to disguise the lack of something to communicate.

produced in-house for a fraction of their former cost. Desktop publishing also saves time. The turnaround time for a publication done on the desktop can be a few days instead of the weeks or months it might take to publish the same thing using traditional channels. Finally, desktop publishing can reduce the quantity of publication errors. Quality control is easier to maintain when documents are produced in house.

The real winners in the desktop publishing revolution might turn out to be not big businesses but everyday people with something to say. With commercial TV networks, newspapers, magazines, and book publishers increasingly controlled by a few giant corporations, many media experts worry that the free press guaranteed by our First Amendment is seriously threatened by *de facto* media monopolies. Desktop publishing technology offers new hope for every individual's right to publish. Writers, artists, and editors whose work is shunned or ignored by large publishers and mainstream media now have affordable publishing alternatives. The number of small presses and alternative, low-circulation periodicals is steadily increasing as publishing costs go down. If, as media critic A.J. Liebling suggested, freedom of the press belongs to the person who owns one, that precious freedom is now accessible to more people than ever before.

Tomorrow's Word Tools

The first books were so difficult to produce that they were considered priceless. They were kept in cabinets with multiple locks so that they couldn't be removed without the knowledge and permission of at least two monks. Today we can print professional-quality publications in short order using equipment that costs less than a used car. But the publishing revolution isn't over yet. Based on current research, several trends are clear.

> **Paper**, often underrated as a communication medium, **will not be eliminated** by the growth of electronic media. It remains **inexpensive**, extremely **portable**, and **capable** of carrying very high-resolution images.
>
> —Mark Duchesne, Vice President, *AM Multigraphics*

Paperless Publishing and the Web

> At the [*San Jose*] *Mercury News*, we spend **$60 million per year** for newsprint. ***Nothing*** on the Internet costs $60 million.
>
> —Robert Ingle, vice president for new media at Knight Ridder

A common prediction is that desktop publishing—and paper publishing in general—will be replaced by paperless electronic media. Paper still offers advantages for countless communication tasks. Reading printed words on pages is easier on the eyes than reading from a screen. Paper documents can be read and scribbled on almost anywhere, with or without electricity. And there's no electronic equivalent for the aesthetics of a beautifully designed, finely crafted book. Predictions aside, the printed word isn't likely to go away anytime soon.

Still, digital media *are* likely to eclipse paper for many applications. Email messages now outnumber post office deliveries of letters. CD-ROM encyclopedias briskly outsell their overweight paper counterparts. Adobe's *PDF (Portable Document Format)* enables documents of all types to be stored, viewed, or modified on any Windows or Macintosh computer, making it possible for many organizations to reduce paper flow. And the World Wide Web offers unprecedented mass publishing possibilities to millions of Internet users.

Programs as diverse as Microsoft Word, AppleWorks, and Page-Maker can save documents in HTML formats, so they can be published on the World Wide Web. Other programs, specifically designed for Web publishing, offer advanced capabilities for graphics, animation, and multimedia publishing. (We'll explore some of these tools in later chapters when we discuss multimedia and the Web in greater depth.)

Never before has a communication medium made it so easy or inexpensive for an individual to reach such a wide audience. For a few dollars a month—or for free, in many cases—an Internet service provider can provide you with space to publish your essays, stories, reviews, and musings. It doesn't matter whether you're a student, a poet, an artist, a government official, a labor organizer, or a corporate president—on the Web all URLs are created equal.

Of course, the most popular commercial Web sites cost their owners more than a few dollars a month. A typical Web storefront costs a million dollars just to build. And one of the biggest challenges in Web publishing is attracting people to your site once it's online. Copyright protection is another problem for Web publishers; anything that's published on the Web for all of the world to see is also available for all of the world to copy. How can writers and editors be paid fairly for their labors if their works are so easy to duplicate?

Still, the Web is far more accessible to small-budget writers and publishers than any other mass medium. And many experts predict that Web technology will eventually include some kind of mechanism for automatic payment to authors whose works are downloaded. In any case, the free flow of ideas may be more significant than the flow of money. In the words of writer Howard Rheingold, the World Wide Web "might be important in the same way that the printing press was important. By expanding the number of people who have the power to transmit knowledge, the Web might trigger a power shift that changes everything."

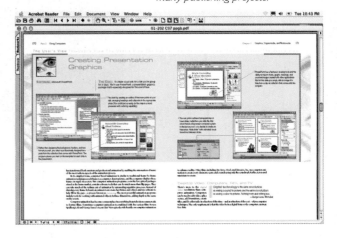

Adobe Acrobat is a cross-platform software program that enables the electonic sharing of PDF documents, eliminating the need for paper in many publishing projects.

Mountains of waste paper like this one should be less common as paperless publishing grows in popularity.

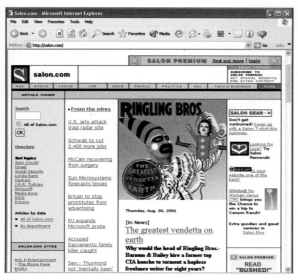

Many popular periodicals, from Newsweek *to* Rolling Stone, *publish electronic versions on the Web.* Salon *is an example of a popular magazine that publishes exclusively on the Web.*

Electronic Books and Digital Paper

▌ **The worth of a book** is to be measured by **what you can carry away** from it.

—James Bryce

Science fiction writers have long predicted the **electronic book**, or **ebook**—a handheld device that can contain anything from today's top news stories to an annotated edition of *War and Peace*. Until recently, these types of devices have been commercial failures for two reasons: First, the screens were hard to read and second, content for them was not easily accessible.

LCD technology has made great strides in recent years, and screens are brighter and easier to read than ever before. Recent advances in font technologies from Microsoft and Adobe should help, too. Microsoft's ClearType enhances the clarity of text on flat-panel LCD screens, reducing pixel "blockiness." Adobe has developed a similar technology called Precision Graphics. Easy-on-the-eyes ebooks are likely to take advantage of these technologies soon.

An ebook like this one can replace a stack of textbooks, plus a novel for relaxing, in a student backpack

To make it easier for ebook owners to find content—books, periodicals, and other software to download into their devices—several companies are cooperating to develop an open ebook standard. Once industry-wide standards are in place, electronic book publishing will be more practical—and popular. Future students may download texts rather than carry them out of bookstores. Everybook CEO Daniel Munyan predicts that college freshmen will load their ebooks with their notes and texts for the next four years and receive future updates via the Internet.

Ebooks today are mostly read on devices with rigid LCD screens—laptop computers, handheld computers, and special-purpose ebook readers that resemble tables. But researchers may soon perfect a form of digital paper that will enable ebooks (as well as e-magazines and e-newspapers) to look and feel more like their paper counterparts. **Electronic paper**, or **epaper**, is a flexible, portable, paper-like material that can dynamically display black-and-white text and images on its surface. Unlike traditional paper, digital paper can erase itself and display new text and images as the reader "turns" the page. A busy commuter might soon be able to carry a complete morning newspaper and several important business documents in a sheet of digital paper stuffed in his pocket!

Electronic paper is currently under development by several companies; this demo suggests that practical products aren't too far into the future.

Word Processing without a Keyboard

▌ I think that the **primary means of communication** with computers in the next millennium will be **speech**.

—Nicholas Negroponte, director of MIT's Media Lab

Changes in output devices—graphic screens and high-resolution printers—have had a tremendous impact on writing and publishing software in the last decade. As a result, the major bottlenecks in most modern desktop publishing systems occur on the input side. Many experts predict that the next big advances will occur as a result of emerging input devices.

In today's computers, the mouse has taken over many of the functions of the keyboard. For a small but growing population, pen-based systems provide an alternative tool for entering text. Handwriting recognition doesn't come easy to computers; it requires sophisticated software that can interpret pen movements as characters and words. The diversity in handwriting makes it impossible for today's programs to translate all of our scribbles into text. Popular pen-based systems like the Palm devices work reliably because they require users to print characters using a carefully defined system that minimizes errors. Future pen devices will undoubtedly be more flexible, learning how their users write rather than requiring that their users learn new ways to write.

Ultimately, though, most writers long for a computer that can accept and reliably process *speech* input—a *talkwriter*. With such a system, a user can *tell* the computer what to type—and how to type it—by simply talking into a microphone. The user's speech enters the computer as a digital audio signal. **Speech-recognition software** looks for patterns in the sound waves and interprets sounds by locating familiar patterns, segmenting input sound patterns into words, separating commands from the text, and passing those commands on to the word processing software.

Speech recognition software enables this scientist to dictate his notes to his computer while he works.

Speech-recognition software systems have been around for many years, but until recently, most were severely limited. It takes a great deal of intelligence to understand the complexities of human speech. Most current commercial systems need to be trained to recognize a particular person's voice before they can function reliably. Even then, many systems require that the user speak slowly in a quiet environment and use a small, predefined vocabulary. Otherwise the machine might interpret, say, "recognize speech" as "wreck a nice beach." Research in speech recognition today focuses on overcoming these limitations and producing systems that can accomplish the following tasks:

▶ Recognize words without being trained to an individual speaker, an ability known as *speaker independence*

▶ Handle speech without limiting vocabulary

▶ Handle continuous speech—natural speech in which words run together at normal speed

Researchers are making great strides toward these goals. Several companies have developed programs that can achieve two of these goals. No one has yet developed a system that consistently achieves all three goals, the human body excepted.

While it's not yet trouble free or error free, PC speech-recognition software is growing in popularity, especially for people who can't use keyboards because of physical disabilities or job restrictions. As the technology improves, the microphone may become the preferred input device for PC users. Future pocket-sized personal digital assistants may become digital dictation machines.

Intelligent Word Processors

> The **real technology**—behind all of our other technologies—is **language**. It actually creates the **world our consciousness lives in**.
> —Norman Fischer, Abbot, Green Gulch Farm Zen Center

Speech recognition is just one aspect of artificial intelligence research that's likely to end up in future word processors. Many experts foresee word processors that are able to anticipate the writer's needs, acting as an electronic editor or coauthor. Today's grammar and style checkers are primitive forerunners of the kinds of electronic writing consultants that might appear in a few years.

Here are some possibilities:

▶ As you're typing a story, your word processor reminds you (via a pop-up message on the screen or an auditory message) that you've used the word *delicious* three times in the last two paragraphs and suggests that you choose an alternative from the list shown on the screen.

▶ Your word processor continuously analyzes your style as you type, determines your writing habits and patterns, and learns from its analysis. If your writing tends to be technical and formal, the software modifies its thesaurus, dictionary, and other tools so they're more appropriate for that style.

▶ You're writing a manual for a large organization whose documentation has specific style guidelines. Your word processor modifies your writing as you type so that it conforms to the organizational style.

▶ You need some current figures to support your argument on the depletion of the ozone layer. You issue a command, and the computer does a quick search of the literature on the Web and quickly reports back to you with several relevant facts.

All of these examples are technically possible now. The trend toward intelligent word processors is clear. Nevertheless, you're in for a long wait if you're eager to buy a system with commands such as Clever Quote, Humorous Anecdote, and Term Paper.

CrossCurrentsCrossCurrentsCrossCurrents **CrossCurrents**

Labor of Love

Christopher Locke

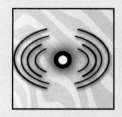

Thanks to the World Wide Web, a writer can reach an audience of millions without going through traditional publishing channels. This is good news for freedom-of-speech advocates and bad news for information monopolies and political tyrants. But there's bad news, too. In this article, first published in the March, 2001, issue of Publish, Cluetrain Manifesto *author Cristopher Locke discusses the down side of this publishing revolution.*

The Web is divided into three parts. From IBM and Intel to a welter of dotcoms and porn sites, there are, for one, the commercial sites that sell products and services. A second category includes media portals. From *The New York Times* to obscure trade magazines, these have come online with existing audiences in tow, seeking to sell advertising. Search engines and directories, such as AltaVista and Yahoo, form a newer subcategory, but the underlying business model is the same: to aggregate "eyeballs" for advertisers.

These two categories may seem the most significant elements of the Web. However, both adhere to a top-down broadcast model, which the Internet has endangered if not made obsolete. And neither is where the Web began.

A third category predates both e-commerce and mainstream media sites. These are the lowely home pages of individuals who realized that, unlike broadcast media, the Web offers few hurdles to direct participation. Owing to substantial entry costs, newspapers, magazines, radio and television stations all must make a compelling prelaunch business case as to how large an audience they will be able to attract.

Not so online. With a modicum of HTML savvy, anyone can create a Web site. And millions did—long before corporations took the Internet seriously. The attraction the Web itself exerted on such creative individuals established the audience that later attracted business.

But how creative were these efforts, really? Everyone knows the Web is awash in garbage—endless lists of favorite links, pet pages, stale jokes and resumes (the last two often overlapping). Some personal sites are nearly as boring and content-free as the obscenely expensive Web monstrosities created by Fortune 500 corporations.

And a significant subcategory is the online journal. Most are naïve and embarrassing. Will Billy ask Suzie out? Will Suzie say yes? Will the boss ever realize what a jerk he is? But the inclination to create a journal is the same inspiration that gives us the word journalism—the drive to impart a personal perspective to events and to make sense of an otherwise confusing world. Whether it comes from *USA Today* or Joe's Way Cool Web Page, the result is still news. But is Joe's news "real" news? Does it really make sense? Online, readers will decide, not some global media conglomerate.

The real difference between *USA Today* and Joe's page is not the inflated notion of "objectivity," but production budget and ROI. Joe doesn't have a business plan. He doesn't need one. With

Web entry costs so low, return on investment is immaterial. Such sites are labors of love, produced nights and weekends by impassioned individuals who make their living elsewhere.

Most personal journals appeal only to doting relatives, but some are attracting significant audiences. Closer to journalism per se, these have been dubbed webzines from their similarity to traditional magazines. The similarities end, however, with the question of what constitutes a "significant audience."

A handful of zines, such as Salon and Feed, are professionally produced and include the work of many journalists. These zines emulate the "controlled circulation" model of offline publications—subscription is free, with costs and profits covered by advertising. These sites have had a hard go of it, as this model requires a relatively mass audience.

In contrast, low-budget bottom-feeder zines don't worry much about size of readership. With little investment at risk, the primary motive is personal gratification—seldom profit—and the style of such zines is therefore often quirky and experimental. If there's an audience that clicks with the material, it shows up via word of mouth. The process works bottom-up, by attraction, not top-down and intrusively, like demographic segmentation and targeting. An entirely new class of markets—small, but often growing fast—are forming around such sites today.

Microsoft's Slate represents an interesting wrinkle in the zine model: corporate patronage. The company owns and underwrites the considerable costs of producing the site. But this begs the age-old journalistic question of corporate influence. For instance, how credible is Slate in reporting on the Microsoft antitrust case? Ownership isn't everything. In fact, it can be an impediment. What if, instead, Microsoft had bankrolled an indie zine with a proven track record and then adopted and ironclad hands-off policy with respect to editorial content?

If corporations underwrote externally produced webzines and were careful to preserve site independence, the resulting sites could be far more credible attractors than are most current corporate Web pages. This sort of enlightened patronage first appeared in the Renaissance when the Medici banking family supported artists like Michelangelo and Leonardo da Vinci. Strangely perhaps, it could work again today, financially rewarding quality site producers and enabling companies to better connect with emergent Web micromarkets.

DISCUSSION QUESTIONS

1. Do you think Web publications are less trustworthy than newspapers, magazines, and television news broadcasts? Be specific.
2. Do you think "enlightened patronage" suggested by the author can make the Web more trustworthy? Explain your answer.

Summary

Even though the computer was originally designed to work with numbers, it quickly became an important tool for processing text. Today the word processor has all but replaced the typewriter as the tool of choice for committing words to paper.

Word processing is far more than typing text into a computer. Word processing software enables the writer to use commands to edit text on the screen, eliminating the chore of retyping pages until the message is right. Other commands enable the writer to control the format of the document: typefaces, spacing, justification, margins, columns, headers, footers, and other visual components. WYSIWYG word processors make it possible to see the formatted pages on the screen before printing them on paper. Most professional word processing programs automate footnoting, hyphenation, and other processes that are particularly troublesome to traditional typists.

Many advanced word processing functions are available as part of modern word processing programs or as stand-alone special-purpose applications. Outlining software turns the familiar outline into a powerful, dynamic organizational tool. Spelling checkers and grammar and style checkers partially automate the proofreading process, although they leave the more difficult parts of the job to literate humans. Online thesauruses, dictionaries, and other computer-based references automate reference work. Production of specialized documents, such as personalized form letters and full-length illustrated books, can be simplified with other word processing tools.

As word processors become more powerful, they take on many of the features previously found only in desktop publishing software. Still, many publishers use word processors and graphics programs to create source documents that can be used as input for page-layout programs. The combination of the graphical user interface (GUI), desktop publishing software, and the high-resolution printer has revolutionized the publishing process by enabling publishers and would-be publishers to produce professional-quality text-and-graphics documents at a reasonable cost. Amateur and professional publishers everywhere use desktop publishing technology to produce everything from comic books to reference books.

The near-overnight success of desktop publishing may foreshadow other changes in the way we communicate with words as new technologies emerge. Computer networks in general and the World Wide Web in particular have made it possible for potential publishers to reach mass audiences without the problems associated with printing and distributing paper documents. Typing may no longer be a necessary part of the writing process as handwriting and speech-recognition technologies improve, and word processing software that incorporates other artificial intelligence technologies may become as much a coach as a tool for future writers.

Chapter Review

▼ Key Terms

automatic correction (autocorrect) (p. 135)

automatic footnoting (p. 135)

automatic formatting (autoformat) (p. 135)

automatic hyphenation (p. 135)

camera-ready (p. 143)

Clipboard (p. 136)

copying text (p. 133)

cut-and-paste (p. 136)

deleting text (p. 133)

desktop publishing (DTP) (p. 142)

drag-and-drop (p. 136)

editing (p. 132)

electronic book (ebook) (p. 148)

electronic paper (epaper) (p. 148)

find command (p. 133)

find and replace (search and replace) (p. 133)

font (p. 133)

footer (p. 135)

formatting (p. 133)

grammar and style checker (p. 141)

groupware (p. 142)

header (p. 135)

inserting text (p. 133)

justification (p. 134)

mail merge (p. 141)

master pages (p. 144)

monospaced font (p. 133)

moving text (p. 133)

navigating (p. 133)

opening a document (p. 132)

outliner (p. 139)

page-layout software (p. 143)

PDF (portable document format) (p. 147)

point size (p. 133)

proportionally spaced font (p. 133)

sans-serif font (p. 133)

saving a document (p. 132)

scrolling (p. 133)

selecting text (p. 136)

serif font (p. 133)

service bureau (p. 143)

source document (p. 143)

speech recognition software (p. 149)

spelling checker (batch or interactive) (p. 140)

style sheet (p. 135)

template (p. 143)

thesaurus (p. 139)

typeface (p. 133)

wizard (p. 135)

word wrap (p. 132)

WYSIWYG (p. 132)

▼ Interactive Quiz Questions

1. The *Computer Confluence* CD-ROM contains self-test quiz questions related to this chapter, including multiple choice, true or false, and matching questions.
2. The *Computer Confluence* Web site, **www.prenhall.com/beekman**, contains self-test exercises related to this chapter. Follow the instructions for taking a quiz. After you've completed your quiz, you can email the results to your instructor.

   The Web site also contains open-ended discussion questions called Internet Explorations. Discuss one or more of the Internet Exploration questions at the section for this chapter.

▼ Review Questions

1. Define or describe each of the key terms listed in the "Key Terms" section. Check your answers in the glossary.
2. How is word processing different from typing?
3. What happens to your document when you turn the computer off? What should you do if you want to work on the document later?
4. Explain the difference between text editing and text formatting. Give several examples of each.
5. What is scrolling, and how is it useful?
6. When do you use the Enter or Return key in word processing?
7. How many different ways can a paragraph or line of text be justified? When might each be appropriate?
8. How is working with an outliner (or idea processor) different from working with a word processor?
9. What is a font, and how is it used in word processing and desktop publishing?
10. Describe three different ways a spelling checker might be fooled.
11. How does desktop publishing differ from word processing?
12. List several advantages of desktop publishing over traditional publishing methods.
13. What are the most important components of a desktop publishing system?
14. Is it possible to have a computer publishing system that is not WYSIWYG? Explain.
15. An automated speech-recognition system might have trouble telling the difference between a "common denominator" and a "comedy nominator." What must the speaker do to avoid confusion? What other limitations plague automated speech-recognition systems today?

▼ Discussion Questions

1. Which of the word processing features and software categories described in this chapter would be the most useful to you as a student? How do you think you would use them?
2. What do you think of the arguments that word processing reduces the quality of writing because (1) it makes it easy to write hurriedly and carelessly and (2) it puts the emphasis on the way a document looks rather than on what it says?
3. Many experts fear that desktop publishing technology will result in a glut of unprofessional, tacky-looking publications. Others fear that it will result in a glut of slick-looking documents full of shoddy ideas and dangerous lies. How do you feel about each of these fears?
4. Like Gutenberg's development of the movable-type printing press more than 500 years ago, the development of desktop publishing puts powerful communication tools in the hands of more people. What impact will desktop publishing technology have on the free press and the free exchange of ideas guaranteed in the United States Constitution? What impact will the same technology have on free expression in other countries?
5. Discuss Question 4, substituting Web publishing for desktop publishing.

▼ Projects

1. Using advertisements, hands-on demonstrations, and personal experience, compare the features of two or more popular word processing programs. (You may include the word processing modules of integrated software packages like ClarisWorks in your comparison.) What are the advantages and disadvantages of each program from a student's point of view?

2. Research one or more of your favorite local or national publications to find out how computers are used in their production.

3. Use a word processing system or a desktop publishing system to produce a newsletter, brochure, or flyer in support of an organization or cause that is important to you.

 # Sources and Resources

Books

Most word processing and desktop publishing books are hardware- and software-specific, that is, they're designed to be used with a specific version of a specific program on a specific machine running a specific operating system. If you need a book to get you started, choose one that fits your system. Make sure the book is an introductory tutorial, not a reference manual or a collection of "power user" tips. If possible, browse before you buy.

The Non-Designer's Design Book, by Robin Williams (Berkeley, CA: Peachpit Press, 1994). In this popular book, Robin Williams provides a friendly introduction to the basics of design and page layout in her popular, down-to-earth style. The first half of the book illustrates the four basic design principles (proximity, alignment, repetition, and contrast). The second half focuses on using type as a design element. This book is highly recommended for anyone new to graphic design.

The Non-Designer's Type Book, by Robin Williams (Berkeley, CA: Peachpit Press, 1998). This followup to *The Non-Designer's Design Book* focuses on fonts and typography. It uses lots of examples and conversational prose to clearly illustrate many ways type can be used to enhance publications.

The Non-Designer's Scan and Print Book, by Sandee Cohen and Robin Williams (Berkeley, CA: Peachpit Press, 1999). Desktop publishers must wear at least two hats, because publishing involves both design and production. This book focuses on the production part of the process. It's packed with information and tips on paper, printers, scanners, color, file formats, fonts, and more. Like the other Non-Designer books, it's easy to read, beautifully designed, and informative.

Looking Good in Print, Fourth Edition, by Roger C. Parker and Patrick Berry (Scottsdale, AZ: Coriolis, 1998). This book covers the non-technical side of desktop publishing. Now that you know the mechanics, how can you make your work look good? Parker and Berry clearly describe the basic design tools and techniques and then apply them in sample documents ranging from brochures to books.

Stop Stealing Sheep and Find Out How Type Works, Second Edition, by Eric Spiekermann and E. M. Ginger (Mountain View, CA: Adobe Press, 2001). This beautiful little book isn't so much a how-to text as a celebration of type as an art form. You'll see printed text differently after you read this book, and you'll have a deeper understanding of how to use it to communicate. The new edition deals with onscreen typography in addition to printed text.

The Official Adobe Print Publishing Guide: The Essential Resource for Print Publishing (San Jose: Adobe Press, 1998). This colorful book covers the entire publication process, from design and construction to proofing and printing. It can be a valuable reference tool for anyone serious about desktop publishing.

The Official Adobe Electronic Publishing Guide: The Essential Resource for Electronic Publishing (San Jose: Adobe Press, 1998). This companion to *The Official Adobe Print Publishing Guide* focuses on the "brave new world" of paperless publishing. Like the print guide, this book uses rich color illustrations and clear, concise explanations to illuminate the entire publishing process.

Adobe PDF with Acrobat 5 Visual Quickstart Guide, by Jennifer Alspach (Berkeley, CA: Peachpit Press, 2001). Adobe's PDF has become a standard for platform-neutral publishing in print and on screen. This little book shows you how to work with PDF using Acrobat, a tool for creating, editing, and viewing PDF files.

Bugs in Writing, by Lynn Dupre (Reading, MA: Addison-Wesley, 1998). This entertaining little book is designed to help computer science and computer information systems students—who presumably already know how to debug their programs—debug their prose. It's a friendly, readable tutorial that can help almost anybody to be a better writer.

The Elements of Style, Fourth Edition, by William Strunk, Jr., and E.B. White (Needham Heights, MA: Allyn & Bacon, 1999). If you want to improve your writing, this book is a classic.

Wired Style: Principles of English Usage in the Digital Age, by Constance Hale and Jessie Scanlon (San Francisco: Broadway Books, 2000). Should an email address be italicized when it's included in a paragraph of text? For that matter, is it E-mail, e-mail, or email? Do you back up files or backup files? When you write about IBM, should you use its unabbreviated name? Digital communication changes our language quickly, and the classic grammar and style manuals don't always have the answers. In this sometimes controversial guidebook, the editors of *Wired* answer these questions, explain their writing and editing philosophies, and provide tips for writing about rapidly evolving technologies and ideas. If you like the informal future-focused style of *Wired*, you'll appreciate this book.

The Microsoft Manual of Style for Technical Publications, Second Edition (Redmond, WA: Microsoft Press, 1998). This style guide isn't as much fun to read as *Wired*'s, and it doesn't offer much in the way of guidance or philosophy. But it's a useful alphabetical reference when you need to write about computer hardware and software.

Scrolling Forward: Making Sense of Documents in the Digital Age, by David M. Levy (Arcade Publishing, 2001). How are computers, the Internet, and digital technology in general changing the notion of documents? The future of books, paper, copyrights, and libraries are discussed in this thought-provoking book.

Periodicals

Publish! This monthly provides cover-to-cover desktop publishing coverage. (The brand-specific magazines like *PC* and *Macworld* mentioned at the end of Chapter 1, "Computer Currents: From Calculation to Connection," also regularly discuss word processing and desktop publishing.)

World Wide Web Pages

The Web is full of fascinating resources for publishers, writers, and page designers. Some, like **http://www.adobe.com**, are obvious; others are harder to find but no less useful. Check the *Computer Confluence* Web site at **www.prenhall.com/beekman** for links to the best pages.

6 | Calculation, Visualization, and Simulation

After you read this chapter you should be able to:

Describe the basic functions and applications of spreadsheet programs

Explain how computers can be used to answer "what if?" questions

Show how spreadsheet graphics can be used and misused as communication tools

Describe other software tools for processing numbers and symbols on personal computers, workstations, and mainframes

Explain how computers are used as tools for simulating mechanical, biological, and social systems

▼ **In this chapter:**

Why spreadsheet programs opened the office door for PCs

How spreadsheet software can answer "what if" questions

How charts and graphs can illuminate—or hide—the truth

Simulations: good news, bad news

. . . and more.

▼ **On the CD-ROM:**

A scientific computing activity

A spreadsheet activity

Instant access to glossary and key word references

Interactive self-study quizzes

. . . and more.

▼ **On the Web:**

www.prenhall.com/beekman

Links to resources for working with numbers, charts, and graphs

Online simulation games and visualization tools

Examples of state-of-the-art scientific simulations and visualizations

Self-study exercises

. . . and more.

Dan Bricklin and Mitch Kapor Count on Computers

In terms of the **success** of VisiCalc,
I don't feel I have to **repeat it**.
But it **is** nice to be able to realize
you've done **something very worthwhile**.

—Dan Bricklin

In 1978 Harvard graduate student Dan Bricklin watched his professor continually erase and recalculate rows and columns of numbers on a blackboard during classroom exercises in corporate financial planning. He envisioned a computer program that would do the calculations and recalculations automatically on the screen of his Apple II. With the help of his friend Bob Frankston, an MIT student, he developed VisiCalc, the first computer spreadsheet program. Almost overnight this revolutionary software changed the world of personal computing. Before VisiCalc, personal computers were used mostly to mimic the functions of mainframes. But VisiCalc was a unique tool—one that provided managers with capabilities they never had before. Financial projections, budgetary reports, and other documents that might have taken days before could be created in minutes, and just as quickly modified if the results weren't satisfactory. VisiCalc was responsible for the

Dan Bricklin

early success of the Apple II, and the desktop computer in general, in the business world. Because of VisiCalc, managers and executives could see the value and power of those early machines.

After IBM introduced the IBM PC in 1981, many VisiCalc-inspired spreadsheet programs were competing for the software dollars of businesses. One of those programs was developed by Mitch Kapor, an idealistic young entrepreneur who had worked for a VisiCalc distributor and tested a release of VisiCalc. In 1983 Kapor's start-up company, Lotus, released a powerful, easy-to-use integrated spreadsheet/graphics package called 1-2-3 that quickly established itself as the standard spreadsheet on IBM-compatible computers. By backing a solid software product with an expensive marketing campaign and a support program that made it easier for nontechnical corporate users to get training and help, Lotus established new standards for software

Mitch Kapor

success. Lotus 1-2-3 quickly became the most successful software product the computer industry had ever seen.

Today 1-2-3 has been eclipsed by Microsoft Excel, a graphical spreadsheet program originally developed for the Macintosh. The original VisiCalc program was purchased by Lotus and discontinued. After an unsuccessful trade-secret-theft lawsuit against Lotus, VisiCalc's parent company faded into obscurity. In 1995 IBM purchased Lotus and began bundling Lotus products with its computers.

What happened to Bricklin and Kapor? Both left their original companies for other computer ventures. Bricklin still develops innovative software, including pen-based systems and multimedia authoring tools. Kapor became the cofounder of and spokesperson for the Electronic Frontier Foundation, an organization dedicated to protecting human rights and the free flow of information on the Internet. ▶

Computers were originally created to calculate, and today's machines are still widely used for numeric computations. Numbers are at the heart of applications ranging from accounting to statistical analysis. The most popular number-crunching application is the spreadsheet, conceived by Bricklin and institutionalized by Lotus. Executives, engineers, scientists, and others use the spreadsheet for the same reason: It enables them to create and work with simulations of real-world situations.

A well-designed simulation, whether constructed with a spreadsheet or with another software application, can help people achieve a better understanding of the world outside the computer. Computer simulations have their limitations and risks, too. In this chapter we explore the world of number manipulation and computer simulation, starting with the spreadsheet.

The Spreadsheet: Software for Simulation and Speculation

Compare the **expansion of business** today to the **conquering of the continent** in the nineteenth century.
The spreadsheet in that comparison is like the **transcontinental railroad**. It **accelerated the movement,** made it possible, and **changed the course** of the nation.

—Mitch Kapor

More than any other type of standalone PC software, the spreadsheet has changed the way people do business. In the same way a word processor can give a computer user control over words, **spreadsheet software** enables the user to take control of numbers, manipulating them in ways that would be difficult or impossible otherwise. A spreadsheet program can make short work of tasks that involve repetitive calculations: budgeting, investment management, business projections, grade books, scientific simulations, checkbooks, and so on. A spreadsheet can also reveal hidden relationships between numbers, taking much of the guesswork out of financial planning and speculation.

The Malleable Matrix

The goal was that it had to be better than **the back of an envelope**.

—Dan Bricklin

Almost all spreadsheet programs are based on a simple concept: the malleable matrix. A spreadsheet document, called a **worksheet**, typically appears on the screen as a grid of numbered **rows** and alphabetically lettered **columns**. The box representing the intersection of a row and a column is called a **cell**. Every cell in this grid has a unique **address** made up of a row number and column letter. For example, the cell in the upper-left corner of the grid is called cell A1 (column A, row 1). All the cells are empty in a new worksheet; it's up to the user to fill them. Each cell can contain a numeric value, an alphabetic label, or a formula representing a relationship between numbers in other cells.

Values (numbers) are the raw material the spreadsheet software uses to perform calculations. Numbers in worksheet cells can represent wages, test scores, weather data, polling results, or just about anything that can be quantified.

To make it easier for people to understand the numbers, most worksheets include **labels** at the tops of columns and at the edges of rows, such as "Monthly Wages," "Midterm Exam 1," "Average Wind Speed," or "Final Approval Rating." To the computer, these labels are meaningless strings of characters. The label "Total Points" doesn't tell the computer to calculate the total and display it in an adjacent cell; it's just a road sign for human readers.

The worksheet may be bigger than what appears on your screen. The program enables you to scroll horizontally and vertically to view the larger matrix. (After Z, columns are labeled with double letters: AA, AB, and so on.)

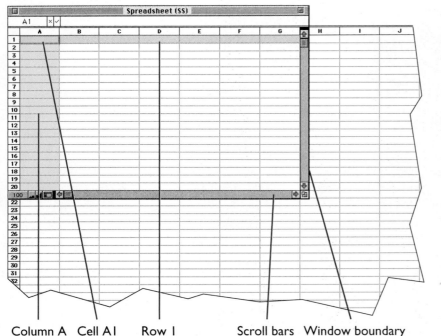

Column A   Cell A1   Row 1   Scroll bars   Window boundary

To calculate the total points (or the average wind speed or the final approval rating), the worksheet must include a **formula**—a step-by-step procedure for calculating the desired number. The simplest spreadsheet formulas are arithmetic expressions using +, −, *, and / to represent addition, subtraction, multiplication, and division, respectively. For example, cell B5 might contain the formula =(B2+B3)/2. This formula tells the computer to add the numbers in cells B2 and B3, divide the result by 2, and display the final result in the cell containing the formula, cell B5. You don't see the formula in cell B5; you just see its effect. It doesn't matter whether the numbers represent test scores, dollars, or nothing at all; the computer obediently calculates their average and displays the results. If either number in cell B2 or B3 changes, the number displayed in B5 automatically changes, too. *The User's View* illustrates how you might create a simple worksheet.

Different brands of spreadsheets, such as those included in Microsoft Office, StarOffice, and AppleWorks, are distinguished by their features and their user interfaces. In spite of their differences, all popular spreadsheet programs work in much the same way and share most of these features:

▶ *Automatic replication of values, labels, and formulas.* Most worksheets contain repetition: Budgetary amounts remain constant from month to month; exam scores are calculated the same way for every student in the class; a scheduling program refers to the same seven days each week. Many spreadsheet commands streamline entry of repetitive data, labels, and formulas. **Replication** commands are, in essence, flexible extensions of the basic copy-and-paste functions found in other software. The most commonly used replication commands are the Fill Down and Fill Right commands illustrated in The User's View example. Formulas can be constructed with *relative references* to other cells, as in the example, so they refer to different cells when replicated in other locations, or as *absolute references* that don't change when copied elsewhere.

▶ *Automatic recalculation.* **Automatic recalculation** is one of the spreadsheet's most important capabilities. It not only enables for the easy correction of errors, but also makes it easy to try out different values while searching for solutions. For large, complicated worksheets, recalculation can be painfully slow, so most spreadsheets enable you to turn off the automatic recalculation feature and recalculate the worksheet only when necessary.

▶ *Predefined functions.* The first calculators made computing a square root a tedious and error-prone series of steps. On today's calculators a single press of the square-root button tells the calculator to do all the necessary calculations to produce the square root. Spreadsheet programs contain built-in **functions** that work like the calculator's square-root button. A function in a formula instructs the computer to perform some predefined set of calculations. For example, the formula =SQRT(C5) calculates the square root of the number in cell C5. Modern spreadsheet applications have large libraries of predefined functions. Many, such as SUM, AVERAGE (or AVG), MIN, and MAX, represent simple calculations that are performed often in all kinds of worksheets. Others automate complex financial, mathematical, and statistical calculations that would be extremely difficult to calculate manually. The IF function enables the worksheet to decide what to do based on the contents of other cells, giving the worksheet logical decision-making capability. (For example: If the number of hours worked is greater than 40, calculate pay using the overtime schedule.) Like the calculator's square-root button, these functions can save time and reduce the likelihood of errors.

▶ *Macros.* A spreadsheet's menu of functions, like the menu in a fast-food restaurant, is limited to the most popular selections. For situations in which the built-in functions don't fill the bill, most spreadsheets enable you to capture sequences of steps as reusable **macros**—custom-designed procedures that you can add to the existing menu of options. Some programs insist that you type macros using a special macro language; others enable you to turn on a macro recorder that captures every move you make with the keyboard and mouse, recording those actions in a macro transcript. Later you can ask the computer to carry out the instructions in that macro. Suppose, for example, you use the same set of calculations every month when preparing a statistical analysis of environmental data. Without macros you'd have to repeat the same sequence of keystrokes, mouse clicks, and commands each time you created the monthly report. But by creating a macro called, for instance, Monthstats, you can effectively say, "Do it again" by issuing the Monthstats command.

Creating a Simple Worksheet

SOFTWARE: *Microsoft Excel.*

THE GOAL: *To create a computerized version of a worksheet showing projected expenses for one college student's fall term. The design of the worksheet is based on this hand-drawn planning version.*

1 The first step is to type descriptive labels for the worksheet title and to label the rows and columns. Typing appears in the current or **active cell**—the cell containing the cursor—and in the long window above the worksheet, called the console or formula bar. You move from cell to cell by clicking with the mouse or by navigating with the keyboard.

2 To make room for row labels, you widen the first column by dragging its border to the right.

3 After typing the labels, you type numeric values to represent dollar values for each category in each month.

4 To change cell formats so numbers are displayed with dollar signs, you select the **range** (rectangular block) of cells by dragging between cells B3 and F11, two opposite corners of the rectangle.

5 Choose the Cells command from the Format menu . . .

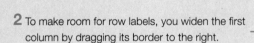

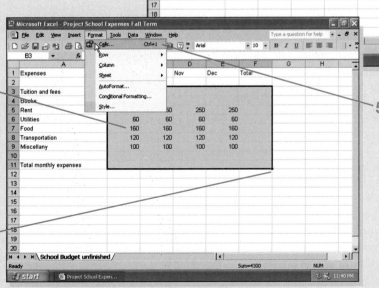

6 . . . and then select the Currency format to change the appearance of all values in the range.

7 You enter a formula to calculate the total expenses for September in cell B11: 5sum(B3:B9). When you press Enter, the formula in the cell is replaced by the calculated value—the sum of the numbers in cells B3 through B9. (The formula is still visible in the formula bar whenever cell B11 is active.)

8 You don't need to repeat this process for the other columns in the worksheet; instead you can replicate this formula in cells C11 through F11. When you select the range of cells from B11 to F11 and apply the Fill Right command, each cell in the block gets a version of this formula automatically adjusted to calculate the total for that cell's column.

9 A similar process (using the Fill Down command) calculates the totals in column F.

10 After you change the format of some cells to make the worksheet more readable, you decide to change numbers in two of December's cells to enable for holiday gifts and travel.

11 The spreadsheet software automatically recalculates all formulas to reflect the revised input data.

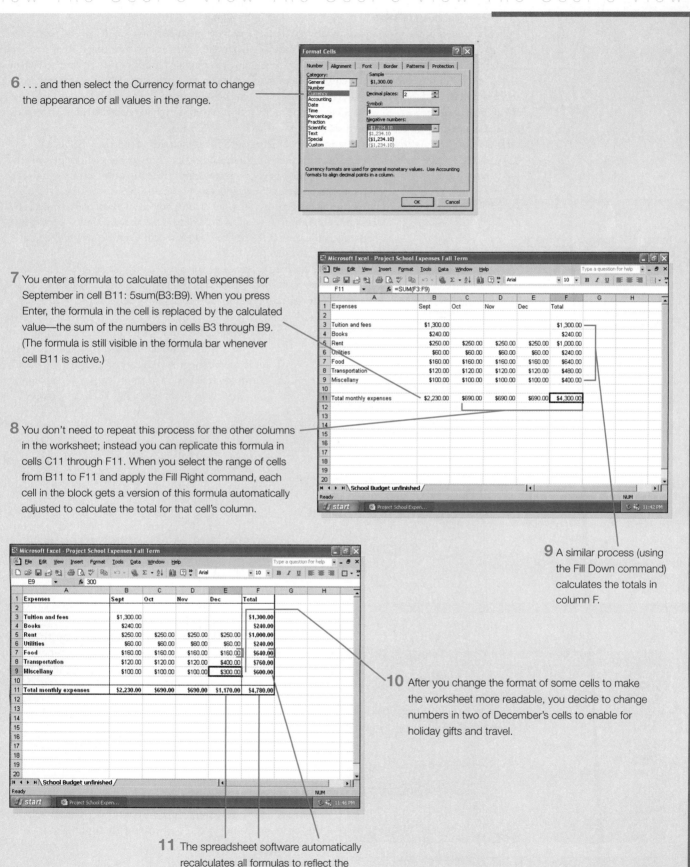

▶ *Formatting.* Most modern spreadsheets enable you to control typefaces, text styles, cell dimensions, and cell borders. They also enable you to include pictures and other graphic embellishments in documents.

▶ *Templates.* Even with functions and macros, the process of creating a complex worksheet from scratch can be intimidating. Many users take advantage of worksheet **templates** that contain labels and formulas but no data values. These reusable templates produce instant answers when you fill in the blanks. Some common templates are packaged with spreadsheet software; others are marketed separately. When templates aren't available, users can create their own or commission programmers to write them. Whatever its origin, a well-designed template can save considerable time, effort, and anguish.

▶ *Linking.* Sometimes a change in one worksheet produces changes in another. For example, a master sales summary worksheet for a business should reflect changes in each department's sales summary worksheet. Most spreadsheet programs can create **automatic links** between worksheets so when values change in one, all linked worksheets update automatically. Some programs can create three-dimensional worksheets by stacking and linking several two-dimensional sheets. Some spreadsheet programs can create links to Web pages so data can be downloaded and updated automatically.

All of these worksheets are linked together into a single 3-D worksheet.

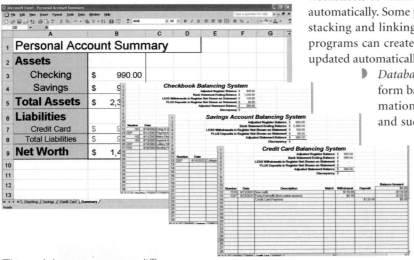

▶ *Database capabilities.* Many spreadsheet programs can perform basic database functions: storage and retrieval of information, searching, sorting, report generation, mail merge, and such. With these features a spreadsheet can serve users whose database needs are modest. For those who require a full-featured database management system, spreadsheet software might still be helpful; many spreadsheet programs support automatic two-way communication with database software.

"What If?" Questions

> The purpose of computation is not **numbers** but **insight**.
>
> —R. W. Hamming

This worksheet compares two different car loans for total interest expense: a five-year loan at 7.61 percent and a four-year loan at 9.15 percent. The cells in which contents appear in color (blue or red) contain formulas that compute results based on the contents of the worksheet. The four-year loan, even though it has a higher interest rate, is a slightly better choice.

A spreadsheet program is a versatile tool, but it's especially valuable for answering **"what if?" questions**: "What if I don't complete the third assignment? How will that affect my chances for getting an A?" "What if I put my savings in a high-yield, tax-sheltered IRA account with a withdrawal penalty? Will I be better off than if I leave it in a low-yield passbook account with no penalty?" "What if I buy a car that gets only 10 miles per gallon instead of a car that gets 40? How much more will I pay altogether for fuel over the next four years?" Because it enables you to change numbers and instantly see the effects of those changes, spreadsheet software streamlines the process of searching for answers to these questions.

Some spreadsheet programs include **equation solvers** that turn "what if?" questions around. Instead of forcing you to manipulate data values until formulas give you the numbers you're looking for, an equation solver enables you to define an equation, enter your target value, and watch while the computer determines the necessary data values. For example, an investor might use an equation solver to answer the question "What is the best mix of these three stocks for minimizing risk while producing a 10 percent return on my investment?"

Avoiding Spreadsheet Pitfalls

Spreadsheet errors are easy to make and easy to overlook. When creating a worksheet, you can minimize errors by following a few basic guidelines:

- **Plan the worksheet before you start entering values and formulas.** Think about your goals, and design the worksheet to meet those goals.
- **Make your assumptions as accurate as possible.** Answers produced by a worksheet are only as good as the assumptions built into the data values and formulas. A worksheet that compares the operating costs of a gas guzzler and a gas miser must make assumptions about future trips, repair costs, and, above all, gasoline prices. The accuracy of the worksheet is tied to all kinds of unknowns, including the future of Middle East politics. The more accurate the assumptions, the more accurate the predictions.
- **Double-check every formula and value.** Values and formulas are input for worksheets, and input determines output. Computer professionals often describe the dark side of this important relationship with the letters *GIGO—garbage in, garbage out*. One highly publicized spreadsheet transcription error for Fidelity Investments resulted in a $2.6 billion miscalculation because of a single missing minus sign! You may not be working with values this big, but it's still important to proofread your work carefully.

- **Make formulas readable.** If your software can attach names to cell ranges, use meaningful names in formulas. It's easier to create and debug formulas when you can use readily understandable language like payrate*40+1.5*payrate* (hours worked–40) instead of a string of characters like C2*40+1.5*C2*(D2-40).
- **Check your output against other systems.** Use another program, a calculator, or pencil and paper to verify the accuracy of a sampling of your calculations.
- **Build in cross-checks.** Compare the sum of row totals with the sum of column totals. Does everything add up?
- **Change the input data values and study the results.** If small input adjustments produce massive output changes, or if major input adjustments result in little or no output changes, something may be wrong.
- **Take advantage of preprogrammed functions, templates, and macros.** Why reinvent the wheel when you can buy a professionally designed vehicle?
- **Use a spreadsheet as a decision-making aid, not as a decision-maker.** Some errors aren't obvious; others don't show up immediately. Stay alert and skeptical.

Spreadsheet Graphics: From Digits to Drawings

> **Our work** . . . is to present things that are **as they are**.
> —Frederick II (1194–1250), King of Sicily

Most spreadsheet programs include charting commands that can turn worksheet numbers into charts and graphs automatically. Standalone charting programs create charts from any collection of numbers, whether stored in a worksheet or not. The process of creating a chart is usually as simple as filling in a few blanks in a dialog box.

The growth in election campaign spending seems more real as a line shooting toward the top of a graph than as a collection of big numbers on a page. The federal budget makes more (or less?) sense as a sliced-up dollar pie than as a list of percentages. The correct chart can make a set of stale figures come to life, awakening our eyes and brains to trends and relationships that we might not have otherwise seen.

Most spreadsheet and charting programs offer a variety of basic chart types and options for embellishing charts. The differences among these chart types are more than aesthetic; each chart type is well suited for communicating particular types of information.

Pie charts show the relative proportions of the parts to a whole. **Line charts** are most often used to show trends or relationships over time or to show relative distribution of one variable through another. (The classic bell-shaped normal curve is a line chart.) **Bar charts** are similar to line charts, but they're more appropriate when data falls into a few categories. Bars can be

Charting with a Spreadsheet

SOFTWARE: *Microsoft Excel.*

THE GOAL: *To create a chart to bring your budget into focus.*

1 To chart the breakdown totals from your budget, you'll use two ranges of cells: One contains the column of totals (F3 through F9) . . .

2 . . . another contains the category names for those totals (A3 through A9).

3 After selecting both ranges, you click the Chart Wizard icon on the button bar. Chart Wizard walks you through the process of creating a chart by presenting a series of dialog boxes.

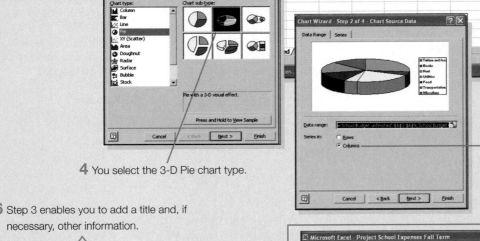

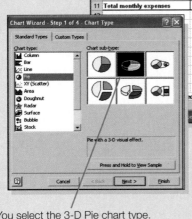

4 You select the 3-D Pie chart type.

5 Step 2 lets you verify the data range and specify that the data is in columns, not rows.

6 Step 3 enables you to add a title and, if necessary, other information.

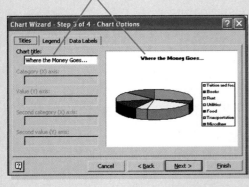

7 You can use the program's graphics tools to fine-tune the chart's appearance.

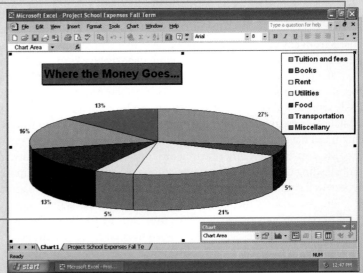

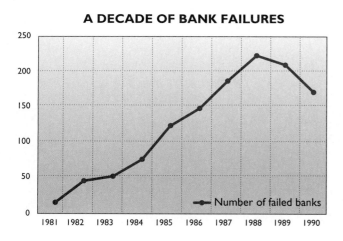

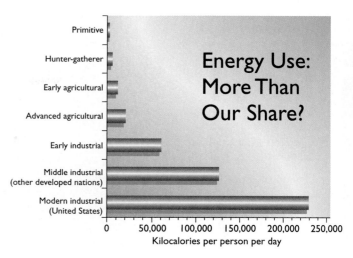

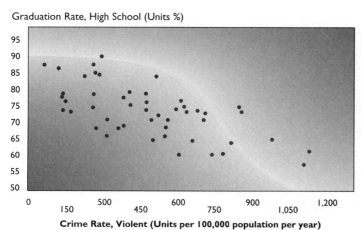

Line charts and bar charts (above) show trends over time or distribution over categories. Scatter charts (left) show relationships between variables.

stacked in a **stack chart** that shows how proportions of a whole change over time; the effect is similar to a series of pie charts. **Scatter charts** are used to discover, rather than display, a relationship between two variables. A well-designed chart can convey a wealth of information, just as a poorly designed chart can confuse or mislead.

Tomorrow's Spreadsheet?

As revolutionary as VisiCalc was when it was introduced in 1979, it simply couldn't meet the demands of today's spreadsheet user. Even the original 1-2-3 looks primitive next to modern graphic spreadsheets. It's unlikely that spreadsheets have reached the end of their evolutionary path. What's next?

Spreadsheets are beginning to incorporate artificial intelligence to guide users through complex procedures. (The wizard shown in the charting User's View box is a simple example.) To help users check complex worksheets for consistency of entries and formula logic, future spreadsheets are likely to include *validators*—the equivalent of spelling and grammar checkers for calculations.

Further down the road, spreadsheets may disappear into the background along with other applications. Smaller software tools that can be combined into custom applications may replace today's feature-laden spreadsheets. Users will work with words, numbers, and other types of data without having to think about separate word processors, spreadsheets, and other applications. The program components, like the data they use in their calculations, might be spread across a network—or the entire Internet. From the user's point of view, the focus will be more on the problem solution than on tools.

Microsoft Office's Help system attempts to answer questions written in English, but the answers aren't always relevant.

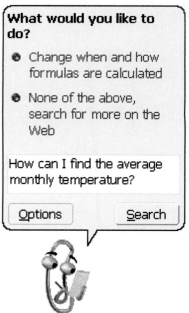

Making Smart Charts

A chart can be a powerful communication tool if it's designed intelligently. If it's not, the message may miss the mark. Here are some guidelines for creating charts that are easy to read and understand.

▶ **Choose the right chart for the job.** Think about the message you're trying to convey. Pie charts, bar charts, line charts, and scatter charts are not interchangeable.

▶ **Keep it simple, familiar, and understandable.** Use charts in magazines, books, and newspapers as models.

▶ **Strive to reveal the truth, not hide it.** Whether accidentally or intentionally, many computer users create charts that convey misinformation. Changes in the scale or dimensions of a chart can completely transform the message, turning information into propaganda.

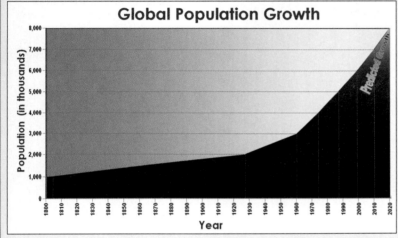

These charts are based on identical data, but only the first one clearly illustrates the data relationships. The second chart distorts the relationship by changing the vertical axis. The third chart hides the relationship with an inappropriately chosen pie chart.

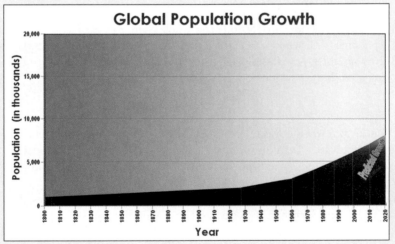

Statistical Software: Beyond Spreadsheets

Spreadsheet software is remarkably versatile, but no program is perfect for every task. Other types of number-manipulation software are available for those situations in which spreadsheets don't quite fit the job.

> **Science** is what we understand well enough to explain to a computer; **art** is everything else.
>
> —Donald Knuth, author of *The Art of Computer Programming*

Money Managers

Spreadsheet software has its roots in the accountant's ledger sheets, but spreadsheets today are seldom used for accounting and bookkeeping. Accounting is a complex concoction of rules, formulas, laws, and traditions, and creating a worksheet to handle the details of the process is difficult and time-consuming. Instead of relying on general-purpose spreadsheets for accounting, most businesses (and many households) use professionally designed **accounting and financial management software**.

Whether practiced at home or at the office, accounting involves setting up **accounts**—monetary categories to represent various types of income, expenses, assets, and liabilities—and keeping track of the flow of money between those accounts. An accountant routinely records *transactions*—checks, cash payments, charges, and other activities—that move money from one account to another. Accounting software, such as Intuit's popular Quicken, automatically adjusts the balance in every account after each transaction. What's more, it records every transaction so that you can retrace the history of each account step by step. This *audit trail* is a necessary part of business financial records, and it's one reason accountants use special-purpose accounting packages rather than spreadsheet programs.

In addition to keeping records, financial management software can automate check writing, bill paying, budgeting, and other routine money matters. Periodic reports and charts can provide detailed answers to questions such as "Where does the money go?" and "How are we doing compared to last year?"

The Internet has made it possible for programs such as Quicken to expand beyond the boundaries of the PC. Through an Internet connection, a home accounting program can recommend investments based on up-to-the-hour performance statistics, track investment portfolios, comparison shop for insurance and mortgages, and link to specialized online calculators and advisors. Hundreds of financial institutions now offer **online banking** services, making it possible to pay bills, check account balances, and transfer funds using software.

Inexpensive financial management programs for homes and small businesses make the accounting process easier to understand by simulating checks and other familiar documents on the screen. Quicken enables you to track cash, check, and credit card transactions, and use the data in a variety of ways. Pocket Quicken enables you to record transactions on a handheld computer when you're away from your desk and upload those transactions into your desktop machine later.

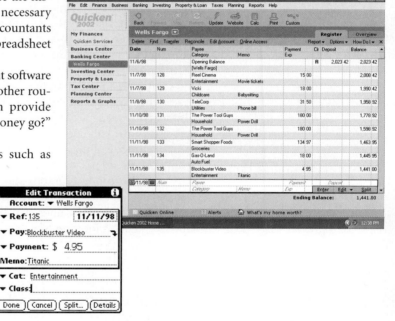

Most accounting and financial management programs don't calculate income taxes, but they can export records to programs that do. **Tax preparation software** works like a prefabricated worksheet. As you enter numbers into the blanks in onscreen forms, the program automatically fills in other blanks. Every time you enter or change a number, the bottom line is recalculated automatically. When the forms are completed, they're ready to print, sign, and mail to the Internal Revenue Service. Some taxpayers bypass paper forms altogether by sending the completed forms electronically to the IRS.

Automatic Mathematics

Most of us seldom do math more complicated than filling out our tax forms. But higher mathematics is an essential part of the work of many scientists, researchers, engineers, architects, economists, financial analysts, teachers, and other professionals. Mathematics is a universal language for defining and understanding natural phenomena as well as a tool used to create all kinds of products and structures. Whether or not we work with it directly, our lives are constantly being shaped by mathematics.

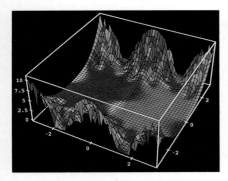

An abstract mathematical relationship is easier to understand when turned into a visible object with high-level mathematical software. (Software: Mathematica.)

Many professionals and students whose mathematical needs go beyond the capabilities of spreadsheets depend on symbolic **mathematics processing software** to grapple with complex equations and calculations. Mathematics processors make it easier for mathematicians to create, manipulate, and solve equations, in much the same way word processors help writers. Features vary from program to program, but a typical mathematics processor can do polynomial factoring, symbolic and numeric calculus, real and complex trigonometry, matrix and linear algebra, and three-dimensional graphics.

Mathematics processors generally include an interactive question-and-answer mode, a programming language, and tools for creating interactive documents that combine text, numerical expressions, and graphics. Although mathematics processors have only been available for a few years, they've already changed the way professionals use mathematics and the way students learn it. By handling the mechanics of mathematics, these programs enable people to concentrate on the content and implications of their work.

Statistics and Data Analysis

> Yet **to calculate** is not in itself **to analyze**.
> —Edgar Allan Poe, 1841

One branch of applied mathematics that has become more important in the computer age is **statistics**—the science of collecting and analyzing data. Modern computer technology provides us with mountains of data—census data, political data, consumer data, economic data, sports data, weather data, scientific data, and more. We often refer to the data as statistics. ("The government released unemployment statistics today.") But the numbers by themselves tell only part of the story. The analysis of those numbers—the search for patterns and relationships among them—can provide meaning for the data. ("Analysts note that the rise in unemployment is confined to cities most heavily impacted by the freeze on government contracts.") Statisticians in government, business, and science depend on computers to make sense of raw data.

Do people who live near nuclear power plants run a higher cancer risk? Does the current weather pattern suggest the formation of a tropical storm? Are rural voters more likely to support small-town candidates? These questions can't be answered with absolute certainty; the element of chance is at the heart of statistical analysis. But **statistical analysis software** can suggest answers to questions such as these by testing the strength of data relationships. Statistical software can also produce graphs showing how two or more variables relate to each other. Statisticians can often uncover trends by browsing through two- and three-dimensional graphs of their data, looking for unusual patterns in the dots and lines that appear on the screen. This kind of visual exploration of data is an example of a type of application known as *scientific visualization*.

Scientific Visualization

> The wind blows over the lake and **stirs the surface** of the water. Thus, **visible effects of the invisible** are manifested.
> —The I Ching

Scientific visualization software uses shape, location in space, color, brightness, and motion to help us understand relationships that are invisible to us. Like mathematical and statistical software, scientific visualization software is no longer confined to mainframes and supercomputers; some of the most innovative programs have been developed for use on high-end personal computers and workstations, working alone or in conjunction with more powerful computers.

Scientific visualization takes many forms, all of which involve graphical representation of numerical data. The numbers can be the result of abstract equations, or they can be data gleaned from the real world. Either way, turning the numbers into pictures enables researchers and students to see the unseeable, and sometimes, as a result, to know what was previously unknowable. Here are two examples:

▶ Astronomer Margaret Geller of Harvard University created a 3-D map of the cosmos from data on the locations of known galaxies. While using her computer to "fly through" this three-dimensional model, she saw something that no one had seen before: the mysterious clustering of galaxies along the edges of invisible bubbles.

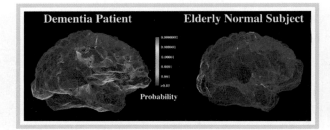

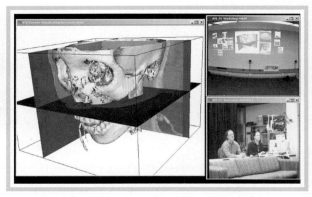

These two visualizations, created at the Laboratory of Neuro Imaging (LONI), map physical differences between a normal human brain and one with a form of dementia (left). Using a tool called Access Grid, researchers work with a shared visualization called the Visible Human (right).

▶ Dr. Mark Ellisman of the University of California, San Diego, School of Medicine used a 30-foot electron microscope to collect data from cells of the brain and enter it into a supercomputer, which rendered a 3-D representation of the brain cell. When Ellisman's team displayed the data on a graphic workstation, they saw several previously undiscovered aberrations in brains of patients who had Alzheimer's disease—aberrations that may turn out to be clues for discovering the cause and cure for this disease.

In these examples and hundreds of others like them, visualization helps researchers see relationships that might have been obscure or even impossible to grasp without computer-aided visualization tools.

Calculated Risks: Computer Modeling and Simulation

> We have the ability to **model**—to prototype—
> **faster, better, and cheaper** than ever before.
> The old back-of-the-envelope is becoming **supercomputer driven** louver!
>
> —Michael Schrage, author of *Serious Play*

Whether part of a simple worksheet or a complex set of equations, numbers often symbolize real-world phenomena. Computer modeling—the use of computers to create abstract models of objects, organisms, organizations, and processes—can be done with spreadsheets, mathematical applications, or standard programming languages. Most of the applications discussed in this chapter are examples of computer modeling. A business executive who creates a worksheet to project quarterly profits and losses is trying to model the economic world that affects the company. An engineer who uses a mathematics processor to test the stress capacity of a bridge is modeling the bridge mathematically. Even a statistician who starts by examining data collected in the real world creates statistical models to describe the data.

Computer models aren't always serious; most computer games are models. Chess boards, pinball games, battlefields, sports arenas, ant colonies, cities, medieval dungeons, interplanetary cultures, and mythological societies have all been modeled in computer games. Students use computer models to travel the Oregon Trail, explore nuclear power plants, invest in the stock market, and dissect digital frogs.

Whether it's created for work, education, or play, a computer model is an abstraction—a set of concepts and ideas designed to mimic some kind of system. But a computer model isn't static; you can put it to work in a computer simulation to see how the model operates under certain conditions. A well-designed model should behave like the system it imitates.

Suppose, for example, an engineer constructs a computer model of a new type of airplane to test how the plane will respond to human commands. In a typical flight simulation, the "pilot" controls the plane's thrust and elevator angle by feeding data to the model plane. The model responds by adjusting air speed and angle of ascent or descent, just as a real plane would. The pilot responds to the new state of the aircraft by adjusting one or more of the controls,

6.1
Scientific Computing

Computers have long been used to analyze and visualize scientific data collected through experiments and observation. A computer can also serve as a virtual laboratory that simulates a physical process without real-world experiments. Of course, an inaccurate simulation can give incorrect results.

The problem of accurate simulation helped initiate the study of chaos and fractals. Chaos is now a vast field of study with applications in many disciplines.

The "Chaos Game" illustrates how computers can quickly complete repetitive tasks in experiments that would otherwise be impractical or impossible. You could perform the first few steps of such an experiment with pencil, paper, and ruler, like this:

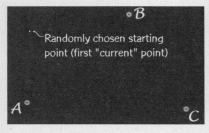

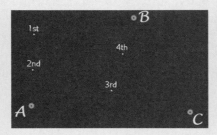

1 Draw three widely separated points on the paper to form a triangle; label the points A, B, and C. Draw a random starting point anywhere on the paper. This will be the first "current" point.

2 Repeat the following process four times: randomly choose from among points A, B, and C, and draw a new point halfway (on an imaginary straight line) between the current point and the chosen point. The newly drawn point then becomes the new current point.

3 If you use a simple computer program to plot 100,000 repeats of step 2 (excluding the first few points from the drawing), you'll see a pattern emerge rather than a solid mass of dots. This pattern, called a Sierpinski gasket, is a fractal—an object in which pieces are miniatures of the whole figure. You will see a pattern like this.

Because some fractal formulas mimic the patterns of natural objects, such as coastlines and mountains, chaos has found applications in computer-generated scenery and special effects for movies and television shows.

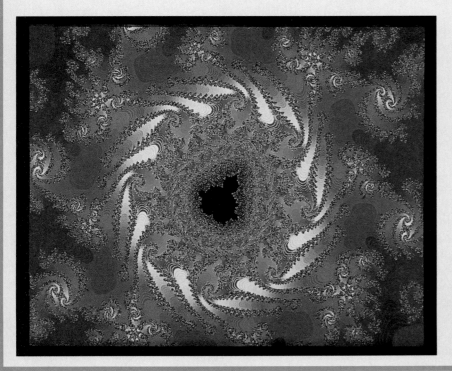

The Mandelbrot set, discovered by the mathematician Benoit Mandelbrot (who coined the term fractal) while he was working at IBM's Thomas J. Watson Research Facility, is one of the most famous fractals to emerge from the theory of chaos.

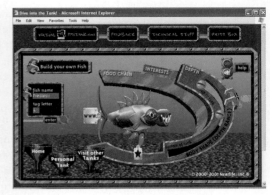

Consumer-oriented simulations enable people to live their fantasies and experiment with artificial realities. The Sims, which enables you to control and observe a household populated with virtual people, combines education with entertainment. Virtualfishtank.com is a Web site that enables you to design artificial fish and watch them interact in a virtual environment.

which causes the system to respond by revising the aircraft's state again. This **feedback loop**, where plane and pilot react to data from each other, continues throughout the simulation.

A flight simulator might have a graphical user interface that makes the computer screen look and act like the instrument panel of a real plane so that human pilots can run it intuitively. Or it might display nothing more than numbers representing input and output values, and the input values might be generated by a simulated pilot—another computer model! Either way, it can deliver a wealth of information about the behavior of the plane, provided the model is accurate.

Computer Simulations:
The Rewards

We are reaching the stage where **problems** that we must solve are going to become **insolvable** without computers. **I do not fear computers;** I fear the lack of them.
—Isaac Asimov, scientist and science fiction writer

Computer simulations are widely used for research in the physical, biological, and social sciences and in

Flight simulator games for home computers such as A-10 X-Plane (left) are simplified versions of flight simulators used to train military pilots (right). Both varieties enable users to test their wings without risking their necks.

engineering. Schools, businesses, and the military also use simulations for training. There are many reasons:

▶ *Safety.* While it's safer to learn piloting skills sitting in front of a computer than actually flying in the air, it's still possible to learn to fly without a computer simulation. Some activities, however, are so dangerous that they aren't ethically possible without computer simulations. How, for example, can scientists study the effects of a nuclear power plant meltdown on the surrounding environment? Unless a meltdown occurs, there's only one practical answer: computer simulation.

▸ *Economy*. It's far less expensive for an automobile manufacturer to produce a digital model of a nonexistent car than to build a prototype out of steel. The company can test the computer model for strength, handling, and efficiency in a series of simulations before it builds and tests a physical prototype. The cost of the computer model is small when compared with the possible expense of producing a defective car.

▸ *Projection*. Without computers, it could take decades for biologists to determine whether the rising deer population on an island threatens other species, and by the time they discover the answer, it would be too late to do anything about it. A computer model of the island's ecosystem could speed up natural biological processes so scientists could measure their effects over several generations in a matter of minutes. A computer simulation can, in effect, serve as a time machine for exploring one or more possible futures.

▸ *Visualization*. Computer models make visualization possible, and visualization enables researchers and students to see and understand relationships that might otherwise go unnoticed. Computer models can speed time up or slow it down; they can make subatomic particles big and the universe small.

▸ *Replication*. In the real world, it can be difficult or impossible to repeat a research project with slightly different conditions. But this kind of repetition is an important part of serious research. An engineer needs to fine-tune dimensions and angles to achieve peak performance. A scientist studies the results of one experiment and develops a new hypothesis that calls for further testing. An executive needs to test a business plan under a variety of economic scenarios. If the research is conducted on a computer model, replication is just a matter of changing input values and running a new simulation.

Computer Simulations: The Risks

All information is **imperfect**.
—Jacob Bronowski

The downside of computer simulation can be summed up in three words: Simulation isn't reality. The real world is a subtle and complex place, and capturing even a fraction of that subtlety and complexity in a computer simulation is a tremendous challenge.

GIGO Revisited

The accuracy of a simulation depends on how closely its mathematical model corresponds to the system being simulated. Mathematical models are built on assumptions, many of which are difficult or impossible to verify. Some models suffer from faulty assumptions; others contain hidden assumptions that may not even be obvious to their creators; still others go astray simply because of clerical or human errors.

The daily weather report is the result of a complex computer model. Our atmosphere is far too complex to capture exactly in a computer model; that's why the weather forecast is wrong so often. Occasionally simulation errors produce disastrous results. Faulty computer models have been responsible for deadly flooding of the Colorado River, the collapse of the roof of a Salt Lake City shopping mall, and the crash of a test plane on its first flight. These kinds of disasters are rare. It's much more common for computer models to help avert tragedies by pointing out design flaws. In fact, sometimes things go wrong because people ignore the results of accurate simulations. Still, *garbage in, garbage out* is a basic rule of simulation.

Making Reality Fit the Machine

Simulations are computation intensive. Today's personal computers can run modest simulations, but they're hopelessly underpowered for medium to large simulations. Most scientists and engineers who work extensively with mathematical models depend on workstations, mainframes, or supercomputers to run simulations.

Some simulations are so complex that researchers need to simplify models and streamline calculations to get them to run on the best hardware available. Even when there's plenty of computing power available, researchers face a constant temptation to reshape reality for the convenience of the simulation. In one classic example a U.S. Forest Service computer model reduced complex old-growth forests to "accumulated capital." Aesthetics, ecological diversity, and other hard-to-quantify factors didn't exist in this model.

Sometimes this simplification of reality is deliberate; more often it's unconscious. Either way, information can be lost, and the loss may compromise the integrity of the simulation and call the results into question.

The Illusion of Infallibility

Risks can be magnified because people take computers seriously. For many people, information takes on an air of respectability if it comes from a computer. People tend to emphasize computer-generated reports, often at the expense of other sources of knowledge. Executives use worksheets to make decisions involving thousands of jobs and millions of dollars. Politicians decide the fate of military weapons and endangered species based on summaries of computer simulations. Doctors use computer models to make life-and-death decisions involving new drugs and treatments. All of these people, in some sense, are placing their trust in computer simulations. Many of them trust the data precisely because a computer produced it.

A computer simulation, whether generated by a PC spreadsheet or churned out by a supercomputer, can be an invaluable decision-making aid. The risk is that the people who make decisions with computers will turn over too much of their decision-making power to the computer. The Jedi Master in *Star Wars* understood the danger when he encouraged Luke Skywalker in the heat of battle to turn off his computer simulation rather than let it overpower his judgment. His admonition was simple: "Trust your feelings."

Getting It Right in the OR

Ellen Goodman

Simulations have long been used to train military pilots, nuclear plant workers, and others whose jobs involve risks. In this syndicated column, first published in January of 2000, Boston Globe writer Ellen Goodman discussed the potential benefits of using simulations to train doctors and other health workers.

It's 2 p.m., and Nancy is being prepped for surgery. On the medical chart, she is listed as a 28-year-old with renal disease and asthma who's come for an appendectomy. Her voice can be heard complaining about a pain in her side while the anesthesiologist reassures her, "We'll get going soon."

But it has not been a good day in this operating room. Earlier, one patient went into anaphylactic shock. Another was in need of oxygen when the supply ran out. Soon, all hell will break loose again.

This is not an episode of "ER." Nor is this operating room suffering from bad karma or incompetence. This is the Center for Medical Simulation. Here, on the fifth floor of a Boston building, another handful of residents in anesthesiology has come for a day of training in crisis management with the staff and, of course, the most patient of patients.

Nancy, you see, is a dummy. A very, very smart dummy. This computer-driven mannequin, whose name and illness change several times a day, is a teaching tool. She's programmed for one problem after another. The software makes her breathe and move her arms, makes her heart rate go up and her blood pressure soar and crash. Let us be frank: This dummy has had some near-death experiences.

I'm here because there is suddenly a spotlight on medical errors in this country. Late in November the Institute of Medicine came out with a report titled honestly and ominously, "To Err Is Human."

We learned that the number of people who die in medical accidents equals two jumbo jets a week. The president has appointed a task force that will soon report on threats to patient safety, and we have already set a goal of cutting mistakes in half.

The easy fix will be to devise systems that reduce prescription drug errors. But the hard fix will be to promote an entire culture of safety. That's what they are working on here.

The most safety-conscious industries from aviation to nuclear energy all use simulations to replicate actual conditions. As Mitchell Rabkin, a former hospital chief standing beside me in Nancy's control room, remarks about pilots, "Nobody says, 'Well, you read the book on the 727, now take it up.'"

Yet in medicine, the first real crisis often involves real people. So here and in a few places like it across the country, sophisticated simulation is getting the sort of medical attention it deserves.

Back in the operating room, the computer has just clicked in, and Nancy is headed for trouble. The tube in her throat gets clogged. Then power in the O.R. goes off. A teacher playing the role of surgeon frantically demands the one flashlight. The anesthesiologist needs it to check Nancy's airway. No one can locate the right plugs for the auxiliary power.

In the mayhem of this scene, Jeff Cooper, the biomedical engineer who runs this center, quietly points out the underlying problems: Communication. Teamwork. Leadership styles.

These are not simple problems of individual human error but of the culture. Indeed, after studying errors and accidents for decades, Cooper thinks most medical mistakes are not just a matter of wrong diagnoses or faulty judgment. They are flaws in the systems.

"We use simulators," he says, "as a vehicle to get people to talk about subtle issues." And later, in the conference room, as the staff and young doctors review the videotape, something unusual happens. The residents and staff talk openly about those subtler subjects in ways that doctors rarely do when reputation and liability are on the line.

They note the small, treacherous failures. Critical information was passed on to a doctor who couldn't hear because he had the stethoscope in his ears. A resident couldn't interact, even in a crisis, with an obnoxious surgeon-actor. No one took the task of calming down a frenzied operating room.

"We're not trying to lay blame," explains Cooper. "We want to give people experiences where they can not just practice but observe themselves on videotape and get a message of deeper cultural change." At the same time, he bets, none of today's residents will ever again forget to notice where the emergency power plugs are in an O.R.

A culture of safety is still the long-term goal. But here in an all-too-realistic O.R., a society that is focusing on medical mistakes can glimpse how much better off we'd be if most of the mishaps happened to Nancy.

DISCUSSION QUESTIONS

1. Do you think simulations can help beginning doctors to avoid mistakes? Explain your answer.

2. Is there a downside to the use of simulations by doctors? Explain your answer.

Summary

Spreadsheet programs, first developed to simulate and automate the accountant's ledger, are widely used today in business, science, engineering, and education. Spreadsheet software can be used for tracking financial transactions, calculating grades, forecasting economic conditions, recording scientific data—just about any task that involves repetitive numeric calculations. Spreadsheet documents, called worksheets, are grids with individual cells containing alphabetic labels, numbers, and formulas. Changes in numeric values can cause the spreadsheet to update any related formulas automatically. The responsiveness and flexibility of spreadsheet software make it particularly well suited for providing answers to "what if?" questions.

Most spreadsheet programs include charting commands to turn worksheet numbers into a variety of graphs and charts. The process of creating a chart from a spreadsheet is automated to the point where human drawing isn't necessary; the user simply provides instructions concerning the type of chart and the details to be included in the chart, and the computer does the rest.

Number crunching often goes beyond spreadsheets. Specialized accounting and tax preparation software packages perform specific business functions without the aid of spreadsheets. Symbolic mathematics processors can handle a variety of higher mathematics functions involving numbers, symbols, equations, and graphics. Statistical analysis software is used for data collection and analysis. Scientific visualization can be done with math processors, statistical packages, graphics programs, or specialized programs designed for visualization.

Modeling and simulation are at the heart of most applications involving numbers. When people create computer models, they use numbers to represent real-world objects and phenomena. Simulations built on these models can provide insights that might be difficult or impossible to obtain otherwise, provided that the models reflect reality accurately. If used wisely, computer simulation can be a powerful tool to help people understand their world and make better decisions.

Chapter Review

▼ Key Terms

account (p. 167)
accounting and financial management
    software (p. 167)
active cell (p. 160)
address (p. 158)
automatic link (p. 162)
automatic recalculation (p. 159)
bar chart (p. 163)
cell (p. 158)
column (p. 158)
console (p. 160)
equation solvers (p. 162)
feedback loop (p. 171)
formula (p. 159)

formula bar (p. 160)
function (p. 159)
label (p. 158)
line chart (p. 163)
macro (p. 159)
mathematics processing software
    (p. 168)
modeling (p. 169)
online banking (p. 167)
pie chart (p. 163)
range (p. 160)
replication (p. 159)
row (p. 158)
scatter chart (p. 165)

scientific visualization software
    (p. 168)
simulation (p. 169)
spreadsheet software (p. 158)
stack chart (p. 165)
statistical analysis software (p. 168)
statistics (p. 168)
tax preparation software (p. 167)
template (p. 162)
value (p. 158)
"what if?" question (p. 162)
worksheet (p. 158)

▼ Interactive Quiz Questions

1. The *Computer Confluence* CD-ROM contains self-test quiz questions related to this chapter, including multiple choice, true or false, and matching questions.
2. The *Computer Confluence* Web site, **www.prenhall.com/beekman**, contains self-test exercises related to this chapter. Follow the instructions for taking a

quiz. After you've completed your quiz, you can email the results to your instructor.

The Web site also contains open-ended discussion questions called Internet Explorations. Discuss one or more of the Internet Exploration questions at the section for this chapter.

▼ Review Questions

1. Define or describe each of the key terms listed in the Key Terms section. Check your answers using the glossary.
2. In what ways are word processors and spreadsheet programs similar?
3. What are some advantages of using a spreadsheet over using a calculator to maintain a budget? Are there any disadvantages?
4. If you enter 5B21C2 in cell B1 of a worksheet, the formula is replaced by the number 125 when you press the Enter key. What happened?
5. Using the worksheet from Question 4, you change the number in cell B2 from 55 to 65. What happens to the number in cell B1? Why?

6. Explain the difference between a numeric value and a formula.
7. What is a spreadsheet function, and how is it useful?
8. What is the difference between a spreadsheet program and a financial management program?
9. Describe or draw examples of several different types of charts, and explain how they're typically used.
10. Describe several software tools used for numeric applications too complex to be handled by spreadsheets. Give an example of an application of each.
11. List several advantages and disadvantages of using computer simulations for decision-making.

▼ Discussion Questions

1. Spreadsheets are sometimes credited with legitimizing the personal computer as a business tool. Why do you think they had such an impact?
2. Why do you think errors in spreadsheet models go undetected? What can you do to minimize the risk of spreadsheet errors?
3. The statement "Computers don't make mistakes, people do" is often used to support the reliability of computer output. Is the statement true? Is it relevant?
4. Are computer simulations misused? Give some examples, and explain your answer.

5. Before spreadsheets, people who wanted to use computers for financial modeling had to write programs in complex computer languages to do the job. Today spreadsheets have replaced those programs for many financial applications. Do you think spreadsheets will be replaced by some easier-to-use software tool in the future? If so, try to imagine what it will be like.
6. Discuss the advantages and disadvantages of computer simulation as a tool for research and education.

▼ Projects

1. Use a spreadsheet or a financial management program to develop a personal budget. Try to keep track of all your income and outgo for the next month or two, and record the transactions with your program. At the end of that time, evaluate the accuracy of your budget, and discuss your reactions to the process.
2. Use a spreadsheet to search for answers to a "what if" question that's important to you. Possible questions: What if I lease a car instead of buying it—am I better off? What if I borrow money for school—how much does it cost me in the long run?
3. Develop a multiple-choice questionnaire for determining public attitudes on an issue that's important to you. Use a

computer to analyze, summarize, and graphically represent the results, trying to be as fair and accurate in your summary as you can.
4. Use a spreadsheet to track your grades in this (or another) class. Apply weightings from the course syllabus to your individual scores, calculating a point total based on those weightings.
5. Choose a controversial issue—environmental, economic, or other—and locate numeric data related to the issue. Develop a set of charts and graphs that argues effectively for one point of view. Using the same data, create visuals to support the other point of view. Compare audience reactions (and your reactions) to both presentations.

Sources and Resources

Books

Books covering basic spreadsheet operations number in the hundreds—far too many to review here. Almost all of these books are software and hardware specific. Some are intended to be used as reference manuals; some are collections of tips, hints, and shortcuts; others are collections of sample documents that can be used as templates; still others are overviews or hands-on tutorials for beginners. If you're new to spreadsheets, start with a book in the last category. Look for one that fits your system and that's readable and easy to understand.

How to Lie with Statistics, by Darrell Huff (New York: Norton, 1954). This 45-year-old book has more relevance in today's computer age than it did when it was written.

The Sum of Our Discontent: Why Numbers Make Us Irrational, by David Boyle (Texere, 2001). Computers, television, and other media bombard us with more numbers than most of us can digest. Boyle argues that all those numbers make it harder, not easier, to undertand what's going on around us.

Designing Infographics, by Eric K. Meyer (Indianapolis: Hayden Books, 1997). This book provides an excellent overview of the theory and the practice of designing graphs, charts, and other informative illustrations. It covers tools, techniques, forms, and applications of quantitative and informative graphics; there's even a section on statistical ethics.

The Visual Display of Quantitative Information, Envisioning Information, and **Visual Explanations: Images and Quantities, Evidence and Narrative,** by Edward R. Tufte (Cheshire, CT: Graphics Press, 1987, 1990, and 1997, respectively). These three beautiful books make a powerful case for intelligent design of charts, graphics, and other visual aids. Many of the examples in these books show how graphs and charts can be both creative and informative.

Elements of Graph Design, by Stephen M. Kosslyn (New York: W. H. Freeman and Company, 1993). This handy book is smaller, more affordable, and more accessible than the Tufte books. It's packed with useful tips for designing charts and graphs that communicate clearly, with plenty of examples comparing charts done the wrong way with charts done correctly.

Serious Play: How the World's Best Companies Simulate to Innovate, by Michael Schrage (Cambridge, MA: Harvard Business School Press, 1999). "When talented innovators innovate, you don't listen to the specs they quote. You look at the models they've created," says Michael Schrage, MIT Media Lab fellow and *Fortune* magazine columnist. In this book, Schrage looks at the kind of "serious play" being done at innovative companies such as Disney, 3M, Sony, and Hewlett Packard.

World Wide Web Pages

The Internet was created as a tool for scientific researchers and engineers. Today the Web is filled with sites that deal with mathematics, statistics, scientific visualization, and simulation. The *Computer Confluence* Web pages include links to many of the best sites in government, education, and private corporations.

7 | Graphics, Hypermedia, and Multimedia

After you read this chapter you should be able to:

▼

Compare and contrast several types of computer graphics programs used by artists, photographers, designers, and others

Explain how computers are changing the way professionals and amateurs work with video, animation, audio, and music

Describe several ways that computers are used to create multimedia materials in the arts, entertainment, education, and business

Explain the relationship between hypermedia and multimedia, describing applications of each

Describe several present and future applications for multimedia technology

▲

▼ **In this chapter:**

Computer graphics, from illustration to digital photography

Dynamic digital media: animation, video, and audio

Hypermedia and multimedia: emerging art forms

Data compression, how and why

. . . and more.

▼ **On the CD-ROM:**

An activity on data compression

Doug Engelbart's history-making Augment presentation

Creating a graphical presentation: an interactive walk-through

Compression technology: an animated example

Dynamic computer art and animation examples

A presentation software activity

. . . and more.

▼ **On the Web:**

www.prenhall.com/beekman

More on Doug Engelbart's groundbreaking work

Links to outstanding art, animation, video, and audio Web sites

Resources for creating your own audio, video, graphic, and multimedia works

Self-study exercises

. . . and more.

Doug Engelbart Explores Hyperspace

If you **look out in the future,**
you can see how best to
make right choices.

—Doug Engelbart

On a December day in 1950, Doug Engelbart looked into the future and saw what no one had seen before. Engelbart had been thinking about the growing complexity and urgency of the world's problems and wondering how he could help solve those problems. In his vision of the future Engelbart saw computer technology augmenting and magnifying human mental abilities, providing people with new powers to cope with the urgency and complexity of life.

Doug Engelbart

Engelbart decided to dedicate his life to turning his vision into reality. Unfortunately, the rest of the world wasn't ready for Engelbart's vision. His far-sighted approach didn't match the prevailing ideas of the time, and most of the research community denounced or ignored Engelbart's work. In 1951 there were only about a dozen computers in the world, and those spent most of their time doing military calculations. It was hard to imagine ordinary people using computers to augment their personal productivity. So Engelbart put together the Augmentation Research Center at the Stanford Research Institute to create working models of his visionary tools.

In 1968, he demonstrated his Augment system to an auditorium full of astonished computer professionals and changed forever the way people think about computers. A large screen showed a cascade of computer graphics, text, and video images, controlled by Engelbart and a coworker several miles away. "It was like magic," recalls Alan Kay, one of the young computer scientists in the audience. Augment introduced the mouse, video display editing (the forerunner to word processing), mixed text and graphics, windowing, outlining, shared-screen video conferencing, computer conferencing, groupware, and hypermedia. Although Engelbart used a large computer, he was really demonstrating a futuristic "personal" computer—an interactive multimedia workstation for enhancing individual abilities.

Doug Engelbart's visionary 1968 presentation showed the world how computers could be used as collaborative tools.

Today many of Engelbart's inventions and ideas are commonplace. He is widely recognized for one small part of his vision: the mouse. But Engelbart hasn't stopped looking into the future. He now heads the Bootstrap Institute at Stanford University, a nonprofit think tank dedicated to helping organizations make decisions with the future in mind. In a world where automation can dehumanize and eliminate jobs, Engelbart is still committed to replacing automation with augmentation. But now he focuses more on the human side of the equation, helping people chart a course into the future guided by intelligent, positive vision. He talks about turning organizations into "networked improvement communities" and demonstrates ways to "improve the improvement process." If anyone understands how to build the future from a vision, Doug Engelbart does.

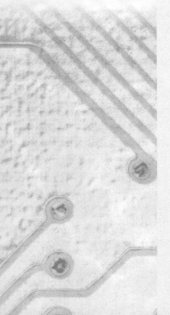

By combining live-action video with long-distance text editing and idea processing, Doug Engelbart showed that the computer could be a multiple-media communication tool with fantastic potential. Today's PC is living up to that potential. Graphics programs allow artists, designers, engineers, publishers, and others to create and edit visual images. Hypermedia documents guide users through information along uniquely personal trails rather than traditional start-to-finish paths. Interactive multimedia tools combine text, graphics, animation, video, and sound in computer-controlled packages. In this chapter we look into these cutting-edge technologies and see how they can augment human abilities.

Focus on Computer Graphics

Mastering technology is only part of what it means to be an artist in the twenty-first century. The other hurdle is **mastering creative expression**, so that art has something substantial to say. **Expression** has been **the one constant** among artists from the Stone Age until now. The only thing that has changed is the **technology**.

—Steven Holtzman, author of *Digital Mantras*

The last chapter demonstrated how spreadsheet programs, statistical programs, and other mathematical software create *quantitative* graphics—charts and graphs generated from numbers. These programs help businesspeople, scientists, and engineers who lack the time or talent to create high-quality drawings by hand. But computer graphics today go far beyond pie charts and line graphs. In this section, we explore a variety of graphical applications, from simple drawing and painting tools to complex programs used by professional artists and designers.

Painting: Bitmapped Graphics

Everything you **imagine** is real.
—Pablo Picasso

An image on a computer screen is made up of a matrix of **pixels**—tiny dots of white, black, or color arranged in rows. The words, numbers, and pictures we see are nothing more than patterns of pixels created by software. Most of the time, the user doesn't directly control those pixel patterns; software creates the patterns automatically in response to commands. For example, when you press the e key while word processing, software constructs a pattern that appears on the screen as an e. Similarly, when you issue a command to create a bar chart from a spreadsheet, software automatically constructs a pixel pattern that looks like a bar chart. Automatic graphics are convenient, but they can also be restrictive. When you need more control over the details of the screen display, another type of graphics software might be more appropriate.

Painting software enables you to "paint" pixels on the screen with a pointing device. A typical painting program accepts input from a mouse, joystick, trackball, touch pad, or pen, translating the pointer movements into lines and patterns onscreen. A professional artist might prefer to work with a pen on a pressure-sensitive tablet because it can, with the right software, simulate a traditional paintbrush more accurately than other pointing devices can.

A painting program typically offers a **palette** of tools onscreen. Some tools mimic real-world painting tools, while others can do things that are difficult, even impossible, on paper or canvas.

Painting programs create **bitmapped graphics** (or, as they're sometimes called, **raster graphics**)—pictures that are, to the computer, simple maps showing how the pixels on the screen should be represented. For the simplest bitmapped graphics, a single bit of computer memory represents each pixel. Since a bit can contain one of two possible values, 0 or 1, each pixel can display one of two possible colors, usually black or white.

Allocating more memory per pixel, so each pixel can display more possible colors or shades, produces even higher-quality graphics. *Gray-scale graphics* allow each pixel to appear as black, white, or one of several shades of gray. A program that assigns 8 bits per pixel allows up to 256 different shades of gray to appear on the screen—more than the human eye can distinguish.

When it's used with compatible software, a pen on a pressure-sensitive tablet can simulate the feel of a paintbrush on paper. As the artist presses harder on the tablet, the line becomes thicker and denser on the screen.

Realistic color graphics require more memory. Many older computers have hardware to support 8-bit color, allowing 256 possible colors to be displayed on the screen at a time—enough to display rich images, but not enough to exactly reproduce most photographs. Photorealistic color requires hardware that can display millions of colors at a time—24 or 32 bits of memory for each pixel on the screen.

The number of bits devoted to each pixel—called **color depth** or **bit depth**—is one of two technological factors limiting an artist's ability to create realistic onscreen images with a bitmapped graphics program. The other factor is **resolution**—the density of the pixels, usually described in *dots per inch*, or *dpi*. Not surprisingly, these are also the two main factors controlling image quality in monitors, as described in Chapter 3. But some graphics images are destined for the printer after being displayed on screen, so the printer's resolution comes into play, too. When displayed on a 72-dpi computer screen—on a Web page, for example—a 72-dpi picture looks fine. But when printed on paper, that same image lacks the fine-grain clarity of a photograph. Diagonal lines, curves, and text characters have tiny "jaggies"—jagged, stair-step-like bumps that advertise the image's identity as a collection of pixels.

Professional painting programs like Synthetik's Studio Artist allow artists and nonartists alike to use tools that work like real-world painting tools.

Painting programs get around the jaggies by allowing you to store an image at 300 dots per inch or higher, even though the computer screen can't display every pixel at that resolution and normal magnification. Of course, high-resolution pictures demand more memory and disk space. But for printed images, the results are worth the added cost. The higher the resolution, the harder it is for the human eye to detect individual pixels on the printed page.

Practically speaking, resolution and bit-depth limitations are easy to overcome with today's hardware and software. Artists can use paint programs to produce works that convincingly simulate watercolors, oils, and other natural media, and transcend the limits of those media. Similarly, bitmapped image-editing software can be used to edit photographic images.

Digital Image Processing: Photographic Editing by Computer

Like a picture created with a high-resolution paint program, a digitized photograph or a photograph captured with a digital camera is a bitmapped image. Digital **image processing software** enables the user to manipulate photographs and other high-resolution images with tools similar to those found in paint programs. Digital image processing software, such as Adobe Photoshop, is in many ways similar to paint software—both are tools for editing high-resolution bitmapped images.

> The aim of every artist is to **arrest motion**, which is life, by artificial means and **hold it fixed** so that a hundred years later, when a stranger looks at it, **it moves again** since it is life.
>
> —William Faulkner

Digital image processing software makes it easier for photographers to remove unwanted reflections, eliminate red eye, and brush away facial blemishes—to perform the kinds of editing tasks that were routinely done with magnifying glasses and tiny brushes before photographs were digitized. But digital photographic editing is far more powerful than traditional photo-retouching techniques. With image processing software, it's possible to distort and combine photographs, creating fabricated images that show no evidence of tampering. Supermarket gossip tabloids routinely use these tools to create sensationalistic cover photos. Many experts question whether photographs should be allowed as evidence in the courtroom now that they can be doctored so convincingly. See The User's View box.

Drawing: Object-Oriented Graphics

Because high-resolution paint images and photographs are stored as bit maps, they can make heavy storage and memory demands. Another type of graphics program can economically store pictures with virtually *infinite* resolution, limited only by the capabilities of the output device. **Drawing software**

> Actually, a root word of technology, **techne**, originally meant **"art."** The ancient Greeks never separated **art** from **manufacture** in their minds, and so never developed **separate words** for them.
>
> —Robert Pirsig, in *Zen and the Art of Motorcycle Maintenance*

Editing Photographic Images

SOFTWARE: *Adobe Photoshop with a scanner plug-in.*

THE GOAL: *To create a cover for a forthcoming CD from an obscure but enthusiastic band.*

1 You select your favorite photo of the band from the prints of a recent photo shoot, as well as a photo of a conga drum which you captured with a digital camera. The cover concept combines the band and the drum. The first step is to import the photos—the band photo using a scanner, and the digital camera image by transferring the file from your camera to your computer—and save each of them as Photoshop documents.

2 You want to isolate the drum from its background, so you trace around it with the magnetic lasso. You don't have to trace the exact profile of the drum, because the magnetic lasso automatically snaps to the nearest edges.

3 You create a mask, which hides everything except the selected drum.

4 The drum photo can now be placed in front of another background as if it were a set of paper dolls. You drag the drum photo into the window with the band photo, which pastes it into a new layer so it can be moved and modified independently.

5 You notice that the light in the drum image appears to fall from the opposite direction as the light which falls on the band in the other photo. To create the illusion of uniform lighting for the photos, you flip the drum image along its horizontal axis.

6 You resize the canvas to the dimensions of a standard CD booklet. You also resize the drum layer, squashing, stretching, and distorting it to create the illusion that the viewer is standing just over the drum.

7 One of the band member's faces appears washed out. To correct this problem, you use the digital equivalent of a dark-room tool, the Burn tool, to simulate the process of selectively over-exposing portions of the image.

8 You select the closest part of the drum with the lasso, and tell Photoshop to apply a blur effect to add a sense of depth to the image.

9 You add a title and resize it to match the drum head. You apply a bulge effect to the text and give it a horizontal slant, so that it matches the perspective of the drum head.

10 You print the final document on a high resolution printer.

This image served as the cover art for a Herbie Hancock album called Dis is de Drum. Photographer Sanjay Kothari created the image through the process of digital photographic manipulation. Several of the photographs used in the final photocollage are shown along the right side of the larger image. The three small images at the bottom of the screen show several of the steps in the process of combining the images using Adobe's Photoshop.

stores a picture not as a collection of dots, but as a collection of lines and shapes. When you draw a line with a drawing program, the software doesn't record changes in a pixel map. Instead, it calculates and remembers a mathematical formula for the line. A drawing program stores shapes as shape formulas and text as text. Because pictures are collections of lines, shapes, and other objects, this approach is often called **object-oriented graphics** or **vector graphics**. In effect, the computer is remembering "a blue line segment goes here and a red circle goes here and a chunk of text goes here" instead of "this pixel is blue and this one is red and this one is white. . . ."

Many drawing tools—line, shape, and text tools—are similar to painting tools in bitmapped programs. But the user can manipulate objects and edit text without affecting neighboring objects, even if the neighboring objects overlap. On the screen, an object-oriented drawing looks similar to a bitmapped painting. But when it's printed, a drawing appears as smooth as the printer's resolution allows. (Of course, not all drawings are designed to be printed. You may, for example, use a drawing program to create images for publication on a Web page. Because many Web browsers recognize only bitmapped images, you'll probably convert the drawings to bit maps before displaying them.) See The User's View box.

Many professional drawing programs, including Adobe Illustrator and Macromedia Freehand, store images using **PostScript**—a standard **page-description language** for describing text fonts, illustrations, and other elements of the printed page. PostScript is built into many laser printers and other high-end output devices, so those devices can understand and follow PostScript instructions. PostScript-based drawing software constructs a PostScript program as the user draws. This program provides a complete set of instructions for reconstructing the picture at the printer. When the user issues a Print command, the computer sends PostScript instructions to the printer, which uses those instructions to construct the grid of microscopic pixels that will be printed on each page. Most desktop publishing software uses PostScript in the same way.

Object-oriented drawing and bitmapped painting each offer advantages for certain applications. Bitmapped image-editing programs give artists and photo editors unsurpassed control over textures, shading, and fine detail; they're widely used for creating screen displays (for example, in video games, multimedia presentations, and Web pages), for simulating natural paint media, and for embellishing photographic images. Object-oriented drawing and illustration programs are a better choice for creating printed graphs, charts, and illustrations with clean lines and smooth shapes. Some integrated programs, including Corel Draw and AppleWorks, contain both drawing and painting modules, allowing you to choose the right tool for each job. Some programs merge features of both in a single application, blurring the distinction and offering new possibilities for amateur and professional illustrators.

3-D Modeling Software

Working with a pencil, an artist can draw a three-dimensional scene on a two-dimensional page. Similarly, an artist can use a drawing or painting program to create a scene that appears to have depth on a two-dimensional computer screen. But in either case, the drawing lacks true depth;

Drawing with a Computer

SOFTWARE: *Macromedia Freehand.*

THE GOAL: *To find the best way to fit your furniture into the space available in your new room. Your furniture is heavy, but you can easily create digital scale models that weigh nothing. It's easier to drag these drawings around a floor plan than to move their real-world counterparts.*

1 After creating a new Freehand document, you turn on the Page Rulers option so you can scale your drawing at 2 feet per inch.

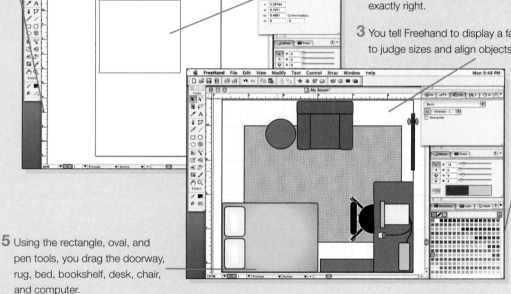

2 Using the rectangle tool from the toolbox, you drag diagonally to draw a rectangle representing the room's floor. Square handles allow you to adjust the shape of this rectangle until it's exactly right.

3 You tell Freehand to display a faint rectangular grid so it's easy to judge sizes and align objects anywhere on the page.

4 Freehand includes a color mixer so you can create custom colors. For this project it's easier to use colors from a standard color palette—in this case a palette of colors normally used for Web graphics. You choose to display all 216 color chips without names so you can easily drag the colors you need onto the objects you draw.

5 Using the rectangle, oval, and pen tools, you drag the doorway, rug, bed, bookshelf, desk, chair, and computer.

6 The Group command allows you to group several objects so you can manipulate them as a single object. You group the desk, chair, and computer into a single object so you can rotate it and move it around in the room.

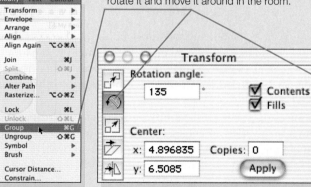

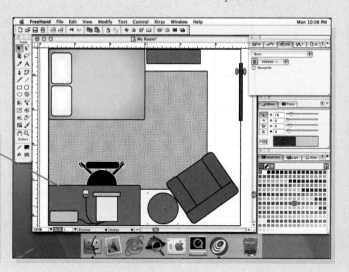

Pixels versus Objects
How do you edit a picture? It depends on what you're doing and how the picture is stored.

The task . . .	Using bit-mapped graphics	Using object-oriented graphics
Moving and removing parts of pictures	Easier to work with regions rather than objects (note), especially if those objects overlap	Easier to work with individual objects or groups of objects, even if they overlap
Working with shapes	Shapes stored as pixel patterns can be edited with eraser and drawing tools	Shapes stored as math formulas can be trans-formed mathematically
Magnification	Magnifies pixels for fine detail editing	Magnifies objects, not pixels
Text handling	Text "dries" and can't be edited, but can be moved as a block of pixels When paint text "dries" it can't be edited like other text	Text can always be edited Draw text always can be changed
Printing	Resolution of printout can't exceed the pixel resolution of the stored picture	Resolution is limited only by the output device
Working within the limits of the hardware	Photographic quality is possible but requires considerable memory and disk storage	Complex drawings require considerable computational power for reasonable speed

it's just a flat representation of a scene. With **3-D modeling software** graphic designers can create 3-D objects with tools similar to those found in conventional drawing software. You can't touch a 3-D computer model; it's no more real than a square, a circle, or a letter created with a drawing program. But a 3-D computer model can be rotated, stretched, and combined with other model objects to create complex 3-D scenes.

Illustrators who use 3-D software appreciate its flexibility. A designer can create a 3-D model of an object, rotate it, view it from a variety of angles, and take two-dimensional "snap-shots" of the best views for inclusion in final printouts. Similarly, it's possible to "walk through" a 3-D environment that exists only in the computer's memory, printing snapshots that show the

Rules of Thumb Rules of Thumb Rules of Thumb Rules of Thumb

Creating Smart Art

Modern graphics software isn't just for professional artists. Just about anybody can use it to create pictures and presentations. Here are some guidelines to help you make the most of the computer as a graphic tool:

▶ **Reprogram yourself . . . relax.** For many of us the hardest part is getting started. We are all programmed by messages we received in our childhood, which for many of us included "You aren't creative" and "You can't draw." Fortunately, a computer can help us overcome this early programming and find the artist that's locked within us. Most drawing and painting programs are flexible, forgiving, and fun. Allow yourself to experiment; you'll be surprised at what you can create if you're patient and playful.

▶ **Choose the right tool for the job.** Is your artwork to be displayed on the computer screen or printed? Does your output device support color? Would color enhance the finished work? Your answers to these questions will help you determine which software and hardware tools are most appropriate. As you're thinking about options, don't rule out low-tech tools. The best approach may not involve a computer, or it may involve some combination of computer and nonelectronic tools.

▶ **Borrow from the best.** Art supply stores sell *clip art*—predrawn images that artists can legally cut out and paste into their own pictures or posters. Computer artists have hundreds of digital clip art collections to choose from, with a difference: Computer clip art images can be cut, pasted, and edited electronically. Some computer clip art collections are in the public domain (that is, they are free); others can be licensed for a small fee. Computer clip art comes in a variety of formats, and it ranges from simple line drawings to scanned color photographs. If you have access to a scanner, you can create your own digitized clip art from traditional photos and drawings.

▶ **Don't borrow without permission.** Computers, scanners, and digital cameras make it all too easy to create unauthorized copies of copyrighted photographs, drawings, and other images. There's a clear legal and ethical line between using public domain or licensed clip art and pirating copyrighted material. If you use somebody else's creative work, make sure you have written permission from the owner.

▶ **Protect your own work.** Copyright laws aren't just to protect other people's work. If you've created something that's marketable, consider copyrighting it. The process is easy and inexpensive, and it might help you to get credit (and payment) where credit is due. For more information, go to the U.S. Copyright Office Web Site: **http://lcweb.loc.gov/copyright/**

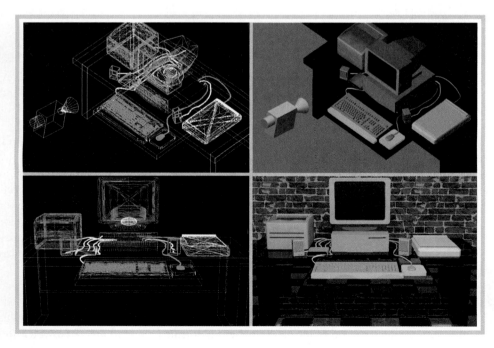

This personal computer system is a 3-D model created on a Macintosh using Strata Studio Pro 3-D modeling software. The images are shown in wireframe view; the ones on the right have been fully rendered to add surface textures.

Animated 3-D figures using technology from LifeFX can simulate human expressions for Internet communication.

simulated space from many points of view. For many applications, the goal is not a printout but an animated presentation on a computer screen or videotape. Animation software, presentation graphics software, and multimedia authoring software (all described later in this chapter) can display sequences of screens showing 3-D objects being rotated, explored, and transformed. Many modern television and movie special effects involve combinations of live action and simulated 3-D animation. Techniques pioneered in *Jurassic Park*, *Final Fantasy*, *Monsters, Inc.*, and other films continually push computer graphics to new levels of realism.

CAD/CAM: Turning Pictures into Products

Three-dimensional graphics also play an important role in the branch of engineering known as **computer-aided design** (CAD)—the use of computers to design products. CAD software allows engineers, designers, and architects to create designs onscreen for products ranging from computer chips to public buildings. Today's software goes far beyond basic drafting and object-oriented graphics. It allows users to create three-dimensional "solid" models with physical characteristics like weight, volume, and center of gravity. These models can be rotated and viewed from any angle. The computer can evaluate the structural performance of any part of the model by applying imaginary force to the object. Using CAD, an engineer can crash-test a new model of an automobile before it ever leaves the computer screen. CAD tends to be cheaper, faster, and more accurate than traditional design-by-hand techniques. What's more, the forgiving nature of the computer makes it easy to alter a design to meet project goals.

Engineers use CAD software to design everything from microscopic electronic circuits to massive structures.

Computer-aided design is often linked to **computer-aided manufacturing (CAM)**. When the design of a product is completed, the numbers are fed to a program that controls the manufacturing of parts. For electronic parts, the design translates directly into a template for etching circuits onto chips. The emergence of CAD/CAM has streamlined many design and manufacturing processes. The combination of CAD and CAM is often called **computer-integrated manufacturing (CIM)**; it's a major step toward a fully automated factory.

Presentation Graphics: Bringing Lectures to Life

One common application for computer graphics today is the creation of visual aids—slides, transparencies, graphics displays, and handouts—to enhance presentations. While drawing and painting programs can create these aids, they aren't as useful as programs designed with presentations in mind.

Presentation graphics software helps to automate the creation of visual aids for lectures, training sessions, sales demonstrations, and other presentations. Presentation graphics programs are most commonly used for creating and displaying a series of onscreen "slides" to serve as visual aids for presentations. Slides might include photographs, drawings, spreadsheet-style charts, or tables. These different graphical elements are usually integrated into a series of **bullet charts** that list the main points of a presentation. Slides can be output as 35mm color slides, overhead transparencies, or handouts. Presentation graphics programs can also display "slide shows" directly on computer monitors or LCD projectors, including animation and video clips along with still images. Some can convert presentations into Web pages automatically.

Because they can be used to create and display onscreen presentations with animated visual effects and video clips, presentation graphics programs, such as Microsoft's PowerPoint, are sometimes called *multimedia presentation tools*. These programs *do* make it easy for nonartists to combine text, graphics, and other media in simple multimedia presentations. But as you'll see,

Making Powerful Presentations

Presentation graphics programs such as PowerPoint make it easy to create dynamic, lively presentations. They also make it easy to create ugly, boring presentations. These suggestions will help you to ensure that your presentations aren't snoozers.

▶ **Remember your goal.** Know what you're trying to communicate. Keep your goal in mind throughout the process of creating the presentation.

▶ **Remember your audience.** How much do they know about your topic? How much do they need to know? Do key terms need to be defined?

▶ **Outline your ideas.** If you can't express your plan in a clear, concise outline, you probably won't be able to create a clear, concise presentation. Once your outline is done, you can import it into your presentation graphics software and massage it into a presentation.

▶ **Be stingy with words.** Avoid big words, long sentences, complex lists, and tiny type. Keep your prose lively and to the point.

▶ **Keep it simple.** Avoid useless decorations and distractions. Avoid fancy borders and backgrounds.

▶ **Use a consistent design.** Make sure all of your slides look like they belong together. Use the same fonts, backgrounds, and colors throughout your presentation. If you don't trust your design skills, use predesigned templates.

▶ **Be smart with art.** Don't clutter your presentation with random clip art. Make sure each illustration contributes to your message. Use simple data graphs if they can support your main points. When you do use clip art or illustrations, make sure they coordinate with the colors and design of the rest of the presentation.

▶ **Keep each slide focused.** Each screen should convey one idea clearly, possibly with a few concise supporting points.

▶ **Tell them what you're going to tell them, then tell them, then tell them what you told them.** It's the speechmaker's fundamental rule, and it applies to presentations, too.

true multimedia authoring tools are more flexible and powerful than are basic slide presentation programs.

We now turn our attention to several types of media that go beyond the limitations of the printed page or the static screen; then we look at how *multimedia authoring* software can combine these diverse media types to produce dynamic, interactive documents.

Dynamic Media: Beyond the Printed Page

Most PC applications—painting and drawing programs, word processors, desktop publishers, and so on—are designed to produce paper documents. But many types of modern media can't be reduced to pixels on printouts because they contain dynamic information—information that changes over time or in response to user input. Today's multimedia computers enable us to create and edit animated sequences, video clips, sound, and music along with text and graphics. Just as words and pictures serve as the raw materials for desktop publishing, dynamic media like animation, video, audio, and hypertext are important components of interactive multimedia projects.

> The world is **complex, dynamic, multidimensional;** the paper is static, flat. How are we to represent the **rich visual world** of experience and measurement on mere **flatland**?
> —Edward R. Tufte, in *Envisioning Information*

Animation: Graphics in Time

Creating motion from still pictures—this illusion is at the heart of all **animation**. Before computers, animated films were hand-drawn, one still picture, or **frame**, at a time. Modern computer graphics technology

> We're on the threshold of a moment in cinematic history that is unparalleled. **Anything** you can **imagine** can be done. If you can draw it, if you can describe it, **we can do it.** It's just a matter of cost.
> —James Cameron, Filmmaker

Creating Presentation Graphics

SOFTWARE: *Microsoft PowerPoint.*

THE GOAL: *To create visual aids for a talk you're giving for a class. You'll use PowerPoint, a presentation graphics package that's especially designed for this kind of task.*

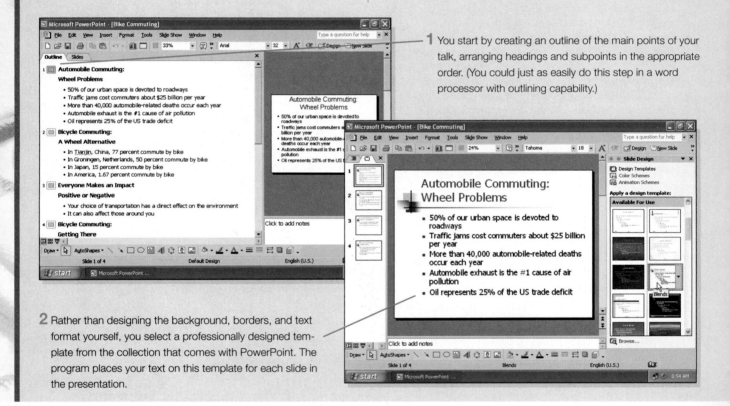

1 You start by creating an outline of the main points of your talk, arranging headings and subpoints in the appropriate order. (You could just as easily do this step in a word processor with outlining capability.)

2 Rather than designing the background, borders, and text format yourself, you select a professionally designed template from the collection that comes with PowerPoint. The program places your text on this template for each slide in the presentation.

has transformed both amateur and professional animation by enabling the automation of many of the most tedious aspects of the animation process.

In its simplest form, computer-based animation is similar to traditional frame-by-frame animation techniques; each frame is a computer-drawn picture, and the computer displays those frames in rapid succession. But computer animation programs, even the low-priced packages aimed at the home market, contain software tools that can do much more than flip pages. They can take much of the tedium out of animation by automating repetitive processes. Instead of drawing every frame by hand, an animator can create key frames and objects and use software to help fill in the gaps—a process known as *tweening*. The most powerful animation programs include tools for working with animated objects in three dimensions, adding depth to the scene on the screen.

Computer animation has become commonplace in everything from television commercials to feature films. Sometimes computer animation is combined with live-action film; Steven Spielberg's *AI* and George Lucas's recent *Star Wars* episodes rely heavily on computer animation

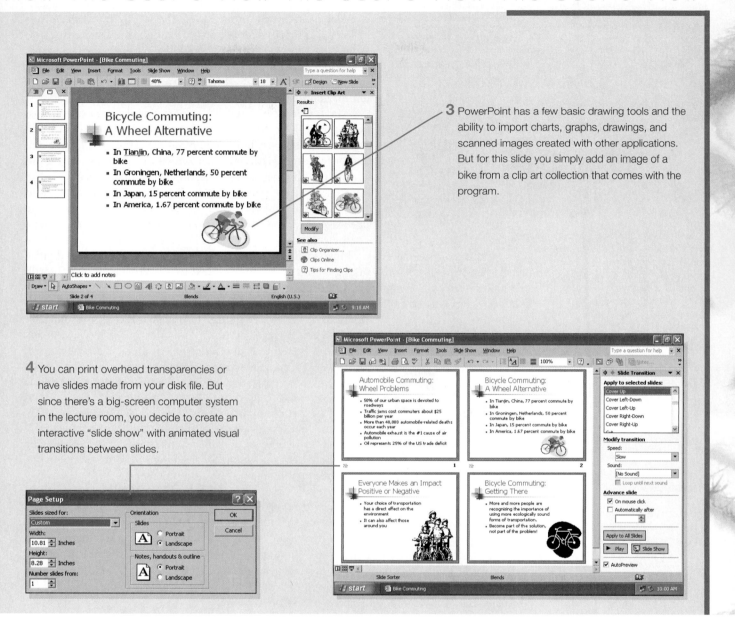

3 PowerPoint has a few basic drawing tools and the ability to import charts, graphs, drawings, and scanned images created with other applications. But for this slide you simply add an image of a bike from a clip art collection that comes with the program.

4 You can print overhead transparencies or have slides made from your disk file. But since there's a big-screen computer system in the lecture room, you decide to create an interactive "slide show" with animated visual transitions between slides.

to enhance reality. Other films, including *Toy Story*, *Shrek*, and *Monsters, Inc.*, use computer animation to create every character, scene, and event, leaving only the soundtrack for live actors and musicians to create.

Desktop Video: Computers, Film, and TV

There's more to the **digital video** revolution than computer animation. Computers can be used to edit video, splice scenes, add transitions, create titles, and do other tasks in a fraction of the time—and at a fraction of the cost—of precomputer techniques. The only requirement is that the video be in a digital form so the computer can treat it as data.

> **Digital technology** is the same **revolution** as adding **sound** to pictures and the same **revolution** as adding **color** to pictures. Nothing more and nothing less.
> —George Lucas, Filmmaker

Macromedia's Director is a popular multi-media program with powerful animation capabilities. The frames in the Cast window (below) show several different views of an object as it moves through the time-line shown in the Score window (below).

Digital video image

Video camera

Video can be easily transferred from a tape in a video camera to a computer's memory. If the camcorder is digital, the video data can be copied through FireWire cable. If the camcorder is analog, the tape signals must be converted to digital data by a digitizer.

Analog and Digital Video

Conventional television and video images are stored and broadcast as analog (smooth) electronic waves. A **video digitizer** can convert analog video signals from a television broadcast or videotape into digital data. Most video digitizers must be installed as add-on cards or external devices that plug into serial or USB ports. Broadcast-quality digitizers are relatively expensive; low-cost models are available for hobbyists who can settle for less-than-perfect images.

Many video digitizers can import signals from televisions, videotapes, video cameras, and other sources and display them on the computer's screen in *real time*—at the same time they're created or imported. The computer screen can serve as a television screen or, with a network connection, a viewing screen for a live video teleconference. For many applications, it's not important to display digitized images in real time; the goal is to capture entire video sequences and convert them into digital "movies" that can be stored, edited, and played on computer screens without external video equipment.

Video professionals and hobbyists who use *digital video cameras* don't need to digitize their video footage before working with it in a computer, because it's already in digital form. Digital video cameras capture and store all video footage as digital data. Most digital video cameras have FireWire (IEEE 1394) ports (see Chapter 3, "Hardware Basics: Peripherals") that can be used to copy raw video footage from tape to a computer and later copy the edited video back from computer to tape. Because digital video can be reduced to a series of numbers, it can be copied, edited, stored, and played back without any loss of quality. Digital video will soon replace analog video for most applications.

Video Production Goes Digital

A typical video project starts with an outline and a simple *story-board* describing the action, dialog, and music in each scene. The storyboard serves as a guide for shooting and editing scenes.

Today most video editing is done using *nonlinear editing* technology. For nonlinear editing, video and audio clips are stored in digital form on a computer's hard disk. These digital clips can be organized, rearranged, enhanced, and combined using onscreen tools and commands. Nonlinear editing is faster and easier than older editing techniques, and it allows filmmakers to do things that aren't possible without computers. Video editing makes massive storage and memory demands on a computer. Until recently, nonlinear editing technology was only available to professionals. But falling hardware prices and technological advances make it possible for hobbyists to edit video with inexpensive desktop machines.

Video editing software (such as Adobe Premiere, Adobe After Effects, and Apple iMovie) makes it easy to eliminate extraneous footage, combine clips from multiple takes into coherent scenes, splice together scenes, insert visual transitions, superimpose titles, synchronize a soundtrack, and create special effects. Editing software can combine live action with computer animation. Software can also create **morphs**—video clips in which one image metamorphoses into another. Photoshop-style tools allow artists to, for example, paint one or two frames with a green polka-dotted sky and then have those painting effects automatically applied to the other frames.

After it's edited, the video clip can be "printed" on a videotape. The process is simplest and most effective in an all-digital system using FireWire and a digital camcorder. Systems that use inexpensive digitizers may not be able to produce satisfactory videotapes. With a DVD-R drive and software such as Apple's iDVD, video footage can be pressed onto a DVD, complete with menus and special features not available on tape.

Edited video doesn't need to be exported to tape or DVD. Many digital clips end up in multimedia presentations. Onscreen digital movies can add realism and excitement to educational, training, presentation, and entertainment software. Video clips are also common on the Web. System extensions such as Apple's cross-platform QuickTime make it possible for any multimedia-capable computer to display digital video clips without additional hardware.

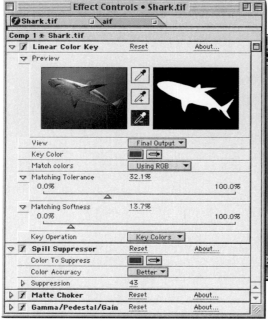

Software can turn a desktop or laptop computer into a video editing and production machine. Video professionals use programs like Apple's Final Cut Pro (top) and Adobe's After Effects (center) to edit video footage and add special effects. Apple's iMovie and iDVD (bottom) are designed to make nonlinear video editing and DVD production simple and intuitive for non-professionals.

7.1

Data Compression

A full-screen 256-color photograph or painting takes about a megabyte of storage—the same as the complete text from a typical paperback book! Graphic images, digital video, and sound files can consume massive amounts of storage space on disk and in memory; they can also be slow to transmit over computer networks. Data compression technology allows large files to be temporarily squeezed so they take less storage space and network transmission time. Before they can be used, compressed files must be decompressed. (In the physical world, many companies "compress" goods to

save storage and transportation costs: When you "just add water" to a can of concentrated orange juice, you're "decompressing" the juice.)

All forms of compression involve removing bits; the trick is to remove bits that can be replaced when the file can be restored. Different compression techniques work best for different types of data.

Suppose you want to store or transmit a large text file. Your text compression software might follow steps similar to those shown here:

1 Each character in the uncompressed ASCII file occupies 8 bits; a seven-character word—invoice, for example—requires 56 bits of storage.

i n v o i c e

(space) p a y a b l e

2 A 2-byte binary number can contain code values ranging from 0 to 65,535—enough codes to stand for every commonly used word in English. This partial code dictionary shows the code values for a few words, including invoice and payable.

Portion of a dictionary		
A	○○○○○○○○	○○○○○○○●
a	○○○○○○○○	○○○○○○●○
aback	○○○○○○○○	○○○○○○●●
abacus	○○○○○○○○	○○○○○●○○
. . .		
invoice	○○●○○●○●	○○●●●○○●
invoiced	○○●○○●●○	○○●●●○●○
invoke	○○●○○●●●	○○●●●○●●
. . .		
pay	○●○○●○●●	●○●○○○●○
payable	○●○○●●○○	●○●○○○●●
. . .		
zygote	●●●●●●●○	●●●●●●●●

3 To compress a file using a code dictionary, the computer looks up every word in the original file; in this example, invoice and payable. It replaces each word with its 2-byte code value. In this example they are % 9 and V ú. The seven-character word now takes up only 16 bits—less than one-third of its original size.

4 In a compressed file, these 2-byte code values would be used to store or transmit the information for invoice and payable, using fewer bits of information either to increase storage capacity or to decrease transmission time.

%   9   V   ú

5 To reverse the process of compression, the same dictionary (or an identical one on another computer) is used to decompress the file, creating an exact copy of the original. All the tedious dictionary lookup is performed quickly by a computer program.

Compression programs usually work on patterns of bits rather than English words. One type of digital video compression stores values for pixels that change from one frame to the next; there's no need to repeatedly store values for pixels that are the same in every frame. For example, the only pixels that change in these two pictures are the ones that represent the unicycle and the shadows.

*In general, compression works because most raw data files contain redundancy that can be "squeezed out." **Lossless compression** systems allow a file to be compressed and later decompressed without any loss of data; the decompressed file will be an identical copy of the original file. Popular lossless compression systems include ZIP/PKZIP (DOS/Windows), StuffIt (Macintosh), tar (UNIX), and GIF (general graphics). A **lossy compression** system can usually achieve better compression than a lossless one but*

may lose some information in the process; the decompressed file isn't always identical to the original. This is tolerable in many types of sound, graphics, and video files but not for most program and data files. JPEG is a popular lossy compression system for graphics files.

*MPEG is a popular compression system for digital video. An MPEG file takes just a fraction of the space of an uncompressed video file. Because decompression programs demand time and processing power, playback of compressed video files can sometimes be jerky or slow. Some computers get around the problem with MPEG hardware boards that specialize in compression and decompression, leaving the CPU free for other tasks. **Hardware compression** is likely to be built into most computers as multimedia becomes more commonplace.*

The original photographic image (above) is clear with an uncompressed size of 725 KB. The image on the right shows the visible lossy effect of aggressive JPEG compression. But the size of the compressed file is only 19 KB.

Many CD-ROMs combine digital video with animation and interactivity. In Steven Speilberg's Survivors: Testimonies of the Holocaust, *four Holocaust survivors tell their stories in illustrated video presentations that emphasize the importance of tolerance in everyday life.*

Many Web sites deliver streaming video content to viewers with fast Internet connections.

Data Compression

Digital movies can make heavy hardware demands; even a short full-screen video clip can quickly fill a large hard disk or CD-ROM. To save storage space and allow the processor to keep up with the quickly changing frames, digital movies designed for the Web or CD-ROM are often displayed in small windows with fewer than the standard video rate of 30 frames per second. In addition, data **compression** software and hardware squeezes data out of movies so they can be stored in smaller spaces, usually with a slight loss of image quality. General data compression software can be used to reduce the size of almost any kind of data file; specialized *image compression software* is generally used to compress graphics and video files. System extensions, such as QuickTime and Windows Media Player, include several common software compression schemes. But the best compression schemes involve specialized hardware as well as software.

Even highly compressed video clips gobble up storage space quickly. As compression and storage technologies continue to improve, digital movies will become larger, longer, smoother, and more common in everyday computing applications. In fact, compression hardware may soon become standard equipment in multimedia computers.

Professionals in the motion picture, television, and video industries create their products using graphics workstations that cost hundreds of thousands of dollars. Today it's possible to put together a Windows- or Macintosh-based system that can perform most of the same functions for a fraction of the cost. These systems might not meet all of Steven Spielberg's needs, but they satisfy thousands of individuals, schools, and small businesses with smaller budgets. Low-cost systems will transform the film and video industry in the same way that desktop publishing has revolutionized the world of the printed word.

The Synthetic Musician: Computers and Audio

It's **easy** to play any musical instrument: all you have to do is **touch** the right key at the right time and **the instrument will play itself**.

—J. S. Bach

Sound and music can turn a visual presentation into an activity that involves the ears, the eyes, and the whole brain. For many applications, sound puts the *multi* in *multimedia*. Computer sounds can be digitized—digitally recorded—or **synthesized**—synthetically generated. Windows PCs (using sound cards; see Chapter 3, "Hardware Basics: Peripherals") and

Macintoshes (which have sound hardware already built in) can produce sounds that go far beyond the basic beeps of early computers; most of them can also digitize sounds.

Digitized Sounds as Computer Data

Any sound that can be recorded can be captured with an **audio digitizer** and stored as a data file on a disk. Digitized sound data, like other computer data, can be loaded into the computer's memory and manipulated by software. Sound-editing software can change a sound's volume and pitch, add special effects such as echoes, remove extraneous noises, and even rearrange musical passages. Sound data is sometimes called *waveform audio* because this kind of editing often involves manipulating a visual image of the sound's waveform. To play a digitized sound, the computer must load the data file into memory, convert it to an analog sound, and play it through a speaker.

Recorded sound can consume massive amounts of space on disk and in memory. As you might expect, higher quality sound reproduction generally requires more memory. The difference is due in part to differences in *sampling rate*—the number of sound "snapshots" the recording equipment takes each second. A higher sampling rate produces more realistic digital sounds in the same way that higher resolution produces more realistic digital photographs—it allows for more accurate modeling of the analog source. The number of bits per sample, usually 8 or 16, also affects the quality of the sound; this is similar to a digital photograph's bit depth.

Music is digitized on audio CDs at a high sampling rate and bit depth—high enough that it's hard to tell the difference between the original analog sound and the final digital recording. But CD audio is memory intensive; a 3-minute song takes about 30 megabytes of space on a compact disc. Files that large are expensive to store and slow to transmit through networks. That's why most computer sound files are recorded at a lower sampling rate and bit depth—and therefore don't have the sound quality of an audio CD recording. Sound data compression, like image compression, can make a file even smaller.

Until recently, high-quality sounds required large files, and compact files compromised quality. But a relatively new method of compression called **MP3** (for MPEG Audio Layer 3) can squeeze a music file to a fraction of its original CD-file size with only a slight loss of quality. MP3 makes it practical to transmit songs and other recordings through the Internet, store them on hard disks, and play them on pocket-sized devices without disk or tape. MP3 files are available for free on hundreds of Web sites. Many are contributed by undiscovered musicians who want exposure; others are copied from copyrighted CDs and distributed illegally. Ethical and legal issues raised by MP3 will be discussed in more detail in Chapter 11, "From Internet to Information Infrastructure," and Chapter 12, "Computer Security and Risks."

You can edit Waveform audio files in a variety of ways using software tools such as Peak, from Bias, Inc. Here a section of a musical recording has been selected so that it can be copied and pasted elsewhere in the recording.

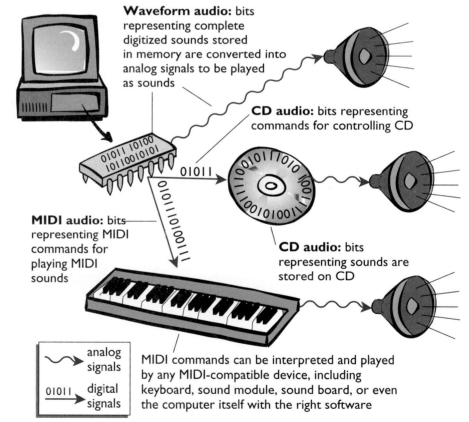

Waveform audio: bits representing complete digitized sounds stored in memory are converted into analog signals to be played as sounds

CD audio: bits representing commands for controlling CD

MIDI audio: bits representing MIDI commands for playing MIDI sounds

CD audio: bits representing sounds are stored on CD

analog signals

digital signals

MIDI commands can be interpreted and played by any MIDI-compatible device, including keyboard, sound module, sound board, or even the computer itself with the right software

Computers can generate sound using waveform digital audio, CD audio, or MIDI audio.

In the modern music studio, computer keyboards and music keyboards often sit side by side.

CD Audio and MIDI: Sounds on Command

A computer can also play sounds from standard audio CDs using a CD-ROM or DVD-ROM drive connected to headphones or amplified speakers. Sounds are stored on CDs, not in the computer's memory. When the sounds are stored on CDs, software needs to contain only *commands* telling the drive what to play and when to play it.

Multimedia computers can also control a variety of electronic musical instruments and sound sources using MIDI (Musical Instrument Digital Interface)—a standard interface that allows electronic instruments and computers, regardless of type or brand, to communicate with each other and work together. In the same way that PostScript is the common language of desktop publishing hardware, MIDI is the universal language of electronic music hardware. MIDI is used to send commands to instruments and sound sources—commands that, in effect, say "play this sound at this pitch and this volume for this amount of time. . . ."

MIDI commands can be interpreted by a variety of music *synthesizers* (electronic instruments that synthesize sounds using mathematical formulas), *samplers* (instruments that can digitize, or sample, audio sounds, turn them into notes, and play them back at any pitch), and hybrid instruments that play sounds that are part sampled and part synthesized. But most multimedia PCs can also interpret and execute MIDI commands using sounds built into their sound cards or stored in software form. Whether the sounds are played back on external instruments or internal devices, the computer doesn't need to store the entire recording in memory or on disk; it just has to store commands to play the notes in the proper sequence. A MIDI file containing the MIDI messages for a song or soundtrack requires only a few kilobytes of memory.

Nonmusicians can use ready-to-play *clip music* MIDI files for multimedia productions. But anyone with even marginal piano-playing skills and sequencing software can create MIDI music files. Sequencing software turns a computer into a musical composition, recording, and editing machine. The computer records MIDI signals as a musician plays each part on a keyboard. The musician can use the computer to layer instrumental tracks, substitute instrument sounds, edit notes, cut and paste passages, transpose keys, and change tempos, listening to each change as it's made. The finished composition can be played by the sequencing software or exported to any other MIDI-compatible software, including a variety of multimedia applications.

With the appropriate software a computer can be used as an aid for composing, recording, performing, music publishing, and music education. Just as computer graphics technology has changed the way many artists work, electronic music technology has transformed the world of the musician. What's more, computer music technology has the power to unleash the musician in the rest of us.

Hypertext and Hypermedia

> Human Beings are naturally predisposed **to hear, to remember, and to tell stories**. The **problem**—for teachers, parents, government leaders, friends, and **computers**—is to have **more interesting stories** to tell.
>
> —Roger Schank et al, in *Tell Me a Story: Narrative and Intelligence*

Word processors, drawing programs, and most other applications today are WYSIWYG—what you see (on the screen) is what you get (on the printed page). But as Doug Engelbart has demonstrated for decades, WYSIWYG isn't always necessary or desirable. If a document doesn't need to be printed, it doesn't need to be structured like a paper document. If we want to focus on the relationship of ideas rather than the layout of the page, we may be better off with another kind of document—a dynamic, cross-referenced super document that takes full advantage of the computer's interactive capabilities.

Since 1945 when President Roosevelt's science advisor, Vannevar Bush, first wrote about such an interactive cross-referenced system, computer pioneers like Doug Engelbart and Ted Nelson (who coined the term "hypertext") pushed the technology toward that vision. Early efforts were called **hypertext** because they allowed textual information to be linked in *nonsequential* ways. Conventional text media like books are linear, or *sequential*: They are designed to be read from beginning to end. A hypertext document contains *links* that can lead readers quickly to other parts of the document or to other related documents. Hypertext invites readers to cut their own personal trails through information.

Hypertext first gained widespread public attention in 1987, when Apple introduced HyperCard, a **hypermedia** system that could combine text, numbers, graphics, animation, sound effects, music, and other media in hyperlinked documents. (Depending on how it's used, the term *hypermedia* might be synonymous with *interactive multimedia*.) Today millions of Windows and Macintosh users routinely use hypertext whenever they consult online Help files. But the biggest hotbed of hypertext/hypermedia activity is the World Wide Web. Hypertext on the Web enables readers to jump between documents all over the Internet.

But in spite of its popularity hypertext isn't likely to replace paper books any time soon. Web users and others who use hypertext have several legitimate complaints:

Music publishing software can turn a MIDI file into a musical score ready for publishing. For many musicians and publishers, this kind of software has eliminated the tedious and error-prone process of transcribing musical scores by hand. (Software: Overture from Cakewalk.)

▶ Hypermedia documents can be disorienting and leave readers wondering what they've missed. When you're reading a book, you always know where you are and where you've been in the text. That's not necessarily true in hypermedia.

▶ Hypermedia documents don't always have the links readers want. Hypermedia authors can't build every possible connection into their documents, so some readers are frustrated because they can't easily get "there" from "here."

▶ Hypermedia documents don't encourage scribbled margin notes, highlighting, or turned page corners for marking key passages. Some hypermedia documents provide controls for making "bookmarks" and text fields for adding personal notes, but they aren't as friendly and flexible as traditional paper markup tools.

▶ Hypermedia hardware can be hard on humans. Most people find that reading a computer screen is more tiring than reading printed pages. Many complain that extended periods of screen-gazing cause eyestrain, headache, backache, and other ailments. It's not always easy to stretch out under a tree or curl up in an easy chair with a Web-linked computer.

▶ The art of hypermedia is still in its infancy. Every new art form takes time to develop. How can writers develop effective plot lines if they don't know what path their readers will choose through their stories? This is just one of the hundreds of questions with which hypermedia authors are struggling.

Some music applications enable nonmusicians to exercise their musical creativity. Mixman Studio simulates DJ turntables, allowing users to create real-time dance music from digital samples.

Still, hypermedia is not all hype. As the art matures, advances in software and hardware design will take care of many of these problems. Even today hypermedia documents provide extensive cross-referencing, flexibility, and instant keyword searches that simply aren't possible with paper media.

Interactive Multimedia:
Eye, Ear, Hand, and Mind

> The hybrid or the meeting of two media is **a moment of truth and revelation** from which a **new form** is born.
>
> —Marshall McLuhan, in *Understanding Media; The Extensions of Man*

We live in a world rich in sensory experience. Information comes to us in a variety of forms: pictures, text, moving images, music, voice, and more. As information-processing machines, computers are capable of delivering information to our senses in many forms. Until recently, computer users could work with only one or two forms of information at a time. Today's multimedia computers allow users to work with information-rich documents that intermix a variety of audiovisual media.

Interactive Multimedia: What Is It?

The term **multimedia** generally means using some combination of text, graphics, animation, video, music, voice, and sound effects to communicate. By this definition an episode of *Sesame Street* or the evening news might be considered multimedia. In fact, computer-based multimedia tools are used heavily in the production of *Sesame Street*, the evening news, and hundreds of other television programs. Entertainment industry professionals use computers to create animated sequences, display titles, construct special video effects, synthesize music, edit sound

Interactivity and multiplicity: the two dimensions of multimedia.

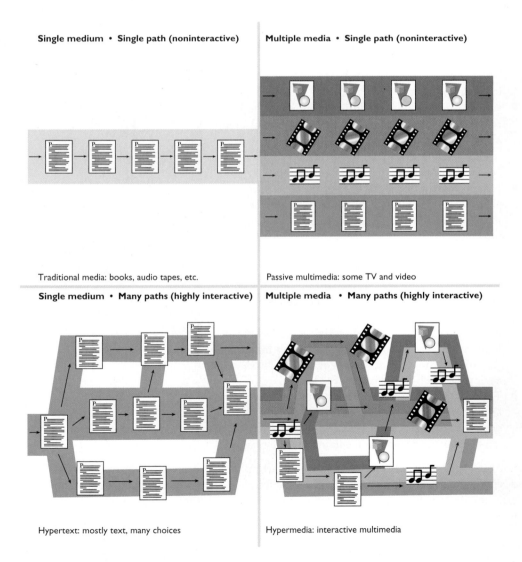

Single medium • Single path (noninteractive)

Multiple media • Single path (noninteractive)

Traditional media: books, audio tapes, etc.

Passive multimedia: some TV and video

Single medium • Many paths (highly interactive)

Multiple media • Many paths (highly interactive)

Hypertext: mostly text, many choices

Hypermedia: interactive multimedia

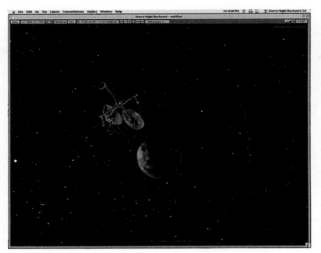

Interactive multimedia CD-ROMs and DVDs can combine education with entertainment. For example, Starry Night Backyard from Sienna turns a computer into a virtual planetarium.

tracks, coordinate communication, and perform dozens of other tasks crucial to the production of modern television programs and motion pictures.

So when you watch a typical TV program, you're experiencing a multimedia product. With each second that passes, you are bombarded with millions of bits of information. But television and video are *passive media*—they pour information into our eyes and ears while we sit and take it all in. We have no control over the information flow. Modern computer technology allows information to move in both directions, turning multimedia into **interactive multimedia**. Unlike TV, radio, and video, interactive multimedia allow the viewer/listener to take an active part in the experience. The best interactive multimedia software puts the user in charge, allowing that person to control the information flow.

Interactive multimedia software is delivered to consumers on a variety of platforms. Multimedia computers—Macintosh and Windows machines with fast processors, large memories, CD-ROM or DVD-ROM drives, speakers, and sound cards—are everywhere. Thousands of education and entertainment multimedia programs are available on CD-ROM and DVD-ROM for these machines. Many more multimedia software titles are designed to be used with television sets and controlled by game machines and other *set-top boxes* from Nintendo, Sony, Microsoft, and other companies. Many multimedia documents are created for use in kiosks in stores, museums, and other public places. A typical multimedia kiosk is a PC-in-a-box with a touch screen instead of a keyboard and mouse for input.

Interactive multimedia materials are all over the Web, too. But multimedia on the Web today is full of compromises, because today's Web pipelines can't deliver large media files quickly enough. Still, Web technology is improving rapidly, making many experts wonder whether disk-based multimedia will eventually be unnecessary.

Multimedia Authoring: Making Mixed Media

Multimedia authoring software is used to create and edit multimedia documents. Like desktop publishing, interactive multimedia authoring involves combining source documents—including graphics, text files, video clips, and sounds—in an aesthetically pleasing format that communicates with the user. Multimedia authoring software, like page layout software, serves as glue that binds documents created and captured with other applications. But since a multimedia document can change in response to user input, authoring involves specifying not just *what?* and *where?* but also *when?* and *why?* Some authoring programs are designed for professionals. Others are designed for children. Many are used by both.

> **Style** used to be an interaction between **the human soul** and **tools** that were **limiting**. In the digital era, it will have to come from **the soul alone**.
>
> —Jaron Lanier, virtual reality pioneer

Some authoring programs, including HyperStudio and MetaCard, use the card-and-stack user interface originally introduced with Apple's HyperCard. According to this metaphor, a multimedia document is a stack of cards. Each screen, called a card, can contain graphics, text, and **buttons**—"hot spots" that respond to mouse clicks. Buttons can be programmed to transport

Making Interactive Multimedia Work

Whether you're creating a simple presentation or a full-blown multimedia extravaganza, your finished product will communicate more effectively if you follow a few simple guidelines:

▶ **Be consistent.** Group similar controls together, and keep a consistent visual appearance throughout the presentation.

▶ **Make it intuitive.** Use graphical metaphors to guide viewers, and make your controls do what they look like they should do.

▶ **Strive for simplicity.** A clean, uncluttered screen is more inviting than a crowded one—and easier to understand, too.

▶ **Keep it lively.** If your presentation doesn't include motion, sound, and user interaction, it probably should be printed and distributed as a paper.

▶ **The message is more important than the media.** Your goal is to communicate information, not saturate the senses. Don't let the bells and whistles get in the way of your message.

▶ **Put the user in the driver's seat.** Include controls for turning down sound, bypassing repetitive animation, and turning off annoying features. Provide navigation aids, search tools, bookmarks, online help, and "Where am I?" feedback. Never tell the user "You can't get there from here."

▶ **Let real people test your presentation.** The best way to find out if your presentation works is to test it on people who aren't familiar with the subject. If they get lost or bored or lost, find out why, fix the problem, and test it again.

---

the user to another card, play music, open dialog boxes, launch other applications, rearrange information, perform menu operations, send messages to hardware devices, or do other things. Some authoring programs, including ToolBook, use a similar user interface with a book-and-page metaphor: A book replaces the stack and a page replaces the card. The World Wide Web uses metaphorical pages to represent screens of information; many authoring tools are designed specifically to create Web pages. The most widely used professional multimedia authoring tool, Macromedia's Director, has a different kind of user interface. A Director document is a *movie* rather than a stack of cards or a book of pages. A button can transport a user to another frame of a movie rather than another card or page. Macromedia Flash, a popular tool for adding multimedia to the Web, is based on an interface similar to Director's. Some authoring tools, such as Authorware, use flowcharts as tools for constructing documents.

The authoring tool's interface metaphor is important to the person creating the multimedia document, but not to the person viewing the finished document, who sees only the user interface that was built into the document by the author. When you're using a well-designed multimedia document, you can't tell whether it was created by Director, Authorware, ToolBook, or another authoring tool.

With the growing interest in the Internet, many people expect the Web to replace CD-ROMs for most multimedia delivery. Most multimedia authoring tools can create Web-ready multimedia documents. For example, documents created by Authorware and Director can

Multimedia authoring software glues together media captured and created with other applications.

be converted into Web documents using Macromedia's Shockwave technology. Shockwave software compresses multimedia documents so they can appear and respond more quickly on the Web. But even with compression, the Internet isn't fast enough to deliver the high-quality audio and video that's possible with CD-ROM and DVD-ROM. On the other hand, the contents of a disk are static; they can't be continually updated like a Web site. And CD-ROMs don't offer opportunities for communication with other people the way a Web site can. Many multimedia manufacturers today produce *hybrid disks*—media-rich CD-ROMs and DVD-ROMs that automatically draw content and communication from the Web. Hybrid disks hint at the types of multimedia experiences that will be possible without disks through tomorrow's faster Internet.

Multimedia authoring software today puts a great deal of power into the hands of computer users, but it doesn't solve all of the technical problems in this new art form. Many of the problems with hypertext and hypermedia outlined earlier are even more serious when multiple media are involved. What's more, current technology hasn't lived up to the hype; multimedia consumers spend far too much time installing, loading, and waiting, and the results often aren't worth the wait. Still, the best multimedia productions transcend these problems and show the promise of this emerging technology.

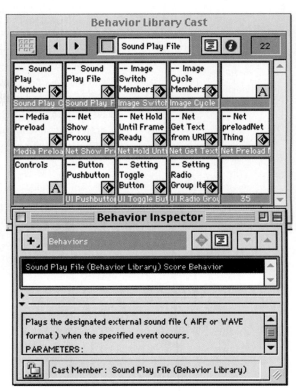

Multimedia authoring involves programming objects on the screen to react, or behave, in particular ways under particular circumstances. Macromedia's Director, the most popular cross-platform multimedia authoring tool, includes prewritten behaviors that can be attached to buttons, images, or other onscreen objects. These behaviors make it possible to create sophisticated multimedia documents without actually writing scripts or programs.

Interactive Media: Visions of the Future

> For most of recorded history, the **interactions** of humans with their media have been **primarily passive** in the sense that marks on paper, paint on walls, even motion pictures and television, **do not change** in response to the viewer's wishes. [But computers can] **respond** to queries and experiments—so that the message may involve the learner in a **two-way conversation**.
>
> —Alan Kay

For hundreds of thousands of years, two-way interactive communication was the norm: One person talked, another responded. Today television, radio, newspapers, magazines, and books pour information into billions of passive people every day. For many people one-way passive communication has become more common than interactive discourse.

According to many experts, interactive multimedia technology offers new hope for turning communication back into a participatory sport. With interactive multimedia software the audience is a part of the show. Interactive multimedia tools can give people control over the media—control traditionally reserved for professional artists, filmmakers, and musicians. The possibilities are far-reaching, especially when telecommunication enters the picture. Consider these snapshots from a not-too-distant future:

▶ Instead of watching your history professor flip through overhead transparencies, you control a self-paced interactive presentation complete with video footage illustrating key concepts.

▶ In your electronic mailbox you find a "letter" from your sister. The letter shows her performing all of the instrumental parts for a song she composed, followed by a request for you to add a vocal line.

▶ Your favorite TV show is an interactive thriller that allows you to control the plot twists and work with the main characters to solve mysteries.

▶ While working on a biology project in the field, you come across an unusual bird with a song you don't recognize. Using a pocket-sized digital device, you record some audio/video footage of the bird as it sings. Using the same device, you dial your project partner's phone number and send the footage directly to her computer for editing and analysis.

▶ You share your concerns about a proposed factory in your hometown at the televised electronic town meeting. Thousands of others respond to questions from the mayor by pressing buttons on their remote control panels. The overwhelming citizen response forces the city council to reconsider the proposal.

204 Part 2   Using Computers

Of course, the future of interactive multimedia may not be all sunshine and roses. Many experts fear that these exciting new media possibilities will further remove us from books, other people, and the natural world around us. If television today can mesmerize so many people, will tomorrow's interactive multimedia TVs cause even more serious addiction problems? Or will interactive communication breathe new life into the media and the people who use them? Will interactive electronic media make it easier for abusers of power to influence and control unwary citizens, or will the power of the push button create a new kind of digital democracy? Will interactive digital technology just turn "sound bites" into "sound bytes," or will it unleash the creative potential in the people who use it? For answers, stay tuned.

Digital Revolution in Retrospect

Bruce Sterling

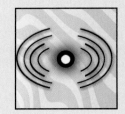

Bruce Sterling is well known for his dark, thoughtful science fiction works about the impact of technology and bureaucracy on our future. But Sterling is more than a cyberpunk writer. In this essay, written for the 50th anniversary of the Association for Computing Machinery, and published in the anniversary issue of Communications of the ACM, Sterling points out one of the hidden problems of modern computer and multimedia technology. If we're putting our creative works in digital form on the Web and CD-ROMs, how can we be sure that anyone will be able to experience them in the future?

After 50 years of the ACM, it's clear that computers have become history. We now live in the Information Age. This is a lovely situation, but it won't last. We're extremely good at transforming "ages" into mere history now—the Radio Age, the Aviation Age, the Atomic Age, the Space Age . . . all of these so called "ages" are history. Soon our much-trumpeted "Information Age" will have that same archaic ring.

The Information Age has accomplished great work during its span on the historical stage, dissolving jobs, transforming industries, frenetically building and destroying great fortunes. Computers have revolutionized the working lives of doctors and artists and clerks, generals and engineers, and politicians. It's delightful to look back and realize how little harm has been done by this transformative tide of computers. By comparison to other ages, we've been lucky. After 50 years of development of the Aviation Age, the Luftwaffe had blitzed London, and Dresden was a giant firestorm. For its part, the so-called Atomic Age never even began to live up to its hype (thank goodness). The Information Age has been much gentler with us. We may dare to hope that trend continues.

The Information Age doesn't always keep its promises—what age ever does?—but computers do change things. The extent and the rate of this quiet immolation have been enormous. The victims of obsolescence are sadly little recognized. In fact, many victims don't even know yet that they're victims. The World-Wide Web has become the great pop hit of late '90s global culture, but there are no formal archives anywhere for the Web. In five years, there will probably be no way to access a contemporary Web page, and in 50 years, the very idea of a "Web page" will seem as arcane as a magic-lantern slide.

There are few archives for computer-generated texts, programs, computer art, or computer-generated cultural activity of any kind. Almost every manifestation of what we call "new media" would be much better described as "temporary media." None of it has any place to hide, no zone of safety from the searing pace of innovation. Everything done by, through, or with a computer is desperately vulnerable.

Computers swallow whatever they can touch, and everything they swallow is forced to become as unstable as they are. With the soaring and brutal progress of Moore's Law, computer systems have become a series of ever-faster, ever more complex, and ever more elaborate coffins.

In the 1990s, we produce computers that are high-tech sarcophagi with the working life span of hamsters. The contemporary computer industry has the production values, and the promotional values, and even the investment structure of the couture industry. This may be why computers are the first truly arcane technology that has become deeply and genuinely glamorous.

We are very glamorous now, but we are building on sand, and the quicker we build, the quicker that sand becomes. In 50 years, however, we will have gotten over this. We'll have put it behind us. We'll have developed other obsessions and other problems. And then perhaps we will really know the full extent of the price we have paid for the revolution.

DISCUSSION QUESTIONS

1. Do you agree with the author's statement that "computer systems have become a series of ever-faster, ever more complex, and ever more elaborate coffins"?
2. Are we creating artistic and intellectual works that will be lost to future generations because of their digital nature?
3. What do you think the author means by "[c]omputers swallow whatever they can touch, and everything they swallow is forced to become as unstable as they are"?

Summary

Computer graphics today encompass more than quantitative charts and graphs generated by spreadsheets. Bitmapped painting programs enable users to "paint" the screen with a mouse, pen, or other pointing device. The software stores the results in a pixel map, with each pixel having an assigned color. The more possible colors there are and the higher the resolution (pixel density) is, the more the images can approach photorealism. Object-oriented drawing programs also allow users to draw on the screen with a pointing device, with the results stored as collections of geometric objects rather than as maps of computer bits.

Bitmapped graphics and object-oriented graphics each offer advantages in particular situations; trade-offs involve editing, and ease of use. Both types of graphics have applications outside the art world. Bitmapped graphics are used in high-resolution digital image processing software for onscreen photo editing. Object-oriented graphics are at the heart of 3-D modeling software and computer-aided design (CAD) software used by architects, designers, and engineers. Presentation graphics software, which may include either or both graphics types, automates the process of creating slides, transparencies, handouts, and computer-based presentations, making it easy for nonartists to create visually attractive presentations.

Computers today aren't limited to working with static images; they're widely used to create and edit documents in media that change over time or in response to user interaction. For animation and digital video work PCs mimic many of the features of expensive professional workstations at a fraction of the cost. Similarly, today's personal computers can perform a variety of sound and music editing tasks that used to require expensive equipment and numerous musicians.

The interactive nature of the personal computer makes it possible to create nonlinear documents that enable users to take individual paths through information. Early nonlinear documents were called hypertext because they could contain only text. Today we can create or explore hypermedia documents—interactive documents that mix text, graphics, sounds, and moving images with onscreen navigation buttons—on disk and on the World Wide Web.

Multimedia computer systems make a new kind of software possible—software that uses text, graphics, animation, video, music, voice, and sound effects to communicate. Interactive multimedia documents are available for desktop computers, video game machines, set-top boxes connected to televisions, and networks. Regardless of the hardware, interactive multimedia software enables the user to control the presentation rather than just watch or listen passively. Only time will tell whether these new media will live up to their potential for enhancing education, training, entertainment, and cultural enrichment.

Chapter Review

▼ Key Terms

animation (p. 189)
audio digitizer (p. 197)
bitmapped (raster) graphics (p. 180)
bullet chart (p. 188)
button (p. 201)
clip art (p. 187)
color depth (bit depth) (p. 181)
compression (p. 196)
computer-aided design (CAD) (p. 188)
computer-aided manufacturing
    (CAM) (p. 188)
computer-integrated manufacturing
    (CIM) (p. 188)
digital video (p. 191)

drawing software (p. 181)
frame (p. 189)
hypermedia (p. 199)
hypertext (p. 199)
image processing software (p. 181)
interactive multimedia (p. 201)
MIDI (p. 198)
morph (p. 192)
MP3 (p. 197)
multimedia (p. 200)
multimedia authoring software
    (p. 201)
object-oriented (vector) graphics
    (p. 184)

page-description language (p. 184)
painting software (p. 180)
palette (p. 180)
pixel (p. 180)
PostScript (p. 184)
Presentation graphics software
    (p. 188)
resolution (p. 181)
sequencing software (p. 198)
synthesized sound (p. 196)
3-D modeling software (p. 186)
video digitizer (p. 192)
video editing software (p. 192)
WYSIWYG (p. 198)

▼ Interactive Quiz Questions

1. The *Computer Confluence* CD-ROM contains self-test quiz questions related to this chapter, including multiple choice, true or false, and matching questions.
2. The *Computer Confluence* Web site, **www.prenhall.com/beekman**, contains self-test exercises related to this chapter. Follow the instructions for taking a quiz. After you've completed your quiz, you can email the results to your instructor.

The Web site also contains open-ended discussion questions called Internet Explorations. Discuss one or more of the Internet Exploration questions at the section for this chapter.

▼ Review Questions

1. Define or describe each of the key terms listed in the "Key Tems" section. Check your answers using the glossary.
2. What is the difference between bitmapped graphics and object-oriented graphics? What are the advantages and disadvantages of each?
3. What two technological factors limit the realism of a bitmapped image? How are these related to storage of that image in the computer?
4. How is digital image processing of photographs related to bitmapped painting?
5. Describe several practical applications for 3-D modeling and CAD software.
6. Why is image compression an important part of digital video technology?
7. Describe three different technologies for adding music or other sounds to a multimedia presentation. Describe a practical application of each sound source.
8. How do hypertext and other hypermedia differ from linear media?
9. Describe several practical applications for hypermedia.
10. What are the main disadvantages of hypermedia when compared with conventional media such as books and videos?
11. Is it possible to have hypermedia without multimedia? Is it possible to have multimedia without hypermedia? Explain your answers.
12. How does presentation graphics software differ from multimedia authoring software? Give an example of a practical application of each.

▼ Discussion Questions

1. How does modern digital image processing technology affect the reliability of photographic evidence? How does digital audio technology affect the reliability of sound recordings as evidence? How should our legal system respond to this technology?
2. Scanners, video digitizers, and audio digitizers make it easier than ever for people to violate copyright laws. What, if anything, should be done to protect intellectual property rights of the people who create pictures, videos, and music? Under what circumstances do you think it's acceptable to copy sounds or images for use in your own work?
3. Do you think hypermedia documents will eclipse certain kinds of books and other media? If so, which ones and why?
4. Thanks to modern electronic music technology, one or two people can make a record that would have required dozens of musicians 20 years ago. What impact will electronic music technology ultimately have on the music profession?
5. Try to answer each of the questions posed at the end of the section called "Interactive Media: Visions of the Future."

▼ Projects

1. Draw a familiar object or scene using a bitmapped painting program. Draw the same object or scene with an object-oriented drawing program. Describe how the process changed using different software.
2. Create visual aids for a speech or lecture using presentation-graphics software. In what ways did the software make the job easier? What limitations did you find?
3. Compose an original music composition using a synthesizer, a computer, and a sequencer. Describe the experience.
4. Review several interactive multimedia titles. Discuss their strengths and weaknesses as communication tools. In what ways did their interactivity enhance their usefulness? (Extra challenge: Make your review interactive.)

Sources and Resources

Books and CD-ROMs

Most of the best graphics, video, music, and multimedia applications books are software specific. When you decide on a software application, choose books based on your chosen software and on the type of information you need. If you want quick answers with a minimum of verbiage, you'll probably be delighted with a book from Peachpit's Visual Quickstart series. Most of the titles in the following list aren't keyed to specific applications.

Bootstrapping: Douglas Engelbart, Coevolution, and the Origins of Personal Computing, by Thierry Bardini (Stanford University Press, 2000). This long-overdue book shines a spotlight on the visionary, revolutionary work of Douglas Englebart at SRI.

The New Drawing on the Right Side of the Brain: A Course in Enhancing Creativity and Artistic Confidence, by Betty Edwards (Los Angeles: J. P. Tarcher, 1999). If you're convinced you have no artistic ability, give this book a try; you might surprise yourself.

Tech TV's Digital Camera and Imaging Guide, by Less Freed with Sumi Das (Que, 2002). This book offers a good introduction to digital photography, including lots of tips for choosing and using the tools of the trade.

Graphic Communications Dictionary, by Daniel J. Lyons (Upper Saddle River, NJ: Prentice Hall, 2000). This is an excellent alphabetic reference for anyone wrestling with the terminology of graphic design.

Real World Digital Photography: Industrial Strength Techniques, by Deke McClelland and Katrin Eismann (Berkeley, CA: Peachpit Press, 1999). This book covers everything from shopping for a digital camera to creating immersive virtual reality environments with QuickTime VR. The authors have lots of experience and they communicate clearly.

Visual Quickstart Guide: Photoshop 6 for Windows and Macintosh, by Elaine Weinmann and Peter Lourekas (Berkeley, CA: Peachpit Press, 2001). Peachpit's Visual Quickstart Guides are popular because they provide maximum instruction for a minimal investment of time. This Photoshop guide is exemplary. Using lots of pictures and few words, it unlocks the secrets of the program that is the industry standard for professional photo and bitmap editing software.

The Arts and Crafts Computer: Using Your Computer as an Artist's Tool, by Janet Ashford (Berkeley, CA: Peachpit Press, 2001). This lavishly illustrated book covers basic principles of drawing, painting, photography, typography, and design with computers. But unlike other books on computer art, this one goes beyond the computer screen and the printed page as output possibilities. If you want to create original fabric art, greeting cards, labels, decals, bumper stickers, toys, you'll find a wealth of ideas here.

Looking Good in Presentations: Third Edition, by Molly W. Joss and Roger C. Parker (Scottsdale, AZ: Coriolis Group, 1999). Programs like PowerPoint can help nondesigners create stylish presentations, but they're not foolproof. (How many ugly, boring computer-enhanced presentations have you had to sit through?) This is a great book for anyone creating presentations, from simple slide shows to full-featured multimedia extravaganzas. Starting with "How To Not Be Boring" in Chapter 1, you'll find plenty of tips to make your presentations shine.

Animation on the Web, by Sean Wagstaff (Berkeley, CA: Peachpit Press, 1999). From simple scrolling banners to 3-D digital video, animation is everywhere on the Web. This "Guide to Webtop Publishing" is a great resource for beginners who want to learn the basics of animation and for experienced animators who want to learn about the technology that can put their works on the Web.

QuickTime Pro 5 for Macintosh and Windows Visual Quickstart Guide, by Judith Stern and Robert Letteieri (Berkeley, CA: Peachpit Press, 1999). QuickTime is a cross-platform multimedia standard for digital video, but it's also a tool for working with audio, interactive media, virtual reality, and more. This book is a good introduction to this powerful software technology.

The Little Digital Video Book, by Michael Rubin (Berkeley, CA: Peachpit Press, 2001). This compact book should be included with every digital camcorder. It's packed with helpful tips for choosing and organizing equipment, preparing a project, shooting quality footage, editing clips, adding soundtracks, and polishing productions. Highly recommended.

Digital Guerrilla Video: A Grassroots Guide to the Revolution, by Avi Hoffer (San Francisco: Miller Freeman Books, 1999). Digital video technology is spawning a revolution—for the first time in history, small-budget operations can produce big-time video productions. This book is as much about the creative process as it is about the technology. After you learn the basics, this book can provide professional advice and a creative kick.

Producing Great Sound for Digital Video, by Jay Rose (San Francisco: Miller Freeman Books, 1999). The soundtrack is often the difference between a good video and a great one. This book provides a wealth of information and advice on capturing, creating, and using sound in your video and multimedia projects.

Audio on the Web: The Official IUMA Guide, by Jeff Patterson and Ryan Melcher (Berkeley, CA: Peachpit Press, 1998). This book is an excellent resource for learning the basics of digital audio and its applications on the Web. It includes easy-to-understand explanations of technology and techniques, plus a cross-platform CD-ROM.

MP3 Underground, by Ron White and Michael White (Indianapolis: Que, 2001). This book covers the basics of MP3 from a consumer's point of view, describing software, Web sites, and techniques for taking advantage of MP3 music technology. A Windows CD-ROM is included.

The Little iTunes Book, by Bob LeVitus (Berkeley, CA: Peachpit Press, 2001). If you're using a late-model Mac, most of your basic music software needs can be handled by iTunes, a program that came with the computer. This book serves as a worthy manual for iTunes.

The Computer Music Tutorial, by Curtis Roads (Cambridge, MA: The MIT Press, 1996). Not for the fainthearted, this highly technical 12,001 page book covers nearly every aspect of creating music on the computer. The focus is on the mathematics and algorithms behind various computer synthesis techniques.

The Dictionary of Multimedia: Terms and Acronyms, by Brad Hansen (Chicago: Fitzroy Dearborn Publishers, 1999). If you want to keep a book handy for those times when you need to know the difference between MPC-1 and MPC-2, or what JPEG stands for, this is a good choice. It includes appendices on HTML standards organizations and (surprisingly) DOS commands.

Theoretical Foundations of Multimedia, by Robert S. Tannenbaum (New York: W.H. Freeman, 1998). Multimedia is an ideal profession for a modern Renaissance person. To be truly multimedia literate, a person needs to understand concepts from fields as diverse as computer science, physics, design, law, psychology, and communication. This introductory text/CD-ROM surveys each of these fields from the multimedia perspective, providing valuable conceptual background with practical value.

Understanding Media: The Extensions of Man, by Marshall McLuhan (Cambridge, MA: MIT Press, 1994.) This classic, originally published in 1964, explores the relationship of mass media to the masses. The new introduction in this 30th Anniversary reissue reevaluates McLuhan's visionary work 30 years later.

net_condition: art and global media (Electronic Culture: History, Theory, and Practice), edited by Peter Weibel and Timothy Druckery (Cambridge, MA: MIT Press, 2001). This bold, colorful book surveys the global landscape of digital art and its impact on our culture.

Multimedia: From Wagner to Virtual Reality, edited by Randall Packer and Ken Jordan (New York: Norton, 2001). This collection of essays by William Burroughs, John Cage, Tim Berners-Lee, and others, offers a broad overview of the historical roots of multimedia.

Film

CyberWorld 3D. This film, shown at Imax theaters, uses 3D goggles and a massive screen to create an experience that's closer to virtual reality than Hollywood has gone before. A silly sci-fi plot loosely ties together several dazzling graphical short pieces.

Audio CD

Wired Music Futurists (Rhino). Digital technology doesn't just make it easier for musicians to do what they've always done; it makes it possible for them to do things that haven't been done before. This CD from *Wired* offers a wide variety of examples of new music for a digital culture, with tracks from Sun Ra, Steve Reich, Laurie Anderson, Brian Eno, Beck, Sonic Youth, DJ Spooky, and others.

Periodicals

Artbyte. This stylish magazine explores the world and culture of digital art and design.

DV and **AV Video & Multimedia Producer.** These days video producers have to pay attention to the world of computers and multimedia. These two publications provide current coverage of the converging worlds of video and multimedia.

Keyboard and **Electronic Musician.** These two magazines are among the best sources for up-to-date information on computers and music synthesis.

World Wide Web Pages

The Web is known as the multimedia part of the Internet, and there are plenty of Web sites for learning about—and experiencing firsthand—a variety of mixed media. The *Computer Confluence* Web pages will link you to multimedia hardware and software companies and pages that demonstrate state-of-the-art multimedia on the Web.

8 | Database Applications and Implications

After you read this chapter you should be able to:

▼

Explain what a database is and describe its basic structure

Identify the kinds of problems that can be best solved with database software

Describe different kinds of database software, from simple file managers to complex relational databases

Describe database operations for storing, sorting, updating, querying, and summarizing information

Explain how databases threaten our privacy

▲

▼ In this chapter:

The basics of databases

Database applications large and small

The future of database technology

How databases threaten your privacy

. . . and more.

▼ On the CD-ROM:

Video clip of Bill Gates

An interactive game based on database logic

Instant access to glossary and key word references

Interactive self-study quizzes

. . . and more.

▼ On the Web:

www.prenhall.com/beekman

Links to major database companies

Resources for database users

Resources to help you protect your personal privacy

Self-study exercises

. . . and more.

Bill Gates Rides the Digital Wave

The goal is **information at your fingertips.**

—Bill Gates

In the early days of the personal computer revolution, Bill Gates and Paul Allen formed a company called Microsoft to produce and market a version of the Basic programming language for microcomputers. Microsoft Basic quickly became the standard language installed in virtually every microcomputer.

Microsoft's biggest break came when IBM went shopping for an operating system for its PC. Gates purchased an operating system from a small company, reworked it to meet IBM's specifications, named it MS-DOS (for Microsoft Disk Operating System), and offered it to IBM. The IBM PC became an industry standard, and Microsoft found itself owning the operating system that kept most of the PCs in the world running.

Today Bill Gates and Microsoft dominate the PC software industry, selling operating systems, programming languages, and applications programs. Software has made Gates the richest man on earth.

Bill Gates

Bill Gates and Paul Allen as students

Microsoft's desktop dominion was threatened in the mid-1990s by the Internet explosion. For many people, computers became little more than portals into the Internet. Gates responded by making the Internet a critical part of its software strategy. Today Microsoft's Internet Explorer Web browser is a central component of the Windows OS; Microsoft desktop applications have links to the Internet, and Microsoft has partnerships with dozens of Web-related businesses worldwide.

According to writer Steven Levy, Gates "has the obsessive drive of a hacker working on a tough technical dilemma, yet has an uncanny grasp of the marketplace, as well as a firm conviction of what the future will be like and what he should do about it." The future, says Gates, will be digital. To prepare for this all-digital future, Microsoft is extending its tentacles beyond software into all kinds of information-related business ventures, from online banking and shopping to the MS-NBC cable TV network.

Many competitors and customers insist that Microsoft uses unethical business practices to ruthlessly—and sometimes illegally—stomp out competition and choice. In 1998, 20 states joined the U.S. government in a widely publicized lawsuit against Microsoft's anticompetitive practices. That same year the European Union filed two antitrust lawsuits against the company. Microsoft responded with arrogant denials and a massive P. R. campaign; one state official received pro-Microsoft form letters from hundreds o f people, including some who had died years before.

In 2000, a federal judge ruled that Microsoft had, indeed, operated as an illegal monopoly, and that Microsoft's crimes had hurt consumers as well as other businesses. The ruling was confirmed by an appeals court in 2001, but the government settled out of court in exchange for minor concessions from Microsoft. Microsoft's legal troubles were far from over, though. Several states refused to go along with the settlement, Microsoft faced several international lawsuits, and new questions were being raised about the legality of some features in Windows XP.

In recent years, Bill Gates and Microsoft have given billions of dollars to public schools, AIDS research, and other charities. Cynics argue that these gifts are calculated to improve the company's public image in the face of legal troubles. Others suggest that fatherhood and family life have made Gates more generous. Whatever the motivation, the donations are helping people all over the world.

In early 2000, Gates stepped aside as CEO of Microsoft to become Chief Software Architect for the company. But few doubt that Gates, who is still Microsoft's Chairman, is the power behind the company. Bill Gates is poised to become one of the most powerful people on Earth, with more practical influence on our lives than most elected officials. In a future where we have all kinds of information at our fingertips, Microsoft wants to be the source of that information. ▶

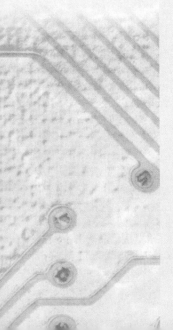

211

We live in an information age. We're bombarded with information by television, radio, newspapers, magazines, books, and computers. It's easy to be overwhelmed by the sheer quantity of information we're expected to deal with each day. Computer applications such as word processors and spreadsheets can aggravate the problem by making it easier for people to generate more documents full of information.

A *database program* is a data manager that can help alleviate information overload. Databases make it possible for people to store, organize, retrieve, communicate, and manage information in ways that wouldn't be possible without computers. To control the flood of information, people use databases of all sizes and shapes—from massive mainframe database managers that keep airlines filled with passengers to computerized appointment calendars on palmtop computers and public database kiosks in shopping malls.

First the good news: Information at your fingertips can make your life richer and more efficient in a multitude of ways. Ready cash from street-corner ATMs, instant airline reservations from any telephone, catalog shopping with overnight mail-order delivery, exhaustive Web searches in seconds—none of these conveniences would be possible without databases.

Now the bad news: Much of the information stored in databases is your data, and you have little or no control over who has it and how it is used. Ironically, the database technology that liberates us in our day-to-day lives is, at the same time, chipping away at our privacy. We explore both sides of this important technology in this chapter.

The Electronic File Cabinet: Database Basics

The next best thing to knowing something is knowing **where to find it**.
—Samuel Johnson

We start by looking at the basics of databases. Like word processors, spreadsheets, and graphics programs, database programs are applications—programs for turning computers into productive tools. If a word processor is a computerized typewriter and a spreadsheet is a computerized ledger, you can think of a database program as a computerized file cabinet.

Internet auctions and other forms of online shopping wouldn't be possible without database technology.

While word processors and spreadsheets generally are used to create printed documents, database programs are designed to maintain *databases*—collections of information stored on computer disks. A database can be an electronic version of a phone book, a recipe file, a library's card catalog, an inventory file stored in an office file cabinet, a school's student grade records, a card index containing the names and addresses of business contacts, or a catalog of your compact disc collection. Just about any collection of information can be turned into a database.

What Good Is a Database?

Why do people use computers for information-handling tasks that can be done with index cards, three-ring binders, or file folders? Computerized databases offer several advantages over their paper-and-pencil counterparts:

▸ *Databases make it easier to store large quantities of information.* If you have only 20 or 30 compact discs, it makes sense to catalog them in a notebook. If you have 2,000 or 3,000, your notebook may become as unwieldy as your CD collection. The larger the mass of information, the bigger the benefit of using a database.

▸ *Databases make it easier to retrieve information quickly and flexibly.* While it might take a minute or more to look up a phone number in a card file or telephone directory, the same job can be done in seconds with a database. If you look up 200 numbers every week, the advantage of a database is obvious. That advantage is even greater when your search doesn't match your file's organization. For example, suppose you have a phone number on a scrap of paper and you want to find the name and address of the person with that number. That kind of search may take hours if your information is stored in a large address book or file alphabetized by name, but the same search is almost instantaneous with a computerized database.

▶ *Databases make it easy to organize and reorganize information.* Paper filing systems force you to arrange information in one particular way. Should your book catalog be organized by author, by title, by publication date, or by subject? There's a lot riding on your decision, because if you decide to rearrange everything later, you will waste a lot of time. With a database, you can instantly switch between these organizational schemes as often as you like; there's no penalty for flexibility.

▶ *Databases make it easy to print and distribute information in a variety of ways.* Suppose you want to send letters to hundreds of friends inviting them to your post-graduation party. You'll need to include directions to your place for out-of-towners but not for home-towners. A database, when used with a word processor, can print personalized form letters, including extra directions for those who need them, and print preaddressed envelopes or mailing labels in a fraction of the time it would take you to do it by hand and with less likelihood of error. You can even print a report listing invitees sorted by Zip code so you can suggest possible car pools. (If you want to bill those who attend the party, your database can help with that, too.)

Database Anatomy

As you might expect, a specialized vocabulary is associated with databases. Unfortunately, some terms take on different meanings depending on their context, and different people use these words in different ways. We'll begin by charting a course through marketing hype and technical terminology to find our way to the definitions most people use today.

For our purposes, a **database** is a collection of information stored in an organized form in a computer, and a **database program** is a software tool for organizing storage and retrieval of that information. A variety of programs fit this broad definition, ranging from simple address book programs to massive inventory-tracking systems. We explore the differences between types of database programs later in the chapter, but for now we treat them as if they are more or less alike.

Many terms that describe the components of database systems grew out of the file cabinet terminology of the office. A database is composed of one or more files. A **file** is a collection of related information; it keeps that information together the way a drawer in a file cabinet does. If a database is used to record sales information for a company, separate files might contain the relevant sales data for each year. For an address database, separate files might hold personal and business contacts. It's up to the designer of the database to determine whether information in different categories is stored in separate files on the computer's disk.

The term *file* sometimes causes confusion because of its multiple meanings. A disk can contain application programs, system programs, utility programs, and documents, all of which are, from the computer's point of view, files. But for database users, the term file usually means a file that is part of a database—a specific kind of file. In this chapter *file* refers specifically to a data file created by a database program.

A database file is a collection of records. A **record** is the information relating to one person, product, or event. In the library's card catalog database a record is equivalent to one card. In an address book database a record contains information about one person. A compact disc catalog database would have one record per CD.

Each discrete chunk of information in a record is called a **field**. A record in the library's card catalog database would contain fields for author, title, publisher, address, date, and title code number. Your CD database could break records into fields by title, artist, and so on.

The type of information a field can hold is determined by its *field type* or *data type*. For example, the author field in the library database would be defined as a text field, so it could contain text. The field specifying the number of copies of a book would be defined as a *numeric field*, so it could contain only numbers—numbers that can be used to calculate totals and other arithmetic formulas, if necessary. A date-of-purchase field might be a *date field* that could contain only dates. In addition to these standard field types, many database programs allow fields to contain graphics, digitized photographs, sounds, or video clips. **Computed fields** contain formulas similar to spreadsheet formulas; they display values calculated from values in other numeric fields. For example, a computed field called GPA might contain a formula for calculating a student's grade point average using the grades stored in other fields.

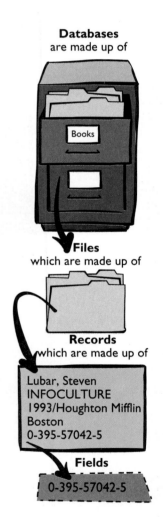

Databases
are made up of

Books

Files
which are made up of

Records
which are made up of

Lubar, Steven
INFOCULTURE
1993/Houghton Mifflin
Boston
0-395-57042-5

Fields

0-395-57042-5

Most database programs provide you with more than one way to view the data, including *form views*, which show one record at a time, and *list views*, which display several records in lists similar to a spreadsheet. In any view, fields can be rearranged without changing the underlying data.

Database Operations

Information has **value**, but it is as **perishable** as fresh fruit.
—Nicholas Negroponte, founder and director of the MIT Media Lab

Once the structure of a database is defined, it's easy to get information in; it's just a matter of typing. Typing may not even be necessary if the data already exists in some computer-readable form. Most database programs can easily **import** or receive data in the form of text files created with word processors, spreadsheets, or other databases. When information changes or errors are detected, records can be modified, added, or deleted.

These two windows show the list and form views of a database.

Browsing

The challenging part of using a database is retrieving information in a timely and appropriate manner. Information is of little value if it's not accessible. One way to find information is to **browse** through the records of the database file just as you would if they were paper forms in a notebook. Most database programs provide keyboard commands, onscreen buttons, and other tools for navigating quickly through records. But this kind of electronic page turning offers no particular advantage over paper, and it's painfully inefficient for large files. Fortunately, most database programs include a variety of commands and capabilities that make it easy to get the information you need when you need it.

Database Queries

The alternative to browsing is to ask the database for specific information. In database terminology, an information request is called a **query**. A query may be a simple **search** for a specific record (say, one containing information on Abraham Lincoln) or a request to **select** *all* the records that match a set of criteria (for example, records for all U.S. presidents who served more than one term). Once you've selected a group of records, you can browse through it, produce a printout, or do just about anything else you might do with the complete file.

Sorting Data

Sometimes it's necessary to rearrange records to make the most efficient use of data. For example, a mail-order company's customer file might be arranged alphabetically by name for easy reference, but it must be rearranged in order by Zip code to qualify for postal discounts on catalog mailings. A **sort** command allows you to arrange records in alphabetic or numeric order based on values in one or more fields.

Printing Reports, Labels, and Form Letters

In addition to displaying information on the screen, database programs can produce a variety of printouts. The most common type of database printout is a **report**—an ordered list of selected records and fields in an easy-to-read format. Most business reports arrange data in tables with rows for individual records and columns for selected fields; they often include summary lines containing calculated totals and averages for groups of records.

Database programs can also be used to produce mailing labels and customized form letters. Many database programs don't actually print letters; they simply **export data** or transmit the necessary records and fields to word processors with **mail merge** capabilities, which then take on the task of printing the letters. See The User's View box on the facing page.

Building a Database

SOFTWARE: *FileMaker Pro.*

THE GOAL: *To create an Addresses database file to replace your tattered address book, the bundle of business cards in your desk drawer, and the scribbled list of numbers posted by your phone.*

1 To create a new Addresses database file, you must first define fields by typing a name and specifying a field type for each one. In addition to including text fields for last name, first name, and other information, you add two date fields: one for birthday and one that will automatically display the most recent modification date for each record. You also include a picture field and two value lists—restricted fields that can only contain values from lists specified by you.

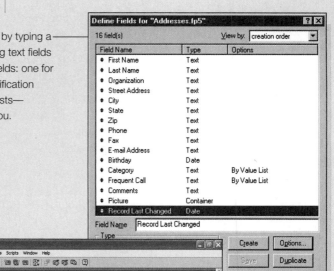

2 The program creates a standard form-style layout for data entry, but it could be easier to use.

3 You modify the layout by rearranging fields and labels and changing their formats.

4 You type information into the first record of the reformatted layout, using the Tab key to move from field to field.

5 The Category and Frequent Call fields use mouse clicks to select the appropriate values.

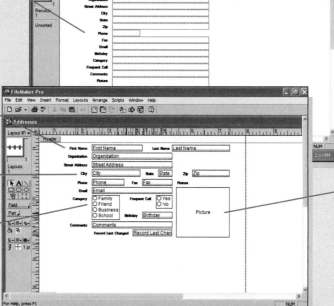

6 You can fill in the Picture field later with a scanned photograph.

7 When you're through, you use the New Record command to store this record in the data file and replace it on the screen with a new empty record.

Selecting, Sorting, and Reporting

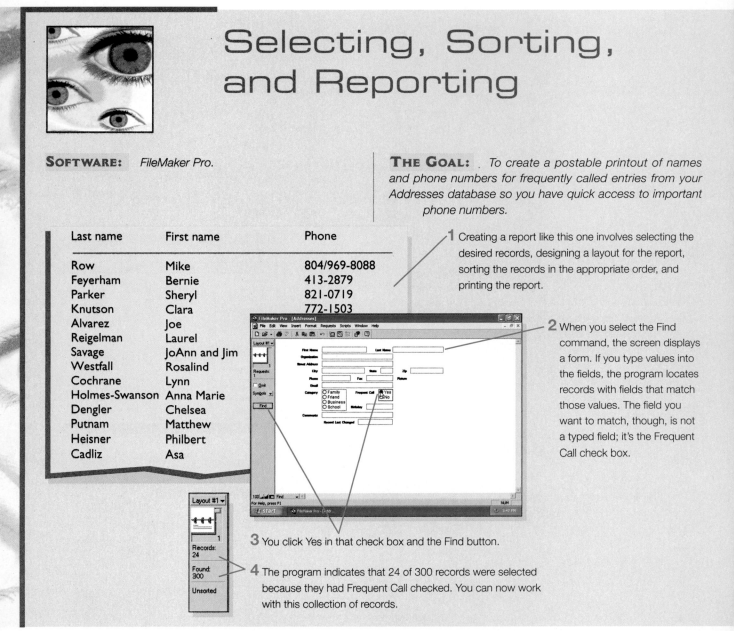

SOFTWARE: *FileMaker Pro.*

THE GOAL: *To create a postable printout of names and phone numbers for frequently called entries from your Addresses database so you have quick access to important phone numbers.*

Last name	First name	Phone
Row	Mike	804/969-8088
Feyerham	Bernie	413-2879
Parker	Sheryl	821-0719
Knutson	Clara	772-1503
Alvarez	Joe	
Reigelman	Laurel	
Savage	JoAnn and Jim	
Westfall	Rosalind	
Cochrane	Lynn	
Holmes-Swanson	Anna Marie	
Dengler	Chelsea	
Putnam	Matthew	
Heisner	Philbert	
Cadliz	Asa	

1 Creating a report like this one involves selecting the desired records, designing a layout for the report, sorting the records in the appropriate order, and printing the report.

2 When you select the Find command, the screen displays a form. If you type values into the fields, the program locates records with fields that match those values. The field you want to match, though, is not a typed field; it's the Frequent Call check box.

3 You click Yes in that check box and the Find button.

4 The program indicates that 24 of 300 records were selected because they had Frequent Call checked. You can now work with this collection of records.

Complex Queries

Queries may be simple or complex, but either way they must be precise and unambiguous. With appropriate databases, queries could be constructed to find the following:

- In a hospital's patient database, the names and locations of all of the patients on the hospital's fifth and sixth floors
- In a database of airline flight schedules, the least expensive way to fly from Boston to San Francisco on Tuesday afternoon
- In a politician's database, all voters who contributed more than $1,000 to last year's legislative campaign and who wrote to express concern over gun control laws since the election

These may be legitimate targets for queries, but they aren't expressed in a form that most database programs can understand. The exact method for performing a query depends on the user interface of the database software. Most programs enable the user to specify the rules of the search by filling in a dialog box or a blank onscreen form. Some require the user to type the

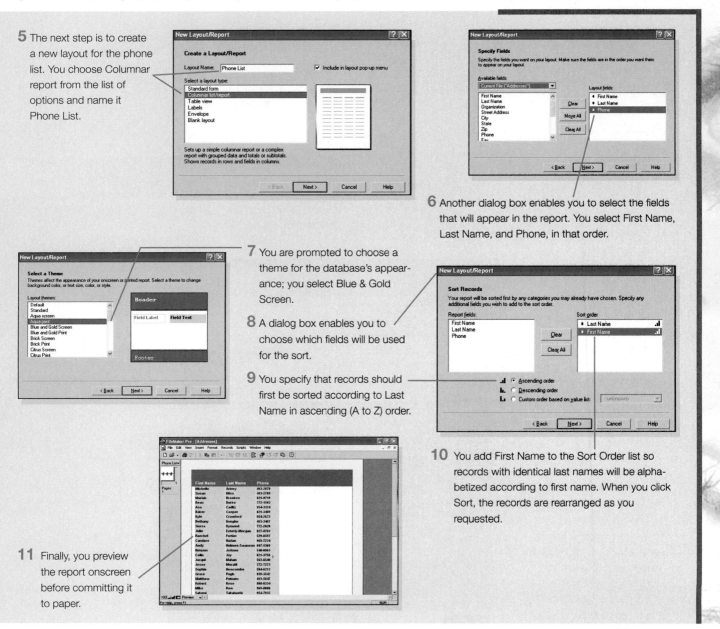

5 The next step is to create a new layout for the phone list. You choose Columnar report from the list of options and name it Phone List.

6 Another dialog box enables you to select the fields that will appear in the report. You select First Name, Last Name, and Phone, in that order.

7 You are prompted to choose a theme for the database's appearance; you select Blue & Gold Screen.

8 A dialog box enables you to choose which fields will be used for the sort.

9 You specify that records should first be sorted according to Last Name in ascending (A to Z) order.

10 You add First Name to the Sort Order list so records with identical last names will be alphabetized according to first name. When you click Sort, the records are rearranged as you requested.

11 Finally, you preview the report onscreen before committing it to paper.

request using a special **query language** that's more precise than English. For example, to view the records for males between 18 and 35, you might type

```
Select * From Population Where
    Sex = M and Age = 18 and Age = 35
```

Many database programs include programming languages, so queries can be included in programs and performed automatically when the programs are executed. While the details of the process vary, the underlying logic is consistent from program to program.

Most modern database management programs support a standard language for programming complex queries called **SQL** (from *Structured Query Language*). Because SQL is available for many different database management systems, programmers and sophisticated users don't need to learn new languages when they work with different hardware and software systems. Users are usually insulated from the complexities of the query language by graphical user interfaces that allow point-and-click queries.

Querying a Web Search Database

SOFTWARE: *Internet Explorer.*

THE GOAL: *To search current news articles for stories about a new method for recycling laser printer toner cartridges. You'll use your Web browser to search newspapers, wires, and transcripts on the Northern Lights Web search engine database.*

1 You don't want to search for anything on the Web about recycling toner cartridges; you're just interested in tracking down a recent news story, so you select "Newspapers, Wires, and Transcripts."

2 You want to search for two key words, so you type *recycle* OR *toner* to indicate that you want to locate all records that have either of those two key words in their subject field; then you click Search.

3 In a few seconds the search reveals that 12,159 records contain at least one of your two target words in the subject field. Your search strategy was flawed. Most of the articles listed for recycle probably have nothing to do with toner cartridges, so you've selected a large collection of mostly irrelevant titles.

4 You replace the OR with AND in the Search field and click Search again to request records that contain both recycle AND toner.

5 The search reveals 69 records that contain both words in the subject field, driving home the importance of choosing every word carefully when defining a database query.

6 You can now browse through the abstracts for relevant articles. Of course, there's no guarantee that you've found all the references on these subjects: You can only be sure that you've found all the articles that had both words listed in their subject fields. If you don't find what you're looking for in this list, you might need to try different search strategies or different databases.

Special-Purpose Database Programs

> The **best** way to organize information is
> **the way that reveals** what we want to communicate.
> —Richard Saul Wurman, author of *Information Anxiety 2*

Specialized database software is preprogrammed for specific data storage and retrieval purposes. Users of special-purpose databases don't generally need to define file structures or design forms, because these details have been taken care of by the designers of the software. In fact, some special-purpose database programs are not even sold as databases; they have names that more accurately reflect their purposes.

Directories and Geographic Information Systems

For example, an *electronic phone directory* can pack millions of names and phone numbers onto a single CD-ROM or Web site. Using an electronic phone directory for the United States, you can track down phone numbers of people and businesses all over the country—even if you don't know where they are. You can look up a person's name if you have the phone number or street address. You can generate a list of every dentist in town—any town. Then using another type of specialized database, an *electronic street atlas*, you can pinpoint each of your finds on a freshly printed map. Many street atlases are designed to work with GPS (global positioning system) receivers on laptop, handheld, or automobile-based computers. GPS satellites feed location information to GPS receivers; mapping software uses that information to provide location feedback for travelers and mobile workers.

Geographical information systems (GISs) go beyond simple mapping and tracking programs. A GIS allows a business to combine tables of data such as customer sales lists with demographic information from the U.S. Census Bureau and other sources. The right combination can reveal valuable strategic information. For example, a stock brokerage firm can pinpoint the best locations for branch offices based on average incomes and other neighborhood data; a cable TV company can locate potential customers who live close to existing lines. Because GISs can display geographic and demographic data on maps, they enable users to see data relationships that might be invisible in table form.

Personal Information Managers

One type of specialized database program is often called a personal information manager (PIM). This type of program can automate some or all of the following functions:

▶ *Address/phone book*. Software address books provide options for quickly displaying specific records and printing mailing labels, address books, and reports. Some include automatic phone-dialing options and fields for recording phone notes.

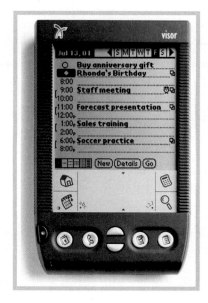

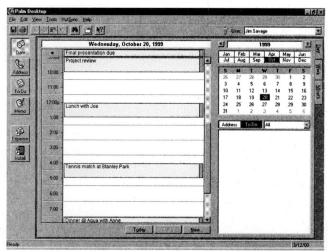

Personal information management software can help you keep track of appointments, phone numbers, and to-do lists. The information is readily accessible as long as your computer is nearby or you can find a way to carry the data with you. Handheld computers like this Palm III can share information with PC and Macintosh programs, so you can carry the essentials with you as you move through your day.

8.1
The Language of
Database Queries

Years ago the number of incompatible database languages made it difficult for people using different applications to access the same database. In the mid-1970s, IBM's E. F. Codd proposed a standardized Structured English Query Language, which evolved into SQL. With SQL, users and programmers can employ the same language to access databases from a wide variety of vendors.

SQL combines the familiar database concepts of tables, rows (records), and columns (fields) and the mathematical idea of a set. Here we illustrate a simple SQL command using the Rental Vehicles database from Clem's Transportation Rental ("If it moves, we rent it."). Here's a complete listing of the database records:

Vehicle_ID	Vehicle_Type	Transport_Mode	Num_Passengers	Cargo_Capacity	Rental_Price
1062	Helicopter	Air	6	500	$1,250.00
1955	Canoe	Water	2	30	$5.00
2784	Automobile	Land	4	250	$45.00
0213	Unicycle	Land	1	0	$10.00
0019	Minibus	Land	8	375	$130.00
3747	Balloon	Air	3	120	$340.00
7288	HangGlider	Air	1	5	$17.00
9430	Sailboat	Water	8	200	$275.00
8714	Powerboat	Water	4	175	$210.00
0441	Bicycle	Land	1	10	$12.00
4759	Jet	Air	9	2300	$2,900.00

▶ *Appointment calendar.* A typical PIM calendar enables you to enter appointments and events and display or print them in a variety of formats, ranging from one day at a time to a monthly overview. Many include built-in alarms for last-minute reminders.

▶ *To-do list.* Most PIMs enable users to enter and organize ongoing lists of things to do and archive lists of completed tasks.

▶ *Miscellaneous notes.* Some PIMs accept diary entries, personal notes, and other hard-to-categorize tidbits of information.

PIMs have long been popular among people with busy schedules and countless contacts. They're easier to understand and use than general-purpose database programs, and they're faster and more flexible than their leather-bound paper counterparts. For people on the go, PIMs work

A typical SQL statement filters the records of a database, capturing only those that meet the specific criteria. For example, suppose you wanted to list the ID numbers and types of the vehicles that travel on land and cost less than $20.00 per day. The SQL statement to perform this task would look like this:

```
SELECT Vehicle_ID, Vehicle_Type
FROM Rental_Vehicles
WHERE Transport_Mode = 'Land' AND
Rental_Price 20.00 ;
```

In English this SQL statement says "Show me (from the Rental Vehicles database) the vehicle IDs and vehicle types for those vehicles that travel by land and cost less than $20.00 per day to rent."

Two rows in the database meet these criteria, the unicycle and bicycle:

```
0213 Unicycle
0441 Bicycle
```

The selection rules for SQL are consistent and understandable whether queries are simple or complex. This simple example is designed to give you an idea of how they work.

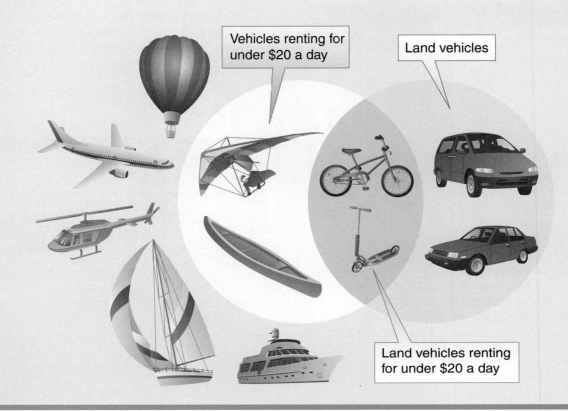

Vehicles renting for under $20 a day

Land vehicles

Land vehicles renting for under $20 a day

especially well with notebook computers or handheld computers. In fact, the market for PIM software has been eclipsed by an even larger market for handheld computers and personal digital assistants with built-in PIM software. For example, software that's built into the Palm OS accepts a pocket-sized device to *hot-sync* with the PIM software on a desktop PC or Mac. This instant data linking makes it easy to keep up-to-date personal information both in and out of the office.

In many organizations, PIMs have been replaced by enterprise information systems such as Microsoft Outlook, part of Microsoft Office. These systems enable networked coworkers to easily share calendars and contacts and often include email and other communication tools along with basic PIM features. The Web offers another alternative: Several Web sites provide free PIM software that can be accessed from any Web-accessible computer; many of these allow for workgroups to share calendars and other information.

Exporting and Transporting Data

SOFTWARE: *FileMaker Pro and Microsoft Outlook for the PC and Address Book for Palm OS.*

THE GOAL: *To move your personal address book into a Palm handheld organizer so you can carry it with you and add to it wherever you go.*

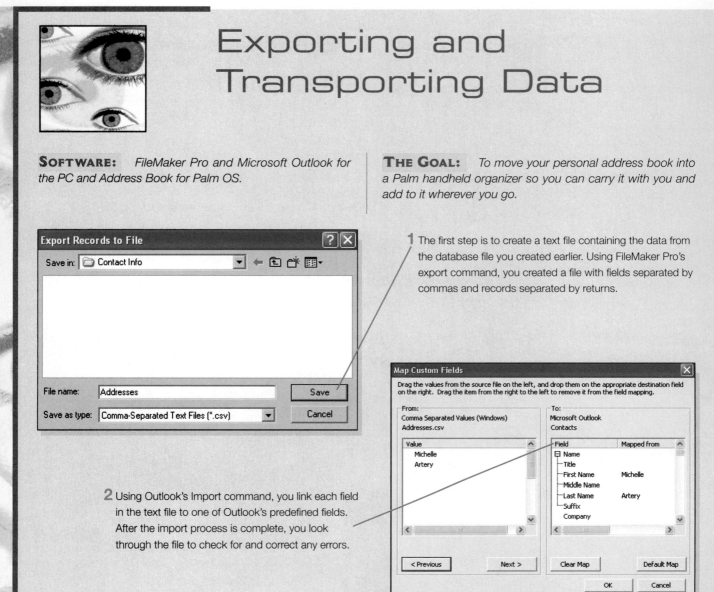

1 The first step is to create a text file containing the data from the database file you created earlier. Using FileMaker Pro's export command, you created a file with fields separated by commas and records separated by returns.

2 Using Outlook's Import command, you link each field in the text file to one of Outlook's predefined fields. After the import process is complete, you look through the file to check for and correct any errors.

Beyond the Basics: Database Management Systems

When we try to pick out **anything**, we find it hitched to **everything else in the universe**.

—John Muir, first director of the National Park Service

So far we've used simple examples to illustrate concepts common to most database programs. This oversimplification is useful for understanding the basics, but it's not the whole story. In truth database programs range from simple mailing label programs to massive financial information systems, and it's important to know a little about what makes them different as well as what makes them alike.

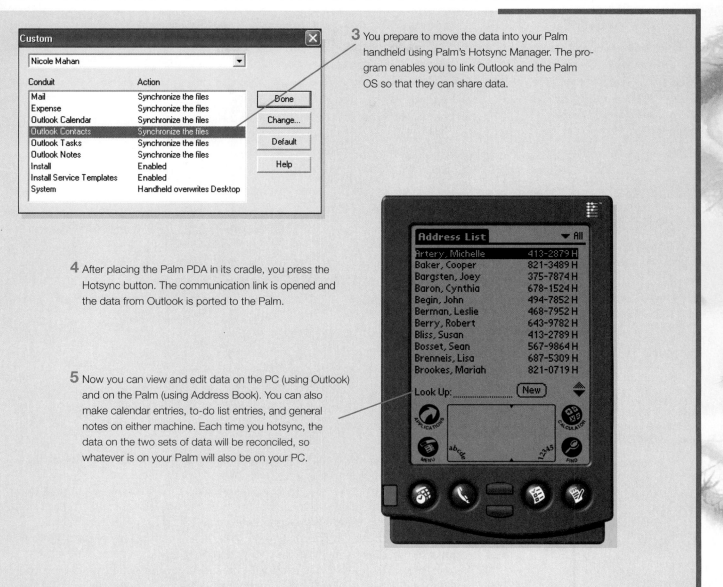

3 You prepare to move the data into your Palm handheld using Palm's Hotsync Manager. The program enables you to link Outlook and the Palm OS so that they can share data.

4 After placing the Palm PDA in its cradle, you press the Hotsync button. The communication link is opened and the data from Outlook is ported to the Palm.

5 Now you can view and edit data on the PC (using Outlook) and on the Palm (using Address Book). You can also make calendar entries, to-do list entries, and general notes on either machine. Each time you hotsync, the data on the two sets of data will be reconciled, so whatever is on your Palm will also be on your PC.

From File Managers to Database Management Systems

Technically speaking, many consumer databases and PIM programs aren't really database managers at all; they're file managers. A **file manager** is a program that enables users to work with one file at a time. A true **database management system (DBMS)** is a program or system of programs that can manipulate data in a large collection of files—the database—cross-referencing between files as needed. A DBMS can be used interactively, or it can be controlled directly by other programs. A file manager is sufficient for mailing lists and other common data management applications. But for many large, complex jobs there's no substitute for a true database management system.

Consider, for example, the problem of managing student information at a college. It's easy to see how databases might be used to store this information: a file containing one record for

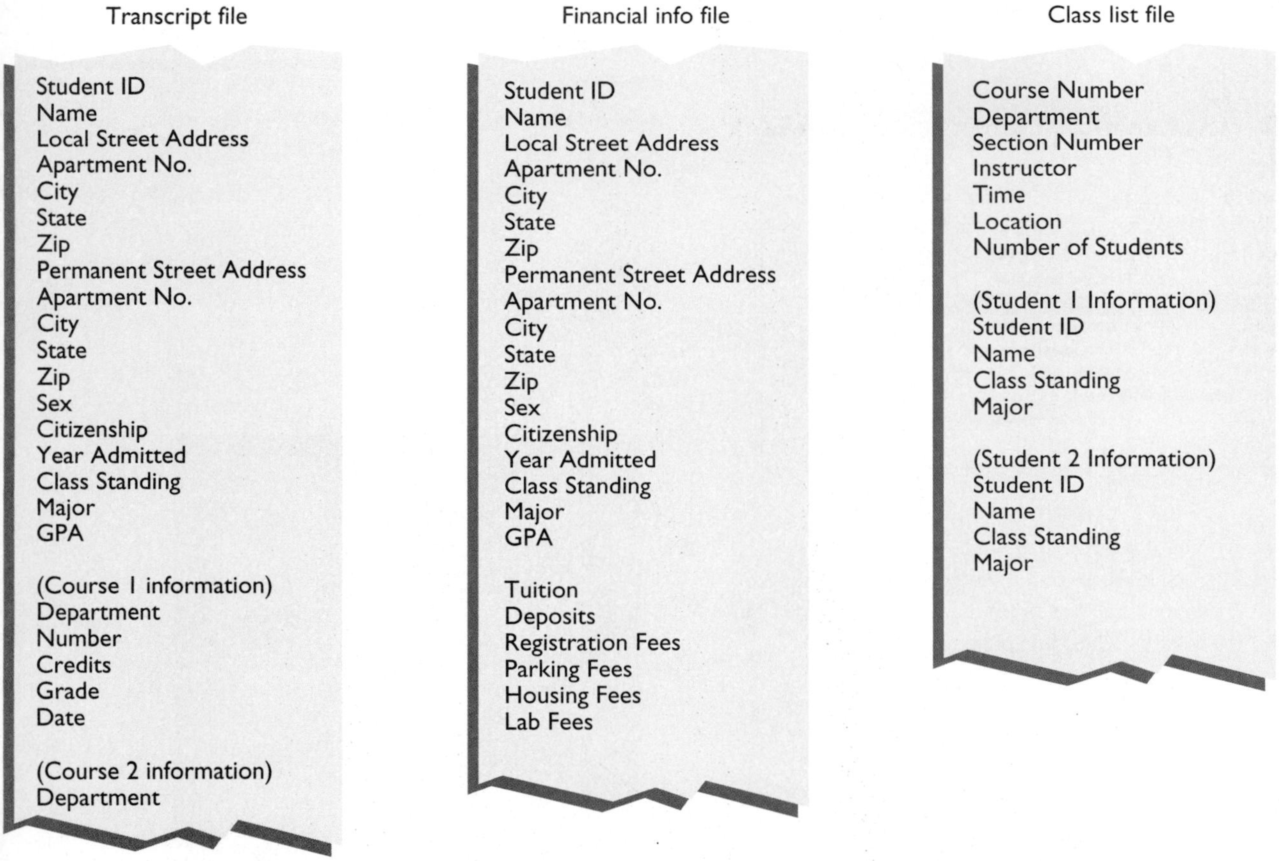

Transcript file

Student ID
Name
Local Street Address
Apartment No.
City
State
Zip
Permanent Street Address
Apartment No.
City
State
Zip
Sex
Citizenship
Year Admitted
Class Standing
Major
GPA

(Course 1 information)
Department
Number
Credits
Grade
Date

(Course 2 information)
Department

Financial info file

Student ID
Name
Local Street Address
Apartment No.
City
State
Zip
Permanent Street Address
Apartment No.
City
State
Zip
Sex
Citizenship
Year Admitted
Class Standing
Major
GPA

Tuition
Deposits
Registration Fees
Parking Fees
Housing Fees
Lab Fees

Class list file

Course Number
Department
Section Number
Instructor
Time
Location
Number of Students

(Student 1 Information)
Student ID
Name
Class Standing
Major

(Student 2 Information)
Student ID
Name
Class Standing
Major

Student information is duplicated in several different files of this inefficient, error-prone database.

each student, with fields for name, student ID number, address, phone, and so on. But a typical student generates far too much information to store practically in a single data file.

Most schools choose to keep several files containing student information: one for financial records, one for course enrollment and grade transcripts, and so on. Each of these files has a single record for each student. In addition, a school must maintain class enrollment files with one record for each class and fields for information on each student enrolled in the class. Three of these files might be organized as shown in the above figure.

In this database, each of the three separate files contains basic information about every student. This redundant data not only occupies expensive storage space, but also makes it difficult to ensure that student information is accurate and up to date. If a student moves to a different address, several files must be updated to reflect this change. The more changes, the greater the likelihood of a data-entry error.

With a DBMS there's no need to store all of this information in every file. The database can include a basic student file containing demographic information—information that's unique for each student. Because the demographic information is stored in a separate file, it doesn't need to be included in the financial information file, the transcript file, the class list file, or any other file. The student ID number, included in each file, serves as a *key field*; it unlocks the relevant student information in the student file when it's needed elsewhere. The student ID field is, in effect, shared by all files that use data from this file. If the student moves, the change of address need only be recorded in one place. Databases organized in this way are called relational databases.

What Makes a Database Relational?

To most users a **relational database** program is one that allows files to be related to each other so that changes in one file are reflected in other files automatically. To computer scientists, the term *relational database* has a technical definition related to the underlying structure of the data and the rules specifying how that data can be manipulated.

The structure of a relational database is based on the relational model—a mathematical model that combines data in tables. Other kinds of database management systems are based on different theoretical models, with different technical advantages and disadvantages. But the majority of DBMSs in use today, including virtually all PC-based database management systems, use the relational model. So from the average computer user's point of view, the distinction between the popular and technical definitions of relational is academic.

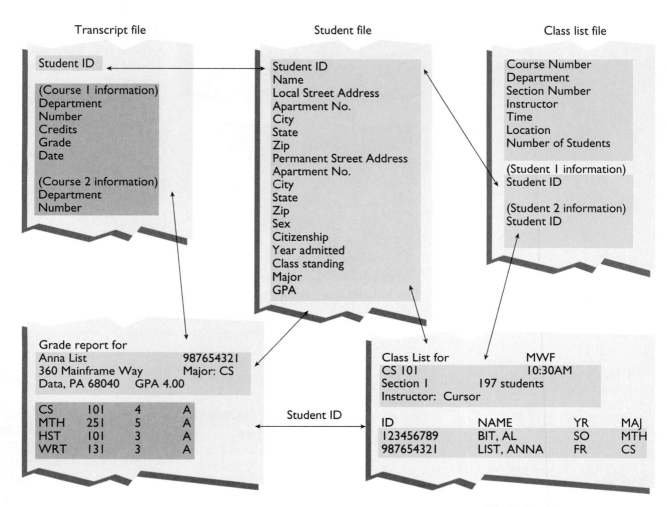

The Student file serves as a reference when grade reports and class lists are created. The Student ID fields in the Transcript file and the Class List file are used as a key for locating the necessary student information in the Student file.

The Many Faces of Databases

Large databases can contain hundreds of interrelated files. This maze of information could be overwhelming to users if they were forced to deal with it directly. Fortunately, a database management system can shield users from the complex inner workings of the system, providing them with only the information and commands they need to get their jobs done. In fact, a well-designed database puts on different faces for different classes of users.

Retail clerks don't need to be able to access every piece of information in the store's database; they just need to enter sales transactions on point-of-sale terminals. Databases designed for retail outlets generally include simple, straightforward terminal interfaces that give the clerks only the information, and the power, they need to process transactions. Managers, accountants, data processing specialists, and customers see the database from different points of view because they need to work with the data in different ways.

Clerk's view

Video rental view used by clerks to access renter information, scan bar codes on videos, and print rental invoices

Video store database

Manager's view

- Inventory-tracking view used by managers to check on rental history and inventory for individual movies
- Policy view used by managers to change pricing, membership, and other policies

Technician/programmer's view

Technical view used by programmer to create other user interfaces and custom queries

Clerks, managers, programmers, and customers see different views of a video rental store's database. Customers can browse through listings and reviews of available movies using a touch-screen kiosk. The clerk's view allows only for simple data-entry and check-out procedures. The manager, working with the same database, has control over pricing, policies, and inventory, but can't change the structure or user interface of the database. The programmer can work under the hood to fine-tune and customize the database so it can better meet the needs of other employees and customers.

Database Trends

It is better to ask **some of the questions** than to know **all of the answers.**
—James Thurber, in *Fables for Our Time*

Database technology isn't static. Advances in the last two decades have changed the way most organizations deal with data, and current trends suggest even bigger changes in the near future.

Real-Time Computing

The earliest file management programs could do only **batch processing**, which required users to accumulate transactions and feed them into computers in large batches. These batch systems weren't able to provide the kind of immediate feedback we expect today. Questions like "What's the balance in my checking account?" or "Are there any open flights to Denver next Tuesday?" were likely to be answered "Those records will be updated tonight, so we'll let you know tomorrow."

Today, disk drives, inexpensive memory, and sophisticated software have allowed **interactive processing** to replace batch processing for most applications. Users can now interact with data through terminals, viewing and changing values online in **real time**. Batch processing is still used for printing periodic bills, invoices, and reports and for making backup copies of data files—jobs for which it makes sense to do a lot of transactions at once. But for applications that demand immediacy, such as airline reservations, banking transactions, and the like, interactive, multiuser database systems have taken over.

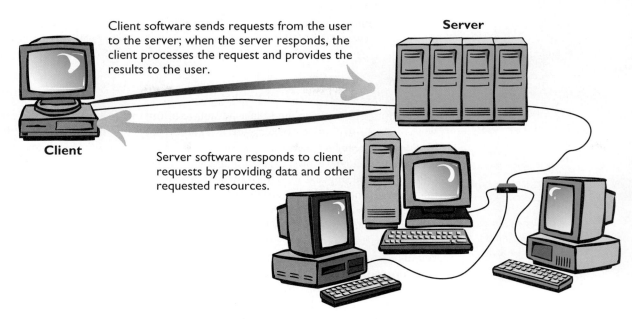

Client software sends requests from the user to the server; when the server responds, the client processes the request and provides the results to the user.

Server

Client

Server software responds to client requests by providing data and other requested resources.

Client/server computing involves two-way communication between client and server programs.

This trend toward real-time computing is accelerated by the Internet, which makes it possible to have almost instant access to information anywhere on Earth, inside or outside the boundaries of the enterprise.

Downsizing and Decentralizing

In the pre-PC days, most databases were housed in mainframe computers accessible only to information-processing personnel. But the traditional hard-to-access **centralized database** on a mainframe system is no longer the norm.

Today many businesses use a **client/server** approach: *Client* programs in desktop (or laptop) computers send information requests through a network to server databases on mainframes or desktop computers; the *servers* process queries and send the requested data back to the client. A client/server system enables users to take advantage of the PC's simple user interface and convenience, while still having access to data stored on large server systems.

Some corporations keep copies of all corporate data in integrated **data warehouses**. In some respects, data warehouses are similar to old-style systems: They're large, relatively expensive, and centralized. But unlike older centralized systems, data warehouses give users more direct access to enterprise data. Data warehouses are most commonly found in large corporations and government departments.

Some companies use **distributed databases**, where data is strewn across networks on several different computers rather than stored in one central site. Many organizations have both data warehouses and distributed databases. From the user's point of view the differences between these approaches may not be apparent. Connectivity software, sometimes called *middleware*, links the client and server machines, hiding the complexity of the interaction between those machines. Wherever the data is stored, the goal is to provide quick and easy access to important information.

Data Mining

Today's technology makes it easy for a business to accumulate masses of information in a database. Many organizations are content to retrieve information using the queries, searches, and reports. But others are finding that there's gold hidden in their large databases—gold that can only be extracted using a new technology called data mining. **Data mining** is the discovery and extraction of hidden predictive information from large databases. It uses statistical methods and artificial intelligence technology to locate trends and patterns in data that would have been overlooked by normal database queries. For example, a grocery chain used data mining to discover differences between male and female shopping patterns so they could create gender-specific marketing campaigns. (In an industry ad they announced that some men habitually buy beer and diapers every Friday!) In effect, data-mining technology enables users to "drill down" through masses of data to find valuable veins of information.

Databases and the Web

Many businesses are retooling to take advantage of Internet technology on their internal networks. These *intranets* enable employees to access corporate databases using the same Web browsers and search engines they use to access information outside the company networks. As Internet tools rapidly evolve, database access should become easier and more transparent.

HTML, the language used to construct most Web pages, wasn't designed to build database queries. But a newer, more powerful language called **XML** is designed with industrial-strength database access in mind. Database manufacturers are currently retooling their products so they can process data requests in XML. Because XML can serve as both a query language and a Web page construction tool, it's likely to open up all kinds of databases to the Web, making it easy for you to request and receive information.

For many organizations, Web database strategies revolve around *directories*. Directories were originally little more than repositories for user phone numbers, addresses, and passwords, and they were commonly buried inside network operating systems. But the explosive growth of the Internet and e-commerce have expanded the roles of directories for many organizations. Directories can be used to store basic employee and customer information, along with access policies, identity proof, payment information, and security information. Directories are at the heart of many *customer relationship management (CRM)* systems—software systems for organizing and tracking information on customers.

The Web makes it possible for employees and customers alike to have instant access to databases, opening up all kinds of rapid-response e-commerce possibilities. But this kind of broad real-time database access also increases the probability of data errors—and the importance of eliminating those errors as quickly as possible. High data quality is a critical factor in successful e-commerce. Most large databases use data-checking routines whenever data is entered. But many organizations also depend on data cleansing tools to correct errors that make it through the entry-checks. For errors that aren't corrected by automated cleansing tools, the last wall of defense is typically a human customer service representative who can provide rapid response to customers complaints.

Object-Oriented Databases

Some of the biggest changes in database technology in the next few years may take place under the surface, where they may not be apparent to most users. For example, many computer scientists believe that the relational data model will be supplanted in the next decade by an object-oriented data model and that most future databases will be **object-oriented databases** rather than relational databases. Instead of storing records in tables and hierarchies, object-oriented databases store software *objects* that contain procedures (or instructions) along with data. Object-oriented databases often are used in conjunction with object-oriented programming languages. Experts suggest that object technology will make construction and manipulation of complex databases easier and less time consuming. Users will find databases more flexible and responsive as object technology becomes more widespread, even if they aren't aware of the underlying technological reasons for these improvements. Today many companies are experimenting with databases that combine relational and object concepts into hybrid systems.

Multimedia Databases

Today's databases can efficiently store all kinds of text and numeric data. But today's computers are multimedia machines that routinely deal with pictures, sounds, animation, and video clips. Multimedia databases can handle graphical and dynamic data along with text and numbers. Multimedia professionals use databases to catalog art, photographs, maps, video clips, sound files, and other types of media files. Media files aren't generally stored in databases because they're too large. Instead, a multimedia database serves as an *index* to all of the separately stored files.

Dealing with Databases

Whether you're creating an address file with a simple file manager or retrieving data from a full-blown relational database management system, you can save yourself a great deal of time and grief if you follow a few commonsense rules:

▶ **Choose the right tool for the job.** Don't invest time and money in a programmable relational database to computerize your address book, and don't try to run the affairs of your multinational corporation with a $99 file manager.

▶ **Think about how you'll get the information out before you put it in.** What kinds of files, records, and fields will you need to create to make it easy to find things quickly and print things the way you'll want them? For example, use separate fields for first and last name if you want to sort names alphabetically by last name and print first names first.

▶ **Start with a plan, and be prepared to change your plan.** It's a good idea to do a trial run with a small amount of data to make sure everything works the way you think it should.

▶ **Make your data consistent.** Inconsistencies can mess up sorting and make searching difficult. For example, if a database includes residents of Minnesota, Minn., and MN, it's hard to group people by state.

▶ **Databases are only as good as their data.** When entering data, take advantage of the data-checking capability of your database software. Does the first name field contain non-alphabetic characters? Is the birth date within a reasonable range? Automatic data checking is important, but it's no substitute for human proofreading or for a bit of skepticism when using the database.

▶ **Query with care.** In the words of Aldous Huxley, "People always get what they ask for; the only trouble is that they never know, until they get it, what it actually is that they have asked for." Here's a real example: A student searching a database of classic rock albums requested all records containing the string "Dylan," and the database program obediently displayed the names of several Bob Dylan albums . . . plus one by Jimi Hendrix called Electric Ladyland. Why? Because "dylan" is in Ladyland! Unwanted records can go unnoticed in large database selections, so it's important to define selection rules very carefully.

▶ **If at first you don't succeed, try another approach.** If your search doesn't turn up the answers you were looking for, it doesn't mean the answers aren't there; they may just be wearing a disguise. For example, if you search a standard library database for "Vietnam War" references, you might not find any. Why? Because the government officially classifies the Vietnam War as a conflict, so references are stored under the subject "Vietnam Conflict." Technology meets bureaucracy!

Multimedia databases have applications in law enforcement, medicine, entertainment, and other professions where information needs go beyond words and numbers. In one high-profile example, IBM and Sony are transferring 115,000 hours worth of CNN videotape into a digital database. This database enables CNN producers to work more efficiently with archived clips, but it also opens up the possibility of pay-per-view Web access by consumers through the Internet and wireless devices.

Natural Language Databases

Ultimately, database technology will all but disappear from the user's view as interfaces become simpler, more powerful, and more intelligent. Future databases will undoubtedly incorporate more artificial intelligence technology. We're already seeing databases and data mining software that can respond to simple *natural language* queries—queries in English or some other human language. Many help sites and search engines on the Web can accept queries in English, German, French, Japanese, and several other languages. Today's natural-language technology is far from perfect, but it's getting better quickly. It won't be long before you'll be able to ask for data using the same language you use when addressing a human being.

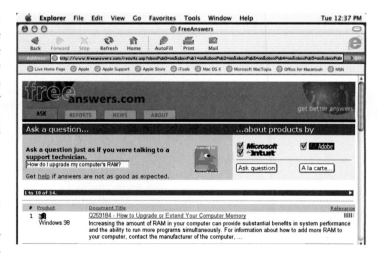

www.freeanswers.com enables users to ask questions about computers by stating their queries in plain English—and other natural languages.

No Secrets: Computers and Privacy

Advanced technology has created **new opportunities** for America as a nation,but it has also created the possibility for **new abuses** of the individualAmerican citizen. Adequate safeguards must always **stand watch**so that man remains **master** and never the **victim of the computer**.

—Richard Nixon, 37th president of the United States, Feb. 23, 1974

Instant airline reservations, all-night automated banking, overnight mail, instant library searches, Web shopping—databases provide us with conveniences that were unthinkable a generation ago. But convenience isn't free. In the case of databases the price we pay is our privacy.

The Internal Revenue Service workers shown here enter taxpayers' personal financial information into massive computer databases. When you shop by phone, respond to a survey, or fill out a warranty card, it's likely that a clerk somewhere will enter that data into a computer.

Personal Data: All About You

We live in an information age, and data is one of the currencies of our time. Businesses and government agencies spend billions of dollars every year to collect and exchange information about you and me. More than 15,000 specialized marketing databases contain 2 billion consumer names, along with a surprising amount of personal information. The typical American consumer is on at least 25 marketing lists. Many of these lists are organized by characteristics like age, income, religion, political affiliation, and even sexual preference—and they're bought and sold every day.

Marketing databases are only the tip of the iceberg. Credit and banking information, tax records, health data, insurance records, political contributions, voter registration, credit card purchases, warranty registrations, magazine and newsletter subscriptions, phone calls, passport registration, airline reservations, automobile registrations, arrests, Internet explorations—they're all recorded in computers, and we have little or no control over what happens to most of those records once they're collected.

For most of us this data is out of sight and out of mind. But lives are changed because of these databases. Here are three representative stories:

▌ When members of Congress investigated ties between President Jimmy Carter's brother Billy and the government of Libya, they produced a report that detailed, among other things, the exact time and location of phone calls placed by Billy Carter in three different states. The phone records, which revealed a great deal about Billy Carter's activities, were obtained from AT&T's massive network of data-collecting computers. Similar information is available on every phone company customer.

▌ When a credit bureau mistakenly placed a bankruptcy filing in the file of a St. Louis couple, banks responded by shutting off loans for their struggling construction business, forcing them into real bankruptcy. They sued but lost because credit bureaus are protected by law from financial responsibility for "honest" mistakes!

▌ A Los Angeles thief stole a wallet and used its contents to establish an artificial identity. When the thief was arrested for a robbery involving murder, the crime was recorded under the wallet owner's name in police databases. The legitimate owner of the wallet was arrested five times in the following fourteen months and spent several days in jail before a protracted court battle resulted in the deletion of the record.

▌ In a more recent, more typical example of **identity theft**, an imposter had the mail of an innocent individual temporarily forwarded to a post office box so he could easily collect credit card numbers and other personal data. By the time the victim discovered an overdue Visa bill, the thief had racked up $42,000 in bogus charges. The victim wasn't liable for the charges, but it took the better part of a year to correct all of the credit bureau errors.

Privacy violations aren't new, and they don't always involve computers. The German Nazis, the Chinese Communists, and even Richard Nixon's 1972 campaign committee practiced surveillance without computers. But the privacy problem takes on a whole new dimension in the age of high-speed computers and databases. The same characteristics that make databases more efficient than other information storage methods—storage capacity, retrieval speed, organizational flexibility, and ease of distribution of information—also make them a threat to our privacy.

The Privacy Problem

What has taken me **a lifetime to build** —my trust, my integrity and my **identity**—has been **tainted**. I **don't know** if I'm dealing with a **14-year-old messing around** with a computer or if I'm dealing with **organized crime**.

—Identity theft victim

In George Orwell's *1984*, information about every citizen was stored in a massive database controlled by the ever-vigilant Big Brother. Today's data warehouses in many ways resemble Big Brother's database. Data-mining techniques can be used to extract information about individuals and groups without their knowledge or consent. And databases can be easily sold or used for purposes other than those for which they were collected. Most of the time this kind of activity goes unnoticed by the public. Here are some examples where public knowledge changed privacy policy:

▶ In 1998 CVS drug stores contracted with Elensys, a Massachusetts direct marketing company, to send reminders to customers who had not renewed their prescriptions. While some customers undoubtedly appreciated the reminders, others objected to this commercial use of their private medical records. CVS terminated the practice as a result of protests.

▶ In many states driver's license information is considered public record, available to anyone for a fee. In 1998 Florida's legislature voted to make driver's license photographs available on the same basis. But after a public outcry, Florida, along with several other states, ended its practice of selling driver's license photos to private companies.

▶ In 1999 Amazon.com introduced "Purchase Circles"—a feature that allowed customers to see which books, CDs, tapes, and videos are most popular within particular companies, schools, government organizations, and cities. Amazon didn't make individual purchase information available to the public, but it used that information to create customer profiles for groups. Using these Purchase Circle profiles, Amazon's Web site might tell you the most popular books and videos among Microsoft employees, Stephens College students, or residents of Hays, Kansas, for example. In response to protests, Amazon decided to give customers the option of being excluded from Purchase Circles.

▶ In 1999 online advertising agency DoubleClick acquired a direct marketing firm along with its database of 90 million households. The company intended to combine supposedly anonymous data on Web user activity with personal information from the massive consumer database, creating data files rich with personal data about consumers. In March, 2000, in response to outcries from consumers and privacy watchdog groups, DoubleClick backed away from the data-matching plan, calling it a "big mistake" to try to match information in that way before government or industry standards could be put into place.

▶ Prior to February, 2001, N2H2, an Internet filtering software company, sold "class clicks" marketing research based on Web usage patterns of children to other companies. The company insists that its data didn't threaten any individual's privacy. Still, in response to protests, it stopped selling its data.

Centralized data warehouses aren't necessary for producing computerized dossiers of private citizens. With networked computers, it's easy to compile profiles by combining information from different database files. As long as the files share a single unique field, such as a Social Security number field, **record matching** is trivial and quick. And when database information is combined, the whole is often far greater than the sum of its parts.

Sometimes the results are beneficial. Record matching is used by government enforcement agencies to locate criminals ranging from tax evaders to mass murderers. Because credit bureaus collect data about us, we can use credit cards to borrow money wherever we go. But these benefits come with at least three problems:

▶ *Data errors are common.* A study of 1,500 reports from the three big credit bureaus found errors in 43 percent of the files.
▶ *Data can become nearly immortal.* Because files are commonly sold and copied, it's impossible to delete or correct erroneous records with absolute certainty.
▶ *Data isn't secure.* A *Business Week* reporter demonstrated this in 1989 by using his computer to obtain then Vice President Dan Quayle's credit report. Had he been a skilled criminal, he might have been able to change that report.

Protection against invasion of privacy is not explicitly guaranteed by the U.S. Constitution. Legal scholars agree that the **right to privacy**—freedom from interference in the private sphere of a person's affairs—is implied by other constitutional guarantees, although debates rage about what this means. Federal and state laws provide forms of privacy protection, but most of those laws were written years ago. Most European countries have had strong privacy protection laws for years. The 1998 European Data Protection Directive guarantees that all countries in the European Union will guarantee a basic set of privacy rights to citizens—rights that go far beyond those of American citizens. The directive allows citizens to have access to all personal data, to know where that data originated, to have inaccurate data rectified, to seek recourse in the event of unlawful processing, and to withhold permission to use their data for direct marketing. The American legislature has refused to pass similar laws because of intense lobbying by business interests. When it comes to privacy violation in America, technology is far ahead of the law.

Big Brother and Big Business

> If **all records** told the same tale,
> then **the lie** passed into history and **became truth**.
> —George Orwell, in *1984*

Database technology clearly poses a threat to personal privacy, but other information technologies amplify that threat:

▶ Networks make it possible for personal data to be transmitted almost anywhere instantly. The Internet is particularly fertile ground for collecting personal information about you. And the Web makes it alarmingly easy for anyone with a connected computer to examine your personal information.
▶ Microsoft's Passport, part of .Net and the Windows XP operating system, collects passwords, credit card numbers, and other consumer information in a central database controlled by Microsoft. The company's stated goal is to make it easier for its customers to take advantage of the Web's many services, but the potential for abuse of this technology may outweigh any possible gains in convenience.
▶ Workplace monitoring technology, described in Chapter 15, "Computers at Work," enables managers to learn more than ever before about the work habits and patterns of workers.
▶ Surveillance cameras, increasingly used for nabbing routine traffic violations and detecting security violators, can be combined with picture databases to locate criminals—and others. Florida law enforcement officials came under fire from privacy groups because they used cameras, face-recognition software, and criminal databases to find and arrest several attendees of the 2001 Super Bowl. After the terrorist attacks of September 11, 2001, surveillance cameras were installed in hundreds of businesses and government agencies to guard against future attacks.
▶ Surveillance satellites can provide permanent peepholes into our lives for anyone willing to pay the price.
▶ Cell phones will soon be required by law to include technology to determine and transmit their locations to emergency personnel responding to 911 calls. Privacy advocates point out that the same technology can easily be used for less noble purposes.
▶ Smart cards and other intelligent personal devices, discussed in the last three chapters of this book, enable us to trade personal privacy for convenience.

In George Orwell's *1984* personal privacy was the victim of a centralized Communist police state controlled by Big Brother. Today our privacy is threatened by many Big Brothers—with new threats emerging almost every day. As Simson Garfinkel says in *Database Nation*, "Over the next 50 years, we will see new kinds of threats to privacy that don't find their roots in totalitarianism, but in capitalism, the free market, advanced technology, and the unbridled exchange of electronic information."

Democracy depends on the free flow of information, but it also depends on the protection of individual rights. Maintaining a balance is not easy, especially when new information technologies are being developed at such a rapid pace. With information at our fingertips it's tempting to think that more information is the answer. But in the timeless words of populist philosopher Will Rogers, "It's not the things we don't know that get us into trouble, it's the things we do know that ain't so."

Your Private Rights

Sometimes computer-aided privacy violations are nuisances; sometimes they're threats to life, liberty, and the pursuit of happiness. Here are a few tips for protecting your right to privacy.

▶ *Your Social Security number is yours—don't give it away.* Since your SSN is a unique identifier, it can be used to gather information about you without your permission or knowledge. For example, you could be denied a job or insurance because of something you once put on a medical form. Never write it (or your driver's license number or phone number, for that matter) on a check or credit card receipt. Don't give your SSN to anyone unless they have a legitimate reason to ask for it.

▶ *Don't give away information about yourself.* Don't answer questions about yourself just because a questionnaire or company representative asks you to. When you fill out any form—coupon, warranty registration card, survey, sweepstakes entry, or whatever—think about whether you want the information stored in somebody else's computer.

▶ *Say no to direct mail, phone, and email solicitations.* Businesses and political organizations pay for your data so they can target you for mail, phone, and email campaigns. You can remove yourself from many lists using forms from the Direct Mail Marketing Association (www.the-dma.org). If this doesn't stop the flow, you might want to try a more direct approach. Send back unwanted letters along with "Take me off your list" requests in the postage-paid envelopes that come with them. When you receive an unsolicited phone marketing call, tell the caller "I never purchase or donate anything as a result of phone solicitations," and ask to be removed from the list. If they call within 12 months of being specifically told not to, you can sue and recover up to $500 per call according to the Telephone Consumer Protection Act of 1991. Unfortunately, there's no comparable federal law to protect you against junk email yet, so you should be especially careful about giving out your email address if you don't like receiving unsolicited email.

▶ *Say no to sharing your personal information.* If you open a private Internet account, tell your Internet service provider that your personal data is not for sale. If you don't want your state's Department of Motor Vehicles selling information about you, notify them. A relatively new federal law gives you more control over DMV use of personal data. If you don't want credit agencies sharing personal information, let them know. The Federal Trade Commission's Privacy Web site

(www.ftc.gov/privacy) includes clear guidelines and forms for contacting your DMV and credit agencies. The Financial Modernization Act of 1999 allows you to tell your banks and other financial institutions not to share your personal information with other institutions; check with those institutions for details.

▶ *Say no to pollsters.* Our political system has been radically transformed by polling; most of our "leaders" check the polls before they offer opinions on controversial issues. If you and I don't tell the pollsters what we're thinking, politicians will be more likely to tell us what they're thinking.

▶ *If you think there's incorrect or damaging information about you in a file, find out.* The Freedom of Information Act of 1966 requires that most records of U.S. government agencies be made available to the public on demand. The Privacy Act of 1974 requires federal agencies to provide you with information in your files relating to you and to amend incorrect records. The Fair Credit Reporting Act of 1970 allows you to see your credit ratings—for free if you have been denied credit—and correct any errors. The three big credit bureaus are Equifax (www.equifax.com), Trans Union (www.tuc.com), and Experian (www.experian.com).

▶ *To maximize your privacy, minimize your profile.* If you don't want a financial transaction recorded, use cash. If you don't want your phone number to be public information, use an unlisted number. If you don't want your mailing address known, use a post office box.

▶ *Know your electronic rights.* Privacy protection laws in the United States lag far behind those of other high-tech nations, but they are beginning to appear. For example, the 1986 Electronic Communications Privacy Act provides the same protection that covers mail and telephone communication to some—but not all—electronic communication. The 1988 Computer Matching and Privacy Protection Act regulates the use of government data in determining eligibility for federal benefits.

▶ *Support organizations that fight for privacy rights.* If you value privacy rights, let your representatives know how you feel, and support the American Civil Liberties Union, Computer Professionals for Social Responsibility, the Electronic Frontier Foundation, Electronic Privacy Information Center, Center for Democracy and Technology, Private Citizen, and other organizations that fight for those rights.

Counterfeit Freedom

Randall E. Stross

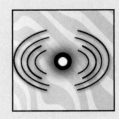

After the terrorist attacks of September 11, 2001, security jumped to the forefront of the political landscape. This article, first published in the October 8 Issue of U.S. News and World Report, *argues that increased security justified a loss of personal privacy and civil liberties. This controversial point of view was rarely heard before the September 11 massacre.*

If we were self-sufficient farmers in a sparsely populated land, or misanthropic hermits, we would not be so vulnerable to the horrors that the few can visit upon the many. But we have become, and will remain, an urban nation, living and working, traveling and spectating, in physical proximity, our exposure to unspeakable violence shared. Until September 11, we had gone about our daily business, cheek by jowl, as strangers to one another, without thinking much about our shared vulnerability. But now we must. And Larry Ellison, the CEO of Oracle, has helped us with a proposal that we adopt a national identification card, with digitized photograph and thumbprint, and tied to a central database, for which Oracle would provide the software for free.

Ellison presented his proposal as a means of improving airline security. We all know that this measure alone is anything but a panacea, that a suicidal terrorist who had entered the country legally and maintained a clean criminal record would not be stopped. Still, would we not feel better when boarding if counterfeit-proof digital ID were required of everyone? We know viscerally that no community has ever deliberately entrusted its well-being to anonymous strangers.

Our current patchwork of ID systems is based on easily forged paper documents and scattered government databases that can't connect with one another. Whether we use Oracle software is unimportant, but the rest of Ellison's proposal incorporates the crucial elements that we must put in place with all possible speed: First, we must insist on biometric authentication, using unique physical characteristics like a fingerprint. This would eliminate identity theft, which increased 16-fold in the mid-1990s, expanding to an estimated 700,000 instances to date. It would also spare law-abiding citizens from wrongful arrest. The Saudi Arabian government complained last month that at least five innocent Saudi citizens had been wrongly identified as suicide bombers.

False choice. Second, we must maintain a single database of identities. The Immigration and Naturalization Service, State Department, Social Security Administration, FBI, IRS, state driver's license bureaus—each could still track different kinds of information. But for a person's physical identity, each should draw upon a single repository. When asked his opinion of the Ellison proposal, Robert Post, a constitutional law professor at the University of California-Berkeley, warned that we should not allow "a terrorist attack to destroy forms of freedom that we have enjoyed." Post

did not specify what "freedom" was at risk. We must identify ourselves for any number of activities of daily life, so the only freedom that would be lost with the advent of improved ID technology is the freedom to falsify one's legal identity. I'm sorry, what's the rationale again for that latitude?

If there's prolonged debate about national identity cards, I hope it will not run along the old ruts, the individual's interests versus the state's. This vital matter is really between citizen and fellow citizen, the obligations of community members to one another. In 1620, the residents of Plymouth did not need to carry ID cards; all knew one another. Thus was born the first American ID database, stored not in silicon but in every resident's head.

By the time of the Revolution, the Colonies' largest city, Philadelphia, was a teeming mass of 25,000, and only 5 percent of the population lived in cities. Yet even then, the young country's leaders saw need for government to help citizens do what the individual could no longer do on his own: identify the newcomers swelling the rapidly expanding U.S. community. The first census, in 1790, recorded the names and addresses of heads of families.

Fast-forward to the present. Instead of the 4 million residents of 1790, we are a nation of 285 million, with 30 million foreign visitors a year. Our borders are so porous and the document requirements for employment so flimsy that we also host 6 million to 12 million illegal aliens. One wonders why we haven't furloughed the border guards and swung the gates open, conceding we have effectively lost control of those who come in and, legally speaking, disappear.

Does a national ID card seem Orwellian? Alternatively, we can build biometric authentication into every state-issued driver's license, require similar ID cards of nondrivers and all foreign visitors, and have states share a central database of identities. Uncomfortable with the picture of that database holding your precious identity? Too late. Your identity, plus your phone calls, medical records, bank transactions, credit problems, and minutely detailed listings of purchases all are on file in digital form, as the private sector has embraced databases enthusiastically (making Ellison a very wealthy man). Yet these are outside our oversight. A federal identity database, however, would be ours, accountable to us, governed by rules that we the public direct. We are all inhabitants of a continent-size village. Knowing one another a bit better is a communal necessity.

DISCUSSION QUESTIONS

1. Do you agree that the advantages of a national ID card justify the threat to personal privacy? Explain your answer.
2. What kinds of laws, if any, should be in place to protect your privacy if a national ID card is adopted?

Summary

Database programs enable users to quickly and efficiently store, organize, retrieve, communicate, and manage large amounts of information. Each database file is a collection of records, and each record is made up of fields containing text strings, numbers, and other chunks of information. Database programs enable users to view data in a variety of ways, sort records in any order, and print reports, mailing labels, and other custom printouts. A user can search for an individual record or select a group of records with a query.

While most database programs are general-purpose tools that can be used to create custom databases for any purpose, some are special-purpose tools programmed to do a particular set of tasks. Geographical information systems, for example, combine maps and demographic information with data tables to provide new ways to look at data. Personal information managers provide automated address books, appointment calendars, to-do lists, and notebooks for busy individuals.

Many database programs are, technically speaking, file managers because they work with only one file at a time. But technically, a true database is a collection of files. Database management systems (DBMSs) can work with several files at once, cross-referencing information among files when appropriate. A DBMS can provide an efficient way to store and manage large quantities of information by eliminating the need for redundant information in different files. A well-designed database provides different views of the data to different classes of users so each user sees and manipulates only the information necessary for the job at hand.

The trend today is clearly away from large, centralized databases accessible only to data processing staff. Instead, most organizations are moving toward a client/server approach that enables users to have access to data stored in servers throughout the organization's network.

The accumulation of data by government agencies and businesses is a growing threat to our right to privacy. Massive amounts of information about private citizens are collected and exchanged for a variety of purposes. Today's technology makes it easy to combine information from different databases, producing detailed profiles of individual citizens. While there are many legitimate uses for these procedures, there's also a great potential for abuse.

Chapter Review

▼ Key Terms

batch processing (p. 226)
browse (p. 214)
centralized database (p. 227)
client/server (p. 227)
computed field (p. 213)
data mining (p. 227)
data warehouse (p. 227)
database (p. 213)
database management system
   (DBMS) (p. 223)
database program (p. 213)
distributed database (p. 227)
export data (p. 214)

field (p. 213)
file (p. 213)
file manager (p. 223)
geographical information system
   (GIS) (p. 219)
identity theft (p. 230)
import data (p. 214)
interactive processing (p. 226)
mail merge (p. 214)
object-oriented database (p. 228)
personal information manager
   (PIM) (p. 219)
query (p. 214)

query language (p. 217)
real time (p. 226)
record (p. 213)
record matching (p. 231)
relational database (p. 224)
report (p. 214)
right to privacy (p. 232)
search (p. 214)
select (records) (p. 214)
sort (p. 214)
SQL (p. 217)
XML (p. 228)

▼ Interactive Quiz Questions

1. The *Computer Confluence* CD-ROM contains self-test quiz questions related to this chapter, including multiple choice, true or false, and matching questions.
2. The *Computer Confluence* Web site, **www.prenhall.com/beekman**, contains self-test exercises related to this chapter. Follow the instructions for taking a quiz. After you've completed your quiz, you can email the results to your instructor.

The Web site also contains open-ended discussion questions called Internet Explorations. Discuss one or more of the Internet Exploration questions at the section for this chapter.

▼ Review Questions

1. Define or describe each of the key words listed in the "Key Words" section. Check your answers in the glossary.
2. What is the difference between a file manager and a database management system? How are they similar?
3. Describe the structure of a simple database. Use the terms *file*, *record*, and *field* in your description.
4. What is a query? Give examples of the kinds of questions that might be answered with a query.
5. What steps are involved in producing a standard multicolumn business report from a database?
6. What are the advantages of personal information management software over paper notebook organizers? What are the disadvantages?
7. What does it mean to sort a data file?
8. How can a database be designed to reduce the likelihood of data-entry errors?
9. Describe how record matching is used to obtain information about you. Give examples.
10. Do we have a legal right to privacy? On what grounds?
11. Why are computers important in discussions of invasion of privacy?

▼ Discussion Questions

1. Grade books, checkbooks, and other information collections can be managed with either a database program or a spreadsheet program. How would you decide which type of application is most appropriate for a given job?
2. What have you done this week that directly or indirectly involved a database? How would your week have been different in a world without databases?
3. "The computer is a great humanizing factor because it makes the individual more important. The more information we have on each individual, the more each individual counts." Do you agree with this statement by science fiction writer Isaac Asimov? Why or why not?
4. Suppose you have been incorrectly billed for $100 by a mail-order house. Your protestations are ignored by the company, which is now threatening to report you to a collection agency. What do you do?
5. What advantages and disadvantages does a computerized law enforcement system have for law-abiding citizens?
6. In what ways were George Orwell's "predictions" in the novel *1984* accurate? In what ways were they wrong?

▼ Projects

1. Design a database for your own use. Create several records, sort the data, and print a report.
2. Find out as much as you can about someone (for example, yourself or a public figure) from public records like tax records, court records, voter registration lists, and motor vehicle files. How much of this information were you able to get directly from the Web? How much was available for free?
3. Find out as much as you can about your own credit rating.
4. The next time you order something by mail or phone, try encoding your name with a unique middle initial so you can recognize when the company sells your name and address to other companies. Use several different spellings for different orders if you want to do some comparative research.
5. Determine what information about you is stored in your school computers. What information are you allowed to see? What information are others allowed to see? Exactly who may access your files? Can you find out who sees your files? How long is the information retained after you leave?
6. Keep track of your purchases for a few weeks. If other people had access to this information, what conclusions might they be able to draw about you?

Sources and Resources

Books

Like word processors, spreadsheet software, and multimedia programs, databases have inspired hundreds of how-to tutorials, user's guides, and reference books. If you're working with a popular program, you should have no trouble finding a book to help you develop your skills.

Database Design for Mere Mortals: A Hands-On Guide to Relational Database Design, by Michael J. Hernandez (Reading, MA: Addison-Wesley, 1997). This book can save time, money, and headaches for anyone who's involved in designing and building a relational database. After defining all of the critical concepts, the author clearly outlines the design process using case studies to illustrate important points.

The Practical SQL Handbook: Using Structured Query Language, Third Edition, by Judith S. Bowman, Sandra L. Emerson, and Marcy Darnovsky (Reading, MA: Addison-Wesley, 1996). If you want to learn to communicate with relational databases using the standard database query language, this book can help you learn the language.

Object Technology: A Manager's Guide, Second Edition, by David A. Taylor (Reading, MA: Addison-Wesley, 1998). This book clearly explains the basics of object technology in nontechnical terms. The author explores object-oriented databases, object-oriented programs, and object-oriented software on networks.

Data Smog: Surviving the Information Glut, by David Shenk (New York: HarperEdge, 1997). It's possible to have too much information at your fingertips. David Shenk's book clearly describes the hazards to individuals and society of all this information.

Surveillance Society: Monitoring Everyday Life (Issues in Society), by David Lyon (Open University Press, 2001). This book intelligently analyzes the deterioration of personal privacy in our information society without getting bogged down in jargon.

Database Nation: The Death of Privacy in the 21st Century, by Simson Garfinkel (Cambridge, MA: O'Reilly, 2000). This is a frightening, sobering account of the erosion of our personal privacy as a result of misuse of technology—databases, on-the-job monitoring, data networks, biometric devices, video surveillance, and more. Simson skillfully mixes chilling true stories and futuristic scenarios with practical advice for reclaiming our individual and collective rights to privacy. Highly recommended.

The Unwanted Gaze: The Destruction of Privacy in America, by Brian Doherty (New York: Random House, 2000). This book ties together the impeachment of President Clinton with the threat computers present to our control over personal information. The unifying thread is the deterioration of the private space earlier generations of Americans enjoyed.

Ben Franklin's Web Site: Privacy and Curiosity from Plymouth Rock to the Internet, by Robert Ellis Smith (Privacy Journal, 2000). This book, by the Editor of the *Privacy Journal*, reviews the twisted evolution of privacy law in the US.

The Transparent Society: Will Technology Force Us to Choose Between Freedom and Privacy?, by David Brin (Cambridge, MA: Perseus Press, 1998). Brin, a mathematician and award-winning science fiction writer, presents a compelling case that personal privacy is doomed by technology. He argues that our best hope is to provide equal access to all information, rather than let the biggest brothers have the only windows into our lives. Compelling reading.

You'll find several other books that deal with privacy issues listed in later chapters of this book.

Videos

Many popular films and television shows, from *Clear and Present Danger* to *The X-Files*, deal directly or indirectly with issues related to privacy and technology. One recent action film, *Enemy of the State*, used those issues as central themes. There's plenty of fantasy in this non-stop thriller about a man on the run and a government that can watch his every move. But there's a good deal of truth here, too.

Periodical

The Privacy Journal (**www.privacyjournal.net**). This widely quoted monthly newsletter covers all issues related to personal privacy.

Organizations

Privacy Foundation (**www.privacyfoundation.org**). The Privacy Foundation isn't an advocacy group; its mission is to report on technology-based privacy threats and circulate alerts.

Computer Professionals for Social Responsibility (**www.cpsr.org**). CPSR provides the public and policy makers with realistic assessments of the power, promise, and problems of information technology. Much of their work deals with privacy-related issues. Their newsletter is a good source of information.

The Electronic Frontier Foundation (**www.eff.org**). EFF strives to protect civil rights, including the right to privacy, on emerging communication networks.

Electronic Privacy Information Center (**www.epic.org**). EPIC serves as a watchdog on government efforts to build surveillance capabilities into the emerging information infrastructure.

American Civil Liberties Union (**www.aclu.org**). The ACLU tirelessly defends constitutional rights, including privacy rights.

Private Citizen (**www.private-citizen.com**). This organization can help keep you off junk phone lists—for a price.

Web Pages

Check the *Computer Confluence* Web site for links to many of the organizations listed above, along with links to other database and privacy-related sites.

Part 3
Exploring with Computers
Networks and Gateways

Networking and Telecommunication

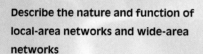

Arthur C. Clarke's Magical Prophecy

1. If an elderly but distinguished scientist says that something is possible he is almost **certainly right**, but if he says that it is impossible he is **very probably wrong.**

2. The only way to find the **limits of the possible** is to go beyond them into the impossible.

3. Any sufficiently advanced technology is **indistinguishable from magic.**

—Clarke's Three Laws

Besides coining Clarke's laws, British writer Arthur C. Clarke has written more than 100 works of science fiction and nonfiction. His most famous work was the monumental 1968 film *2001: A Space Odyssey,* in which he collaborated with movie director Stanley Kubrick. The film's villain, a faceless English-speaking computer with a lust for power, sparked many public debates about the nature and risks of artificial intelligence.

Arthur C. Clarke

HAL, the rebellious computer in the movie 2001: A Space Odyssey

But Clarke's most visionary work may be a paper published in 1945 in which he predicted the use of *geostationary* communications satellites—satellites that match the Earth's rotation so they can hang in a stationary position relative to the spinning planet below, relaying wireless transmissions between locations on the planet below. Clarke's paper pinpointed the exact height of the orbit required to match the movement of the satellite with the planetary rotation. He also suggested that these satellites could replace many telephone cables and radio towers, allowing electronic signals to be beamed across oceans, deserts, and mountain ranges, linking the people of the world with a single communications network.

A decade after Clarke's paper appeared, powerful rockets and sensitive radio receiving equipment made communications satellites realistic. In 1964 the first synchronous TV satellite was launched, marking the beginning of a billion-dollar industry that has changed the way people communicate.

Today Clarke is often referred to as the father of satellite communications. He lives in Sri Lanka, where he continues his work as a writer, but now he uses a personal computer and beams his words around the globe to editors using the satellites he envisioned half a century ago. ▶

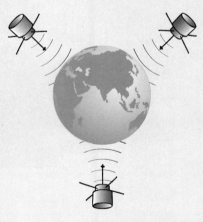

Geostationary communication satellites

The Battle of New Orleans, the bloodiest battle of the War of 1812, was fought two weeks after the war officially ended; it took that long for the cease-fire message to travel from Washington, D.C., to the front line. In 1991, 179 years later, six hard-line Soviet communists staged a coup to turn back the tide of democratic and economic reforms that were sweeping the U.S.S.R. Within hours messages zipped between the Soviet Union and Western nations on telephone and computer networks. Cable television and computer conferences provided up-to-the-minute analyses of events—analyses that were beamed to computer bulletin boards inside the Soviet Union. Networks carried messages among the resistors, allowing them to stay steps ahead of the coup leaders and the Soviet military machine. People toppled the coup and ultimately the Soviet Union—not with guns, but with courage, will, and timely information.

Telecommunication technology—the technology of long-distance communication—has come a long way since the War of 1812, and the world has changed dramatically as a result. After Samuel Morse invented the telegraph in 1844, people could, for the first time, send long-distance messages instantaneously. Alexander Bell's invention of the telephone in 1876 extended this capability to the spoken voice. Today systems of linked computers enable us to send data and software across the room or around the world. The technological transformation has changed the popular definition of the word *telecommunication*, which today means long-distance electronic communication in a variety of forms.

In this chapter we look at the computer as part of a network rather than as a self-contained appliance, and we discuss ways in which such linked computers are used for communication and information gathering. We also consider how networks are changing the way we live and work. In the next chapter we'll delve deeper into the Internet—the global computer network at the heart of the next telecommunication revolution.

Linking Up: Network Basics

All the **most promising technologies** making their debut now are chiefly due to communication between computers— that is, to **connections** rather than to **computations**. And since **communication is the basis of culture**, fiddling at this level is indeed **momentous**.

—Kevin Kelly, former *Wired* Executive Editor

A student uses a terminal in the library to connect with an online information source.

A computer network is any system of two or more computers that are linked together. Why is networking important? The answers to this question revolve around the three essential components of every computer system:

▶ *Hardware.* Networks enable people to share computer hardware, reducing costs and making it possible for more people to take advantage of powerful computer equipment.
▶ *Software.* Networks enable people to share data and software programs, increasing efficiency and productivity.
▶ *People.* Networks enable people to work together in ways that are otherwise difficult or impossible.

Important information is hidden in these three statements. But before we examine them in more detail, we need to look at the hardware and software that make computer networks possible.

Basic Network Anatomy

The most desirable interaction with a network is one in which **the network itself is invisible and unnoticeable**. Planners often forget that people do not want to use systems at all—easy or not. What people want is to **delegate** a task and **not to worry about how** it is done.

—Nicholas Negroponte, director of MIT's Media Lab

In Chapter 2, you saw how information travels among the CPU, memory, and other components within a computer as electrical impulses that move along collections of parallel wires called buses. A network extends the range of these information pulses, allowing them to travel to other computers. A computer may have a **direct connection** to a network—for example, it might be one of many machines linked together in an office—or it might have **remote access** to a network through a phone line, a television cable system, or a satellite link. Either way, the computer needs some specialized hardware to complete the connection. To connect directly, the computer needs a network interface card; for a remote connection it generally needs a modem or similar device.

The Network Interface

Chapter 2 described personal computer **ports**—sockets that enable information to pass in and out. *Parallel ports*, commonly used to connect older printers to a computer, enable bits to pass through in groups of 8, 16, or 32. *Serial ports*, on the other hand, require bits to pass through one at a time. Most PCs have at least one of each. Macintoshes don't have built-in parallel ports. Older Macs have multipurpose serial ports for connecting to printers, modems, and some networks. The standard serial port on an IBM-compatible computer is designed to attach peripherals such as modems—not to connect directly to networks. Modern Macs and PCs have *USB* and *FireWire (IEEE 1394)* ports that are much faster and more flexible than traditional serial and parallel ports.

A **network interface card** (NIC) adds an additional serial port to the computer—one that's especially designed for a direct network connection. The network interface card controls the flow of data between the computer's RAM and the network cable. At the same time it converts the computer's internal low-power signals into more powerful signals that can be transmitted through the network. The type of card depends on the type of network connection needed. The most common types of networks today require some kind of Ethernet card in each computer. **Ethernet** is a popular networking architecture developed in 1976 at Xerox. (Most Macintoshes and some PCs include an Ethernet port on the main circuit board and don't need an additional card to connect to an Ethernet network.) Details vary—and there are *many* details—but the same general principles apply to all common network connections.

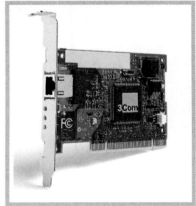

A network interface card allows a PC to connect to a network.

In the simplest networks two or more computers are linked by cables. But direct connection is impractical for computers that are miles or oceans apart. For computers to communicate over long distances, they need to transmit information through other paths.

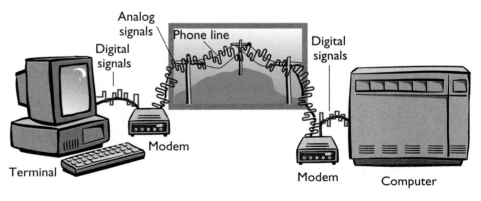

Communication á la Modem

The world is outfitted with plenty of electronic communication paths: An intricate network of cables, radio transmitters, and satellites enables people to talk by telephone between just about any two places on the planet. The telephone network is ideal for connecting remote computers, too, except it was designed to carry sound waves, not streams of bits. Before a **digital signal**—a stream of bits—can be transmitted over a standard phone line, it must be converted to an **analog signal**—a continuous wave. At the receiving end the analog signal first must be converted back into the bits representing the original digital message. Each of these tasks is performed by a **modem** (short for modulator/demodulator)—a hardware device that connects a computer's serial port to a telephone line.

A modem converts digital signals from a computer or terminal into analog signals. The analog waves are transmitted through telephone lines to another modem, which converts them back into digital signals.

An internal modem is installed on a circuit board inside the computer's chassis. An external modem sits in a box linked to a serial port. Both types use phone cables to connect to the telephone network through standard modular phone jacks. Modems differ in their transmission speeds, measured in **bits per second (bps)**. Many people use the term *baud rate* instead of bps, but bps is technically more accurate for high-speed modems. Modems today commonly transmit at 28,800 bps to 56.6K (56,600) bps over standard phone lines. In general, communication by

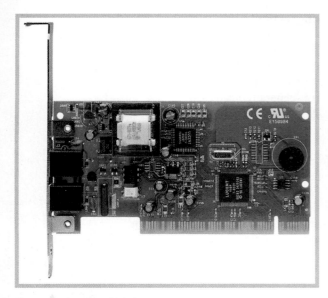

An external modem (right) connects to the computer's serial port. An internal modem (left) is installed inside the computer's chassis.

modem is slower than communication between computers that are directly connected on a network. High-speed transmission isn't usually critical for text messages, but it can make a huge difference when the data being transmitted includes graphics, sound, video, and other multimedia elements—the kinds of data commonly found on the Web.

Faster Modem Alternatives

For faster remote connections, many businesses and homes bypass standard modems and use some kind of high-speed alternative. Several competing technologies are available to computer users in many areas: DSL, cable modems, and satellite modems.

▶ DSL uses standard phone lines and is provided by phone companies in many cities.
▶ Cable modems provide fast network connections through cable television networks in many areas.
▶ High-speed wireless connections can connect computers to networks using radio waves rather than wires.
▶ Satellite dishes can deliver fast computer network connections as well as television programs.

These technologies, sometimes called *broadband* technologies, are discussed in more detail later in this chapter and the next chapter.

Networks Near and Far

Imagine how useful an office would be without a door.
—Doug Engelbart, Internet pioneer, the importance of network connections

A LAN can contain a variety of computers and peripherals that are connected.

Computer networks come in all shapes and sizes, but most can be categorized as either local-area networks or wide-area networks.

A **local-area network (LAN)** is a network in which the computers are physically close to each other, usually in the same building. A typical LAN includes a collection of computers and peripherals; each computer and networked peripheral is an individual *node* on the network. Nodes are connected by cables, which serve as pathways for transporting data between machines. Some LAN cables, known as *twisted pair*, resemble the copper wires in standard telephone cables. Another type of cable, *coaxial cable*, is the same type of cable used to trans-

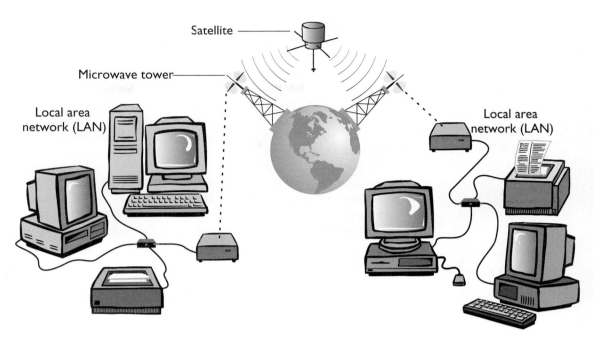

Satellite

Microwave tower

Local area
network (LAN)

Local area
network (LAN)

WANs are often made up of LANs linked by phone lines, microwave towers, and communication satellites.

port television signals. Some networks, mostly in homes, use existing household electrical or telephone wiring to transmit data.

In a **wireless network** each node has a tiny radio or infrared transmitter connected to its network port so it can send and receive data through the air rather than through cables. Wireless network connections are especially convenient for workers who are constantly on the move. They're also used for creating small networks in homes and small businesses because they can be installed without digging or drilling.

All computers on a LAN do not have to use the same operating system. For example, a single network might include Macintoshes, Windows PCs, and UNIX workstations. The computers can be connected in many different ways, and many rules and industry-defined standards dictate what will and won't work. Most organizations depend on network administrators to take care of the behind-the-scenes details so others can focus on using the network. For *enterprise network systems*—large, complex networks with hundreds of computers—network administrators depend on network management system software to help them track and maintain healthy networks.

A *metropolitan area network (MAN)* is a service that links two or more LANs within a city. MAN service is typically provided by a telephone or telecommunications company. With a MAN, a company can keep employees linked even if they're blocks away from each other.

A **wide-area network (WAN)**, as the name implies, is a network that extends over a long distance. In a WAN each network site is a node on the network. Data is transmitted long-distance between networks on a collection of common pathways known as a *backbone*. Large WANs are possible because of the web of telephone lines, microwave relay towers, and satellites that span the globe. Most WANs are private operations designed to link geographically dispersed corporate or government offices.

In today's internetworked world, communication frequently happens between LANs and WANs. **Bridges** and **gateways** are hardware devices that can pass messages between networks and, in some cases, translate messages so they can be understood by networks that obey different software protocols. **Routers** are hardware devices or software programs that route messages as they travel between networks via bridges and gateways.

Communication Software

Whether connected by cables, radio waves, or a combination of modems and telephone lines, computers need some kind of **communication software** to interact. To

Pretty soon you'll have no more idea of **what computer you're using** than you have an idea of **where your electricity comes from**.

—Danny Hillis, computer designer

communicate with each other, two machines must follow the same protocol—a set of rules for the exchange of data between a terminal and a computer or between two computers. One such protocol is transmission speed: If one machine is "talking" at 56,600 bps and the other is "listening" at 28,800 bps, the message doesn't get through. (Most modems can avoid this particular problem by adjusting their speeds to match each other.) Protocols include prearranged codes for messages such as "Are you ready?" "I am about to start sending a data file," and "Did you receive that file?" For two computers to understand each other, the software on both machines must be set to follow the same protocols. Communication software establishes a protocol that is followed by the computer's hardware.

Communication software can take a variety of forms. For users who work exclusively on a local-area network, many communication tasks are taken care of by a network operating system (NOS) such as Novell's Netware or Microsoft's Windows XP Server. Just as a personal computer's operating system shields the user from most of the nuts and bolts of the computer's operation, a NOS shields the user from the hardware and software details of routine communication between machines. But unlike a PC operating system, the NOS must respond to requests from many computers and must coordinate communication throughout the network. Today many organizations are replacing their specialized PC-based NOSs with intranet systems—systems built around the open standards and protocols of the Internet, as described in more detail in the next chapter.

The function and location of the network operating system depend in part on the LAN model. Some LANs are set up according to the client/server model, a hierarchical model in which one or more computers act as dedicated servers and all the remaining computers act as clients. Each server is a high-speed, high-capacity computer containing data and other resources to be shared with client computers. Using NOS server software, the server fulfills requests from clients for data and other resources. In a client/server network the bulk of the NOS resides on the server, but each client has NOS client software for sending requests to servers.

Many small networks are designed using the peer-to-peer model (sometimes called *p-to-p* or *P2P*) which enables every computer on the network to be both client and server. In this kind of network every user can make files publicly available to other users on the network. Some desktop operating systems, including many versions of Windows and the Mac OS, include all the software necessary to operate a peer-to-peer network. In practice many networks are hybrids, combining features of the client/server and peer-to-peer models.

Outside of a LAN one of the most common types of communication software is terminal emulation software, which enables a personal computer to function as a character-based "dumb" terminal—a simple input/output device for sending messages to and receiving messages from the host computer. A terminal program handles phone dialing, protocol management, and the miscellaneous details necessary for making a PC and a modem work together. With terminal software and a modem, a personal computer can communicate through phone lines with

Client/server computing involves two-way communication between client and server programs.

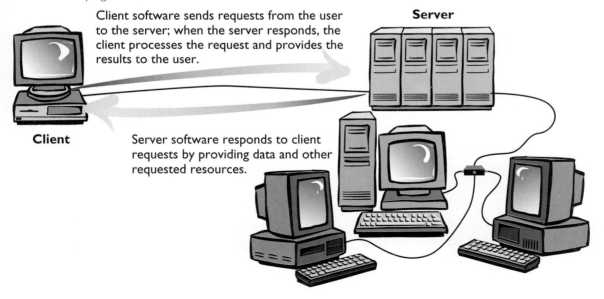

Client software sends requests from the user to the server; when the server responds, the client processes the request and provides the results to the user.

Client

Server software responds to client requests by providing data and other requested resources.

Server

another PC, a network of computers, or, more commonly, a large multiuser computer. The Windows operating system package includes a terminal emulation program.

Basic terminal emulators are fine for bare-bones computer-to-computer connections, but their character-based user interfaces can be confusing to people who are used to point-and-click GUIs. What's more, they can't be used to explore media-rich destinations on and off the World Wide Web. That's why most online explorers today use Web browsers and other specialized graphical client software instead of generic terminal programs.

At the other end of the line the communication software is usually built into the multiuser operating system of the **host system**—the computer that provides services to multiple users. This software enables a timesharing computer to communicate with several other computers or terminals at once. The most widely used host operating system today is UNIX, the 30-year old OS that has many variants, including the non-commercial Linux OS discussed in Chapter 4, "Software Basics: The Ghost in the Machine."

Servers like these can provide software and data for hundreds of networked computers.

The Network Advantage

A network becomes more valuable as

it reaches more users.

—Metcalf's Law, by Bob Metcalf, inventor of Ethernet

With this background in mind let's reconsider the three reasons people use networks:

▸ *Networks enable people to share computer hardware, reducing costs and making it possible for more people to take advantage of powerful computer equipment.* When computers and peripherals are connected in a LAN, computer users can share expensive peripherals. Before LANs the typical office had a printer connected to each computer. Today it's more common to find a small number of high-quality networked printers shared by a larger group of computers and users. In a client/server network, each printer may be connected to a *print server*—a server that accepts, prioritizes, and processes print jobs. While it may not make much sense for users to try to share a printer on a wide-area network, WAN users often share other hardware resources. Many WANs include powerful mainframes and supercomputers that can be accessed by authorized users at remote sites.

▸ *Networks enable people to share data and software programs, increasing efficiency and productivity.* In offices without networks people often transmit data and software by sneakernet—that is, by carrying disks between computers. In a LAN one or more computers can be used as **file servers**—storehouses for software and data that are shared by several users. With client software a user can get software and data from any server on the LAN without taking a step. A large file server is typically a dedicated computer that does nothing but serve files. But a peer-to-peer approach, allowing any computer to be both client and server, can be an efficient, inexpensive way to share files on small networks. Of course, sharing computer software on a network can violate software licenses (see Chapter 4) if not done with care. Many, but not all, licenses allow the software to be installed on a file server as long as the number of simultaneous users never exceeds the number of licensed copies. Some companies offer **site licenses** or **network licenses**, which reduce costs for multiple copies or remove restrictions on software copying and use at a network site. (Software copying is discussed in more detail in Chapter 11, "From Internet to Information Infrastructure.") Networks don't eliminate compatibility differences between different computer operating systems, but they can simplify data communication between machines. Users of Windows-compatible computers, for example, can't run Macintosh applications just because they're available on a file server. But they can, in many cases, use data files and documents created on a Macintosh and stored on the server. For example, a poster created with Adobe Illustrator on a Macintosh could be stored on a file server so it can be opened, edited, and printed by users of Illustrator on Windows PCs. File sharing isn't always that easy. If users of different systems use programs with incompatible file formats, they need to use *data translation software* to read and modify each other's files. On WANS the transfer of data and software can save more than shoe leather; it can save time. There's no need to send disks or CDs by overnight

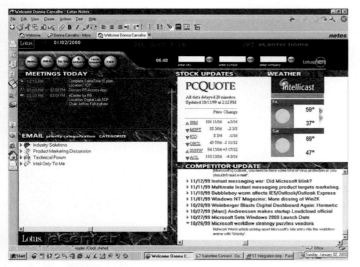

Lotus Notes, the most widely used groupware application, combines distributed databases, email, and document management to facilitate information sharing and workgroup collaboration. Lotus Notes is a client/server application that works on all major operating systems. Notes is compatible with many Internet protocols and services. (Lotus Notes® is a registered trademark of Lotus Development Corporation.)

mail between two sites if both sites are connected to the same network. Typically, data can be sent electronically between sites in a matter of minutes.

▶ *Networks enable people to work together in ways that are difficult or impossible without network technology.* Some software applications can be classified as **groupware**—programs designed to enable several networked users to work on the same documents at the same time. Groupware programs include multi-user appointment calendars, project-management software, database-management systems, and software for group editing of text-and-graphics documents. Many groupware programs today, such as Lotus Notes, are built on Internet protocols, so group members can communicate and share information using Web browsers and other standard Internet software tools.

Workgroups can benefit from networks without groupware packages. Most groupware features—email, message posting, calendars, and the rest—are generally available through Web and PC applications. Still, for large organizations a full-featured groupware package can be easier to manage than a collection of separate programs.

For many LAN and WAN users, network communication is limited to sending and receiving messages. As simple as this might sound, electronic messaging profoundly changes the way people and organizations work. In the next section we take a close look at the advantages and implications of interpersonal communication with computers.

Email, Teleconferences, and Instant Messaging: Interpersonal Computing

New technology gives us two kinds of **newfound freedom**:
The ability to **reach each other** 24/7—
and the chance to **avoid one another** as never before.
—Lori Gottlieb, Author of *Stick Figure*

Whether you're connected to a LAN, a WAN, a timesharing mainframe, or the Internet, you probably have access to some kind of **email** system that enables you to send and receive messages to others on the network. Chapter 0, ReadMe, covered the basics of email and illustrated a simple email session.

As explained in that chapter, most email messages are plain ASCII text; formatted documents, pictures, multimedia documents, and other computer files are typically sent as **attachments** that accompany messages. Newer email programs can (optionally) send, receive, edit, and display email messages formatted in HTML, the formatting language used in most Web pages. HTML email messages can include multiple typeface sizes and styles, and the text can be formatted in a variety of ways. The email client software hides the HTML from the sender and the recipient; they just see the formatted message. If the recipient views a formatted message with a mail program that doesn't recognize HTML, the formatting doesn't appear.

A variation of email is the **teleconference**—an online meeting between two or more people. Many teleconferencing systems enable users to communicate in real time, just as they would by telephone. In a typical **real-time teleconference** each participant sits at a computer or terminal, watching the messages appear on the screen as they're typed by other participants and typing comments for others to see immediately. Because of their give-and-take, informal nature, public real-time teleconferences are often called **chat rooms**. Whatever they're called, they tend to be chaotic, and typing responses can seem painfully slow to participants watching the process on the screen. Still, many people enjoy the immediacy of real-time communication.

Instant messaging (IM) adds spontaneity by allowing an online user to create a "buddy list" to determine who on the list is logged on at any given time, and start an instant keyboard conversation with anyone who's available from the list. Instant messaging was popularized by America Online as an entertaining way for members to chat with each other and with others on the Internet. IM services from AOL, Microsoft, and others are extremely popular today. Many businesses now use instant messaging to keep employees connected. IM technology is even built into many mobile phones.

In an **asynchronous teleconference** (sometimes called a *delayed teleconference*), participants type, post, and read messages at their convenience. In effect, participants in a delayed teleconference share an email box for messages related to the group's purposes. The Internet's Usenet *newsgroups*, discussed in the next chapter, are popular examples of asynchronous teleconferences.

Email, instant messaging, and other types of online communication can replace many memos, letters, phone calls, and face-to-face meetings, making organizations more productive and efficient.

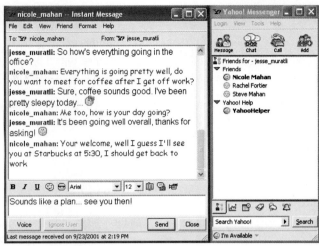

Instant messaging systems allow people to carry on real-time text-based conversations whenever they're online.

The Postal Alternative

The number of email messages now exceeds the number of letters sent through the U.S. Postal Service each year. Most experts expect email to take an even bigger chunk of the post office's business in coming years. Here's why:

▶ *Email is fast.* A typical email message takes no more than a few minutes from the time it's conceived until it reaches its destination—across the office or across the ocean. Email users often refer to traditional mail as "snail mail."

▶ *Email doesn't depend on location.* If you send someone an electronic message, that person can log in and read it from a computer at home, at the office, or anywhere in the world.

▶ *Email facilitates group communication.* In most email systems it's no harder and no more expensive to send a message to several people than to send it to one person. Most systems enable groups to have named distribution lists (sometimes called *aliases)* so a mail message addressed to an alias name (like faculty, office, or sales) is sent automatically to everyone in the group.

▶ *Email messages are digital data that can be edited and combined with other computer-generated documents.* Because the messages you receive by email are stored in your computer electronically, you can edit text and numbers without having to retype the entire document and without wasting paper. You can easily add text from other documents stored on your computer. When you're finished, you can forward the edited document back to the original sender or to somebody else for further processing.

Bypassing the Telephone

Email and teleconferencing also offer advantages over telephones:

▶ *Online communication is less intrusive than the telephone.* A ringing phone can interrupt concentration, disrupt a meeting, and bring just about any kind of activity to a standstill. Instead of shouting "Answer me now!" an email message waits patiently in the mailbox until the recipient has the time to handle it.

▶ *Online communication allows time shifting.* Email users aren't plagued by busy signals, unanswered rings, and message machines. You can receive email messages when you're busy, away, or asleep, and they'll be waiting for you when you have the time to pick them up. Time zones are largely irrelevant to email users.

Minimizing Meetings

Teleconferences and email can drastically reduce the amount of time people spend traveling to and participating in meetings. They offer several advantages for group decision-making:

▶ *Teleconferences and email enable decisions to evolve over time.* A group can discuss an issue electronically for hours, days, or weeks without the urgency of getting everything settled in a single session. New information can circulate when it's current rather than at the next meeting. Participants have time to think about each statement before responding. When organizations use teleconferences for discussion and information dissemination, meetings tend to be infrequent, short, and to the point.

> ◗ *Teleconferences and email make long-distance meetings possible.* Teleconferences can include people from all over the world, and nobody needs to leave home to participate. In fact, a growing number of programmers, writers, and other information workers literally work at home, communicating with colleagues by modem.
>
> ◗ *Teleconferences and email emphasize the message over the messenger.* In companies that rely on email and teleconferences for much of their communication, factors like appearance, race, gender, voice, mannerisms, and title tend to carry less weight than they do in other organizations. Status points go to people with good ideas and the ability to express those ideas clearly in writing.

Online Issues: Reliability, Security, Privacy, and Humanity

Well there's egg and bacon; egg, sausage and bacon; egg and **spam**; bacon and **spam**; egg, bacon, sausage and **spam**; **spam**, bacon, sausage and **spam**; **spam**, egg, **spam**, **spam**, bacon and **spam**; **spam**, **spam**, **spam**, egg and **spam**; **spam**, **spam**, **spam**, **spam**, **spam**, **spam**, baked beans, **spam**, **spam**, **spam** and **spam**; or lobster thermidor aux crevettes with a mornay sauce garnished with truffle paté, brandy, and a fried egg on top of **spam**.

—Waitress in *Monty Python's Flying Circus*

Any new technology introduces new problems, and online communication is no exception. Here are some of the most important:

> ◗ *Email and teleconferencing are vulnerable to machine failures, network glitches, human errors, and security breaches.* A system failure can cripple an organization that depends on email for critical communications. Internet users have experienced email blackouts caused by power outages, satellite failures, system overloads, and other technological breakdowns. Email attachment viruses like 2000's Love Bug have caused billions of dollars worth of damage worldwide. (See the Chapter "Computer Security and Risks" for more on viruses.)
>
> ◗ *Email can be overwhelming.* Many people receive hundreds of messages a day. Sifting through all those messages can consume hours of time that could have been used in other ways. Email overload has become such a serious problem that some businesses have implemented email-free Fridays to give their employees time to catch up on other work.
>
> ◗ *Email can be unsolicited.* Because it's easy, fast, and free, email is often used to send blanket messages to masses of people without permission. Some of this unsolicited mail is innocent (and not-so-innocent) humor. Some is designed to spread the word for a good cause. (Some "good cause" campaigns are, in fact, fraudulent or misinformed; even so, they continue to circulate.) Most unsolicited email is designed to sell something—weight-loss plans, insurance, vacation homes, cigarettes, pornography, cheap loans, political campaigns, or just about anything that people can pay for with a credit card. Junk email is known as spam because it can be just as annoying and repetitive as the menu in the Monty Python skit quoted above. But spam can also be a security risk, as you'll see in the next two chapters.
>
> ◗ *Email can pose a threat to privacy.* The U.S. Postal Service has a centuries-old tradition of safeguarding the privacy of first-class mail. Electronic communication is not grounded in that tradition. While most email messages are secure and private, there's always a potential for eavesdropping by an organization's system administrators and crafty system snoopers. Many businesses routinely monitor email sent by employees. In 1999 an online bookseller was found guilty of intercepting a competitor's email to gain market advantage. That same year users of Microsoft's popular HotMail service learned that their private email messages and address books could be easily accessed by anyone with a basic knowledge of how Web addresses work. Microsoft corrected the problem, but questions of email security remain.
>
> ◗ *Email can be faked.* Email forgery can be a serious threat on a surprising number of email systems. Some systems have safeguards against sending mail using someone else's ID, but none completely eliminates the threat. In time, it's likely that a digital signature will be encoded into every email message (using cryptography technology described in the Chapter "Computer Security and Risks."). Until then, forgery is a problem.

▶ *Email works only if everybody plays.* Just as the postal system depends on each of us checking our mailboxes daily, an email system can work only if all subscribers regularly log in and check their mail. Most people develop the habit quickly if they know important information is only available online.

▶ *Email and teleconferencing filter out many "human" components of communication.* When Bell invented the telephone, the public reaction was cool and critical. Businesspeople were reluctant to communicate through a device that didn't allow them to look each other in the eye and shake hands. While this reaction might seem strange today, it's worth a second look. When people communicate, part of the message is hidden in body language, eye contact, voice inflections, and other nonverbal signals. The telephone strips visual cues out of a message, and this can lead to misunderstandings. Most online communication systems peel away the sounds as well as the sights, leaving only plain words on a screen—words that might be misread if they aren't chosen carefully. What's more, email and teleconferences seldom replace casual "water cooler conversations"—those chance meetings that result in important communications and connections.

Problems notwithstanding, email and electronic messaging have become fixtures in businesses, schools, and government offices everywhere.

Converging Communication Technologies: From Messages to Money

The Internet is at the heart of the telecommunications explosion that's going on today. But many telecommunication services and technologies—online information services, fax machines, voice mail, GPS devices, mobile phones, video teleconferencing systems, ATMs, and more—aren't dependent on the Internet. Each of these applications is built around digital computer technology, and the boundaries that separate them are growing fuzzy as communication technologies converge.

Never in history has distance meant less.
—Alvin Toffler, in *Future Shock*

Online Information Services

A decade ago, when the Internet was the domain of researchers, thousands of electronic bulletin board systems (BBS) served as modem destinations for online explorers. Most BBSs were small operations operated out of homes. Visitors could post messages and read messages left by others with similar interests, send and receive email, and share software. Today most BBSs have been replaced by Web sites that offer the same services, and more, via the Internet. The same fate has befallen most online databases. Customers who used to connect directly to database services such as Dow Jones News Retrieval Service now retrieve the same information through Web sites on the Internet.

Commercial **online services**—America Online, CompuServe, and Prodigy—can still be accessed without venturing onto the Internet. Subscribers have access to a variety of services: news, research tools, shopping, banking, games, chat rooms, bulletin boards, email, instant messaging, software libraries. Subscribers can **download** software—copy it from the host computer to their computers—and **upload** software—post it on the host system so it's available for others. (Software sharing is part of the community spirit networks, but it's not without problems. Two of these problems, software piracy and viruses, are discussed in the Chapter "Computer Security and Risks.")

The Internet has forced online services to change the way they do business. Customers who used to be content within the confines of a particular service now want to have access to the World Wide Web. Many information services have responded to the Web's popularity by becoming part of it. Before the Web, CompuServe was the largest online information service. In 1997, after several consecutive years of declining enrollment, it converted to a fee-based subscription outpost on the Web. Not long afterward it was purchased by America Online (AOL), now the largest private online service.

AOL's customers use special client software rather than a Web browser to connect and use its services. But the AOL client software includes a Web browser so AOL users can explore the entire Web—not just the offerings inside AOL. AOL also provides space for customers to build

Online services such as AOL offer a variety of services in a privately controlled environment.

My Places
- Customize My Places
- Greetings
- Horoscopes
- Local News
- Maps & Directions
- My Portfolios
- People Directory
- Sports Scores
- Stock Quotes
- What's New on AOL
- White Pages

Have You Tried?
- AOL Anywhere
- People Directory

- AOL Help
- Go to Internet
- Parental Controls

AOL Keyword: Welcome

Rules of Thumb Rules of Thumb Rules of Thumb Rules of Thumb

Online Survival Tips

Whether you log into an information service or the Internet, you're using a relatively new communication medium with new rules. Here are some suggestions for successful online communication:

▶ **If your online service is metered, do what you can offline.** *Do your homework before you log in so you don't have to look things up while the meter is running. Compose, edit, and address messages before you log on. Plan your strategy before you connect.*

▶ **Avoid peak hours.** *Online traffic comes in waves. If you avoid the peaks, you'll save time and aggravation.*

▶ **Let your system do as much of the work as possible.** *If your email program can sort mail, filter mail, or automatically append a signature file to your mail, take advantage of those features. If you send similar messages over and over, store them, and recycle the relevant text. If you find yourself sending messages to the same group of people repeatedly, create an alias that includes all of those people—a distribution list that can save you the trouble of typing or selecting all those names each time. If you can automate repetitive processes like logging in and downloading mail, do it; the time you invest will be paid back over and over.*

▶ **Store names and addresses in an online address book.** *Email addresses aren't always easy to remember and type correctly. If you mistype even a single character, your mes-*sage will probably either go to the wrong person or **bounce**—come back to you with some kind of undeliverable mail message. An online address book enables you to select addresses without typing them each time you use them.

▶ **Protect your privacy.** *Miss Manners said it well in a 1998 Wired interview: "For email, the old postcard rule applies. Nobody else is supposed to read your postcards, but you'd be a fool if you wrote anything private on one."*

▶ **Cross-check online information sources.** *Don't assume that every information nugget you see online is valid, accurate, and timely. If you "hear" something online, treat it with the same degree of skepticism that you would if you heard it in a cafeteria or coffee shop.*

▶ **Be aware and awake.** *It's easy to lose track of yourself and your time online. In his book Virtual Community, Howard Rheingold advises, "Rule Number One is to pay attention. Rule Number Two might be: Attention is a limited resource, so pay attention to where you pay attention."*

▶ **Avoid information overload.** *When it comes to information, more is not necessarily better. Search selectively. Don't waste time and energy trying to process mountains of online information. Information is not knowledge, and knowledge is not wisdom.*

---

and display personal Web pages. By including Internet email and Web services in its package, AOL has become the largest Internet service provider.

Many experts question whether everything-under-one-roof services like AOL can successfully compete with the free-for-all World Wide Web. Others believe there'll always be a place for services that can simplify the online experience. One thing is certain: The Internet will continue to bring changes to these services, and the changes will come rapidly.

Video Teleconferencing

A **video teleconference** enables people to communicate face to face over long distances by combining video and computer technology. In its simplest form video teleconferencing is like two-way television. Each participant sits in a room equipped with video cameras, microphones, and television monitors. Video signals are beamed between sites so that every participant can see and hear every other participant on television monitors. Video teleconferencing is mainly practiced in special conference rooms by groups that meet too often to travel. But some businesses now use video telephones that transmit pictures as well as words through phone lines.

With the addition of a video camera, an interface, and a high-speed network connection, a telephone-capable desktop computer can be used for video teleconferencing. These systems enable callers to see each other on their computer screens while they carry on phone

Video conferencing hardware and software make this long-distance business meeting possible.

A fax modem (left) enables a personal computer to communicate with a fax machine (right).

conversations over high-speed computer networks, including the Internet. Some enable them to view and edit shared documents while they talk. Today most PC-based video teleconferencing systems suffer from erratic video transmission, but the technology is getting better quickly.

Fax Machines and Fax Modems

A **facsimile (fax) machine** is a fast and convenient tool for transmission of information stored on paper. When you send a fax of a paper document, the sending fax machine scans each page, converting the scanned image into a series of electric pulses and sending those signals over phone lines to another fax machine. The receiving fax machine uses the signals to construct and print black-and-white facsimiles or copies of the original pages. In a sense the two fax machines and the telephone line serve as a long-distance photocopy machine.

A computer can send onscreen documents through a fax modem to a receiving fax machine. The **fax modem** translates the document into signals that can be sent over phone wires and decoded by the receiving fax machine. In effect, the receiving fax machine acts like a remote printer for the document. A computer can also use a fax modem to receive transmissions from fax machines, treating the sending fax machine as a kind of remote scanner. A faxed letter can be displayed on screen or printed to paper, but it can't be immediately edited with a word processor the way an email message can. Like a scanned document, the digital facsimile is nothing more than a collection of black-and-white dots to the computer. Before a faxed document can be edited, it must be processed by optical character recognition (OCR) software.

Voice Mail and Computer Telephony

"Hi. This is Anita Chen. I'm either away from my desk or on another line. Please leave your name, number, and a message. If you prefer to talk to a receptionist, press zero." The **voice mail** system that delivers this recorded message is more than an answering device; it's a voice messaging system with many of the features of an email system.

Your response is recorded in Anita's voice mailbox. When she dials the system number from any telephone and enters her ID number or password on the phone's keypad, she can listen to her messages, respond to them, forward copies to others, and delete unneeded messages. She can do just about anything she could do with an email message except edit messages electronically and attach computer documents.

In spite of its growing popularity, voice mail has detractors. Many people resent taking orders from a machine rather than being able to talk to a human operator. Many callers are frustrated by having to wade through endless voice menus before they can speak to a real person. Office workers often complain about the time-consuming processes of recording and listening to messages.

Voice mail is a familiar example of a growing trend toward *computer telephony integration (CTI)*—the linking of computers and telephones to gain productivity. Many PCs have **telephony** software and hardware that allow them to serve as speakerphones, answering machines, and complete voice mail systems. A typical computer telephony system connects to a standard phone line through a modem capable of handling voice conversations. But it's also possible to

The Kyocera Smartphone is a cell phone and a PDA that uses the Palm OS. Integrated software makes it easy to call contacts from the address book, record notes about phone conversations, and connect to the Internet.

send voice signals through a LAN, a WAN, or the Internet, bypassing the phone companies (and their charges) altogether. So far this kind of network telephony isn't as simple or reliable as commercial phone services, but it may soon pose a threat to phone company profits.

On the mobile front, the line between computers and telephones is especially fuzzy. Many mobile phones can connect to the Internet, do instant messaging, upload and download short email messages, and display miniature Web pages. Handheld PDAs from Palm, Handspring, Compaq, and other companies can do the same things, but with larger screens and friendlier input devices. These handheld computers use software to integrate the functions of a PDA, a phone, and an Internet terminal. Hybrid PDAs and phones involve tradeoffs—do you want to use a boxy PDA as a phone or type email on a tiny phone keypad? But most analysts expect rapid advances in these converging technologies over the next few years—advances such as reliable speech recognition—that will make these devices much more useful for people on the go.

The Global Positioning System

The U.S. Department of Defense **Global Positioning System (GPS)** includes 24 satellites that circle the Earth, carefully spaced so that they can pinpoint any location on the planet. The satellites are positioned so that from any point on the planet, at any time, four satellites will be above the horizon. Each satellite contains a computer, an atomic clock, and a radio. On the ground, a *GPS receiver* can use signals broadcast by three or four visible satellites to determine its position. Handheld GPS receivers can display locations, maps, and directions on small screens; GPS receivers can also be embedded in automobile navigation systems or connected to laptop computers. Members of the U.S. military use GPS receivers to keep track of where they are, but so do scientists, engineers, motorists, hikers, boaters, and others. Many mobile phones include GPS receivers so they can be located quickly when used for emergency calls.

E-Money

When you strip away the emotional trappings, money is just another form of information. Dollars, yen, pounds, and rubles are all just symbols that make it easy for people to exchange goods and services. Money can be just about anything, provided people agree to its value. During the last few centuries, paper replaced metal as the major form of money. Today paper is being replaced by digital patterns stored in computer media. Most major financial transactions take place inside computers, and most money is stored on computer disks and tapes instead of in wallets and safe deposit boxes.

A GPS receiver helps this hiker produce an extremely accurate map of the Colorado trail.

Money, like other digital information, can be transmitted through computer networks. That's why it's possible to withdraw cash from your checking account using an *automated teller machine (ATM)* at a bank, airport, or shopping mall thousands of miles from your home bank. An ATM (not to be confused with the communication protocol with the same initials) is a specialized terminal linked to a bank's main computer through a commercial banking network.

An ATM isn't necessary for *electronic fund transfer* to take place. Many people have paychecks deposited automatically in checking or savings accounts and have bills paid automatically out of those accounts. These automatic transfers don't involve cash or checks; they're done inside computer networks. Many banks allow you to use your home computer or your touch-tone phone to transfer money between accounts, check balances, and pay bills. Electronic fund transfer is one component of *electronic commerce,* or *e-commerce*—commercial activity that takes place through networked computers. E-commerce will be discussed in more detail in later chapters.

Emerging Communication Technologies: Beyond Wires

After more than a century of electric technology, we have **extended our central nervous system** itself in a global embrace, **abolishing both space and time** as far as our planet is concerned.

—Marshall McLuhan, in *Understanding Media*

Until recently, most computer networks depended on wires to transmit electrical signals between computers. But the last decade has seen enormous growth in network technology that carries bits in other ways. In this section, we'll focus on two types of network technology that are dramatically changing the ways people communicate: fiber optic cables and wireless technology. But first, a few words about bandwidth.

Building Bandwidth

Computer networks transmit text, numbers, pictures, sounds, speech, music, video, and money as digital signals. The World Wide Web is fertile ground for mixing of these diverse media. Video on demand, pay-by-the-song music shopping, interactive multiplayer games, real-time auctions, picture phones, customized news feeds, and more are available on the Web—if you don't mind putting up with small, jerky videos, grainy images, and (especially) long waits.

Every day stock traders move billions of dollars in funds electronically through world markets.

The cause of most of these problems on the Internet and other networks is a lack of bandwidth at some point in the path between the sending computer and the receiving computer. The word has a technical definition, but in the world of computer networks **bandwidth** generally refers to the quantity of information that can be transmitted through a communication medium in a given amount of time. In general, increased bandwidth means faster transmission speeds. Bandwidth is typically measured in kilobits (thousands of bits) or megabits (millions of bits) per second. (Since a byte is 8 bits, a megabit is 1/8 of a megabyte. The text of this chapter is about 1/16 megabyte, or a half megabyte of information. A physical medium capable of transmitting 100 megabits per second could theoretically transmit this chapter's text 200 times in one second.) Bandwidth can be affected by many factors, including the physical media that make up the network, the amount of network traffic, the software protocols of the network, and the type of network connection.

Some people find it easier to visualize bandwidth by thinking of a network cable as a highway. One way to increase bandwidth in a cable is to increase the number of parallel wires in that cable—the equivalent of adding more lanes to a freeway. Another way is to increase the speed with which information passes through the cable; this is the same as increasing the speed of the vehicles on the freeway. Of course, it's easier and safer to increase highway speed limits if you have a traffic flow system that minimizes the chance of collisions and accidents; in the same way, more efficient, reliable software can increase network bandwidth. But increasing a highway's throughput doesn't help much if cars pile up at the entry and exit ramps; in the same way, a high-bandwidth network seems like a low-bandwidth network if you're connected through a slow modem.

Fiber Optic Connections

> These are the days of **lasers in the jungle**
> **Lasers in the jungle** somewhere. . . .
> —Paul Simon, in "The Boy in the Bubble"

Broadband network connections such as cable modems and DSL are faster than standard modems because they have greater bandwidth. But DSL and cable modems have nowhere near the bandwidth of **fiber optic cables** that are gradually replacing copper wires in the worldwide telephone network. Fiber optic cables use light waves to carry information at blinding speeds. A single fiber optic cable can transmit half a gigabit (500 *million* bits) per second, replacing 10,000 standard telephone cables!

All-digital fiber optic networks improve the sound quality of phone calls and the speed of long-distance phone response while cutting costs for callers. More importantly, a fiber optic network can rapidly and reliably transmit masses of multimedia data at the same time it's handling voice messages.

Digital fiber optic networks now connect major communication hubs around the world. Many large businesses and government institutions are connected to the global fiber optic network. But most small businesses and homes still depend on copper wires for the "last mile," as it's often referred to in the industry—the link to the closest on-ramp to the fiber optic freeway. Fiber optic communication lines will eventually find their way into most homes, radically changing our lives in the process. These cables will provide two-way links to the outside world for our phones, televisions, radios, computers, and a variety of other devices.

The lines that separate the telephone industry, the computer industry, and the home entertainment industry will blur as voices, video, music, and messages flow back and forth on light waves. Many services we take for granted today—video rentals, cable TV, newspapers, and magazines, for example—will be transformed or replaced by digital high-bandwidth interactive delivery systems of the future. At the same time, entirely new forms of communication are likely to emerge.

Wireless Communication Takes Off

Wireless technology is a **liberating force**. It will make possible **human-centered computers**. This wasn't possible before because we were **anchored to a PC**, and we had to go to it like going to a temple to **pay our respects**.

—Michael Dertouzos, Director, MIT Laboratory for Computer Science

A lightning-fast network connection to your desktop is of little use if you're away from your desk most of the time. When bandwidth is less important than mobility and portability, wireless technology can provide practical solutions.

Infrared wireless technology has been around for many years. Many laptops and handheld computers have infrared ports that can send and receive digital information short distances. Infrared technology isn't widely used in networks because of distance and line-of-sight limitations. Still, infrared technology has practical applications—especially for mobile users. For example, Palm users routinely share programs and data by beaming them through infrared links.

One popular wireless LAN technology is known in the industry as **Wi-Fi** or *802.11b*. (Apple refers to its brand of 802.11b as Airport.) This client/server technology allows multiple computers to connect to a LAN through a base station up to 150 feet away. Wi-Fi isn't as fast as a hard-wired Ethernet connection, but it's fast enough for most applications, including multimedia Web downloads. A home Wi-Fi network allows computers to connect from any room without cables. Wi-Fi base stations are showing up in airports, coffee shops, and other public places. On some campuses Wi-Fi networks allow students to effortlessly connect their laptops to the Internet from dorm rooms, classrooms, or tree-lined gardens.

Another type of wireless technology is **Bluetooth**, named for a Danish king who overcame his country's religious differences. Bluetooth technology

Different types of networks are built with different physical media; the media play critical roles in determining network performance. The two most important performance variables on the physical layer are bandwidth—the amount of information that can be transmitted in a given amount of time—and maximum operating distance.

NETWORKS ARE BUILT ON PHYSICAL MEDIA

Type		Principal Uses	Maximum Operating Distance (without amplification)	Cost
Twisted pair		Small LANS	300 feet	Low
Coaxial cable		Large LANS	600–2,500 feet	Medium
Fiber optic		Network backbones; WANS	1–25 miles	High
Wireless/infrared		LANS	3–1,000 feet (line of sight)	Medium
Wireless/radio		Connecting things that move	Varies considerably	High

overcomes differences between mobile phones, handheld computers, and PCs, making it possible for all of these devices to communicate with each other regardless of operating system. Bluetooth uses radio technology similar to Wi-Fi, but its transmissions are limited to about 30 feet. In some ways Bluetooth competes with Wi-Fi, but it has the potential to complement a Wi-Fi network. With Bluetooth it's possible to create a *personal area network (PAN)*—a network that links a variety of personal electronic devices so they can communicate with each other. Bluetooth technology is still in the early stages of development. When it becomes widely available and affordable, it will open up all kinds of possibilities:

This University of Tennessee student can connect to the Internet using the campus wireless network.

▶ A pacemaker senses a heart attack and notifies the victim's mobile phone to dial 911.
▶ A car radio communicates with parking-lot video cameras to find out where spaces are available.
▶ A pen scans business cards and sends the information to a PDA inside a briefcase.
▶ A medical wristband transmits an accident victim's vital information to a doctor's handheld computer.
▶ A cell phone tells you about specials on clothes (available in your size) as you walk past stores in a mall. (Many fear that this technology will usher in a new era of wireless spam.)

Wi-Fi and Bluetooth aren't part of mainstream culture yet, but wireless communication through mobile phones certainly is. In two decades, mobile phones have gone from simple analog systems to powerful digital devices that can handle Internet data along with voice traffic. In the United States, mobile phones are seldom used to connect to the Internet. Mobile Internet connections are more common in Europe and Asia. In Japan, people routinely use their phones to send and receive email, exchange instant messages, check news headlines, shop, play games, and even do karaoke. The next generation of mobile wireless technology, often called *3G*, promises high-bandwidth connections that will support true multimedia, including real-time video.

The convenience of wireless technology carries a price in security. Wireless networks are far more vulnerable to eavesdropping, data snooping, and hacking than wired networks. Many techniques and tools can help preserve privacy and security, but none of them so far is foolproof. These problems are discussed in more detail in the security chapter.

Many Japanese students use their mobile phones regularly for instant messaging and multiplayer games.

Digital Communication in Perspective

Fiber optic networks and wireless networks are already changing our lives, and the changes will accelerate as these technologies spread. We'll explore these changes in the next chapter as we focus on the Internet—the network of networks at the center of the communication revolution.

Before we do, let's step back and put electronic communication in a larger perspective. As futurist Stewart Brand reminded us in his groundbreaking book, *The Media Lab*:

We can be grateful for the vast dispersed populations of peasant and tribal cultures in the world who have never used a telephone or a TV, who walk where they're going, who live by local subsistence skills honed over millennia. You need to go on foot in Africa, Asia, South America to realize how many of these people there are and how sound they are. If the world city goes smash, they'll pick up the pieces, as they've done before. Whatever happens, they are a reminder that electronic communication may be essential to one kind of living, but it is superfluous to another.

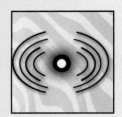

Time To Do Everything Except Think

David Brooks

Is there a downside to the digital communication explosion? In this lighthearted article, first published in the April 30, 2001 issue of Newsweek, *David Brooks raises some serious questions about being over-connected. Brooks is the author of* Bobos in Paradise.

Somewhere up in the canopy of society, way above where normal folks live, there will soon be people who live in a state of perfect wirelessness. They'll have mobile phones that download the Internet, check scores and trade stocks. They'll have Palm handhelds that play music, transfer photos and get Global Positioning System readouts. They'll have laptops on which they watch movies, listen to baseball games and check inventory back at the plant. In other words, every gadget they own will perform all the functions of all the other gadgets they own, and they will be able to do it all anywhere, any time.

Wireless Woman will do a full day's work on the beach in her bikini: her personal digital assistant comes with a thong clip so she can wear it on her way to the pina colada stand. Her phones beep, her pagers flash red lights; when they go off, she looks like a video arcade. Wireless Man will be able to put on his performance underwear, hop in his SUV and power himself up to the top of a Colorado mountain peak. He'll be up there with his MP3 device and his carabiners enjoying the view while conference-calling the sales force, and playing MegaDeath with gamers in Tokyo and Sydney. He'll be smart enough to have enough teeny-tiny lithium batteries on hand to last weeks, and if he swallows them they'd cure depression for life. He's waiting for them to develop a laptop filled with helium that would actually weigh less than nothing, and if it could blow up into an inflatable sex doll he'd never have to come down.

So there he sits in total freedom on that Rocky Mountain peak. The sky is blue. The air is crisp. Then the phone rings. His assistant wants to know if he wants to switch the company's overnight carrier. He turns off his phone so he can enjoy a little spiritual bliss. But first, there's his laptop. Maybe somebody sent him an important email. He wrestles with his conscience. His conscience loses. It's so easy to check, after all . . .

Never being out of touch means never being able to get away. But Wireless Man's problem will be worse than that. His brain will have adapted to the tempo of wireless life. Every 15 seconds there is some new thing to respond to. Soon he has this little rhythm machine in his brain. He does everything fast. He answers emails fast and sloppily. He's bought the fastest machines, and now the idea of waiting for something to download is a personal insult. His brain is operating at peak RPMs.

He sits amid nature's grandeur and says, "It's beautiful. But it's not moving. I wonder if I got any new voice mails." He's addicted to the perpetual flux of the information networks. He craves his next data fix. He's a speed freak, an info junkie. He wants to slow down, but can't.

Today's business people live in an overcommunicated world. There are too many Web sites, too many reports, too many bits of information bidding for their attention. The successful ones are forced to become deft machete wielders in this jungle of communication. They ruthlessly cut away at all the extraneous data that are encroaching upon them. They speed through their tasks so they can cover as much ground as possible, answering dozens of emails at a sitting and scrolling past dozens more. After all, the main scarcity in their life is not money; it's time. They guard every precious second, the way a desert wanderer guards his water.

The problem with all this speed, and the frantic energy that is spent using time efficiently, is that it undermines creativity. After all, creativity is usually something that happens while you're doing something else: when you're in the shower your brain has time to noodle about and create the odd connections that lead to new ideas. But if your brain is always multitasking, or responding to techno-prompts, there is no time or energy for undirected mental play. Furthermore, if you are consumed by the same information loop circulating around everyone else, you don't have anything to stimulate you into thinking differently. You don't have time to read the history book or the science book that may actually prompt you to see your own business in a new light. You don't have access to unexpected knowledge. You're just swept along in the same narrow current as everyone else, which is swift but not deep.

So here's how I'm going to get rich. I'm going to design a placebo machine. It'll be a little gadget with voice recognition and everything. Wireless People will be able to log on and it will tell them they have no messages. After a while, they'll get used to having no messages. They'll be able to experience life instead of information. They'll be able to reflect instead of react. My machine won't even require batteries.

DISCUSSION QUESTIONS

1. Do you think Wireless Woman and Wireless Man are realistic? Explain.
2. Do you agree that speed and efficiency undermine creativity? Explain.

Summary

Networking is one of the most important trends in computing today. Computer networks are growing in popularity because they allow computers to share hardware, allow computers to send software and data back and forth, and enable people to work together in ways that would be difficult or impossible without networks.

LANs are made up of computers that are close enough to be directly connected with cables or wireless radio transmitters/receivers. Most LANs include shared printers and file servers. WANs are made up of computers separated by considerable distance. The computers are connected to each other through the telephone network, which includes cables, microwave transmission towers, and communication satellites. Before it can be transmitted on a phone network, a computer's digital signal is converted to an analog signal using a modem.

Communication software takes care of the details of communication between machines—details like protocols that determine how signals will be sent and received. Network operating systems typically handle the mechanics of LAN communication. Terminal programs enable personal computers to function as character-based terminals when connected to other PCs or to timesharing computers. Other types of specialized client programs have graphical user interfaces and additional functionality. Timesharing operating systems enable multiuser computers to communicate with several terminals at a time.

Email and teleconferencing are the two most common forms of communication between people on computer networks. Email and teleconferencing offer many advantages over traditional mail and telephone communication and can shorten or eliminate many meetings. But because of several important limitations email and teleconferencing cannot completely replace older communication media.

A modem can link a computer to online services that offer shopping, banking, teleconferencing, software downloading, email, games, and other features. But online services are being overshadowed and transformed by the Internet, the global network that provides the same services and many more.

Other kinds of telecommunication, including fax, voice mail, GPS, video teleconferencing, and electronic fund transfer, are built on computer technology. The conversion of the global phone network to fiber optic cables with digital switching makes it possible for phone lines to transmit all kinds of digital data along with phone calls. Increased bandwidth increases communication options on and off the Internet. The lines that separate the telephone, computer, and home entertainment industries will blur as new communication options blossom.

Chapter Review

▼ Key Terms

analog signal (p. 245)
asynchronous teleconference (p. 251)
attachment (p. 250)
bandwidth (p. 257)
bits per second (bps) (p. 245)
bluetooth (p. 258)
bounce (p. 254)
bridges (p. 247)
chat room (p. 250)
client/server model (p. 248)
communication software (p. 247)
digital signal (p. 245)
direct connection (p. 245)
download (p. 253)
electronic commerce (e-commerce) (p. 256)
electronic mail (email) (p. 250)
Ethernet (p. 245)

facsimile (fax) machine (p. 255)
fax modem (p. 255)
fiber optic cable (p. 257)
file server (p. 249)
gateways (p. 247)
Global Positioning System (GPS) (p. 256)
groupware (p. 250)
host system (p. 249)
instant messaging (p. 250)
local-area network (LAN) (p. 246)
modem (p. 245)
network interface card (NIC) (p. 245)
network license (p. 249)
network operating system (NOS) (p. 248)
online service (p. 253)
peer-to-peer model (p. 248)

port (p. 245)
protocol (p. 248)
real-time teleconference (p. 250)
remote access (p. 245)
router (p. 247)
server (p. 248)
site license (p. 249)
spam (p. 252)
telecommunication (p. 244)
teleconference (p. 250)
telephony (p. 255)
terminal emulation software (p. 248)
upload (p. 253)
video teleconference (p. 254)
voice mail (p. 255)
wide-area network (WAN) (p. 247)
Wi-Fi (p. 258)
wireless network (p. 247)

▼ Interactive Quiz Questions

1. The *Computer Confluence* CD-ROM contains self-test quiz questions related to this chapter, including multiple choice, true or false, and matching questions.
2. The *Computer Confluence* Web site, **www.prenhall.com/beekman**, contains self-test exercises related to this chapter. Follow the instructions for taking a

quiz. After you've completed your quiz, you can email the results to your instructor.

The Web site also contains open-ended discussion questions called Internet Explorations. Discuss one or more of the Internet Exploration questions at the section for this chapter.

▼ Review Questions

1. Define or describe each of the key terms listed in the "Key Terms" section. Check your answers using the glossary.
2. Give three general reasons for the importance of computer networking. (*Hint*: Each reason is related to one of the three essential components of every computer system.)
3. How do the three general reasons listed in Question 2 relate specifically to LANs?
4. How do the three general reasons listed in Question 2 relate specifically to WANs?
5. Under what circumstances is a modem necessary for connecting computers in networks? What does the modem do?
6. Describe at least two different kinds of communication software.

7. How could a file server be used in a student computer lab? What software licensing issues would be raised by using a file server in a student lab?
8. What are the differences between email and instant messaging systems?
9. Describe some things you can do with email that can't be done with regular mail.
10. Describe several potential problems associated with email and teleconferencing.
11. "Money is just another form of information." Explain this statement, and describe how it relates to automated teller machines and electronic fund transfer.
12. Wi-Fi and Bluetooth wireless technologies are designed to serve different purposes than mobile phone technology. Explain this statement.

▼ Discussion Questions

1. Suppose you have an important message to send to a friend in another city, and you can use the telephone, email, real-time teleconference, fax, or overnight mail service. Discuss the advantages and disadvantages of each. See if you can think of a situation for each of the five options in which that particular option is the most appropriate choice.

2. Some people choose to spend several hours every day online. Do you see potential hazards in this kind of heavy modem use? Explain your answer.
3. In the quote at the end of the chapter, Stewart Brand points out that electronic communication is essential for some of the world's people and irrelevant to others. What distinguishes these two groups? What advantages and disadvantages does each have?

▼ Projects

1. Find out about your school's computer networks. Are there many LANs? How are they connected? Who has access to them? What are they used for?

2. Spend a few hours exploring an online service like AOL. Describe the problems you encounter in the process. Which parts of the service are the most useful and interesting?

 Sources and Resources

Books

The Communications Miracle: The Telecommunication Pioneers from Morse to the Information Superhighway, by John Bray (New York: Plenum, 1995). This book gives the communication revolution a historical perspective by mixing technical explanations with human stories.

How Networks Work, Millennium Edition, by Frank J. Derfler, Jr., and Les Freed (Indianapolis, IN: Que, 2000). Follows the model popularized with the *How Computers Work* series. It uses a mix of text and graphics to illuminate the nuts and bolts of PC networks.

The Little Network Book, by Lon Poole and John Rizzo (Berkeley, CA: Peachpit Press, 1999). Networking isn't just for professionals anymore. Today's operating systems and network hardware make it (almost) easy to set up a network in a home or small business. This little book clearly explains options, techniques, and technology for setting up and using a network of PCs, Macs, or both.

Networking: A Beginner's Guide, Second Edition, by Bruce Hallberg (Berkeley, CA: Osborne McGraw-Hill, 2001). This book is written for people who know a fair amount about bits and bytes inside a computer but want to learn the ins-and-outs of transmitting those bits and bytes between computers. It's clearly written, but probably too technical for *true* beginners.

The Essential Guide to Networking, by James Edward Keogh (Upper Saddle River, NJ: Prentice Hall, 2000). This book is part of a series of technical *Essential* books for non-technical professionals. This one provides a broad overview of network technology, from LANs and WANs to the Internet and wireless networks.

The Essential Guide to Telecommunications, Third Edition, by Annabel Z. Dodd (Prentice Hall, 2002). This popular book presents a clear, comprehensive guide to the telecommunications industry and technology, including telephone systems, cable systems, wireless systems, and the Internet. If you want to understand how the pieces of our communication networks fit together, this book is a great place to start.

Computer Networks and Internets, Third Edition, by Douglas E. Comer, CD-ROM by Ralph Droms (Upper Saddle River, NJ: Prentice Hall, 2001). This text answers the question, "How do computer networks and internets operate?" Coverage includes LANs, WANs, Internet packets, digital telephony, protocols, client/server interaction, network security, and the underpinnings of the World Wide Web. A CD-ROM and a companion Web site supplement the text.

Telecommunications Systems and Technology, by Michael Khader and William E. Barnes (Upper Saddle River, NJ: Prentice Hall, 2000). This text is a technical overview of telecommunications systems, with in-depth discussions of modems, telephony systems, multimedia communication, TCP/IP, and many other topics.

Wireless Nation: The Frenzied Launch of the Cellular Revolution, by James B. Murray (Perseus Books, 2001). The mobile phone explosion and the PC both burst into our culture in the last decades of the twentieth century, and they came together through the Internet. This book chronicles the rise of mobile communication technology.

Jargon Watch: A Pocket Dictionary for the Jitterati, as overheard by Gareth Branwin (San Francisco: HardWired, 1997). Hard-core computer networkers speak a language all their own—a language rich with opaque acronyms and shorthand descriptors for complex concepts. This tiny book leaves the technical definitions for other references. It focuses instead on "geek speak, exec lingo, and memo slang." If you have any doubt that computers are changing our language, you'll be convinced by reading this collection of colorful, often hilarious phrases. To keep abreast of this ever-changing new language, check the column of the same name in *Wired* magazine.

Telecosm: How Infinite Bandwidth Will Revolutionize Our World, by George Gilder (Free Press, 2000). The thesis of this book is in the title. Gilder is a well-known pundit with a colorful writing style and grand optimism concerning our technological future.

Tyranny of the Moment: Fast and Slow Time in the Information Age, by Thomas Hylland (Pluto Press, 2001). In an age when instantaneous communication has never been easier, time is one of our scarcest commodities. Hylland explores this paradox, and discusses the social and political implications of the evaporation of "slow time.".

F2f, by Phillip Finch (New York: Bantam, 1997). As communities form on computer networks, they bring with them many of the problems found in other communities. This suspense thriller captures some of the potential risks of online communities in an exciting, tightly written story.

Film

You've Got Mail. This light comedy, named for AOL's ubiquitous greeting, points out the power of electronic communication to build strong emotional bonds.

Periodicals

Network Magazine focuses on networks with a business perspective.

Computer Telephony and **CTI** are two magazines that cover the rapidly changing territory where computers and telephones meet. Both periodicals are aimed at professionals and include a fair amount of technical material.

Web Pages

Computer networking technology is changing faster than publishers can print books and periodicals about it. The *Computer Confluence* Web site can connect you to up-to-date networking information all over the Internet.

10 | Inside the Internet and the Web

After you read this chapter you should be able to:

Explain how and why the Internet was created

Describe the technology that's at the heart of the Internet

Describe the technology that makes the Web work as a multimedia mass medium

Discuss the tools people use to build Web sites

▼ **In this chapter:**

The roots of the Internet

Why nobody controls the Internet

How the Internet works

Publishing pages on the Web

. . . and more.

▼ **On the CD-ROM:**

A 3-D model of a global information network

Animated demonstration showing how a Web browser works

Important access to glossary and key word references

Interactive self-study quizzes

. . . and more.

▼ **On the Web:**

www.prenhall.com/beekman

Articles and books on the Internet's history, structure, and use

Tools for exploring the Internet

Resources for building and publishing multimedia Web pages

Self-study exercises

. . . and more.

ARPANET Pioneers Build an Unreliable Network . . . on Purpose

It's a bit like **climbing a mountain**.
You don't know how far you've come until you **stop and look back**.

—Vint Cerf, ARPANET pioneer and first president of the Internet Society

In the 1960s, the world of computers was a technological Tower of Babel—most computers couldn't communicate with each other. When people needed to move data from one computer to another, they carried or mailed a magnetic tape or a deck of punch cards. While most of the world viewed computers only as giant number crunchers, J. C. R. Licklider, Robert Taylor, and a small group of visionary computer scientists saw the computer's potential as a communication device. They envisioned a network that would enable researchers to share computing resources and ideas.

U.S. military strategists during those Cold War years had a vision, too: They foresaw an enemy attack crippling the U.S. government's ability to communicate. The Department of Defense wanted a network that could function even if some connections were destroyed. They provided a million dollars to Taylor and other scientists and engineers to build a small experimental network. The groundbreaking result, launched in 1969, was called ARPANET, for Advanced Research Projects Agency NETwork. When a half dozen researchers sent the first historic message from UCLA to Doug Engelbart's lab at the Stanford Research Institute, no one even thought to take a picture.

ARPANET was built on two unorthodox assumptions: The network itself was unreliable, so it had to be able to overcome its own unreliability, and all computers on the network would be equal in their ability to communicate with other network computers. In ARPANET there was no central authority because that would make the entire network vulnerable to attack. Messages were contained in software "packets" that could travel independently by any number of different paths, through all kinds of computers, toward their destinations.

The team that built the Internet included, from front to back: Bob Taylor, Vint Cerf, Frank Heart, Larry Roberts, Len Kleinrock, Bob Kahn, Wes Clark, Doug Engelbart, Barry Wessler, Dave Walden, Severo Ornstein, Truett Thach, Roger Scantlebury, Charlie Herzfeld, Ben Barker, Jon Postel, Steve Crocker, Bill Naylor, and Roland Bryan.

ARPANET grew quickly into an international network with hundreds of military and university sites. In addition to carrying research data, ARPANET channeled debates over the Vietnam War and intense discussions about Space War, an early computer game. ARPANET's peer-to-peer networking philosophy and protocols were copied in other networks in the 1980s. Vint Cerf and Bob Kahn, two of the original researchers, developed the protocols that became the standard computer communication language, allowing different computer networks to be linked.

In 1990 ARPANET was disbanded, having fulfilled its research mission and spawned the Internet. In a recent interview, Cerf said about the network he helped create, "It was supposed to be a highly robust technology for supporting military command and control. It did that in the Persian Gulf War. But, along the way, it became a major research support infrastructure and now has become the best example of global information infrastructure that we have."

The ARPANET pioneers have gone on to work on dozens of other significant projects and products. In the words of Bob Kahn, "Those were very exciting days, but there are new frontiers in every direction I can look these days." ▶

The team that designed ARPANET suspected they were building something important. They couldn't have guessed, though, that they were laying the groundwork for a system that would become a universal research tool, a hotbed of business activity, a virtual shopping mall, a popular social hangout, a publisher's clearinghouse of up-to-the-minute information, and one of the most talked about institutions of our time.

The Internet is a technology, a tool, and a culture. Computer scientists originally designed it for computer scientists, and other scientists and engineers are continually adding new features. Consequently, the vocabulary of the Internet often seems like a flurry of technobabble to the rest of us. You don't need to analyze every acronym to make sense of the Internet, but your Net experiences can be far more rewarding if you understand the concepts at the heart of basic netspeak terminology. In this chapter we delve a little deeper into the Internet to make those concepts clearer.

Inside the Internet

It shouldn't be too much of a surprise that the Internet has evolved into a force **strong enough** to reflect the **greatest hopes and fears** of those who use it. After all, it was designed to **withstand nuclear war**, not just the **puny huffs and puffs** of politicians and religious fanatics.

—Denise Caruso, digital commerce columnist, *New York Times*

The Internet includes dozens of national, statewide, and regional networks, hundreds of networks within colleges and research labs, and thousands of commercial sites. Most sites are in the United States, but the Internet has connections in almost every country in the world.

The Internet provides hundreds of millions of people with services that include email, network newsgroups, instant messaging, Web publishing, shopping, banking, and research. Many of these services are similar to those provided by America Online and other online services. But the Internet is far bigger than any single network or online service. America Online is, in essence, a members-only club that occupies a tiny corner of the public Internet; members use their AOL accounts to explore the rest of the Web as well as the private AOL areas. More importantly, the Internet is not controlled by any one government, corporation, individual, or legal system. Several international advisory organizations develop standards and protocols for the evolving Internet, but no one has the power to control the Net's operation or evolution. The Internet is, in a sense, a massive anarchy unlike any other organization the world has ever seen.

Cyber cafes around the world, like this one in China, enable travelers to stay connected to their homes—and the rest of the world. Customers pay by the minute to log into their home servers, keep up with email, and explore the Web.

Counting Connections

No **LAN** is an **island**.

—Karyl Scott, *InfoWorld* writer

In its early days, the Internet connected only a few dozen computers at U.S. universities and government research centers, and the government paid most of the cost of building and operating it. Today it connects millions of computers in almost every country in the world, and costs are shared by thousands of connected organizations. It's impossible to pin down the exact size of the Internet for several reasons:

▶ The Internet is growing too fast to track. Millions of new users connect to the Internet every year in the United States alone, and the rest of the world is adding new connections by the minute.

▶ The Internet is decentralized. There's no Internet Central that keeps track of user activity or network connections. To make matters worse for Internet counters, some parts of the Internet can't be accessed by the general public; they're sealed off to protect private information.

▶ The Internet doesn't have hard boundaries. There are several ways to connect to the Internet (described later in this chapter); these different types of connections offer different classes of services and different degrees of interactivity. As choices proliferate, it's becoming harder to know exactly what it means to "belong to the Internet."

This last point is worth a closer look. It's easier to understand the different types of Internet access if you know a little bit about the protocols that make the Internet work.

Internet Protocols

The protocols at the heart of the Internet are called **TCP/IP** (Transmission Control Protocol/Internet Protocol). They were developed as an experiment in **internetworking**—connecting different types of networks and computer systems. The TCP/IP specifications were published as **open standards**, not owned by any company. As a result TCP/IP became the "language" of the Internet, allowing cross-network communication for almost every type of computer and network. These protocols are generally invisible to users; they're hidden deep in software that takes care of communication details behind the scenes. They define how information can be transferred between machines and how machines on the network can be identified with unique addresses.

The TCP protocols define a system similar in many ways to the postal system. When a message is sent on the Internet, it is broken into *packets*, in the same way you might pack your belongings in several individually addressed boxes before you ship them to a new location. Each packet has all the information it needs to travel independently from network to network toward its destination. Different packets might take different routes, just as different parcels might be routed through different cities by the postal system. The host systems that use software to decide how to route Internet transmissions are called *routers*, although sometimes less flexible hardware *switches* can do the same routing work faster. Regardless of the route they follow, the

> The most important quality of the Internet is that it lends itself to **radical reinvention**.... In another 10 years, the **only part** of the Internet as we know it now that will have survived will be **bits and pieces** of the underlying Internet protocol. . . .
>
> —Paul Saffo, director of the Institute for the Future

Packet switching gets the message through.

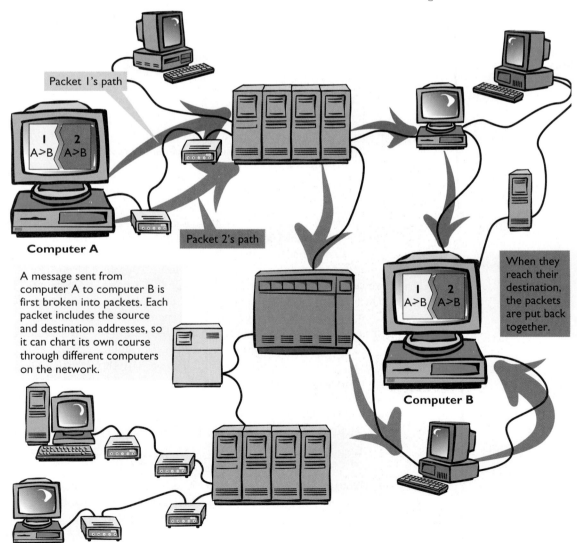

Computer A

Packet 1's path

Packet 2's path

A message sent from computer A to computer B is first broken into packets. Each packet includes the source and destination addresses, so it can chart its own course through different computers on the network.

Computer B

When they reach their destination, the packets are put back together.

packets eventually reach their destination, where they are reassembled into the original message. This **packet-switching** model is flexible and robust, allowing messages to get through even when part of the network is down.

The other part of TCP/IP—the IP part—defines the addressing system of the Internet. Every host computer on the Internet has a unique *IP address*: a string of four numbers separated by periods, or, as they say in netspeak, dots. A typical IP address might look like this: 123.23.168.22 ("123 dot 23 dot 168 dot 22"). Every packet includes the IP address of the sending computer and the receiving computer.

Internet Addresses

In practice, people seldom see or use numerical IP addresses, because the Internet's *domain name system (DNS)* translates the IP address into something that's easier for humans to read and remember. The DNS uses a string of names separated by dots to specify the exact Internet location of the host computer.

Internet addresses are classified by *domains*. In the United States the most widely used top-level domains are general categories that describe types of organizations:

- .edu   Educational sites
- .com   Commercial sites
- .gov   Government sites
- .mil   Military sites
- .net   Network administration sites
- .org   Nonprofit organizations

The Internet Ad Hoc Committee recently created seven additional top-level domain names:

- .aero   Air transport organizations
- .biz   Businesses
- .coop   Cooperative businesses such as credit unions
- .info   Information services
- .museum   Museums
- .name   Personal registration by name
- .pro   Licensed professionals, including lawyers, doctors, and accountants

Some of these domains, including .com, .net, .org, and .info, are open to anyone without restriction. For example, you could have a Web site or an email address in the .net domain whether or not you're part of a nonprofit organization. Other domains, including .edu and .mil, are restricted so only people in the designated organizations can use them. Outside (and occasionally inside) the United States top-level domains are two-letter country codes, such as .jp for Japan, .th for Thailand, .au for Australia, .uk for United Kingdom, and .us for United States.

The top-level domain name is the last part of the address. The other parts of the address, when read in reverse, provide information that narrows down the exact location on the network. The words in the domain name, like the lines in a post office address, are arranged hierarchically from little to big. They might include the name of the organization, the name of the department or network within the organization, and the name of the host computer.

The domain naming system is used in virtually all email addresses and Web URLs. In a Web address, the URL specifies the IP address of the Web server that houses the page. In an email address, domain name system is used to pinpoint the Internet location of the host computer that contains the user's mail server. The email address includes the user name and the host address, as illustrated at the top of the next page.

Here are some other examples of email addresses using the domain name system:

- president@whitehouse.gov   User *president* whose mail is stored on the host *whitehouse* in the government domain
- crabbyabby@AOL.com   User called *crabbyabby* whose mail is handled by AOL, a commercial service provider
- hazel_filbert@admin.gmcc.ab.ca   User *hazel_filbert* at the *admin* server for Grant MacEwan Community College in Alberta, Canada

benjamin@cs.orst.edu

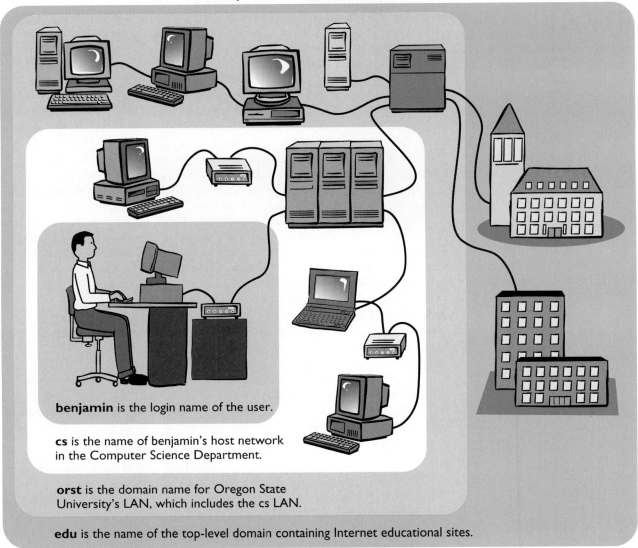

benjamin is the login name of the user.

cs is the name of benjamin's host network in the Computer Science Department.

orst is the domain name for Oregon State University's LAN, which includes the cs LAN.

edu is the name of the top-level domain containing Internet educational sites.

Anatomy of an email address.

Internet Access Options

> The **grand design** keeps getting grander.
> A **global computer** is taking shape, and we're all connected to it.
> — Stewart Brand, in *The Media Lab*

Computers connect to the Internet through three basic types of connections: direct connections, dial-up connections through modems, and broadband connections through high-speed alternatives to modems.

Direct Connections

In many schools and businesses the computers have a direct (dedicated) connection to the Internet through a LAN and have their own IP addresses. A direct connection offers several advantages: You can take full advantage of Internet services without dialing in; your files are stored on your computer, not on a remote host; and response time is much faster, making it possible to transfer large files (like multimedia documents) quickly. Direct connect digital lines come in many varieties, including *T1* connections, which can transmit voice, data, and video at roughly 1.5Mbps, and *T3*, which is even faster. (On some continents a technology called E1 is used instead of T1.)

Dial-up Connections

If your computer isn't directly connected to the Internet, you can temporarily connect to an Internet host through a **dial-up connection**—a connection using a modem and standard telephone lines. The time-honored method—one that works even with ancient equipment and questionable phone lines—is called dial-up terminal emulation. *Terminal emulation software* makes your computer act as a dumb terminal—an input/output device that enables you to send commands to and view information on the host computer. Email messages and other files are stored on the host computer, not your PC. Many Internet services, including most of the Web, are off limits with this kind of connection because of the character-based, command-line interface. Graphics and multimedia files must be specially encoded before they can be transmitted or received.

Software that uses *PPP* (point-to-point protocol) allows a computer connected via modem and phone line to have full Internet access temporarily and a temporary IP address. *Full-access dial-up connections* offer most of the advantages of direct connection, including Web access, but response time is limited by the modem's speed. A typical connection through a modem and *POTS* (plain old telephone service) is much slower (and often less reliable) than a direct Internet connection. While modern modems are theoretically capable of delivering data at 56Kb or faster, they're often much slower when connected to typical noisy phone lines. Modem connections are sometimes called **narrowband connections** because they don't offer much bandwidth when compared to other types of connections.

Broadband Connections

Until a few years ago, a slow dial-up connection was the only alternative to direct Internet for homes and small businesses. Today millions of Internet users connect via DSL, cable modems, and satellites. These modem alternatives are often called **broadband connections** because they have much higher bandwidth than standard modem connections. In some cases, broadband connections offer data transmission speeds comparable to direct connection speeds. Many broadband services offer another big advantage: They're always on. Users of these services don't need to dial in; the Internet is instantly available anytime, like television or radio. The most common broadband alternatives are based on the following different technologies:

▶ *DSL.* Many phone companies offer **DSL (digital subscriber line),** a technology for bringing high-bandwidth connections to homes and small businesses over ordinary copper telephone lines. (*Jargon alert*: There are several variants of DSL. The term xDSL is sometimes used to refer to all forms of DSL. DSL is faster and cheaper than *ISDN*, a digital service offered by phone companies in the 1990s. Most experts believe ISDN will soon be obsolete.) DSL customers must be geographically close to phone company service hubs. DSL transmission speeds vary considerably. *Downstream traffic*—information from the Internet to the subscriber—sometimes approaches T1 speeds. A graphics-heavy Web page that takes minutes to download through a conventional modem will load in seconds through a DSL connection. *Upstream traffic*—data traveling from the home computer to the Internet—typically travels much slower, but still much faster than standard modem transmission. A DSL signal can share a standard telephone line with voice traffic, so it can remain on without interfering with telephone calls. DSL connections are only available in limited areas, and installation can be complicated and expensive. But DSL's high-speed, always-connected signal brings the advantages of a direct Internet connection to homes and small businesses.

▶ *Cable modem connections.* Some cable TV companies offer ultra-high-speed Internet connections through **cable modems.** Cable modems allow Internet connections using the same network of coaxial cables that delivers television signals to millions of homes. Like DSL, cable modem service isn't available everywhere. Cable modem speeds can theoretically exceed DSL speeds both downstream and upstream. But because a single cable is shared by an entire neighborhood, transmission speeds can go down when the number of users goes up. What's more, cable modems come from cable TV companies, which often receive them over T1 lines. In the end, cable modem users typically experience data transmission speeds in roughly the same range as high-speed DSL connections.

Some airports have Wi-Fi wireless networks that enable travelers to connect to the Internet while they wait for their flights.

INTERNET CONNECTION SPEEDS

Connection type		Downstream		Upstream
		Potential	Typical	Typical
Dial-up modems: connection modem (56 K)		56 Kbps	42 to 53 Kbps	33.6 Kbps
T1/E1		1.544 Mbps	1.544 Mbps	1.544 Mbps
T3		44.736 Mbps	44.736 Mbps	44.736 Mbps
ISDN		128 Kbps	64 Kbps to 128 Kbps	64 Kbps to 128 Kbps
DSL/xDSL		6.1 Mbps	512 Kbps to 1.544 Mbps	128 Kbps
Cable modem		27 Mbps	1.5 to 3 Mbps	500 Kbps to 2.5 Mbps
Satellite connection		1.2 Mbps	150 Kbps to 1000 Kbps	50 Kbps to 150 Kbps
Wireless broadband (802.11b)		20 Mbps	5.5 or 11 Mbps	5.5 or 11 Mbps

Speeds vary widely for different types of Internet connections.

▶ *Satellite connections.* **Satellite Internet connections** are available through many of the same satellite dishes that provide television channels to viewers. Downstream satellite transmission is much faster than conventional modem traffic, although not quite as fast as DSL or cable modem service. For some satellite services, upstream traffic goes through phone lines at standard modem rates. Some newer services use satellites for both upstream and downstream traffic. For many homes and businesses outside of urban centers, satellites provide the only high-speed Internet access options available.

▶ *Wireless broadband connections.* People packing portable computers can, in some places, temporarily connect to the Internet through **wireless broadband connections**. The wireless broadband technology with the most industry support is referred to by its IEEE certification number, *802.11b*, but also called *Wi-Fi*. This technology, described in the last chapter, allows multiple computers to connect to a base station using short-range radio waves. This technology is used in many homes and offices for sharing Internet connections without cables. Using the same technology, students can connect to the Internet while they move around a wireless-equipped campus, travelers can make Web connections while waiting in some airports, and coffee shops can become Internet cafes for people with wireless receivers in their laptops.

There are many ways to connect a PC to the Internet.

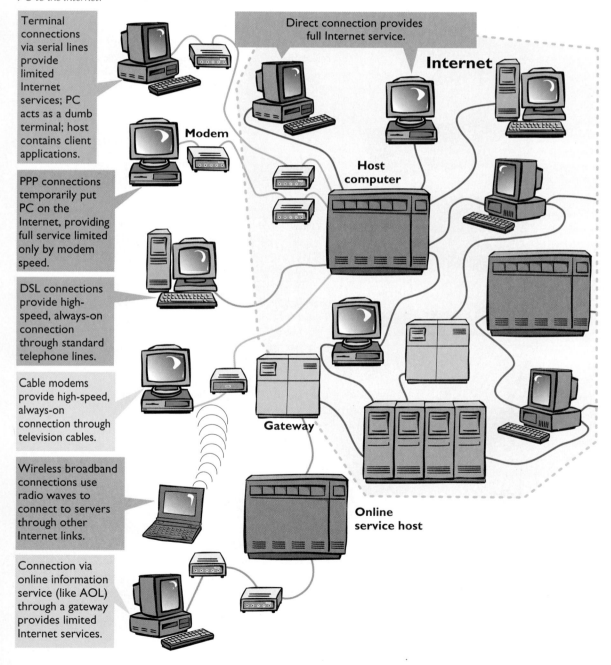

Terminal connections via serial lines provide limited Internet services; PC acts as a dumb terminal; host contains client applications.

PPP connections temporarily put PC on the Internet, providing full service limited only by modem speed.

DSL connections provide high-speed, always-on connection through standard telephone lines.

Cable modems provide high-speed, always-on connection through television cables.

Wireless broadband connections use radio waves to connect to servers through other Internet links.

Connection via online information service (like AOL) through a gateway provides limited Internet services.

Direct connection provides full Internet service.

Internet

Modem

Host computer

Gateway

Online service host

None of these broadband technologies is widely available, but each is rapidly expanding its area of coverage. In the future, many homes and small businesses will have direct connection to the Internet via fiber optic cables. But for now, most Internet users must settle for modem speeds or choose from broadband services available in their areas.

Internet Service Providers

Internet service providers (ISPs) generally offer several connection options at different prices. Local ISPs are local businesses with permanent connections to the Internet. They provide connections to their customers, usually through local telephone lines, along with other services. For example, an ISP might provide an email address, a server for customers to post Web pages, and technical help as part of a service package. National ISPs such as EarthLink offer similar services on a nationwide scale. National ISPs have local telephone numbers in most major cities so travelers can dial into the Net on the road without paying long-distance charges. In some cities inexpensive or free access to the Internet is available through a freenet—a local ISP designed to provide community access to online forums, announcements, and services.

Many private networks and online services (including America Online, CompuServe, and Prodigy) provide Internet access through **gateways**. A gateway is a computer connected to two networks—in this context the Internet and an outside network—that translates communication protocols and transfers information between the two. Some online services, such as MSN, have been rebuilt so they use the same protocols and framework as the Internet; subscribers use standard Web browsers and email programs to access services. Others, such as AOL and CompuServe, use proprietary client software to give subscribers access to their services and to the Internet. These services also enable members to use standard Internet software tools to connect to the Web and check email. Whatever their underlying architecture, online services are essentially ISPs that offer extra services to subscribers.

Inside Internet Applications: The Client/Server Connection

Internet applications, like PC applications, are software tools for users. But working with Internet applications is different from working with word processors or spreadsheets because of the distributed nature of the Internet and the **client/server model** used by most Internet applications. In the client/server model, a client program asks for information, and a server program fields the request and provides the requested information from databases and documents. The client program hides the details of the network and the server from the user.

Different people might access the same server using different client applications with different user interfaces. For example, a user with a direct connection might be using a Web browser with a point-and-click interface to explore a particular server, while another user with a dial-up terminal connection might be typing UNIX commands and seeing only text on screen. A third user might be viewing the same data, a few words at a time, on the tiny screen of a handheld PDA or mobile phone.

Many Internet applications use specialized servers. Some of the most common server types include the following:

▶ *Email servers.* An **email server** acts like a local post office for a particular Internet host—a business, an organization, or an ISP. For example, a college might have an email server to handle the mail of all students, faculty and staff; their email addresses point to that server. The email server receives incoming mail, stores it, and provides it to the email client programs of the addressees when they request it. Similarly, the email server collects mail from its subscribers and sends those messages toward their Internet destinations. Basically, the email server handles local client requests of two types: "Give me my mail," and "Pick up my mail and send it."

▶ *File servers.* File servers are common within LANs, but they're also used to share programs, media files, and other computer data across the Internet. The Internet's **file transfer protocol (FTP)** enables users to **download** files from remote servers (sometimes called FTP servers) to their computers—and to **upload** files they want to share from their computers to these archives. When you click a Web link that downloads a file, the Web browser's request is probably handled using FTP. Most files in Net archives are compressed—made smaller using special encoding schemes. File **compression** saves storage space on disk and saves transmission time when files are transferred through networks. (See Chapter 7, "Graphics, Hypermedia, and Multimedia," for more on compression.) Once files are downloaded to a PC, they have to be decompressed before they can be used. You don't need to know how compression works to take advantage of it; software makes the process automatic and transparent.

▶ *Application servers.* An **application server** stores applications—PC office applications, databases, or other applications—and makes them available to client programs that request them. An application server might be used within a large company to keep PCs updated with the latest software. Each PC might have a client program that regularly sends requests for updates to the server. The application server might also be housed at an **application service provider (ASP)**—a company that manages and delivers application services on a contract basis. Users of ASPs don't buy applications; they rent them, along with service contracts. Some application servers supply platform-neutral, Web-centered applications rather than OS-specific PC applications. Many industry watchers believe ASPs will eventually provide most of the software we use. For some companies ASPs are part of larger Web-services strategies. Web services are discussed in later chapters.

▶ *Web servers.* A **Web server** stores Web pages and sends them to client programs—Web browsers—that request them. It may also store and send Web media, including graphics, audio, video, and animation. We'll turn our attention now to the technology behind the Web.

Inside the Web

> The dream behind the Web is of a **common information space** in which we **communicate by sharing** information.
> —Tim Berners-Lee, creator of the World Wide Web

The **World Wide Web (WWW)** is a distributed browsing and searching system originally developed at CERN (European Laboratory for Particle Physics) by Tim Berners-Lee, a visionary scientist who is profiled in the next chapter. He designed a system for giving Internet documents unique addresses, wrote the HTML language for encoding and displaying documents, and built a software browser for viewing those documents from remote locations. Since it was introduced in 1991, the Web has become phenomenally popular as a system for exploring, viewing, and publishing all kinds of information on the Net.

Web Protocols: HTTP and HTML

> The Web was built by millions of people simply **because they wanted it**, without need, greed, fear, hierarchy, authority figures, ethnic identification, advertising, or any form of manipulation. **Nothing like this ever happened** before in history. We can be blasé about it now, but it is **what we will be remembered for**. We have been made aware of a **new dimension** of human potential.
> —Jaron Lanier, virtual reality pioneer

The Web is built around a naming scheme that allows every information resource on the Internet to be referred to using a **uniform resource locator** or, as it's more commonly known, URL. Here's a typical URL:

```
http://weatherunderground.com/satellite/vis/1k/US.html/
```

The first part of this URL refers to the protocol that must be used to access information; it might be FTP, news, or something else. It's most commonly *http*, for *hypertext transfer protocol*, the protocol used to transfer Web pages. The second part (the part following the //) is the address of the host containing the resource; it uses the same domain-naming scheme used for email addresses. The third part, following the dot address, describes the path to the particular resource on the host—the hierarchical nesting of directories (folders) that contain the resource.

Most Web pages are created using a language called **HTML (hypertext markup language)**. An HTML *source document* is a text file that includes codes that describe the format, layout, and logical structure of a hypermedia document. HTML is not WYSIWYG (What You See Is What You Get); the HTML codes embedded in the document make it look cryptic and nothing like the final page displayed on the screen. But these codes enable a Web browser to translate an HTML source document into that finished page. Because it's a text file, an HTML document can be easily transmitted from a Web server to a client machine anywhere on the Internet.

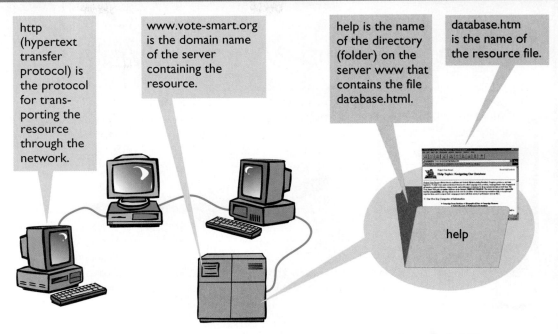

http://www.vote-smart.org/help/database.html

http (hypertext transfer protocol) is the protocol for transporting the resource through the network.

www.vote-smart.org is the domain name of the server containing the resource.

help is the name of the directory (folder) on the server www that contains the file database.html.

database.htm is the name of the resource file.

help

Anatomy of a URL.

HTML codes tell the Web browser how to format the text when it's displayed on screen.

Publishing on the Web

You can create a Web page with any word processor or text editor; you just type the HTML commands along with the rest of the text. But you don't need to write HTML code to create a Web page. Many programs, including Microsoft Word, PowerPoint, and FileMaker Pro, can automatically convert basic formatting features (including character styles, indentation, and justification) into HTML codes. Some Web authoring software, including Macromedia Dreamweaver, Adobe GoLive, and Microsoft FrontPage

> By expanding the number of people who have **the power to transmit knowledge**, the Web might trigger a power shift that **changes everything**.
> —Howard Rheingold, author of *Virtual Communities*

10.1
The World Wide Web

1 When you type a URL into the address box of your Web browser, the browser sends a message through the Internet to the server with the specified domain name www.requestfiles.com.

www.xyz123.com

2 The server responds by sending the specified file to the client browser. The file is an HTML file containing the text contents of the requested Web page along with HTML codes for formatting and adding other elements to the page. Because HTML files are all text, they're small and easy to transmit through the Internet.

<H1> xyz123 </H1> <IMG

3 The browser reads the HTML file and interprets the HTML commands, called *tags*, embedded in angle brackets <like this>. It uses the formatting tags to determine the look and layout of the text on the page. For example, <H1> indicates a level-one heading to be displayed in large text; <1> indicates italics, and so on.

Server

4 The HTML file doesn't contain pictures; it's a text file. But it does contain a tag specifying where a picture file is stored and where in the page it is to be displayed. The server responds to this tag by sending the requested graphics files.

Server

5 The HTML file also contains a tag indicating a hyperlink to another document with a URL on another server. When the user clicks that link, a message is sent to the new server; and the process of building a Web page in the browser window starts anew.

work like page layout programs that desktop publishers use. You can lay out text and graphics exactly the way you want them to look, and the authoring program creates an HTML document that looks like your original layout when viewed through a Web browser. The best of these Web authoring programs enable you to manage entire Web sites using tools that can automate repetitive edits, apply formatting styles across pages, and check for bad links. Some have tools for connecting large sites to databases containing critical, rapidly changing content.

Once an HTML document is completed, it needs to be uploaded onto a Web server before it's visible on the Web. Many ISPs provide Web server space as part of their subscription service; other companies rent Web server space to individuals and organizations. By default, most Web pages have URLs that include the ISP or Web server domain names—names like **http://hometown.aol.com/shjoobedebop/index.htm**. Many businesses, organizations, and individuals pay an annual fee to a *domain name registry* company for names that match and are easier to remember and use. Many customized domain names resemble company or product names—for example, **www.prenhall.com** or **www.computerconfluence.com**.

From Hypertext to Multimedia

Way back in the early 1990s (!) the first Web pages were straight hypertext. Within a couple of years graphics were common, and a few cutting-edge Web sites enabled browsers to download scratchy video and audio clips to their hard disks. Today color graphics and animation are everywhere, and a typical Web site can contain any or all of these:

> We are still a **multimedia organism**. If we want to push the envelope of complexity further, we have to use **all of our devices** for accessing information—not all of which are **rational**.
>
> —Psychologist Mihaly Csikszentmihalyi

- ▶ *Tables*—spreadsheet-like grids whose rows and columns contain neatly laid out text and graphical elements. Tables with invisible cell borders are often used as simple alignment tools.
- ▶ *Frames*—subdivisions of a Web browser's viewing area that enable visitors to scroll and view different parts of a page—or even multiple pages—simultaneously.
- ▶ *Forms*—pages that visitors who want to order goods and services, respond to questionnaires, enter contests, express opinions, or add comments to ongoing discussions can fill in.
- ▶ *Animation*—based on a variety of technologies, from simple repetitive GIF animations to complex interactive animations created with authoring tools such as Flash.
- ▶ *Search engines*—tools for locating what you're looking for on a site. Most of these site-specific search engines are based on the same technology as Web-wide search engines. Many site builders license search engines from search engine companies.
- ▶ *Downloadable audio* clips—compressed sound files that you must download onto your computer's hard disk before the browser or some other application can play them. Some types of audio compression cause significant sound quality degradation. The MP3 compression format is popular because compressed music files sound almost the same as uncompressed originals. MP3 files can be played using a variety of software programs and portable MP3 players. The next two chapters discuss applications and implications of MP3 technology.
- ▶ *Downloadable video* clips—compressed video files that you can download and view on a computer. Many are small, short, and jerky, but quality is rapidly improving as new video compression technologies mature.
- ▶ *Streaming audio* files—sounds that play without being completely downloaded to the local hard disk. Some streaming files play automatically while you view a page providing background music and sound effects. Others, such as sound samples at music stores, play on request. Unlike downloaded media files, you can view or hear streaming media files within seconds, because they play while you're downloading them. For the same reason, streaming media files don't need to be limited to short clips. Concert-length streaming programs are common. High-quality streaming music requires a fast connection and can be interrupted by Internet traffic jams.
- ▶ *Streaming video* files—video clips that play while you're downloading them. Streaming video is even more dependent on high-bandwidth connection than streaming audio.
- ▶ *Real-time streaming audio* broadcasts, or Webcasts—streaming transmission of radio broadcasts, concerts, news feeds, speeches, and other sound events as they happen.
- ▶ *Real-time streaming video* Webcasts—similar to streaming audio Webcasts, but with video.
- ▶ *3-D environments*—drawn or photographed virtual spaces you can explore with mouse clicks.

Building a Web Site

SOFTWARE: *Macromedia Dreamweaver and Microsoft Internet Explorer.*

THE GOAL: *To create a Web site to represent a small service business.*

1 The first step in publishing, whether on paper or on the Web, is to plan the layout for the publication. Since a Web site is a hypertext document, a flowchart can make it easier to plan the links between pages.

2 A sketch can help you crystallize your ideas for the layout of each page.

3 Once the plan is complete, you collect, digitize, and edit the source documents—the images, articles, and other elements that will make up the finished publication.

4 Because your Web site will contain only standard HTML code, you could create the site using any text editor, inserting appropriate HTML codes into the text. But you use Dreamweaver, a Web authoring tool that enables you to design the page with a WYSIWYG editor that automatically creates HTML code.

5 After you define a directory (folder) as the temporary home for your site, you create a new page. Using the Page Properties command, you define the basic characteristics of the page: name, location, default fonts, text link colors, and background color. You select colors that match the dominant colors in your most important graphical images.

6 Your sketch calls for a column of links on the left side of the page, so you create a table, which enables you to align pictures and text neatly in rows and columns.

7 You select the table and change its background color to green from the Properties palette.

8 You type the titles for your navigation banner. You format the text using commands similar to those of a word processor. Dreamweaver converts your commands to HTML codes.

9 You select a title in your navigation banner, and specify the file name for the new page that will be linked to that text.

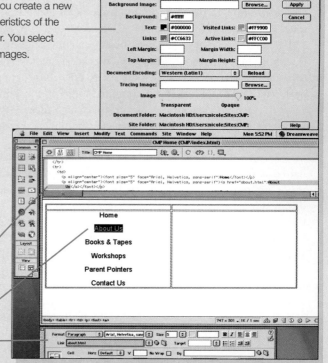

10 You create links for the rest of the titles in the column, and place an image you created earlier above the links.

11 You realign the borders of the table and make them invisible. The dotted line borders are visible in the Dreamweaver editor, but they won't show up when the page is displayed in a Web browser.

12 You select the two empty cells, change their background color to white, and merge them, leaving you with one large cell to contain the content specific to each page of your site.

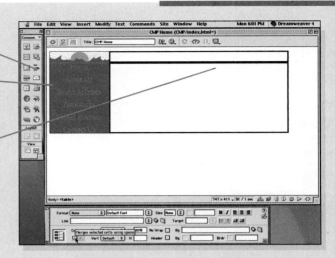

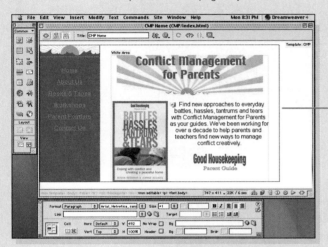

13 You want all the pages in the site to share the elements you have created so far, so you save a copy of the page, which you'll use as the starting point for all the pages in your site.

14 You place another image in the empty cell of the home page, then type a welcome message beneath it.

15 To begin work on the next page, you make another copy of your template file, and rename it with the name that you entered into the Link bar earlier. You add images, text, and other elements to the page, just as you did on the home page.

16 After you complete the pages, you preview them in a browser, which uses the HTML codes to construct a page that's similar to the design you created. You make sure to test the links before loading the entire site onto the Web server so they can be viewed by the world.

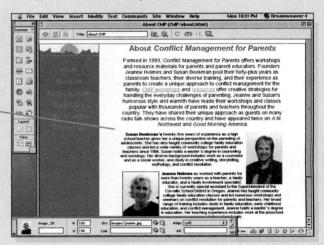

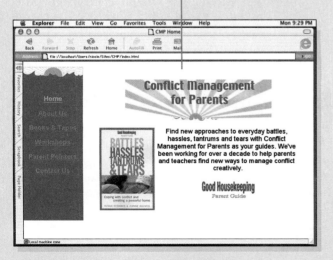

17 After thoroughly testing the site with different browsers, you compare this site map, created by Dreamweaver, with the original design. You're ready to load the site onto your Web server so the world can view it.

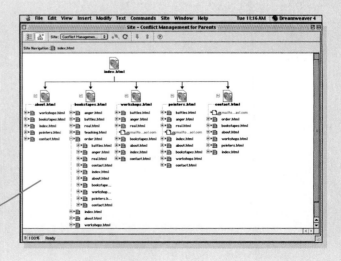

Streaming media are available from a variety of Web sites. rollingstone.com (left) offers music videos on request. live365.com (right) provides live audio feeds from hundreds of radio stations around the word.

▶ *Personalization*—customization of content made possible because sites can remember information about guests from visit to visit. Some sites use login names and passwords to remember visitors. Others track and remember using cookies—small files deposited on the visitor's hard disk. Cookies can make online shopping and other activities more efficient and rewarding, but they can also pose a threat to personal privacy.

Today new Web ideas appear at an astounding rate—so fast that browser makers have trouble keeping up. Fortunately, the most popular browsers can be enhanced with plug-ins—software extensions that add new features. When a company introduces a Web innovation—say, a new type of animation—it typically makes a free browser plug-in available to users. Once you download the plug-in and install it in your browser, you can take advantage of any Web pages that include the innovation. Popular plug-ins become standard features in future browser versions, so you don't need to download and install them. Even if a browser can't play or display a particular type of graphics, animation, audio, or video by itself, it might be able to offload the task to a helper application—a separate program designed to present that particular media type.

The most popular free cross-platform plug-ins and helper applications include the following:

This 3D pool game is one of many interactive multimedia Web applications provided at shockwave.com

▶ RealPlayer (Real) is one of the most popular programs for playing streaming audio and video, including live Webcasts. RealPlayer movies and sound files are encoded in proprietary formats so they can't be played with other media players.
▶ Windows Media Player (Microsoft) is a direct competitor to RealPlayer, delivering streaming media in proprietary formats that aren't compatible with other players.
▶ QuickTime (Apple) also delivers cross-platform streaming media in proprietary formats. But QuickTime excels at providing high-quality multimedia for CD-ROMs, broadband downloads, and other delivery systems where bandwidth is less of an issue.
▶ Shockwave/Flash (Macromedia) plug-ins enable Web browsers to present compressed interactive multimedia documents and animations created with Flash, Director, and other authoring tools.
▶ Acrobat (Adobe) displays documents in *Portable Document Format (PDF)* so they look the same

Weaving Winning Web Sites

It's easy to create a Web site—just about anybody with an Internet connection can do it. It's not so easy to create an effective Web site—one that communicates clearly, attracts visitors, and achieves its goals. Here are a few pointers for making your Web publications work.

▶ **Start with a plan.** The Web is littered with Web sites that seem pointless. Many of those sites were probably constructed without clear plan or purpose. Start with clear goals and design your entire site with those goals in mind.

▶ **Write for the Web.** Most people won't read long, scrolling documents on computer screens. Limit each page to a couple of screens worth of text. Provide clearly marked links to pages with more details for people who need them. And don't forget to check your spelling and grammar.

▶ **Keep it simple.** Web pages that are cluttered with blinking text, busy backgrounds, repetitive animations, and garish graphics tend to lose their visitors quickly. Stick with clean lines and clear design if you want people to stick around.

▶ **Keep it consistent.** Every page in your site should look like it's related to the other pages in your site. Fonts, graphical elements, colors, buttons, and menus should be consistent from page to page.

▶ **Make it obvious.** Your visitors should be able to tell within a few seconds how your site works. Unless you're building a puzzle palace, make sure the buttons and structure of your site are intuitive.

▶ **Keep it small.** Large photographs, complex animations, video clips, and sounds can make your Web site big and slow to load. People with standard modem connections won't want to wait two minutes for your graphically heavy Web page to load. If you need lots of pictures, use an image-editing program to optimize them for the Web.

▶ **Keep it honest.** Anybody can publish a Web site, without the benefit of an editor. Check your facts before you share your pages with the world.

▶ **Offer contact information.** Web communication shouldn't be one-way. Provide an email address or a form to enable your visitors to contact you.

▶ **Think like a publisher and a multimedia designer.** The rules of publishing and design, discussed in earlier chapters, apply to Web publishing, too.

▶ **Test before you publish.** Show your work to others—preferably people in your target audience—and watch their reactions carefully. If they get lost, confused, bored, or upset, you probably have more work to do before launching the final site.

▶ **Think before you publish.** It's easy to publish Web pages for the world—at least that part of the world that uses the Web. Don't put anything on your Web pages that you don't want the world to see; you may, for example, be asking for trouble if you publish your home address, your work schedule, and a photo of the expensive computer system in your study.

▶ **Keep it current.** It's easy to build a Web site, and it's even easier to forget to keep it up to date. If your Web site is worth visiting, it's worth revising. If the contents of your site are constantly in need of revision, consider using a database to house the data so you can automatically update the site when the data changes.

on the screen as on paper, even if the documents are viewed on computers that don't have the same fonts installed.

HTML was originally designed to share scientific research documents—not to deliver media-rich documents in which design is as important as content. By popular demand, the HTML standard has been revised several times to incorporate new features. Newer versions of HTML, sometimes called *dynamic HTML*, allow HTML code to modify itself automatically under certain circumstances. Dynamic HTML supports cascading style sheets that can define formatting and layout features that aren't recognized in older versions of HTML.

Dynamic HTML also recognizes *scripts*—short programs—that can add interactivity, animation, and other dynamic features to Web pages. One common use of scripts is to add *rollovers* to onscreen buttons, so they visibly change when the pointer rolls over them. Scripts are typically written in **JavaScript**, a scripting language developed by Netscape. Microsoft's *VBScript* is also used for writing scripts, but VBScript code doesn't work on non-Microsoft browsers. Web pages that take advantage of the latest dynamic HTML features can be more interesting and interactive, but only if they are viewed with newer full-featured browsers. Unscrupulous Web programmers can use scripts to embed viruses and other unwanted elements into your computer. We'll explore these risks in the Security chapter.

Dynamic Web Sites: Beyond HTML

If you thought a Web site consisted of **HTML** pages organized as a directory, **go back to the 20th century**. A successful Web site today consists primarily of **XML** code and a **database**.

—Dana Blankenhorn, coauthor of *Web Commerce: Building a Digital Business*

HTML is flexible, but it's designed for page layout, not programming. By itself, it can't support online shopping, financial transaction processing, library catalogs, daily newspapers, search engines, and other applications with masses of rapidly changing data. This kind of dynamic Web site requires two things that HTML can't easily deliver: a database to store the constantly changing content of the site, and custom programming to make the appropriate data available to visitors through the Web site. A **database-driven Web site** can display dynamic, changeable content without having constantly redesigned pages. For example, an online store's Web site doesn't have a separate HTML page for each catalog item. Instead, it has pages that are coded to display product information drawn from a database that can be continually updated. The Web site is a *front end* for the database; it serves as the visitor's window into the database.

The REI.com Web site uses a massive database to store catalog items, inventory information, customer data, and transaction information. The dynamic Web site displays data based on visitor input.

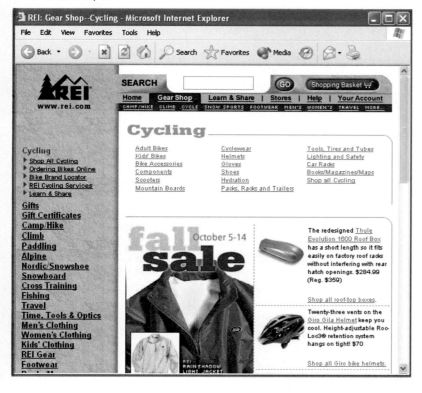

Programmers use a variety of programming languages for creating dynamic Web sites. The Perl language is particularly popular for programming Web servers. **Java**, an object-oriented programming language developed by Sun Microsystems, is probably the best-known language for Web programming. (Java and JavaScript have little in common except their names. JavaScript is a simple scripting language for enhancing HTML Web pages; Java is a full-featured cross-platform programming language.) Small Java programs are called *applets* because they're like tiny applications. Java applets can be automatically downloaded onto your client computer through almost any modern Web browser. A Java applet is platform independent; it runs on a Windows PC, a Mac, a UNIX workstation, or anything else as long as the client machine has Java Virtual Machine (JVM) software installed. This JVM software is built into most modern browsers and is available for free download.

Microsoft offers several alternatives to Java. The oldest is *ActiveX*, a collection of programming technologies and tools for creating *controls* or *components*—programs that are similar in many ways to Java applets. ActiveX components require a compatible browser, such as Internet Explorer, to run properly. Another Microsoft technology, *C#*, is a programming language similar to Java in many ways, but it lacks Java's cross-platform capabilities.

Many experts expect **XML (extensible markup language)**, which includes all of HTML's features plus many additional, powerful programming extensions to replace HTML. XML enables Web developers to control and display data the way they now control text and graphics. Forms, database queries, and other data-intensive operations that can't be completely constructed with standard HTML are much easier with XML. In effect, XML combines a programming language with a page layout language. XML is at the heart of Microsoft's .NET and other competing strategies for developing Web services. Web services will be discussed in later chapters.

XML isn't the only markup language that's emerging to go beyond the capabilities of HTML. *XHTML*, a sort of cross between HTML and XML, is backward compatible with HTML, making it easier to upgrade older sites. A subset of XHTML called XHTML basic is especially designed to work with phones, PDAs, and other small-screen wireless devices. XHTML and XHTML basic are designed to work together, so that sites designed with XHTML automatically work on handheld devices. XHTML isn't yet widely used, but it has strong support from the wireless industry and from the World Wide Web Consortium (W3C), an organization that sets standards for the Web. W3C is also developing a standard for *SMIL (synchronized multimedia integration language)*, an HTML-like language designed to make it possible to link time-based streaming media so, for example, sounds, video, and animation can be tightly integrated with each other.

Putting Protocols to Work

In this chapter we've examined the technology that makes the Internet tick. Of course, we've only scratched the surface—the technology of the Internet is far too complex to cover in detail in an overview like this one. Still, it's satisfying to know that everything you do with the Internet is based on technological foundations described in this chapter. In the next chapter we'll survey the ways people are putting this technology to work to enhance communication, connection, and commerce. We'll also look at some of the ethical, legal, and social issues raised by the Internet as it grows and changes.

Machine Net

Cathy Benko

Networks aren't just for people anymore. Advances in networking technology, including wireless technology, are making it practical to connect machines so they can communicate directly with each other. In this article, first published in the February 7, 2000 issue of The Industry Standard, *Cathy Benko of Deloitte Consulting discusses the machine-to-machine network revolution.*

"In the bowling alley of tomorrow, there will even be machines that wear rental shoes and throw the ball for you. Your sole function will be to drink beer."

Dave Barry

A lot of people have predicted that a time will come when machines become more important than humans. What few predicted was that machines would seize power on the Net.

In fact, more and more machines are using sophisticated artificial intelligence programs to talk to one another online—without human interference. Until now, the Net has been the most human-centric technology ever. Starting with the browser, every new Internet development has made it easier to send email, surf the Web, shop online and conduct business. Few technologies have worked so hard to be human-friendly.

Now it's the machines' turn to catch up. Within the next few years, Internet connections between machines will outnumber the connections made by man.

Just as the Net has reshaped business, so it will reshape relationships between machines. Air conditioners will send messages to the electric company. Truck fleets will stay linked to headquarters. Wired VCR clocks will set themselves.

Sending simple messages from one machine to another is just the beginning. At the experiment stage is a gizmo that reads email for U.S. congressmen and summarizes the correspondence by issue—a clever device that elected officials probably wouldn't want to boast about.

Such newly empowered machines suggest the Net is headed in a direction we haven't previously considered. The growing adoption of handheld devices has made it possible to think in terms of communicating through the Net anywhere, anytime. What may be more revolutionary is the notion of machines and databases communicating without our help.

Want to make a virtual visit to the future? Visit **www.echelon.com/demo**, where you can use your mouse to pull down the blinds and turn on a lamp in a mock living room at the headquarters of network control designer **Echelon** (ELON) in Palo Alto, Calif. It's a first step toward a future where you can log on at work to see if you left the iron on in your bedroom—and turn it off if you did. And it's not far from there to putting refrigerators, cars and phones online.

Industrial and commercial applications involving power may be the first to market. GE Lighting, for instance, is exploring "intelligent office" control systems, connecting lighting; heating, ventilation and air conditioning; fire and security; and electrical systems. Expect IT managers to find themselves in charge of utilities, too.

The current incarnation of the Net is all about bringing information to us. But as machines demand more online time, and then become the most voracious users of bandwidth, the Net will reconfigure itself to cater to their needs.

This opens an immense and still embryonic market. Surging demand will surface for products that let machines do things better and faster than we can. With increasingly advanced artificial intelligence software, vending machines will let delivery vans know when they need to be replenished; copy machines will notify overnight delivery computers when an order is ready for pickup; manufacturers' shop floors will use digital cameras and the Internet to coordinate production schedules. In homes, simple devices will set electricity use based on time of day and temperature. For consumers, these new machines will make user-friendly PCs seem hostile by comparison.

Who—or what—uses the Net won't be the only change. It has long been the conventional wisdom that the Internet was primarily about people—and until now, that has largely been true. The Internet's playing field, however, is about to become a lot more crowded and complex.

For many apps, the PC remains a slow, complex tool. A machine-to-machine dialogue promises to change that. A customer-friendly era is coming online—and some of those customers will be machines.

DISCUSSION QUESTIONS

1. Do you think these predictions are realistic? Explain your answer.
2. How do you think these changes will effect your life? Will there be both negative and positive effects?

Summary

The Internet is a network of networks that connects all kinds of computers around the globe. It grew out of a military research network designed to provide reliable communication even if part of the network failed. The Internet uses standard protocols to allow internetwork communication to occur. No single organization owns or controls the Internet.

You can connect to the Internet in any of several ways; these ways provide different degrees of access to Internet services. A direct connection provides the most complete and fastest service, but users can also access most Internet information through modem connections. Broadband connections approach direct connection speeds, but they aren't universally available. Several online services have gateways to the Internet; these gateways enable users to access Internet information resources and send and receive Internet mail.

Most Internet applications are based on the client/server model. The user interface for these applications varies depending on the type of connection and the type of client software used by the user. A user might type UNIX commands to a host computer or use point-and-click tools on a personal computer.

Millions of people use Web browsers to explore interconnected Web pages published by private companies, public institutions, and individuals. The earliest Web pages were simple hypertext pages; today the Web contains thousands of complex, media-rich structures that offer visitors a wealth of choices. The World Wide Web uses a set of protocols to make a variety of Internet services and multimedia documents available to users through a simple point-and-click interface. Web pages are generally constructed using a language called HTML. Many Web authoring tools automate the coding of HTML pages, making it easy for nonprogrammers to write and publish their own pages. Other languages and techniques are being developed to extend the power of the Web in ways that go beyond the capabilities of HTML. Today, most large interactive Web sites are database-driven, so content can be updated automatically.

Chapter Review

▼ Key Terms

application server (p. 274)
application service provider (ASP) (p. 274)
broadband connection (p. 270)
cable modem (p. 270)
client/server model (p. 273)
compression (p. 273)
cookies (p. 280)
database-driven web site (p. 282)
dial-up connection (p. 270)
direct (dedicated) connection (p. 269)
download (p. 273)
DSL (digital subscriber line) (p. 270)
email server (p. 273)

extensible markup language (XML) (p. 282)
file transfer protocol (FTP) (p. 273)
gateway (p. 273)
helper application (p. 280)
HTML (hypertext markup language) (p. 274)
Internet service provider (ISP) (p. 273)
internetworking (p. 267)
Java (p. 282)
JavaScript (p. 281)
narrowband connection (p. 270)
open standards (p. 267)
packet switching (p. 268)

plug-in (p. 280)
satellite connections (p. 272)
streaming audio (p. 277)
streaming video (p. 277)
TCP/IP (p. 267)
upload (p. 273)
uniform resource locator (URL) (p. 274)
WWW (p. 274)
web-authoring software (p. 275)
Web server (p. 274)
wireless broadband connection (p. 272)

▼ Interactive Quiz Questions

1. The *Computer Confluence* CD-ROM contains self-test quiz questions related to this chapter, including multiple choice, true or false, and matching questions.
2. The *Computer Confluence* Web site, **www.prenhall.com/beekman**, contains self-test exercises related to this chapter. Follow the instructions for taking a

quiz. After you've completed your quiz, you can email the results to your instructor.

   The Web site also contains open-ended discussion questions called Internet Explorations. Discuss one or more of the Internet Exploration questions at the section for this chapter.

▼ Review Questions

1. Define or describe each of the key terms listed in the "Key Terms" section. Check your answers using the glossary.
2. Why is it hard to determine how big the Internet is today? Give several reasons.
3. Why are TCP/IP protocols so important to the functioning of the Internet? What do they do?
4. How does the type of Internet connection influence the things you can do on the Internet?

5. Explain the relationship between the client/server model and the fact that different users might experience different interfaces while accessing the same data.
6. What do email addresses and URLs have in common?
7. Why is file compression important on the Internet?
8. Briefly describe several software tools that can be used to develop Web pages.

▼ Discussion Questions

1. How did the Internet's Cold War origin influence its basic decentralized, packet-switching design? How does that design affect the way we use the Net today? What are the political implications of that design today?

2. Why is the World Wide Web important as a publishing medium? In what ways is the Web different from any publishing medium that's ever existed before?

▼ Projects

1. Search the Web for articles related to the history and evolution of the Internet. Create a summary report on paper or on the Web.

2. Create a Web site on a subject of interest to you and link it to other Web sites. (When you're trying to decide what information to include in your home page, remember that it will be accessible to millions of people all over the world.)

Sources and Resources

Books

There are thousands of books on the Internet. Many of them promise to simplify and demystify the Net, but they don't all deliver. The Internet is complex and ever-changing. The following list contains a few particularly good titles, but you should also look for more current books released since this book went to press.

When Wizards Stay Up Late, by Katie Hafner and Matthew Lyon (New York: Simon and Schuster, 1998). If you want to learn more about the birth of the Internet, this book is a great place to start. The authors describe the people, challenges, and technical issues in clear, entertaining prose.

The Whole Internet: The Next Generation, by Kiersten Conner-Sax and Ed Krol (Sebastapol, CA: O'Reilly, 1999). In 1992 Ed Krol turned his online Internet guide into one of the first true guidebooks to the Net. It provided explorers with the technical knowledge necessary to get around on the pre-Web Internet. This completely rewritten edition is less technical, but just as practical. It's packed with useful information and advice on everything from shopping at auctions to stopping spam.

How the Internet Works, Millennium Edition, by Preston Gralla (Indianapolis: Que, 1999). If you like the style of *How Computers Work*, you'll appreciate *How the Internet Works*. You won't learn how to use the Net, but you'll get a colorful tour of what goes on behind the scenes when you connect. There's a surprising amount of technical information in this graphically rich, approachable book.

TCP/IP Clearly Explained, Third Edition, by Pete Loshin (Boston: AP Professional, 1999). If you want to dig deeper into the protocol that makes the Internet tick, this book, by a former *Byte* magazine editor, should help.

HTML 4 for the World Wide Web Visual QuickStart Guide, Fourth Edition, by Elizabeth Castro (Berkeley, CA: Peachpit Press, 2000). There are dozens of books on HTML, but few offer the clear, concise, comprehensive coverage of this bestseller. Castro does a marvelous job of presenting just enough information on each topic, and presenting it in an understandable way. If you want to build your own Web pages, this is a great place to start. Even if you know the basics of HTML, you'll appreciate the coverage of "advanced" topics like DHTML and CGI. Once you've read it, you'll almost certainly want to keep it as a reference.

Perl and CGI for the World Wide Web Visual QuickStart Guide, by Elizabeth Castro (Berkeley, CA: Peachpit Press, 1999). When you fill out a form on a Web page, it's likely that your input is processed by a script that's written in PERL following the CGI protocol. Castro's book takes up where her popular HTML book leaves off, introducing the basics of PERL and CGI for first-time scripters.

JavaScript for the World Wide Web Visual QuickStart Guide, Third Edition, by Tom Negrino and Dori Smith (Berkeley, CA: Peachpit Press, 1999). JavaScript is the most popular cross-platform scripting language for Web pages. A little bit of JavaScript can turn a static Web page into a dynamic interactive page. This book provides a quick introduction to the language, including applications involving forms, frames, files, graphics, and cookies. If you're ready to move beyond basic HTML, this book can help.

HTML: The Complete Reference, Second Edition, by Thomas A. Powell (Berkeley, CA: Osborne/McGraw Hill, 1999). This massive book includes a well-designed, in-depth tutorial and a comprehensive reference section. It covers beginning HTML and many more advanced topics.

Philip and Alex's Guide to Web Publishing, by Philip Greenspun (San Francisco: Morgan Kaufmann Publishers, Inc., 1999). This is a quirky, wordy, opinionated, and informative exposition on creating Web sites that work. Greenspun covers a great deal of territory here, including building a site, tracking users, publicizing a site, interfacing with relational databases, and handling finances. The author's color photos allow this book to hold its own on the coffee table. (Alex, the author's dog, appears on the cover; beyond that, it's not clear what he contributed to the book.)

Web Style Guide: Basic Design Principles for Creating Web Sites, by Patrick J. Lynch and Sarah Horton (New Haven: Yale University Press, 1999). Yale University was one of the first institutions to publish a Web style guide on the Web. This book, like that site, offers a clear, thoughtful discussion of techniques for designing effective Web sites.

The Non-Designer's Web Book, by Robin Williams and John Tollett (Berkeley, CA: Peachpit Press, 1997). Web publishing, like desktop publishing, can be hazardous if you don't have a background in design. Robin Williams and John Tollett provide a crash course in design for first-time Web authors. They assume you're using an authoring tool that hides the nuts and bolts of HTML; if you're not, you'll need to learn HTML elsewhere.

Great Web Architecture, by Clay Andres (Sebastapol, CA: IDG Books, 1999). There's more to Web design than making pretty pages. This book explores and explains the underlying structure of successful Web sites.

Community Building on the Web, by Amy Kim (Berkeley, CA: Peachpit Press, 2000). Some of the most successful Web sites today offer more than information—they offer a sense of community. In this book the designer of some of the best Web community sites shares strategy, philosophy, and technology secrets for building a successful Web community. If you want your Web site to be a satisfying group experience for visitors, read this book.

World Wide Web: Beyond the Basics, edited by Dr. Marc Abrams (Upper Saddle River, NJ: Prentice Hall, 1998). If you already know how to build Web pages and use search engines, and want to learn more about the technical side of the Web, this book can help. It covers history, technology, security, and other topics with academic depth that goes beyond typical Web books.

Periodicals

Inter@ctive Week. This weekly publication provides comprehensive coverage of all things interactive and online, with a special focus on the Web.

Internet World. This news magazine is aimed at Webmasters and others who make a business of the Internet.

Internet Week. This weekly also covers the Internet from a professional business perspective.

Web Techniques. This technical monthly goes into detail on constructing Web sites that work.

Web Pages

The World Wide Web is especially good at providing information about itself. Whether you want to learn HTML, see the latest Web traffic reports, or explore the technological underpinnings of the Net, you'll find Web links at the *Computer Confluence* Web site (**www.prenhall.com/beekman**) that can help.

11

From Internet to Information Infrastructure

After you read this chapter you should be able to:

▼

Describe several software tools for navigating and using the Internet

Discuss several important social and political issues raised by the Internet

Explain how the Internet and other telecommunication technologies are evolving into an all-encompassing information infrastructure

Discuss the future of the Internet in particular and cyberspace in general

▲

▼ **In this chapter:**

Internet communication beyond email

How Napster changed the Net

The dark side of the Internet

Publishing pages on the Web

Next generation Internet and beyond

. . . and more.

▼ **On the CD-ROM:**

Video clips featuring Web pioneers

Animated demonstration of peer-to-peer computing

Access to glossary and key word references

Interactive self-study quizzes

. . . and more.

▼ **On the Web:**

www.prenhall.com/beekman

Tools for exploring the Internet

Resources for communicating through the Internet

Discussions of important Internet issues

Self-study exercises

. . . and more.

Tim Berners-Lee Weaves the Web for Everybody

*The whole idea you can have some idea and **make it happen** means that **dreamers** all over the world should **take heart** and **not stop**.*

—Tim Berners-Lee, creator of the World Wide Web

Tim Berners-Lee

The Internet has long been a powerful communication medium and a storehouse of valuable information. But until recently, few people mastered the cryptic codes and challenging languages that were required to unlock the Internet's treasures. The Net was effectively off limits to most of the world's people. Tim Berners-Lee changed all that when he single-handedly invented the World Wide Web and gave it to all of us.

Tim Berners-Lee was born in London in 1955. His parents met while programming the Ferranti Mark I, the first commercial computer. They encouraged their son to think unconventionally. He developed a love for electronics, and even built a computer out of spare parts and a TV set when he was a physics student at Oxford.

Berners-Lee took a software engineering job at CERN, the European Particle Physics Laboratory in Geneva, Switzerland. While he was there, he developed a program to help him track all of his random notes. He tried to make the program, called Enquire, deal with information in a "brain like way." Enquire was a primitive hypertext system that allowed related documents on his computer to be linked with numbers rather than mouse clicks. (In 1980 PCs didn't have mice.)

Berners-Lee wanted to expand the concept of Enquire so he could link documents on other computers to his own. His idea was to create an open-ended distributed hypertext system with no boundaries, so scientists everywhere could link their work together.

The World Wide Web was born at CERN in Geneva, Switzerland

Over the next few years he single handedly built a complete system to realize his dream. He designed the URL scheme for giving every Internet document a unique address. He developed HTML, the language for encoding and displaying hypertext documents on the Web. He created HTTP, the set of rules that allow hypertext documents to be linked across the Internet. And he built the first software browser for viewing those documents from remote locations.

When he submitted the first paper describing the Web to a conference in 1991, the conference organizers rejected it because the Web seemed too simple to them. They thought that Berners-Lee's ideas would be a step backward when compared to hypertext systems that had been developed by Ted Nelson, Doug Engelbart, and others over the previous 25 years. It's easy to see now that the simplicity of the Web was a strength, not a weakness.

Rather than trying to own his suite of inventions, Berners-Lee made them freely available to the public. Suddenly, vast tracts of the Internet were open to just about anyone who could point and click a mouse. The Web's popularity spread like a virus, and the Internet was forever changed.

When he created the Web, Tim Berners-Lee turned the Internet into a mass medium. Few people in history have had so great an impact on the way we communicate. In the words of writer Joshua Quittner, Tim Berners-Lee's accomplishments are "almost Gutenbergian."

Tim Berners-Lee now works in an unassuming office at MIT, where he heads the World Wide Web Consortium (W3C). The W3C is a standards-setting organization dedicated to helping the Web evolve in positive directions rather than disintegrating into incompatible factions. The work of Tim Berners-Lee and the W3C will help ensure that the World Wide Web continues to belong to everyone.

In the last chapter, we looked at the hardware, software, and protocols at the core of the Internet and the Web. People have built an amazing variety of powerful, useful, and novel applications on top of these core technologies. In this chapter we'll examine some of those applications and the ways people use them. Later in this chapter we'll survey some of the issues raised by this rapidly evolving technology. We'll end the chapter with a look into the future—a future in which the Internet is much more intimately involved in our lives.

Internet Applications: Communication and Connection

No other medium gives every participant the capability to communicate **instantly** with thousands and thousands of people.

—Tracy LaQuey, in The Internet Companion

We'll begin our survey of Internet applications by examining Web search engines and portals in a little more detail. Then we'll review several types of interpersonal communication tools on the Net. Next we'll take a look at peer-to-peer computing, grid computing, and push technology, and the ways people are using those technologies. Finally, we'll look at e-commerce applications, including Web services, and their impact on business.

Search Engines

With its vast storehouses of information, the Web is like a huge library. Unfortunately, the Web is a poorly organized library; you might find information on a particular topic almost anywhere. (What can you expect from a library where nobody's in charge?) That's why search engines are among the Web's most popular tools.

You're probably familiar with at least one Web search engine, but you may not know much about how it works. All search engines are designed to make it easier to find information on the Web, but they don't all function the same way. A typical search engine uses *web crawlers* or *spiders*—software robots that systematically explore the Web, retrieve information about pages, and index the retrieved information in a database. Different search engines use different search and indexing strategies. For example, one search engine might record detailed information about keywords in documents, while another might pay more attention to links to and from other documents. For some search engines, researchers organize and evaluate Web sites in databases; other search engines are almost completely automated.

Most search engines enable you to type queries using keywords, just as you might locate information in other types of databases. You can construct complex queries using *Boolean logic* (for example, American AND Indian BUT NOT Cleveland), quotations, and other tools for refining queries. Some search engines enable you to narrow your search repeatedly by choosing subcategories from a hierarchical *directory* or *subject tree*, as described in Chapter 0. Whatever search technique you use, you're eventually presented with a rank-ordered list of Web pages. A page might go undetected by one search engine and appear at the top of a list on another. That's why many researchers use *meta-search engines* such as MetaCrawler, OneSeek, and Apple's Sherlock—software tools that conduct parallel searches using several different search engines and directories. Of course, getting more hits isn't necessarily better. The best search engines provide you with relatively few high-quality results rather than overwhelming you with marginally relevant links.

Some popular search engines are designed to search for specific types of information. Specialized search engines can help you locate email addresses and phone numbers; others can help you find the lowest prices on the Web. These specialized search engines generally use technology that's very similar to general search engine technology.

Most search engines have access to less than one percent of the pages on the Web. The rest are out of reach of the public or stored in databases that can't be searched by conventional search engines. Some newer search engines, including **invisibleweb.com**, can provide access to information in those databases. Web search technology continues to evolve with the Web.

Sherlock 2, a meta-search engine built into the Mac OS, coordinates searches using multiple search engines.

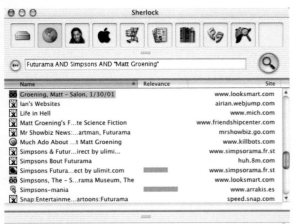

Portals

Many Web sites that started out as search engines have evolved into **portals**—Web entry stations that offer quick and easy access to a variety of services. Popular general-interest portals include Yahoo!, Excite, Lycos, AltaVista, Netscape Netcenter, and MSN. *Consumer portals* includes search engines, email services, chat rooms, references, news and sports headlines, shopping malls, other services, and advertisements—many of the same things found in online services such as AOL. You can personalize many of the portals so they automatically display local weather and sports scores, personalized TV and movie listings, news headlines related to particular subjects, horoscopes, and ads to meet your interests. Most browsers enable users to choose a home page that opens by default when the browser is launched; portals are designed with this feature in mind.

In addition to these general interest portals, the Web has a growing population of specialized portals. *Corporate portals* on intranets serve the employees of particular corporations. *Vertical portals*, or *vortals*, like vertical market software (Chapter 4) target members of a particular industry or economic sector. For example, **webmd.com** is a portal for medically minded consumers and health-care professionals. A growing number of specialized portals are competing to be your browser's home page.

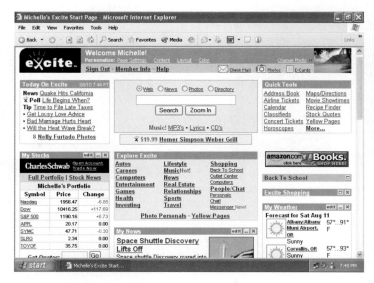

Like other portals, Excite can be personalized to highlight weather, news, sports, and financial headlines the user specifies.

Email on the Internet

The most popular Internet application is one of the oldest—email. There's no single way to send and receive Internet mail. What you see on the screen depends on the type of Internet connection you have and the mail program you use. If you have a dial-up connection to a UNIX-based host, you might send and receive mail using the UNIX mail program Pine, an easy-to-use program developed at the University of Washington. Because it's character-based, Pine works with almost any kind of Internet connection. Users with full Internet connections have many more mail software options, including graphical programs such as Microsoft Outlook Express and Qualcomm Eudora Pro. These programs enable PCs to download and handle mail locally rather than depending on a host as a post office. Many email services, including several free ones, are designed to be accessed through Web browsers rather than separate email client programs.

Email programs have a variety of user interfaces. Pine (top) is a character-based UNIX program that can be used on a terminal or PC. Eudora (bottom left) is a cross-platform commercial email program that is powerful and easy to use. Hotmail is a free email service that is accessible through Web browsers.

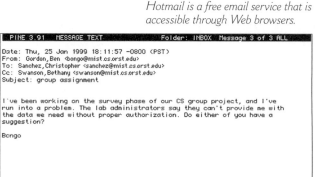

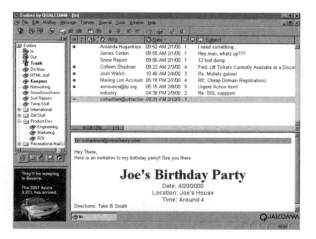

Working the Web

The Web is so easy to navigate that it's tempting to just dive in. But like a large library, the Web has more to offer if you learn a few tricks and techniques. Your goals should dictate your Web strategy.

▶ **Get to know your search engines.** Try several, choose your favorites, and learn the more advanced search features so you can minimize the time it takes to find what you're looking for. Searchenginewatch (www.searchengingwatch.com) is a good source of information about search engines.

▶ **Be specific when you search.** A search engine is more likely to give you the answer you're looking for if you search for "Epson USB scanner" than if you just type "scanner".

▶ **Know your plusses and minuses.** In most search engines you can use a plus sign to signify that you want pages that contain all words. For example, "+Alaska +oil +wildlife" searches pages that contain all three words. On the other hand, a minus sign usually means "not". For example, "cancer –astrology" locates pages that contain "cancer" but not "astrology". When you use these symbols, you're using basic Boolean algebra—the logical basis of database queries.

▶ **Be selective.** As Robert P. Lipshutz wrote in *Mobile Computing*, "A few tidbits of accurate, timely and useful information are worth much more than a ream of random data, and bad information is worse than no information at all." When you're assessing a Web page's credibility, consider the author, the writing, the references, and the page sponsor's objectivity and reliability. Be aware that many of the most popular search engines charge companies to be listed prominently in their directories, and that some give top billing to their own services and partners.

▶ **Triangulate.** A traditional navigation technique for sailors, triangulation involves using two points, other than yourself, to establish location. Xerox Chief Scientist John Seely Brown suggests that the same concept should be applied to the turbulent waters of the Web. Don't assume something is true because one Web source tells you so, unless you're sure the source is rock solid.

▶ **Organize your favorites.** When you find a page worth revisiting, record it on your list of favorites or bookmarks. Browsers enable you to organize your lists by category—a strategy that's far more effective than just throwing them all in a digital shoebox.

▶ **Protect your privacy.** Many Web servers keep track of all kinds of data about you: what site you visited before you came, where you clicked, and more. When you fill out forms to enter contests, order goods, or leave messages, you're providing more data for your hosts. Don't divulge any private information about yourself. And make sure you don't leave tracks that you're ashamed of as you hip-hop around the Web.

▶ **Be conscious of cookies and bugs.** Many Web servers send **cookies** to your browser when you visit them or perform other actions. Cookies are tidbits of information about your session that can be read later; they enable Web sites to remember what they know about you between sessions. Cookies make personalized portals and customized shopping experiences possible. Unfortunately, Cookies can also provide all kinds of possibilities for snoopers who want to know how you spend your time online. By default, most browsers don't tell you when they leave a cookie. It's easy to change browser settings so your browser will refuse all cookies, accept cookies only from selected sites, or ask you, on a cookie-by-cookie basis, whether to accept or refuse cookies. Unfortunately, you can't easily turn off *Web bugs*—one-pixel graphic images that are programmed to send information about your Web use back to their creators.

▶ **Online shopping isn't always better.** In increasing numbers shoppers are abandoning brick-and-mortar stores for click-and-mortar Web stores. Online shops and auctions can save you money, especially if you comparison shop. But when a product doesn't work as advertised, or when you have after-sale questions, a Web merchant might not be as helpful as a local shopkeeper. Some don't even accept phone queries. If your purchase will require person-to-person communication before or after the sale, you're probably better off patronizing a local merchant.

▶ **Shop with bots.** Bots are software robots, or agents, that can explore the Web and report back their findings. Several bots (such as mySimon at www.mySimon.com) are designed to help you find low prices by searching the databases of hundreds of merchants.

▶ **Shop with care.** The Web, like the nondigital world, has its share of less-than-honest merchants. Use services such as bizrate (www.bizrate.com) to evaluate questionable merchants before you lay your digital money down. If you're dealing with a private party or an unknown merchant, consider using a transaction service such as Paypal (www.paypal.com) to serve as a safe temporary depository for funds until the purchased product reaches you.

▶ **Remember why you're there.** The Web's extensive hyperlinks make it all too easy to wander off course when you're searching for important information. If you're using the Web to save time, stay focused or you may find that the Web costs more time than it saves.

Standard Internet mail messages are plain ASCII text. Plain text messages can be viewed with any mail client program, including those in email-capable PDAs and phones. Many email programs can also send and receive documents formatted with HTML—the language commonly used to create Web pages. HTML messages can include text formatting, pictures, and links to Web pages. But not all email programs can handle HTML email, and not all email users *want* HTML email. HTML encoding can slow down an email program. An HTML email message can also carry a *Web bug*—an invisible piece of code that silently notifies the sender about when the message was opened and may report other information about their machine or email software at the same time. Web bugs, which operate through specially encoded one-pixel graphics files, are increasingly common in commercial Web pages as well as HTML email messages.

Most email programs can send and receive formatted word processor documents, pictures, and other multimedia files as **attachments** to messages. Attachments need to be temporarily converted to ASCII text using some kind of encoding scheme before they can be sent through Internet mail. Most modern email programs take care of the encoding and decoding automatically. Of course, attachments aren't practical with many PDAs, cell phones, and other text-only email devices. And attachments can contain viruses and other unwelcome surprises, as described in the next chapter.

The Handspring Treo is a wireless device designed to send and receive email without a PC. The Treo also serves as a PDA, a wireless phone, and a wireless Web browser.

Mailing Lists

Email is a valuable tool for communicating one-to-one with individuals around the globe, but it's also useful for communicating one-to-many. **Mailing lists** enable you to participate in email discussion groups on special-interest topics. Lists can be small and local, or large and global. They can be administered by a human being or automatically administered by programs with names like Listserv and Majordomo. Each group has a mailing address that looks like any Internet address.

You might belong to one student group that's set up by your instructor to carry on discussions outside of class, another group that includes people all over the world who use Macromedia Flash to animate Web pages, a third that's dedicated to saving endangered species in your state, and a fourth for customers of an online bookstore. When you send a message to a mailing list address, every subscriber receives a copy. And, of course, you receive a copy of every mail message sent by everyone else to those lists.

Subscribing to a busy list might mean receiving hundreds of messages each day. To avoid being overwhelmed by incoming mail, many list members sign up to receive them in daily digest form; instead of receiving many individual messages each day, they receive one message that includes all postings. But digest messages can still contain lots of repetitive, silly, and annoying messages. Some lists are *moderated* to ensure that the quality of the discussion remains high. In a moderated group, a designated moderator acts as an editor, filtering out irrelevant and inappropriate messages and posting the rest.

Network News

You can participate in special-interest discussions without overloading your mailbox by taking advantage of **newsgroups**. A newsgroup is a public discussion on a particular subject consisting of notes written to a central Internet site and redistributed through a worldwide newsgroup network called Usenet. You can check into and out of a newsgroup discussion whenever you want; all messages are posted on virtual bulletin boards for anyone to read anytime. There are groups for every interest and taste . . . and a few for the tasteless. Newsgroups are organized hierarchically, with dot names like rec.music.makers.percussion and soc.culture.french. You can explore network newsgroups through several Web sites, including Google, or with a newsreader client program.

Many newsgroups contain the same kind of free-flowing discussions you'll find in Internet mailing lists, but there are two important differences:

▶ Listserv mail messages are delivered automatically to your mailbox, but you have to seek out information in newsgroups.

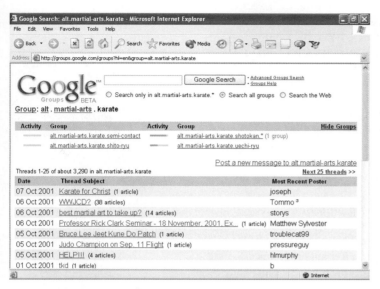

Google.com's newsreader enables you to view newsgroups by category (top) and view messages posted within those categories (bottom).

Mailing list messages are sent to a specific group of people, whereas newsgroup messages are available for anyone to see . . . for years to come.

Newsgroup discussions can get bogged down by repetitive questions from newcomers, childish rants, off-topic trivia, and other counterproductive messages. *Moderated newsgroups* contain only messages that have been filtered by designated moderators. The moderator discards inappropriate messages, making it easier for others to find the information they're looking for. Yahoo, MSN, AOL, and other portals and information services have discussion groups that are similar to Usenet newsgroups; the main difference is that they aren't distributed as widely.

Real-Time Communication

For **time** is the **longest distance** between two points.

—Tennessee Williams

Mailing lists and newsgroups are delayed or **asynchronous communication** because the sender and the recipients don't have to be logged in at the same time. The Internet offers programs for **real-time communication**, too. **Instant messaging** has been possible since the days of text-only Internet access. Internet relay chat (IRC) and Talk enable UNIX users to exchange instant messages with their online friends and coworkers. But newer, easier to use messaging systems from AOL/Netscape, Microsoft, Yahoo, ICQ, and others have turned instant messaging into one of the most popular Internet activities. Instant messaging programs enable users to create buddy lists, check for "buddies" who are logged in, and exchanged typed messages and files with those who are. Most of these programs are available for free.

Some chat rooms and multiplayer games on the Web use graphics to simulate real-world environments. Participants can represent themselves with *avatars*—graphical "bodies" that might look like simple cartoon sketches, elaborate 3-D figures, or exotic abstract icons.

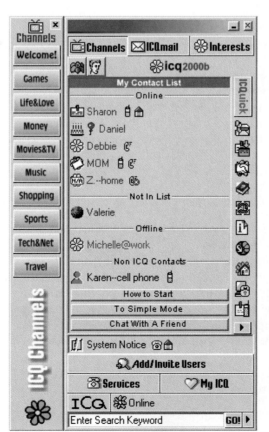

ICQ, one of the most popular instant messaging services on the Internet, enables users to communicate in real time with friends and colleagues.

For more conventional communication, many programs enable you to use a computer's microphone and speaker to turn the Internet into a toll-free long-distance telephone service. Most **Internet telephony (IP telephony)** programs work only when both parties are running the same program at the same time, and they're not nearly as trouble-free as traditional long-distance service. Still, many experts predict that this kind of technology will soon pose a serious competitive threat to the current telephone infrastructure.

Several programs make it possible to carry on two-way **video teleconferences**—provided you have a video camera and a high-speed Internet connection for each computer. With high-powered hardware, it's even possible to have multiperson videoconferences through the Web. The video images may be small, grainy, and jerky, but they're bound to get better as the technology matures.

Netiquette

The Internet is a new type of community that uses new forms of communication. Like any society the Net has rules and guidelines of acceptable behavior. If you follow these rules of **netiquette**, you'll be doing your part to make life on the Net easier for everybody—especially yourself.

▶ ***Say what you mean, and say it with care.*** Once you send something electronically, there's no way to call it back. Compose each message carefully, and make sure it means what you intend it to mean. If you're replying to a message, double-check the heading to make sure your reply is going only to those people you intend to send it to. Even if you took only a few seconds to write your message, it may be broadcast far and wide and be preserved forever in online archives.

▶ ***Keep it short.*** Include a descriptive subject line, and limit the body to a screen or two. If you're replying to a long message, include a copy of the relevant part of the message—but not the whole message. Remember that many people receive hundreds of email messages each day and they're more likely to read and respond to short ones.

▶ ***Proofread your messages.*** A famous *New Yorker* cartoon by Peter Steiner shows one dog telling another, "On the Internet no one knows you're a dog." You may not be judged by the color of your hair or the clothes you wear when you're posting messages, but that doesn't mean appearances aren't important. Other people will judge your intelligence and education by the spelling, grammar, punctuation, and clarity of your messages. If you want your messages to be taken seriously, present your best face.

▶ ***Don't assume you're anonymous.*** Your messages can say a lot about you, Those messages might be seen by more than your intended audience, and they won't necessarily go away when you want them to. Researcher Jonathan G.S. Koppell suggests a more contemporary caption for the *New Yorker* cartoon mentioned above: "On the Internet, everyone knows you're an aging, overweight, malamute-retriever mix living in the southwest, and with a preference for rawhide."

▶ ***Learn the "nonverbal" language of the Net.*** A simple phrase like "Nice job!" can have very different meanings depending on the tone of voice and body language behind it. Since body language and tone of voice can't easily be stuffed into a modem, online communities have developed text-based substitutes, sometimes called ***emoticons***. Here are a few:

:-)	These three characters represent a smiling face. (To see why, look at them with this page rotated 90° to the right.) "Smilie" suggests the previous remark should not be taken seriously. (The dash is optional.)
;-)	This winking smilie usually means the previous remark was flirtatious or sarcastic.
:-(	This frowning character suggests something is bothering the author—probably the previous statement in the message.
:-I	This character represents indifference.
:-.	This usually follows an extremely biting sarcastic remark.
:-P	This one is sticking its tongue out as if to say, "I'm grossed out!"
<g>	People who don't like smilies use this to say "grin."
ROTFL	This is short for "rolling on the floor laughing"; it's one of hundreds of keystroke-saving acronyms.

BTW	This one means "by the way."
IMHO	This one says "in my humble opinion."
Flame on	This statement, inspired by a comic book hero, warns readers that the following statements are inflammatory.
Flame off	This means the tirade is over.
<rant>	The angle brackets make this emoticon look like HTML, the page description language of the Web; this one means "beginning of rant."
</rant>	Using the HTML convention, this means "end of rant."

▶ ***Keep your cool.*** Many otherwise timid people turn into raging bulls when they're online. The facelessness of Internet communication makes it all too easy to shoot from the hip, overstate arguments, and get caught up in a digital lynch-mob mentality. There's nothing wrong with expressing your emotions, but broadside attacks and half-truths can do serious damage to your online relationships. Online or off, freedom of speech is a right that carries responsibility.

▶ ***Don't be a source of spam.*** It's so easy to send multiple copies of email messages that it's tempting broadcast too widely. Target your messages carefully; if you're trying to sell tickets to a local concert or advertise your garage sale, don't tell the whole world. If you *do* send a mass mailing, hide the recipient list to protect the privacy of your recipients. One way is to send the message to yourself and put everyone else in the bcc (blind carbon copy) field. And if you send repeated mass mailings, make sure you *always* include a message telling people how they can get off your list.

▶ ***Send no-frills mail.*** Even if your email program makes it easy to use fancy formatting, embed HTML, and include attachments, it's usually better to err on the side of simplicity. Graphics and fancy formatting make message files bigger and slower to download. Many people turn off the HTML capabilities of their email programs to protect themselves from Web bugs (HTML code that sends messages back to the sender). And many email veterans fear attachments because of the risk of email viruses. If you don't need the extra baggage, why not leave it out?

▶ ***Lurk before you leap.*** People who silently monitor mailing lists and newsgroups without posting messages are called ***lurkers***. There's no shame in lurking, especially if you're new to a group—it can help you to figure out what's appropriate. After you've learned the culture and conventions of a group, you'll be better able to contribute constructively and wisely.

▶ ***Check your FAQs.*** Many newsgroups and mailing lists have **FAQs** (pronounced "facks")—posted lists of **frequently asked questions**. These lists keep groups from being cluttered with the same old questions and answers, but only if members take advantage of them.

▶ ***Give something back.*** The Internet includes an online community of volunteers who answer beginner questions, archive files, moderate newsgroups, maintain public servers, and provide other helpful services. If you appreciate their work, tell them in words and show them in actions—do your part to help others in the Internet community.

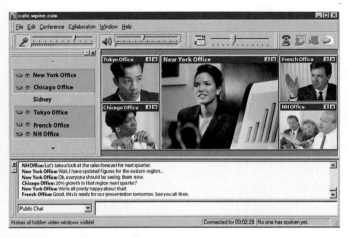

CU-SeeMe enables real-time audio/visual communication over the Internet.

Push Technology

We think we "surf" the Web now, but what we really do is hopscotch across fragile stepping-stones of texts, or worse, spelunk in a vast unmapped cave of documents. Only when **waves of media** begin to cascade behind our screens—huge swells of unbrowsable stuff—will we truly surf.

—Kevin Kelly and Gary Wolf, former Wired editors

The Web was built with **pull technology**—browsers on client computers pull information from server machines. With pull technology the browser needs to initiate a request before any information is delivered. But for some applications, it makes more sense to have information delivered automatically to the client computer. That's the way **push technology** works. (Microsoft used the term *Webcasting* for their brand of push technology. But today Webcasting more commonly refers to streaming audio and video feeds from radio stations, TV stations, and others on the Web.) With push technology you subscribe to a service or specify the kinds of information you want to receive and the server delivers that information periodically and unobtrusively. Maybe you want up-to-the-minute weather maps displayed in a small window in the corner of your screen. You might prefer to see news headlines (on subjects of your choice) scroll across the top of your screen. You may want to automatically receive new product descriptions from selected companies. Or you might like to have the software on your hard disk automatically upgraded when upgrades are posted on the Web. All of this is possible with push technology.

Technically speaking, today's push technology is really pull technology in disguise. Your computer quietly and automatically pulls information from selected Web servers based on your earlier requests or subscriptions. As convenient as they are, push programs have the same basic problem as Web search engines: They give you what they think you want, but they may not be very smart. Their ability to deliver what you really need—without bombarding you with unwanted data—will get better as artificial intelligence technology improves. In the meantime, push technology is used mostly for in-house delivery of information on intranets. Email continues to be the single form of push technology that has been embraced by almost all Internet users.

Peer-to-Peer and Grid Computing

The genie does not go back in the bottle—**period**.

—Tom Peters, business guru and best-selling author

Of all the companies that came out of nowhere during the dot-com boom of the late '90s, Napster generated the most conversation—and controversy. When 19-year-old college student Shawn Fanning put a friendly user interface and a fresh spin on decades-old file-sharing technology, he created a virtual swap meet for students and others who wanted to share MP3 music files. Almost overnight Napster became one of the hottest Internet destinations, with millions of users downloading and sharing MP3s daily using Napster's software. In May of 2000, a tech company hired by the rock band Metallica revealed that 322,000 Napster users were illegally distributing their music. The Recording Industry Association of America sued the company because its software enabled users to download copyrighted recordings without paying the record companies or artists.

The Napster servers didn't contain those illegal recordings—it just displayed links to recordings scattered all over the Net. People who used Napster practiced **peer-to-peer (P2P) computing**—or, more specifically, *peer-to-peer file sharing*—by making music files on their hard drives available to others rather than posting them on central servers. In April of 2001, a U.S. District Judge ruled that Napster was violating federal copyright law and forced the company to change its software so that users no longer had free access to copyrighted recordings. Napster changed its software and its business model, but the peer-to-peer music exchange lived on through other programs and Web sites. The popular Gnutella file-sharing system avoids Napster's legal problems by allowing users to share music, movies, and other files without going through a central directory. According to some experts, Gnutella's rapid growth suggests that it may become a Web standard.

Technologies like Gnutella make it difficult—or impossible—for laws to contain the peer-to-peer file-sharing phenomenon. Recording artists are divided on the issue; some encourage fans to share their music, while others fear that sharing will make it difficult for many musicians to support themselves. (Copyright and intellectual property issues are discussed in more detail in the next chapter.)

Music sharing is just one application of peer-to-peer computing. The technology is being applied to a growing number of diverse applications. Books, movies, and computer software are shared using Napster-like technology—and with the same legal and ethical concerns. Businesses use P2P for group collaboration, for Web searches, and for sharing updates to virus-control software, among other things.

The SETI@Home program starts after a PC sits idle for a few minutes; this animated screensaver shows the program in action.

A related technology—**grid computing**—is, like P2P, a form of *distributed computing*. But grid computing isn't about sharing files; it's about sharing processing power. The best-known example is SETI@Home (**setiathome.ssl.berkeley.edu/**), a program that puts PCs all over the Internet together into a sort of virtual supercomputer that analyzes space telescope data in the search for extraterrestrial life. The SETI@Home program, when installed on a PC, uses the computer's idle time to do calculations and send the results back to SETI headquarters. Millions of PCs around the world can do the work of a million-dollar supercomputer in much less time. A similar program called FightAIDS@home (**fightaidsathome.com**) enables PCs to contribute spare processing cycles to the fight against AIDS.

Grid computing may soon extend far beyond these processor-sharing programs to a new Internet model that resembles a utility grid. IBM and other companies are supporting initiatives to build a grid computing environment where anyone can plug in from anywhere and rent processing power and software from anywhere on the Net. Grid computing applications are currently being used by the U.S. Department of Defense, the U.S. Department of Energy, NASA, the U.K National Grid, and a variety of academic and scientific communities.

Intranets, Extranets, and Electronic Commerce

> Our customers are moving at **Internet speed**. They need us to respond at Internet speed.
> —Laurie Tucker, Federal Express vice president

For many businesses, Internet protocols and software are almost as important as the Net itself. Members of these organizations communicate through **intranets**—self-contained intraorganizational networks that are designed using the same technology as the Internet. A typical intranet offers email, newsgroups, file transfer, Web publishing, and other Internet-like services, but not all of these services are available to people outside the organization. For example, an intranet Web document might be accessible only to company employees—not to the entire Internet community. If an intranet has a gateway connection to the Internet, the gateway probably has some kind of *firewall* to prevent unauthorized communication and to secure sensitive internal data.

Some private TCP/IP networks are designed for outside use by customers, clients, and business partners of the organization. These networks, often called **extranets**, are typically for **electronic commerce (e-commerce)**—business transactions through electronic networks. Most use *electronic data interchange (EDI)*—a decade-old set of specifications for ordering, billing, and paying for parts and services over private networks.

Some extranets are **virtual private networks** that use encryption software (described in the next chapter) to create secure "tunnels" through the public Internet. Others use their own lines or lease lines that aren't subject to the traffic and security problems of the public Internet. Extranets are especially useful for **business-to-business (B2B)** e-commerce—transactions that involve businesses providing goods or services to other businesses.

Business-to-consumer (B2C) e-commerce generally involves transactions that take place on the Internet, rather than an extranet, because consumers don't have access to private extranets. The Internet has spawned a wide variety of B2C businesses, including

- *Online catalog sales.* Online catalogs save paper, but they offer other advantages for consumers, including search engines, immediate availability reports, custom orders, and instant updates. But some types of merchandise don't lend themselves to online sales, and online customers can be frustrated by confusing user interfaces and minimal customer support.
- *Auctions.* The Internet makes long-distance auctions practical, allowing people to bid on all kinds of items. Some retail outlets use auctions to move clearance merchandise; some sites sell everything through auctions.
- *Reverse auctions.* Some sites allow customers to request goods or services and have merchants bid on prices. Everything from airline tickets to legal services is offered through reverse auctions.
- *Comparison shopping.* Specialized search engines search the Web for the lowest prices.
- *Financial services.* Checks, credit cards, stocks are all available online.

B-to-C sites can offer a high degree of personalization—for example, suggesting products similar to the ones already ordered by a customer, or remembering a customer's personal preferences and sizes between visits. But personalization raises privacy and security concerns in many customers. (Security issues are discussed in detail in the next chapter.)

E-commerce is changing the way many companies do business. But e-commerce isn't cheap or easy. Profits have proven to be elusive for many online companies. Like the brick-and-mortar world, the Internet presents challenges along with opportunities for enterprising business people.

Web Services

> The **network** is the **computer**.
> —advertising slogan used by Sun Microsystems, Inc., in the 1990s

Software costs can be daunting for companies that have to build e-commerce sites from the ground up. Several of the computer industry's biggest companies, including IBM, Hewlett Packard, Microsoft, Oracle, and Sun, are developing software tools to make e-commerce solutions easier to build and maintain. These systems have different names and features, but they all fall into a software category called **Web services**. Web services involve new kinds of Web-based applications that can be assembled quickly using existing *software components*. Component technology can, for example, make it easy to plug a shopping-cart component into an existing Web site, or to design applications that can be accessed through a variety of Web-enabled devices. XML plays an important role in most Web services systems currently under development.

Unfortunately, the industry hasn't agreed on the details of this emerging technology. Sun, Hewlett Packard, and IBM are using Java to build their cross-platform service tools. Microsoft's .NET is being built using C#, a proprietary language that (so far) runs only on Windows platforms. The Free Software Foundation is working on a UNIX version of Microsoft's .NET technology, hoping to keep .NET from being a proprietary system. Meanwhile, the W3C is attempting to create standards that the entire industry can embrace.

Complete Web Services systems are still many years away. But they offer great hope for companies struggling with the challenges of creating successful e-commerce sites.

The Evolving Internet

> In the short term, the **impact** of new technologies like the Internet will be **less than the hype** would suggest. But in the long term, it will be vastly **larger than we can imagine** today.
> —Paul Saffo, director of the Institute for the Future

The Internet started as a small community of scientists, engineers, and other researchers who staunchly defended the noncommercial, cooperative charter of the network. Today the Net has swollen into a community of millions, including everybody from children to corporate executives. The rate of growth is so great that it raises questions about the Internet's ability to keep up; the amount of information transmitted may eventually be more than the Net can handle.

The U.S. government no longer assumes primary responsibility for Internet expansion. Many funding and administrative duties have been passed on to private companies, allowing businesses to commercialize the Net. In 1995, for the first time, the number of commercial host sites on the Net exceeded the number of noncommercial sites. In the 3-year period that followed, the Net experienced a hundredfold increase in monthly traffic.

Internet2 and the Next Generation Internet

As the Internet evolves into the network of the masses, congestion becomes more problematic for the scientists and researchers who made up the original Internet community. The U.S. government, working in conjunction with several large corporations, launched **Internet2** in 1998 to provide faster network communications for universities and research institutions. A related effort from DARPA, the *Next Generation Internet (NGI)*, will consist of a nationwide web of optical fiber integrated with intelligent management software to maintain high-speed connections.

Internet2 will eventually be capable of transmitting data at 9.6 billion bits per second—enough to send all 30 volumes of the Encyclopedia Britannica in 1 second. Internet2 isn't available for commercial or recreational use; it is reserved for research and academic work. Participating universities are building virtual laboratories, digital libraries, telemedicine research facilities, and distance learning applications that take advantage of its tremendous bandwidth. The rest of us will undoubtedly inherit the technologies developed for Internet2.

Internet Issues: Ethical and Political Dilemmas

The Internet still hasn't figured out how to **conduct itself in public**. . . . Everybody is trying to **develop the rules** by which they can conduct themselves in order to keep a **civil operation** going and not **self-destruct**.

—George Lucas, filmmaker

The commercialization of the Internet has opened a floodgate of new services to users. People are logging into the Internet to view weather patterns, book flights, buy stocks, sell cars, track deliveries, listen to radio broadcasts from around the world, conduct videoconferences, coordinate disaster recovery programs, and do countless other private and public transactions. The Internet saves time, money, and lives, but it brings problems, too.

Computer Addiction

For a few hard-core networkers the world on the other side of the modem is more real and more interesting than the everyday physical world. One Alaskan reader wrote to advice columnist Ann Landers: "Computer chat lines can become every bit as addictive as cocaine. I have been hooked on both, and it was easier to get off coke." While this may seem strange, it's not unique. Many people feel the same way about television, spectator sports, or romance novels. Internet addiction, like any addiction, can be a serious problem—for individuals and for society. The problem is growing as more people go online, and no quick fixes are in sight.

Freedom's Abuses

Commercialization has brought capitalism's dark side to the Internet. Electronic junk mail scams, get-rich-quick hoaxes, online credit-card thefts, email forgery, child pornography hustling, illegal gambling, Web site sabotage, online stalking, and other sleazy activities abound. The Internet has clearly lost its innocence.

Some of these problems have at least partial technological solutions. Concerned parents and teachers can now install **filtering software** that, for the most part, keeps children out of Web sites that contain inappropriate content. Commercial Web sites routinely use encryption so customers can purchase goods and services without fear of having credit-card numbers stolen by electronic eavesdroppers. Several software companies and banks are developing systems for circulating **digital cash** on the Internet to make online transactions easier and safer. To protect against email forgery, many software companies are working together to hammer out standards for *digital signatures* using encryption techniques described in the next chapter.

Many problems associated with the rapid growth and commercialization of the Internet are social problems that raise important political questions. Online hucksterism and pornography have prompted government controls on Internet content, including the 1996 Communications Decency Act. Opponents to this law and other proposed controls argue that it's important to preserve the free flow of information; they stress the need to protect our rights to free speech and privacy on the Net. In 1996 the U.S. Supreme Court declared the Communications Decency Act unconstitutional, arguing that "the interest in encouraging freedom of expression in a democratic society outweighs any theoretical but unproven benefit of censorship." Nevertheless, the legal battle is certain to continue.

In December of 2000, Congress passed the Children's Internet Protection act. The act requires public libraries and schools that receive certain types of federal funding install content filters on computers with Internet access. Like the Communications Decency Act, the Children's Internet Protection Act faces legal challenges based on the First Amendment to the Constitution.

Questions about human rights online probably won't be resolved by legislators and judges, though. The Internet's global reach makes it nearly impossible for a single government to regulate it. Even if the governments of the world agree to try to restrict information flow, the Net seems to have developed a mind of its own. The same decentralized, packet-switching technology that was designed to protect government messages from enemy attack today protects civilian messages from government or corporate control. In the words of Internet pioneer John Gilmore, "The Net interprets censorship as damage and routes around it."

Universal Access Issues

During the 1990s the U.S. government pushed for the development of a National Information Infrastructure (NII)—an affordable, secure, high-speed network to provide "universal service" for all Americans. Probably the biggest roadblock to realizing the dream of NII is the **digital divide** that separates computer haves from have-nots.

As part of the nonprofit Tech Corps program, these computer professionals volunteer their time and skills to help students and teachers put technology to good use.

Today a little more than half of the U.S. population has easy access to the Internet—a subset of America that excludes most poor people and minorities. Government programs to wire schools, libraries, and other public facilities have increased access for disadvantaged populations. But many Internet services that used to be free for all are now available to only paying customers. Families can't buy computers or Internet service if they're having trouble paying the rent. The problem of equal access isn't likely to go away without combined efforts of governments, businesses, and individuals.

Even if America achieves a universal access NII, access issues still confront the rest of the world. The Internet is a global infrastructure, but huge populations all over the world are locked out. Many experts fear that we'll leave those populations behind as we move further into the information age. This kind of information stratification could be harmful to all of us unless we find ways to unlock the Internet for everybody who wants it.

Internet Everywhere: The Invisible Information Infrastructure

In the future, **everything with a digital heartbeat** will be connected to the Internet.

—Scott McNealy, CEO of Sun Microsystems

Where is it all heading? Vint Cerf, one of the Internet's founders, thinks it's headed for space. He's putting much of his time and energy into a project called InterPlaNet, which he hopes will extend the Internet to the other planets in our solar system. According to the plan, electronic "post offices" will orbit other planets, routing messages between space explorers, both human and robot.

Back on Earth, technology forecaster Paul Saffo suggests a blurring of the boundaries between the Web and interpersonal communication applications. When we visit a Web site that's being explored by hundreds of other people, we'll actually be able to experience their presence and interact with them in ways that go beyond today's simple chat rooms. In Saffo's words, "We're going to shift away from a model of people accessing information to a model of people accessing other people in an information-rich environment. The information will become the wallpaper surrounding conversational space."

We may be sharing Web space with more people in the future, but we'll also be sharing it with all kinds of gadgets. Today we think of the Web as a network of computers, but the Web isn't just for PCs, mainframes, and servers anymore. A variety of Internet appliances, network computers, set-top boxes, PDAs, mobile phones, and other devices are being connected to the Internet in offices and homes. Everything from coffee makers to traffic lights may be routinely connected to the Web soon. Consider the possibilities:

You tell your alarm clock to wake you in time to catch the 8:00 A.M. flight to Washington. At 5:00 A.M. the clock checks the airline's Web site and determines that the flight has been delayed an hour. It also checks online traffic reports and finds that traffic is light. The clock resets your wakeup time accordingly, giving you an extra hour of sleep. As usual, it turns on the heat and the coffee maker 10 minutes before it wakes you. On the way to the airport, your car routes you around a congested construction spot. When you arrive at the airport, it tells you where to find a vacant parking spot close to the terminal.

Whether you consider this future fantasy appealing or appalling, the technology is on the horizon. One thing is clear: The Web is changing so fast it's impossible for anybody to predict exactly what it will look like even a few months from today.

Cyberspace: The Electronic Frontier

> Cyberspace. **A consensual hallucination** experienced daily by billions of legitimate operators, **in every nation**, by children being taught mathematical concepts. . . .
> A graphic representation of data abstracted from the banks of
> **every computer in the human system**.
> **Unthinkable complexity**. Lines of light ranged in the nonspace of the mind, clusters and constellations of data. Like city lights, receding. . . .
>
> —William Gibson, in *Neuromancer*

Science fiction writers suggest that tomorrow's networks will take us beyond the Internet into an artificial reality that has come to be known as **cyberspace**, a term coined by William Gibson in his visionary novel *Neuromancer*.

In *Neuromancer*, as in earlier works by Vernor Vinge and others, travelers experience the universal computer network as if it were a physical place, a shared virtual reality, complete with sights, sounds, and other sensations. Gibson's cyberspace is an abstract, cold landscape in a dark and dangerous future world. Vinge's novella *True Names* takes place in a network hideaway where adventurous computer wizards never reveal their true names or identities to each other. Instead, they take on mythical identities with supernatural abilities.

Today's computer networks are still light-years from the futuristic visions of Vinge and Gibson. But the Net today *is* a primitive cyberspace—a world where messages, mathematics, and money can cross continents in seconds. People from all over the planet meet, develop friendships, and share their innermost thoughts and feelings in cyberspace.

John Perry Barlow, co-founder of the Electronic Frontier Foundation has called the online world an "electronic frontier," suggesting parallels to America's Old West. Until recently the electronic frontier was populated mostly by free-spirited souls willing to forgo creature comforts. These digital pioneers built the roads and towns that are used today by less adventurous settlers and business interests.

In spite of its rapid commercialization, the electronic frontier is far from tame. Network nomads pick digital locks and ignore electronic fences. Some explore nooks and crannies out of a spirit of

Cindy Price and Josh Marquis met on an AOL message board devoted to the O. J. Simpson murder trial in 1995. They married in 1996.

adventure. Others steal and tamper with private information for profit or revenge. Charlatans and hustlers operate outside the law. Law enforcement agencies and lawmakers occasionally overreact.

There's a strong sentiment on the Net toward keeping controls to a minimum. Netizens commonly argue that the Web will always be free of control because of the way it's constructed. It's true that governments have so far had trouble regulating many Internet activities. But there's no guarantee that the free-spirited Internet will always remain that way.

In *The Code and Other Laws of Cyberspace*, Lawrence Lessig claims that, because of commerce and other forces, an architecture of control is being built into the Net—control by government and by businesses intent on maximizing Net profits. Lessig argues that the code—the way the Net is programmed—will determine how much freedom we have in the future Internet. "We can build, or architect, or code cyberspace to protect values we believe are fundamental, or we can build, or architect, or code cyberspace to allow those values to disappear. There is no middle ground. There is no choice that does not include some kind of *building*."

There are parallels in the nondigital world. Many city planning experts argue that industrialized nations have systematically (if not consciously) rebuilt their cities so that, in many places, it's just about impossible to live without a car. These car-centered cities have generated revenue for businesses and governments, and they've brought a new sense of freedom to many citizens. But for the poor, the disabled, the young, the old, and others who can't drive, these cities are anything but free. At the same time, other cities have thriving masses of car-free people. Design choices (and nonchoices) made decades ago determine the livability of our cities today.

In the same way, the design decisions being made today by software architects, corporate managers, government officials, and concerned citizens will determine the nature of our Internet experiences in the future. Will portals guide us to corporate-approved information sources? Will netizens feel free to express controversial opinions and criticize powerful institutions without fear of lawsuits and prosecution? Will paths through cyberspace be accessible to everyone? As Mark Stefik says in *Internet Dreams: Archetypes, Myths, and Metaphors,* "Different versions of [cyberspace] support different kinds of dreams. We choose, wisely or not."

The Day I got Napsterized

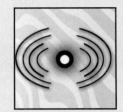

Steven Levy

Steven Levy has eloquently written for years about free speech and privacy on the Internet. In this article, first published in the May 28, 2001 issue of Newsweek, *Levy brings the discussion to a personal level.*

As a spectator, I found it easy to be sanguine about the raging Internet intellectual-property debates. I'd tempered my ecstasy during the heady exultations of the "information wants to be free"-bies, and kept my emotional powder dry as apocalyptic content owners warned that wanton file-sharing would mean the death of creativity. Basically, my take was that the Net had simply opened up a powerful mode of distribution, most fully realized in the Napsterlike peer-to-peer (P2P) model, where everybody could help spread the word (and the music). Artists and merchants alike would eventually figure out how to reap bucks from that bounty, and until then I'd sit back and enjoy the fun as Metallica and Courtney Love duked it out.

That was before I got P2P'd. And like facing a hangman's noose, being pirated on the Net has a way of focusing one's attention.

I first got wind of my own Napsterish problem a few months back when I stumbled on a message posted in an Internet discussion group that mentioned my 1984 book *Hackers*. Some helpful soul informed the group that one could get the whole tome free, simply by going to a certain Web site. Huh?

Indeed, the entire text of *Hackers* was posted for all the world to download. And the Web address revealed a most unexpected host for the giveaway: Stanford University. How did my copyrighted work find its way there? A few minutes of clicking revealed that this particular server had some connection to the chair of the university's program in history and philosophy of science, Tim Lenoir. So I called him to ask if he'd any idea who'd done this.

"I scanned your book," he said. Then came the apologies. The professor professed to be a big fan of my work, and (erroneously) assuming that it was out of print, spent a few hours to suck the words from each page of my book, submit it to a program that converted it to text and posted it for the benefit of his students only. The fact that anyone in the world could get to it, he said, was a mistake: he had not intended Stanford University to become an unofficial global distributor of *Hackers*, charging nothing and, of course, paying no royalties. Lenoir promised to remove the book from the site, and we had a pretty good conversation about what might be fair use of electronic texts in an educational setting. By the time I hung up the phone, I felt somewhat less violated. Still, I wondered whether his "mistake" had cost me book sales.

My benign outlook dissolved about a week later when I received an email from an English reader informing me that "in some kind of ironic but illegal turn, your book *Crypto* has been . . . posted onto the newsgroup alt.binaries.e-book." This was the work I had published just weeks before, still selling briskly at $25.95 a pop! I knew all too well where the aforementioned irony came from. One topic I'd discussed in *Crypto* was the use of cyberanonymity, a means of cloaking the origin of an electronic missive. The purloiner of my own book called himself Stormysky, and carefully hid his tracks. Using those techniques, a number of Internet repositories had emerged as thriving underground book dumps where free-riders could download the texts of hundreds of recent tomes. Author Harlan Ellison calls the alt-scanners "rodents without ethic or understanding." A talk with my publisher's lawyer was even more dispiriting. "We're seeing this problem all the time," he moaned; he'd had little success in stemming the tide of purloined works by the likes of Tom Clancy. (So what were my chances?)

Though the technologies of anonymity wouldn't let me trace this particular rodent, it was possible to send him email. Stormysky replied promptly, assuring me that he'd posted my book not to hurt me but to express his notion that the Internet was about sharing—and also as a protest against the intention of publishers to lock up intellectual property on the Net. If publishers have their way, Stormysky warned, they would limit the uses of books so that traditional consumer rights—lending a book to a friend, or even getting access to the book after a specified period—might be lost.

I actually agree with those sentiments, but also think I'm entitled to some payment for my work—and wonder what will happen when electronic reading devices become more convivial, and downloaders of these files won't pay a penalty in eyestrain. Unfortunately, my new friend's protest contradicted his belief that "authors should receive monetary compensation for their creations." Grappling with this concept, he graciously agreed not to post any more of my work to newsgroups.

Forgive me, Stormy, if I'm feeling less than grateful. But I do appreciate the wake-up call. For authors like me—as musicians have already learned—the intellectual-property wars cannot be a spectator sport. I need to speak up more forcefully on the issues, and petition vociferously for creative business models—even if they require drastically altering the ones that have evolved over decades. Publishers mainly want control, and the consumers mainly want convenience and value, if not freebies. But it's the artists who are on the firing line, eager to win audiences but concerned about maintaining our credit ratings. We have to muscle our way into the center of the quest for a solution that somehow exploits the distribution power of the Net while assuring that our audiences pay us something for the experience. Otherwise, we'll just be P'd on.

DISCUSSION QUESTIONS

1. What do you think of Stormysky's argument that the Internet should be about sharing?
2. Under what circumstances would it be okay, in your opinion, to scan a book and post it? To download it?.

Summary

A variety of applications are built on the protocols of the Internet and the World Wide Web. For example, people who use the Web depend on search engines to find the information they need. Search engines use a combination of automated searching and indexed databases to catalog Web resources.

The most popular Internet communication service, email, uses a standard email addressing scheme so users on different networks can communicate. Mailing lists and newsgroups enable group discussions, debates, and information sharing on particular subjects. Other communication tools enable real-time instant messaging, voice communication, and even video teleconferencing.

Peer-to-peer computing was popularized by Napster, but its applications go beyond music sharing. Many businesses are exploring ways to apply P2P technology. Grid computing goes beyond P2P computing by enabling people to share processor power with others. Some organizations are working to build a grid-computing model that would make the Internet work like a shared utility.

E-commerce is built on Internet technology. Businesses use the Internet and the Web for business-to-business and business-to-customer communication. Many businesses have private networks, called intranets, based on Internet technology. Extranets are also private networks based on the same technology; extranets enable businesses to connect with their partners and customers without going through public Internet channels.

As the Internet grows and changes, issues of privacy, security, censorship, criminal activity, universal access, and appropriate Net behavior are surfacing. Even more questions will arise when all kinds of electronic devices are attached to the Web, communicating with each other from our homes, our offices, and our vehicles. We have many questions to answer as the Internet evolves from an electronic frontier into a futuristic cyberspace.

Chapter Review

▼ Key Terms

asynchronous communication (p. 294)
attachment (email) (p. 293)
business-to-business (B2B) (p. 298)
business-to-consumer (B2C) (p. 298)
cookies (p. 292)
cyberspace (p. 301)
digital cash (p. 299)
digital divide (p. 300)
electronic commerce (e-commerce) (p. 297)
extranet (p. 297)

FAQ (frequently asked question) (p. 295)
filtering software (p. 299)
grid computing (p. 297)
instant messaging (p. 294)
Internet telephony (p. 294)
Internet2 (p. 299)
intranet (p. 297)
mailing list (p. 293)
netiquette (p. 295)
newsgroup (p. 293)

peer-to-peer (P2P) computing (p. 296)
portal (p. 291)
pull technology (p. 296)
push technology (p. 296)
real-time communication (p. 294)
video conferences (p. 294)
virtual private networks (p. 298)
Web services (p. 298)

▼ Interactive Quiz Questions

1. The *Computer Confluence* CD-ROM contains self-test quiz questions related to this chapter, including multiple choice, true or false, and matching questions.
2. The *Computer Confluence* Web site, **www.prenhall.com/beekman**, contains self-test exercises related to this chapter. Follow the instructions for taking a quiz. After you've completed your quiz, you can email the results to your instructor.

   The Web site also contains open-ended discussion questions called Internet Explorations. Discuss one or more of the Internet Exploration questions at the section for this chapter.

▼ Review Questions

1. Define or describe each of the key terms listed in the "Key Terms" section. Check your answers using the glossary.
2. Why is netiquette important? Give some examples of netiquette.
3. How might you use remote login while visiting another school? What about file transfer? How might the Web make remote login unnecessary?
4. Why is file compression important on the Internet?
5. Why is the World Wide Web important as a publishing medium? In what ways is the Web different from any publishing medium that has ever existed before?
6. Briefly describe several software tools that can be used to develop Web pages.
7. How does push technology differ from standard Web page delivery techniques? How is it used?
8. What new services are available as a result of the commercialization of the Internet? What new problems are arising as a result of that commercialization?

▼ Discussion Questions

1. As scientists, engineers, and government officials develop plans for the future of the Internet, they wrestle with questions about who should have access and what kinds of services to plan for. Do you have any ideas about the kinds of things they might want to consider?
2. Do you know anyone who has experienced Internet addiction? If so, can you describe the experience?
3. How do you think online user interfaces will evolve as bandwidth and processing power increase? Describe what cyberspace will feel like in the year 2010, in the year 2050, and beyond.

▼ Projects

1. Research peer-to-peer and grid-computing applications to determine how they're used. Write a report summarizing your findings.
2. Read several books and articles about cyberspace, and write a paper comparing them. Better yet, write a hypertext document, and publish it on the Web.

Sources and Resources

Books

These books, along with the ones listed in the last chapter, represent a sampler of good Internet resources.

Weaving the Web, by Tim Berners-Lee. (San Francisco: Harper San Francisco, 1999). This is the story of the creation of the Web straight from the word processor of the man who did it. Few people in history have had more impact on the way we communicate than this unassuming man.

How the Web Was Born, by James Gillies and Robert Cailliau. (London: Oxford University Press: 2000). This book provides another account of the events leading up to and following the creation of the Web. The authors provide a context that helps explain how Englishman Tim Berners-Lee made critical decisions in shaping the Web.

The World Wide Web: A Mass Communication Perspective, by Barbara K. Kaye and Norman J. Medoff (Mountain View, CA: Mayfield Publishing Company, 1999). This book examines the relationship of the Web to radio, TV, newspapers and other mass media and discusses issues raised by the emergence of Web communication.

From Anarchy to Power: The Net Comes of Age, by Wendy M. Grossman (New York University Press, 2001). The Internet has gone through a radical transition in just a few years. This book chronicles the changes and comments on the profound social and political impact of those changes.

Search Engines for the World Wide Web Visual QuickStart Guide, Third Edition, by Alfred and Emily Glossbrenner (Berkeley, CA: Peachpit Press, 2001). There's plenty of information on the Web; the trick is finding what you need when you need it. This little book tells you what you need to choose and use search engines efficiently and effectively. It covers the big six general-purpose Web search engines along with a healthy sampling of specialty sites for locating anything from automobiles to Zip codes. Highly recommended.

The Invisible Web: Uncovering Information Sources Search Engines Can't See, by Gary Prince and Chris Sherman (CyberAge Books, 2001). If the information you need is stowed in a Web database, a standard search engine can't find it. This book will tell you what you need to know to track down the Web's hidden treasures.

Harley Hahn's Internet and Web Yellow Pages, 2002 Edition, by Harley Hahn (Berkeley, CA: Osborne/McGraw Hill, 2001). Many books attempt to catalog the contents of the Web, but most of them can't compete with the currency and convenience of online Web search tools. Harley Hahn's popular directory combines solid research and a careful selection process with useful tips, clever insights, and amusing asides. The result is a book that's both fun and informative. The built-in CD-ROM contains the text in clickable hypertext format.

Stopping Spam: Stamping Out Unwanted Email and News Postings, by Alan Schwartz and Simson Garfinkel (Cambridge: O'Reilly, 1998). Spam can be a serious problem for casual computer users and systems administrators alike. This book outlines the problem and provides guidance for anyone who wants a spam-free Internet diet.

Sending Your Government a Message: Email Communication Between Citizens and Government, by C. Richard Neu, Robert H. Anderson, and Tora K. Bikson (Santa Monica, CA: Rand, 1999) and **Universal Access to E-Mail,** by Robert H. Anderson, Tora K. Bikson, Sally Ann Law, and Bridger M. Mitchell (Santa Monica, CA: Rand, 1999). These two books, from the influential Rand research organization, address the critical issue of email access. *Sending Your Government a Message* focuses on citizen access to U.S. government's agencies; *Universal Access* deals with email access in general. Both books discuss current public policy and make recommendations for future policy. *Sending Your Government a Message* includes a list of government email addresses. Both texts are available online, along with other Rand publications, at www.rand.org/publications/electronic.

Peer-to-Peer: Harnessing the Power of Disruptive Technologies, edited by Andy Oram (O'Reilly and Associates, 2001). This collection of essays discusses the philosophy, applications, and implications of peer-to-peer technology, from music sharing to CPU sharing and beyond.

The Code and Other Laws of Cyberspace, by Lawrence Lessig (New York: Basic Books, 1999. This important book presents a strong argument that we might lose our liberty on the Internet unless we consciously work to preserve it. The way we build the Net today will determine what's possible in cyberspace tomorrow. Lessig, a lawyer, is an excellent writer with something important to say.

Crypto Anarchy, Cyberstates, and Pirate Utopias, edited by Peter Ludlow (MIT Press, 2001). This lively, thought-provoking collection of essays presents a cyberspace made up of virtual communities that are outside of the circles of corporate and political power.

True Names: and the Opening of the Cyberspace Frontier, by Vernor Vinge and James Frenkel (New York: Tor Books, 2000). In 1981 (three years before the original publication of *Neuromancer*) Vernor Vinge's critically acclaimed novella, *True Names,* described a virtual world inside a computer network. Vinge didn't use the term "cyberspace," but his visionary story effectively invented the concept. This book includes the wonderful original *True Names* novella and a collection of articles by cyberspace pioneers about the past, present, and future of cyberspace.

Neuromancer, by William Gibson (New York: Ace Books, 1995). Gibson's 1984 cyberpunk classic spawned several sequels, dozens of imitations, and a new vocabulary for describing a high-tech future. Gibson's future is gloomy and foreboding, and his futuristic slang isn't always easy to follow. Still, there's plenty to think about here.

Snow Crash, by Neal Stephenson (New York: Bantam, 1992). This science fiction novel lightens the dark, violent cyberpunk future vision a little with Douglas Adams–style humor. Characters regularly jack into the Metaverse, a shared virtual reality network that is in many ways more real than the physical world where they live. The descriptions of this alternate reality heavily influenced the design of many VR-like Web sites today.

Periodicals

Yahoo! Internet Life. This monthly magazine attempts to keep readers abreast of the technology and culture of the Internet. Of course, many Internet travelers aren't satisfied reading paper news that's two or three months old when they can get up-to-the-minute information online.

Net Economy. This monthly covers the impact of the Internet on business and the economy.

Web Pages

To learn more about the Web, turn to the Web. Emerging technologies and applications abound; you'll find links at the *Computer Confluence* Web site (**www.prenhall.com/beekman**).

12 | Computer Security and Risks

▼ **In this chapter:**

Who are the real computer criminals?

Who owns information?

How to protect your computer from viruses and other attacks

Ethics and the law—where are the gaps?

Can we really have security?

... and more.

▼ **On the CD-ROM:**

An interactive look at cryptography

An animated illustration of viruses in action

Instant access to glossary and key word references

Interactive self-study quizzes

... and more.

▼ **On the Web:**

www.prenhall.com/beekman

Articles and books on computer crime, hackers, and law enforcement

Tips for protecting yourself from electronic mischief and malice

Discussions of intellectual property and other legal issues related to information technology

Self-study exercises

... and more.

Kempelen's Amazing Chess-Playing Machine

Check.

—The only word ever spoken by
Kempelen's chess-playing machine

In 1760 Wolfgang Kempelen, a 49-year-old Hungarian inventor, engineer, and advisor to the court of Austrian Empress Maria Theresa, built a mechanical chess player. This amazing contraption defeated internationally renowned players and earned its inventor almost legendary fame.

A Turkish-looking automaton sat behind a big box that supported a chessboard and chess pieces. The operator of the machine could open the box to "prove" there was nothing inside but a network of cogwheels, gears, and revolving cylinders. After every 12 moves, Kempelen wound the machine up with a huge key. Of course, the chess-playing machine was actually a clever hoax. The real chess player was a dwarf-sized person, who controlled the mechanism from inside and was concealed by mirrors when the box was opened. The tiny player couldn't see the board, but he could tell what pieces were moved by watching magnets below the chessboard.

Kempelen's chess-playing machine

Kempelen had no intention of keeping the deception going for long; he thought of it as a joke and dismantled it after its first tour. But he became a slave to his own fraud, as the public and the scientific community showered him with praise for creating the first "machine-man." In 1780 the Emperor Joseph II ordered another court demonstration of the mechanical chess player, and Kempelen had to rebuild it. The chess player toured the courts of Europe, and the public became more curious and fascinated than ever.

After Kempelen died in 1804, the machine was purchased by the impresario Maelzel, who showed it far and wide. In 1809 it challenged Napoleon Bonaparte to play. When Napoleon repeatedly made illegal moves, the machine-man brushed the pieces from the table. Napoleon was delighted to have unnerved the machine. When he played the next game fairly, Napoleon was badly beaten.

The chess-playing machine came to America in 1826, where it attracted large, paying crowds. In 1834 two different articles—one by Edgar Allen Poe—revealed the secrets of the automated chess player. Poe's investigative article was insightful but not completely accurate; one of his 17 arguments was that a true automatic player would invariably win.

After Maelzel's death in 1837, the machine passed from hand to hand until it was destroyed by fire in Philadelphia in 1854. During the 70 years that the automation was publicly exhibited, its "brain" was supplied by 15 different chess players, who won 294 of 300 games. ▶

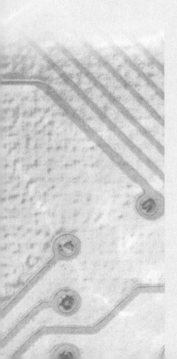

With his elaborate and elegant deception, Kempelen might be considered the forerunner of the modern computer criminal. Kempelen was trapped in his fraud because the public wanted to believe that the automated chess player was real. Desire overtook judgment in thousands of people, who were captivated by the idea of an intelligent machine.

More than two centuries later, we're still fascinated by intelligent machines. In 1997 people all over the world watched (many via the Web) as IBM's Deep Blue computer trounced Garry Kasparov, the reigning international chess champion. But modern computers don't just play games; they manage our money, our medicine, and our missiles. We're expected to trust information technology with our wealth, our health, and even our lives. The many benefits of our partnership with machines are clear. But blind faith in modern technology can be foolish and, in many cases, dangerous. In this chapter we examine some of the dark corners of our computerized society: legal dilemmas, ethical issues, and reliability risks. All of these issues are tied to a larger question: How can we make computers more secure so that we can feel more secure in our daily dealings with them?

Online Outlaws: Computer Crime

> Computers are **power**, and **direct contact** with power can bring out the **best** or **worst** in a person.
> —Former computer criminal turned corporate computer programmer

Like other professions, law enforcement is being transformed by information technology. The FBI's National Crime Information Center provides police with almost instant information on crimes and criminals nationwide. Investigators use PC databases to store and cross-reference clues in complex cases. Using pattern recognition technology, automated fingerprint identification systems locate matches in minutes rather than months. Computers routinely scan the New York and London stock exchanges for connections that might indicate insider trading or fraud. Texas police use an intranet to cross-reference databases of photographs, fingerprints, and other crime-fighting information. *Computer forensics* experts use special software to scan criminal suspects' hard disks for digital "fingerprints"—traces of deleted files containing evidence of illegal activities. All of these tools help law enforcement officials ferret out criminals and stop criminal activities.

Like guns, people use computers to break laws as well as uphold them. Computers are powerful tools in the hands of criminals, and computer crime is a rapidly growing problem.

A police officer uses his mobile computer to check records in a central crime database.

The Computer Crime Dossier

> Some will rob you with a **six gun**, and some with a **fountain pen**.
> —Woody Guthrie, in "Pretty Boy Floyd"

Today the computer has replaced both the gun and the pen as the weapon of choice for many criminals. **Computer crime** is often defined as any crime accomplished through knowledge or use of computer technology.

Nobody knows the true extent of computer crime. Many computer crimes go undetected. Those that are detected often go unreported because businesses fear that they can lose more from negative publicity than from the actual crimes.

According to a 2001 survey of more than 500 companies and government agencies by the FBI and the Computer Security Institute, 85 percent detected computer security breaches in the preceding 12 months. These breaches included system penetration by outsiders, theft of information, changing data, financial fraud, vandalism, stealing of passwords, and preventing legitimate users from gaining access to systems. According to the survey, financial losses due to security breaches topped $377 million. By conservative estimates, businesses and government institutions lose billions of dollars every year to computer criminals.

The majority of computer crimes are committed by company insiders who aren't reported to authorities, even when they are caught in the act. To avoid embarrassment, many companies cover up computer crimes committed by their own employees and managers. These crimes are typically committed by clerks, cashiers, programmers, computer operators, and managers who have no extraordinary technical ingenuity. The typical computer criminal is a trusted employee with no criminal record who is tempted by an opportunity such as the discovery of a loophole in system security. Greed, financial worries, and personal problems motivate this person to give in to temptation.

Of course, not all computer criminals fit this profile. Some are former employees seeking revenge on their former bosses. Some are high-tech pranksters looking for a challenge. A few are corporate or international spies seeking classified information. Organized crime syndicates are turning to computer technology to practice their trades. Sometimes entire companies are found guilty of computer fraud. For example, Equity Funding, Inc., used computers to generate thousands of false insurance policies that later were sold for over $27 million.

The 2001 survey suggests that the explosive growth of Internet commerce is changing the demographics of computer crime: 70 percent reported that Internet connections were frequent points of attack; only 31 percent said that internal systems were frequent points of attack.

Comparing this survey with previous annual surveys shows unmistakable trends: Internet security breaches are on the rise, internal security breaches are on the rise, and computer crime in general is on the rise. All of these increases are happening in spite of increased security and law-enforcement efforts.

Theft by Computer

Theft is the most common form of computer crime. Computers are used to steal money, goods, information, and computer resources. Here are a few examples:

> Every system has **vulnerabilities**.
> Every system can be **compromised**.
> —Peter G. Neumann, in *Computer Related Risks*

▌ A part-time college student used his touch-tone phone and personal computer to fool Pacific Telephone's computer into ordering phone equipment to be delivered to him. He started a business, hired several employees, and pilfered about a million dollars' worth of equipment before he was turned in by a disgruntled employee. (After serving two months in jail, he became a computer security consultant.)

▌ A former automated teller machine repairman illegally obtained $86,000 out of ATMs by spying on customers while they typed in passwords and then creating bogus cards to use with the passwords.

▌ In 1988 several million dollars of assets at a major U.S. bank were illegally transferred to a private Swiss bank account. The transfer was noticed because a computer glitch on that particular day forced employees to check transactions manually; the automated procedure normally used wouldn't have noticed the suspicious transaction.

▌ In 1999 the *London Times* revealed that several London banks had paid millions of pounds in ransoms to hackers who threatened to cripple their computer systems if they didn't pay. The banks paid rather than admitting publicly that their systems weren't secure against attack.

▌ In 1999 two brothers in China were sentenced to death for using computers to redirect about $30,000 to bank accounts they controlled.

▌ In 1999 an employee of PairGain posted an anonymous announcement on a Yahoo stock board; the message claimed that PairGain was about to be purchased by another company for nearly twice its current market value. Investors drove the stock price up about 40 percent before they learned they had been bilked out of thousands of dollars by a bogus message. An FBI task force retraced the perpetrator's electronic footprints and arrested him for stock manipulation a week later. This kind of pump-and-dump stock manipulation has been committed dozens of times since the PairGain crime.

▌ In 2000 intruders broke into Creditcards.com, stole 55,000 credit card numbers, and held them for ransom. When their extortion attempt failed, they posted the numbers on the Web. The company has since created a more secure Web site.

▌ In 2001 two young Russian men were arrested for breaking into several U.S. company networks, stealing sensitive information, and demanding ransom for it. The FBI captured the pair by using a fake computer security company as bait. When they demanded payment from the bogus company, FBI agents agreed. The two men were arrested when they landed in the United States to collect their bounty.

▌ In May of 2001 Operation Cyber Loss, the FBI's crackdown on Internet fraud, netted 88 people in 10 days. According to the FBI, 56,000 people were defrauded of more than $117 million during the scams.

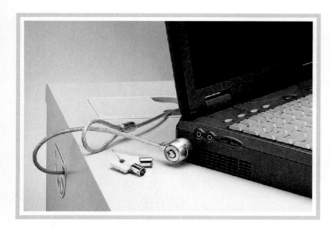

A portable computer is easy prey for a thief unless it's locked to something solid and stationary.

Some types of computer crime are so common that they've been given names. A common student scam uses a process called **spoofing** to steal passwords. The typical spoofer launches a program that mimics the mainframe computer's login screen on an unattended terminal in a public lab. When an unsuspecting student types an ID and password, the program responds with an error message and remembers the secret codes.

Sometimes thieves use computers and other tools to steal whole *identities*. By collecting personal information—credit-card numbers, driver's license numbers, Social Security numbers, and a few other tidbits of data—a thief can effectively pose as someone else, even committing crimes in that person's name. **Identity theft** doesn't require a computer; many identity thieves get sensitive information by dumpster diving—rummaging through company and personal trash. But computers generally play a role in the process. Identity theft often involves **social engineering**—slang for the use of deception to get individuals to reveal sensitive information.

The steady increase in electronic commerce has been accompanied by an increase in online fraud. Online auctions seem to be particularly fertile grounds for criminals. "The ePrivacy and Security Report" from market-research company eMarketer.com estimated that 87 percent of online fraud cases in 2000 were related to online auctions, with the average cost per victim being around $600.

One common type of computer theft today is the actual theft of computers. Laptop and handheld computers make particularly easy prey for crooks—especially in airports and other high-traffic, high-stress locations.

All of these crimes are expensive—for businesses, law enforcement agencies, and taxpayers and consumers who ultimately must pay the bills. But as crimes go, the types of theft described so far are relatively uncommon. The same can't be said of the most widely practiced type of computer-related theft: software piracy.

Software Piracy and Intellectual Property Laws

> Information wants to be free. Information also wants to be expensive.
> **Information wants to be free** because it has become so cheap to distribute, copy, and recombine—**too cheap to meter**.
> **It wants to be expensive** because it can be **immeasurably valuable** to the recipient.
> **That tension will not go away**.
>
> —Stewart Brand, in *The Media Lab*

Software piracy—the illegal duplication of copyrighted software—is rampant. Millions of computer users have made copies of programs they don't legally own. Now that many software companies have given in to user demands and removed physical copy protection from their products, copying software is as easy as duplicating a cassette tape or photocopying a book. Unfortunately, many people aren't aware that copying software, recorded music, and books can violate federal laws protecting intellectual property.

The Piracy Problem

The software industry, with a world market of more than $50 billion a year, loses billions of dollars every year to software pirates. The Business Software Alliance (BSA) estimates that more than one-third of all software in use is illegally copied, costing the software industry tens of thousands of jobs. Piracy can be particularly hard on small software companies. Developing software is just as difficult for them as it is for big companies like Microsoft and Oracle, but they often lack the financial and legal resources to cover their losses to piracy.

Software industry organizations, including the BSA and SPA Anti-Piracy (a division of the Software & Information Industry Association), work with law enforcement agencies to crack down on piracy. At the same time they sponsor educational programs to make computer users aware that piracy is theft, because laws can't work without citizen understanding and support.

Software piracy is a worldwide problem, with piracy rates highest in developing nations. In China approximately 95 percent of all new software installations are pirated; in Vietnam the piracy rate is 97 percent. A few Third World nations refuse to abide by international copyright laws. They argue that the laws protect rich countries at the expense of underdeveloped nations. In 1998, the Argentine Supreme Court ruled that the country's copyright laws don't apply to computer software.

Intellectual Property and the Law

Legally, the definition of intellectual property includes the results of intellectual activities in the arts, science, and industry. Copyright laws have traditionally protected forms of literary expression; patent law has protected mechanical inventions, and contract law has covered trade secrets. Software doesn't fit neatly into any of these categories under the law. Copyright laws protect most commercial software programs, but a few companies have successfully used patent laws to protect software products.

The purpose of intellectual property laws is to ensure that mental labor is justly rewarded and to encourage innovation. Programmers, inventors, scientists, writers, editors, filmmakers, and musicians depend on ideas and the expression of those ideas for their incomes. Ideas are information, and information is easy to copy. Intellectual property laws are designed to protect these professionals and encourage them to continue their creative efforts so society can benefit from their future work.

In this 1999 scene, Moscow police attempted to make a dent in the illegal software market by destroying mountains of pirated software.

Most of the time, these laws help to achieve their goals. A novelist can devote two or three years of her life to writing a masterpiece, confident that she won't find bootleg copies for sale on street corners when she finishes it. A movie studio can invest millions of dollars in a film, knowing that the investment will be returned, a little at a time, through ticket sales and video rentals. An inventor can work long hours to create a better mousetrap and know that MegaMousetrap City won't steal her idea.

But sometimes intellectual property laws are applied in such a way that they may stifle the innovation and creativity they're designed to protect. In 1999 Amazon.com was awarded a controversial patent for "one-click shopping." Similarly, SightSound patented all paid downloads of "desired digital video or digital audio signals," RealNetworks patented streaming audio and video, and British Telecom claims to hold a 1976 patent that covers every Web hyperlink! Most experts agree that these ideas are too simple and broad to be owned by one company. And in many cases, the patent owner isn't the inventor of the concept—Douglas Engelbart demonstrated hyperlinking as early as 1967 at Stanford Research Institute. Such broad patents generally end up in court, where legal experts and technology experts debate the merits and scope of the ideas and the laws designed to protect them. Meanwhile, legislators attempt to update the laws.

Most existing copyright and patent laws, which evolved during the age of print and mechanical inventions, are outdated, contradictory, and inadequate for today's information technology. Many laws, including the Computer Fraud and Abuse Act of 1984, clearly treat software piracy as a crime. The NET (No Electronic Theft) Act of 1997 closed a narrow loophole in the law that allowed people to give away software on the Internet.

The Digital Millennium Copyright Act (DMCA) of 1998 represents the most comprehensive reform of U.S. copyright law in a generation. The DCMA includes several controversial provisions that need to be clarified by the courts. According to the law, it is illegal to write a program that circumvents copy protection schemes, whether or not that program is used to copy DVDs, electronic books, or other protected material illegally. The DMCA also makes it a crime to share information about how to crack copy protection. Critics argue that the law suppresses freedom of speech, academic freedom, and the principle of *fair use*—the time-honored right to make copies of copyrighted material for personal and academic use and for other noncompetitive purposes.

In matters of software, the legal system is sailing in uncharted waters. Whether dealing with issues of piracy or monopoly, lawmakers and judges must struggle with difficult questions about innovation, property, freedom, and progress. The questions are likely to be with us for quite a while.

Software Sabotage: Viruses and Other Invaders

The American government can stop me from going to the U.S., but they **can't stop my virus**.

—Virus creator

Another type of computer crime is sabotage of hardware or software. The word **sabotage** comes from the early days of the Industrial Revolution, when rebellious workers shut down new machines by kicking wooden shoes, called sabots, into the gears. Modern computer saboteurs commonly use software rather than footwear to do destructive deeds. The names given to the saboteurs' destructive programs—viruses, worms, and Trojan horses—sound more like biology than technology, and many of the programs even mimic the behavior of living organisms.

Trojan Horses

A **Trojan horse** is a program that performs a useful task while at the same time carrying out some secret destructive act. As in the ancient story of the wooden horse that carried Greek soldiers through the gates of Troy, Trojan horse software hides an enemy in an attractive package. Trojan horse programs are often posted on shareware Web sites with names that make them sound like games or utilities. When an unsuspecting bargain hunter downloads and runs such a program, it might erase files, change data, or cause some other kind of damage. Some network saboteurs use Trojan horses to pass secret data to other unauthorized users.

One type of Trojan horse, a **logic bomb**, is programmed to attack in response to a particular logical event or sequence of events. For example, a programmer might plant a logic bomb that is designed to destroy data files if the programmer is ever listed as terminated in the company's personnel file. A logic bomb might be triggered when a certain user logs in, a special code is entered in a database field, or a particular sequence of actions is performed by the user. If the logic bomb is triggered by a time-related event, it is called a *time bomb*. A widely publicized virus included a logic bomb that was programmed to destroy PC data files on Michelangelo's birthday.

Trojan horses can cause serious problems in computer systems of all sizes. To make matters worse, many Trojan horses carry software viruses.

Viruses

A biological virus is unable to reproduce by itself, but it can invade the cells of another organism and use the reproductive machinery of each host cell to make copies of itself; the new copies leave the host and seek out new hosts to repeat the process. A software **virus** works in the same way: It spreads from program to program, or from disk to disk, and uses each infected program or disk to make more copies of itself. Virus software is usually hidden in the operating system of a computer or in an application program. Some viruses do nothing but reproduce; others display messages on the computer's screen; still others destroy data or erase disks.

A virus is usually operating-system specific. Windows viruses invade only Windows disks, Macintosh viruses invade only Macintosh disks, and so on. There are exceptions: *Macro viruses* attach themselves to documents that contain *macros*—embedded programs to automate tasks. Macro viruses can be spread across computer platforms if the documents are created and spread using cross-platform applications—most commonly the applications in Microsoft Office. Macro viruses can be spread through innocent-looking email attachments. Viruses spread through email are sometimes called *email viruses*.

One of the most widely publicized email viruses was 1999's Melissa virus. Melissa's method of operation is typical of email viruses: An unsuspecting computer user receives an "Important message" from a friend: "Here is that document you asked for . . . don't show it to anyone else ;-)." The attached Microsoft Word document contains a list of passwords for Internet pornography sites. It contains something else: a macro virus written in Microsoft Office's built-in Visual Basic scripting language. Once the document is opened, the macro virus goes to work, sending a copy of the email message and infected document to the first 50 names on the user's Outlook address book. Within minutes, 50 more potential Melissa victims receive messages apparently from someone they know—the user of the newly infected computer. Melissa spread like wildfire among Windows systems, infecting 100,000 systems in just a few days. Melissa wasn't designed to do damage to systems, but the flurry of messages brought down some email servers. A nationwide search located the probable author of the Melissa virus, a 30-year-old New Jersey resident with a fondness for a topless dancer named Melissa.

Shortly after Melissa faded from the headlines, a similar, but more destructive, virus named Chernobyl infected more than 600,000 computers worldwide. South Korea alone suffered 300,000 attacks; about 15 percent of their PCs were damaged by the virus, at a cost of $250 million. In May of 2000, a Melissa-like virus called Love Bug spread from a PC in the Philippines around the world through innocent-looking "I Love You" email message attachments. In a matter of hours, the Love Bug caused billions of dollars in lost productivity and damage to computer systems.

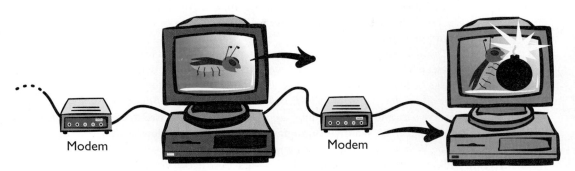

Origination
A programmer writes a tiny program—the virus—that has destructive power and can reproduce itself.

Transmission
Most often, the virus is attached to a normal program; unknown to the user, the virus spreads to other software.

Reproduction
The virus is passed by disk or network to other users who use other computers. The virus remains dormant as it is passed on.

Infection
Depending on how it is programmed, a virus may display an unexpected message, gobble up memory, destroy data files or cause serious system errors.

How a virus works.

Worms

Like viruses, **worms** (named for tapeworms) use computer hosts to reproduce themselves. But unlike viruses, worm programs travel *independently* over computer networks, seeking out uninfected workstations in which to reproduce. A worm can reproduce until the computer freezes from lack of free memory or disk space. A typical worm segment resides in memory rather than on disk, so the worm can be eliminated by shutting down all of the workstations on the network.

The first headline-making worm was created as an experiment by a Cornell graduate student in 1988. The worm was accidentally released onto the Internet, clogging 6,000 computers all over the United States, almost bringing them to a complete standstill and forcing operators to shut them all down so every worm segment could be purged from memory. The total cost, in terms of work time lost at research institutions, was staggering. The student was suspended from school and was the first person convicted of violating the Computer Fraud and Abuse Act.

In the summer of 2001, a worm called Code Red made worldwide headlines. Code Red didn't attack PCs; its target was Internet servers running Microsoft server software. The U.S. government and Microsoft issued warnings about the worm and made free software patches available to protect servers. Even so, many servers were crippled by the repeated attacks from the worm, including servers owned and operated by Microsoft.

Virus Wars

The popular press usually doesn't distinguish among Trojan horses, viruses, and worms; they're all called computer viruses. Whatever they're called, these rogue programs make life more complicated and expensive for people who depend on computers. Researchers have identified more than 18,000 virus strains, with 200 new ones appearing each month. At any given time, about 250 virus strains exist in the wild—in circulation.

Modern viruses can spread faster and do more damage than viruses of a few years ago for several reasons. The Internet, which speeds communication all over the planet, also speeds virus

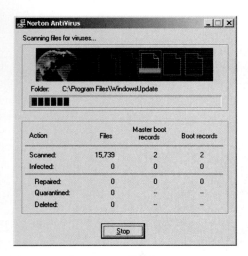

Antivirus software scans files for viruses; updates with new virus "signatures" are downloadable from the software company's Web site.

transmission. Web pages, macros, and other technologies give virus writers new places to hide their creations. And increased standardization on Microsoft applications and operating systems has made it easier for viruses to spread. Just as natural mixed forests are more resistant to disease than are single-species tree farms, mixed computing environments are less susceptible to crippling attacks than is an organization in which everyone uses the same hardware and software.

When computers are used in life-or-death situations, as they are in many medical and military applications, invading programs can even threaten human lives. The U.S. government and several states now have laws against introducing these programs into computer systems.

Antivirus programs (also called *vaccine* or *disinfectant programs*) are designed to search for viruses, notify users when they're found, and remove them from infected disks or files. Most antiviral programs continually monitor system activity, watching for and reporting suspicious virus-like actions. But no antivirus program can detect every virus, and these programs need to be frequently revised to combat new viruses as they appear. Most antivirus programs can automatically download new virus-fighting code from the Web as new virus strains appear. But it can take several days for companies to develop and distribute patches for new viruses—and destructive viruses can do a lot of damage in that time.

The virus wars continue to escalate as virus writers develop new ways to spread their works. After a rash of 1999 email viruses, most users learned not to open unidentified email attachments. But before the year was over, a worm called BubbleBoy (named for an episode of TV's *Seinfeld*) demonstrated that a system could be infected by email even if the mail wasn't opened. Some viruses have even been developed to infect HTML code in Web pages or HTML email messages. HTML viruses can't (so far) infect your computer if you're viewing an infected Web page on another computer; the infected HTML code must be downloaded onto your machine. Still, HTML viruses are reminders that the virus wars are far from over.

Hacking and Electronic Trespassing

The Hacker Ethic

Access to computers—and anything which might teach you something about the way the world works—should be **unlimited** and **total**. Always yield to the **Hands-on Imperative**.

1. All information should be **free**.
2. **Mistrust Authority—Promote Decentralization**.
3. Hackers should be judged by their **hacking**, not bogus criteria such as degrees, age, race, or position.
4. You can create **art and beauty** on a computer.
5. Computers can **change your life** for the better.

—Steven Levy, in *Hackers: Heroes of the Computer Revolution*

I don't drink, smoke, or take drugs. I don't steal, assault people, or vandalize property. **The only way** in which I am really **different** from most people is in my fascination with the ways and means of learning about **computers that don't belong to me**.

—Bill "The Cracker" Landreth, in *Out of the Inner Circle*

In the late 1970s, timesharing computers at Stanford and MIT attracted informal communities of computer fanatics who called themselves *hackers*. In those days a hacker was a person who enjoyed learning the details of computer systems and writing clever programs, referred to as hacks. Hackers were, for the most part, curious, enthusiastic, intelligent, idealistic, eccentric, and harmless. Many of those early hackers were, in fact, architects of the microcomputer revolution.

Over the years the idealism of the early hacker communities was at least partly overshadowed by cynicism, as big-money interests took over the young personal computer industry. At the same time the term hacking took on a new, more ominous connotation in the media. While many people still use the term to describe software wizardry, it more commonly refers to unauthorized access to computer systems. Old-time hackers insist that this electronic trespassing is really *cracking*, or criminal hacking, but the general public and popular media don't recognize the distinction between hackers and crackers. Today's stereotypical hacker, like his early counterparts, is a young, bright, technically savvy, white, middle-class male who, in addition to programming his own computer, may break into others.

Of course, not all young computer wizards break into systems, and not all electronic trespassers fit the media stereotype. Still, hackers aren't just a media myth; they're real, and there are lots of them. Electronic trespassers enter corporate and government computers using stolen passwords and security holes in operating system software. Sometimes they use modems to dial up the target computers directly; in other cases they "travel" to their destinations through the Internet and other networks.

Many hackers are merely motivated by curiosity and intellectual challenge; once they've cracked a system, they look around and move on without leaving any electronic footprints. Some hackers claim to be acting in the public good by pointing out security problems in commercial software products. Some malicious hackers use Trojan horses, logic bombs, and other tricks of the trade to wreak havoc on corporate and government systems. A growing number of computer trespassers are part of electronic crime rings intent on stealing credit-card numbers and other sensitive, valuable information. This kind of theft is difficult to detect and track because the original information is left unchanged when the copy is stolen.

Cliff Stoll discovered an international computer espionage ring because of a 75-cent accounting error.

According to the FBI, an Internet hack happens every 30 seconds. Hackers have defaced the Web sites of the White House, the U.S. Senate, the Department of the Interior, presidential candidates, countless online businesses, and even a hacker's conference. Sometimes Web sites are simply defaced with obscene or threatening messages; sometimes they're replaced with satirical substitutes; sometimes they're vandalized so they don't work properly. *Webjackers* hijack legitimate Web pages and redirect users to other sites—anywhere from pornographic sites to fraudulent businesses.

Denial of service (DoS) attacks bombard servers and Web sites with so much bogus traffic that they're effectively shut down, denying service to legitimate customers and clients. In a *distributed denial of service (DDoS) attack* the flood of messages comes from many compromised systems distributed across the Net. In a single week in February, 2000, Yahoo, E*TRADE, eBay, and Amazon Web sites were crippled by denial of service attacks, costing their owners millions of dollars in business. Two months later a 15-year-old Canadian boy nicknamed "Mafia Boy" was arrested after he bragged online about causing the breakdowns. His expensive pranks didn't require any special expertise; he reportedly downloaded all of the software he used from the Internet.

The most famous case of electronic trespassing was documented in Cliff Stoll's best-selling book, *The Cuckoo's Egg*. While working as a system administrator for a university computer lab in 1986, Stoll noticed a 75-cent accounting error. Rather than letting it go, Stoll investigated the error. He uncovered a system intruder who was searching government, corporate, and university computers across the Internet for sensitive military information. It took a year and some help from the FBI, but Stoll eventually located the hacker—a German computer science student and part of a ring of hackers working for the KGB. Ironically, Stoll captured the thief by using standard hacker tricks, including a Trojan horse program that contained information on a fake SDI Net (Strategic Defense Initiative Network).

This kind of online espionage is becoming commonplace as the Internet becomes a mainstream communication medium. A more recent front-page-story-turned-book involved the 1995 capture of Kevin Mitnick, the hacker who had stolen millions of dollars' worth of software and credit-card information on the Net. By repeatedly manufacturing new identities and cleverly concealing his location, Mitnick successfully evaded the FBI for years. But when he broke into the computer of computational physicist Tsutomu Shimomura, he inadvertently started an electronic cat-and-mouse game that ended with his capture and conviction. Shimomura was able to defeat Mitnick because of his expertise in computer security—the protection of computer systems and, indirectly, the people who depend on them.

Computer Security: Reducing Risks

In the **old world**, if I wanted to attack something physical, there was **one way to get there**. You could put guards and guns around it, **you could protect it**. But a database—or a control system—usually has multiple pathways, **unpredictable routes to it**, and seems intrinsically **impossible to protect**. That's why most efforts at computer security have been **defeated**.

—Andrew Marshall, military analyst

With computer crime on the rise, computer security has become an important concern for system administrators and computer users alike. **Computer security** refers to protecting computer systems and the information they contain against unwanted access, damage, modification, or destruction. According to a 1991 report of the Congressional Research Service, computers have two inherent characteristics that leave them open to attack or operating error:

1. A computer does exactly what it is programmed to do, including reveal sensitive information. Any system that can be programmed can be reprogrammed by anyone with sufficient knowledge.
2. Any computer can do only what it is programmed to do. "[I]t cannot protect itself from either malfunctions or deliberate attacks unless such events have been specifically anticipated, thought through, and countered with appropriate programming."

Computer owners and administrators use a variety of security techniques to protect their systems ranging from everyday low-tech locks to high-tech software scrambling.

Physical Access Restrictions

One way to reduce the risk of security breaches is to make sure that only authorized personnel have access to computer equipment. Organizations use a number of tools and techniques to identify authorized personnel. Computers can perform some security checks; human security guards perform others. Depending on the security system, you might be granted access to a computer based on

▶ *Something you have*—a key, an ID card with a photo, or a *smart card* containing digitally encoded identification in a built-in memory chip
▶ *Something you know*—a password, an ID number, a lock combination, or a piece of personal history, such as your mother's maiden name
▶ *Something you do*—your signature or your typing speed and error patterns
▶ *Something about you*—a voice print, fingerprint, retinal scan, facial feature scan, or other measurement of individual body characteristics; these measurements are collectively called **biometrics**.

Because most of these security controls can be compromised—keys can be stolen, signatures can be forged, and so on—many systems use a combination of controls. For example, an employee might be required to show a badge, unlock a door with a key, and type a password to use a secured computer.

In the days when corporate computers were isolated in basements, physical restrictions were sufficient for keeping out intruders. But in the modern office, computers and data are almost everywhere, and networks connect computers to the outside world. In a distributed, networked environment, security is much more problematic. It's not enough to restrict physical access to mainframes when personal computers and network connections aren't restricted. Additional security techniques—most notably passwords—are needed to restrict access to remote computers.

Passwords

Passwords are the most common tool used to restrict access to computer systems. Passwords are effective, however, only if they're chosen carefully. Most computer users choose passwords that are easy to guess: names of partners, children, or pets; words related to jobs or hobbies; and consecutive characters on keyboards. One survey found that the

Biometric devices provide high levels of computer and network security because they monitor human body characteristics that can't be stolen. The U-Match Bio-Link Mouse (top) checks the thumbprint of the user against a database of prints approved for access. IriScan's PC Iris (bottom) can compare the patterns in the iris of the user against a database of employees or other legitimate network users.

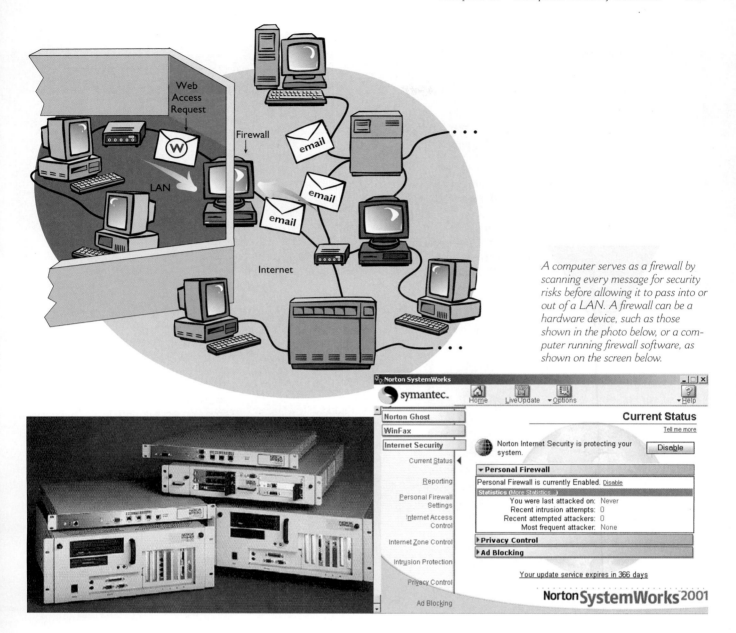

A computer serves as a firewall by scanning every message for security risks before allowing it to pass into or out of a LAN. A firewall can be a hardware device, such as those shown in the photo below, or a computer running firewall software, as shown on the screen below.

two favorite passwords in Britain were "Fred" and "God"; in America they were "love" and "sex." Hackers know and exploit these clichés; cautious users avoid them. Many security systems refuse to enable users to choose any real words or names as passwords so hackers can't use dictionary software to guess them systematically. Even the best passwords should be changed frequently.

Access-control software doesn't need to treat all users identically. Many systems use passwords to restrict users so they can open only files related to their work. In many cases, users are given read-only access to files that they can see but not change.

To prevent unauthorized use of stolen passwords by outsiders, many companies use callback systems. When a user logs in and types a password, the system hangs up, looks up the user's phone number, and calls back before providing access.

Firewalls, Encryption, and Audits

Many data thieves do their work without breaking into computer systems; instead, they intercept messages as they travel between computers on networks. Passwords are of little use for hiding email messages when they're traveling through phone lines or Internet gateways. Still, Internet communication is far too important to sacrifice in the name of security. Many organizations use **firewalls** to keep their internal networks secure while enabling communication with the rest of

12.1
Cryptography

If you want be sure that an email message can be read only by the intended recipient, you must either use a secure communication channel or secure the message.

Mail within many organizations is sent over secure communication channels—channels that can't be accessed by outsiders. But you can't secure the channels used by the Internet and other worldwide mail networks; there's no way to shield messages sent through public telephone lines and airwaves. In the words of Mark Rotenberg, director of the Electronic Privacy Information Center, "Email is more like a postcard than a sealed letter."

If you can't secure the communication channel, the alternative is to secure the message. You secure a message by using a crypto-system to encrypt it—scramble it so it can be decrypted (unscrambled) only by the intended recipient.

Almost all cryptosystems depend on a key—a password-like number or phrase that can be used to encrypt or decrypt a message. Eavesdroppers who don't know the key have to try to decrypt it by brute force—by trying all possible keys until the right one is guessed.

Some cryptosystems afford only modest security: A message can be broken after only a day or week of brute force cryptanalysis on a supercomputer. More effective systems would take a supercomputer billions of years to break the message.

The traditional kind of cryptosystem used on computer networks is called a symmetric secret key system. With this approach the sender and recipient use

Secret Key System

the Internet. The technical details of firewalls vary considerably, but they're all designed to serve the same function: to guard against unauthorized access to an internal network. In effect, a firewall is a gateway with a lock—the locked gate opens only for information packets that pass one or more security inspections. Firewalls aren't just for large corporations anymore. Without firewall hardware or software installed, a home computer with an always-on DSL or cable modem connection can be easy prey for Internet snoopers.

The sender creates, encrypts, and sends the message.

The encrypted message is transmitted through the network.

The message is received and decrypted.

The encryption process.

the same key, and they have to keep the shared key secret from everyone else.

The biggest problem with symmetric secret key systems is key management. If you want to communicate with several people and ensure that each person can't read messages intended for the others, then you'll need a different secret key for each person. When you want to communicate with someone new, you have the problem of letting them know what the key is. If you send it over the ordinary communication channel, it can be intercepted.

In the 1970s, cryptographers developed public key cryptography to get around the key management problems. The most popular kind of public key cryptosystem, RSA, is being incorporated into most new network-enabled software. Phillip Zimmerman's popular shareware utility called PGP (for Pretty Good Privacy) uses RSA technology.

Each person using a public key cryptosystem has two keys: a private key known only to the user and a public key that is freely available to anyone who wants it. Thus a public key system is asymmetric: A different key is used to encrypt than to decrypt. Public keys can be published in phone directories, Web pages, and advertisements; some users include them in their email signatures.

If you want to send a secure message over the Internet to your friend Sue in St. Louis, you use her public key to encrypt the message. Sue's public key can't decrypt the message; only her private key can do that. The private key is specifically designed to decrypt messages that were encrypted with the corresponding public key.

Since public/private key pairs can be generated by individual users, the key distribution problem is solved. The only keys being sent over an insecure network are publicly available keys.

You can use the same technology in reverse (encrypt with the private key, decrypt with the public key) for message authentication: When you decrypt a message, you can be sure that it was sent from a particular person on the network. In the future, legal and commercial documents will routinely have digital signatures that will be as valid as handwritten ones.

Public Key System

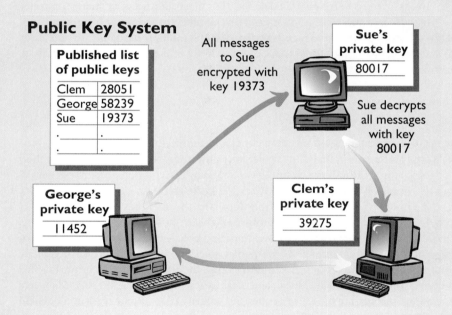

Published list of public keys	
Clem	28051
George	58239
Sue	19373
.	.
.	.

All messages to Sue encrypted with key 19373

Sue's private key
80017

Sue decrypts all messages with key 80017

George's private key
11452

Clem's private key
39275

Of course, the firewall's digital drawbridge has to let some messages pass through; otherwise there could be no communication with the rest of the Internet. How can those messages be secured in transit? To protect transmitted information, many organizations and individuals use **encryption** software to scramble their transmissions. When a user encrypts a message by applying a secret numerical code, called an *encryption key*, the message can be transmitted or stored as an indecipherable garble of characters. The message can be read only after it's been reconstructed with a matching key.

For the most sensitive information, passwords, firewalls, and encryption aren't enough. A diligent spy can "listen to" the electromagnetic signals that emanate from the computer hardware and, in some cases, read sensitive information. To prevent spies from using these spurious broadcasts, the Pentagon has spent hundreds of millions of dollars on a program called Tempest to develop specially shielded machines.

Audit-control software is used to monitor and record computer transactions as they happen so auditors can trace and identify suspicious computer activity after the fact. Effective audit-control software forces every user, legitimate or otherwise, to leave a trail of electronic footprints. Of course, this kind of software is of little value unless someone in the organization monitors and interprets the output.

An uninterruptible power supply (UPS) protects against both power surges and momentary power failures.

Backups and Other Precautions

Even the tightest security system can't guarantee absolute protection of data. A power surge or a power failure can wipe out even the most carefully guarded data in an instant. An **uninterruptible power supply (UPS)** can protect computers from data loss during power failures; inexpensive ones can protect even home computers from short power dropouts. *Surge protectors* don't help during power failures, but they can shield electronic equipment from dangerous power spikes.

Of course, disasters come in many forms. Sabotage, human errors, machine failures, fire, flood, lightning, and earthquakes can damage or destroy computer data along with hardware. Any complete security system should include a plan for recovering from disasters. For mainframes and PCs alike, the best and most widely used data recovery insurance is a system of making regular **backups**. For many systems data and software are backed up automatically onto disks or tapes, usually at the end of each workday. Most data processing shops keep several *generations* of backups so they can, if necessary, go back several days, weeks, or years to reconstruct data files. For maximum security, many computer users keep copies of sensitive data in several different locations. A storage device called a *RAID (redundant array of independent disk)* enables multiple hard disks to operate as a unit. RAID systems can, among other things, automatically *mirror* data on multiple disks, effectively creating instant backups.

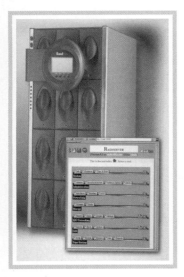

A RAID such as this NAS RAID server stores redundant copies of data so that the data can be saved even if a disk crashes.

Human Security Controls: Law, Management, and Ethics

Security experts are constantly developing new technologies and techniques for protecting computer systems from computer criminals. But at the same time, criminals continue to refine their craft. In the ongoing competition between the law and the lawless, computer security generally lags behind. In the words of Tom Forester and Perry Morrison in *Computer Ethics,* "Computer security experts are forever trying to shut the stable door after the horse has bolted."

Ultimately, computer security is a human problem that can't be solved by technology alone. Security is a management issue, and a manager's actions and policies are critical to the success of a security program. An alarming number of companies are lax about computer security. Many managers don't understand the problems and don't think they are at risk. It's important for managers to understand the practical, ethical, and legal issues surrounding security. Managers must make their employees aware of security issues and security risks. If managers don't defend against security threats, information can't be secure.

Security, Privacy, Freedom, and Ethics: The Delicate Balance

> In this age of advanced technology, **thick walls** and **locked doors** cannot guard our **privacy** or safeguard our **personal freedom**.
> —Lyndon B. Johnson, 36th president of the United States, February 23, 1974

It's hard to overstate the importance of computer security in our networked world. Destructive viruses, illegal interlopers, crooked coworkers, software pirates, and cyber-vandals can erode trust, threaten jobs, and make life difficult for everyone. But sometimes computer security measures can create problems of their own. Complex access procedures, virus-protection programs, intellectual property laws, and other security measures can, if carried too far, interfere with people getting their work done. In the extreme, security can threaten individual human rights.

When Security Threatens Privacy

As we've seen in other chapters, computers threaten our personal privacy on several fronts. Corporate and government databases accumulate and share massive amounts of information about us against our will and without our knowledge. Internet-monitoring programs and software snoopers track our Web explorations and read our electronic mail. Corporate managers use monitoring software to measure worker productivity and observe their onscreen activities. Government security agencies secretly monitor telephone calls and data transmissions.

When security measures are used to prevent computer crime, they usually help protect privacy rights at the same time. When a hacker invades a computer system, legitimate users of the system might have their private communications monitored by the intruder. When an outsider breaks into the database of a bank, the privacy of every bank customer is at risk. The same applies to government computers, credit bureau computers, and any other computer containing data on private citizens. The security of these systems is important for protecting people's privacy.

But in some cases security and law enforcement can pose threats to personal privacy. Here are some examples:

▹ In 1990 Alana Shoar, email coordinator for Epson America, Inc., found stacks of printouts of employee email messages in her boss's office—messages that employees believed were private. Shortly after confronting her boss, she was fired for "gross misconduct and insubordination." She filed a class-action suit, claiming that Epson routinely monitored all email messages. Company officials denied the charges but took a firm stand on their right to any information stored on, sent to, or taken from their business computers. The courts ruled in Epson's favor. Since then, many other U.S. court decisions have reinforced a company's right to read employee email stored on company computers.

▹ In 1995 the U.S. government passed legislation requiring new digital phone systems to include additional switches that allow for electronic surveillance. This legislation protects the FBI's ability to wiretap at the expense of individual privacy. Detractors have pointed out that this digital "back door" could be abused by government agencies and could also be used by savvy criminals to perform illegal wiretaps. Government officials argue that wiretapping is a critical tool in the fight against organized crime.

▹ The digital manhunt that led to the arrest of the programmer charged with authoring the Melissa virus was made as a direct result of information provided by America Online Inc. A controversial Microsoft document identification technology—the Global Unique Identifier, or GUID—may also have played a role. While virtually everyone was happy when the virus's perpetrator was apprehended, many legal experts feared that the same techniques will be used for less lofty purposes.

▹ In 2000 the U.S. government found Microsoft guilty of gross abuses of its monopolistic position in the software industry. The government's case included hundreds of private email messages between Microsoft employees—messages that contradicted Microsoft's public testimony.

▹ A 2001 U.S. law required that future mobile phones include GPS technology for transmitting the phone's location to a 911 operator in the case of an emergency call. Privacy activists fear that government agents and criminals will use this E911 technology to track the movements of phone owners.

▹ In response to the terrorist attacks of September 11, 2001, the U.S. Congress quickly drafted and passed the USA Patriot Act, a sweeping act that redefined terrorism and the government's authority to combat it. The act defined "cyberterrorism" to include computer crimes that cause at least $5,000 in damage or destroy medical equipment. It increased the FBI's latitude to use wiretap technology to monitor suspects' Web browsing and email without a judge's order. Critics argued that this law could easily be used to restrict the freedom and threaten the privacy of law-abiding citizens.

One of the best examples of a new technology that can simultaneously improve security and threaten privacy is the **active badge** (sometimes called the *smart badge*). Researchers at the University of Cambridge and nearby Olivetti Research Center are developing and wearing microprocessor-controlled badges that broadcast infrared identification codes every 15 seconds. Each badge's code is picked up by a nearby network receiver and transmitted back to a badge-location database that is constantly being updated. Active badges are used for identifying, finding, and remembering:

▹ *Identifying.* When an authorized employee approaches a door, the door recognizes the person's badge code and opens. Whenever anyone logs into a computer system, the badge code identifies the person as an authorized or unauthorized user.

▶ *Finding.* An employee can check a computer screen to locate another employee and find out with whom that person is talking. With active badges there's no need for a paging system, and "while you were away" notes are less common.

▶ *Remembering.* At the end of the day, an active-badge wearer can get a minute-by-minute printout listing exactly where he's been and whom he's been with.

Is the active badge a primitive version of the communicator on TV's *Star Trek* or a surveillance tool for Big Brother? The technology has the potential to be either or both; it all depends on how people use it. Active badges, like other security devices and techniques, raise important legal and ethical questions about privacy—questions that we, as a society, must resolve sooner or later.

Justice on the Electronic Frontier

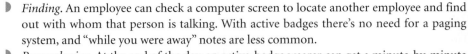

Through our scientific genius, we have **made this world a neighborhood**; now through our moral and spiritual development, we must **make of it a brotherhood**.

—The Rev. Martin Luther King, Jr.

An active badge transmits signals that enable a network to identify, locate, and track the badge wearer. This active badge from Versus Technology also includes a button that can be programmed to send a message to a pager, open a door, or perform another task.

Federal and state governments have responded to the growing computer crime problem by creating new laws against electronic trespassing and by escalating enforcement efforts. Hackers have become targets for nationwide anti-crime operations. Dozens of hackers have been arrested for unauthorized entry into computer systems and for the release of destructive viruses and worms.

Many have been convicted under federal or state laws. Others have had their computers confiscated with no formal charges filed.

Some of the victims of these sting operations claim that they broke no laws. In one case a student was arrested because he published an electronic magazine that carried a description of an emergency 911 system allegedly stolen by hackers. Charges were eventually dropped when it was revealed that the "stolen" document was, in fact, available to the public.

Cases like this raise questions about how civil rights apply in the "electronic frontier." How does the Bill of Rights apply to computer communications? Does freedom of the press apply to online magazines in the same way it applies to paper periodicals? Can an electronic bulletin board operator or Internet service provider be held responsible for information others post on a server? Can online pornography be served from a house located in a neighborhood with anti-porn laws?

Laws like the Telecommunications Act of 1996 attempt to deal with these questions by outlining exactly what kinds of communications are legal online. Unfortunately, these laws generally raise as many questions as they answer. Shortly after passage a major section of the Telecommunications Act, called the Communications Decency Act, was declared unconstitutional by the Supreme Court. The debates continue inside and outside of the courts.

The Digital Millennium Copyright Act of 1998 (discussed earlier in this chapter) hasn't (so far) been found unconstitutional, but it has resulted in several lawsuits that raise serious human rights questions. In the summer of 2001, a Russian programmer and graduate student named Dmitry Sklyarov was arrested by the FBI after he spoke at a computer security conference in Las Vegas. His alleged crime was writing—not using—a program that cracks Adobe's copy protection scheme for e-books. After a Web-wide demonstration against the arrest and Adobe, the company publicly came out in favor of freeing Sklyarov.

The same law was used to silence Professor Edward Felton in 2001. The Princeton University computer scientist was threatened with a lawsuit from the Recording Industry Association of America if he presented a paper analyzing the system that encodes digital music; he withdrew the paper. Several months later Felton published the paper and the RIAA recanted its threat—but not its right to threaten similar suits in the future.

The DMCA was even used to file a suit against *2600* magazine because of a single Web site link. A Norwegian 15-year-old had written code allowing DVD movies to be played on Linux

Rules of Thumb Rules of Thumb Rules of Thumb **Rules of Thumb**

Safe Computing

Even if you're not building a software system for the DOJ or the FBI, computer security is important. Viruses, disk crashes, system bombs, and miscellaneous disasters can destroy your work, your peace of mind, and possibly your system. Fortunately, you can protect your computer, your software, and your data from most hazards.

▶ *Share with care.* A computer virus is a contagious disease that spreads when it comes in contact with a compatible file or disk. Viruses spread rapidly in environments where disks and

files are passed around freely, as they are in many student computer labs. To protect your data, keep your disks to yourself, and don't borrow disks from others. When you do share a 3.5-inch disk, physically

Write-protect opening

write-protect it (by moving the plastic slider to uncover the square hole) so a virus can't attach to it.

▶ *Beware of email bearing gifts.* Many viruses hide in attachments to email messages that say something like "Here's the document you asked for. Please don't show anyone else." Don't open unsolicited email attachments; just throw them away.

▶ *Handle shareware and freeware with care.* Other viruses enter systems in Trojan horse shareware and freeware programs. Treat public domain programs and shareware with care; test them with a disinfectant program before you install them on your hard disk. Contrary to popular belief, you can't get a virus by reading an email message. But a virus can be embedded in an email attachment, so scan attached files before opening them.

▶ *Don't pirate software.* Even commercial programs can be infected with viruses. Shrink-wrapped, virgin software is much less likely to be infected than pirated copies. Besides, software piracy is theft, and the legal penalties can be severe.

▶ *Disinfect regularly.* Virus protection programs are available for all kinds of systems, often for free. Use up-to-date virus pro-

tection software regularly if you work in a high-risk environment like a public computer lab.

▶ *Treat your removable disks as if they contained something important.* Keep them away from liquids, dust, pets, and (especially) magnets. Don't put your disks close to phones, speakers, and other electronic devices that contain hidden magnets. (Magnets won't harm CD-ROMs or DVD-ROMs, but scratches can make them unusable.)

▶ *Take your passwords seriously.* Choose a password that's not easily guessable, not in any dictionary, and not easy for others to remember. Don't post it by your computer, and don't type it when you're being watched. Change your password occasionally—immediately if you have reason to suspect it has been discovered.

▶ *If it's sensitive, lock it up.* If your computer is accessible to others, protect your private files with passwords and/or encryption. Many operating systems and utilities include options for adding password protection and encrypting files. If others need to see the files, lock them so they can be read but not changed or deleted. If secrecy is critical, don't store the data on your hard disk at all. Store it on removable disks and lock it away in a safe place.

▶ *If it's important, back it up.* Regularly make backup copies of every important file on different disks than the original. Keep copies of critical disks in different locations so that you have backups in case disaster strikes.

▶ *If you're sending sensitive information through the Internet, consider encryption.* Use a utility or a program like freeware PGP (Pretty Good Privacy) to turn your message into code that's almost impossible to crack.

▶ *Don't open your system to interlopers.* If you've got an always-on Internet connection—T1, DSL, or cable modem—consider using firewall hardware or software to detect and lock out snoopers. Set your file sharing controls so access is limited to authorized visitors.

▶ *Prepare for the worst.* Even if you take every precaution, things can still go wrong. Make sure you aren't completely dependent on the computer for really important things.

computers—code that broke the DVD copy protection scheme. *2600*'s Web site included a link to another site containing the program. (*The New York Times* Web site contained a link to the same site, but was not sued by the recording industry.)

When Congress passed the Telecommunications Act of 1996 and the Digital Millennium Copyright Act of 1998, they were attempting to make U.S. law more responsive to the issues of the digital age. But each of these laws introduced new problems by threatening rights of citizens—problems that have to be solved by courts and by future lawmakers. These laws illustrate the difficulty lawmakers face when protecting rights in a world of rapid technological change.

Computer Ethics

Ethics is moral philosophy—philosophical thinking about right and wrong. Many people base their ethical beliefs on religious rules such as the Ten Commandments or the Buddhist Eightfold Path. Others use professional codes such as the doctor's Hippocratic Oath, which includes the often quoted "First do no harm." Still others use personal philosophies with principles such as "It's okay if a jury of observers would approve." But in today's changing world, deciding how to apply the rules isn't always easy. Sometimes the rules don't seem to apply directly, and sometimes they contradict each other. (How should you "Honor thy father" if you learn that he's using the home computer to embezzle money from his employer? Is it okay to allow a friend who's broke to borrow your Microsoft Office CD for a required class project?) These kinds of *moral dilemmas* are central questions in discussions of ethics. Information technology poses moral dilemmas related to everything from copying software to reporting a coworker's sexually explicit screen saver or racist email.

Computer ethics can't be reduced to a handful of rules—the gray areas are always going to require thought and judgment. But principles and guidelines can help to focus thinking and refine judgments when dealing with technology-related moral dilemmas. The ACM **Code of Ethics**, reprinted in the Appendix of this book, is the most widely known code of conduct specifically for computer professionals. The ACM Code is worth understanding and applying even if you don't plan to be a "computer professional." Who shouldn't "Contribute to Society and Human Well-Being" or "Honor Confidentiality"? But these principles take on new meaning in an age of email and databases.

Here are some other guidelines that might help you to decide how to "do the right thing" when faced with ethical dilemmas at school, at work, or at home:

▶ *Know the rules and the law.* Many laws, and many organizational rules, are reflections of moral principles. For example, almost everyone agrees that *plagiarism*—presenting somebody else's work as your own—is wrong. It's also a serious violation of rules in most schools. And if the work is copied without permission, plagiarism can become copyright infringement,

a serious legal offense . . . whether or not the work explicitly says that it is copyrighted.

▶ *Don't assume that it's okay if it's legal.* Our legal system doesn't define what's right and wrong. How can it, when we don't all agree on morality? The law is especially lax in areas related to information technology, because the technology changes too fast for lawmakers to keep up. It's ultimately up to each individual to act with conscience.

▶ *Think scenarios.* If you're debating between different actions, think about what might happen as a result of your actions. If you suspect your employer is falsifying spreadsheets to get around environmental regulations, what's likely to happen if you snoop around on his computer and blow the whistle on him? What's likely to happen if you don't? What are your other alternatives?

▶ *When in doubt, talk it out.* Discuss your concerns with people you trust—ideally, people with wisdom and experience dealing with similar situations. For example, if you're unsure about the line between getting computer help from a friend and cheating on homework, ask an instructor.

▶ *Make yourself proud.* How would you feel if you saw your actions on the front page of *The New York Times*, your company newsletter, or your family's hometown newspaper? If you'd be embarrassed or ashamed, you probably should choose another course of action.

▶ *Remember the golden rule: Do unto others as you would have them do unto you.* This universal principle is central to every major spiritual tradition, and it is amazingly versatile. One example: Before you download that bootleg MP3 file of that up-and-coming singer, think about how you'd feel about bootleggers if you were the singer.

▶ *Take the long view.* It's all too easy to be blinded by the rapid-fire rewards of the Internet and computer technology. Consider this guiding principle from a Native American tradition: In every deliberation, consider the impact of your decision on the next seven generations.

Security and Reliability

If the automobile had followed the same development cycle as the computer, a **Rolls Royce would today cost $100**, get a million miles per gallon, and **explode once a year**, killing everyone inside.

—Robert X. Cringely, *InfoWorld* columnist

So far our discussion of security has focused mainly on protecting computer systems from trespassing, sabotage, and other crimes. But security involves more than criminal activity. Some of the most important security issues have to do with creating systems that can withstand software errors and hardware glitches.

Bugs and Breakdowns

Computer systems, like all machines, are vulnerable to fires, floods, and other natural disasters, as well as breakdowns caused by failure of hardware components. But in modern computers, hardware problems are relatively rare when compared with software failures. By any measure bugs do more damage than viruses and computer burglars put together. Here are a few horror stories:

▶ On November 20, 1985, the Bank of New York's computer system started corrupting government securities transactions. By the end of the day, the bank was $32 billion overdrawn with the Federal Reserve. Before the system error was corrected, it cost the bank $5 million in interest.

▶ In September, 1999, the Mars Climate Orbiter burned up as it approached Mars because controllers had mixed up British and metric units. Three months later, the Mars Polar Lander went silent 12 minutes before touchdown. Investigators suspect software errors are at least partly responsible for this spectacular mission failure.

▶ Programs on NASA observation satellites in the 1970s and 1980s rejected ozone readings because the programmers had assumed when they wrote the programs that such low numbers could not be correct. It wasn't until British scientists reported ozone-level declines that NASA scientists reprocessed the data and confirmed the British findings that the earth's ozone layer was in danger.

▶ The Therac 25 radiation machine for tracking cancers was thoroughly tested and successfully used on thousands of patients before a software bug caused massive radiation overdoses, resulting in the partial paralysis of one patient and the death of another.

▶ On January 15, 1990, AT&T's 30-year-old signaling system software failed, bringing the long-distance carrier's network to its knees. Twenty million calls failed to go through during the next 18 hours before technicians found the problem: a single incorrect instruction hiding among a million lines of code.

▶ On February 25, 1991, 28 American soldiers were killed and 98 others wounded when an Iraqi Scud missile hit a barracks near Dhahran, Saudi Arabia. A tiny bug in a Patriot missile's software threw off its timing just enough to prevent it from intercepting the Scud. Programmers had already fixed the bug, and a new version of the software was being shipped to Dhahran when the attack occurred.

Every year brings new stories of breakdowns and bugs with catastrophic consequences. But it wasn't until 1999 that a computer bug—the Y2K (year 2000) bug, or millennium bug—became an international sensation. For decades programmers commonly built two-digit date fields into programs to save storage space, thinking "Why allow space for the first two digits when they never change?" But when 1999 ended, those digits did change, making many of those ancient programs unstable or unusable. Programmers knowledgeable in COBOL, FORTRAN, and other ancient computer languages repaired many of the programs. But others couldn't be repaired and had to be completely rewritten.

Businesses and governments spent more than 100 billion dollars trying to head off Y2K disasters. Many individuals bought generators and guns, stockpiled food and water, and prepared for a collapse of the computer-controlled utility grids that keep our economy running. When the fateful day arrived, the Y2K bug caused many problems, ranging from credit card refusals to malfunctioning spy satellites. But for most people, January 1, 2000, was business as usual. It's debatable whether disasters were averted by billions of dollars worth of preventive maintenance, or whether the Y2K scare stories were overblown. The truth is undoubtedly somewhere between these two extremes. In any event, Y2K raised public consciousness about their dependence on fickle, fragile technology.

Given the state of the art of programming today, three facts are clear:

1. It's impossible to eliminate all bugs. Today's programs are constructed of thousands of tiny pieces, any one of which can cause a failure if it's incorrectly coded.

These South Koreans, like people all around the world, stocked up on food and cooking gas cans to prepare for possible emergency shortages as a result of Y2K computer failures.

2. Even programs that appear to work can contain dangerous bugs. Some bugs are easy to detect and correct because they're obvious. The most dangerous bugs are difficult to detect and may go unnoticed by users for months or years.

3. The bigger the system, the bigger the problem. Large programs are far more complex and difficult to debug than small programs, and the trend today is clearly toward large programs. For example, Microsoft Windows 95 has 11 million lines of code, and was considered huge at the time; Windows 2000 has close to 29 million!

As we entrust complex computerized systems to do everything from financial transaction processing to air traffic control, the potential cost of computer failure goes up. In the last decade, researchers have identified hundreds of cases in which disruptions to computer system operations posed some risk to the public, and the number of incidents has doubled every two years.

Computers at War

> Massive networking makes the U.S. the
> ## world's most vulnerable target.
> —John McConnell, former NSA director

Nowhere are the issues surrounding security and reliability more critical than in military applications. To carry out its mission effectively, the military must be sure its systems are secure against enemy surveillance and attack. At the same time, many modern military applications push the limits of information technology farther than they've ever been before.

Smart Weapons

The United States has invested billions of dollars in the development of smart weapons—missiles that use computerized guidance systems to locate their targets. A command-guidance system enables a human operator to control the missile's path while watching a missile's-eye view of the target on a television screen. A missile with a homing guidance system can track a moving target without human help, using infrared heat-seeking devices or visual pattern recognition technology. Weapons that use "smart" guidance systems can be extremely accurate in pinpointing enemy targets under most circumstances. In theory smart weapons can greatly reduce the amount of civilian destruction in war if everything is working properly.

One problem with high-tech weapons is that they reduce the amount of time people have to make life-and-death decisions. As decision-making time goes down, the chance of errors goes up. In one tragic example, an American guided missile cruiser on a peacetime mission in the Persian Gulf used a computerized Aegis fleet defense system to shoot down an Iranian Airbus containing 290 civilians. The decision to fire was made by well-intentioned humans, but those humans had little time—and used ambiguous data—to make the decision.

Autonomous Systems

Even more controversial is the possibility of people being left out of the decision-making loop altogether. Yet the trend in military research is clearly toward weapons that demand almost instantaneous responses—the kind that only computers can make. An autonomous system is a complex system that can assume almost complete responsibility for a task without human input, verification, or decision making.

In today's weapon systems, such as those based on the North America Aerospace Defense Command (NORAD) Cheyenne Mountain Complex in Colorado Springs, Colorado, computers are critical components in the command and control process.

The most famous and controversial autonomous system is the Strategic Defense Initiative (SDI)—former President Ronald Reagan's proposed "Star Wars" system for shielding the United States from nuclear attack. The SDI system, as planned, would have used a network of laser-equipped satellites and ground-based stations to detect and destroy attacking missiles shortly after launch, before they had time to reach their targets. SDI weapons would have to be able to react almost instantaneously, without human intervention. If they sensed an attack, these system computers would have no time to wait for the president to declare war, and no time for human experts to analyze the perceived attack.

SDI generated intense public debates about false alarms, hardware feasibility, constitutional issues, and the ethics of autonomous weapons. But for many who understand the limitations of computers, the biggest issue is software reliability. SDI's software system would require tens of millions of lines of code. The system couldn't be completely tested in advance because there's no way to simulate accurately the unpredictable conditions of a global war. Yet to work effectively, the system would have to be absolutely reliable. In a tightly coupled worldwide network, a single bug could multiply and expand like a speed-of-light cancer. A small error could result in a major disaster. Many software engineers have pointed out that absolute reliability simply isn't possible now or in the foreseeable future.

In spite of years of political haggling, system failures, and cost overruns, an SDI-like system is still in the works, and systems reliability issues remain. Supporters of automated missile-defense systems argue that the technical difficulties can be overcome in time, and the U.S. government continues to invest billions in research toward that end. Whether or not a "smart shield" is ever completed, it has focused public attention on critical issues related to security and reliability.

Warfare in the Digital Domain

Even as the U.S. government spends billions of dollars on smart missiles and missile defense systems, many military experts suggest that future wars may not be fought in the air, on land, or at sea. The front lines of the future may, instead, be in cyberspace. By attacking through vast interconnected computer networks, an enemy could conceivably cripple telecommunications systems, power grids, banking and financial systems, hospitals and medical systems, water and gas supplies, oil pipelines, and emergency government services without firing a shot.

Several recent examples highlight our vulnerability:

▶ In 1994 Swedish hackers broke into telecommunications systems in central Florida and blocked several 911 systems by automatically dialing their numbers repeatedly. Anyone who called 911 with a legitimate emergency was greeted with a busy signal until the attack ended.

▶ In 1996 a juvenile hacker disabled a key phone computer servicing a Massachusetts airport, paralyzing the airport control tower for six hours.

▶ In 1998 Israeli police working with the FBI, the U.S. Air Force, and NASA arrested three Israeli teens who successfully hacked into Department of Defense computers in both countries.

▶ During the 2000 U.S. election, dozens of politically motivated Web attacks occurred for various causes, parties, and countries. The attacks included Web site vandalism, denial of service attacks, and system snooping.

None of these crimes resulted in serious damage or injury. But terrorists, spies, or criminals might use the same techniques to trigger major disasters.

Recognizing the growing threat of system sabotage, Attorney General Janet Reno created the *National Infrastructure Protection Center* in early 1998. The NIPC's state-of-the-art command center is housed at FBI headquarters. The center includes representatives of various intelligence agencies (the departments of defense, transportation, energy, and treasury), and representatives of several major corporations.

Corporate participation is critical because private companies own many of the infrastructure systems that are most vulnerable to attack. Unfortunately, many businesses are slow to recognize the potential threat to their systems. They embrace the efficiency that networks bring, but they don't adequately prepare for attack through those networks.

In the wake of the terrorist attacks of September, 2001, George W. Bush formed The President's Critical Infrastructure Board consisting of cabinet members and top presidential aids. The cyberterrorism panel was designed to protect utilities and critical public services that depend on information networks.

Network attacks are all but inevitable, and such attacks can have disastrous consequences for all of us. In a world where computers control everything from money to missiles, computer security and reliability are too important to ignore.

Is Security Possible?

Computer thieves. Hackers. Software pirates. Computer snoopers. Viruses. Worms. Trojan horses. Wiretaps. Hardware failures. Software bugs. When we live and work with computers, we're exposed to all kinds of risks that didn't exist in the precomputer era. These risks make computer security especially important and challenging.

Because computers do so many amazing things so well, it's easy to overlook the problems they bring with them and to believe that they're invincible. But like Kempelen's chess-playing machine, today's computers hide the potential for errors and deception under an impressive user interface. This doesn't mean we should avoid using computers, only that we should remain skeptical, cautious, and realistic as we use them. Security procedures can reduce but not eliminate risks. In today's fast-moving world absolute security simply isn't possible.

Now, Weapons of Mass Disruption?

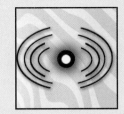

George F. Will

The terrorist attacks of September 11, 2001, used passenger airliners as crude, but powerful, weapons of mass destruction. In this article, first published in the October 29, 2001, issue of Newsweek, George Will tells us to expect a wave of terrorism that uses hardware, software, and computer expertise as weapons.

Americans have received their marching orders. They have been told to stiffen their sinews, summon up their blood—and go to the mall. And a movie. This summons to normality is akin to the rallying cry on the eve of Agincourt. However, energetic everydayness, even lightheartedness, is suddenly a serious duty. Just as there is at all times a moral obligation to be intelligent, there is today an obligation to be cheerful.

It would be irrational for Americans to begin acting as though terrorists are capable of making daily life hazardous for Americans generally. Acting that way would cripple the country's social and economic vigor, its defining assets. And an even more important reason for not allowing current problems to knock America off its normally jaunty stride is that the nation's equilibrium may soon be tested by even bigger problems.

When in 1820 the argument about the admission of Missouri to the Union as a slave state aggravated sectional animosities, Jefferson called the crisis a "fire bell in the night," awakening the nation to the possibility of worse to come. Last week's fire bell was anthrax, a small sample of what can be called the terrorism of substances, biological and chemical. There have been hearings, reports and books on these subjects, but complacent democracies are educated primarily by events, not exhortations—the British did not bring Churchill to power until Hitler approached the English Channel ports.

What might be the next alarm bell to ring? Of course, a truck bomb would intensify national nervousness by making things that are ubiquitous—trucks—seem ominous. And high explosives directed against, say, Hoover Dam would not only complicate life in the Southwest, it would underscore the unsettling message that even big things can be pulverized. However, it is time to think about attacks using things not solid and directed against things not as solid as skyscrapers or dams.

Consider cyberterrorism, assaults that can be undertaken from anywhere on the planet against anything dependent on or directed by flows of information. Call this soft terrorism. Although it can put lives in jeopardy, it can do its silent, stealthy work without tearing flesh or pulverizing structures. It can be a weapon of mass disruption rather than mass destruction, as was explained by the President's Commission on Critical Infrastructure Protection in its 1997 report on potential cyberattacks against the "system of systems" that is modern America.

"Life is good in America," the report says, "because things work. When we flip the switch, the lights come on. When we turn the tap, clean water flows." Now suppose a sudden and drastic shrinkage of life's "taken for granted" quotient. The report notes that terrorist attacks have usually been against single targets—individuals, crowds, buildings. But today's networked world of complexity and interconnectedness has vast new vulnerabilities with a radius larger than that of any imaginable bomb blast.

Terrorists using computers might be able to disrupt information and communications systems and, by doing so, attack banking and financial systems, energy (electricity, oil, gas) and the systems for the physical distribution of America's economic output.

Hijacked aircraft and powdered anthrax—such terrorist tools are crude and scarce compared with computers, which are everywhere and inexpensive. Wielded with sufficient cunning, they can spread the demoralizing helplessness that is terrorism's most important intended byproduct. Computers as weapons, even more than intercontinental ballistic missiles, render irrelevant the physical geography—the two broad oceans and two peaceful neighbors—that once was the basis of America's sense of safety.

A threat is a capability joined with a hostile intent. In early summer 1997 the U.S. military conducted a threat-assessment exercise, code-named Eligible Receiver, to test the vulnerabilities of "borderless cyber geography." The results confirmed that in a software-driven world, an enemy need not invade the territory, or the air over the territory, of a country in order to control or damage that country's resources.

The attack tools are on sale everywhere: computers, modems, software, telephones. The attacks can shut down services or deliver harmful instructions to systems. And a cyberattack may not be promptly discovered. The report says, "Computer intrusions do not announce their presence the way a bomb does."

Already "subnational" groups—terrorists, organized crime—are taking advantage of legal and widely available "strong encryption" software that makes their communications invulnerable to surveillance. How invulnerable? John Keegan, the British military analyst, quotes William Crowell, former deputy director of the largest U.S. intelligence agency, the National Security Agency: "If all the personal computers in the world were put to work on a single [strongly encrypted] message, it would still take an estimated 12 million times the age of the universe to break a single message."

Now suppose a state or group or state-supported group used similar cybermarvels to attack, say, U.S. banking and financial systems, or the production and distribution of electric power. Americans know how impotent, and infuriated, they feel when a thunderstorm knocks out electrical power for even a few hours. The freezer defrosts, the Palm handheld cannot be recharged, "SportsCenter" is missed. War is hell. And speaking of war:

. . . If we are supposed to stiffen our sinews and summon up our blood for a battle, it would be well to remember that the Battle of Agincourt, for which Shakespeare's Henry V exhorted the stiffening and summoning, was won in 1415 by the skill of English archers wielding longbows, the high technology of the day.

DISCUSSION QUESTIONS

1. The author seems to be arguing that computer technology will be the major weapon in the next wave of terrorism. Do you agree? Explain your answer.
2. What do you think we should do to prepare to defend ourselves against cyberterrorism?

Summary

Computers play an ever-increasing role in fighting crime. At the same time, law enforcement organizations are facing an increase in computer crime—crimes accomplished through special knowledge of computer technology. Most computer crimes go undetected, and those that are detected often go unreported. But by any estimate computer crime costs billions of dollars every year.

Some computer criminals use computers, modems, and other equipment to steal goods, money, information, software, and services. Others use Trojan horses, viruses, worms, logic bombs, and other software tricks to sabotage systems. According to the media, computer crimes are committed by young, bright computer wizards called hackers. Research suggests, however, that hackers are responsible for only a small fraction of computer crimes. The typical computer criminal is a trusted employee with personal or financial problems and knowledge of the computer system. The most common computer crime, software piracy, is committed by millions of people, often unknowingly. Piracy is a violation of intellectual property laws, which, in many cases, lag far behind the technology.

Because of rising computer crime and other risks, organizations have developed a number of computer security techniques to protect their systems and data. Some security devices, such as keys and badges, are designed to restrict physical access to computers. But these tools are becoming less effective in an age of personal computers and networks. Passwords, encryption, shielding, and audit-control software are all used to protect sensitive data in various organizations. When all else fails, backups of important data are used to reconstruct systems after damage occurs. The most effective security solutions depend on people at least as much as on technology.

Normally, security measures serve to protect our privacy and other individual rights. But occasionally, security procedures threaten those rights. The trade-offs between computer security and freedom raise important legal and ethical questions.

Computer systems aren't just threatened by people; they're also threatened by software bugs and hardware glitches. An important part of security is protecting systems—and the people affected by those systems—from the consequences of those bugs and glitches. Since our society uses computers for many applications that put lives at stake, reliability issues are especially important. In modern military applications, security and reliability are critical. As the speed, power, and complexity of weapons systems increase, many fear that humans are being squeezed out of the decision-making loop. The debate over high-tech weaponry is bringing many important security issues to the public's attention for the first time.

Chapter Review

▼ Key Terms

access-control software (p. 319)
active badge (p. 323)
antivirus program (p. 316)
audit-control software (p. 321)
autonomous system (p. 328)
backup (p. 322)
biometrics (p. 318)
code of ethics (p. 326)
computer crime (p. 310)
computer security (p. 318)
contract (p. 313)

copyright (p. 313)
denial of service (DoS) attacks (p. 317)
encryption (p. 321)
ethics (p. 326)
firewall (p. 319)
hacker (p. 316)
identity theft (p. 312)
intellectual property (p. 313)
logic bomb (p. 314)
password (p. 318)

patent (p. 313)
query language (p. 351)
sabotage (p. 314)
social engineering (p. 312)
smart weapon (p. 328)
software piracy (p. 312)
uninterruptible power supply (UPS) (p. 322)
virus (p. 314)
worm (p. 315)

▼ Interactive Quiz Questions

1. The *Computer Confluence* CD-ROM contains self-test quiz questions related to this chapter, including multiple choice, true or false, and matching questions.
2. The *Computer Confluence* Web site, **www.prenhall.com/beekman**, contains self-test exercises related to this chapter. Follow the instructions for taking a quiz. After you've completed your quiz, you can email the results to your instructor.

   The Web site also contains open-ended discussion questions called Internet Explorations. Discuss one or more of the Internet Exploration questions at the section for this chapter.

▼ Review Questions

1. Define or describe each of the key terms listed in the "Key Terms" section. Check your answers using the glossary.
2. Why is it hard to estimate the extent of computer crime?
3. Describe the typical computer criminal. How does he or she differ from the media stereotype?
4. What is the most common computer crime? Who commits it? What is being done to stop it?
5. What are intellectual property laws, and how do they apply to software?
6. Describe several different types of programs that can be used for software sabotage.
7. What are the two inherent characteristics of computers that make security so difficult?
8. Describe several different computer security techniques, and explain the purpose of each.
9. Every afternoon at closing time, the First Taxpayer's Bank copies all the day's accumulated transaction information from disk to tape. Why?
10. In what ways can computer security protect the privacy of individuals? In what ways can computer security threaten the privacy of individuals?
11. What are smart weapons? How do they differ from conventional weapons? What are the advantages and risks of smart weapons?

▼ Discussion Questions

1. Are computers morally neutral? Explain your answer.
2. Suppose Whizzo Software Company produces a program that looks, from the user's point of view, exactly like the immensely popular BozoWorks from Bozo, Inc. Whizzo insists that it didn't copy any of the code in Bozo-Works; it just tried to design a program that would appeal to BozoWorks users. Bozo cries foul and sues Whizzo for violation of intellectual property laws. Do you think the laws should favor Bozo's arguments or Whizzo's? Why?
3. What do you suppose motivates people to create computer viruses and other destructive software? What do you think motivates hackers to break into computer systems? Are the two types of behavior related?
4. Some people think all mail messages on the Internet should be encrypted. They argue that, if everything is encrypted, the encrypted message won't stand out, so everybody's right to privacy will be better protected. Others suggest that this would just improve the cover of criminals with something to hide from the government. What do you think, and why?
5. Would you like to work in a business where all employees were required to wear active badges? Explain your answer.
6. How do the issues raised in the debate over SDI apply to other large software systems? How do you feel about the different issues raised in the debate?

▼ Projects

1. Talk to employees at your campus computer labs and computer centers about security issues and techniques. What are the major security threats according to these employees? What security techniques are used to protect the equipment and data in each facility? Are these techniques adequate? Report on your findings.

2. Perform the same kind of interviews at local businesses. Do businesses view security differently than your campus personnel?

 # Sources and Resources

Books

A Gift of Fire: Social, Legal, and Ethical Issues in Computing, by Sara Baase (Upper Saddle River, NJ: Prentice-Hall, 1997). This book offers a thorough, easy-to-read overview of the human questions facing us as a result of the computer revolution: privacy, security, reliability, accountability, and the rest. A revised edition should be available by the time you read this.

Cyberethics: Morality and Law in Cyberspace, by Richard Spinello (Jones and Bartlett, 2000). This book surveys most of the big issues of computer ethics: intellectual property, privacy, security, free speech, and others. Case studies help make theoretical concepts concrete.

Readings in CyberEthics, edited by Richard A. Spinello and Herman T. Tavani (Jones and Bartlett, 2001). This collection of papers and articles includes sections on freedom of expression, property, privacy, and other critical subjects related to information technology.

Computer Network Security and CyberEthics, by Joseph Migga Kizza (McFarland & Co., 2001). This book clearly analyzes the causes, cost, and consequences of computer crime and cracking.

Web Security: A Step-by-Step Reference Guide, by Lincoln D. Stein (Reading, MA: Addison-Wesley, 1997). The explosive growth of the Web has created a variety of new security problems and risks. This book explains in clear language many of the technical problems related to Web security. It also offers practical advice for Web administrators and users who want to protect themselves from attacks and privacy violations.

Secrets and Lies: Digital Security in a Networked World, by Bruce Schneier (New York: Wiley, 2000). Mathematician and computer security expert Schneier tells you in clear, lively prose how to think like a computer thief so you can protect yourself and your organization from that thief.

The Hundredth Window: Protecting Your Privacy and Security in the Age of the Internet, by Charles Jennings and Lori Fena (Free Press, 2000). The Internet is only as secure as its weakest link. This practical book can help you to understand where the weakest links are and how to protect your privacy online.

Virtual Private Networks for Dummies, by Mark Merkow (Foster City, CA: IDG Books, 1999). In spite of its title, this book provides a great deal of technical information on setting up secure Internet connections and communications. Coverage includes cryptography, privacy, reliability, and e-commerce.

Internet Cryptography, by Richard E. Smith (Reading, MA: Addison-Wesley, 1997). Cryptography is the most effective tool for protecting privacy and preserving security on the Internet. This book explains the ins and outs of cryptography, with plenty of practical details for people who need to protect their data as it moves around on the Net.

Cyberwars: Espionage on the Internet, by Jean Guisnel (New York: Plenum, 1997). If you need proof that the Internet has graduated from its role as a research assistant, read Cyberwars. Guisnel, a respected French journalist, exposes the emerging online battle zones where spies, saboteurs, government agents, drug traffickers, and others wage virtual wars. Even though we can't see them happening, we're all victims of the fallout from these dangerous battles.

Digital Copyright Protection, by Peter Wayner (Boston: AP Professional, 1997). This somewhat technical book provides information and advice on several ways of protecting digital information on the Web and elsewhere.

Hackers: Heroes of the Computer Revolution, by Steven Levy (New York: Delta, 1994). This book helped bring the word "hackers" into the public's vocabulary. Levy's entertaining account of the golden age of hacking gives a historical perspective to today's anti-hacker mania.

The Cuckoo's Egg, by Cliff Stoll (New York: Pocket Books, 1989, 1995). This best-selling book documents the stalking of an interloper on the Internet. International espionage mixes with computer technology in this entertaining, engaging, and eye-opening book.

Takedown: The Pursuit and Capture of Kevin Mitnick, America's Most Wanted Computer Outlaw—by the Man Who Did It, by Tsutomu Shimomura with John Markoff (New York: Hyperion Books, 1996) and *The Fugitive Game*, by Jonathon Littman (New York: Little, Brown and Co., 1997). These two books chronicle the events leading up to and including the capture of Kevin Mitnick, America's number one criminal hacker. Takedown presents the story from the point of view of the security expert who captured Mitnick. The Fugitive Game is written from a more objective journalistic point of view.

Cyberpunk—Outlaws and Hackers on the Computer Frontier, Updated Edition, by Katie Hafner and John Markoff (New York: Simon & Schuster, 1995). This book profiles three hackers whose exploits caught the public's attention: Kevin Mitnick, a California cracker who vandalized corporate systems; Pengo, who penetrated U.S. systems for East German espionage purposes; and Robert Morris, Jr., whose Internet worm brought down 6,000 computers in a matter of hours.

The Hacker Crackdown: Law and Disorder on the Electronic Frontier, by Bruce Sterling (New York: Bantam Books, 1992). Famed cyberpunk author Sterling turns to nonfiction to tell both sides of the story of the war between hackers and federal law enforcement agencies. The complete text is available online along with rest-of-the-story updates.

Computer-Related Risks, by Peter Neumann (Reading, MA: Addison-Wesley, 1995). Neumann runs the popular and eye-opening comp.risks forum on the Internet. This book draws on that forum and Neumann's expertise, providing an exhaustive technical survey of the risks we face as a result of our dependence on computer technology. The hundreds of documented examples range from humorous to horrifying, and they're tied together with Neumann's intelligent assessment of the broader problems and possible solutions.

Ender's Game, by Orson Scott Card (New York: Tor Books, 1999). This award-winning, entertaining science fiction opus has become a favorite of the cryptography crowd because of its emphasis on encryption to protect privacy.

The Blue Nowhere, by Jeffery Deaver (New York: Simon & Schuster, 2001). This suspenseful thriller involves a sadistic hacker who invades his victim's computers, meddles with their lives, and lures them to their deaths. Though fictional, the novel presents a terrifyingly accurate analysis of the lack of privacy and security on the internet.

The Postman, by David Brin (New York: Bantam, 1990). This entertaining science fiction novel weaves a tale of the future that raises many of the same issues raised by Kempelen's chess-playing machine. The disappointing 1997 movie bears little resemblance to the novel.

Periodicals

Many popular magazines, from *Newsweek* to *Wired*, provide regular coverage of issues related to privacy and security of digital systems. Most of the periodicals listed here are newsletters of professional organizations that focus on these issues.

Information Security (www.infosecuritymag.com). This magazine focuses on security problems and solutions. Some of the articles are technical, but most are accessible to anyone with an interest in security issues.

The CPSR Newsletter, published by Computer Professionals for Social Responsibility (P.O. Box 717, Palo Alto, CA 94302, 415/322-3778, fax 415/322-3798, email: cpsr@csli.stanford.edu). An alliance of computer scientists and others interested in the impact of computer technology on society, CPSR works to influence public policies to ensure that computers are used wisely in the public interest. Their newsletter has intelligent articles and discussions of risk, reliability, privacy, security, human rights, work, war, education, the environment, democracy, and other subjects that bring together computers and people.

EFFector, published by the Electronic Frontier Foundation (155 Second St., Cambridge, MA 02141, 617/864-0665, fax 617/864-0866, email: effnews-request@eff.org). This electronic newsletter is distributed by EFF, an organization "established to help civilize the electronic frontier." EFF was founded by Mitch Kapor (see Chapter 6) and John Perry Barlow to protect civil rights and encourage responsible citizenship on the electronic frontier of computer networks.

Ethix: The Bulletin of the Institute for Business, Technology, and Ethics (www.ethix.org, email: contact@ethix.org). The IBTE is a relatively new nonprofit corporation working to transform business through appropriate technology and ethical values.

Web Pages

As you might suspect, the Net is the best source of up-to-the-minute information on computer security and related issues. Public and commercial organizations maintain Web pages devoted to these issues, and dozens of newsgroups contain lively ongoing discussions on controversial topics. Check the *Computer Confluence* Web site for the latest links.

Managing Computers

Information Systems at Work

13 Systems and Organizations in the Information Age

After reading this chapter, you should be able to:

Discuss the roles of information workers and computers in the information economy

Describe the social responsibilities of information workers and organizations

Describe the components of a system

Describe the value chain model

Discuss a business organization as a system by using the value chain model

Describe the components of an information system

Explain how transaction processing systems are used to support business processes

Discuss how computers are used to support automated manufacturing and design

▼ In this chapter:

The roles and responsibilities of information workers in the information economy

How to apply systems thinking to organizations

The components of an information system

How information systems are used to support business transactions

. . . and more.

▼ On the CD-ROM:

Video clip showing how computers are used in medical imaging

Video clip showing how virtual reality can cure fear of flying

Video clip of robots in action at a Mazda auto assembly line

Instant access to glossary and key word references

Interactive self-study quizzes

. . . and more.

▼ On the Web:

www.prenhall.com/beekman

Articles on systems thinking and a variety of information system topics

Links to important organizations for social responsibility, information ethics, and information professionals

Resources for exploring business organizations and transaction processing systems

Self-study exercises

. . . and more.

Marshall McLuhan: The Medium Is the Message

The new **electronic interdependence**
recreates the world in the image of a **global village**.

—Marshall McLuhan

Marshall McLuhan was a popular theorist of mass communications in the 1950s and 1960s. He probed and he predicted trends, and his ideas stimulated thousands of artists, intellectuals, and professionals throughout the world. He was an English professor at the University of Toronto where he directed the Centre for Culture and Technology located in a tiny 19th century coach-house on the university's campus. McLuhan devoted himself to studying the effect of electronic technology on the human community.

McLuhan's most well-known books are *The Mechanical Bride* (1951), *The Gutenberg Galaxy* (1962), and *Understanding Media* (1964). In *The Mechanical Bride* McLuhan analyzed modern popular culture through the satirical juxtaposition of text and images from contemporary advertising and media. In *The Gutenberg Galaxy* he introduced the phrase "global village" as a metaphor for contemporary society and examined how the inventions of the phonetic alphabet and of typography were primary forces behind the shaping of Western culture and values. He outlined his general

Marshall McLuhan

theoretical framework in *Understanding Media* including his famous notions of 'the medium is the message' and 'hot and cool media.' McLuhan used a wide definition of the term "media" and, as such, covered a diverse range of subjects in his analysis, including clocks, clothing, automobiles, weapons, games, radio and television, the typewriter and telephone, and many other technologies.

McLuhan was a well-paid consultant for academia, mass media, and big business. He told executives at General Motors that automobiles were obsolete, and he told executives at Bell Telephone that they didn't really understand the function of the telephone. McLuhan was even engaged by Canada's Prime Minister Pierre Trudeau to help improve Trudeau's television image.

McLuhan's statements, which he referred to as "probes," were designed to yield further information and insight about a company's work processes. However, his probes were sometimes difficult to understand. For example, he would make statements such as "the electric light is pure information" and "people don't actually read newspapers—they get into them every morning like a hot bath." Of his own work, McLuhan remarked playfully in a 1969 Playboy magazine interview "I don't pretend to understand it. After all, my stuff is very difficult."

Despite his metaphors and puns, McLuhan's basic idea was relatively simple—that all forms of technology, innately and independently of the messages they communicate, exert a compelling influence on individuals and society. Individuals in prehistoric, or tribal, society existed in a harmonious balance of the senses, perceiving the world through hearing, smell, touch, sight, and taste. But technological innovations, which are extensions of human abilities and senses, have altered this balance. This sensory alteration, in turn, has reshaped the society that created the technology.

McLuhan saw the powerful impact of technological change on the world and showed us a new way to explain our world and society. Today, such McLuhan coinages as "sensory impact," "the global village," and "the medium is the message" have become part of our language. His ideas have re-emerged with the advent of the World Wide Web. *Wired* magazine adopted him as its "patron saint." New editions of his work have been published, and several new books about McLuhan and his ideas have appeared. A whole new generation of students is finding relevance and inspiration in the life and work of Marshall McLuhan. ❱

Marshall McLuhan liked to point out that any technology gradually creates a totally new human environment. Indeed, information technology has changed the way millions of people live and work by providing new choices and opportunities. For other less fortunate persons, technology has taken away choices and opportunities. In this chapter and the following three, we'll see how computers are changing the ways people work. We'll start in this chapter by examining the roots and characteristics of the modern information economy. Then we'll explore information systems in general and see how they apply to modern businesses. In the next two chapters, we'll focus on information systems for management and electronic commerce. This section will close with a detailed look at the process for developing the systems that have become so vital to businesses today.

Into the Information Age

It is the business of the future to be **dangerous**. . . .
The **major advances in civilization** are processes
that all but **wreck** the **societies** in which they occur.
—Alfred North Whitehead

Every so often civilization dramatically changes course. Events and ideas come together to transform radically the way people live, work, and think. Traditions go by the wayside, common sense is turned upside down, and lives are thrown into turmoil until a new order takes hold. Humankind experiences a paradigm shift—a change in thinking that results in a new way of seeing the world. Major paradigm shifts take generations because individuals have trouble changing their assumptions about the way the world works.

Before the 21st century, humanity experienced two major paradigm shifts directly related to the world of work: the agricultural revolution and the industrial revolution. It's helpful to glance backward at these two shifts for perspective before we focus on the information revolution—the paradigm shift that's affecting us today.

Three Monumental Changes

Prehistoric people were mostly hunters and gatherers. They lived tribal, nomadic lives, tracking animals and gathering wild fruits, nuts, and grains. Anthropologists speculate that some prehistoric people spent as few as 15 hours per week satisfying material needs and devoted the rest of their time to cultural and spiritual pursuits.

The Agricultural Economy
As the human population grew, people learned to domesticate animals, grow their own grains, and use plows and other agricultural tools. The transformation to an agricultural economy took place over several centuries around 10,000 years ago. The result was a society in which most people lived and worked on farms, exchanging goods and services in nearby towns. The agricultural age lasted until about a century ago, when technological advances triggered what has come to be known as an *industrial revolution*.

The Industrial Economy
In the first half of the 20th century, the world was dominated by an industrial economy in which more people worked in urban factories than on farms. Factory work promised a higher material standard of living for a growing population, but not without a price. Families who had worked the land on sustainable farms for generations found it necessary to take low-wage factory jobs for survival. As work life became separate from home life, fathers were removed from day-to-day family life, and those mothers who didn't have to work in factories assumed the bulk of domestic responsibilities. As towns grew into cities, crime, pollution, and other urban problems grew with them.

The Information Economy
Twentieth-century information technology produced what's been called a second industrial revolution as people turned from factory work to information-related work. In today's information economy (sometimes called a *post-industrial economy*) clerical workers outnumber factory workers, and most people earn their living working with words, numbers, and ideas. Instead of planting corn or making shoes, most of us shuffle bits in one form or another. As we roar into the information age 21st century, we're riding a wave of social change that rivals any that came before.

Technology was central to each of these transformations. The agricultural economy grew from the plow; the industrial revolution was sparked by machines, and the information age is so dependent on computers that it's often called the *computer age*.

The information revolution is a global phenomenon, but it is taking hold at different rates in different countries; the United States is one of many countries at the forefront of the movement toward an information economy. Today approximately 70 percent of workers in the United States information economy are **information workers** whose jobs require them to create, process, use, or distribute information. There are two types of information workers: knowledge workers and data workers. Knowledge workers, such as scientists, architects, engineers, and some managers, create new information. Data workers, including salespersons, accountants, clerks, and some managers, use and distribute information. Noninformation workers include service workers, such as waiters and hairdressers, who provide services; and goods workers, including machinists and construction workers, who work with and manipulate physical objects. Many noninformation workers process information in the course of their jobs, but information isn't the main focus of their work.

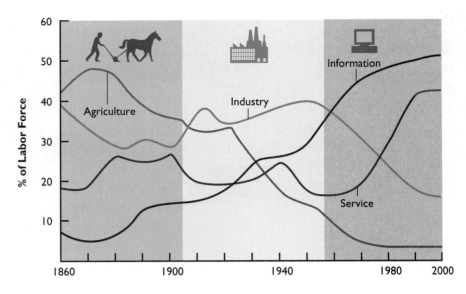

In the last century, the majority of the workforce has moved from the farm, to the factory, and then to the office.

Where Computers Work

Just as people and organizations in prior agricultural and industrial ages used technologies in new ways to improve their productivity and quality of life, information technologies are being used in the information age to improve work practices. It's becoming harder all the time to find jobs that haven't been changed in some way by computers. Consider these examples:

> All those ones and zeros we've been passing around—the **fuel that fans the digital fire**—have reached critical mass and ignited, **big time**.
> —Steven Levy

▶ *Entertainment.* The production of television programs and movies involves computer technology at every stage of the process. Scriptwriters use specialized word processors to write and revise scripts, and they use the Internet to beam the scripts between Hollywood and New York. Artists and technicians use graphics workstations to create special effects, from simple scene fadeouts and rolling credits to giant creatures and intergalactic battles. Musicians compose soundtracks using synthesizers and sequencers. Sound editors use computer-controlled mixers to blend music with digital sound effects and live-action sound. Even commercials—*especially* commercials—use state-of-the-art computer graphics, animation, and sound to keep you watching the images instead of changing the channel with your remote control.

Portable computers are standard equipment for journalists today.

▶ *Publishing.* The newspaper industry is being radically transformed by computer technology. Reporters scan the Internet for facts, write and edit stories on location using notebook computers, and transmit those stories by modem to central offices. Artists design charts and drawings

A growing number of newspapers and magazines are published on the World Wide Web.

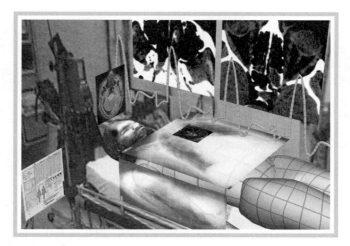

Medical students and professionals use this virtual emergency room to simulate processes of collecting vital signs and other patient data.

with graphics software. Photo retouchers use computers instead of brushes and magnifying glasses to edit photographs. Production crews assemble pages with computers instead of type-setting machines and paste-up boards. Many newspapers produce Web editions in addition to traditional paper publications.

▶ *Medicine.* High-tech equipment plays a critical role in the healing arts, too. Hospital information systems store patient medical and insurance records. LANs enable doctors, nurses, technicians, dietitians, and office staff to view and update information throughout the hospital. For patients who are outside the hospital walls in remote locations, doctors use the Web to practice telemedicine. Computers monitor patient vital signs in intensive care units in hospitals, at home, and on the street with portable units that analyze signals and transmit warnings when problems arise. Databases alert doctors and pharmacists to the problems and possibilities of prescribed drugs. A variety of digital devices enable doctors to see inside our bodies. Every day computers provide medical researchers with new ways to save lives and reduce suffering.

▶ *Airlines.* Without computers, today's airline industry simply wouldn't fly. Designers use CAD (computer-aided design) software to design aircraft. Engineers conduct extensive computer-simulations to test them. Pilots use computer-controlled instruments to navigate their planes,

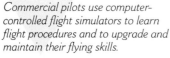

Commercial pilots use computer-controlled flight simulators to learn flight procedures and to upgrade and maintain their flying skills.

monitor aircraft systems, and control autopilots. Air traffic controllers on the ground use computerized air traffic control systems to keep track of incoming and outgoing flights. And, of course, computerized reservation systems make it possible for all those planes to carry passengers.

▶ *Science.* From biology to physics, computers have changed every branch of science. Scientists collect and analyze data using remote sensing devices, notebook computers, and statistical analysis programs. They catalog and organize information in massive databases, many of which are accessible through the World Wide Web. They use supercomputers and workstations to create computer models of objects or environments that would otherwise be out of reach. They communicate with colleagues all over the world through the Internet. It's hard to find a scientist today who doesn't work with computers.

Neurosurgeons use a computer-controlled robot arm called a MagicWand to locate and surgically remove small brain tumors.

Systems and Organizations

> The machines that are **first invented** to perform any particular **movement** are always the most complex.
>
> —Adam Smith, in The Wealth of Nations

Information technology is at the center of the information revolution; the productivity of information workers depends on computers, networks, and other information technologies. But the role and impact of information technology in business can be complex and confusing without the help of clearly defined concepts. The relationships between computers, networks, and organizations are easier to understand if we consider them as systems.

Earlier in the book, we discussed computer systems, operating systems, simulation systems, and other systems without paying much attention to the nature of a system. The remaining sections explore the concepts that define systems in general and business information systems in particular.

Anatomy of a System

A **system** is a set of interrelated parts that work together to accomplish a purpose. To accomplish its purpose, a system performs three basic functions: *input*, *processing*, and *output*. During input, needed materials are gathered and organized. During processing, the input materials are manipulated to produce the desired output, such as a product or service. During output, the result is transferred or delivered to customers, clients, or other systems.

Does this definition sound familiar? In Chapter 2, "Hardware Basics: Inside the Box," the description of a basic computer included each of these functions along with

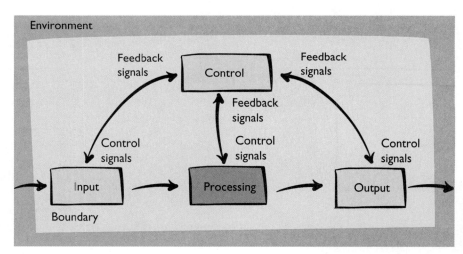

a storage function for saving and retrieving data for processing. By this definition, then, a computer is a system.

A system is a group of interrelated or interacting elements working together toward a common goal.

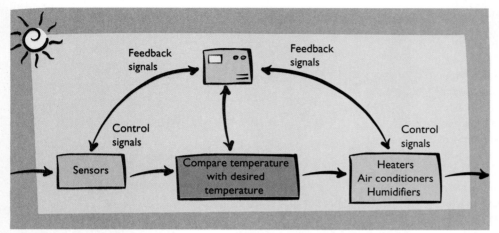

A building's climate control system uses feedback from the environment to determine how to adjust temperature and humidity controls.

A ski resort uses sensors on the slopes that monitor weather to help employees know when and how long to operate snow-making equipment.

A system has two additional functions: *feedback* and *control*. Feedback measures the performance of the input, processing, and output functions of the system and provides the measurement data to the control function. Control evaluates the feedback data and adjusts the system's input and processing functions to ensure the desired output is produced.

Every system has a *boundary* that defines its limits; anything outside the system's boundary is part of the system's *environment*. The system's environment provides input resources to the system and uses the output from the system.

A system can be a part, or a *subsystem*, of a larger system. For example, a personal computer can be a subsystem of a LAN, which might be a subsystem of a larger WAN, which could be a subsystem of the Internet. When the output of one subsystem is used as input for another subsystem, the two systems have a shared boundary, or interface. A large system (like the Internet or a corporation) can have many interfacing subsystems.

Let's bring these abstract definitions down to earth with concrete examples. A computerized climate control system in a modern office building is designed by engineers to continually maintain a comfortable temperature and humidity for the office workers—that's the purpose of the system. The system accepts input from human operators that tell it what ideal temperature and humidity to maintain. The system also accepts regularly timed input from sensors that tell it what the actual temperature and humidity are in the building. If temperature or humidity is significantly different than the target value, the system sends output signals to heaters, air conditioners, or humidifiers to adjust conditions accordingly. The monitoring sensors provide feedback from the environment; the system controller processes the feedback and responds by adjusting output signals.

Similarly, a ski resort might use a computer system to maintain an adequate snow level on its ski slopes. Sensors gather temperature and other weather data at several locations around the slopes. The computer processes this information, and the ski resort staff uses the information to decide when to turn the snow-making equipment on or off.

Robots as Systems

Another example of a system that's becoming increasingly common in today's workplace is the robot. As exotic as they might seem, robots are similar to other kinds of computer systems people use every day. While a typical computer performs mental tasks, a **robot** is a computer-controlled machine designed to perform specific manual, or mechanical, tasks. A robot's central processor might be a microprocessor embedded in the robot's shell, or it might be a supervisory computer that controls the robot from a distance. In any case, the processor is functionally identical to the processor found in a personal computer, a workstation, or a mainframe computer.

The most important hardware differences between robots and other computers are the input and output peripherals. Instead of sending output to a screen or a printer, a robot sends commands to joints, arms, and other moving parts. The first robots had no corresponding input devices to monitor their movements and the surrounding environment. They were effectively deaf, blind, and in some cases dangerous—at least one Japanese worker was killed by an early sightless robot. Most modern robots include some kind of input sensors. These sensing devices allow robots to correct or modify their actions based on feedback from the outside world.

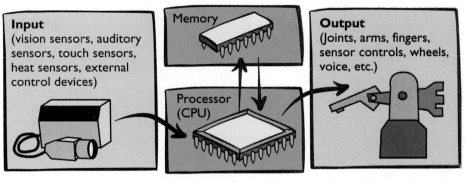

Input
(vision sensors, auditory sensors, touch sensors, heat sensors, external control devices)

Memory

**Processor
(CPU)**

Output
(Joints, arms, fingers, sensor controls, wheels, voice, etc.)

A robot is, in effect, a computer with exotic peripherals.

Industrial robots seldom have the human-inspired anatomy of Hollywood's science fiction robots. Instead they're designed to accomplish particular tasks in the best possible way. Robots can be designed to see infrared light, rotate joints 360 degrees, and do other things that aren't possible for humans. Today hundreds of thousands of industrial robots do welding, part fitting, painting, and other repetitive tasks in factories all over the world. In most automated factories, robots work alongside humans, but in some state-of-the-art factories, the only function of human workers is to monitor and repair robots. On the other hand, robots are constrained by the limitations of software and still can't compete with people for jobs that require exceptional perceptual or fine-motor skills.

Robots are practical for a variety of jobs, especially in harsh environments. The robot Jason Jr. (bottom right) was used to explore the sunken Titanic. The Viking space probe robot (bottom left) was used to collect soil samples on the surface of Mars. Robots are widely used in manufacturing, especially in the automotive industry to weld cars on assembly lines (upper left).

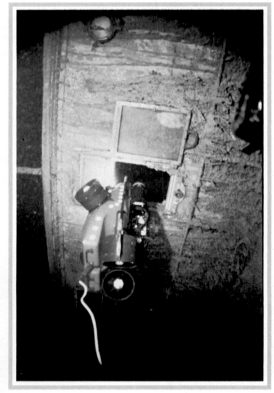

Business Organizations as Systems

In every **business**, however large or small, every person must have a **broad vision** and a sense of place in that vision.

—Sir David Scholey

While the concept of a system can be (and often is) used to describe biological and other natural phenomena, the systems we're discussing here are designed and used by people. A **business organization** is a system designed for the purpose of creating products and services for customers. A business organization is commonly referred to also as a company or a firm. When we view a company as a system within an environment, each of the basic system concepts takes on a specific meaning.

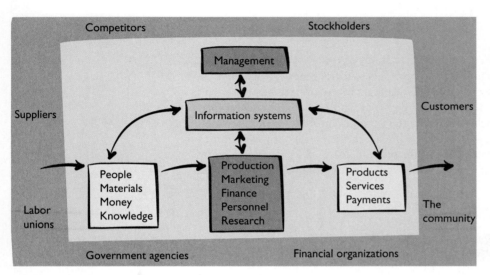

The firm's environment is made up of customers, stockholders, and other organizations such as competitors, suppliers, banks, and government agencies. From the environment, a company acquires people, materials, money, knowledge, and other resources as input. These resources are used in work processes such as manufacturing, marketing and sales, accounting and finance, all of which are needed to produce desired outputs for customers. These outputs include products and services as well as dividends, taxes, and information that are transferred to entities in the environment. The firm's managers perform the control function to ensure that the input, processing, and output func-

A business organization is a system that uses a variety of resources to produce produces and services for customers.

tions perform properly. Information systems, which will be discussed later in this chapter, play a key role in the feedback and control functions, collecting data from each of the primary activities and processing the data into information needed by managers.

The Value Chain Model of a Business Organization

Art is the **beautiful** way of doing things.
Science is the **effective** way of doing things.
Business is the **economic way of doing things**.

—Elbert Hubbard, U.S. author

A good way to help you understand a business organization as a system is to use the value chain model, developed by Harvard professor Michael E. Porter. According to the **value chain model**, an organization performs a series of activities to provide products and services for customers. Each activity adds something valuable to the production of the product or service. The value chain model divides the activities of an organization into two types—primary activities and support activities. There are five primary activities in an organization's value chain:

▶ Inbound logistics receives and stores supplies and materials from the firm's environment and distributes them when and where they are needed in the organization.
▶ Operations uses the supplies and materials to create or manufacture the organization's products and services.
▶ Outbound logistics delivers the products and services when and where needed by customers.
▶ Marketing and sales investigates customer needs and promotes the value of and sells the products and services in the environment (marketplace).
▶ Service maintains and enhances the usefulness of the product or service to customers through, for example, training and maintenance.

The value chain model includes four support activities of an organization to ensure that the primary activities can function efficiently and effectively:

▶ Management and other administrative services (for example, accounting, finance, and legal) comprise the general management structure of the organization that deals with banks, government agencies, and other organizations in the firm's environment.

▶ Human resources recruits, hires, trains, and develops the people in the firm.

▶ Research and technology development creates new products and services and looks for ways to improve the efficiency and effectiveness of the company's primary activities.

▶ Procurement interacts with the organization's suppliers and vendors to ensure high-quality supplies and materials are available to the organization.

The value chain model shows the activities in an organization that make a product or service more valuable to customers.

Each of the primary and support activities can be viewed as a subsystem of the organization. The activities interact by exchanging their inputs and outputs, the output of one activity being the input to another activity. The specific combination of primary and support activities an organization uses to accomplish a specific objective is often referred to as a *business process.* More specifically, a **business process** is a related set of primary and support activities that uses people, information, and other resources (such as information technology) to create valuable products and/or services for customers. For example, a typical business process is a sale-purchase transaction with customers—the people in marketing and sales take an order from a customer and give the order to the operations employees; the operations people may order supplies to produce the product to fill the order; the outbound logistics people receive the filled order and ship the requested product. The accounting and finance support people receive the filled customer order and send a bill or invoice to the customer.

A business process, such as a sale-purchase transaction with customers, is the interaction of primary and support activities in the organization's value chain.

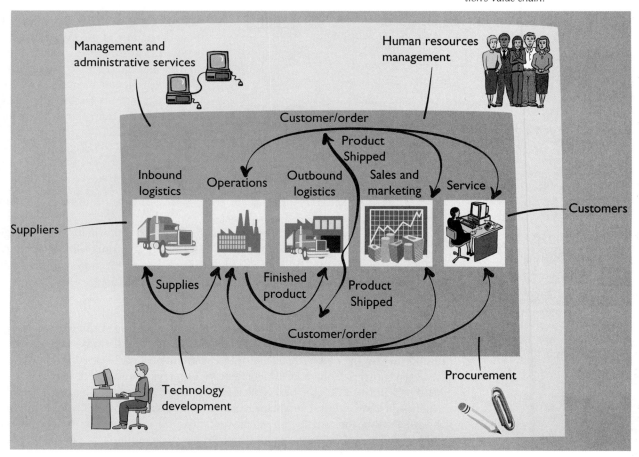

Generally speaking, we can think of three major types of business processes in organizations—transaction-oriented, communications, and decision-making processes. In today's business world, information and information technology play important key roles in each of these three types of business processes of an organization. We will next examine the concept of *information systems* and how information systems are used in transaction-oriented business processes. (We'll consider how information systems are used in communications and decision making in the next chapter).

Information Systems

Information is the oxygen of the modern age.
It seeps through the walls topped by barbed wire,
it wafts across the electrified borders.
—Ronald Reagan, 40th President of the United States

We can think of an **information system** as a subsystem that supports the information needs of other business processes within an organization. The overall purpose of an information system is to help people in the organization gather and use information, communicate with other people within and outside the organization, and make effective decisions.

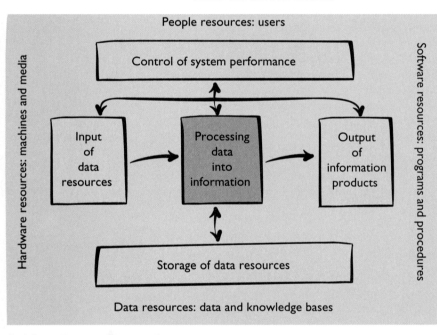

An Information system uses people, hardware, and data resources for input, processing, output, storage, and control activities to produce valuable information for users

Like other systems, an information system performs input, processing, and output functions, and contains feedback and control functions. The output of an information system is an information product of some kind—for example, a report or other document. The input of an information system is data, or raw facts, about other subsystems in the business or other systems in the environment, such as descriptions of customer needs, materials purchased, and sales transactions. The processing function organizes and arranges the data in ways that people can understand and use. An information system also has a storage function to save data and information products for future use. The control function assures that the information product outputs are of high quality and are useful to the information users for problem solving and decision making.

Elements of an Information System

We now mass produce information
the way we used to mass produce cars.
—John Naisbitt, in *Megatrends*

An information system involves people using information and information technologies to perform business processes, or tasks, that are important for the mission and objectives of the organization within a business environment. Let's examine some of the important terms in that sentence.

People

All members of an organization need to use information to perform their jobs. As a group these persons are referred to as information system users or end-users. Think of employees in an organization as forming a hierarchical management structure of users: clerical and production workers at the basic level; operational managers who supervise production, clerical, and other nonmanagement workers at the next level; middle managers who are responsible for programs and facilities on another level ; and managers who are responsible for the organization performance as a whole at the top. Another set of end-users is people in the organization's environment who utilize the firm's information products and services, such as suppliers and customers.

The structure and design of an information system is defined by another group of people—the system designers. They attempt to design the system to maximize its usefulness and value to the system users. Another group of people in the organization—managers—decide how money, time, and other resources should be allocated to design, implement, and maintain the organization's information systems. These three groups of people—users, designers, and managers—are all important for the successful utilization of information technologies in an organization.

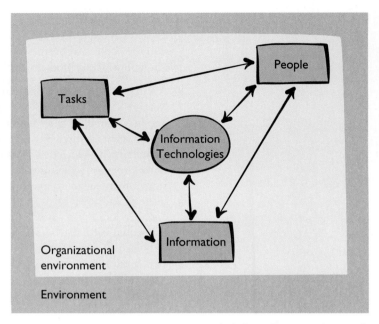

An information system is a set of information technologies that enable people in an organization to accomplish tasks effectively by providing access to information.

Tasks

As described previously a business process is a related set of value chain activities performed by a person or group to achieve an objective. When you think about a particular business process in more detail, you can describe it as a sequence of activities, or tasks. For example, when you go shopping you usually perform certain tasks in sequence, such as entering the store, locating items in the store, selecting the items you'd like to buy, purchasing the items, and then carrying your purchases to your car. Similarly, Many tasks are simple and straightforward, such as typing a memo to a colleague. Other tasks are complex—creating an advertising campaign for a product, for example.

Information

Information is an important resource that people in organizations use to accomplish tasks. Information has two dimensions: physical or digital representation and human cognition. As a commodity, information refers to facts, statistics, or other data that are valuable or useful to a person for accomplishing a task. These valuable pieces of information are organized and represented in some physical or digital form—a newspaper, email message, or report, for example. You can also think of information as the cognitive state of a person being aware of and knowledgeable about the tasks to be performed. From a cognitive point of view, people need information to be able to answer questions such as what, when, where, who, how and why. Information does not exist independently of a person who gives it meaning and somehow acts upon it.

Organization

A business, or other organization such as a college, can be defined by its purpose, the tasks or activities that it performs, and its structure. As we saw earlier in this chapter, the purpose of an organization is usually to provide or sell a product or service to its clients or customers. An organization that produces physical products, such as automobiles or computers, is called a manufacturing organization. A firm that provides a service, such as legal or medical advice, is called a service organization. Although business organizations operate for a profit, not-for-profit organizations, such as charitable organizations and government agencies, provide goods and services without the intent of making a profit. Both profit and not-for-profit organizations usually comprise several departments, such as accounting, finance, and marketing to accomplish the tasks in the organization's value chain. Often the people within one or several departments are organized into workgroups to accomplish a specific task.

Environment

The global, competitive business environment presents problems and opportunities that a business organization must cope with to thrive. Today many firms need to conduct trade and coordinate with their suppliers and distributors on a global scale. Customers can shop in a worldwide marketplace, so firms must do business in open, unprotected worldwide markets. More powerful technology, such as the Internet, is now more accessible by small and large organizations alike.

Information Technology

You've already seen and read about a wide variety of information technologies in previous chapters. In the context of business, these technologies when used in information systems perform five functions: acquisition, processing, storage and retrieval, presentation, and transmission.

▶ **Acquisition** is a process of capturing data about an event that is important to the organization. Managers, clerks, or other users expect the data to be useful later. The data can be text, numbers, graphics, sound, or other sensory input. An example of acquisition is the identification of each grocery item captured by a scanning device during checkout at a grocery store.

▶ **Processing** is an activity that manipulates and organizes information in ways that adds value to the information so it is useful to users. For example, one function of data processing in a grocery store is to calculate the total grocery bill during checkout.

▶ **Storage and retrieval** is an activity that systematically accumulates information for later use and then locates the stored information when needed. For example, a grocery information system would use a database to store revised information about inventory levels of grocery items after each customer has checked out.

▶ **Presentation** is the process of showing information in a format and medium useful to the user. A grocery receipt given to a customer is one example; a summary report displayed on a manager's screen is another.

▶ **Transmission** is the process of sending and distributing data and information to various locations. For example, a grocery store may send information about inventory levels and sales to headquarters frequently. Telecommunications, LANs in a computer laboratory, intranets within an organization, and the Internet are examples of information transmission media.

Benefits of Information Systems

A firm can reap many benefits by using information technology creatively to extend people's natural ability to cope with tasks and to improve the performance of the organization. Consider the following benefits:

▶ *High-quality information.* Information workers can accomplish tasks more quickly and accurately when they use information that is more accurate, precise, complete, and up to date.

▶ *Access to information.* Information workers' productivity improves when information is easier to obtain and manipulate and is presented in a useful format.

▶ *Utilization of information.* Information technology enables workers to innovate and learn new work practices, and generally be more highly productive, motivated, and satisfied on the job.

▶ *Performance of organizational work efficiently.* A company can do its work more quickly and reliably, with reduced costs, by using information technology to eliminate wasted time and resources, and to reorganize or automate work flows.

▶ *Better communication and decision making.* Information workers, especially managers, can use information technologies to improve exchanging information with their colleagues to identify, analyze, and solve problems more quickly and effectively.

▶ *Better products and services for customers.* You probably expect quick service made possible by computer-based information systems, such as point-of-sale systems in grocery stores and automated teller machines located conveniently. Because we expect quality service, companies must improve their products and services continually. As you will see in Chapter 14, "Information Technology in Management," a company can use information technology to provide a product or service that competing companies may not be able to match, thus creating a *competitive advantage* for the company.

In the remainder of this chapter, we look at how information systems are used in the transaction-oriented and operational business processes of an organization.

Information Systems for Business Transactions

Being good in **business** is the most fascinating kind of **art**. . . .
—Andy Warhol

Many business processes handle transactions between the company and its customers, suppliers, or other organizations. A **transaction** is an event that occurs in any of the primary activities of the companyæmanufacturing, marketing, sales, and accounting. A transaction might be a sale to a customer, a purchase from a supplier or vendor, or a payroll payment to an employee. An organization can use an information system to track transactions in order to operate efficiently.

Information systems that support the transaction-based business processes of a firm are called transaction processing systems. A **transaction processing system (TPS)** is a firm's basic accounting and record-keeping system that keeps track of routine daily transactions necessary to conduct business. Examples of transaction processing systems include sales-order entry, ticket and hotel reservations, payroll, accounts receivable, and inventory. Transaction processing systems are important in any organization, because they make it possible to control the various business processes intelligently based on accurate information. For example, by tracking the number of cars a dealership sells a week, a manager can make a fairly accurate assessment of the number of cars to order from the manufacturer. Similarly, by tracking the number of students that enroll in an introduction to computers course each fall semester a university can determine the number of books it needs to order.

Transaction processing systems typically involve large amounts of data stored in large databases; they require high processing speeds to manipulate large volumes of data. These systems capture data users and managers use to produce documents and reports. Many systems enable people to retrieve information from files and databases interactively through database query systems, groupware applications, and intranet Web pages. A transaction processing system must ensure a high level of accuracy and security of the data.

The Transaction Processing Cycle

Transaction processing is a cyclical process with five steps:

1. *Data entry*. This first step in TPS is to enter the transaction data into machine-readable form. This involves online data entry (typing at a terminal, scanning bar codes, or other direct input into the computer), or transcribing paper source documents into an electronic format acceptable to a computer. Data entry can also use **Electronic Data Interchange (EDI)** to electronically exchange business transactions between companies using standard document formats for purchase orders, invoices, and shipping notices.

2. *Processing the data*. A typical transaction processing system organizes and sorts the data and performs calculations, including totals and subtotals. Data can be processed in two ways: **batch processing** involves gathering and manipulating all the data to be processed for a particular time period; **real-time processing** involves processing each transaction as it occurs. Batch processing is used when processing is needed periodically, such as monthly payroll or checking account statements. Real-time processing is appropriate when users need the data immediately, as with bank ATM machines.

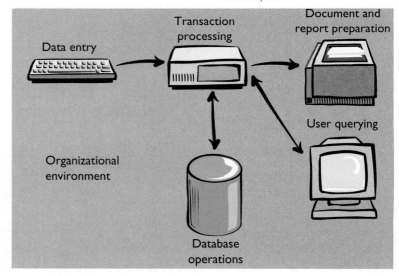

A transaction processing cycle consists of the same steps as in other systems: input, processing, storage, and output.

3. *Storing and updating the data*. This step involves storing the transaction data in database files so the data can be retrieved later in processing some future transaction. For example, the amount you paid on this month's phone bill is used in calculating the amount you're billed next month. Many large organizations use **data warehousing** software to create and maintain large databases containing data on all aspects of the company. For example, Harrah's Entertainment developed a data warehouse to store all the company's customer information that enables it to track particular customers use of Harrah's facilities on a national basis.

4. *Document and report preparation*. A transaction processing system produces several types of action documents and reports. An **action document** initiates an action by the recipient

or verifies for the recipient that a transaction has occurred. For example, a billing statement produced by your phone company is intended to trigger an action on your part, namely to make a payment. A sales receipt verifies the details of a purchase you make. Other examples of action documents are payroll checks, invoices, warehouse packing lists, and sales receipts. Reports are used by management to monitor the transactions that occur over a period of time. Reports can contain detailed information about specific transactions or summary information about a group of transactions, such as totals and averages. These reports are customized for their specific users.

5. *User inquiry*. Managers and other workers can use a database query language to ask questions and retrieve information about any transaction activity. The responses can be presented on the screen or in hard-copy form. User inquiry enables a worker to search for specific information when it's needed.

The transaction processing cycle repeats regularly with output from one cycle serving as input to the next cycle. Each transaction system is a subsystem of the business as a whole, and these subsystems can interact in a variety of ways.

Enterprise Resource Planning

Transaction processing systems exist in all functional areas of a business' value chain. Most early computer applications in business were designed to maintain accurate and up-to-date records of business transactions; today's accounting systems perform the same function. Typically, an accounting system is made up of a number of subsystems that keep track of the revenues, expenditures, and cash requirements of a business. Typical subsystems include order processing, inventory control, accounts receivable, accounts payable, payroll, and general ledger. Each subsystem is itself a transaction processing system. The subsystems exchange information; the output of one subsystem is the input to another subsystem.

Many managers in organizations look for ways to create cross-functional information systems by reengineering, or combining and integrating two or more transaction processing systems. Careful reengineering can increase the efficiency and effectiveness of a business process by reducing wasted time, paperwork, and unnecessary work procedures. Work practices can also be restructured to minimize costs and maximize worker effectiveness. One example of a successful reengineering of a transaction processing system happened at Ford Motor Company. Ford used database and telecommunications information technologies to revamp the accounts-payable transaction system resulting in more accurate purchase orders, faster exchange of invoice and payment information between Ford and its suppliers, and reduced labor costs.

Ford updated its accounts payable transaction processing system. The jagged lines in the new process show that pieces of the system have been replaced with information technology using an online database. To meet the different needs of Ford's many suppliers, purchase orders and payments are done either with paper or electronically. With the new system, accuracy improved and head count was reduced by 75 percent.

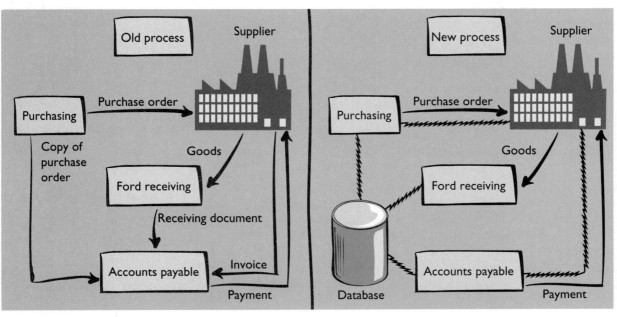

This approach of creating information systems to support an organization's operational business processes is referred to as **enterprise resource planning (ERP)**. An ERP system links, simplifies, and speeds up a company's entire transaction processing cycle. The primary focus is to improve customer service and the ultimate goal is to make it easier for both suppliers and customers to do business with the company. A typical ERP system collects transaction data from various business processes in the organization and stores the data in a single database, or data warehouse, that consolidates the organization's information consistently so that all business processes can deal with the same unified set of data. Once stored in the database, the data can be shared automatically between business processes and retrieved by managers in all parts of the organization in a precise and timely manner to help coordinate the daily operations of the firm.

The emphasis of ERP is to improve the free flow of information between different parts of the firm. A company can also use ERP to improve the coordination of its value chain logistics activities and the logistics activities of its supplier and customers, a concept called **supply chain management**.

Several ERP software vendors exist, including Peoplesoft, Baan, Oracle, J. D. Edwards, and SAP. SAP is a German-based multinational company and the largest of the ERP vendors with sales in 50 countries although the majority of its sales are in the United States. The company's name is an abbreviation of its original name Systems, Applications, and Products in Data Processing.

ERP systems are usually large and complex and take a lot of time and money to implement. A recent survey of 63 companies—including small, medium, and large companies in a range of industries—the average total cost of an ERP was $15 million (the highest was $300 million and lowest was $400,000).

Because of the complexity involved in planning and implementing ERP systems, many companies have had difficulty implementing ERP systems successfully the first time they tried. For example, Whirlpool's initial ERP implementation crippled the shipping system, leaving appliances stacked on loading docks—and therefore not delivered to paying customers—for a full eight weeks. Another example was Hershey Foods that had a 19 percent drop in earnings caused by an incompetent ERP implementation that wreaked distribution havoc during one of its most profitable seasons: Halloween. And a new ERP system at Volkswagen resulted in significant delays in parts shipments, causing product inventories to build up to costly levels.

ERP software is evolving quickly to support the growing need of organizations to conduct their business transactions over the Internet; some examples of Web-based ERP are described in Chapter 14, "Information Technology in Management."

Automated Information Systems for Design and Manufacturing

Automation does not make **optimism** obsolete.

—George Keith Funston, President, New York Stock Exchange

Two types of information technologies, computer-aided design (CAD) and computer-aided manufacturing (CAM), are used to support design and manufacturing business processes within the organization's value chain. (See Chapter 7, "Graphics, Hypermedia, and Multimedia," for more information about these technologies.) Manufacturing transforms raw materials into a finished product. Design refers to creating and developing both new products and new ways of manufacturing those products. The overall objective of automation systems is to increase the productivity of the manufacturing and design processes to increase product quality and customer satisfaction.

Computer-Aided Design (CAD)

Product designers and engineers use **computer-aided design (CAD)** with computer workstations and software to draw product or process designs on the screen. They can draw objects that make up the design, change the dimensions, and make other modifications to the design quickly and easily. They can show the design in three dimensions and rotate it to see it from

13.1
The Information Flow Through a Company's Transaction Processing System

Running a nursery business involves selling to customers, keeping track of inventory and ordering from vendors, paying employees, and keeping track of income and expenses.

1 Sales transaction processing system. When a customer buys a plant, the clerk enters the information into a cash register, and the customer receives a receipt.

2 Inventory control transaction processing system. The sale of the plant is recorded for inventory control by reading the UPC code on the price tag. This allows the buyers for the nursery to know how much stock for any plant is available and when to order more.

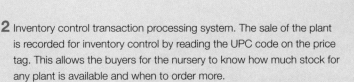

3 Accounts receivable transaction processing system. The nursery keeps records of amounts owed by customers. The clerk prepares accurate and timely invoices to credit customers.

6 General ledger transaction processing system. The income and expenses are organized in reports so that the nursery's owners know the "health" of the company.

4 Accounts payable transaction processing system. When an account needs to be paid, the clerk can print the check. In accounts payable, the nursery knows how much to pay each vendor and when to send the check.

7 Payroll transaction processing system. The nursery keeps track of the time each employee works and produces paychecks and other payroll statements.

5 Purchasing transaction processing system. When new stock needs to be purchased, the vendors' bills for the new inventory moves to accounts payable.

CAD enables product designers to "build" product prototypes and "test" them as computer objects.

every imaginable perspective. When they save the design as a disk file, they can retrieve, edit, and print the design any time. All the design files are a CAD database containing detailed product and process design specifications and other information.

A wide variety of industries use CAD. A good example of the importance of CAD is its use in the design of the Boeing 777, the first commercial airplane to be designed entirely with CAD software. More than 5000 engineers and other technical employees used more than 2000 workstations and 8 mainframe computers in the Boeing CAD system. CAD proved to be an important productivity tool because it enabled everyone on the design team equal access to consistent design drawings, which in turn fostered coordinated design improvements.

Computer-Aided Manufacturing (CAM)

Computers and other information technologies are used to automate the manufacturing process with **computer-aided manufacturing (CAM)**. The software in a CAM system retrieves the design specifications of the product from the CAD database; controls specific tools, machines, and robots on the factory floor to manufacture the product; and monitors the overall physical process of manufacturing the product. CAM is used in flexible manufacturing; it improves the overall efficiency of the manufacturing process by reducing the time needed to set up machines or robots for the next production run. CAM makes it possible for a company to respond to a customer's unique needs by making the product to order and delivering it in a short time, rather than making a large number of the products and storing them in inventory. For example, Panasonic uses CAD to take a customer's order for a custom-made bicycle, faxes the design file to the manufacturing plant, and uses CAM to set up the production run and produce the bicycle, all in just a few hours.

The assembly line for manufacturing computer chips is highly automated.

Computer-Integrated Manufacturing (CIM)

Computer-integrated manufacturing (CIM) is a concept, or management philosophy, emphasizing the coordination of CAD and CAM systems along with other information systems in the company. CIM automates the information flow between design, manufacturing, and other functional areas in a company, and it simplifies and automates as many manufacturing processes as possible. As a result, CIM improves product consistency, lowers the amount of waste in producing the product, makes more accurate reporting possible and improves overall quality and flexibility of the manufacturing process.

Social Responsibility in the Information Age

As an information worker, you must learn how to use information and information technologies to do your job effectively. But you must also use that information and technology in a socially responsible way. Using computers in a socially responsible way is a key concern in business today because of the many ways an information worker's actions can affect other people.

> In the 20th century B.C. the Code of Hammurabi declared that if a house collapsed and killed its owner, the **builder of the house was to be put to death**. In the 20th century A.D. many builders of computer software would **deny responsibility** and pass the *entire risk* to the user.
>
> —Helen Nissenbaum

Social responsibility refers to both legal and ethical behavior. Laws define a society's proper, or legal, behavior and outline the actions a government can take in response to improper behavior. Ethics are sets of principles or moral standards that help guide behavior, actions, and choices. Ethical dilemmas are difficult choices involving conflicting goals, responsibilities, and loyalties that may or may not be covered by laws. As an information worker, you will face many situations in which you will have to decide what the ethical and legal ways to behave are. Here are a few situations to consider:

- Making an extra backup of your software just in case both the copy you are using and the primary backup fail from some reason
- Accessing and viewing files or the email of people in your department or on your project team
- Making a recommendation to sell mailing lists of your company's customers to other businesses
- Using a browser during working hours to find entertaining Web sites unrelated to your job
- Copying a substantial portion of another employee's report and inserting it in a report you are writing
- Telling your project manager's boss that you are dissatisfied with the way a new software system was designed and that it should not be distributed to customers even though it has no obvious bugs
- Helping to implement a system that will result in five people losing their jobs

Social responsibility applies to a company as a whole as well as to individuals. A company that is socially responsible attempts to balance the interests of its various stakeholder groups—including employees, suppliers, customers, stockholders, and the local community. Basically, a company has a social contract with the community to enhance the material well-being of all the community's members, even if it means lower than maximized profits for its stockholders or higher than the lowest prices for its customers. Depending on circumstances, a socially responsible company might donate money to local charities or the arts, give employees time off to do volunteer work, avoid any fraud or deception of the public, or play an active role establishing and supporting community programs.

Regarding its own employees, a company is obliged to treat them with personal respect, healthy working conditions, fair wages, and employment continuity. Within this context, a socially responsible company can provide a stable and predictable ethical working environment by establishing policies and procedures, called a **code of ethics**, to guide the behavior of its information workers. Companies have developed codes of ethics covering issues such as email privacy, software licenses and copyrights, access to hardware and files, and data and intellectual property ownership.

In the Rules of Thumb box in Chapter 12, "Computer Security and Risks," you learned about several guidelines that can help you determine what is and is not ethical behavior. Here are some additional ethical guidelines for information professionals that were developed by Donn B. Parker, a leading expert on computer ethics:

- *Informed consent*. If you are in doubt about the ethics or laws of a particular action, inform those whom your action will affect of your intentions and obtain their consent before proceeding.
- *The higher ethic*. You should take the action that achieves the greater good for everyone involved.
- *Most restrictive action*. When you are deciding to take or avoid taking and action, assume that the most severe damage that could happen will happen.

Considering Computer Careers

Until recently, people who wanted to work with computers were forced to choose between a few careers, most of which required highly specialized training. But when computers are used by everybody from fast-food sales clerks to graphic artists, just about anybody can have some kind of "computer career." Still, many rewarding and high-paying computer-related careers require a fair amount of specialized education. If you're interested in a computer-related job, consider the following tips:

▶ **Learn touch-typing.** Computers that can read handwriting and understand spoken English are probably in your future, but not your immediate future. Several low-cost typing tutorial programs can help you to teach your fingers how to type. The time you invest will pay you back quickly. The sooner you learn, the sooner you'll start reaping the rewards.

▶ **Use computers regularly to help you accomplish your immediate goals.** Word process your term papers. Use spreadsheets and other math software as calculation aids. Use databases for research work. Computers are part of your future. If you use them regularly, they'll become second nature, like telephones and pencils. If you don't own a computer, find a way to buy one if you can.

▶ **Don't forsake the basics.** If you want to become a programmer, a systems analyst, a computer scientist, a computer engineer, or some other kind of computer professional, don't focus all your attention on computers. A few young technical

wizards become successful programmers without college degrees. But if you're not gifted and lucky, you'll need a solid education to land a good job. Math and communication skills (written and oral) are extremely important, even in highly technical jobs. Opportunities abound for people who can understand computers and communicate clearly.

▶ **Combine your passions.** If you like art and computers, explore computer art. If you love ecology and computers, find out how computers are used by ecologists. People who can speak the language of computers and the language of a specialized field have opportunities to build bridges.

▶ **Ask questions.** The best way to find out more about computer careers is to ask the people who do them. Most people are willing to talk about their jobs if you're willing to listen.

▶ **If you can't find your dream job, build it yourself.** Inexpensive computer systems provide all kinds of entrepreneurial opportunities for creative self-starters: Desktop publishing service bureaus, multimedia video production, custom programming, commercial art and design, freelance writing, consulting . . . the jobs are there for the making if you have the imagination and initiative.

▶ **Prepare for change.** In a rapidly changing world, lifelong careers are rare. Be prepared to change jobs several times. Think of education as a lifelong process. In Marshall McLuhan's words, "The future of work consists of learning a living."

▶ *Universality rule*. If an action or a failure to act is not right for everyone to commit, then it is not right for anyone to commit.

▶ *"Change in" rule*. You should consider that many small losses may be acceptable individually, but when added together they may result in an unacceptable total loss.

▶ *Owner's conservative rule*. You should assume others will consider your assets as in the public domain, and so you should show explicitly, in reasonable and visible ways, that the products of your efforts and your property are either private or public.

▶ *User's conservative rule*. You should assume that any tangible or intangible item belongs to somebody else unless an explicit identifier shows it as being in the public domain or authorized for your use.

Several professional organizations exist for information workers. These organizations have formulated codes of ethics regarding the use of computers and the handling of information. These organizations and their Web sites are listed in the "Sources and Resources" section at the end of this chapter.

The Laws of Nature

By Tom Davenport

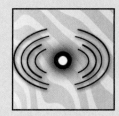

It's not enough to use the hottest technologies to build a company's information systems. You have to think about how people will use them. In this Darwin magazine article, Tom Davenport unveils his Ten Commandments for using computers in organizations.

My first consulting mentor, Chuck Gibson, introduced me to the sad fact that information systems—even the ones with all the right technologies—often fail for reasons related to human behavior and culture. Information itself—or more specifically, how it is given meaning—is a highly social construction…Maybe you've heard of Moore's law about the increase in processor speeds or Metcalfe's law about the increase in the number of computers in a network. But where are the laws that deal with the organizational and human side of computing? I'd like to try to articulate some here. Call them The Ten Commandments of Organizational Computing.

1. Thou shalt not expect humans to act like computers. Computers largely proceed according to their algorithms. Humans, however, often depart from their algorithms, or the business processes they are supposed to follow. People can be counted on to have their own agendas, and they are notoriously resistant to engineering or reengineering.

2. Thou shalt not assume that because information comes from a computer that it's correct. This fallacy is almost as old as the original Ten Commandments, but we still suffer from it. The current variation involves information on the Internet; if it can be found through a search engine, the story goes, it's worth including in your report or presentation. But almost all information ultimately derives from human activity, and laundering it through a computer or a network doesn't make it clean.

3. Thou shalt not attempt to sucketh knowledge out of humans and put it into a computer. For at least a couple of decades "knowledge engineers" have been trying to extract knowledge from the human brain and put it into a software program. Successes have been rare. The problem is that knowledge is both social—embedded in groups, not individuals—and also tacit. In many cases people can't even express much of what they know.

4. Thou shalt not build a system without consulting a focus group of likely users. Of course, many systems have token user representation, but they are usually consulted only at the beginning of the project and are asked only what their requirements are.

5. Thou shalt not blindly build IT products without some evidence that anyone actually wants or needs said products…In the IT industry . . . . . .the dominant cultural ethos is to follow your technical muse, throw a bunch of products against the wall and see what sticks. This is enormously inefficient. Of course, technologists will say that people often don't know what they want from technology. This is sometimes true but usually a rationale for not doing enough market research.

6. Thou shalt not ask what information a person needeth to build an IT product because he hath not a clue. Technologists have for years assumed that if you want to find out what information a person needs, all you have to do is ask. But people find it extremely difficult to determine what information they need. This is one reason why the art of systems prototyping—quickly developing a version of a system and then getting user reaction—is so valuable.

7. Thou shalt not presuppose that because a person has access to vast realms of online information and knowledge that he will actually use said knowledge in making decisions or taking actions. The Stanford organizational behavior guru James March once coauthored an article on this subject called "Information in Organizations as Signal and Symbol." The upshot was that people surround themselves with information in order to appear rational, but they often make decisions on biases or gut feelings.

8. Thou shalt not assume rational decision making. Even when humans do actually use information to make a decision, the process won't necessarily be a rational one. One of the leading schools of managerial decision making is called the "garbage can" model. It posits that the managerial brain is full of unorganized trash and that what's on the top of the pile may inordinately influence a decision.

9. Thou shalt not assume that because the company wants the information, those who have it will give it to said company. For example, many companies that implement so-called sales-force automation systems quickly install the call reporting and customer information applications. Sales managers want to know where the salespeople are spending their time, and they want the company, not the salesperson, to own key knowledge about the customer. But it's amazing how many ways sales folks can find to avoid putting in accurate information.

10. Thou shalt not take information gathered for one purpose and use it for another. The organizational context for which information was amassed is usually specific and idiosyncratic enough to make the information unsuited for other purposes. Customer information gathered for warranty administration, for example, probably won't be well-suited for marketing.

DISCUSSION QUESTIONS

1. Based on your experience with using Web sites, how strongly do you agree or disagree with each of Davenport's commandments?

2. Based on your experience using computer systems, can you think of examples for Commandments 7 and 8?

3. Do you believe we should be optimistic or pessimistic about the use of information technology in organizations and in our society?

Summary

Our civilization is in the midst of a transition from an industrial economy to a post-industrial information economy. The transition, or paradigm shift, is having a profound influence on the way we live and work, and it is likely to challenge many of our beliefs, assumptions, and traditions. Computers and other information technologies are central to these changes and have become critical to the efficient functioning of profit and not-for-profit organizations; it's hard to find a workplace that isn't computerized in some way. Along with this transition to an information economy comes new social responsibilities for information workers. Several professional organizations have formulated codes of ethics regarding the use of computers and information by information workers and companies.

To understand the role of information technologies in organizations, you must understand the concept of a system. A system is a set of interrelated parts that work together to accomplish a goal by performing three basic functions: input, processing, and output. A system has two additional functions: feedback, which provides measurements of the system's input, processing, and output; and control, which evaluates the feedback data and adjusts the system's input and processing functions to ensure the desired output is produced. Everything outside the system's boundary is called the environment. A system can be a subsystem of another system and may interact with other systems in its environment. Users, designers, and managers all play a role in defining the system's purpose, its boundaries, and its subsystems.

Computers are systems. Robots are computer systems with specialized peripherals and software that enable them to perform manual tasks. Business organizations can also be viewed as systems.

The value chain model defines a business organization as a system. According to the value chain model, the organization is a sequence, or chain, of activities, each adding something valuable to the production of a product or service. The value chain model divides the activities of an organization into five primary activities and four support activities. Each of the primary and support activities is a subsystem with inputs and outputs; these subsystems interact with each other to create the overall performance of the organization.

As a subsystem of a larger business organization, an information system is a set of interrelated parts that work together to produce, distribute, and use information products. One purpose of an information system is to provide information in the feedback and control functions of a larger system. An information system involves people using information and information technologies to perform tasks that are important for the mission and objectives of the organization within a business environment. Information systems provide many benefits to an organization including higher-quality information used to improve work flows, communications, decision making, and products and services.

Information systems that support the transaction-based business processes of a firm are called transaction processing systems. Transaction processing is by nature cyclical. The cycle might be based on income, expenditures, production, or cash management, but in every case transaction processing goes through a series of five steps repeatedly: data entry, processing the data, storing and updating the data, document and report preparation, and user inquiry. Integrated operations management uses software to automate many transaction processing applications of a company. CAD, CAM, and CIM systems represent other types of information systems that are especially well suited for manufacturing environments.

Chapter Review

▼ Key Terms

acquisition (p. 350)
action document (p. 351)
batch processing (p. 351)
business organization (p. 346)
business process (p. 347)
code of ethics (p. 357)
Computer-aided Design (CAD) (p. 353)
Computer-aided Manufacturing (CAM) (p. 356)
Computer-integrated Manufacturing (CIM) (p. 356)

data warehousing (p. 351)
Electronic Data Interchange (EDI) (p. 351)
Enterprise Resource Planning (ERP) (p. 353)
information economy (p. 340)
information system (p. 348)
information worker (p. 341)
paradigm shift (p. 340)
presentation (p. 350)
processing (p. 350)
real-time processing (p. 351)

robot (p. 344)
social responsibility (p. 357)
storage and retrieval (p. 350)
supply chain management (p. 353)
system (p. 343)
transaction (p. 350)
transaction processing system (TPS) (p. 351)
transmission (p. 350)
value chain model (p. 346)

▼ Interactive Quiz Questions

1. The *Computer Confluence* CD-ROM contains self-test quiz questions related to this chapter, including multiple choice, true or false, and matching questions.
2. The *Computer Confluence* Web site, **www.prenhall.com/beekman**, contains self-test exercises related to this chapter. Follow the instructions for taking a quiz. After you've completed your quiz, you can email the results to your instructor.

   The Web site also contains open-ended discussion questions called Internet Explorations. Discuss one or more of the Internet Exploration questions at the section for this chapter.

▼ Review Questions

1. Define or describe each of the key terms in the "Key Terms" section. Check your answers using the glossary.
2. What are the types of information workers in our information economy?
3. What are the social responsibilities of information workers?
4. What are the major components of a system? What is the difference between a system and a subsystem?
5. What distinguishes a robot from a desktop computer?
6. What are the components of the value chain model?
7. What are the basic systems components of an information system?
8. How would you describe the conceptual context within which information systems exist in an organization?
9. What are the five information activities that information technologies perform in a system?
10. What is the purpose of a transaction processing system?
11. What are the steps in a transaction processing cycle?
12. What are the relationships between computer-aided design, computer-aided manufacturing, and computer-integrated manufacturing?

▼ Discussion Questions

1. Use system terminology to describe a real-world situation, such as organizing a sporting event or looking for a job. Does the systems model increase your understanding of the situation or make it more confusing?
2. Many companies are trying to improve the quality of their products and services for customers. How can you use the value chain model to identify what business processes to change so as to improve quality?
3. Use information systems terminology to describe a real-world situation. In what ways, if any, does the information systems model clarify the situation?
4. Discuss the types of transactions and transaction cycles that occur in an organization. What types of transaction processing systems would be helpful in these situations?
5. Why are transaction processing systems important in an organization? Discuss the impact on an organization if one of its transaction processing systems fails or does not work properly.
6. How can computer-aided design and computer-aided manufacturing improve the quality of products and services to customers of an organization?
7. Describe some of the social responsibilities of information workers in an organization with which you are familiar, such as a bank, police station, retail store, or a government office.

▼ Projects

1. Scan through a newspaper or magazine and pick a situation that is interesting to you. Describe the situation as a system and identify the information activities in the situation. Think about how the situation could be improved. Use a word-processing software package to compose a report describing your analysis and recommendations.
2. Use the value chain model to describe the primary and support activities of a business organization you are familiar with, such as a student group, church or volunteer organization, a family-owned business, your favorite restaurant or clothing store, or any other business. Use a predesigned template available with your word processor to write a memo describing your analysis and recommendations. Attach the memo document to an email message and send it to your professor.
3. Interview the owner of a small business, such as a dry cleaners, photo shop, stationary store, or other small business. Describe the important transactions and the five-step transaction processing cycle for the organization. Identify some relevant information ethics issues for the organization. Create a presentation of your findings using a presentation software package such as Microsoft PowerPoint.

4. With a class partner, interview a manager in a large company, such as Wal-Mart. Use the information systems in context model (people, tasks, information, organization, environment, and information technology) to guide your interview. Use a word processor to prepare a two-page report describing the company as a system. Exchange reports with another class group; then read and comment on each other's reports.

5. Use a search engine to find more information about CAD/CAM products and how they are used in manufacturing firms or architectural firms. Use a word processor to compose a short report describing how these information systems are used to improve the quality of the company's products. Share your report with your class via email.

Case studies

United Colors of Benetton

Benetton is one of the world's largest garment companies. Starting from a shop in Venice, Italy, Benetton now operates over 5,000 shops in 75 countries and works with over 200 suppliers worldwide. Located in Castrette (Italy), Benetton's design and manufacturing facility produces over 90 million garments yearly, along with sportswear and sports equipment, footwear, bags, and accessories. Benetton emphasizes quick response, flexibility, low prices to customers, and excellent service.

Benetton uses a variety of technologies to accomplish its goals. For example, it uses proprietary cloth cutting and dyeing equipment that make it possible to respond quickly to changes in garment color preferences. Benetton uses computer networks and computer-aided design systems to plan and coordinate activities among its suppliers and outlets. It also uses a computerized warehouse that services the company's seven factories in Italy.

Its manufacturing system is based on technical innovation and flexibility in manufacturing processes. The plant consists of twin units (one producing cotton garments and shirts, the other tailored garments, skirts, and jeans), an automated distribution center, and a unit dedicated to the production of woolen garments. One of Benetton's most innovative systems is Robostore 2000, an automated packaging and distribution system. Nineteen staff persons manage the system, which handles over 30,000 packages a day, organizing deliveries according to geographical area and individual client. The system, and other automated systems at Benetton, has considerably improved the efficiency and speed of customer service while reducing transport costs.

Benetton is well known for its research into new composite materials and innovative product design. This research has been applied successfully to its sports clothing and sports equipment products of tennis rackets, skis, and snowboards.

The company maintains an efficient transaction processing system. When a customer purchases a sweater, for example, in Boston, Massachusetts, the details of the sale (product color, size, quantity, and so on) are captured with a point-of-sale bar code scanner and transmitted electronically to a computer system in Italy. The sale's details are combined with other transactions from outlets worldwide to determine the daily production schedule at each of the seven factories. The company does not dye its sweaters until it receives information on which retail stores need colors. This manufacturing process allows Benetton to rapidly adjust the product mix to changes in customer demand. After the sweaters are dyed, they are shipped directly from the centralized warehouse to the retail outlets, with quantities of different products determined by the recent sales transactions. Similarly, items that are not selling in each retail outlet are monitored closely and removed on a regular basis.

Benetton maintains so much detailed information in its database that it can fine-tune products to the demographics and tastes of the customers of each store. Colors, styles, and sizes can be adjusted to the specific characteristics of customers for stores only a few blocks apart.

Adapted from the Benetton Web site at http://www.benetton.it.

Discussion Questions

1. Use the system model to describe Benetton as a system. Discuss the purpose of Benetton; its environment, inputs, processes, and outputs; and how it handles feedback.

2. Discuss the primary and support activities in Benetton's value chain.

3. Describe the types of transactions Benetton handles on a day-to-day basis.

4. Discuss the challenges of Benetton's information systems due to its large global presence.

L'Oréal's Data Warehouse

The main distribution facility for cosmetic giant L'Oréal's Retail division in Cranbury, N.J., ships over 200 million hair-care and cosmetic products every year to mass volume retailers and food and drug chains around the country. L'Oréal used to keep shipping and point-of-sale (POS) information locked up in a number of separate databases, making it difficult for employees to retrieve the figures necessary for determining sales, identifying hot products, and determining candidates for advertising campaigns. But now, L'Oréal is developing a data warehousing system to incorporate all sales information under one roof. The system is expected to eliminate inefficiency in data management, improve internal communications, upgrade sales-force automation, and pave the way for the Information Systems department to redefine its role from data processing to strategic leadership.

Prior to the data warehousing system, L'Oréal recorded tremendous amounts of sales and marketing information, but the data was so disorganized that few employees outside the Information Systems department knew how to find it. Net sales figures were in one set of files, while data on returns was somewhere else. If a marketing executive wanted information about shipments and returns on a particular product, he or she had to ask a programmer to produce a custom report. Sometimes, when programmers were preoccupied with other work, such requests would take as long as two weeks to fill. Once employees received their reports, it could take them days to interpret them. Most reports were 32 columns wide and contained more than 50 pages, making it difficult for employees to locate the information they needed.

The new data warehousing system is being implemented on a state-of-the-art NT SQL 7.0 server. The system enables L'Oréal employees to view the data through a Web browser and reduces the wait time on some queries to three seconds.

During the system's development, several users and administrators served as a core team to support the project from a business perspective, and L'Oréal's senior management team formed a governance committee to resolve business issues. These users established procedures to move data from the old shipping systems into the data warehouse so that the data conformed to the new, standard definitions for the data. For example, the term "net sales" used to mean something different to everyone, but now everyone knows the same way to calculate net sales. Having standard definitions of data enables L'Oréal's managers to focus more on understanding the numbers rather than struggling with their meanings. One of the most important aspects of the data warehousing project was to improve interdepartmental communication.

The data warehouse has already come in handy in preparing for the next fiscal year. How many bottles of L'Oréal for Kids shampoo were delivered to Wal-Mart this summer? Of those, how many were sold? Marketing employees can use answers to questions like these to determine advertising and promotional strategies for the new millennium. Users report that the new system is quicker and more efficient than the old one. They also say they appreciate how the system enables them to retrieve data themselves, without calling on the Information Systems department.

It will take another year to complete the data warehouse system project. L'Oréal expects the system to result in speedy delivery of other business applications, faster and better sales-force automation, and the ability to get at data in ways the old system did not allow. L'Oréal employees will be able to use the warehouse not only to see how its products are selling but also to see how L'Oréal products compete with products from other companies.

Adapted from Matt Villano, "Data Gets a Makeover," *CIO Magazine*, October 1, 1999, http://www.cio.com/archive/100199_inprintcio.html; and L'Oreal's Web sites, 2001: www.loreal.com and http://www.lorealpro.net/

Discussion Questions

1. Identify some of the primary and support activities in L'Oréal's value chain.
2. Discuss how L'Oréal's data warehouse system supports the company's transaction processing.
3. Discuss the benefits of L'Oréal's data warehousing system.
4. Identify the roles people play in designing and using L'Oréal's data warehousing system.

Sources and Resources

Books

Understanding Media: The Extensions of Man, by Marshall McLuhan (New York: McGraw-Hill,1964). This is the classic book in which McLuhan explores the way electronic media reflect and influence modern civilization. McLuhan's other best known works are *The Gutenberg Galaxy: The Making of Typographic Man* (Toronto: University of Toronto Press, 1962) in which he introduces the phrase "global village" as a metaphor of contemporary society, and *The Mechanical Bride: Folklore of Industrial Man* (Toronto, Vanguard Press, 1951) the title of which is a typical McLuhan pun.

The Structure of Scientific Revolutions, Second Edition, by Thomas Kuhn (Chicago: University of Chicago Press, 1970). This landmark book shows how scientific progress is built on paradigm shifts—radical new world views that challenge and threaten the status quo. The social dynamics described here apply to business, technology, and countless other human endeavors.

A Better Way to Think About Business: How Personal Integrity Leads to Corporate Success, by Robert C. Solomon (Oxford University Press, 1999). Have you ever thought that business ethics is a contradiction in terms? Solomon doesn't think so. He writes that corporations are members of the larger community and that without a base of shared values and trust, today's national and international business world would fall apart.

The Dilbert Principle, by Scott Adams (New York: HarperBusiness, 1997) and *The Dilbert Future*, by Scott Adams (New York: HarperBusiness, 1998). These books, like the Dilbert comic strip, are packed with irreverent insights into the inner workings of the information age workplace. Adams clearly understands the world he satirizes—he has an MBA from Berkeley and 17 years' experience in a cubicle working for Pacific Bell.

Evolve!; Succeeding in the Digital Culture of Tomorrow, by Rosabeth Moss Kanter (Boston: Harvard Business School Press; 2001). The book challenges the new economy with having had a "lobotomy" about basic business fundamentals. Using examples from both private and public sector companies, Kanter shows how digital innovation can be achieved within a company. She skewers the cliches and uses them to expose the shallow thinking that has led to disaster. She gets beyond the technical whiz bang to look at the human possibilities of a global community.

Mission Critical: Realizing the Promise of Enterprise Systems, by Thomas H. Davenport (Boston: Harvard Business School Press; 2000). As information-dependent companies of all types continually expand and globalize, the need to share critical data between far-flung sites increases dramatically. This text is an introduction to Enterprise Resource Planning systems and how they are useful for organizations. The text is easy to understand and gives real world examples of benefits and pitfalls of different implementation methods and gives you a good idea of the magnitude of an ERP project.

Cyberethics: Social & Moral Issues in the Computer Age by Robert M. Baird, Reagan Mays Ramsower , and Stuart E. Rosenbaum (Editors) (New York: Prometheus Books, 2000). This very readable book explores the moral dilemmas that are arising as computer technology penetrates further into our professional, private, and social lives. The book is an anthology of 26 essays exploring issues such as anonymity, personal identity, and the moral dimensions of creating new personalities; privacy; ownership of intellectual property and copyright law; and the impact of computers on democracy and community.

The Cluetrain Manifesto: The End of Business as Usual, by Christopher Locke, Rick Levine, Doc Searls, David Weinberger (Perseus Books, 2000). *The Cluetrain Manifesto* began as a Web site (www.cluetrain.com) in 1999 when the authors posted 95 theses pronouncing what they felt was the new reality of the networked marketplace. For example, thesis 2: "Markets consist of human beings, not demographic sectors," and thesis 20: "Companies need to realize their markets are often laughing. At them," and thesis 62: "Markets do not want to talk to flacks and hucksters. They want to participate in the conversations going on behind the corporate firewall." The book enlarges on these themes through seven essays filled with dozens of stories and observations about how business gets done in America and how the Internet will change it all.

Periodicals

Computerworld. This weekly newspaper for computer professionals has a section called "Computer Careers" with advice and information on information technology professions.

Business Week. Besides national and international business news, this magazine publishes interesting articles about the information industry and the use of information technologies in companies.

Information Week. This magazine is laid out much like *Business Week* and contains interesting articles covering the information industry. It's a good source for business-related Web sites.

Upside. This magazine is aimed at managers, entrepreneurs, and others who want to track the business side, rather than the technological side, of the computer industry.

Darwin. This magazine's theme is showing how business is evolving in the information age and the individual and social impacts of this evolution.

Professional Organizations for Information Workers

Association for Computing Machinery (ACM)
http://www.acm.org (You'll find the complete text of the ACM's Code of Ethics in the Appendix of this book.)

Association of Information Technology Professionals (AITP)
http://www.aitp.org

Association of Information Systems (AIS)
http://www.aisnet.org/

Institute for Certification of Computer Professionals (ICCP)
http://www.iccp.org/

Institute of Electrical and Electronics Engineers (IEEE)
http://www.ieee.org

International Federation for Information Processing (IFIP)
http://www.ifip.or.at/

Society of Information Management (SIM)
http://www.simnet.org/

The American Society for Information Science
http://www.asis.org

Web Pages

The Web has become a hotbed of business activity in recent years; .com is the fastest growing domain on the Web. Look for links to the best .com sites on the *Computer Confluence* Web site.

14

Information Technology in Management

After reading this chapter, you should be able to:

Describe several aspects of management, the information needs of managers, and the types of decisions managers make

Describe basic communication concepts and several ways that information technologies are used to help managers collaborate and communicate more effectively

Describe several decision-making concepts and ways that information technologies are used to help managers make decisions more effectively

List several strategies business organizations use to succeed in a competitive environment

Discuss how a business organization can use information technologies to counter competitive forces in the environment

Describe how a business organization can use information technologies to compete effectively by improving efficiency and by improving its products and services

Describe the issues that should be included in an organization's information code of ethics

▼ In this chapter:

The types of managers and their information needs

How managers use information technology to communicate and make decisions

How organizations compete with information technology

The elements of an information code of ethics

. . . *and more.*

▼ On the CD-ROM:

Video clip showing how information technology is used to support strategy decisions

Instant access to glossary and key word references

Interactive self-study quizzes

. . . *and more.*

▼ On the Web:

www.prenhall.com/beekman

Articles on the competitive use of information technologies by organizations

Links to various types of communication and decision making technology companies

Resources for exploring decision making and other management activities

Self-study exercises

. . . *and more.*

Andy Grove, the Paranoid Chip Merchant

Only the **paranoid survive**.

—Andrew Grove

The competition in the computer industry is fierce. Andy Grove, cofounder and now chairperson of the board of Intel, is always worrying about big issues affecting the computer industry: Why do people watch so much TV? Why are people so enthralled with PCs if they are frustrating to use? Why were he and Microsoft's Bill Gates and other industry hotshots surprised by the sudden popularity of the Internet?

Grove worries, but he has faith in three principles he uses to manage Intel: Moore's Law, the Cannibal Principle, and his own Grove's Law. Gordon Moore, another cofounder of Intel, observed that the performance of chip technology, as measured against its price, doubles every 18 months or so. This observation, dubbed Moore's Law, explains why computer hardware often seems outdated within months of purchase. The Cannibal Principle, also stated by Moore, says that semiconductor technology absorbs the functions of what previously were discrete electronic components onto a single new chip. That's why computer components can be packed with more and more features at lower and lower cost. Moore's Law and the Cannibal Principle guarantee a wide-open future for the semiconductor industry. But Andy Grove likes to worry about the competition, so he follows a third principle of his own: Only the paranoid survive.

Observing these principles, Grove led Intel to become the world's largest maker of computer chips. He helped start Intel in 1968 and as CEO led Intel from tenth place to the top of the heap in the semiconductor industry. He now serves as Intel's chairman of the board. Intel has built microprocessors that power more than 80 percent of the world's personal computers and has become one of the most profitable companies in America doing it. In 2000, Intel had record sales of $33.7 billion worldwide, with 59 percent of its sales coming from outside the United States. Intel employs more than 70,000 people in more than 40 nations worldwide.

But is Grove satisfied? No! (Remember Grove's Law.) Grove's goal for Intel is to be the global standard for consumer computers. He envisions computers that will incorporate all the features and capabilities of today's best multimedia PCs but as standard equipment and at

Andy Grove

much lower cost. The key is to develop processors, such as the Pentium 4 with advanced video processing capabilities and the soon-to-be-introduced Itanium, the first in a family of 64-bit products from Intel with capabilities of processing terabytes of data, speeding protected online purchases and transactions, and processing complex computations. This strategy challenges Microsoft's primacy and other competitors as well. Grove says that the typical PC doesn't come close to pushing the limits of Intel's microprocessor, primarily because Microsoft's software hasn't kept pace with Intel's designs. Using Moore's Law and the Cannibal Principle, Grove assumes that Intel's processors will improve continuously in performance and take over many functions that now require extra chips, add-on hardware, and extra software. Grove envisions microprocessors of the future subsuming today's game players, TVs, and VCRs and becoming the basis for superb digital entertainment and communication machines.

Grove is always worrying about the issues that face Intel. For example, when Intel introduced the Pentium chip in 1994, customers found a flaw in the chip. After initially down playing the problem, the company was forced by competitive necessity to replace the flawed chips for free and modify its marketing and customer support practices. Grove managed to sell some of the arithmetically challenged chips to jewelry makers for use in cufflinks and earrings. Also, he dreamed up the phenomenally successful "Intel Inside" advertising campaign that helped dampen sales of clones of Intel microprocessors made by competitors.

He has no doubt it is necessary for him and his employees to be paranoid of the industry's competitive forces and be afraid of competitors. But he has no doubt that fear inside the company is harmful. Although Grove's management style is straightforward and results oriented, he believes a leader must be sure that no one in an organization is afraid to express an opinion. He attributes much of the success of Intel to having created a healthy work environment in which mtivated people can flourish. But Grove's Law probably keeps him awake nights, wondering how to push his competitors to the limit. ▶

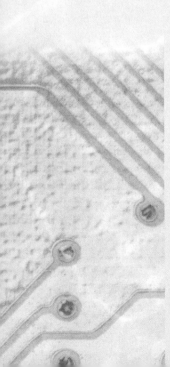

The phenomenal success of Andrew Grove and Intel isn't accidental. Grove's victories in the microprocessor wars are due in large part to his ability to think strategically and to harness information technology to manage Intel well to support his business strategies.

In this chapter, we'll explore the information technologies that support managerial work in an organization. First we'll review some of the characteristics of managerial work and the importance for managers to get the right information, at the right time, in the right form. Then we'll look at various types of information systems managers use to communicate and make decisions. We'll end the chapter with a discussion of how managers use information technology strategically to compete effectively with other companies.

Managing a Business or Organization

> Businessmen go down with their businesses because they like the **old way** so well they cannot **bring themselves to change**.
>
> —Henry Ford

Managers have several functions in an organization, all aimed at accomplishing the goals and objectives of the firm. The functions of management are supported by information technologies discussed in this chapter.

Every organization has limited time, money, and people. To stay in business, an organization must use these resources wisely . **Management** is a set of activities that helps people efficiently use resources to accomplish an organization's goals. Small entrepreneurial companies have at least one person designated as a manager. Large multinational organizations may have hundreds of managers. No matter the size of the organization, managing is a complex job involving many different tasks and information needs.

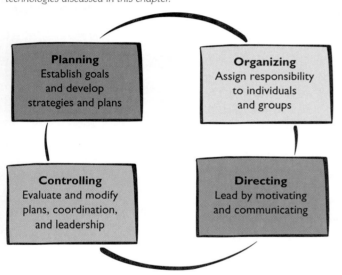

The Functions and Roles of a Manager

> The most **important quality in a leader** is that of being acknowledged as such.
>
> —André Maurois, French author

Managers have several responsibilities in an organization. These responsibilities, referred to as **management functions**, are to plan, organize, direct, and control the various business processes in the company. A manager typically must decide on goals and design plans to accomplish them (plan), delegate authority and responsibility to people in the organization to accomplish the plan (organize), motivate and communicate appropriately with his or her employees (direct), and evaluate the organization's progress toward achieving the desired goals (control).

Managers play several roles in an organization, interacting with other managers, employees, customers, vendors, and other people. At any one time managers may have to assume all three roles expected of them.

Managers also play several roles when they interact with people, both inside and outside the organization. These **management roles** are interpersonal, informational, and decisional. For example, a manager typically uses his or her interpersonal skills to encourage and motivate employees, to speak or preside at dinners or other formal functions, and to interact with vendors, customers, labor union representatives, politicians, and even competitors. Playing an information role, a manager may gather, analyze, and distribute important information about the organization. In a decision-making role, a manager might decide, for example, how to improve a business process, how to react to a new product announced by a competitor, how to allocate resources to different projects, and how to resolve disputes between employees.

Decision-making is important in all managerial functions and roles. In a university organization for example, there are managers at different levels in the university (such as the president, provost, deans, and directors of various administrative offices) that must use information to

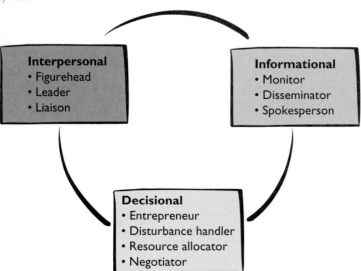

decide how to solve all types of problems. We will now take a quick look at the interplay of managers' information needs for three types of decisions at three levels in an organization.

Types of Management Decisions

> Humans fear reason, but they ought to **fear stupidity**— for reason can be hard, but **stupidity can be fatal.**
> —Goethe, German writer, 1749–1832

Managers use information technology to make effective decisions. To understand how information technologies can be useful, it is important to understand the three types of decisions that managers make: structured, semistructured, and unstructured.

Managers use several methods to solve different types of problems in various decision-making situations.

A manager makes a **structured decision** when he or she understands the situation clearly and uses established procedures and information to resolve the problem. Structured decisions, such as deciding how many inventory items to reorder in a university caféteria, are usually relatively simple and routine and can sometimes be made by a computer. Some structured decisions, such as deciding a university's department course schedule for the semester, can be very complex, because they involve many established procedures and large quantities of information.

A manager makes a **semistructured decision** when there's some uncertainty about a problem and the manager must use his or her judgment. For example, a car dealership manager may need to decide how many of a new model automobile to order for delivery three months in the future but is uncertain about the actual demand for the model.

Decision type	Problem type	Methodology
Structured	Repetitive, routine	Procedures, rules
Semistructured	Partial structure, Partial "fuzzy"	Judgment, procedure
Unstructured	"Fuzzy," complex	Judgment, intuition

Sometimes a manager faces unique circumstances or must anticipate events over a relatively long period of time. In these situations, a manager must make an **unstructured decision** requiring many quantitative and ethical judgments that have no clear answers. For example, a manager may need to decide how the company should respond to a competitor that has introduced an entirely new product line with excellent customer services.

Levels of Management

We have seen that there are three different types of decisions a manager can make: structured, semi-structured, and unstructured. However, not every manager will be involved in making each of these. There are three **management levels** in an organization: operational, tactical, and strategic. Managers have different functions and roles and face different types of decisions at each level.

A manager at the *operational level* is responsible for supervising the day-to-day activities in the organization's value chain (see Chapter 13, "Systems and Organizations in the Information Age," for more on the value chain). Operational level managers are also referred to as lower-level managers, supervisors, and group leaders. They decide on short-term plans, such as production and work schedules, and follow established guidelines and budgets. Most operational-level decisions are structured, but semistructured decisions do occur—for example, resolving a work scheduling disagreement between employees.

A manager at the tactical level is called a middle manager and may be responsible for a large organizational unit, such as a sales region or a production plant. Typically, a middle manager develops short-term plans for the next year or so and then makes

An organization usually has a hierarchy of managers responsible for work at several levels.

Top managers
• plan and control overall organizational direction

Middle managers
• plan and control organizational units

Lower-level mana[
• plan and control da[
business processes

sure his or her employees perform according to the plans. Semistructured decisions are common at this level. Tactical level managers responsible for the development and use of information systems in an organization are called information systems managers.

A manager at the *strategic level* is called a top manager and is responsible for the long-range issues related to the business' growth and development. Top managers include the board of directors, chief executive officers, and vice-presidents. They must cope with situations that require relatively unstructured decisions—for example, new business plans, company reorganizations, and joint ventures with other companies. The top manager responsible for the overall planning of information systems in an organization is called the **chief information officer (CIO)**.

Management Information Requirements

We have advanced to the point where the **means** we use **to communicate are more elegant and important than what we have to say**.

—Andy Rooney, author

Managers need accurate information that corresponds to their function, role, and level of management, the types of decisions they make, and their personal characteristics.

Think of the information requirements of a manager as information characteristics categorized in three dimensions: time, content, and form. The time dimension of information relates to when the information was created, how frequently the information is needed, how often it is updated, and whether the information relates to past, present, or future time periods. The content dimension of information relates to its accuracy and completeness, how relevant the information is, whether the information has a broad or narrow scope, and whether the source of the information is within the organization (internal information) or from the environment (external information). The form dimension of information relates to how the information is arranged and presented in a report, whether the report contains detailed or summary information, and what medium is used to present the information—printed-paper, video display, or a Web page.

An important organizational goal based on these information characteristics is to provide a manager relevant information—the right information (content) at the right time and in the right form—for the situation at hand. For example, an operational manager making a structured

Information has several dimensions and characteristics that can be adjusted to make the information more valuable to a manager.

Dimensions and Characteristics of Information

Dimension	Characteristic	Comment
Time	Timeliness	Information is provided when it is needed
	Currency	Information is up-to-date when it is provided
	Frequency	Information is provided as often as needed
	Time period	Information is provided about past, present, and future time periods depending on the manager's needs
Content	Accuracy	Information is error-free
	Relevance	Information is useful to a manager for a specific situation
	Completeness	All the information that is needed is provided
	Conciseness	Only the information that is needed is given
	Scope	Information has a broad or narrow scope, or an internal or external focus depending on the manager's needs
Form	Clarity	Information is provided in a form that is easy to understand
	Detail	Information is provided at a level of detail that is needed
	Order	Information is arranged in a useful sequence
	Presentation	Information is presented in narrative, numeric, graphic, or other forms
	Media	Information is shown on printed paper, video displays, or on other media

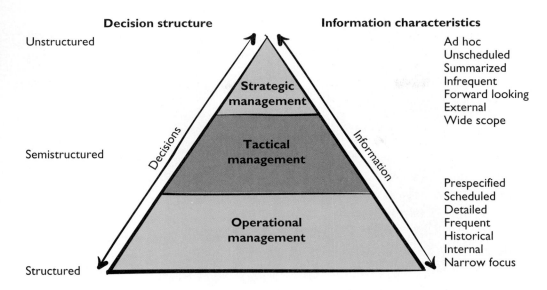

Decision structure   **Information characteristics**

Unstructured

Strategic management

Tactical management

Operational management

Semistructured

Structured

Decisions

Information

Ad hoc
Unscheduled
Summarized
Infrequent
Forward looking
External
Wide scope

Prespecified
Scheduled
Detailed
Frequent
Historical
Internal
Narrow focus

decision would probably need current, accurate, and detailed information to make sure the day-to-day work schedule is being maintained. A middle manager making a semistructured decision about a marketing plan would probably need historical and future-oriented information about the sales performance of particular products. A top manager making an unstructured decision about developing a new product line would need to have both internal and external information presented in an easy-to-understand form.

A manager can easily receive too much relevant information presented awkwardly. Using the information technologies described in this chapter, a manager can *filter* the information by manipulating the time, content, and form dimensions in an indefinite number of ways to make the information more valuable and useful, depending on the situation.

Information Technology to Support Managerial Communications

> Without **communications** there would be no **life**.
> —Norbert Wiener

It is important that managers facilitate the flow of information among themselves and others to achieve a high level of collaboration among employees in the organization. Especially in today's global business environment, with an increasing emphasis on using the Internet, communication is critical for individuals to be able to work together, both in the same and in dispersed locations. Managers spend up to 90 percent of their time communicating with other persons in the organization and in the company's external environment. Part of this time is wasted because of ineffective or inefficient collection, processing, or distribution of information. In a recent survey of over 500 organizations, CEOs answered most frequently that if they could go back and change one thing in their companies it would be the way they communicate with their employees. In this section, we'll examine basic communication concepts and explore ways information technologies can provide more timely communication.

Communication Concepts

Communication is a social process of people exchanging ideas or other messages through some physical medium. For communication to occur a sender must convey the message in some physical form, such as voice, text, or graphics. The message

Communication involves a person expressing an idea (using text, voice, pictures, or other media) and sending it through a channel to another person who interpets the message. Feedback helps to clarify a garbled or unclear message.)

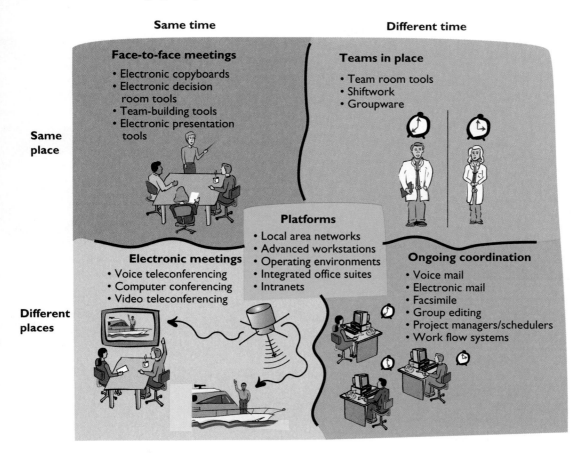

Information technologies can be used to improve communications in several types of situations.

must be transmitted reliably through a communication channel, such as the phone, the mail, or the Internet. A receiver must receive the message and interpret it.

You need to consider several important factors when you use information technology to improve a communication process. The number of people participating in a communication can vary—a person might send a message to one other person, called *one-to-one communication*, or to many other people, called *one-to-many communication*. The physical location of a sender and receiver can vary from being in the same room, called *same-place communication*, to geographically dispersed locations around the globe, called *different-places communication*. The time difference between when a message is sent and when it is received can vary from simultaneous or *same-time communication*, to hours, days, or longer, called *different-time communication*.

Combining the time and place dimensions result in four typical communication situations. Same-time/same-place communication occurs in face-to-face meetings; same-time/different-places communication occurs also in meetings, but where the participants are in different offices or other places; different-times/same-place communication occurs when people work in shifts and leave messages for different shifts; and different-times/different-places communication occurs when the participants are located anywhere and send and receive messages at any time.

All of these variables suggest that there are many ways of using information technology to improve communication processes in an organization. For example, companies are utilizing email technologies to increase the number of messages transmitted to more people who need the information and to make sure messages go only to the people who need to know the information. Increasingly, companies are utilizing high-speed networks to eliminate unnecessary time delays between sending and receiving a message, especially in international situations. And organizations use multimedia technologies, especially virtual reality, to vary the form of messages so the receiver can use them more effectively.

Collaborative Work

 Three **helping one another** will do as much as six **working singly**.

—Spanish proverb

If a company has geographically dispersed offices in different time zones, managers from these different offices can form collaborative workgroups and use information technology to communicate. A workgroup can be a committee, a product design team, an executive board, or any other group of people who act as a single social unit to perform some task. There are many benefits of collaborative work to the organization and to the people in the group. For example, groups are sometimes better than an individual at understanding complex situations, people feel more involved and accountable for decisions in which they participate, and there can be a synergy among group members that results in effective and high-quality work. On the other hand, poor communication, social pressures, inappropriate social dynamics, work shirking, and time wasting can lead to less than effective collaborative work.

Groupware is software that enables groups of users to share calendars, send messages, access data, and work on documents simultaneously. The best groupware applications enable workgroups to do things that would be difficult or impossible otherwise; they actually change the way people work in groups. Many of these applications focus on the concept of *workflow*—the path of information as it flows through a workgroup. With groupware and telecommunication, workgroups don't need to be in the same room, or even the same time zone. For example, a Big Three automaker can get a body design from Germany and an engine design from Japan and combine the two in real-time for review by engineers in a Detroit conference room. During much of the 1990s, Lotus Notes dominated this market, offering a complete, though expensive, workgroup solution for corporations.

However, the advent of the World Wide Web changed the workgroup landscape. The prospect of simultaneous collaboration, across geographies, time zones, and corporate boundaries, has only been possible recently as more companies and vendors take advantage of the lightning capabilities of the Internet. Many of the functions of groupware—email, teleconferencing, shared databases, electronic publishing, and others—are available now for little or no cost through freely available Internet technologies. Corporations are installing *intranets* using HTML, Web browsers, and other Internet technologies that enable managers and employees to access and share the company's internal data and to collaborate on projects easily. And because these intranets are built on standardized protocols like TCP/IP, corporations can open up their intranets to strategic partners and customers, creating *extranets*. Lotus and other groupware manufacturers have responded by rebuilding their applications using standard Internet technologies and protocols, so their customers can have the best of both worlds: computer systems built on universal public standards, and customer support and customization from a groupware specialist. We'll discuss inranets and extranets more fully in the next chapter.

Distributed Computing

In the age of networks, the challenge for a company's chief information officer (CIO) and other information systems managers is to integrate all kinds of computers into a single, seamless system. This approach, often called distributed computing, allows PCs, workstations, network computers, and mainframes to coexist peacefully and complement each other. Many organizations are adding *thin clients—network computers, Internet appliances*, and wireless devices—to the mix. These low-cost, low-maintenance machines enable managers and workers to access critical network information without the overhead of a PC or workstation. Portable wireless devices such as phones, pagers, and computers with mobile modems are becoming the Internet access devices of choice by many companies.

People throughout business organizations use personal computers: Workers use word processing software to generate memos and reports, marketing teams create promotional pieces using desktop publishing tools, and financial departments analyze budgets using spreadsheets. They communicate with each other and with the outside world electronically, sending electronic mail through networks. If a business uses mainframes to house databases, office workers use desktop computers to access that data. In many integrated client/server systems, users view everything, including mainframe data, through a familiar PC interface. If the organization uses intranet technology, users may view corporate data using a standard Web browser. They don't

Workgroup Computing with Lotus Notes

Groupware software, such as Lotus Notes, is used by people in workgroups to organize and share information about projects and other activities. Each group member can create | *documents and access and modify documents created by others in the group.*

2 Group members can organize documents in folders within a database in the same way you can organize documents in folders on your disk.

3 You can use the menu bar to create, save, and print documents, to edit documents, and to change the view of information on the desktop.

1 The Lotus Note's work surface, or desktop, contains menus, tabbed pages, and database icons.

4 Group members can store documents they create and use on a particular topic as a database. Each database is represented as an icon. Group members can create any number of databases and group the database icons on a tabbed page for convenience.

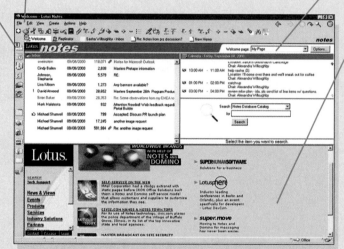

5 You double-click the appropriate database icon to access the documents you want to work with. A group member can leave the databases that are needed most often during the day open on the desktop.

6 Group members can organize documents in folders within a database in the same way you can organize documents in folders on your disk.

7 Group members can collaborate in the process of writing a document, such as a product development proposal. You can scroll through the list of documents in a database to find the document you need. You can open a document that other group members created and modified previously.

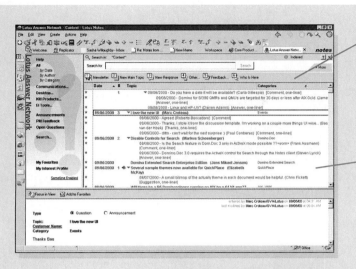

8 Any group member can respond to another group member's message. You click the Responses button to create a response to a selected message. Lotus Notes keeps track of the responses to each message.

9 Group members can use Lotus Notes to brainstorm and exchange ideas informally. You can type comments, ideas, and other information as a document, much like an email message.

10 You can use Lotus Notes to send and receive email and fax messages. You can communicate with other group members, people in other workgroups in your organization, or anyone else on the Internet. You use the toolbar to customize the Mail screen for your convenience.

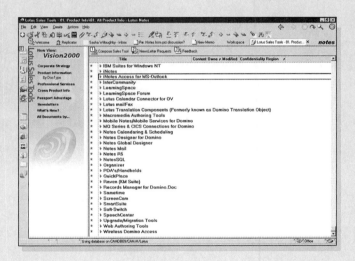

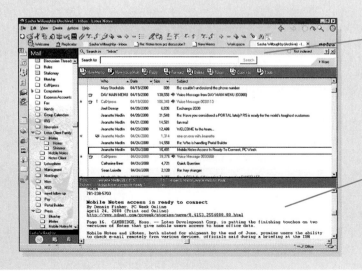

11 Group members can organize their own Inbox folder for private or personal messages from others. You can select an incoming message and view it in the preview window. You can use the toolbar to reply to or forward a message, or store a message to another folder.

12 You can view and edit the document in a preview window. Lotus Notes automatically keeps track of who modified the document and when.

need to know where or how information is stored; the network quietly moves data back and forth to meet user needs.

The Automated Office

If we want our institutions to be more productive, then **we must learn to focus** the power of **information technology** not on the institutions themselves but on the **individuals** inside the institutions.

—John Sculley, in Odyssey

An **automated office** enables individuals, workgroups, and organizations to acquire, process, store, and distribute information electronically, using computers and telecommunication networks. In earlier chapters (especially Chapters 9, "Networking and Telecommunication," and 10, "Inside the Internet and the Web,"), we explored a variety of information technologies that can be used to enable and enhance communication in a modern office and reduce paper flow. Some of these technologies include: electronic and voice mail; facsimile; Internet technologies, such as the intranets and Internet newsgroups; and various types of conferencing technologies. The illustration on page xxx shows the usefulness of these technologies in the time/place communication matrix.

Computer conferencing, voice teleconferencing, and video teleconferencing fall under the general category of **electronic meeting** technologies; they enable members of a workgroup to conduct meetings even when participants are scattered around the world. New multimedia technologies eliminate the need for special video teleconferencing rooms by allowing participants to see and hear each other through personal computers equipped with video cameras and microphones. While participants conduct on-screen discussions, they can view and exchange documents in real time.

Managers find that video teleconferencing with people in different places at the same time can be effective.

Experts have predicted the **paperless office**—an office of the future in which magnetic and optical archives will replace reference books and file cabinets, digital documents will replace letters and memos, and digital publications provided through the Internet and online services will replace newspapers and other periodicals. In the automated, paperless office, people will read computer screens, not paper documents.

All of these trends are real: digital storage media are replacing many paper depositories; computers now deliver more mail messages than postal carriers do; and the World Wide Web has accelerated a trend toward online publishing. But so far, computers haven't reduced the flow of paper-based information. What has changed is the way people tend to use paper in the office. According to Paul Saffo of the Institute for the Future, "We've shifted from paper as storage to paper as interface. It is an ever more volatile, disposable, and temporary display medium."

To reduce the flow of paper, a growing number of organizations are using **document imaging systems** that can scan, store, retrieve, and route bit-mapped images of paper documents. These systems generally include scanners for converting paper pages to digital documents, high-capacity disk drives for storing the document images, and fax machines for sending document images to remote locations.

Interorganizational Information Systems

Another way a company can automate communications and reduce paper flow between itself and its suppliers, customers, and other organizations is through an interorganizational information system. **Interorganizational information systems (IOS)** use networking and telecommunication technologies that enable a company to share business data and exchange transactions

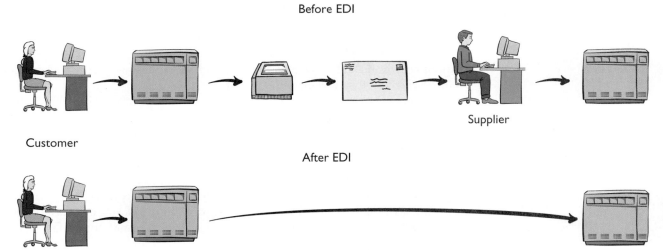

Before EDI

Customer

Supplier

After EDI

with other companies electronically. There are two forms of IOS—electronic data interchange and business alliances.

Electronic Data Interchange (EDI

As we saw in Chapter 13, "Systems and Organizations in the Information Age," Electronic Data Interchange (EDI) is the direct, computer-to-computer exchange of standardized, common business transaction documents, such as purchase orders and invoices, between business partners, suppliers, and customers. EDI uses international standards for data formatting that enable companies to exchange large amounts of information in real time around the world.

EDI systems have been developed for particular business partners in specific industries for several decades. In the retail clothing industry for example, Dillards department store uses EDI to send purchase orders electronically to Haggar, one of its apparel manufacturers. If Haggar doesn't have the cloth to manufacture a needed item of clothing, Haggar uses EDI to place an order electronically with the textile manufacturer Burlington Industries. In the automotive industry, Ford, General Motors, and other car manufacturers use EDI to order parts from their suppliers; in turn, the suppliers must agree to implement EDI and use it for transactions with the car manufacturer. In the federal government arena, all contractors wanting government contracts are required to link into the government's EDI systems.

EDI can integrate the order entry activity of a customer and the order filling activity of a supplier. In this case Dillard's, the customer, orders clothing from Haggar, the supplier. Integration is possible because EDI enables the customer and the supplier to use consistent technical standards and share information about each other's activities. Integration increases efficiency for both the customer and the supplier by eliminating delays and increasing accuracy.

Calyx & Corolla uses information technology to maintain business alliances for selling and delivering flowers to customers directly.

Business Alliances

A **business alliance** is a cooperative arrangement between two or more businesses with complementary capabilities. A good example is Calyx & Corolla, a direct-mail flower company. Calyx & Corolla maintains customer databases, a Web site, and online catalog, and it does all its own marketing. But rather than create its own distribution system, Calyx & Corolla has an agreement with FedEx who handles the logistics of delivering the flowers from the growers to the customers. Similarly, Calyx & Corolla has an agreement with MasterCard and American Express who handle all the credit authorization and paymet activities. Calyx & Corolla also created

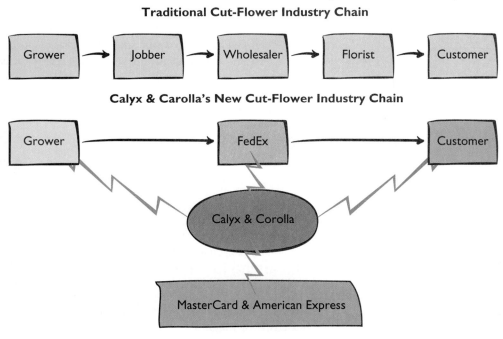

Traditional Cut-Flower Industry Chain

Grower → Jobber → Wholesaler → Florist → Customer

Calyx & Carolla's New Cut-Flower Industry Chain

Grower → FedEx → Customer

Calyx & Corolla

MasterCard & American Express

alliances with independent flower growers worldwide. All of these arrangements are supported with information technology. When a customer order is entered on Calyx & Corolla's Web site, the customer's credit is verified electronically with MasterCard or American Express; the order is sent electronically to the appropriate flower grower and to FedEX; and MasterCard or American Express charges the bill to the customer's account and transmits electronically payments to FedEx, Calyx & Corolla, and the flower grower.

Another example of a business alliance is an *information partnership* in which the companies, usually in different industries, share information for their mutual benefit. For example, United Airlines and MCI WorldCom have an arrangement in which customers receive United Airlines frequent flyer miles for MCI WorldCom services. By sharing information, these types of partnerships help companies gain new customers and subsequently new opportunities for cross-selling and targeting products.

A type of business alliance that is becoming more feasible because of the Internet is *industrial networks* in which the systems of several companies in an industry are linked. An example is the system Procter & Gamble has developed to coordinate its manufacturing facilities and suppliers with grocery store point-of-sale systems, warehouses, and shippers. The system enables Procter & Gamble and its business partners to monitor all its products from raw materials to customer purchase.

International Information Systems

Information technologies, especially networks, telecommunications, and the Internet, have made it economically feasible for a company to do business internationally and conduct its business processes virtually any time and anywhere. Using the appropriate technology, a company can communicate effectively with suppliers and customers located anywhere in the world, employ engineers and designers in a number of different countries, and have production facilities located at cost-effective geographic sites worldwide. Any information system that supports international business activities is called an **international information system.**

The international business environment poses several challenges compared to a purely domestic business environment. An international environment is multilingual and multicultural, has multiple governments, has many different regulations regarding privacy and intellectual property protection, has varying standards for telecommunications and other technologies, and has multiple geographic conditions, time zones, and monetary currencies. All of these factors affect the flow of data between countries, commonly called **transborder data flow.**

Developing an international information system to facilitate transborder data flows is fraught with difficulties and ethical dilemmas. For example, some countries do not allow personal data about employees to leave the country. Many countries have weak, nonexistent, or poorly enforced software copyright laws. Inexpensive labor costs in one country may be the result of what another country considers unethical labor practices. Some countries have poorly maintained and aging telecommunication infrastructures. Even though good business practices make sense around the world, you cannot ignore the issues that are unique to a particular country.

In a broader context, *electronic commerce* (which we'll discuss in the next chapter) characterizes how organizations are conducting business processes using Internet technologies on a global scale.

Information Technology to Support Managerial Decision Making

We are moving very rapidly in all forms of production and services to a **knowledge-based economy** in which what you earn depends on what you can learn. Not only what you know today, but **what you are capable of learning tomorrow**.
—Tracy LaQuey, in *The Internet Companion*

In addition to communication, managerial work requires decision making. In many ways, it is more difficult to make decisions in today's business environment than it has been in the past. How can a manager choose among a large number of alternative solutions made possible by modern technology? Because many modern organizations use large, complex, interconnected systems, the risk—and cost—of making a wrong decision can be massive, especially when you consider the international nature of business today. On the other hand, the benefits can be immense when wise decisions ripple rapidly through a tightly linked organization. Before we look at information technology tools that help managers make decisions more effectively, we'll examine the decision-making process and the most common styles of decision making.

Decision-making Concepts

Decision making is a process that includes four phases—intelligence, design, choice, and implementation. Initially, in the intelligence phase, a manager becomes aware of a problem or opportunity, searches for more information about the situation, and attempts to understand and clarify the problem or opportunity. During the design phase, a manager identifies several feasible approaches to solving the problem or responding to the opportunity. During the choice phase, the manager evaluates the feasible solutions and decides on the best one. Then the proposed solution is implemented in a timely manner.

Managers use conceptual models in decision-making to cope with the complexities of a situation. A **model** is a simplified representation, or abstraction, of reality containing only the most relevant aspects of the real situation. For example, a manager may use: a *mental model* of his or beliefs and assumptions of reality to determine what information is relevant and useful for that situation; a *mathematical model* to represent a situation as numeric relationships among a few important variables, such as a budget spreadsheet or a product sales forecast spreadsheet; a pictorial representation, or *analog model*, such as an organization chart or a stock market graph; and an *iconic model* —a physical replica of reality but on a different scale from the original such as a computer-aided design.

Each person is unique and shows a personal style of decision-making. A manager's **decision style** reflects how that individual approaches decision-making. For example one manager may have a *rational decision style* tending to search for and evaluate as much information as possible, examine as many alternative solutions as possible, and then try to choose the alternative that maximizes the value of the decision. Another manager may prefer a *satisficing decision style* tending to limit the information search and choose the first satisfactory solution.

It is important to pay attention to the individual differences among managers in the context of the general decision-making process. An information system that supports decision-making should be flexible and adaptable enough to support these different decision-making conditions.

Four types of information systems configurations have been developed over the years in response to these decision-making complexities: management information systems, decision support systems, executive support systems, and expert systems. Each information system configuration is designed to provide managers with relevant information and the tools to manipulate that information appropriately.

Management Information Systems

A **management information system (MIS)** gives a manager the information he or she needs to make decisions, typically structured decisions, regarding the operational activities of the company. These decisions require the manager to measure performance and compare that measurement information with predetermined standards of performance. Transaction processing systems (described in Chapter 13, "Systems and Organizations in the Information Age,") provide the MIS with data on the performance of the primary activities of the company. The MIS extracts the relevant data from databases of the transaction processing systems, organizes and summarizes the data in useful ways, and provides the information to the manager in various

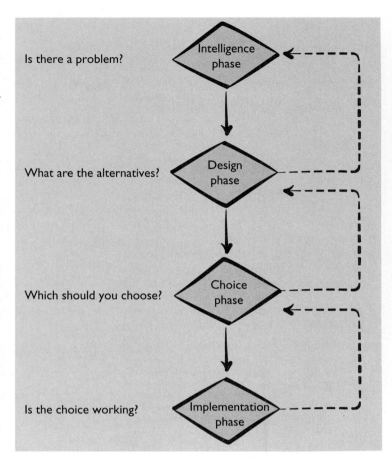

Decision making involves understanding the problem, identifying possible solutions, selecting the most desirable solution, and implementing it.

14.1
Information Flow in a Management Information System

A retail chain processes a tremendous amount of data daily. Depending on how it is handled, this information can be either overwhelming or enlightening. To make the best use of the information, many chains use management information systems to aid in decision making. This example follows the many paths of information through the Frostbyte Outdoor Outfitters Corporation.

Top-level managers use reports that summarize long-term trends to analyze overall business strategies.

When a new shipment arrives, a clerk records it using a terminal; inventory and accounting files are updated automatically.

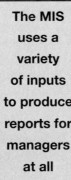

The MIS uses a variety of inputs to produce reports for managers at all levels.

Mid-level managers use summary and exception reports to spot trends and unusual circumstances.

When a clerk punches a sale into the terminal, a database records changes in financial and inventory files.

Low-level managers use detailed reports to keep tabs on day-to-day operations.

On-demand reports integrate information and show relationships. Example: impact of cold weather on ski sales.

Sales Volume vs. Average Temperature as of 6/30/02

	Jan.	Feb.	Mar.	Apr.	May	June
Sales Volume	1798	1700	1609	1532	1302	1216
Sales	$24,398	$24,673	$22,468	$21,003	$18,068	$16,328
Average temperature	24	32	41	48	58	71

Year-End Sales by Item: Top 20 as of 12/31/02

ITEM	SOLD UNITS	RETURNED UNITS	TOTAL UNITS	TOTAL SALES
Beaver Kayaks	58	3	55	$12,375
Possum Packs	1240	212	1028	$20,046
Possum Parkas	1003	323	680	$17,000
Rhinoceros Hiking Boots	1162	429	733	$47,645
Snoreswell Sleeping Bags	923	62	861	$39,175

Summary reports show departmental totals or trends. Example: most popular footwear.

Items Temporarily Out of Stock as of 12/31/02

ITEM	OUT SINCE	DATE AVAILABLE
Fancy Flashlights	10/31/02	1/4/03
Foxy Flannels	10/31/02	1/2/03
Snappy Tents	10/02/02	1/2/03

Exception reports reflect unusual relationships. Example: out-of-stock gear.

Daily Sales Register by Type: 7/31/02

ITEM	UNITS	SALES
Parkas	62	$1209
Flashlights	154	$1540
Tents	2	$500
Hiking Boots	78	$65

Detail reports give complete, detailed information on routine operations. Example: daily orders.

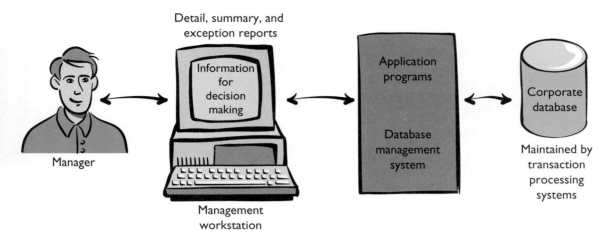

The components of a management information system. Managers can use the system to access information about the company's business processes.

reports. The manager can use the reports in the intelligence phase of decision making to identify any operational problems.

Management information systems are also referred to as **management reporting systems** because their main output is a variety of reports for managers. An MIS provides three types of reports: detailed reports, summary reports, and exception reports. Each type of report typically shows both actual and planned performance measures for certain transactions that allow a manager to compare actual performance with planned performance.

MIS reports are usually distributed to managers routinely as scheduled reports. A manager can also use the query language and report generation capabilities of a newer MIS to retrieve ad-hoc, on-demand reports. Many organizations now have intranet infrastructures that enable managers to use Web browsers to retrieve and view MIS reports.

Typically an MIS provides access to an organization's internal transaction data but not to information external to the organization. An MIS doesn't provide analytic capabilities other than straightforward statistical operations for summary and exceptions reports. As a result, an MIS can supply performance information to managers about the primary activities of the company but is not particularly useful in helping managers decide how to actually improve performance.

Decision Support Systems

> You can lead a **horse to water**, but you can't make him enter **regional distribution codes** in data field 92 to **facilitate regression analysis** on the back end.
>
> —John Cleese, corporate consultant and former member of Monty Python's Flying Circus

The components of a decision support system. Managers can use the syustem interactively to analyze information for decision making.

A **decision support system (DSS)** helps a manager make semistructured decisions, such as budget planning and sales forecasting, and unstructured decisions, such as new product development and contract negotiating. In these types of situations, a manager uses the DSS to

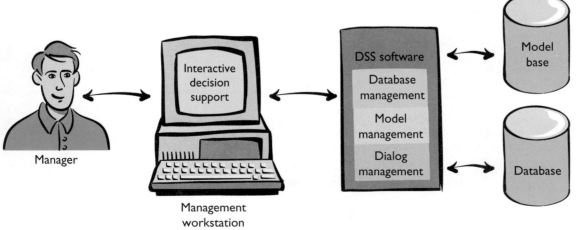

manipulate information for analysis, but must also use his or her intuition and mature judgment to make an effective decision.

The term *decision support system* also refers to a way of thinking about how information systems should be designed to support managerial decision-making. The DSS design philosophy is to provide managers with the tools they need to analyze information they deem relevant for a particular decision or class of decisions. A DSS is designed with the decision style of the managers in mind and provides powerful information access, processing, and reporting capabilities the managers can use in a flexible manner whenever it's needed.

Components of a Decision Support System

A DSS has three major components that a manager uses interactively to retrieve and manipulate relevant data. The *data management* component is a database of relevant internal and external information of the organization. Current and historical internal information is extracted from the company's MIS and transaction-processing applications, and external information, such as stock prices, research data, and company information of customers, competitors, and vendors, is accessed through publicly available databases. Database management software enables the manager to query the database and retrieve relevant information, much like an MIS.

The *model management* component enables the manager to evaluate alternative problem solutions and identify the best or most satisfying solution by using appropriate software, such as spreadsheet and statistical modeling tools. For example, a manager could use a spreadsheet model to learn how product sales correlate with differences in income, age, and other characteristics of consumers; based on this analysis, the manager could use the model to then forecast future sales. The model management component also contains other model-building tools, such as graphics software, that a manager can use to design and implement his or her own customized graphs and charts.

The third DSS component is the user interface, or *dialog management*, through which a manager utilizes the data and modeling capabilities of the DSS easily and effectively. Most DSS user interfaces are graphical interfaces that enable the manager to view information in a variety of forms, including graphs, charts, lists, tables, and reports. Designers of the user interface take the manager's decision-making style into consideration so that the dialog-box procedure is intuitive and straightforward for the manager.

Group Decision Support Systems

Many decisions are made by a team or group of managers. **Group decision support systems (GDSS)** are designed to improve the productivity of decision-making meetings by enhancing the dynamics of collaborative work. Physically the GDSS usually takes the form of a room equipped with computers, DSS database and modeling software, LAN connections, and a large-screen projection of computer output for viewing by the group. The GDSS also includes specific communication-oriented software tools that support the development and sharing of ideas.

During a decision-making meeting, managers can use the GDSS capabilities as if they were using their own DSS to perform an analysis or some other management activity. A manager can show his or her work to the group using the large-screen projection system or keep it confidential. The managers as a group can use the GDSS software tools to brainstorm and organize their ideas, comments, suggestions, criticisms, and other information. A GDSS enables the group members to share information anonymously, encouraging them to participate without risking the counterproductive dynamics of group meetings.

Geographic Information Systems

A **geographic information system (GIS)** is a special type of DSS designed to work with map and other spatial information. A GIS is made up of mapping and

Group decision support systems can enhance the dynamics of face-to-face contact in group meetings.

14.2
Using DSS for Analysis

A decision support system can provide a manager with powerful tools for analysis of information. Different management decisions call for different types of analysis. A DSS handles these four types of analysis:

can use any DSS to ask and answer what-if questions. For example, a manager may want to know what the monthly payment of a product will be for a certain purchase price, loan length, and interest rate. By using an analytic model, a manager can change the value of one or more key input variables or parameters and immediately see the effect on the output variables or proposed solution.

▶ *What if? analysis.* DSSs have been designed to support many types of decision-making applications, including corporate planning and forecasting, product pricing, flight scheduling, transportation routing, and investment analysis. Even though each DSS is designed to solve a specific problem, managers

▶ *Sensitivity analysis.* By varying the value of key input variables systematically, or by asking a sequence of what-if? questions, the manager performs a sensitivity analysis. A sensitivity analy-

Real Estate agents can use a GIS to view property data at various layers such as proximity to schools and shopping, city limits, and owner information.

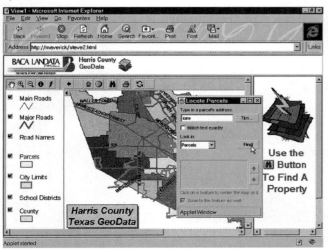

analytic modeling software, databases that contain map images. and geographic and demographic data, and a user interface enabling a manager to query the database interactively and see the results shown on a map. Government agencies such as the U.S. Census Bureau and U.S. Bureau of Labor Statistics, and more than 100 commercial companies produce spatial information databases containing demographic, employment, and consumer-habit information that can be incorporated into a business-oriented GIS.

Managers use GISs to support a wide variety of managerial decisions that involve geographic information. A few examples are identifying the best location site for a new retail store or branch office, analyzing customer buying preferences in a geographical area, planning delivery and service routes, planning sales and marketing campaigns, and realigning sales territories.

Executive Information Systems

An **executive information system** (EIS) combines features of MIS and DSS to support unstructured decision-making by top managers. Executives work in an increasingly global competitive business environment requiring quick and easy access to timely information, both internal and external to the company. A top manager

sis shows the manager the degree of change in the results or output of a model as the value of a key variable or assumption changes incrementally. With a well-designed user interface, a manager can evaluate any number of what-if? questions to do a sensitivity analysis easily and quickly.

desired monthly payment level is found. Some DSSs enable managers to perform goal seeking automatically.

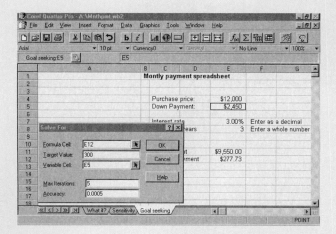

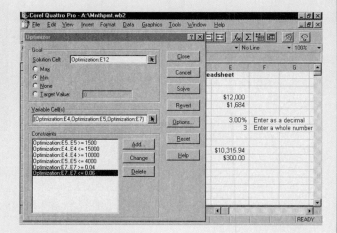

▶ *Goal-seeking analysis.* A variation of sensitivity analysis is goal-seeking analysis, which attempts to find the value of one or more key input variables of a model that will result in a desired level of output. For example, a manager might wish to know what down payment would be necessary to obtain a particular monthly payment. The manager could enter a value for the down payment variable and observe the resulting monthly payment calculation, and then reiterate this process until the

▶ *Optimization analysis.* Another variation of sensitivity analysis is optimization analysis. All decisions are made under certain constraints and limitations, such as a limited budget. Optimization analysis attempts to find the highest or lowest value of one or more variables, given certain limits or constraints. For example, a manager could use an analytic model to calculate the optimal monthly payment on a product, given that the purchase price, the interest rate of the loan, and the down payment cannot exceed certain limits. Spreadsheet software has the ability to perform optimization analysis.

can use an EIS to monitor key indicators of the company's performance, such as profitability, finance and marketing, and human and technology resources. An EIS also makes it easy for a manager to access economic, consumer, and environmental trends affecting the company.

An EIS has similar design components to a DSS. The EIS data-management component provides interactive access to the company's important information, and the model management component provides access to data on the company's critical success factors. The *dialog management component* is the set of human-computer interactive features that enables the executive to select the necessary data and display it in a variety of formats, including summary and exception reports, lists, charts, tables, and graphs.

An EIS enables the executive to *drill down* through the available information to the level of detail needed. For example, an executive may view a summary report and notice that sales in a particular region have declined over the past month, negatively affecting profitability. The executive can retrieve the detailed sales information for that particular sales region. Examining this data, the executive might decide to retrieve information about product sales at a particular store or by a particular salesperson.

Using the database-management capability of an EIS, an executive has access to up-to-the-minute data on internal operations of the company and access to a wide variety of external online information, including news services, financial market databases, economic information, and other publicly available information, especially on the Internet. This ability to access both internal and external information makes an EIS a powerful tool during the intelligence phase of decision-making.

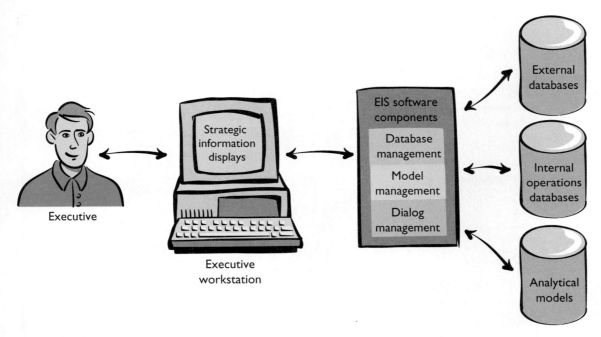

The components of an executive
information system. Managers can
use the system to monitor the important economic and social trends
affecting the organization, as well as
the important performance measures
of the company.

Expert Systems

> An expert is one who **knows more** and more **about less** and less.
>
> —Nicholas Murray Butler

MIS, EIS, and DSS support decision making primarily by providing managers easy access to relevant information; and to analytic tools to manipulate the information. An **expert system (ES)** supports decision making by providing managers with access to computerized expert knowledge. An expert is someone who has mastery of an extraordinary amount of knowledge within a narrow domain. An ES is designed to replicate the decision-making process of a human expert. Today's expert systems are based on years of **artificial intelligence** research devoted to replicating elusive human cognitive abilities in machines.

Components of an Expert System

An ES has three main components—a knowledge base, an inference engine, and a user interface.

A **knowledge base** is similar to the database component in an MIS or DSS. But while a database contains only facts, a knowledge base also contains a system of rules for determining and changing the relationship between those facts. A knowledge base commonly represents knowledge in the form of if-then rules like these:

▶ If the engine will not turn over and the lights do not work, then check the battery.
▶ If checking the battery shows it is not dead, then check the battery connectors.

An expert system may contain hundreds or thousands of rules, depending on the complexity of the topic domain. Most human decision making involves uncertainty, so many ESs include "fuzzy" rules that state conclusions as probabilities rather than certainties. Here's an example from MYCIN, one of the first expert systems designed to capture a doctor's expertise:

```
If (1) the infection is primary-bacteremia, and
   (2) the site of the culture is one of the sterile sites,
       and
   (3) the suspected portal of entry of the organism is the
       gastrointestinal tract, then there is suggestive
       evidence (.7) that the identity of the organism is
       bacteriodes.
```

Along with the knowledge base, a complete ES also includes a user and an inference engine. The **user interface** enables the manager to interact with the system, typically in a question-

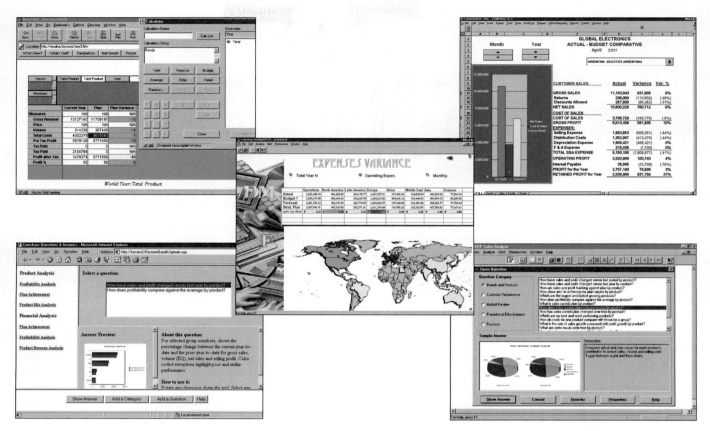

Comshare's Decision modular software can be used as an executive information system and provides the ability to present information in lists, tables, graphs, and other formats.

answer dialog. The interface is designed to enable the user to enter facts that are requested by the system easily, to show the conclusions made by the system, and to query the system about why certain questions are asked and the reasons why particular conclusions were made.

The **inference engine** combines the user input with the knowledge base, applies logical principles, and produces the requested expert advice. The inference engine of an ES is similar to the model base component of a DSS. It processes the facts and rules in the knowledge base following the laws of deductive logic. The inference engine software keeps track of the facts and rules it used to reach a specific conclusion.

Expert systems are difficult to build. To simplify the process, many software companies sell **expert system shells**—generic expert systems containing user interfaces and inference engines. These programs can save time and effort, but they don't include the part that is most difficult to build—the knowledge base. The knowledge base is constructed usually by a *knowledge engineer*—a specialist who interviews and observes experts and painstakingly converts their words and actions into a knowledge base while observing human decision makers doing their jobs. The knowledge engineer may also draw on other sources of expertise, such as government regulations, company guidelines, and statistical databases.

Even with a knowledge base, an ES isn't the machine equivalent of a human expert. Unlike human experts, automated expert systems are poor at planning strategies. Their lack of flexibility makes them less creative than human thinkers. Most importantly, expert systems are powerless outside of their narrow, deep domains of knowledge. While most ES domains can be summarized with a few hundred tidy rules of thumb, the world of people is full of inconsistencies, special cases, and ambiguities that could overwhelm even the best expert systems.

Expert Systems in Action

Expert systems help managers by providing automated data analysis, informed second opinions, and predictions of the likely consequences of a particular situation. Some of the first successful expert systems were developed around medical knowledge and have been successfully designed for many other applications such as pinpointing likely sites for new oil exploration, aiding in automobile and appliance repairs, providing financial-management advice, targeting direct-mail marketing campaigns, detecting problems in computer-controlled machinery, advising air

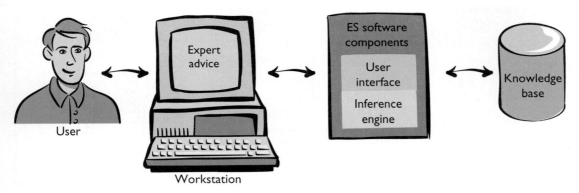

Workstation

The components of an expert system. The software modules perform inferences on a knowledge base built by an expert or both. This provides expert answers to a user's questions in an interactive process.

traffic controllers, predicting weather . . . the list is growing at an astounding rate. Here are a few examples of expert systems in action:

▶ American Express uses an ES to automate the process of checking for fraud and misuses of its no-limit credit card. Credit checks must be completed within 90 seconds while the customer waits, and the cost of making a wrong decision can be high. The company spent 13 months developing the system based on the decision-making expertise of its best credit clerks.

▶ Whirlpool uses an ES named Consumer Appliance Diagnostic System to help handle over 3 million annual telephone inquiries. The customer service representatives use the system to direct customers to a single source of help with little or no delay, thereby improving customer service quality. The system comprises 1000 rules for 12 product lines and was developed by two knowledge engineers, a programmer, and three of the company's best customer service representatives.

▶ Deloitte Touche Tohmatsu, a management consulting firm, developed an ES to provide advice on trade opportunities and licensing requirements for technology products with Central and Eastern European countries. The system was initially used by the company's consultants and is now marketed directly to business traders. The system evaluates the trade opportunities for general classes or specific products, identifies potential buyers and procedures for contacting them, and provides advice on export licensing and instructions about how to complete the required forms.

This ES leads the user through the process of diagnosing problems with malfunctioning cameras.

▶ Blue Cross/Blue Shield of Virginia uses an ES for insurance claim processing. The ES handles up to 200 routine claims each day, enabling human clerks to spend more time on tough situations that require human judgment. The developers of the system extracted diagnostic rules from manuals and watched human claims processors apply those rules.

▶ Boeing Company factory workers use an ES to locate the right parts, tools, and techniques for assembling airplane electrical connectors. The system replaces 20,000 pages of documentation and reduces the average search time from 42 minutes to 5 minutes.

▶ Microsoft Corporation sells a package of utilities to supplement its Windows operating system. The package includes an ES for diagnosing printer network problems.

Information Systems in Perspective

> The sheer **volume** of information **dissolves the information**.
> —Günther Grass, German author

We've described several information system configurations in this chapter—systems to support managerial communication, managementinformation systems (MIS), decision support systems (DSS), executive information systems (EIS), and expert systems (ES). Information systems rarely fall cleanly into just one of these categories. Information systems are tools and should be designed to meet the particular information needs of the people using those tools. Any specific information system can have a mix of communications, MIS, DSS, EIS, and ES design features,

Decision support features	MIS	DSS	EIS	ES
Type of decision maker	Many operational managers	Individual and small groups of tactical managers	Individual strategic manager	Individual strategic, tactical, or operational manager
Type of problem	Structured	Semistructured	Unstructured	Structured
Type of information	Predesigned reports on internal operations	Interactive queries and responses for specific problems	On-line access to internal and external information on many issues	Conclusions and recommendation for a particular complex problem
Type of use	Indirect	Direct	Direct	Direct
Phase of decision making	Intelligence	Design, choice	Intelligence	Implementation

Comparison of design features for MIS, DSS, EIS, and ES.

although one particular design configuration will probably predominate in any given situation. Which design features to incorporate into an information system should be chosen based on the communication and decision making requirements of the managerial users.

Information systems provide critical information and advice, but they aren't without risks. Poorly designed information systems can hamper a manager's ability to make quality decisions. Systems notwithstanding, the human manager always has the responsibility for the quality of every decision. Some managers complain that these systems provide too much information— too many reports, too many printouts, too many summaries, too many details. This malady is known as information overload. Managers who are bombarded with computer output may not be able to separate the best from the rest. What's worse, managers who rely too heavily on computer output run the risk of overlooking more conventional, nondigital sources of insight. Although user training is essential, the best managers know that no computer or information system can replace the human communication and decision-making skills necessary for successful management.

In the remainder of this chapter, we'll focus on information technology as a strategic tool for managers and organizations.

Information Technology to Support Business Strategy

A business competes with other companies based primarily on the cost and value of products and services. You will see in this section how managers use information technology to reduce costs by improving the company's value-chain activities and improve the value of products and services from the customer's perspective. Also, you will see how managers use information technology strategically to interact effectively with customers, suppliers, competitors, and other organizations in the business environment.

> **Business** is a good game—**lots of competition** and a **minimum of rules**. You keep score with money.
>
> —Nolan Bushnell, founder of Atari

Strategy Concepts

In chapter 13, "Systems and Organizations in the Information Age," we saw that a business organization is actually a system in an environment that has customers, stockholders, suppliers, community and government agencies, and other businesses, some of which may be competitors. Managers use a *competitive forces model* to understand the environmental influences that affect the organization's ability to compete successfully.

> All **strategy** depends on **competition**.
>
> —Bruce D. Henderson, American educator

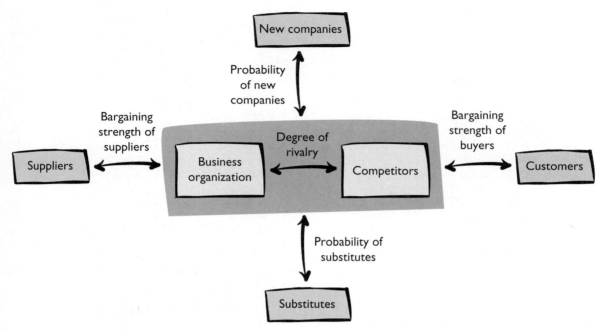

Managers can decide how best to use information technologies by understanding the competitive forces in the business environment.

The **competitive forces model** is a tool used to examine the following five key factors that influence, and often threaten, a company:

▌ *Competition.* The degree of competitive rivalry among firms in an industry
▌ *New Competition.* The probability of new companies entering the industry
▌ *Customers.* The relative bargaining strength of customers
▌ *Suppliers.* The relative bargaining strength of suppliers
▌ *Substitution.* The probability that customers may substitute or switch to other products or services

By identifying the interaction of these five factors in their industry, managers can better formulate a strategy to improve the company's competitiveness.

A **strategy** is an organization's intention to pursue a set of activities over the long term to attain its goals. An organization uses the the competitive forces model to evaluate its environment and choose a strategy that will help it achieve a **competitive advantage**. That is, it will control a significant portion of the market or enjoy larger-than-average profits. Managers use the following three basic strategies to achieve competitive advantage:

▌ A **cost leadership strategy** focuses on providing high-quality products and services at the lowest cost in the industry. Wal-Mart, for example, uses this strategy to compete in the consumer retail industry.
▌ A **differentiation strategy** focuses on providing products and services that are particularly valued and are perceived by customers as uniquely different from the competition. Automotive companies, such as Mercedes and Volkswagen, use differentiation strategies in their product design and marketing to appeal to certain types of customers.
▌ An **innovation strategy** emphasizes finding new ways to restructure business processes for producing or distributing products and services, or developing unique products and services. Many Internet-based companies, such as Amazon.com, E*Trade.com, and Dell Computer Corp., use innovation strategies. Among the many of Dell Computer's innovations is it's build-to-order system enabling customers to select the options they want and order their computer custombuilt to those specifications

Top managers can choose any one of the three strategies to deal with the competitive forces in their industry. For example, a business may try to deal with the bargaining power of customers or suppliers by developing unique relationships with them, making it easy and convenient for them to buy from or sell to the business, and in effect making it more expensive and inconvenient for them to deal with competing companies. Or a company may develop a product

Applying Competitive Strategies to Competitive Forces

Competitive Forces	Competitive Strategies		
	Cost Leadership Strategy	Differentiation Strategy	Innovation Strategy
Customers	Offer lower prices	Provide better quality, features, and service	Provide new products and services
Suppliers	Help suppliers lower costs	Help suppliers improve services	Develop unique services with suppliers
Competitors	Undercut competitors' prices	Make competition more difficult with unique features	Develop products and services unmatched by competitors
New companies	Make cost of entry unattractive	Make entry decision more difficult	Develop products and services provided by potential entrants
Substitutes	Make substitution expensive	Provide features of substitute products	Develop substitutes

Applying competitive strategies to competitive forces.

or service that is difficult for other companies to emulate, thereby making it more difficult for other companies to create a viable substitute product or service. Or a company may be able to lower production costs dramatically or create such a unique product or service that the whole basis of competition changes in an industry.

An important factor common among competitive strategies is time. A company can compete on the basis of time by providing more value to the customer, doing things faster, introducing new products more quickly, responding to customer demand more quickly, and providing faster service. Many companies have reduced the time to design and manufacture a product by more than 50 percent by reorganizing work flows, reorganizing the organization's structure, and using information technology to eliminate redundant work and speed up necessary work. A strategy that emphasizes competition primarily on the basis of time is called a quick response strategy.

Today's business environment is dynamic. Even if managers of a business organization achieve a competitive advantage, they usually find it difficult to sustain a *competitive advantage* for an extended period of time. Market conditions change, customer expectations change, technological innovations emerge, and some competitors always respond with equally effective strategies of their own. Even though they strive for a *sustainable competitive advantage*, most managers must follow a strategy based on *competitive necessity* just to keep abreast of the competition and survive in business. A typical business organization thrives and survives through phases of having a competitive advantage followed by competitive necessity in a continuous cycle through the years.

Strategic Information Systems

> Anyone who believes that the **competitive spirit in America** is dead has never been in a **supermarket** when the cashier opens another **checkout line**.
>
> —Ann Landers, American advice columnist

An information system that is crucial to the company's competitive success is called a strategic information system. Such a system could be a management information system or a decision support system or any of the other types of information systems we've discussed.

Strategic Uses of Information Technology

How can organizations use information technology strategically? Let's consider three examples of how top managers use the competitive forces model to help answer that general question.

▶ *Create entry barriers, switching costs, and new products or services.* An entry barrier is usually an innovative new product or service that is difficult for a competitor to emulate. A classic example is Merrill Lynch, a large financial service firm that developed a system called Cash Management Account that provided customers many new financial, banking, and investment services. The

Small businesses, like this bistro, compete successfully by using information technology to provide new services for their customers.

system was costly and difficult to implement, and it took several years for competing brokerage firms and banking institutions to develop similar products. In the meantime, Merrill Lynch continued to innovate and enhance the product, making it all the harder for competitors to catch up.

▶ **Switching costs** are the time, effort, and money a customer or supplier would have to expend changing to a competitor's product or service. For example, Baxter Healthcare International, Inc., the supplier of nearly two-thirds of all products used by U.S. hospitals, developed an inventory and ordering system that enables hospitals to order online from the Baxter supply catalog using Baxter computer terminals installed in the hospitals. The system handles shipping, billing, invoicing, and inventory information and provides hospitals an estimated delivery date, usually within a day. Participating hospitals become unwilling to switch to another supplier because the system is very economical and convenient to use.

▶ *Modify or enhance a product or service to differentiate it from the competitors' and to increase its value to customers.* For example, a company could enhance its product by including more informational features to make it easier to use, or customize the product to meet a customer's special needs, or improve the service dimension of the product in the eye of the customer. For example, the clothing manufacturer Levi Strauss & Co. provides a microcomputer system named Personal Pair™ Jeans in their own retail stores. A fit specialist enters a customer's measurements and jeans style preference and then transmits that information directly to a special Levi's production plant. The completed jeans are then shipped to the store or directly to the customer's office or home within two or three weeks.

▶ *Emphasize the organization's primary and support activities.* This involves focusing on the activities that add the most value to products and minimizing those activities that do not provide value to the customer. Streamlining or redesigning particular value-chain activities can be done to reduce costs, to enhance existing products and services, or to expand a company's capacity to develop new products and services. A good example is Wal-Mart inventory replenishment system. The system's point-of-sale cash registers record each sales transaction and send orders for new merchandise to suppliers via telecommunications as soon as customers pay for their purchases. The system enables Wal-Mart to minimize the cost of storing merchandise in warehouses. It also enables the company to adjust purchases from suppliers to meet customer demands. Wal-Mart has been able to reduce its overhead expenses, including salaries, advertising, and warehousing, to 15 percent of sales revenues. Other competitors in the retail industry have overhead expenses ranging from 20 to 30 percent of sales revenues.

Competing on Efficiency and Effectiveness

> In business, the **competition will bite you** if you keep running; if you stand still, they will **swallow you**.
>
> —William Knudsen, Jr., Chairman, Ford Motor Company

Another way top managers use information technology strategically is to improve efficiency and effectiveness of the organization. **Efficiency** is how primary and support activities produce desired output with less work or lower costs. **Effectiveness** is how customers evaluate the quality of the output—products and services—of the value chain.

There are several ways to use information technology to improve efficiency: empowering people, eliminating waste, using the best known way to do the work, automating work, and integrating value chain activities within the company and with other organizations.

▶ *Empowering people.* A company can improve employees' abilities to use information technologies for competitive advantage. For example, the competitiveness of CitySoft, a Web development and site management company, has everything to do with the skills of its employees. The company works with neighborhood-based training centers in New York City's Harlem and East Harlem that teach practical courses such as advanced HTML and Web design. The training centers have the goal of creating job opportunities in the tech sector for local residents. CitySoft has primarily hired Web developers who were trained at the centers. A 2001 recipient of the MIT Sloan eBusiness Award for social responsibility, CitySoft has landed Web site design work from companies very much in the economic mainstream-companies such as Accenture, Houghton Mifflin and Reebok.

▶ *Eliminating waste.* It is estimated that 20 to 30 percent of the work done in business organizations is simply waste—a waste of time, a waste of paper or other physical resources, or a waste of effort. Information technologies, compared with paper, can cut waste by making it easier to access, duplicate, transmit, and display information in a variety of formats. For example, many insurance sales representatives use laptop computers to evaluate different insurance plans directly with customers, eliminating the unnecessary steps of going back to the office to do the calculations and then getting back with the customer at a later date.

▶ *Using the best-known way to do the work.* Information technologies can be used to perform the best repeatable, structured procedures that consistently result in high work productivity. For example, bar-code readers record transaction data automatically and thus minimize repetitive record keeping and data handling involved in many jobs.

Information workers are empowered to do their work well by having access to the right information, the right tools, and the right training.

▶ *Automating work.* Work requiring repetition, endurance, and speed is usually highly structured; automating this work results in significant productivity gains. Automated factories and computer-controlled robots are good examples.

▶ *Integrating across functions and organizations.* Information technologies can be used to transmit information between a company's value-chain activities. For example, the tight integration of sales and production activities is common in many companies because the more integrated those activities are, the faster the production activity can respond to new orders from sales. For example, Motorola coordinated its production and sales activities so that production of a customized electronic pager can begin 17 minutes after an order is placed in the field and be sent to the customer within two to three hours.

Effectiveness is related to how customers evaluate the quality of a company's products and services. A company can improve its effectiveness by using information technology to improve how customers interact directly with the company. Some of these interactions include purchasing the product, ensuring that the product fits the customer's requirements, using the product, and maintaining the product.

▶ *Purchasing the product.* Companies use information technology to help customers purchase products through increasing product awareness, improving the availability of a product, and making it easier to pay. For example, many organizations get information about consumer buying patterns contained in marketing databases, and then target their advertising at individuals who are likely to buy their products. Also, many companies, such as Walgreens drug stores for example, use online order entry systems to replenish items in the store quickly so that items are always available. And, many companies are enabling customers to pay for a product by using debit cards to transfer money electronically from the customer's bank account to the company's bank account.

▶ *Fitting the product to customer requirements.* Information technologies are used to match products to customer needs and to customize products based on customer needs. For example, the cosmetic company, Elizabeth Arden, provides computer-based video systems so cosmetologists can try different makeup combinations electronically on video-projected customer images, enabling the customers to see what they'll look like before they buy. Similarly, customers at a Home Depot store can meet with a salesperson and lay out the redesign of a kitchen or bathroom on a computer screen; the salesperson can use the results to make sure the customer purchases the correctly sized cabinets and other fixtures.

▶ *Using the product.* Information technology is used also to provide additional product features so that the product is easier to use or more useful to the customer. For example, including, or embedding, computer semiconductor technology adds data processing and programmability to everyday products, such as kitchen appliances, VCRs, and automobiles. Computerized systems are *essential* components of some products; computerized flight control systems in commercial aircraft provide the pilot with critical information for monitoring and controlling the craft. Also, companies try to make their products easy to use by providing excellent service and providing customers with better information about the products. For example, Avis provides a Web site and an 800 number to answer frequently asked customer questions. It also minimizes the check-in time for returning a car by providing each service representative with a hand-held terminal that records the transaction and prints a receipt without the customer having to go back into the office to handle more paperwork.

▶ *Making the product easier to maintain.* Customers want high-quality products along with maintenance service. Businesses with effective field service operations use information technology as an essential component of their service and repair activities. For example, Otis Elevator manufactures each of its elevators with a modem and microprocessor to report any malfunctions automatically to a dispatching office. Pagers and other communication devices are used to contact a service technician immediately whenever an elevator problem occurs. Each technician uses a hand-held computer to communicate instantly with a central office for technical assistance and job-dispatching information. A complete history of service calls for each elevator is stored in a centralized database that can be used by technicians to diagnose an elevator malfunction easily and by designers to redesign the elevator to eliminate recurring malfunctions.

Many business organizations use the World Wide Web to help customers purchase products and services. A customer can use an organization's Web site to see and read product information and use interactive order entry screens to purchase the product.

An Information Code of Ethics

Each organization should foster an ethical information culture and develop its own information policies and procedures to guide managers and information workers. A company's information code of ethics should address four main topics: privacy, information quality, intellectual property, and access to information.

Privacy—Many organizations and information systems encourage information workers to accumulate information about people, for example, customers' transaction data, the general public's credit information, and employees' email. In the process, a person's privacy could be compromised or other sensitive information revealed. Based on the 1973 Code of Fair Information Practices:

▶ There must be no personal record-keeping systems whose very existence is secret.

▶ There must be a way for persons to find out what information about them is on record and how it is being used.

▶ There must be a way for persons to correct or amend a record of information about them.

▶ There must be a way for persons to prevent information about themselves obtained for one purpose from being used or made available for other purposes without their consent.

▶ An organization must assure the reliability of records that contain identifiable personal data and must take reasonable precautions to prevent misuse of the data.

Information Quality—Databases, including transaction-oriented, text, image, and multimedia, are basic components of today's information systems. As organizations rely increasingly on information in databases, people are more likely to be harmed by inaccuracies in these systems. A company should ensure quality by managing several information characteristics:

▶ *Accuracy.* Control data to ensure information represents what is supposed to represent and to identify likely errors; avoid misrepresentation and misleading information.

▶ *Precision.* Control data to ensure an appropriate level of detail.

▶ *Completeness.* Ensure that available information is adequate for the person and situation; avoid swamping persons with excessive information; do not suppress or hide valid information.

▶ *Age.* Update information frequently enough to be accurate and complete.

▶ *Timeliness.* Provide information quickly enough so that it is useful.

▶ *Source.* Verify the credibility of information sources and analyze information for bias.

▶ *Use.* Ensure that the decisions and actions taken on the basis of quality information is consistent with the overall ethical values of the employees and organization.

Intellectual Property—Information systems embody the ideas, writing, expression, and knowledge of many different information workers. Ownership rights for intellectual property have been protected traditionally in the United States by copyright, patent, and trade secret laws. A company should have explicit guidelines for the following:

▶ *Software copyright.* Policy for determining who owns the copyright of software products developed in the company.

▶ *Software licenses.* Policy for acquiring and monitoring conformance to licenses of using software developed by another company.

▶ *Acquiring information.* Policy for identifying and using sources of information (including any print, image, audio, or electronic sources) and respecting other companies' trade secrets.

▶ *Storing information.* Policy for copying files, software, and other intellectual property within the company and from other organizations.

Access—Information workers need access to intellectual skills, information, and information technologies. Different levels of access relate to power in organizations, employment opportunities, job satisfaction, and other human resource issues. A company should have guidelines for the following:

▶ *Hardware access.* Policy defining the circumstances an employee may use a company's computer and communications hardware.

▶ *File access.* Policy defining the circumstances an employee may access and use information in various files and databases.

▶ *Disseminating information.* Policy for providing information in a timely manner to those persons authorized, and for safeguards against those who do not have a right or need to know.

▶ *Skill acquisition.* Policy for employee training and other professional development

▶ *Job performance.* Policy for providing job-supporting technologies for handicapped information workers.

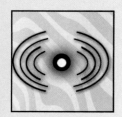

Viewing Ethics Through a Global Lens

Karen D. Loch

In a global economy, corporate computer systems often intercon-nect across borders, creating an ethical chain that affects people internationally. In this excerpt from a Beyond Computing article, Dr. Karen Loch describes several important ethical issues, includ-ing privacy and intellectual property, for companies using the Internet to conduct business globally.

The explosion of the Internet into the workplace has created a global virtual morality unfettered by time and space. Globalization forces companies to interconnect their computer systems to employees, suppliers, distributors and customers, creating an eth-ical chain that can reach around the world. As businesses become more dependent on this electronic lifeline, they are going to en-counter ethical moments of truth that will have a ripple effect—either positive or negative—throughout the chain.

Advances in technologies such as the Internet create new spins on old issues such as privacy, intellectual property and stan-dards of conduct. The geographically dispersed firm has the addi-tional challenge of aligning corporate policies with accepted cul-tural practices in different parts of the world. These issues make it essential for today's businesses to view their information ethics policies from a global perspective.

Business practices vary from country to country. A comparison of attitudes toward privacy, property rights and general standards of conduct illustrates these ethical challenges.

Fundamentally, privacy is about the ability of individuals to con-trol information about themselves. Computers increased the threat to privacy by making it easy to collect and store large volumes of personal data for easy access by anyone. The pervasiveness of web technology has intensified the debate and drawn the lines ever sharper as we cross geographical boundaries.

The free flow of information is considered as American as apple pie, provided it is for commercial (not government) purposes. Companies routinely gather intimate profiles of consumers, cross-reference that data, and sell it to second and third parties. In addi-tion, the use of electronic cookies and other forms of tracking con-sumer activity is justified on the basis of providing better service.

Most American firms follow an "opt out" privacy policy, which requires consumers to explicitly request that their personal infor-mation *not* be used for marketing purposes. Firms operating in Europe confront a different attitude. First, the European Union (EU) Data Protection Directive requires organizations to obtain explicit user permission regarding the collection and movement of per-sonal data. Foreign governments and companies must abide by these guidelines or risk action by European data protection authorities to cut off their access to data. The directive institution-alizes the "opt in" approach to privacy. This means that firms must obtain explicit user permission prior to collecting data, and provide an explicit statement on the usage of that information.

When it comes to employee privacy, a typical company position is that electronic surveillance is needed to ensure productivity, pre-vent unlawful or unethical behavior, and enforce security. However, policies on employee surveillance vary not just by country, but by company. While it is the norm in some firms, it is forbidden in others.

The United States has no formal policy on this issue so enter-prises—and sometimes the courts—have been settling it. The courts maintain that since equipment resources belong to the employer, the employer is entitled to enforce policies on their use, including tracking web behavior and monitoring the contents of e-mail and employees' desktop areas. The EU also protects employ-ees from surveillance. In other parts of the world, however, the government has the ultimate say in what takes place on comput-ers, and monitors incoming and outgoing content on the Internet.

In the West, intellectual property is the property of the person or organization that created it. In countries in which material com-pensation for artistic work has not been the norm, the introduction of software and the international copyright laws have created fric-tion between the old and new ways. While the majority of coun-tries have international copyright laws on their books, enforcement is lax. Consequently, 38 percent of all new business software applications installed worldwide in 1998 were pirated.

The real challenge for global firms is to successfully transfer the home office's corporate culture and ethical attitude toward piracy—or risk damaging their reputation. Companies that don't adopt and enforce the international norm of protection for intellec-tual property may find that potential partners are unwilling to do business with them.

Contrasting cultural viewpoints also are reflected in attitudes toward controlling Internet content—with legal liabilities and potential loss of market for failure to comply with national norms. In America, free speech is highly prized and constitutionally sanc-tioned. In some cultures, however, family and community harmony is valued more highly. So, in many parts of the world, Internet ser-vice providers (ISPs) are expected to control website content. Some countries threaten to ban ISPs that don't block content considered pornographic. And many governments block access to sites that post what they consider unacceptable material, including political content deemed contrary to government inter-ests. However, in the United States, responsibility resides with the individual viewer. Someone who does not wish to receive such information should not log onto a site that provides it.

Formulating a set of ethical guidelines helps a company detect and resolve ethical breaches and potential public missteps. Companies should vigilantly monitor [technology changes] and the potential ethical threats they represent. This will require a coordi-nated effort by the company and its ethical chain partners. Enterprises that are known for their integrity attract business part-ners, customers and employees from around the world. So taking the high road *can* bring a competitive advantage.

DISCUSSION QUESTIONS

1. Do you believe the privacy and intellectual property policies in the United States and Europe are unreasonable for companies using the Internet? Explain.
2. Would copying software and manuals be an ethical problem for you if the practice was the accepted norm in the country you were doing business? Describe your rationale.
3. In what types of situations would you agree that an ISP, such as AOL, should control its Web site content?

Summary

Managers have complicated jobs that involve functions and roles that require communication and decision making. Managers need information to perform these communication and decision-making tasks. A number of information system configurations have been developed to support these managerial needs.

Managers perform planning, organizing, directing, and controlling functions, intelligently using various resources to accomplish an organization's goals. Managers also play interpersonal, informational, and decisional roles in interacting with other employees in the organization and the organization's environment. An organization has three levels of management: operational, tactical, and strategic. Typically operational managers need to make structured decisions; tactical, or middle, managers need to make semistructured decisions; and strategic, or top, managers, need to make unstructured decisions.

Information has three dimensions: time, content, and form. An organizational goal is to provide the right information (content) to a manager at the right time and in the right form so it is the most valuable for the situation at hand.

A number of information technology configurations exist to improve communications within an organization. Collaborative, workgroup computing enables groups of users to access and share information easily. Distributed computing efficiently coordinates the use of PCs, workstations, minicomputers, and mainframes in an organization. An automated office, which uses many types of electronic meeting technologies, enables individuals, workgroups, and organizations to acquire, process, store, and distribute information electronically. Communications between organizations is improved with Electronic Data Interchange, enabling companies to send each other standard business documents electronically, and cooperative arrangements called business alliances.

Decision making is a process that consists of four phases: an intelligence phase, a design phase, a choice phase, and an implementation phase. Individuals have a variety of decision-making styles.

Several types of information system configurations have been developed to support managerial decision making: management information systems (MIS), decision support systems (DSS), executive information systems (EIS), and expert systems (ES).

A manager uses an MIS to make structured decisions at the operational level in an organization. With an MIS a manager can access the internal transaction data of a company in the form of detailed reports, summary reports, and exceptions reports. A manager can receive these reports on a scheduled basis or interactively by using a database query language.

A manager uses a DSS to make semistructured decisions at the tactical level in an organization. With a DSS, a manager can access internal and external information, analytic modeling tools to manipulate the information, and an easy-to-use interface. Group decision support systems (GDSSs) are used to enhance collaborative decision making in teams. Geographic information systems (GIS) support decision making with map and other spatial information.

A manager uses an EIS to make unstructured decisions at the strategic level in an organization. A manager can use an EIS to access internal and external information about key indicators of the company's performance and about business and other environmental trends affecting the company. With an EIS, a manager can drill down through the available information to retrieve the level of detailed information needed.

A manager uses an ES to access computerized expert knowledge. An ES includes a knowledge base, an inference engine for applying logical rules to the facts in a knowledge base, and a user interface. Once the knowledge base is constructed, an ES can provide consultation that rivals human advice in many situations.

Information systems are tools that should be designed to meet the information needs of the people using them. Poorly designed information systems can result in information overload and hamper a manager's ability to communicate effectively or make quality decisions. A company's information code of ethics should address the privacy, intellectual ownership, and the information quality and access policies to guide its managers and information workers, and foster an ethical information culture.

Top managers must understand the business environment of global competition and follow a competitive strategy to ensure the success of their organization. They use a competitive-forces model to help identify where competition may impact their companies.

Top managers choose strategies that address the competitive forces in their industry and enable their organization to sustain a competitive advantage. The three basic competitive strategies are cost leadership, differentiation, and innovation A quick response strategy, which emphasizes competing on the basis of time, is a variation of the other three strategies.

A strategic information system is any information system that is crucial to the company's competitive success. Top managers can focus an information systems strategically on improving the efficiency or the effectiveness of the organization's value chain. Improving efficiency means producing the desired products and services with less work or lower costs; improving effectiveness means increasing the quality of the products and services as perceived by customers.

Chapter Review

▼ Key Terms

artificial intelligence (AI) (p. 386)
automated office (p. 376)
business alliance (p. 377)
chief information officer (CIO) (p. 370)
communication (p. 371)
competitive advantage (p. 390)
competitive forces model (p. 390)
cost leadership strategy (p. 390)
decision style (p. 380)
decision support system (DSS) (p. 382)
differentiation strategy (p. 390)
distributed computing (p. 373)
document imaging system (p. 376)
effectiveness (p. 392)
efficiency (p. 392)
electronic meeting (p. 376)
entry barrier (p. 391)

executive information system (EIS) (p. 384)
expert system (ES) (p. 386)
expert system shell (p. 387)
geographic information system (GIS) (p. 383)
group decision support system (GDSS) (p. 383)
groupware (p. 373)
inference engine (p. 389)
information overload (p. 389)
information system manager (p. 373)
innovation strategy (p. 390)
interorganizational information systems (IOS) (p. 376)
international information system (p. 378)
knowledge base (p. 386)
management (p. 368)

management functions (p. 368)
management information system (MIS) (p. 380)
management levels (p. 369)
management reporting system (p. 382)
management roles (p. 368)
model (p. 380)
paperless office (p. 376)
quick response strategy (p. 391)
semistructured decision (p. 369)
strategic information system (p. 391)
strategy (p. 390)
structured decision (p. 369)
switching costs (p. 392)
transborder data flow (p. 378)
unstructured decision (p. 369)
user interface (p. 386)
workgroup (p. 373)

▼ Interactive Quiz Questions

1. The *Computer Confluence* CD-ROM contains self-test quiz questions related to this chapter, including multiple choice, true or false, and matching questions.
2. The *Computer Confluence* Web site, **www.prenhall.com/beekman**, contains self-test exercises related to this chapter. Follow the instructions for taking a quiz. After you've completed your quiz, you can email the results to your instructor.

   The Web site also contains open-ended discussion questions called Internet Explorations. Discuss one or more of the Internet Exploration questions at the section for this chapter.

▼ Review Questions

1. Define or describe each of the key terms in the "Key Terms" section. Check your answers using the glossary.
2. What are the functions and roles of a manager in an organization?
3. Describe three types of decisions. Which types of decisions are made by different management levels in an organization?
4. Describe the dimensions and several characteristics of information. What information qualities characterize the information needs of managers at different levels in an organization?
5. Describe the basic communication model. How does communication differ depending on time and place?
6. How are collaborative work, distributed computing, automated office, and interorganizational information systems used to improve communication within and between organizations?

7. What are the different phases of the decision-making process? How do models and individual decision styles affect decision making?

8. Describe the characteristics of a MIS. What kinds of reports do they produce?

9. Describe the characteristics of a DSS. What types of information tools do they provide?

10. Describe the characteristics of a GIS. Why would a GIS be useful in a business organization?

11. What are the design features and uses of an EIS?

12. What is a knowledge base? What is an ES? How are the two related?

13. Describe three basic strategies organizations use to compete successfully.

14. How can a strategic information system be used to improve an organization's efficiency? Effectiveness?

▼ Discussion Questions

1.. Managers can have many different information needs. Discuss how managers' information needs would depend on the function or role they are performing in the organization. How would their information needs change depending on the type of decisions they need to make?

2. How important do you think communication is for the success of a modern organization? In what ways does communication improve the quality of products and services provided by an organization to its customers or clients?

3. How could you evaluate whether decisions are made effectively in an organization? What factors or variables would you need to consider in your analysis?

4. If an ES gives you erroneous information, should you be able to sue it for malpractice? If it fails and causes major disruptions or injury, who's responsible? The programmer? The publisher? The owner? The computer?

5. Identify and discuss some of the ethical dilemmas and issues involved with an MIS. A DSS. An ES.

6. How could you evaluate whether an information system could be used strategically to help an organization compete more successfully?

▼ Projects

1. With a class colleague, interview a manager of an organizational unit at your school. Ask the manager to describe the activities he or she performed during the previous workday and the information needed to perform those activities. Discuss the results of the interview with your class colleague and use a word processor to compose a memo to the manager, thanking him or her, and summarizing what you learned.

2. From your personal knowledge and research, identify the various kinds of information systems that are used by your favorite professional sports team. Use a search engine to locate relevant Web sites. Prepare a two-page report using a word processor and distribute it to your class.

3. With a group, visit a service organization in your community, such as a hospital, fire department, church, or restaurant. Interview a manager to identify the information systems he or she uses to support decision-making responsibilities. Present a group oral report to your class describing your findings.

4. Information technology affects human workers and managers positively and negatively. Use email or an electronic chat room to debate the pros and cons of technology with students in your class. Conduct your email discussion over a period of several days.

Case Studies

Venetian Wireless Guest Check-in

The Venetian Hotel in Las Vegas is launching a pilot system that's aimed at using wireless devices to ensure that rooms are ready for arriving guests. Guests will meet hotel clerks at any of several entrances, including the car drop-off area, and be able to show a credit card to check reservations via a wireless LAN connection to a server in real time. Once the reservation has been confirmed, the clerk will be able to encode a room-key card for the guest.

The goal is to eliminate check-in lines at the 3,000-room hotel, which is connected to a casino and conference center. The pilot is expected to cost less than $100,000 and will be deemed a success if it helps business flow and is not a disruption for clerks to handle the devices. Venetian Hotel officials are hoping the system will facilitate guest needs and serve them faster.

Clerks will use rugged handheld computers running the Palm OS operating system, with attached magnetic stripe readers for gathering credit card information. The handheld will be secured with a strap to a clerk's hand, and it will be connected to a separate device on the belt to encode the room-key cards. A short-range radio connection from the handheld to the device on the belt will be used instead of a coiled phone-type cord or an infrared connection, which were considered too awkward in previous trials.

The Venetian Hotel was designed with wireless innovations in mind, including cell towers that permit a variety of cell phones to function. Eventually, guests will be able to check in with their personal cell phones using a password. The hotel's wireless communications network is similar to many that are now being installed by businesses around the world, in places such as in Capetown; South Africa; and Helsinki, Finland.

Adapted from Matt Hamblen, "Las Vegas Hotel to Try Wireless Check-In," *Computerworld*, May 28, 2001; and
http://www.computerworld.com/cwi/story/0,1199,NAV47_STO60898,00.html

Discussion Questions

1. Discuss the communication concepts involved in the Venetian hotel's wireless system.
2. Discuss how the Venetian hotel's wireless applications provide more timely and effective communication between the hotel staff and customers.
3. Are there ethical issues related to the Venetian hotel's use of wireless technologies?

The Knowledge Crunch

It takes more than good flavor and a hearty crunch to sell the salty snacks churned out at Frito-Lay. Corporate executives knew that using corporate information would give employees something they could sink their teeth into. But information was scattered around the company in disparate systems, and there was no easy way for the geographically dispersed sales force to get at it. For example, multiple salespeople would ask the corporate sales, marketing and operations staff for the same types of information and data, such as current private-label trends in their snack category or research on people's shopping behavior. The result was Frito-Lay's support staff ended up performing the same tasks over and over. If that information lived in a central, easily accessible spot, the salespeople could access it as needed.

Additionally, much valuable knowledge was squirreled away on each salesperson's system. There were many idiosyncratic, inefficient methods of capturing information. The sales team also lacked a place for brainstorming and collaboration online. If somebody got a piece of research and wanted to get input from account executives in Baltimore and Los Angeles, the ability to collaborate [online] just wasn't there.

To address these information issues, Frito-Lay designed an information system to be implemented on their corporate intranet. The goals of the system were to streamline knowledge, exploit customer-specific data and foster team collaboration.

The system is a single point of access to multiple sources of information and provides personalized access. The system was designed to give the sales department a central location for all sales-related customer and corporate information and cut down on the time it takes to find and share research. In addition to different types of information about customers—including sales, analysis, and the latest news—the system contains profiles on who's who in the corporation, making finding an internal expert a snap.

Frito-Lay used a consultancy company that built the system in about three months using technologies previously approved by Frito-Lay's IS department, including Lotus Domino, BusinessObjects' WebIntelligence, Java, IBM's DB2 database, and Autonomy, a natural language search engine that enables users to search information in different repositories. The system, known as the Customer Community Portal (CCP), went live in January 2000. Users access the system through a Netscape Navigator browser and enter their name and password on the Frito-Lay intranet.

CCP paid off with increased sales. For example the growth rate of the customer's business in the salty snack category doubled within a year. It also made the sales teams happier. For example, the members of one of the sales team reside in 10 different cities, so the system became extremely valuable for communication and helped cut down on travel. A year after implementing the system, the sales teams were able to share documents concurrently instead of having to send faxes around the country to different offices. They can now manipulate large amounts of data and can look at it online versus having to have somebody physically travel to the retail customer. It's almost a distance-learning tool as much as anything else.

The CCP helped foster a sense of camaraderie and relationship building. For example, the system lists the team members' birthdays. People can also share best practices—on anything under the sun. If someone developed an effective sales presentation for a potential customer in Boston, a salesperson in San Francisco could co-opt the information. Salespeople can also find the latest news about their customers, and there's an automatic messaging feature that informs team members who is online.

Managers use the system for helping them assess employee skill sets, because each salesperson is required to catalog his or her strengths and areas of expertise. It helps managers analyze where people's gaps might be without having to travel to another member's location.

The system has also helped boost employee retention rates. Turnover used to be terrible because salespeople felt pressured

to find vital information and communicate with the rest of the sales team. Salespeople felt frustrated and disconnected because there was no way to collaborate efficiently with the rest of their group unless they flew into a central location.

Adapted from Esther Shein, "The Knowledge Crunch," *CIO Magazine*, May 1, 2001; http://www.cio.com/archive/050101/crunch.html

Discussion Questions

1. Discuss how the CCP system supports communications and decision making at Frito-Lay.
2. Discuss the information needs of the sales persons and managers at Frito-Lay.
3. Discuss the various decision support features of the CCP system.
4. Discuss any information ethical issues related to using the CCP system. What are your suggestions for resolving those issues?
5. Discuss features you would suggest for improving the CCP system.

Weyerhaeuser's Roots

Weyerhaeuser Co. is an $11 million forest products company that uses Internet technology to empower its employees, eliminate waste, and improve the efficiency of its internal business processes. The company operates 28 high-tech sawmills that use laser scanners that position logs to guarantee the best cut. Information about each day's cutting are entered into a database and linked to daily reports which are published on the home page of Weyerhaeuser's intranet, named Roots. The intranet is also used to share real-time production, environmental, personnel, and safety information with workers at locations all over the Northwest.

Roots supports 16,000 workers with email, and 6,500 employees with Netscape Navigator and Microsoft Internet Explorer browsers, and intranet-based applications. Roots is implemented using 40 Web servers that publish 8,000 Web pages that are designed using Microsoft FrontPage. Roots receives about 3,600 hits per day.

Roots is continuously modified and improved to meet corporate goals. Initially, the hierarchical organization of Root's content mirrored that of Weyerhaeuser. The information content is being redesigned based on how subjects and topics relate to one another. Management is still debating whether Weyerhaeuser should give open access to every employee or

restrict access in several ways. Weyerhaeuser's CIO has moved quickly to implement a company-wide process for standardizing on new Internet technology.

(Adapted from Alex Frankel, "New Growth", CIO Web Business, 11(3), 11/1/97, pp 37-41; David Bovet and Joseph Martha, Value Nets: Breaking the Supply Chain to Unlock Hidden Profits. New York, John Wiley & Sons, 2000; and from Weyerhaeuser's Web site at http://www.Weyerhaeuser.com/)

Discussion Questions

1. Which of the three basic strategies—cost leadership, differentiation, or innovation—do you think Weyerhaeuser is following?
2. What competitive advantages does Weyerhaeuser gain by developing and using Internet technologies to improve communications and other business processes?
3. Discuss how Weyerhaeuser's decision-making processes may be improved through their use of Internet technologies.
4. Discuss any ethical issues related to Weyerhaeuser's intranet use by employees.

Sources and Resources

Books

Only the Paranoid Survive: How to Exploit the Crisis Points That Challenge Every Company, by Andrew S. Grove (New York: Bantam Books, 1999). In this widely publicized book, now in paperback, the founder and previous CEO of Intel shares his business philosophy and lots of stories from the front lines of the microprocessor wars.

Competitive Advantage: Creating and Sustaining Superior Performance, by Michael Porter (New York: Simon & Shuster, 1998). In this updated classic text, the author describes the competitive forces affecting how a business organization can survive and thrive in the global competitive business environment.

Harvard Business Review on Managing the Value Chain (Boston: Harvard Business School Press, 2000). This collection of eight essays examines the changing relationship between suppliers, customers, and competitors in the age of technology and globalization, outlining key ideas and providing guidance for incorporating shifts in the value chain into a firm's strategic outlook.

Competing for the Future, by Gary Hamel and C. K. Prahalad (Boston: Harvard Business School Press, 1994). This worldwide bestseller written by a couple of academics is surprisingly readable. The authors claim that to compete successfully, managers must develop an independent point of view about tomorrow's opportunities and build capabilities to take advantage of them. The book is full of examples of how information technology is used strategically in organizations.

The New Science of Management Decision, by Herbert A. Simon (Englewood Cliffs, NJ: Prentice-Hall, 1977). This book is a business classic. Simon describes the process of problem solving in a variety of business and personal settings.

The Nature of Managerial Work, by Henry Mintzberg (New York: Harper & Row, 1973). Another business classic. Mintzberg's description of the various roles of managers in organizations has been the basis of subsequent research and insights into how information systems can be applied to management.

Speed Is Life: Street Smart Lessons from the Front Lines of Business, by Robert Davis (Doubleday & Company, 2001) Bob Davis was the founder and CEO of Lycos. He discusses how quickly companies must act in order to seize new opportunities; explains why size is important in a global economy; and highlights the critical importance of creating and extending a company's brand.

Information Rules : A Strategic Guide to the Network Economy, by Carl Shapiro, Hal R. Varian (Boston: Harvard Business School Press, 1998). One hundred years ago, the emerging telephone and electrical network was transforming business. Today it's the Internet. The authors' main point is that while the circumstances of a particular era may be unique, the underlying principles that describe the exchange of goods in a free-market economy are the same. They offer a deep knowledge of how economic systems work coupled with first-hand experience of today's network economy.

Common Knowledge: How Companies Thrive by Sharing What They Know, by Nancy M. Dixon (Boston: Harvard Business School Press, 2000). The author describes insights into how organizational knowledge is created and how information systems can effectively communicate that knowledge within the organization. The book provides in-depth studies of several organizations-including Ernst & Young, Bechtel, Ford, Chevron, British Petroleum, Texas Instruments, and the U.S. Army-that are leading the field in successful knowledge transfer.

Computer Power and Human Reason (From Judgment to Calculation), by Joseph Weizenbaum (San Francisco: W. H. Freeman, 1995). An MIT computer scientist speaks out on the things computers shouldn't do, even if they can. This classic book is as important now as when it was first published in the 1970s.

Periodicals

Journals like the *MIS Quarterly*, *Journal of Management Information Systems*, *Harvard Business Review*, and *Journal of Organizational Computing and Electronic Commerce* are written primarily for researchers and academics who want to keep up with current research in the field. Articles about information systems research written for managers and the general public are published routinely in magazines and newspapers such as *Business Week*, *Fortune*, the *Wall Street Journal*, *Darwin*, *Upside*, *Information Week*, *CIO (Chief Information Officer),* *Client/Server Computing*, *Beyond Computing*, and *Modern Office Technology*. *Business Geographics* covers the geographic technology revolution in business and is written for managers and the general business reader.

Web Pages

The Web has several sites that are valuable resources for managers. The *Computer Confluence* Web site will help you find them.

15 | Electronic Commerce and E-Business

▼ **In this chapter:**

The growth and impact of electronic commerce

The different forms of electronic commerce

How companies use intranets and extranets

The characteristics of Web sites for electronic commerce

. . . and more.

▼ **On the CD-ROM:**

Video clip showing the impact of electronic commerce

Instant access to glossary and key word references

Interactive self-study quizzes

. . . and more.

▼ **On the Web:**

www.prenhall.com/beekman

Articles about how the Internet is changing business

Links to a variety of e-commerce sites

Resources for exploring e-commerce statistics and Web site design

Self-study exercises

. . . and more.

Jeff Bezos: The Virtual Bookseller

Most people never **have the opportunity**, even in a small way, to make history, which **Amazon.com** is trying to do. It's work hard, **have fun**, **make history**. That's what we're trying to do.

—Jeff Bezos, founder and CEO of Amazon.com

Jeff Bezos was always interested in anything that could be revolutionized by computers; as a child, he wanted to be an astronaut. As an adult intrigued by the amazing growth in use of the Internet, Jeff created a business model that leveraged the Internet's unique ability to deliver huge amounts of information rapidly and efficiently.

Jeff Bezos

He founded Amazon.com, Inc. as an online retailer in 1994. With high ambitions, he initially named the company Cadabra.com before changing it to Amazon.com, after the most voluminous river in the world. Amazon opened its virtual doors in July 1995 with a mission to use the Internet to transform book buying into the fastest, easiest, and most enjoyable shopping experience possible. His mantra, imitated by hundreds of other Internet companies as well, was "get big fast." Amazon did just that, expanding beyond books to become a general store selling music, electronics, household goods, and a myriad of other products. Its growth seemed phenomenal—20 million customers in more than 160 countries bought $2.8 billion worth of merchandise in 2000. Bezos is proud of that performance, which is better than any start-up company in history. Unfortunately, Amazon also lost $1.4 billion doing so.

Fueled by big dreams and seemingly endless cash from investors, Amazon created an unprecedented offering for consumers to use a Web site to purchase merchandise at a low price, with responsive service and quick shipment. When you visit the Amazon.com Web site, you can browse virtual aisles in hundreds of product categories, get instant personalized recommendations based on your prior purchases the moment you log on, receive via email the latest reviews of exceptional new titles in categories that interest you, use other shopping services by linking to other retail Internet sites, and purchase your selections easily using online ordering features.

But the big dreams and investors' cash shriveled quickly during the economic slowdown of 2000. Amazon had formed business alliances with many other Internet retailers (such as Pets.com and Living.com, at the time the largest pet supply and home furnishings companies on the Internet) and other established retailers (such as Borders and Toys "R" Us). Bezos promised investors big returns from agreements to promote these companies on Amazon's Web site. Most of the Internet companies paid Amazon in stock, not cash. During the economic slowdown, many of the Internet companies went out of business, leaving Amazon with worthless stocks. The other retailers suffered their own difficulties, leaving Amazon with greatly reduced revenues.

Bezos acknowledges he underestimated the impact of the economic slowdown on the Internet industry generally and on Amazon's sales in particular. To survive, he analyzed why Amazon loses money. He found, like many of his critics, that Amazon's business model was too complicated, expensive, and inefficient. His new mantra, copied from any number of successful companies, is "march to profitability." Instead of designing flashy new features for its Web site or developing grandiose business strategies, Bezos is focusing on cutting costs and raising revenues. Amazon is undertaking an efficiency drive that includes using a new accounting system that for the first time calculates how much money Amazon makes or loses on each product it sells. Amazon is getting rid of products that are not profitable, cutting the number of errors in its packing and shipping process, moving its call center operations to India, and converting its international warehouses into regional hubs to cut down on inventory levels and delivery times.

Still, Bezos wants Amazon to be the online equivalent of Wal-Mart, with so much sales volume that it has the buying power and efficiency to sell the same products available everywhere, but at low prices, and still make money. What does the future hold for Jeff Bezos? Will Amazon dominate retailing around the world, or will it be the Internet's most spectacular flameout? ▶

Jeff Bezos's Amazon.com is a major player in the global electronic marketplace. Adam Smith, the founding father of Economics, described the market concept in his book *The Wealth of Nations* in 1776, theorizing that "if every buyer knew every seller's price, and if every seller knew what every buyer is willing to pay, everyone in the market would be able to make fully informed decisions and society's resources would be distributed efficiently." The information technologies we describe throughout this book are making a global electronic marketplace possible, coming close to Smith's ideal. The confluence of networking and the Internet especially are revolutionizing the way business is being done. This confluence is electronic commerce.

Electronic Commerce in Perspective

> Firms are increasingly **organized in networks**, both internally and in their **relationships**.
>
> —Manuel Castells, *The Rise of the Network Society*

Electronic commerce (e-commerce) is the process of sharing business information, maintaining business relationships, and conducting business transactions through the use of telecommunications networks. The term e-commerce is relatively new, but the ideas underlying e-commerce have been evolving since computers were first developed for business applications 50 years ago and maybe even since 1845, when Samuel Morse invented the telegraph. Most businesses have used one or more traditional e-commerce tools such as bar coding, fax communication, Electronic Data Interchange, enterprise-wide messaging system, and other private LAN and WAN systems. Since the development of the World Wide Web and the beginning of the commercial use of the Internet in the early 1990s, e-commerce has become Internet based.

Internet-based e-commerce is much more than a set of Internet technologies, however. E-commerce also involves reorganizing internal business processes, fostering external business alliances, and creating new consumer-oriented products and services globally. With e-commerce, companies need to be able to share internal business information and conduct electronic transactions with customers, partners, suppliers, and sometimes even their competitors via the Internet. The term *e-business* is sometimes used interchangeably with the term e-commerce to refer to this broader concept. In this book, the term e-commerce is used in its broadest scope and the term e-business is used to refer to the e-commerce activities of a particular company or organization.

A new aspect of e-commerce is **mobile commerce (m-commerce)**. M-commerce, sometimes also called *m-business*, refers to the use of wireless technologies such as handheld computers, cellular phones, personal digital assistants (PDAs), and two-way pagers. Wireless technologies give users the Internet access they need to conduct e-commerce. Wireless technologies hold tremendous potential for helping workers—be they doctors, home-care nurses, real estate agents, sales managers, or utility representatives—conduct business more effectively outside the office. A Gartner Group study forecasted that by 2004, 65 percent of Global 2000 companies will offer their mobile workers wireless access to perform critical applications. M-commerce revenues are expected to jump from just less than $150 million in 2001 to more than $5 billion by 2004.

The infrastructure of e-commerce, such as the number and distribution of Internet hosts, is not distributed equally worldwide. The growth of e-commerce has been concentrated in North America and Europe.

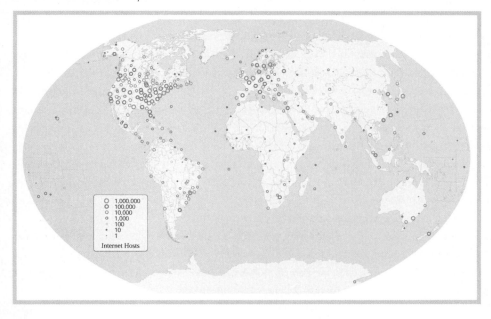

○	1,000,000
○	100,000
○	10,000
○	1,000
·	100
·	10
·	1

Internet Hosts

How E-Commerce Is Transforming Business

E-commerce is all about cycle time, **speed**, globalization, enhanced productivity, **reaching new customers** and sharing knowledge across institutions for **competitive advantage**.

—Lou Gerstner, IBM's CEO

Internet-based electronic commerce continues to develop at a rapid rate despite the economic slowdown in 2000. It's estimated that e-commerce will account for over 8.6 percent of worldwide sales of goods and services within just a few years. Recent surveys by *The Standard* and *InternetWeek*, widely read industry magazines, indicate that there are several thousand Internet-based companies, also referred to as dot coms, that make up only 10 percent to 15 percent of Internet economy revenue and jobs. But the Internet economy has evolved to include the millions of traditional, so-called brick-and-mortar, companies, and a large majority of these better-managed companies utilizing the Internet are operating profitable e-business operations. Fortune 1000 and Global 2000 companies, especially in industries, such as chemicals, energy, financial services, manufacturing, retail and utilities, are pushing ahead aggressively with entire portfolios of e-business projects. And according to another survey by *Interactive Week* magazine, budgets for Internet products and services will continue to rise, in some large companies by as much as 20 percent.

The growth of e-commerce in the United States and Europe is particularly strong. Recent studies by International Data Corporation indicate that spending on goods and services bought over the Internet, either by individuals or companies, in the United States will exceed $1,000 billion, and in Europe will exceed $750 billion by 2004. The spending on the technical and business infrastructure for e-commerce by U.S. companies is forecasted to exceed $900 billion, and by European companies $656 billion by 2004. So by the end of 2004, e-commerce just in the United States may be two trillion dollars and in Europe one-and-a-half trillion dollars.

The longer-term growth of e-commerce is even more robust. Consider that by 2004 e-commerce will account for only about 5 percent of the total U.S. economy. A study by the University of Texas indicates that Internet-related revenue growth is about 20 times the growth rate for the U.S. economy. As part of this growth, companies engaging in e-commerce generate nearly one in five dollars of their revenues from the Internet and directly support 2.476 million workers, including an additional 650,000 jobs. Recent studies by DiamondCluster International, an e-business development consulting company, and by A.T. Kearney, a management consulting firm, show that 70 percent of the more than 200 CEOs surveyed believe the Internet is either essential or important to their company's success. Seventy-two percent said their companies are extremely or moderately active with developing e-business initiatives and strategies. The majority of CEO's said that e-commerce has changed the way they do business by, for example, improving relationships with customers and suppliers, boosting online sales, and bringing efficiency to their supply chain. Most CEO's indicated realistic expectations of what the Internet could do for their businesses. It is the immediate return on investment that drives companies to keep up with technology in those areas. They also believed that about 12 percent of their sales would come via the Internet by 2003, about double current totals.

The expected benefits of e-commerce for a company are enormous. Another University of Texas study indicates that a company selling goods and services over the Internet is three times more likely to see expense reductions, two and a half times more likely to see productivity gains, and more than two and a half times more likely to see market share growth and penetration of new markets as a result of its Internet applications compared with U.S. businesses overall. Such a company can create a competitive advantage by dramatically expanding its market from local to national, to international, and to global. The company can substantially increase the speed and efficiency of business transaction processes, such as order processing, by automating tasks previously performed manually. The company can gather valuable customer information,

Historical and projected e-commerce growth from 2001 to 2005.

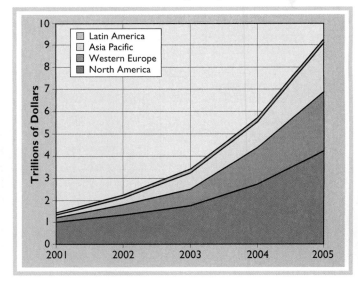

enabling it to form closer interactive relationships with its customers and more accurately anticipate their future purchasing needs. And there is the promise of significant cost savings in conducting business transactions.

E-Commerce Models

Cyberspace has spawned a more resilient type of business. Sans physical plant and inventory, a **Web-based business** can **reinvent itself** in a matter of weeks.

—David Raths, Inc. Technology

The basic idea of e-commerce is that at least two parties—a seller and a buyer—exchange valuable information, products, or services. The exchange, or transaction, can occur between individuals, businesses, and organizations.

There are several forms of e-commerce, or e-commerce models, based on who is involved in the transaction:

Many real estate agencies list available properties on their public Web sites. Links are provided for you to explore specific properties, find information about the community, and communicate via email with the real estate agent.

▶ *Business-to-business (B2B).* The **business-to-business (B2B)** model represents interorganizational information systems in which a company handles transactions within its own value chain and with other businesses and organizations, such as its suppliers, distributors, and bank. For example, Wal-Mart purchases the products it sells in its stores from its vendors over the Internet. B2B is sometimes referred to as **business-to-employee (B2E)** when the focus is primarily on handling the activities that take place within the organization. It is estimated that approximately 70 percent of employees in midsized and large companies have access to internal Web intranet sites. B2B is the most dominant aspect of e-commerce. Jupiter Research estimates that companies worldwide will increase their spending on developing their B2B capabilities from $2.6 billion in 2000 to over $137 billion by 2005. As a result of this investment in B2B infrastructure, the GartnerGroup, a technology research and marketing company, reported that B2B transactions in North America exceeded $433.3 billion in 2000, which comprised 59 percent of the world's share. Asia/Pacific B2B e-commerce totaled $96.8 billion, or 22 percent of the world total, and European B2B was $72.5 billion, or 17 percent of the world total. By 2005, worldwide B2B e-commerce is projected to reach $8 trillion—more than the combined economic output of France, Spain, and Sweden. The Delphi Group, another marketing research firm, surveyed 200 companies of B2B technologies and projected that an overwhelming 50 percent of their transactions conducted online will flow through a B2B marketplace by 2003. And still another market research company, Forrester Research Inc., predicts B2B e-commerce in the United states will grow to $207 trillion in 2004.

Consumers can search for products and purchase them easily online using the catalog display feature of Web sites designed for B2C e-commerce, such as the REI web site.

▶ *Business-to-consumer (B2C).* The **business-to-consumer (B2C)** model represents retailing transactions between a company and individual customers. Examples of B2C are dot-com companies, such as Amazon.com and E*Trade.com, and traditional companies, such as Lands-End and United Airlines, that utilize the Internet to sell to customers via a Web site. B2C is the most visible aspect of e-commerce from a consumer's point of view. According to the Boston Consulting Group, the Web is the fastest-growing retail channel, even though dot-coms declined during the economic slowdown in 2000. They estimated that online retail revenues grew 66 percent in 2000 to $44.5 billion. Much of the retail online sales activity is in the categories of gifts and flowers, entertainment, and computer software and hardware. Worldwide revenues of B2C in 2003 are estimated to be at least $178 billion and of that amount $75 billion in the United States.

▶ *Consumer-to-consumer (C2C).* The **consumer-to-consumer (C2C)** model represents individuals, organizations, or companies that are selling and buying directly with each other via the Internet. A good example of C2C is a Web auction in which individuals or businesses use a Web site to offer items for sale and bid on items to buy. One of the first and most successful consumer auction Web sites is eBay.com with over 29 million registered buyers and sellers.

These e-commerce models apply as well to nonbusiness institutions, such as religious organizations, academic institutions, government agencies, and not-for-profit and social organizations.

In the next three sections, we'll describe intranets, extranets, and public Web sites to support e-commerce transactions in more detail.

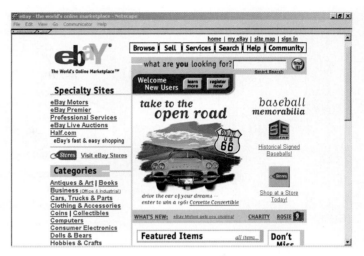

A consumer can use a C2C Web auction site, such as eBay.com, to buy, sell, or trade just about any type of product with other people.

Intranets: E-Commerce to Support Internal Business Processes

> My bottom line is that **intranets** are about **people empowerment**, not technology.
> —Randy J. Hinrichs, Microsoft Corp.

In business-to-employee (B2E) e-commerce, an organization uses Internet technology, organized as an intranet, to support its internal value chain activities as efficiently as possible. Using Internet technology as the basis of intranet design has several benefits, including a cross-platform environment, open standards, reduced hardware and software costs, easy installation, and minimal user training. Most important is that intranets can dramatically improve communications within the organization—any employee can access the organization's intranet from any geographic location by using a Web browser and an Internet connection, provided the employee has the security authorization to use the intranet.

Characteristics of a B2E Intranet

An **intranet** is made up of physical technology and information content. The physical elements of an intranet are a network, a computer with server software installed (including TCP/IF), and other computers with client software installed (including TCP/IP and a Web browser). The physical network can be a LAN or WAN configured using either an Ethernet, or Token Ring, topology. The Ethernet, or Token Ring, topology is the actual hardwire connections between the computers, printers, and other hardware on the network.

The communication software for an intranet includes middleware and TCP/IP. *Middleware* is software that handles the actual physical communications connections between the computers, scanners, printers, and other devices on the network. The TCP/IP software handles the intranet communication protocols for messages transferred between the server and client computers.

Another type of software used in an intranet is security, or **firewall**, software. A firewall protects the intranet against unauthorized access by users on a network external to the organization. Other software used to protect the intranet include user identification and authentication, data encryption, and virus protection.

An intranet for a small company may be a network comprised of only one serve and several client computers.

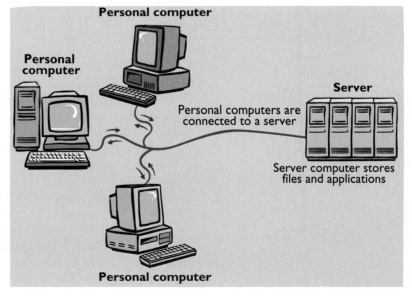

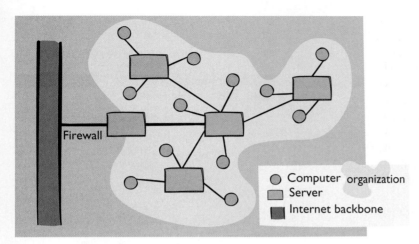

Firewall

Computer organization
Server
Internet backbone

A large company's intranet may be a network comprised of several servers and many client computers. Firewall security guards against unauthorized access to the intranet.

An important goal of an intranet is to provide users within an organization easy access to information. The information content of an intranet is designed just as a public Web site on the Internet. The home page of an intranet typically presents information about what's available on the network and navigational tools—buttons, menus, and navigational maps—to find the information easily. The company establishes guidelines for the design of individual Web pages, and then each department in the organization is responsible for the information it wants to publish on the intranet.

How Organizations Use B2E Intranets

Businesses use intranets to support their internal business processes in three basic ways: to provide employees access to important information for their jobs; to facilitate employees' teamwork and collaboration within and between departments; and to process internal company transactions online.

▌ *Provide access to important information.* Many large companies have massive amounts of information stored in databases that have been placed on their intranets. Any employee with a connection to the intranet can have access to the information with her or his Web browser. For example:

Children's Healthcare Of Atlanta (CHA) has 4,500 employees who use the company's intranet, Careforce Connection, to access current employee data, medical research, and health-care rules and regulations. The intranet has reduced CHA's administrative claims denials and administrative costs, and improved customer service.

Los Alamos National Laboratory publishes several million internal classified, technical, and administrative documents on its intranet. By making this information available electronically, the Los Alamos scientists and managers can access the information quickly and easily, and the organization is saving an estimated $500,000 per year in printing and distribution costs.

Deere & Co. has employees located in 10 countries worldwide who use Deere's intranet to view electronic phone books, read the latest information about the company's pension and benefit plans, review the company's financial position, and work on projects.

General Motors' intranet, named Socrates, lets 100,000 GM employees worldwide search more than 500 internal GM sites, providing news, information, and services related to GM as a whole and their divisions in particular. The site reaches serves up more than 400,000 page views a day.

Newaygo, Michigan, School District's intranet is used by students, teachers, and parents to access all school-related information, including lunch menus, sports and other schedules, daily announcements, attendance records, and much more.

Delta Airlines' intranet, named DeltaNet, houses Delta's aircraft maintenance manuals online. The FAA requires airlines to make sure their manuals are accurate and timely and levies significant fines if they fail. DeltaNet has reduced the labor needed to update the manuals and it has kept Delta from paying those hefty fines.

▌ *Facilitate teamwork and collaboration.* Teamwork and collaboration based on improved communications are becoming the expected way for people to do work in organizations. Intranets play an important role here by making possible the easy access and distribution of information in an organization, no matter where employees are located geographically. For example:

Chrysler's Dashboard intranet provides collaborative workgroup support for its 40,000 employees; employees can access competitive intelligence information, financial modeling tools, and many other work-related information resources.

Engineers at Ford use its intranet to collaborate on car design; the engineers can view computer-generated models of cars to ensure that all the parts fit together correctly.

U.S. West's intranet, named Global Village, enables its employees, who are located in 14 western states, to meet in online chat rooms to discuss ongoing projects and exchange reports and other documents.

Camp Fire Boys & Girls use their intranet, The Camp Fire Café, as the communication link between the national Camp Fire office and more than 125 independent local councils throughout the United States.

▶ *Conduct internal business transactions.* Employees in many organizations can use Web browsers to conduct actual internal business transactions on the organization's intranet. Having employees work electronically on an intranet increases efficiency, reduces paperwork costs, and increases the speed of updating information. For example:

Lucent Technologies, Inc.'s, intranet, named Benefits Central, automates benefit enrollment transactions of nearly 100,000 employees; individual employees are able to use their Web browser to make changes in their health, retirement, and other benefits programs.

The U.S. Department of Health and Human Services' intranet, named Medical Program, is used to do all the agency's health insurance services.

Millipore Corp., a manufacturer of scientific and chemical purification products, uses its intranet, named @Millipore, to support employee self-service pages, including expense reporting, travel booking, and business-card ordering, and uses push technology to distribute to employees information from 120 subscription-based corporate databases.

Rainforest Café, a theme restaurant and retail chain with 25 domestic and 11 international stores, uses its intranet to send daily sales reports from its stores to its Houston headquarters.

PricewaterhouseCoopers, a large accounting and management consulting firm, provides employees an intranet named KnowledgeCurve. Formerly paper-based processes, such as filling out health care reimbursement forms, accessing corporate credit card statements, booking travel, and registering for courses, are now are taken care of online. It's available in 34 countries and has 112,000 users.

E-Commerce to Connect Business Alliances

As an organization uses the Internet and develops its intranet, it may find that its business partners are developing their own intranets. The organizations may come to realize that they could work together more easily and efficiently if they could link their intranet Web sites directly, creating an extranet. Extranets play an important role in the global business strategy of many companies, large and small, enabling them to build alliances with vendors, suppliers, and other organizations internationally. These alliances are sometimes referred to as e-marketplaces.

An extranet, or extended intranet, is a private interorganizational information system connecting the intranets of two or more companies in an e-marketplace. An extranet extends the cross-functional activities between trusted business partners and facilitates their working relationships. Companies using an extranet can place orders with each other, check each other's inventory level, confirm the status of an invoice, and exchange many other types of business information. A good example is Hilton Hotels, which operates a business-to-business extranet to communicate with companies that have contractual agreements to use Hilton's facilities for business travel. Hilton's corporate customers install links to the Hilton Web site on their own intranets, and those links call up customized Web pages with contractual prices and travel limitations.

Characteristics of a B2B Extranet

Organizations can set up an extranet in one of three ways:

▶ A *secure private network* physically attaches the intranets with private leased telephone lines. These types of intranets are relatively expensive because monthly leased line charges can become very costly, especially as additional business partner intranets are added to the network. On the other hand, each business partner can operate inside the system to the full extent of its access and security privileges. Security is relatively high for business transactions because only a limited number of partners have access to the system.

Public network

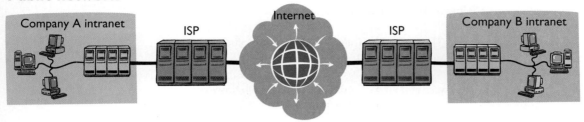

Virtual private network

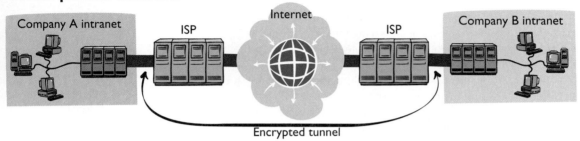

Secure private network

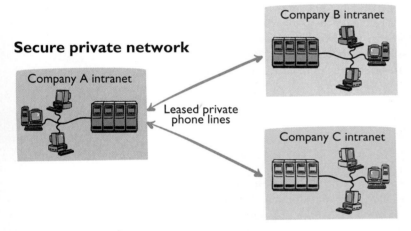

These three types of extranets enable organizations to connect their intranets to facilitate business transactions, communications, and other shared activities.

▌ A *public network* uses a public communications network, such as a public utility telecommunication network or the Internet. These types of intranets are relatively inexpensive to set up and maintain, but security is low. Intranets within a public network extranet are protected only by firewalls and user logon procedures, which are not guarantees that unauthorized users will be blocked from accessing the system.

▌ A **virtual private network** (VPN) uses a public network with special protocols that provide a secure, private "tunnel" across the network between the business partners' intranets. An extranet is called an *Internet VPN* when the public network used is the Internet. VPNs are becoming the preferred method for extranets for a variety of reasons. VPN-based extranets are relatively economical, because companies pay only a flat fee per month plus a fee for the time used for transactions. Privacy and security are good, because data are specially coded—a process called encapsulation—for sending transactions over the Internet; essentially, transactions are conducted via an encrypted channel, or tunnel, between the intranet firewalls of the extranet.

Ensuring secure transactions is a major concern of companies conducting B2B transactions over the Internet, regardless of the type of extranet used. (See Chapter 12, "Computer Security and Risks," to review the many computer security issues with which an organization must cope.)

How Companies Use B2B Extranets

Companies constituting a business alliance use an extranet to achieve certain strategic benefits, such as the following:

▌ Increasing the speed of business-to-business transactions
▌ Reducing errors on intercompany transactions
▌ Reducing costs of telecommunications
▌ Increasing the volume of business with partners
▌ Exchanging business-to-business documents
▌ Checking on inventory and order status from suppliers
▌ Collaborating with business partners on joint projects

Wal-Mart and its suppliers are a good example of companies using a B2B extranet. Wal-Mart built direct software linkages between its suppliers' factories and the cash registers at its stores. One major supplier, Procter & Gamble, can monitor the shelves at Wal-Mart stores through real-time satellite link-ups that send messages to the factory whenever a checkout clerk swipes a Proctor & Gamble item past a scanner at the register. With this kind of minute-to-minute information, Protor & Gamble knows when to make, ship, and display more products at the Wal-Mart stores. The system saves Proctor & Gamble so much in time, reduced inventory, and lower order-processing costs that it can afford to give Wal-Mart "low, everyday prices" without putting itself out of business. As a result, Wal-Mart moves products through its stores more quickly and with less overhead.

The hotel industry is increasingly using extranets. For example, Hilton Hotels is expanding its private supply e-marketplace on a single integrated Web site platform for its 1,600 managed and franchised hotel sites and 3,500 suppliers worldwide.

Another example of a B2B extranet is Caterpillar Inc., a multinational heavy machinery manufacturer. Caterpillar developed extranet applications to reduce the time needed to develop and redesign its vehicle products. The company connected its engineering and manufacturing divisions with its suppliers, distributors, overseas factories, and corporate customers, all in a global extranet. Caterpillar customers, for example, can use the extranet to modify order information while the vehicle is still on the assembly line. This ability to collaborate remotely between the customer and the product developers decreases time delays in redesign work.

Another good example of using an extranet in B2B e-commerce is the automotive industry. The trade association of automotive manufacturers and suppliers has developed an extranet named Automotive Network Exchange (ANX). The extranet was designed as an Internet VPN to provide a global infrastructure for trading partners within the industry, including Chrysler Corp., Ford Motor Co., General Motors Corp., and several dozen major suppliers. One major benefit of ANX is that it reduces telecommunication costs significantly by eliminating the need for manufacturers to have many T1 lines to connect with their suppliers. ANX also reduces the time it takes a supplier to fill an order. Ford, for example, expects to compress some work-order communications from three weeks to five minutes.

FedEx provides services required for shipping and tracking packages worldwide. The shipping status of packages and other critical information is stored on the FedEx extranet which is integrated with the customers' order and warehousing systems.

A company can use an extranet successfully through proper planning and collaboration with its business partners. However, a principal barrier to achieving success is a lack of trust in using the network as the main method for sharing information. As with intranets, extranets work well only if the business partners are willing to share information in an open and consistent manner. In an effort to enhance a climate of trust, 19 corporations from the United States, Europe, and Asia are forming the Global Trading Web Council, a multi-industry corporate alliance that aims to be the world's first international B2B network. Sponsored by CommerceOne, an e-commerce software and services company, the goal is to integrate various e-marketplace extranets into the Global Trading Web where organizations can have marketplace-to-marketplace communication.

B2C for Connecting with Customers on the Internet

As you read in the two preceding sections, intranets are used to support an organization's internal business processes, and extranets are used to support the business-to-business processes of two or more organizations. A third aspect of e-commerce is to conduct business transactions with consumers. To conduct B2C transactions on the Internet, a company provides customers with a public Web site where they can search product catalogs, retrieve product information, order and pay for a product, and look up customer service information. For example, Dell Computer Corporation has unique Web sites for customers in 80 countries and 23 languages, and does $35 million a day in online sales—43 percent of its total revenue. Another good example is the Charles Schwab & Co. Web site, which is used by 3.3 million customers to access their accounts online, encompassing $349 billion in customer assets—roughly half of Schwab's total business.

Characteristics of Effective B2C Web Sites

> You cannot have a **better tomorrow** if you are thinking about yesterday **all the time**.
>
> —Charles F. Kettering, American inventor

A company must develop a well-designed Web site to conduct business effectively with consumers on the Internet. A bad design can cost a Web site 40 percent of repeat traffic. A good design can keep customers coming back. Features of a well-designed Web site include the following:

▶ *Speed of transactions.* As with any business transaction, speed of service is critical for attracting and keeping customers. If a company's Web site is too slow, customers will find and use a competitor's faster Web site.

▶ *Large, up-to-date product selection.* Finding the right product at the right price is a consumer's mantra. Electronic catalogs can hold thousands of pages of product information at low cost for the company compared to printed catalogs and a rich, varied selection for consumers not available in print. In fact, many companies, such as Prentice Hall, a New Jersey–based publisher, have developed entirely new electronic content products that are available only on the Web.

▶ *Ease of use.* The customer should be able to move easily through a business transaction without getting lost or confused. A Web site must be well organized, providing navigation tools and a search engine to find and evaluate product information and well-designed online forms so that the customer can complete a transaction quickly. A good example is Amazon Booksellers, which sells exclusively through its Web site. Customers can search among 2.5 million book titles using Amazon's subject directory and search engine and use an easy-to-read online form to type their address, phone number, and credit card number for billing. However, users can run into trouble even at a well-designed, well-financed site. Several studies have shown that people typically cannot find the information they are seeking on a Web site about 60 percent of the time.

▶ *Secure transactions.* Currently, there are two obstacles to expanding B2C e-commerce: ensuring safe and private transactions technically and consumer perception of whether the Internet is safe or unsafe for credit card usage. Both obstacles are gradually being brought down. Message encryption standards are being developed that use software for authenticating the parties involved in a credit card purchase on the Internet, and transmitting credit card numbers over the Internet using encryption is probably safer now than many people think. As the public's experience grows with using trusted Web sites, people's confidence matures, although they should avoid Web sites of unknown companies unless they can show evidence of good security.

▶ *After-sale features.* After a customer completes a purchase transaction, the Web site should provide the customer after-sale information, including confirmation of the order and online support for customer questions regarding delivery, repairs and maintenance, and warranty.

An organization can conduct business with consumers over the Internet by making its intranet publicly accessible on the Web.

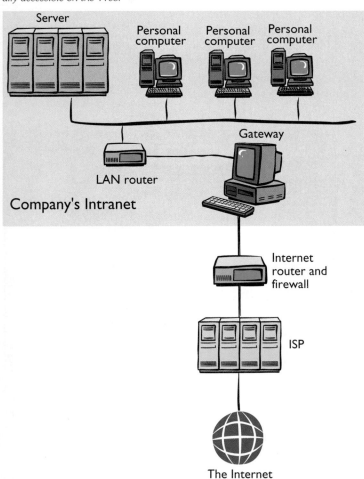

Server

Personal computer

Personal computer

Personal computer

LAN router

Company's Intranet

Gateway

Internet router and firewall

ISP

The Internet

Examples of these after-sales features are common on travel, car, and hotel reservation Web sites.

In addition to the previously mentioned Web site features, a company must also pay attention to two other important issues: how the company should connect their intranet to the Internet for public access and how to design the Web site effectively.

▶ *Connecting to the Internet.* Before a company opens up its intranet or other Web-based business processes to the outside world, it has to be equipped to handle the potential additional network traffic and applications. Customers don't like to wait, so the need for speed is the name of the game here. Based on an evaluation of its intranet's capacity and the potential consumer demand, a company might need to upgrade the size and speed of the network's internal cabling, install additional servers and routers, and install Web server software. Also, the company must decide which Internet Service Provider (ISP) to use to connect to the Internet. An ISP furnishes a dialup, ISDN, T1 line, or cable modem connections to the Internet. It is important far a company to contract with an ISP that provides high-quality, reliable Internet connections at a reasonable cost and that the ISP is a stable business and provides excellent technical support.

▶ *Designing the Web site.* You read about important technical design guidelines of a Web site in Chapter 11, From Internet to Information Infrastructure." Besides technical issues, several managerial questions concern the effectiveness of an organization's B2C Web site. What is it doing for us? Is it helping us compete? Is the site helping us meet corporate goals and improve the bottom line? How can we manage it better?

When a company develops a public Web site, it should be in response to a business need, although many firms have developed sites even though they weren't sure why. The best Internet sites have a well-articulated goal or purpose and target a specific market or customer audience, and their success is measured against the specific objectives. Depending on the objectives, there are many ways to measure the effectiveness of a Web site, and the number of hits a site gets is not necessarily one of them.

Another major issue in Web site design is identifying the content, structure, and design elements of the site. It makes sense for a company to publish electronically catalogs, brochures, and annual reports that it already publishes in print. However, the multimedia and hypertext capabilities of the Web provide the potential for a much richer and varied content customers can search and use. On the other hand, it is easy to throw anything onto the site because it is relatively easy and inexpensive to do so. A key to a good Web site design is to give the user essential information and avoid information overload. Also of critical importance in Web site design is the organization, or structure, of the content so that a user can find relevant information quickly. The Web pages constituting a Web site are usually organized in some combination of hierarchical and sequential structures wherein the most important information can be accessed in no more than three mouse clicks. Still another important consideration is the design elements, such as a logo, colors, and other graphics, which should be used consistently on the Web pages making up the site. A site that has a consistent look and feel is pleasant and easy to use.

A good way to foster customer loyalty for using a Web site is to include interactive features that enable users to provide feedback and comments about their needs, how well the site is filling those needs, and suggestions for improvement. Three interactive features are often included on public Web sites: email, discussion groups, and chat rooms.

Finally, the company must decide where to locate the public Web site physically. Large organizations frequently have the technical know-how and capacity to run the site on their own servers. However, many small- and medium-sized companies opt for Web hosting, or contracting with another company, usually an ISP, to run the site on that company's servers. Web hosting is a popular growing industry. A company should take care to pick a Web host that is a well-run, reliable business and that provides acceptable security, state-of-the-art technology, and excellent customer service.

In addition to selling sheet music, software, and accessories, SchoolMusic.com provides community-building features such as chat room, message boards, and an online magazine. Music teachers from around the country swap lesson plans and curriculum ideas and share the joys of leading the school band.

Some Technical Requirements of E-Commerce

The labyrinth of telecommunications networks that span the globe and all the Web technologies that comprise the Internet infrastructure, described in Chapters 9, "Networking and Telecomunication," and 10, "From Internet to Information Infrastructure," make it possible for any sized organization to engage in e-commerce. However, there are several important Web server requirements and e-commerce software requirements.

Web Server Requirements

A company, organization, or individual who wants to engage in e-commerce must have a *Web server*, including both hardware and software. The server's role is to support an effective, user-friendly Web presence, process and respond to Web client requests, facilitate B2B and B2C online transactions, and support customer service. An important criteria when you build an e-commerce site is the capacity of the server to handle the volume of e-commerce transactions and traffic on the site. For example, a Web site such as Yahoo.com with many thousands of visitors must have a server, or even several servers, with a large processing capacity. Another criteria is the scalability of the Web server, meaning whether the server hardware and software combination can be quickly and easily expanded, or scaled, if the Web site traffic increases.

Most servers run on either Windows NT computers or on Unix-based operating systems. Unix-based machines, such as those that run the Sun Microsystems Solaris operating system, are more popular, especially in large companies that require a high-capacity Web site.

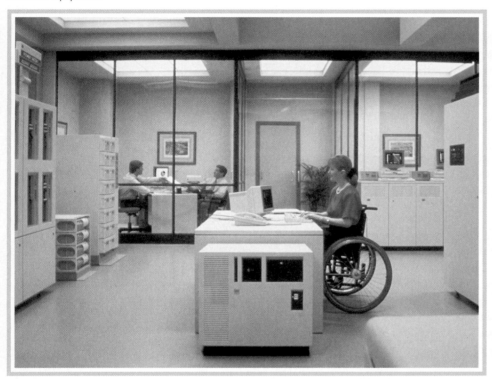

A company that engages in e-commerce must maintain a stable, secure, environmentally sound computer room for its Web site servers and other equipment.

Beside the operating system, there are other important Web server software features. Web server software includes basic capabilities of security, FTP, search engines, and data analysis of visitor information to the site. Web server software also includes site-management capabilities that check for problems and errors, especially link checking, or hyperlinks that do not work. (Linkbot Pro, Big Brother, and Siteinspector are popular types of site-management software.) Other Web server software includes tools to develop Web sites and Web pages, especially pages with dynamic content, or information that changes in response to a Web client's request.

A recent report by Netcraft, a networking consulting company, indicates that companies most often use four Web server software programs: Apache HTTP Server, Microsoft Internet Information Server, Netscape Enterprise Server, and O'Reilly Webster Professional.

Large companies can usually develop an e-commerce site on their own, but many companies, both large and small, and individuals use a third-party ISP as a host provider. A third-

The Yahoo!Shopping site arranges product information as a catalog and provides links to specific merchants' Web sites.

party host provider has the expertise to decide on the best server hardware/software combination and to provide all the management and staffing services for the site. Deciding on the best host provider for you or your company can be risky. The Web Host Guild, a consortium of 40 Web hosting companies, is developing industry standards for all hosting companies and tries to protect consumers from unscrupulous host providers to help identify the honest, legitimate host companies that exist.

E-Commerce Software Requirements

E-commerce software is hosted on a Web server and provides the actual online capabilities for the commercial services provided to consumers and business partners on the Web site.

One type of service that e-commerce software must provide is finding and delivering business information, usually as a catalog display. For example, the Yahoo!Shopping Web site is organized as a catalog arranging items into groups.

Another important e-commerce software capability is providing on-demand customer service. This is done in B2C with a shopping cart capability that keeps track of the items a customer has selected to purchase.

A critical service that e-commerce software must support is transaction processing. The software must be able to do all the typical calculations for a transaction, including computing taxes and shipping costs. The software must also be able to collect payments from customers accurately and securely.

Many large companies in B2B develop their own e-commerce software, but small and midsize businesses in both B2B and B2C use a **Web hosting service**. Similar to a server host provider, a Web hosting service provides the e-commerce software and expertise to run an on-line business. Good examples of these are B-City, Blizland.com, and HyperMart. They provide free space on their servers and easy-to-use templates to set up your business Web pages. A drawback of these free host sites is that customer purchases are handled via email between the hosting service and the merchants, who must handle all the transaction steps, including processing the payment from the customer. A full-service Web hosting service provides comprehensive customer transaction processing along with shopping cart software and better software tools to build and maintain your business Web site, all for a monthly fee and usually some percentage of each customer transaction. Examples of full-service Web hosting services are Yahoo!Store, Virtual Spin Internet Store, ShopBuilder, and GeoShops.

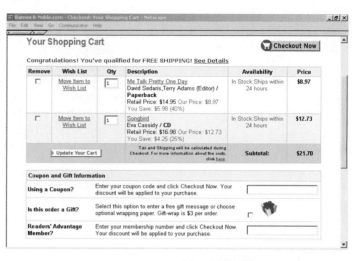

Most B2C Web sites, such as Barnes & Noble, have a shopping cart feature that keeps track of the items you have selected to purchase.

HyperMart is a Web hosting service that provides inexpensive and easy to use tools to individuals and small companies for building and maintaining an e-commerce site

Ethical Issues of E-Commerce

Is it possible to have an **ideal world** in which **ethical awareness** is pervasive? Is such a world even **desirable**?

—Richard O. Mason, information systems professor

Top managers, particularly in large companies, are challenged ethically when they consider using e-commerce, to gain competitive advantage. One difficult ethical issue is gathering information about competitors and monitoring their activities. It is ethical to use publicly available databases to find information about competitors, but managers need to be careful not to use unethical information-gathering practices, such as pressuring a competitor's employees to reveal information or otherwise invading the privacy of individuals.

A major e-commerce ethical issue is top managers' responsibility for their organizations to develop a code of ethics and professional conduct, especially in the area of the Internet. (This is a good time for you to review the information code of ethics we discussed in Chapter 14, "Information Technology in Management.") One of the main challenges is to maintain trust between the people engaging in e-commerce. If that trust is lost, it is difficult to reestablish, and the potential benefits for the company, and for society as a whole, are diminished. Publishing the company's information code of ethics as a link on the company's Web site ensures that users—both the company's information workers and customers—are aware of the company's e-commerce policies. You should look for the following elements in an organization's Web site code of ethics:

▶ A statement of the organization's privacy policy.
▶ A statement that a person's permission must be secured before his or her ID, photo, ideas, or communications are used or transmitted.
▶ A statement on how the company will inform customers of the intended uses of personal information gathered during an online transaction and how to secure permission from customers for those uses.
▶ A statement that addresses issues of ownership with respect to network postings and communications.
▶ A statement of how the company monitors, or tracks, user behaviors on the Web site.

Even though voluntary ethical policies are important, poor practices for handling personal information are a big problem for American businesses and government. Consumers are becoming more impatient with companies and organizations that play fast and loose with the privacy of customer information. Here are some recent well-publicized examples:

▶ Each of Intel's Pentium III computer chips contains a unique electronic personal serial number that can be tracked over the Internet and possibly through e-commerce transactions. Privacy groups have protested, but the ID remains, and the chip may soon be banned in Europe, which has stricter privacy policies.
▶ Online auction house ReverseAuction.com allegedly collected consumers' personal information from competitor eBay and sent emails to those consumers soliciting their business. According to the U.S. Federal Trade Commission (FTC), ReverseAuctions.com signed up at eBay, disregarded the privacy agreement posted on the rival auction site, and copied the information from bidders to send solicitations that were later deemed deceptive by the FTC. ReverseAuctions consented to a settlement but said it did not gather any confidential information from the eBay site.
▶ Interloc, an online bookseller and ISP, was accused of intercepting email messages directed by online bookseller Amazon.com to Interloc's bookseller clients with Interloc email addresses. The company was accused of trying to steal business strategies from its industry competitor. Alibris, the new owner of Interloc, settled the case.
▶ The FTC brought suit against Liberty Financial Companies for violating the privacy rights of children who frequented its data privacyYoung Investor Web site. The FTC alleged that the company had used prizes and contests to encourage children to disclose their names and addresses as well as information such as stock holdings and the amount of weekly allowances that could be used to market to their parents.

Proponents of voluntary self-regulation fear that the more publicity these situations get, the more inclined Congress will be to act. Businesses and trade organizations favor self-regulation fearing that government rules would quash the growth of e-commerce. Privacy fundamentalists and various politicians, however, see rigid privacy legislation as a necessity.

Unlike Canada, Europe, Australia, and even Hong Kong, Americans lack both the legislation that would establish overall privacy standards and a regulatory agency that could advise businesses on acceptable privacy practices. The United States does have many laws relating to the issue of privacy, but they affect only certain industries and consumer segments. For example, Americans have the legal right to see their credit records. Another law prohibits video rental stores from releasing the names of the movies that you rent. The recent Health Insurance Portability and Accountability Act requires health care providers and hospitals to protect the confidentiality of an individual's health information. The Children's Online Privacy Protection Act of 1998 requires certain commercial Web sites to obtain parental consent before collecting, using, or disclosing personal information about children under 13.

Guidelines for Web Site Content

Although the Supreme Court declared unconstitutional the 1996 Communications Decency Act, there still exists a fine line between freedom of expression and irresponsible behavior. Sensitive to social norms, companies struggle to decide what kind of content is and is not acceptable to put on their intranet and public Web sites. From an ethical perspective, persons must realize the effect that a Web site's content may have on others. A company's Web site is a form of communication, and, as with other forms of communication, Web sites work best when they show respect for the people who use them.

The following guidelines will help you design a Web site that meets the overall communications standards of the company:

▶ Decide whether to allow employees to set up their own Web pages on the company intranet. If you do allow it, formulate a general idea of the purpose that individuals' Web pages play in their work. This helps in developing a policy and providing employees with a rationale for that policy.

▶ Decide on standards of acceptable text and graphics. Guidelines should address the unacceptable use of obscenities, nudity, racist language, provocative pictures and jokes, symbols, and other offensive communication.

▶ Ensure that the content standards are explicitly clear and are consistent with other company policies on sexist and racist behavior, offensive material on office walls, and other unacceptable behavior.

▶ Encourage employees to think about who should and shouldn't have access to information before posting the information on the Web site. Employees should be aware of the security risks involved with using the Internet and think carefully about who they give access to what.

▶ Remember that Web site content policies are an extension of other Netiquette guidelines, social etiquette, and common decency.

The United States does not have an overall scheme for dealing with the issues of data privacy. In contrast, the European Union adopted the European Union's Data Protection Directive in October 1998. The directive establishes a high level of legal protection for the privacy of individuals and personal data within the EU. The directive also prohibits companies from transferring personally identifiable information from EU member countries to jurisdictions where that information is not treated with respect by law. Because the United States does not have an umbrella privacy policy, the EU could choose to stop the transfer of all data until a compromise is reached.

As privacy legislation is proposed and regulatory issues unfold, U.S. companies are urged to be active in discussions of how privacy should be handled publicly and within their own corporate structures. IBM and Disney are good examples of self-regulation—both do a great deal of advertising on other Web sites and have a policy that any site they advertise on had better have an ironclad privacy policy. Also, both companies, along with others such as America Online (AOL) and Intel, are working with government groups, such as the FTC's Advisory Committee on Online Access and Security, and industry-sponsored organizations, such as the Online Privacy Alliance and World Wide Web Consortium (W3C).

But compliance with Internet privacy legislation has a long way to go. For example, the Federal Trade Commission (FTC) recently passed the Children's Online Privacy Protection Act (COPPA) providing guidelines for protecting children's privacy on the Internet. A report from the Annenberg Public Policy Center of the University of Pennsylvania revealed that, since COPPA has been in effect, many of the 162 sites with the highest percentage of child visitors under age 13 often did not live up to the spirit and sometimes even the letter behind the rules. A typical finding was that of the sites surveyed, 17 collected information about the users but didn't post links to their privacy policies from the home page. Of those that did have a link, 44 percent followed FTC guidelines by putting the link in a different font; but only 6 percent put the link in a different color and 68 percent put the link at the bottom of the home page.

Researchers Sniffing for Clues on How We Surf the Web

By Matthew Fordahl

How do people find what they're looking for on the World Wide Web? In this newspaper article, Matthew Fordahl describes research being done at Xerox's Palo Alto Research Center (PARC) to develop a program that automatically determines a Web site's usability.

How do people find what they're looking for on the World Wide Web?

Most simply follow the call of the wild. The same theories that describe how animals behave while sniffing for prey also can predict how people ferret out information in the jungle of cyberspace, researchers say. Foraging theories, developed by ecologists decades ago, are now being applied to Internet usage in an attempt to understand how Web sites can be made more intuitive and less like a maze.

Ultimately, researchers hope to develop a program that automatically determines a site's usability, said Ed Chi, a computer scientist at Xerox's Palo Alto Research Center (PARC). The Web site is **http://www. parc.xerox.com**. The key, according to Chi, is understanding Web surfers' basic instincts, so searching for information becomes more intuitive. "We discovered people don't like to think. They'd rather have the thinking done for them," Chi said.

Usability is more important than ever, as both Internet usage and the number of sites soar. Many people have always found it easier for some reason to buy groceries, books and dog food at actual stores. To find out why, computer scientists and psychologists are working together on the project at PARC, where such technologies as the computer mouse, laser printers and Ethernet networking first saw light. At the very least, the team is providing a scientific foundation for Web design, said Jakob Nielsen, a Web usability consultant. His site is **http://www.webuse.com**. "There is an appalling lack of good research in Web usability and fundamental thinking in the field," he said. "Most academics think that the Web is beneath them, that it's too good and it's too practical."

One of the biggest problems is that users are often clueless as where to go next, like tourists who are stuck in a foreign country without knowing the language. To get a better sense of how people use the Web, the scientists asked research subjects to perform simple tasks. They were closely watched, told to talk about what they were doing and connected to a device that tracked their eye movements.

In one chore, the subjects were told to find and buy a poster for the movie "Antz."

Researchers then studied each link and site as the users clicked from search engines like Alta Vista to more specific sites.

By analyzing users' actions, the links and other data, the scientists determined the strength of the information "scent." "You can think of information scent as basically the idea of leaving bread crumbs all over the place in the information environment," Chi said.

In the real world, strong scents lead animals to food. It's an important part of foraging theory, said Peter Pirolli, a cognitive psychologist at PARC. "You're always judging the cues in your environment with respect to your experience, saying what information is relevant to what," he said. "You're continuously making those judgments."

Researchers say the most usable sites provide useful clues to where a link will take a user. Amazon.com's site, for example, generates suggestions based on a user's purchases and previous searches.

The experiments provide insight into other reasons why Web surfers might abandon one site in favor of others. An overabundance of links and confusing presentations are common problems. "They decide to quit not because the information isn't there, but because the amount of cognition it would take is so high," Chi said.

Besides better understanding why some sites are easy and others just plain confusing, the team hopes to finish a program that can figure out how usable a Web site is. Bloodhound, as it's called, analyzes words and links, determining scent based on a formula. It then computes how easy it would be to find information, without having to hire human testers. "Our idea is to take as many people out of the usability loop as much as possible," Chi said.

Nielsen doubts such a program will ever be as effective as watching real people click their way through Web sites—at least until artificial intelligence is available. But, he added, the PARC research does lend scientific credence to good design practices, such as including meaningful descriptions. Though obvious, the rules are not always followed.

"Common sense isn't as common as you think, as proven by how often rules are violated," Nielsen said.

DISCUSSION QUESTIONS

1. Based on your experience using the Web, what do think makes a Web site easy to use?
2. Select a particular Web site that you have used frequently. What suggestion would you make to the designers to improve the useability of the site?

Summary

A major new strategy for conducting business is electronic commerce (e-commerce). E-commerce is the sharing of business information, maintaining business relationships, and conducting business transactions through the use of telecommunications networks, especially the Internet. Internet-based e-commerce is much more than new Internet technologies, however. E-commerce is also about reorganizing internal business processes and external business alliances and creating new consumer-oriented products globally.

Organizations are following a four-step path for using the Internet to conduct business. Typically, a company decides first to use email as a communication tool; then it later decides to create a public Web site, and then later still it decides to develop a private intranet, and finally it learns how to use the Internet to actually conduct business transactions with its customers, suppliers, and other organizations.

There are three main e-commerce configurations using the Internet: intranet, extranet, and public Web sites. An intranet is an internal information system based on Internet client/server technology, including TCP/IP protocols and Web tools, to support the value chain activities between individuals and departments within an organization. An extranet is a private interorganizational information system connecting the intranets of two or more companies in a business alliance. Also, a company can connect its intranet to the Internet and operate a publicly accessible Web site to support business-to-customer transactions.

An intranet comprises physical technology and information content. The physical elements of an intranet are a network, a computer with server software installed including TCP/IP, and other computers with client software installed including TCP/IP and a Web browser. A firewall protects the intranet against unauthorized access by users on a network external to the organization. The company establishes guidelines for the design of individual Web pages, and then each department in the organization is responsible for the information it wants to publish on the intranet. Companies use intranets to provide employees access to important information for their jobs, to facilitate teamwork and collaboration within and between departments, and to process internal company transactions online.

An extranet extends the cross-functional activities between trusted business partners and facilitates their working relationships. Extranets play an important role in the global business strategy of many companies, large and small, enabling them to build alliances with vendors, suppliers, and other organizations internationally. An extranet can be set up either as a secure private network, as a public network, or as a virtual private network (VPN). Each configuration uses a different type of telecommunications technology to connect the intranets comprising the extranet. A major concern of companies conducting business-to-business transactions over an extranet is the guarantee of secure transactions.

A third aspect of e-commerce is to conduct business transactions with customers. A company can connect its intranet to the Internet and operate a publicly accessible Web site. A customer can use a Web browser to connect to the company's internet site and conduct an entire purchasing transaction online—from browsing through product catalogs, retrieving specific product information, and using an online form to order and pay for a product or conduct some other type of transaction. A company's Web site should be easy to use, support speedy and secure transactions, and provide up-to-date product selections.

Although e-commerce has many technical requirements, Web server and e-commerce software requirements are particularly important. The Web server must have the capacity to handle the volume of e-commerce transaction on a company's Web site. Also, appropriate server software must include capabilities of security, FTP, search engines, site management, and tools to develop Web sites and Web pages, especially pages with dynamic content. The e-commerce software requirements include the capability of information search and retrieval, providing on-demand customer service, and supporting customer transaction processing. Several e-commerce Web hosting services are available that provide the software you need to set up your business on the Web.

A company conducting business on the Internet should develop an information code of ethics that ensures that users of the Web site—both the company's information workers and customers—will be aware of the company's e-commerce policies, especially consumer information privacy.

Chapter Review

▼ Key Terms

business-to-business (B2B) (p. 408)
business-to-consumer (B2C) (p. 408)
consumer-to-consumer (C2C) (p. 409)
dot coms (p. 407)
emarketplace (p. 411)

electronic commerce (e-commerce) (p. 406)
e-commerce software (p. 417)
extranet (p. 409)
firewall (p. 409)
intranet (p. 409)

mobile commerce (m-commerce) (p. 406)
virtual private network (VPN) (p. 412)
Web hosting service (p. 417)

▼ Interactive Quiz Questions

1. The *Computer Confluence* CD-ROM contains self-test quiz questions related to this chapter, including multiple choice, true or false, and matching questions.
2. The *Computer Confluence* Web site, **www.prenhall.com/beekman**, contains self-test exercises related to this chapter. Follow the instructions for taking a quiz. After you've completed your quiz, you can email the results to your instructor.

   The Web site also contains open-ended discussion questions called Internet Explorations. Discuss one or more of the Internet Exploration questions at the section for this chapter.

▼ Review Questions

1. Define or describe each of the key terms in the "Key Term: section. Check your answers using the glossary.
2. Define e-commerce. Why is the Internet important for e-commerce?
3. Describe the phases a typical company goes through to incorporate the use of the Internet for business purposes.
4. Describe the three forms of e-commerce.
5. What are the purposes and objectives of an intranet? What are the main characteristics of an intranet?
6. What are the purposes of middleware and a firewall in an intranet?
7. What are three important ways companies use intranets?
8. What are the purposes and objectives of an extranet? What are the main characteristics of an extranet?
9. Describe some of the issues a company must deal with to conduct business with consumers over the Internet successfully.
10. Describe the features of a well-designed company Web site used to conduct business effectively with consumers on the Internet.
11. Describe the purpose of a Web server in an e-commerce company.
12. List the capabilities e-commerce software should provide.
13. Describe the ethical issues involved in electronic commerce.

▼ Discussion Questions

1. Discuss why you believe e-commerce is important in today's business world. What impacts do you think e-commerce is having on consumers?
2. Can you identify examples of e-commerce applications within your college or university? Discuss how your school could use an intranet to improve its internal operations, such as class registration. How could such an intranet be used for competitive advantage for your school?
3. Can you identify opportunities for using an extranet at your college or university? Discuss how your school could form a business alliance with its suppliers (such as book publishers and office suppliers) and use an extranet to conduct its B2B transactions more efficiently? How could such an extranet be used for competitive advantage for your school?
4. Discuss the design characteristics of a B2C Web site. From the consumer's point of view, which characteristics are more important than others? From the business point of view, which characteristics are more important than others?
5. Discuss the issues you would need to consider if you were to create a B2C Web site for a small company.

▼ Projects

1. Find an example of a business organization that is using the Internet and the World Wide Web to increase its competitive advantage in its industry. What competitive strategy is the organization following? Is the Internet being used to decrease costs? Increase value to the customers? Use a word processor to compose a report describing your findings to your teacher.
2. Form a team and visit a local company that has a Web site on the Internet. Interview the manager and others about the company's Internet philosophy. What is the purpose of the company's Web site? Who designed the site? Who maintains the site? Does the company advertise on the Internet? Does the company use an intranet or extranet? What are the company's plans for its future use of the Internet? Use a word processor to prepare a three- to five-page summary of the interview.
3. Create a list of factors, or characteristics, of a well-designed public Web site for conducting business transactions effectively with consumers. Use a search engine to locate the public Web sites of several competitors in the same industry. Then use your list to evaluate the effectiveness of each of the Web sites. Use a word processor to present your findings in a row-column layout.
4. Using a Web browser, visit two Web sites that offer a similar shopping experience, for example, two clothing sites or two bookstore sites. Evaluate how each company handles your security and privacy concerns.
5. Form a team and use Yahoo!Store to create a storefront business. Yahoo!Store enables you to create and save a storefront free for 10 days. Create a small store with only a few items. When you finish building your store, visit it as a customer and print several of your store's Web pages.

Case Studies

Kroger Online

Kroger Co., the nation's largest grocery chain has a two-pronged Internet strategy: moving full-force on its e-marketplace to streamline its supply chain, while taking a patient approach on the still unproven business of online grocery sales.

Kroger Chairman and CEO Joseph Pichler wants to find a profitable online shopping formula. "We're not waiting for somebody else to be successful and then jumping on the bandwagon. We are aggressively testing models, but so far we have not found one that meets the test for ROI (return on investment)."

But other Kroger executives like the success of Kroger's B2B strategy. For example, Kroger participated in four GlobalNetXchange auctions, which were used to procure supplies for stores. Kroger became a partner in GNX, joining founders Carrefour Corp. (France), J Sainsbury (U.K.), METRO AG (Germany), Oracle Corp., and Sears, Roebuck & Co.

Kroger execs think the best is yet to come. GNX is now identifying a supply-chain software provider—likely to be Oracle—to provide CPFR (Collaborative Planning, Forecasting and Replenishment) and other supply-chain applications. Kroger expects the exchange's links to suppliers to increase distribution efficiencies and reduce the cost of purchasing food products.

With more than 2,300 supermarkets in 31 states, Kroger is king of the U.S. food-retailing hill. Its $13 billion merger with Fred Meyer stores helped push annual sales to over $43 billion. And while competitors Albertson's and A&P have had disappointing earnings, Kroger's performance only solidified its position.

Like many of its brick-and-mortar lcompetitors, Kroger has just dipped a toe in e-retailing, with only its King Soopers unit in Colorado offering online grocery shopping. Similarly, Albertson's has pilot online programs in the Dallas and Seattle areas.

Adapted from David Lewis, "Kroger Takes Separate Roads to the Internet," September 18, 2000.

Discussion Questions

1. Describe the type of e-commerce model represented by Kroger. How would you describe Kroger's e-commerce strategy?
2. As a food vendor, what advantages or disadvantages are there to being a supplier to Kroger? What are the advantages or disadvantages to Kroger's customers?
3. What competitive advantages or disadvantages does Kroger have compared to its competitors because of its e-commerce lstrategy?

Foreign Laws Trip Up Another Net Company

Internet companies based in the United States are running into trouble with international laws. A German court ruled that America Online (AOL) is liable for allowing customers to trade pirated music on its service. A similar case in the United States is the recording industry's crusade against music piracy. In a landmark case for the online music industry, Napster is being sued by the Recording Industry Association of America for alleged piracy. Napster's software enables users to share MP3 libraries with others, and RIAA say Napster is building a business on the backs of artists and copyright owners. The case may help settle whether product manufacturers are liable for the ways in which their products are used.

Although phone companies are protected from liability, if someone uses a phone to harass someone, ISPs are not as well protected against their users' infractions. Under the Digital Millennium Copyright Act, ISPs can be liable if they are notified of copyright infringements but fail to take action. The ruling in Germany against AOL means that online services may have to take more seriously the threat of copyright infringements beyond U.S. borders.

The AOL case isn't the only instance of an Internet company butting heads with international laws. A Bavarian court ruled recently that the former top executive of Compuserve's German subsidiary was not guilty of distributing pornography, because he couldn't have done anything to block access to a number of sites effectively. The executive had been convicted, because customers could use the online service to download child pornography from Internet sites in the United States.

"With the global nature of the Web, when you're doing business on the Internet, you are subject to those laws internationally," commented a Washington, D.C., attorney who specializes in e-commerce and intellectual property law. "The lesson is, make sure you comply."

Based on Kathleen Murphy, "Foreign Laws Trip up Another Net Company," *Internet World News*, 2(72), April 13, 2000.

Discussion Questions

1. Discuss the information ethics issues in the case.
2. Discuss how you believe information ethics issues differ between the United States and other areas of the world.
3. Discuss the responsibilities, if any, of an ISP to its customers.

Dr Pepper

Dr Pepper Bottling Co. celebrated its 110th anniversary as the oldest operational bottling plant. Dr Pepper/Seven Up Inc., a $1.5 billion division of $7 billion Cadbury Schweppes, is moving away from a classic, if not chaotic, approach to the way its bottlers send data to retailers. It has developed an extranet, named Bottler Hub/Extranet that automates the communication of pricing data to Dr Pepper's 1,400 independent and franchise bottlers. Dr Pepper's hopes also the extranet will help it keep, if not increase, its 10.6 percent share of the $58 billion soft drink market that is dominated by Coca-Cola Co. and Pepsi Co.

Before deploying Bottler Hub, Dr Pepper/Seven Up bottlers sent voluminous faxes to the main office with pricing, confirmation updates, and profitability reports. A small platoon of workers fielded the faxes—up to 70,000 per year—and directed them to the intended recipients. Although the bottlers set the pricing, retailers such as Wal-Mart had complained about their approach to faxing weekly price changes. Because many bottlers were mom-and-pop organizations and didn't have the resources to modernize the process, Dr Pepper/Seven Up decided to put in a centralized system that would make the information available online to retail outlets

Now, a bottler logs into the system with a Web browser, inputs personalized information, such as price changes negotiated with retailers, and sends the information to Dr Pepper/Seven Up. Dr Pepper/Seven Up collects the pricing information from all the bottlers, because large retailers, such as Wal-Mart, don't want 1,400 bottlers coming to them.

Given the limited resources of independent bottlers and Dr Pepper's need to accommodate its retail customers, the extranet is having immediate benefits for all parties. The extranet is also more efficient at handling pricing data for large retailers as well.

The Bottler Hub/Extranet was developed in Java using IBM's VisualAge developer tools. The Java 2 Enterprise Edition components link to Dr Pepper's SAP financial, manufacturing, and enterprise resource planning applications. The applications connect to Unix-based IBM WebSphere application servers.

Dr Pepper/Seven Up has other plans for the extranet too. The company will begin collecting case sales data online, enabling merchants to report how many cases of soda they sell. The data will be used to measure sales growth and to analyze brands and packages that are sold by a bottler within a territory to the major retail chains.

Dr Pepper/Seven Up plans to give its field sales people Palm-based devices to get real-time information from them. The sales people will use Handspring Visors to gather data for surveys while they are in the field. The sales data can be used for collaborative planning and demand forecasting.

Adapted from Mike Koller, "Bottler Extranet: Just What Dr Ordered," *InternetWeek*, May 28, 2001, pp. 49-50.

Discussion Questions

1. Discuss the ways Dr Pepper is using its extranet to compete with other bottlers. How does the extranet give Dr Pepper a strategic advantage, if any?
2. What kinds of business alliances do Dr. Pepper's extranet make possible?
3. Discuss some of the problems and risks Dr. Pepper faces in further developing its extranet.
4. How would you evaluate the effectiveness of Dr Pepper's extranet?

 # Sources and Resources

Books

Building Successful Internet Businesses: The Essential Sourcebook for Creating Businesses on the Net, by David Elderbrock and Niten Borwankar (Foster City, CA: IDG Books, 1996). This book explores the Internet as a fertile ground for doing business. The book presents informative real-world case studies, complete with business plans and technical explanations. The book includes a Windows/Unix CD and has a companion Web site.

B2B Basics: How to Build a Profitable E-Commerce Strategy, by Michael J. Cunningham (New York: Perseus Publishing, 2001) This book is packed with explanations and a history of the Internet and e-commerce. A good reference to use as a base for building a B2B strategy.

Designing Web Usability, by Jakob Nielsen ((Indianapolis, Indiana: New Riders Publishing, 1999). Creating Web sites that truly meet the needs and expectations of the wide range of online users is not all that simple. The author is a renowned Web usability guru and he shares his insightful thoughts on Web site design in this highly regarded paperback. The book is packed with annotated examples of actual Web sites and describes many of the design precepts all Web developers should follow.

Intranets: What's the Bottom Line?, by Randy J. Hinrichs (Upper Saddle River, NJ: Prentice Hall, 1997). Less of a how-to guide than a why-should-I-care primer, this interesting book describes not only how to create and expand a corporate intranet but also how to make it pay off strategically.

Bum Rate: How I Survived the Gold Rush Years on the Internet, by Michael Wolff (New York: Simon & Schuster, 1998). The author is the founder of Wolff New Media, a major Internet content provider. He tells his own rags-to-riches tale and shares insights on several Internet pioneers, including AOL head Steve Case and *Wired* magazine founders Louis Rossetto and Jane Metcalfe.

e-Business 2.0: Roadmap for Success, by Ravi Kalakota and Marcia Robinson (Reading, MA: Addison-Wesley, 2001). The authors present a survey of how the processes of business have changed as a result of Internet technologies. The emphasis is on companies that sell things to large numbers of consumers. The authors argue convincingly that information technology isn't an end in itself, but a tool that can facilitate valuable changes in business processes.

Electronic Commerce: A Manager's Guide, by Ravi Kalakota and Andrew B. Whinston (Reading, MA: Addison-Wesley, 1997). It seems like everybody's trying to make money on the Internet, but very few are succeeding. This book is designed to provide managers with the technical and organizational background they need to generate revenue through the Internet and intranets.

Electronic Commerce: A Managerial Perspective, by Efraim Turban, Jae Lee, David King, and H. Michael Chung (Upper Saddle River, NJ: Prentice Hall, 2000). This textbook covers the rapidly changing field of e-commerce, including intranets, extranets, marketing, business-to-business transactions, electronic payment, and more. Case studies and examples supplement the theoretical material.

Electronic Commerce, by Gary Schneider and James Perry (Cambridge, MA: Course Technology, 2000). A popular textbook that covers all the important aspects of e-commerce with plenty of actual real-world examples.

Evolve: Succeeding in the Digital Culture of Tomorrow, by Rosabeth Moss Kanter   (Cambridge, MA: Harvard Business School Press, 2001). Much has been written about "e-culture," the unique corporate culture created around the Internet. This book aims to help companies successfully incorporate the principles of this new culture, which include nurturing networks of partners, making connections between online and offline employees, and attracting top talent.

Understanding Groupware in the Enterprise, by Joanne Woodcock (Redmond, WA: Microsoft Press, 1997), *Understanding Intranets*, by Tyson Greer (Redmond, WA: Microsoft Press, 1998), and *Understanding Electronic Commerce*, by David Kosiur (Redmond, WA: Microsoft Press, 1997). These three books are parts of Microsoft Press's Strategic Technology series, designed to provide practical, non-technical explanations for managers and others who need to make decisions about emerging technology. They're generally well written and clear, without getting bogged down in unnecessary detail. As you might expect, they're Microsoft-centric, but they also contain plenty of useful information that's not brand specific.

The Power of Now: How Winning Companies Sense and Respond to Change Using Real-Time Technology, by Vivek RanadivE (New York: McGraw-Hill, 1999). Information technology is forcing businesses to function in a continual state of flux. Real-time businesses are event driven. This book examines how businesses must change to survive in the networked world.

Complete Idiot's Guide to E-Commerce, by Rob Smith, Mark Speaker, Mark Thompson, and Robert S. Smith (Indianapolis, IN Que Education & Training, 2000). This book shows you what makes e-businesses successful and what to consider when starting an online business. An e-commerce business model is included at the end of the book that brings all the content together in one cohesive strategy. Also included are Web site URLs for real examples of e-commerce concepts such as "real-time" supply chain objects or secure electronic payment forms. The book also includes links to e-commerce suppliers, information, and new technology.

Periodicals

There are several periodicals devoted either in whole or in part to electronic commerce topics. Many of these periodicals are available in print and on the Web.

CIO Web Business focuses on management-level information of the Internet economy, e-business strategies, and up-to-date statistics on Web usage. Available on the Web at **webbusiness.cio.com**.

Business 2.0 provides practical, interesting, and in-depth information on how to succeed in the Internet age. Available on the Web at **www.business2.com**.

Internet World is a biweekly newsmagazine aimed at Webmasters and others who make a business of the Internet. Available on the Web at **www.iw.com**.

InternetWeek focuses on news and analysis of the Internet, especially the communications and e-business applications. Available on the Web at **www.internetwk.com**.

eWeek focuses specifically on issues related to building and maintaining dot.com businesses. Available on the Web at **www.eweek.com**.

Interactive Week provides comprehensive coverage of all things interactive and online, with a special focus on the Web. Available on the Web at **www.interactive-week.com**.

Digital Coast Reporter and **Silicon Alley Reporter** are monthly magazines focusing on upbeat Web news and social issues related to the Internet, especially entertainment media. Daily news and updates are available on the Web at **www.digitalcoastdaily.com** and **www.siliconalleyreporter.com**.

Global Technology Business publishes many articles related to e-commerce from an international perspective.

World Wide Web Pages

The Web has several sites that are valuable resources. The *Computer Confluence* Web site will help you find them.

16 | Systems Design and Development

After you read this chapter you should be able to:

▼

Explain the motivation to develop new information systems

Outline the major phases of planning for information technology in a business organization

Outline the steps in the life cycle of an information system

Describe several system development approaches including prototyping, end-user development, and outsourcing

Describe several systems analysis tools and techniques

Describe the process of designing, programming, and debugging a computer program

Explain why there are many different programming languages and give examples of several

Explain why computer languages are built into applications, operating systems, and utilities

Describe the problems faced by system developers and software engineers in trying to produce reliable large systems

Describe several ethical issues related to developing an information system

▲

▼ In this chapter:

The process of developing information systems

The variety of systems development tools and techniques

How software is made

The many languages of programming

Why systems and software don't always work reliably

. . . *and more.*

▼ On the CD-ROM:

Grace Murray Hopper's famous threat

Video clip showing how object-oriented programming is used to create a 3D game

Instant access to glossary and key word references

Interactive self-study quizzes

. . . *and more.*

▼ On the Web:

www.prenhall.com/beekman

Articles and tutorials on a variety of systems analysis, design, and programming topics

Links to the most important organizations of computer professionals

Resources for exploring systems and software development and computer science

Self-study exercises

. . . *and more.*

Grace Murray Hopper Sails on Software

The only phrase I've ever disliked is,
"Why, we've always done it that way."
I always tell young people, **"Go ahead and do it.**
You can always apologize later."

—Grace Murray Hopper

Grace Murray Hopper (1906–1992)

Amazing Grace, the grand old lady of software, had little to apologize for when she died at the age of 85 in 1992. More than any other woman, Grace Murray Hopper helped chart the course of the computer industry from its earliest days.

Hopper earned a Ph.D. from Yale in 1928 and taught math for 10 years at Vassar before joining the U.S. Naval Reserve in 1943. The Navy assigned her to the Bureau of Ordnance Computation at Harvard, where she worked with Howard Aiken's Mark I, the first large-scale digital computer. She wrote programs and operating manuals for the Mark I, Mark II, and Mark III.

Aiken often asked his team, whether they were "making numbers." When she wasn't making numbers, Hopper replied that she was debugging the computer. Today that's what programmers call the process of finding and removing errors, or bugs, from programs. Scientists and engineers had referred to mechanical defects as bugs for decades; Thomas Edison wrote about bugs in his inventions in 1878. But when Hopper first used the term, she was referring to a real bug—a 2-inch moth that got caught in a relay, bringing the mighty Mark II to a standstill! That moth carcass is taped to a page in a log book, housed in a Navy museum in Virginia.

Hopper recognized early that businesses could make good use of computers. After World War II, she left Harvard to work on the UNIVAC I, the first general-purpose commercial computer, and other commercial computers. She played central roles in the development of the first compiler (a type of computer language translator that makes most of today's software possible) and COBOL, the first computer language designed for developing business software.

Throughout most of her career, Hopper remained anchored to the Navy. When she retired from the fleet with the rank of rear admiral at the age of 79, her list of accomplishments filled eight single-spaced pages in her Navy biography. ❯

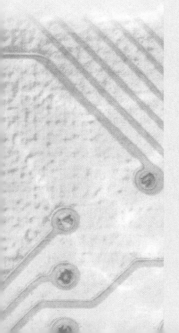

Today's information systems and computer software are so sophisticated that they're almost invisible to the user. For example, just as a great motion picture can make us forget we're watching a movie, word processing software allows us to do our creative work without ever thinking about the instructions and data flowing through the computer's processor as we work. Whether you're writing a paper, using an ATM machine, flying a simulated space shuttle, or exploring the nooks and crannies of the Internet, your imaginary environment stands on an incredibly complex information technology and software substructure. The process of creating information systems and computer software is one of the most intellectually challenging activities ever done by people.

In this chapter, we look at the process of turning ideas into working information systems. First, we consider how an organization develops an overall plan for the successful use of information technology. We look at the life cycle of an information system and examine the tools and techniques systems developers use to analyze, design, and implement a system. We then take a close look at developing computer programs, a critical element in any information system. We examine computer languages and the ways programmers use them to create software. In addition, we see how computer users take advantage of the programming languages built into applications, operating systems, and utilities. We also examine the problems involved with producing reliable software and discuss the ethical issues related to systems development.

Planning for Information Technologies

I firmly believe that any organization, in order to **survive and achieve success**, must have a sound set of beliefs on which it premises all its policies and actions . . . the basic **philosophy, spirit, and drive** of an organization have far more to do with its relative **achievements** than do technological or economic resources . . .

—Thomas Watson, Jr.

In this chapter, we see how information systems and software applications are developed. But to ensure successful systems development, managers must first plan how information technology will be used within the context of the overall mission and goals of their organization.

Any business or organization prepares for the future through planning. Planning is a process of identifying a desired goal or objective and then deciding what will be done to achieve the objective, when it will be done, who will do it, and how it will be done. Since information technology plays an important role at all levels of an organization, information technology planning is a major concern of top management. Information technology planning involves four phases:

- Aligning the information technology (IT) plan with the overall business plan of the organization
- Describing the firm's IT infrastructure
- Allocating resources to specific information systems and projects
- Planning specific information system projects

Description of Information Technology Planning Phases

Major IT Planning Activity	Description
Strategic planning	Align the overall business organization plan with the information technology plan
Information technology infrastructure analysis	Conduct an organizational information infrastructure analysis to identify the desirable features for the information technology infrastructure
Resource allocation	Select the information system projects to invest in
Project planning	Develop the plan schedule and budget for specific information system projects

Aligning the Information Technology Plan with the Overall Business Plan

This first phase of IT planning is referred to as **strategic planning**. The overall, or strategic, plan of a business defines the mission of the company, identifies the company's environment and internal strengths and weaknesses, and defines the competitive strategy of the company. A component of an organization's strategic plan is an IT plan that describes the IT mission within the company, reviews the company's current IT capabilities and applications, and describes the IT strategies and policies to support the organization's overall strategy.

Organizations use several strategic planning frameworks and approaches to make sure IT plans truly reflect business needs. One of the better known frameworks is the critical success factors (CSF) approach. The approach identifies the variables that are crucial for the success of the business from the top managers' point of view and identifies IT plans for systems that provide access to information about those critical success factors. CSFs typically relate to the major competitive forces faced by the company and to business operational problems and opportunities. Examples of CSFs include quality customer service, correct pricing of products and services, tight control of manufacturing costs, and the efficient and effective use of employees.

Describing the Information Technology Infrastructure

The second phase in IT planning is to describe the desirable features for the organization's IT infrastructure. The IT infrastructure comprises all the organization's information systems hardware, software, and telecommunications equipment; the information system department's staff and other personnel; and the organizational structure and procedures that affect accessing, processing, and using information in the company. The IT infrastructure should be designed to support effectively the business operations, communications and decision-making, and competitive strategy of the company.

An approach many companies use to define their IT infrastructure is organizational information requirements analysis, also called *enterprise modeling*. This approach is used to summarize the company's current IT infrastructure, to identify the practical range of business and product strategies based on the current infrastructure, and to identify information system projects that offer the most benefits to the organization.

Allocating Resources

The third phase of information technology planning is resource allocation, a process of selecting the information system projects in which to invest. Every organization has a limited budget, a limited number of people, and limited time. The information system department must decide how to allocate these limited resources to information systems work. Typically resources are allocated proportionally between maintaining or enhancing existing systems; developing new systems for supporting managerial, clerical, and other users; and developing new ideas and techniques for incorporating information technologies into improving business operations, products, and services.

Business organizations use many approaches to make resource allocation decisions. One widely used approach is cost-benefit analysis. Managers use cost-benefit analysis to decide whether an information system project is worthwhile on its own merits and also in comparison with other proposed information system projects. Costs usually relate to hardware and software, salaries of the information system staff, and the ongoing operation and maintenance of a system. Benefits relate to increased efficiency and effectiveness, and are categorized usually as tangible or intangible. Tangible benefits, such as the reduction in the number of customer complaints and the increase in the number of sales orders, can be measured relatively easily. Intangible benefits, such as better employee morale and better supervision, are harder to measure. Top managers often find it difficult to make an honest comparison of proposed information system projects based solely on anticipated costs and benefits.

Project Planning

The fourth phase of IT planning is project planning. The purpose of project planning is to organize a sequence of steps to accomplish a particular project's goals and to keep the project on schedule and within budget. A project plan includes a description of the measurable project goals that are used to evaluate the success of the project. A project goal can relate to the process of building the information system—completing the project by a certain date, for example. The project goal might also relate to business operations after the system is installed—for example, decreasing the time to place an order by a certain amount.

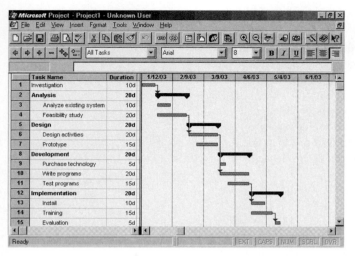

A manager can view a Gantt chart and see at a glance the overall schedule of an information system project.

A project plan describes what needs to be done to accomplish each step in the system's life cycle. (The systems development life cycle is discussed later in this chapter.) The plan specifies what deliverable output is to be produced at the completion of each step in the project. A deliverable can be a report, a computer program, a progress report, or any other tangible output. The plan specifies a schedule identifying how long certain steps are forecasted to take to complete and the forecasted date of completion. The project plan also specifies milestones, or checkpoints, to allow managers to review the project's progress when certain deliverables are produced, after a certain amount of the budget is used, or on a time basis, such as weekly or monthly.

Managers use *project management software* to help coordinate, schedule, and track complex projects. Many project plans use a Gantt chart to represent a project schedule visually. A Gantt chart shows each step or category of steps in a plan, along with their planned and actual start and completion times.

Project managers use the **critical path method (CPM)** to keep track of a project's schedule. CPM is a mathematical model of a project's schedule used to calculate when particular activities will be completed. A project manager first estimates the time needed to complete each activity and then determines the total time required to finish a project by locating the longest path, called the critical path, through the interconnected activities of the project. A critical path chart shows visually the interconnection of steps in a project. Project managers sometimes use a variation of CPM called the *program evaluation and review technique (PERT)*. With PERT, a manager uses three time estimates: an optimistic, a pessimistic, and a most likely time to complete each activity. The appearance of PERT and CPM diagrams is the same—both reflect single times for each activity. In the case of a PERT diagram, the single times are computed from the three estimates.

Managers use Gantt charts and CPM or PERT diagrams to identify bottlenecks in a project and anticipate the impact problems and delays will have on project completion times.

How People Make Systems

All men are system designers . . . For each human, the system he designs is **his life**, i.e., his self.

—C. West Churchman, American philosopher and systems scientist

The critical path through the interconnected activities of a project shows the activities that must be completed on time to finish the whole project on time.

An information system doesn't appear magically; it is developed over a period of time by teams of people using a variety of tools and techniques so that the system will work properly and be useful to the system's users. The process of systems development is important for any organization and requires not only technical skills but also creativity. In your future professional life you will very likely be a member of a system's project team. In this section we examine the guiding principles and tools of the systems development process.

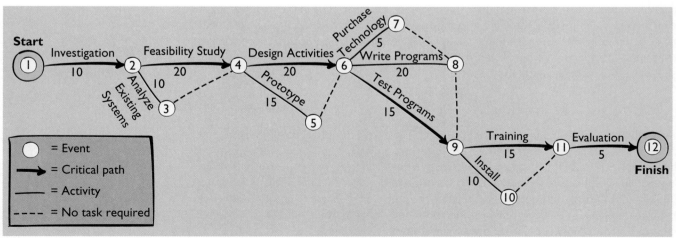

Systems Development

> The first 90 percent of the task **takes 90 percent** of the time. The last 10 percent **takes the other 90 percent.**
>
> —A systems development proverb

Systems development is a problem-solving process of investigating a situation, designing a system solution to improve the situation, acquiring the human, financial, and technological resources to implement the solution, and finally evaluating the success of the solution.

The systems development process begins when someone recognizes that a problem needs to be solved or an opportunity exists that can be taken advantage of. A typical situation might resemble one of these:

▶ mom-and-pop music store needs a way to keep track of instrument rentals and purchases so that billing and accounting don't take so much time.
▶ A college's antiquated, labor-intensive registration system forces students to endure long lines and frequent scheduling errors.
▶ A catalog garden-supply company is outgrowing its small, slow PC-based software system, resulting in shipping delays, billing errors, and customer complaints. At the same time, the company is losing business because competitors now sell on the Web.
▶ The success of an upcoming oceanographic investigation hinges on the ability of scientists to collect and analyze data instantaneously so the results can be fed into remote-control navigation devices.
▶ A software manufacturer determines that its PC graphics program is rapidly losing market share to a competitor with more features and a friendlier user interface.
▶ A small retail store doing business on the Web realizes it can modify its Web site to market to customers internationally.

An organization may face several problems and opportunities, each of which may require the company to develop new applications of information technology. Each new project requires people, money, and other organizational resources, so a steering committee may be formed to decide which projects should be considered first. The steering committee comprises people from each of the functional areas of the organization.

After the steering committee determines that a proposed project is desirable, a project team is formed to develop the system. The participants on the project team include *end-users* and *systems analysts*. An **end-user** is a person who uses the information system directly or uses the information produced by the system. A **systems analyst** is an information professional who develops the system. The project team may have one or several end-users and systems analysts, depending on the size and complexity of the proposed system.

The systems analyst is usually part of the organization's information systems department. But the business organization may choose to contract, or outsource, the systems analyst from an outside consulting firm. **Outsourcing** avoids the need for permanent in-house staff while allowing the organization to hire quality talent for selected activities on a contract basis. In fact, outsourcing has evolved into an entirely new industry of that provides outsourced services for specific applications via the Internet.

A project team comprising only end-users can develop many small scale systems without the direct involvement of a professional systems analyst. This systems development approach, called **end-user development**, is popular in business organizations where end-users have access to and training in the use of Web site development tools, spreadsheet and database management packages, and fourth-generation languages.

The Systems Development Life Cycle

> It has often been observed that we more frequently fail to **face the right problem** than fail to **solve the problem** we face.
>
> —Russell Ackoff, American systems scientist

Whether it's a simple, single-user accounting system for a small business or a Web-based, multi-user management information system for a large organization, a *system has a life cycle*. The **systems development life cycle (SDLC)** is a sequence of seven activities, or phases: investigation, analysis, design, development, implementation, maintenance, and retirement.

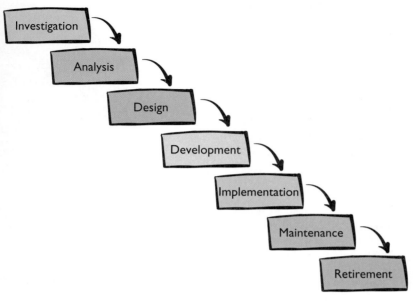

This graphical "waterfall" model of the SDLC shows a basic sequential flow from identifying the right things to do to making sure that things are done right.

Investigation

The purpose of the *investigation* phase is to study the existing business problem or opportunity and determine whether it is feasible to develop a new system or redesign the existing system if one exists. The project team conducts a feasibility study to identify the nature of the business problem or opportunity, to examine the current system to determine how well it meets the needs of the users and the organization, and to assess whether a new or improved information system is a feasible solution.

The project team tries to answer several questions for various types of feasibility:

▶ *Technical*. Can the required hardware and software be purchased or developed? Is the technology reliable? Does the system have sufficient information-processing capacity to handle the number of individuals who will use the system? Does the system provide for accurate, reliable, and secure data?

▶ *Economic*. Will the costs of developing and operating the proposed system be offset by the benefits of using the system? Is the system a good financial investment for the business? Can sufficient money and personnel resources be committed to complete the system's development on time?

▶ *Operational*. Does the proposed system meet the needs of the organization? Are the changes in work procedures required by the proposed system acceptable to the organization? Can the proposed system be developed on a timely schedule?

▶ *Organizational*. Does the proposed system support the goals and strategy of the organization? Are there any legal implications of the system, such as copyrights, patents, or federal regulations?

Based on its investigation, the project team makes one of three recommendations: leave the current system as is, improve or enhance the current system, or develop an entirely new system. The systems analyst documents the findings of the investigation in a written feasibility report that is presented to the steering committee. Based on the feasibility study, the steering committee decides whether to continue with the analysis phase of the SDLC.

Analysis

During the *analysis* phase, the systems analyst gathers documents, interviews users of the current system (if one exists), observes the system in action, and generally gathers and analyzes data to understand the current system and identify new requirements.

A requirement is a feature or capability that must be included in the design of a system to meet the information needs of the users. The systems analyst identifies the requirements related to each subsystem of the proposed system:

▶ *Input/output requirements*. The characteristics of the user interface, including for example the content, format, and timing requirements for data entry screens and managerial reports.

▶ *Processing requirements*. The calculations, decision rules, data processing capacity, and response time needed

▶ *Storage requirements*. The content of records and of databases, the type and frequency for updating databases and for user inquiries and data retrieval.

▶ *Control requirements*. The desired accuracy, validity, and security of the system; for example, to prevent data entry errors and guarantee an easy-to-use, user-friendly system

The systems analyst documents the work done in the analysis phase in a written functional requirements report. The report explains the current business procedures and how the current system works, identifies the problems with the current procedures and system, and describes the requirements for the new or modified system. The steering committee reviews the requirements report and decides whether to proceed with the design phase of the SDLC.

Design

The investigation phase focuses on why; the analysis phase focuses on what, and the *design* phase focuses on how. In the design phase, the systems analyst develops the system specifications that describe how exactly the system requirements, identified in the analysis phase, will be met. The systems analyst considers important how-to questions in three categories:

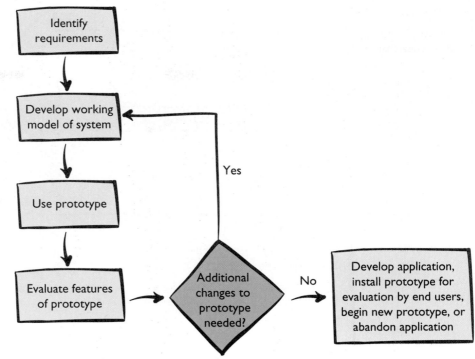

▶ *User interface design.* How will the various outputs of the system be designed? Where will input data come from, and how will it be entered into the system? How will the various windows, menus, and other user-computer dialogue characteristics be designed?

▶ *Database design.* How will the data elements and structure of the files that compose the database be designed?

▶ *Process design.* How will the programs and the procedures for the proposed system be designed? Should the system be centralized in a single computer or distributed through a network of desktop computers?

The systems analyst answers these questions, sometimes proposing several alternative solutions through a design approach called *prototyping*. A **prototype** is a limited working system that gives users and management an idea of how the completed system will work. **Prototyping** is an iterative process in which the systems analyst can modify the prototype until it meets the needs and expectations of the organization. Prototyping makes the design phase faster and easier for the systems analyst, especially for systems where the users' requirements are difficult to define. Once the design is acceptable, the systems analyst can fill in the details of the output, input, data files, processing, and system controls.

Prototyping is used widely by companies to develop their e-commerce applications quickly, especially for designing the human interface components of information systems such as data entry screens and Web pages. By encouraging a lot of end-user involvement in the design phase, prototyping increases the probability the system will satisfy the users' needs. For example, at Tech Data, a computer products distributor, a Rapid Application Development (RAD) team works on small initiatives of its own design to enhance the company's Web site, such as search engine improvements or navigational changes. The RAD group speaks directly with in-house staff and the company's customers who use its Web site to identify the most useful enhancements it can make. The group then quickly prototypes a given change and invites users to come back and evaluate the prototype; RAD then modifies its plans, recodes, and tests again.

Prototyping is an interactive methodology in which the prototype is continually modified and improved until it meets the needs of the end users.

The systems analyst must plan and schedule carefully the activities in the development phase of the SDLC because they can overlap and occur simultaneously.

Development

After the design phase is completed, the actual system development can begin. The *development* phase is a process of turning the design specifications into a real working system. Development includes a complex mix of scheduling; hardware, software, and communications purchasing; documentation; and programming. For most large projects, the development phase involves a team of programmers, technical writers, and clerical people under the supervision of a systems analyst. A large part of the development schedule is devoted to testing the system. Members of the system

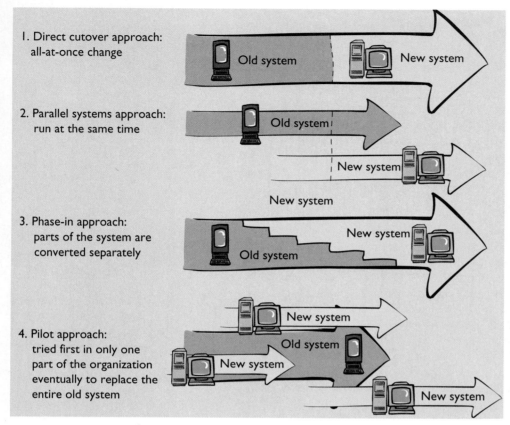

1. Direct cutover approach: all-at-once change
2. Parallel systems approach: run at the same time
3. Phase-in approach: parts of the system are converted separately
4. Pilot approach: tried first in only one part of the organization eventually to replace the entire old system

The systems analyst must choose carefully the system conversion approach that is best for the organization and the end users.

development team perform early testing to locate and eliminate bugs. This initial testing is known as **alpha testing**. Later potential end-users who are willing to work with almost-finished software perform **beta testing** and report bugs to the developers.

Implementation

The *implementation* phase occurs when the testing phase is completed and the new system is ready to replace the old one. For commercial software packages, this phase typically involves extensive training and technical user support to supplement sales and marketing efforts. For large custom systems, implementation includes end-user education and training, equipment replacement, file conversion, and careful monitoring of the new system for problems.

The systems analyst can choose one of four approaches for converting to the new system:

▷ The direct cutover approach simply replaces the old system with the new system. The organization relies fully on the new system with the risk that parts of the new system might not work correctly.

▷ The parallel systems approach operates the old system along with the new system for a period of time. The old system is gradually phased out as users gain skills and confidence that the new system is stable and reliable.

▷ The phase-in approach implements subsystems of the new system gradually over a period of time or, alternatively, the system is implemented in only a few departments, branch offices, or plant locations at a time.

▷ The pilot approach implements the new system in one department or other work site in the organization. The new system is used and modified at this test site until the systems analyst believes the system can be successfully implemented throughout the organization.

Converting from an old system to a new system means that people in the organization need to change as well. Sometimes people resist change by blaming the system for problems it did not actually cause, or they become intimidated, frustrated, or reluctant to familiarize themselves with the new system. Thus end-user training is critical to implementing an information system successfully. During training, clerical and managerial end-users learn to use the features of the new system effectively, become informed about the format and content of reports and workstation displays, and learn how to handle problems that may arise when they use the system. Sometimes clerical and managerial end-users are intimidated by the technology or technical personnel, so it is usually advantageous to have end-user representatives from the project team or from the different departments train the other end-users.

Maintenance

The *maintenance* phase involves monitoring, evaluating, repairing, and enhancing the system throughout the lifetime of the system. Some software problems don't surface until the system has been operational for awhile or the organization's needs change. Systems often need to be adjusted to keep up to date with new products, services, customers, industry standards, and government regulations. Ongoing maintenance enables organizations to deal with those problems and opportunities for improvement when they arise.

Evaluation is an important aspect of maintenance. The system is evaluated periodically to determine whether it is providing the anticipated benefits and meeting organizational needs. Also, evaluation provides the feedback necessary for management to assess whether the system was developed on schedule and within budget, and to identify what adjustments to make in the system development process in the future.

Retirement

Systems are often used for many years. But at some point there is a *retirement* phase in the life of a system. Because of changes in organizational needs, user expectations, available technology, increasing maintenance costs, and other factors, the system may no longer meet the needs of the users or the organization. At that point it's time to phase it out and launch an investigation for a newer system, which begins another round of the systems development life cycle.

As stated in the functional requirements

As outlined in the system specifications

As designed by the systems analyst

As implemented by information services

As operated by the end user

What the end user really needed

This drawing—a common sight on computer center walls—illustrates the importance of end-user involvement in the system development process.

Systems Development Tools and Techniques

> You can **observe** a lot **by just watching**.
> —Yogi Berra

Systems analysts use a variety of tools and techniques in each phase of the systems development life cycle. Some of the tools and techniques are used to gather data; others are used to describe or design the system's features, procedures, and processes, and others are used to document the system in reports. Systems development tools and techniques help the systems analyst be more productive and effective.

Data Collection Techniques

Systems analysts use several data collection techniques, including: document review, interviews, questionnaires, observation, and sampling. These techniques can be used during any phase of the systems development life cycle.

▶ *Document review.* A great deal of information about the current system exists in company documents such as business plans, reports, manuals, correspondence, and systems documentation. The systems analyst can review these documents in the investigation and analysis phases to find out how the current system is designed and how it is supposed to operate.

▶ *Interview.* Systems analysts interview managers, employees, customers, suppliers, and other people to gather information about business processes and problems and to collect ideas and suggestions for improvement. An interview can be structured or unstructured. In a structured interview the systems analyst asks the same questions of each person; whereas in an unstructured interview the systems analyst might vary the questions from person to person.

▶ *Questionnaire.* The systems analyst can collect factual information from a large group of people using a questionnaire. Questionnaires are convenient, and respondents can remain anonymous if desired.

▶ *Observation.* The systems analyst can watch an employee perform a task, or see how people interact with one another, or observe whether procedures work as expected.

16.1
The System
Development Life Cycle

College registration is a complex system involving hundreds of people and masses of information. A registration system must be solidly designed, carefully maintained, and eventually replaced as the needs of the college change. In this example we follow systems analysts at Chintimini College as they guide a registration system through a system life cycle.

1 Investigation. Analysts at the college's Information Processing Center identify several problems with the antiquated manual registration system: long lines, frequent scheduling errors, and expensive labor costs. After studying registration systems at other schools, they determine that a registration-by-phone system might be the best solution to these problems. After a few years the phone registration system has developed problems of its own. The college begins developing a new system that will allow students to register through the World Wide Web. When the new Web registration system reaches the implementation phase of its life cycle, the phone-in system is retired.

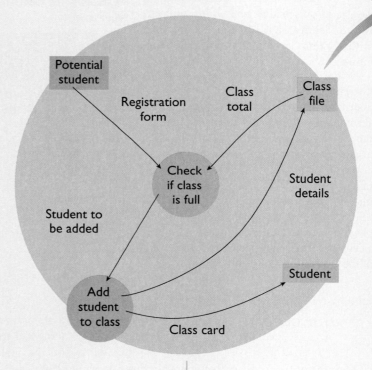

2 Analysis. Analysts use a ***data flow diagram*** to illustrate the flow of data through the old registration system. They'll use the information in this diagram to help them develop the new system.

7 Retirement. After a few years the phone registration system has developed problems of its own. The college begins developing a new system that will allow students to register through the World Wide Web. When the new Web registration system reaches the implementation phase of its life cycle, the phone-in system is retired.

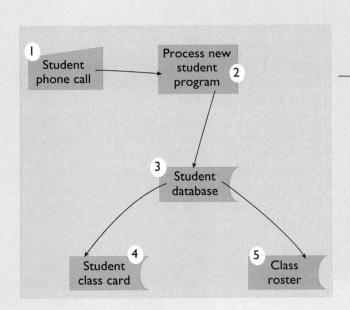

3 Design. Analysts use standard symbols to create a *system flowchart* to show the relationship among programs, files, input, and output in the new system.

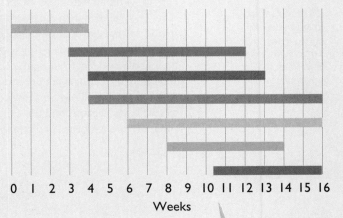

4 Development. Analysts use a **Gantt chart** to plan the schedule deadlines and milestones for creating the new system.

Program specifications
Programming
Unit testing
Documentation
System testing
File conversion
Training

0 1 2 3 4 5 6 7 8 9 10 11 12 13 14 15 16
Weeks

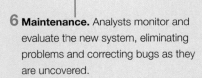

6 Maintenance. Analysts monitor and evaluate the new system, eliminating problems and correcting bugs as they are uncovered.

5 Implementation. Analysts supervise the training, equipment conversion, file conversion, and system conversion as the new system is brought online.

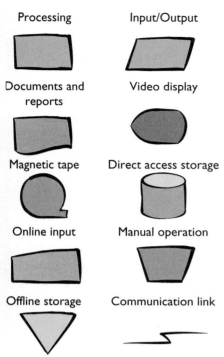

Processing   Input/Output

Documents and   Video display
reports

Magnetic tape   Direct access storage

Online input   Manual operation

Offline storage   Communication link

A systems analyst uses standard symbols to create a system flow chart. Each of the symbols represents the physical components of an information system. You can see an example of a system flow chart in How it Works 16.1.

▶ *Sampling.* If the system is large or has many users, the systems analyst can collect data at prescribed time intervals or from a subset of the users. For example, the systems analyst could interview a sample of 10 percent of the users or observe 5 percent of the transactions of a business to get a sense of how well the current system is working.

Modeling Tools

Modeling tools are graphic representations of a system. Many such tools are available, but the modeling tools most widely used by systems analysts are system flowcharts, data flow diagrams, data dictionaries, and decision tables.

▶ A **system flowchart** is a graphical depiction of the physical system that exists or is proposed. A system flowchart uses standard symbols to show the overall structure of a system, the sequence of activities that take place in the system, and the type of media or technology used at each step. System flowcharts are used both in the analysis and design phases of the SDLC to show the current system and the design for the proposed system.

▶ A **data flow diagram (DFD)** is a simple graphical depiction of the movement of data through a system. A data flow diagram uses four symbols to show the movement of data, the processes that use and produce data, the storage of data, and the people or other entities that originate input or receive output from the system. A system-level DFD depicts the entire system in summary form; a level-one DFD expands the processes in the system-level DFD to show more detail. Processes in the level-one DFD can in turn be expanded to show more detail, and so on to an appropriate level of detail.

▶ A **data dictionary** is a catalog, or directory, that describes all the data flowing through a system. Systems analysts use a data dictionary to keep track of all the system's data elements and data structures. Data elements are the fields stored in the system's databases. Recall from Chapter 8, "Database Applications and Implications," that each field has a field name, field type, and a field length allowance. A **data structure** refers to a set of data elements used together, such as an invoice or other paper or electronic document.

▶ A **decision table** shows, in a row-column format, the decision rules that apply and what actions to take when certain conditions occur. In fact, a decision table shows a set of if-then rules like those in expert systems, as discussed in Chapter 14, "Information Technology in Management."

A systems analyst needs to use only four symbols to create a data flow diagram. You can see how a DFD graphically shows the underlying logical flow of data in a system in How it Works 16.1.

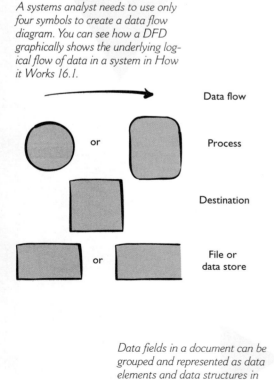

Data flow

Process

Destination

File or
data store

Data fields in a document can be grouped and represented as data elements and data structures in the data dictionary

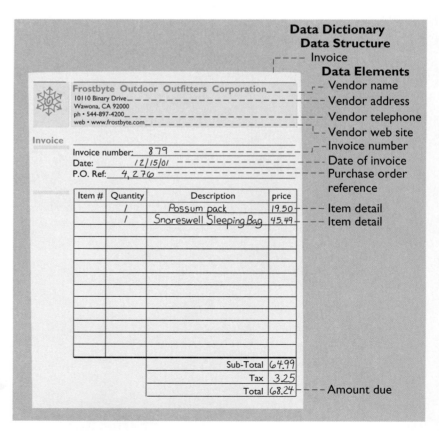

Data Dictionary
Data Structure
---- Invoice
Data Elements
-- Vendor name
--- Vendor address
--- Vendor telephone
-- Vendor web site
-- Invoice number
--- Date of invoice
--- Purchase order
     reference
--- Item detail
--- Item detail
--- Amount due

Frostbyte Outdoor Outfitters Corporation
10110 Binary Drive
Wawona, CA 92000
ph • 544-897-4200
web • www.frostbyte.com

Invoice

Invoice number: 879
Date: 12/15/01
P.O. Ref: 4,276

Item #	Quantity	Description	price
	1	Possum pack	19.50
	1	Snoreswell Sleeping Bag	45.49

	Sub-Total	64.99
	Tax	3.25
	Total	68.24

A systems analyst can describe and analyze a complex procedure more effectively by constructing a decision table than by writing a complicated narrative of all the possible combinations of conditions and actions.

Computer-Aided Systems Engineering (CASE)

Today many of the systems development tools and techniques are included in commercially available software packages referred to as **computer-aided systems engineering (CASE).** Most CASE tools software packages include

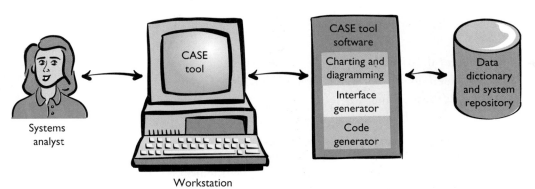

	Decision rules				
	1	2	3	4	5
Conditions If...	No	Yes	Yes	Yes	No
And if...	Yes	Yes	No	Yes	No
And if...	Yes	Yes	No	No	Yes
Actions Then do...	✓				
Then do...			✓		✓
Then do...		✓		✓	

A decision table shows if-then rules in a tabular format. The upper half of the table includes the if conditions, and the lower half shows the then actions. Each numbered column is a decision rule that shows the action(s) to be taken when certain conditions occur. In a real decision table, the leader dots in the left column would be filled in with information specific to the system.

▶ Charting and diagramming tools to draw system flowcharts and data flow diagrams
▶ A centralized data dictionary containing detailed information about all the system components
▶ A user interface generator to create and evaluate many different interface designs
▶ Code generators that automate much of the computer programming to create a new system or application

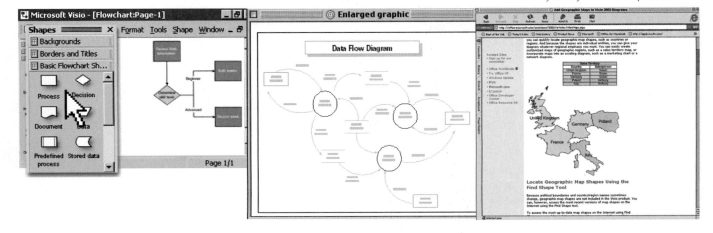

The components of a CASE tool system, Systems analysts can use CASE tools to automate many routine systems development tasks, create clear documentation, and coordinate the project time development efforts.

Some CASE tools software packages contain tools that apply primarily to the analysis and design phases of the systems development life cycle; others contain tools that automate the later phases of systems development, implementation, and maintenance. Integrated CASE tools incorporate the whole spectrum of tools to support the entire systems development life cycle.

But the trend today in the information industry is to run on Internet time with short system development schedules. CASE has an essential niche in the design of large systems. But over the last decade, the tools that worked well migrated out from under the CASE umbrella into other programming tools and suites such as Microsoft's Visual Studio, a development tool suite for building Windows and Web applications, and Microsoft's Visio, an easy-to-use yet powerful charting and diagramming tool. We take a closer look at computer programming in the next section.

You can use Microsoft Visio® to create data flow diagrams, Gantt charts, and many other types of diagrams useful in systems development work.

How People Make Programs

It's the only job I can think of where I get to be both an **engineer** and an **artist**. There's an incredible, rigorous, technical element to it, which **I like** because you have to do very **precise thinking**. On the other hand, it has a wildly creative side where **the boundaries of imagination are the only real limitation.**

—Andy Hertzfeld, co-designer of the Macintosh

Most computer users depend on professionally programmed applications—spreadsheets, image editing programs, Web browsers, and the like—as problem-solving tools. But in some cases it's necessary or desirable to write a program rather than use one written by somebody else. As a human activity, computer programming is a relative newcomer. But **programming** is a specialized form of the age-old process of problem solving. Problem solving typically involves four steps:

1. *Understanding the problem.* Defining the problem clearly is often the most important—and most overlooked—step in the problem-solving process.
2. *Devising a plan for solving the problem.* What resources are available? People? Information? A computer? Software? Data? How might those resources be put to work to solve the problem?
3. *Carrying out the plan.* This phase often overlaps with Step 2, since many problem-solving schemes are developed on the fly.
4. *Evaluating the solution.* Is the problem solved correctly? Is this solution applicable to other problems?

The programming process can also be described as a four-step process, although in practice these steps often overlap:

1. Defining the problem
2. Devising, refining, and testing the algorithm
3. Writing the program
4. Testing and debugging the program

Most programming problems are far too complex to solve all at once. To turn a problem into a program, a programmer typically creates a list of smaller problems. Each of these smaller problems can be broken into subproblems that can be subdivided in the same way. This process, called **stepwise refinement**, is similar to the process of developing an outline before writing a paper or a book. Programmers sometimes refer to this type of design as **top-down design** because the design process starts at the top, with the main ideas, and works down to the details.

The result of stepwise refinement is an **algorithm**—a set of step-by-step instructions that, when completed, solves the original problem. (Recall Suzanne's French toast recipe in Chapter 4, "The Ghost in the Machine.") Programmers typically write algorithms n a form called **pseudocode**—a cross between a computer language and plain English. When the details of an algorithm are in place, a programmer can translate it from pseudocode into a computer language.

From Idea to Algorithm

One programs, just as one writes, not because one understands, but **in order to come to understand**. Programming is an act of design. To write a program is to legislate the laws for **a world one first has to create in imagination**.

—Joseph Weizenbaum, in Computer Power and Human Reason

Let's develop a simple algorithm to illustrate the process. Let's start with a statement of the problem:

A schoolteacher needs a program to play a number-guessing game so students can learn to develop logical strategies and practice their arithmetic. In this game the computer picks a number between 1 and 100 and gives the player seven turns to guess the number. After each incorrect try the computer tells the player whether the guess is too high or too low.

In short, the problem is to write a program that can play a guessing game.

Stepwise Refinement

The first cut at the problem breaks it into three parts: a beginning, a middle, and an end. Each of these parts represents a smaller programming problem to solve.

```
begin game
repeat turn until number is guessed or seven turns are
completed
end game
```

These three steps represent a bare-bones algorithm. In the completed algorithm these three parts are carried out in sequence. The next refinement fills in a few details for each part:

```
begin game
        display instructions
        pick a number between 1 and 100
repeat turn until number is guessed or seven turns are
completed
        input guess from user
        respond to guess
end repeat
end game
        display end message
```

The middle part of our instructions includes a sequence of operations that is repeated for each turn: everything between "repeat" and "end repeat." But these instructions are missing crucial details. How, for example, will the computer respond to a guess? We can replace "respond to guess" with instructions that vary depending on the guessed number:

```
if guess = number, then say so and quit;
else if guess < number, then say guess is too small;
else say guess is too big
```

Finally, we need to give the computer a way of knowing when seven turns have passed. We can set a counter to 0 at the beginning and add 1 to the counter after each turn. When the counter reaches 7, the repetition stops, and the computer displays a message. That makes the algorithm look like this:

```
begin game
        display instructions
        pick a number between 1 and 100
        set counter to 0
repeat turn until number is guessed or counter = 7
        input guess from user
        if guess = number, then say so and quit;
        else if guess < number, then say guess is too small;
        else say guess is too big
        add 1 to counter
end repeat
end game

        display end message
```

Control Structures

A computer can't understand this algorithm, but the pseudocode is clear to any person familiar with **control structures**—logical structures that control the order in which instructions are carried out. This algorithm uses three basic control structures: sequence, selection, and repetition.

A sequence control structure is a group of instructions followed in order from the first through the last. In our algorithm example, as in most computer languages, the sequence is the default structure; that is, it applies unless a statement says otherwise:

```
display instructions
pick a number between 1 and 100
set counter to 0
```

A selection (or decision) control structure is used to make logical decisions—to choose between alternative courses of action depending on certain conditions. It typically takes the form of "If (some condition is true) then (do something) else (do something else)":

```
if guess < number, then say guess is too small;
else say guess is too big
```

A repetition control structure is a looping mechanism. It allows a group of steps to be repeated several times, usually until some condition is satisfied. In this algorithm the indented statements between "repeat" and "end repeat" are repeated until the number is guessed correctly or the counter is equal to 7:

```
repeat turn until number is guessed or counter = 7
input guess from user
...
add 1 to counter
end repeat
```

As our example illustrates, these simple control structures can be combined to produce more complex algorithms. In fact, any computer program can be constructed from these three control structures.

Testing the Algorithm

The next step is **testing** the algorithm. Testing of the completed program will come later; this round of testing is designed to check the logic of the algorithm. We can test it by following the instructions using different sets of numbers. We might, for example, use a target number of 35 and guesses of 15, 72, 52, and 35. Those numbers test all three possibilities in the if–then–else structure (guess is less than target, guess is greater than target, and guess equals target), and they show what happens if the player chooses the correct number. We should also test the algorithm with seven wrong guesses in a row to make sure it correctly ends a losing game.

From Algorithm to Program

> You know, computer science **inverts the normal**. In normal science you're given a world and **your job is to find out the rules**. In computer science, you give the computer the rules and **it creates the world**.
>
> —Alan Kay

When testing is complete, the algorithm is ready to become a program. Because the algorithm has the logical structure of a program, the process of **coding**—writing a program from the algorithm—is simple and straightforward. Statements in the algorithm translate directly into lines of code in whichever programming language best fits the programmer's needs.

A Simple Program

Let's look at the algorithm rewritten in C++, a popular variation of the C programming language. (The name C doesn't stand for anything; the language grew out of a less successful language called B.) This program, like most well-written C++ programs, is organized into three parts, similar to a recipe in a cookbook:

1. The program heading, containing the name of the program and data files (equivalent to the name and description of the dish to be cooked)
2. The declarations and definitions of variables and other programmer-defined items (equivalent to the list of ingredients used in the recipe)
3. The body of the program, containing the instructions, sandwiched between curly braces, { } (equivalent to the cooking steps).

The program listing (next page) looks a little like a detailed version of the original algorithm, but there's an important difference: Because it's a computer program, every word, symbol, and punctuation mark has an exact, unambiguous meaning.

The words highlighted with italics in this listing are key words with predefined meanings in C++. These key words, along with special symbols like 1 and 5, are part of the standard vocabulary of C++. The words number, guess, and counter are defined by the programmer so they become part of the program's vocabulary when it runs. Each of these words represents a *variable*—a named portion of the computer's memory whose contents can be examined and changed by the program.

```cpp
// Game.cpp
//
// by Paul Thurrott and Gary Brent
//
```
PROGRAM HEADING

```cpp
#include <iostream.h>
#include <stdlib.h>
#include <time.h>

// global variables
int number,
guess,
counter = 0;

int
main()


{
```
DECLARATIONS/DEFINITIONS

```cpp
   cout  << "Welcome to the guessing game. I'll pick a number" << endl
         << "between 1 and 100 and you try to guess what it is." << endl
         << "You get 7 tries." << endl;

   // seed the random number generator so that the number is always
   // different. This example uses the current time as a seed.
srand((unsigned) time(NULL));

   // calculate a random number between 1 and 100
   number = abs(rand() % 100) + 1;

   // do this loop for each guess. Leave the loop when the guess is
   // correct or when 7 incorrect guesses have been made
   do
      {
         cout << "What's your guess?" << endl;
         cin >> guess;
         if (guess == number)
            cout << "You guessed it!" << endl;
         else
         if (guess < number)
            cout << "Too small, guess again." << endl;
         else
            cout << "Too big, guess again." << endl;
         ++counter;
      } while ( (counter < 7) && (guess != number) );

   if (guess != number)
      cout << "I fooled you 7 times - the number was "
            << number << "!" << endl;
   return EXIT_SUCCESS;
}
```
PROGRAM BODY

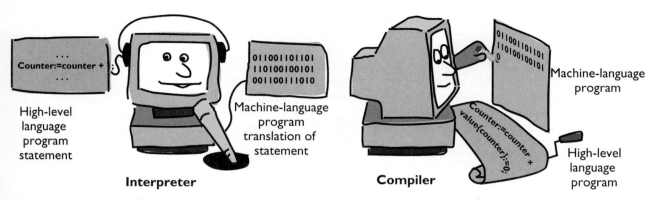

Interpreter

High-level language program statement

Machine-language program translation of statement

An interpreter translates a high-level program to machine language one statement at a time during execution.

Compiler

Machine-language program

High-level language program

A compiler translates an entire high-level program to machine language before executing the program.

As programs go, this C++ program is fairly easy to understand. But C++ isn't English, and some statements occasionally need clarification or further documentation. For the sake of readability most programs include comments—the programmer's equivalent of Post-It Notes. In C++, lines that begin with double slashes (//) contain comments. The computer ignores comments; they're included to help human readers understand (or remember) something about the program.

Into the Computer

The program still needs to be entered into the computer's memory, saved as a disk file, and translated into the computer's native machine language before it can be executed, or run. To enter and save the program, we can use a text editor. A *text editor* is like a word processor without the formatting features required by writers and publishers. Some text editors, designed with programming in mind, provide automatic program indenting and limited error checking while the program is being typed.

To translate the program into machine language, we need translation software. The translation program might be an **interpreter** (a program that translates and transmits each statement individually, the way a United Nations interpreter translates a Russian speech into English) or a **compiler** (a program that translates an entire program before passing it on to the computer, as a scholar might translate the novel *War and Peace* from Russian to English). Most C++ translators are compilers because compiled programs tend to run faster than interpreted programs.

A typical compiler software package today is more than just a compiler. It's an integrated **programming environment**, including a text editor, a compiler, a debugger to simplify the process of locating and correcting errors, and a variety of other programming utilities.

Programming Languages and Methodologies

> If one character, one pause, of the incantation is not strictly in proper form,
> **the magic doesn't work**.
>
> —Frederick Brooks, in *The Mythical Man-Month*

C++ is one of hundreds of computer languages in use today. Some are tools for professional programmers who write the software the rest of us use. Others are intended to help students learn the fundamentals of programming. Still others enable computer users to automate repetitive tasks and customize software applications. Since the earliest days of computing, programming languages have continued to evolve toward providing easier communication between people and computers.

Machine Language and Assembly Language

Every computer has a native language—a *machine language*. Similarities exist between different brands of machine languages: They all have instructions for the four basic arithmetic operations, for comparing pairs of numbers, for repeating instructions, and so on. But like English and French, different brands of machine languages are different languages, and machines based on one machine language can't understand programs written in another.

From the machine's point of view, machine language is all binary. Instructions, memory locations, numbers, and characters are all represented by strings of zeros and ones. Because binary numbers are difficult for people to read, machine-language programs are usually displayed with the binary numbers translated into decimal (base 10), *hexadecimal* (base 16), or some other number system. Even so, machine-language programs have always been hard to write, read, and debug.

The programming process became easier with the invention of *assembly language*—a language that's functionally equivalent to machine language but is easier for people to read, write, and understand. In assembly language, programmers use instructions. Subtract, for example, might be SUB. Of course, SUB means nothing to the computer, which only responds to commands like 10110111. To bridge the communication gap between programmer and computer, a program called an *assembler* translates each assembly-language instruction into a machine-language instruction. Without knowing any better, the computer acts as its own translator.

Because of the obvious advantages of assembly language, few programmers write in machine language anymore. But assembly-language programming is still considered low-level programming; that is, it requires the programmer to think on the machine's level and to include an enormous amount of detail in every program. Assembly language and machine language are *low-level languages*. Low-level programming is a repetitive, tedious, and error-prone process. To make matters worse, a program written in one assembly language or machine language must be completely rewritten before it can be run on computers with different machine languages. Many programmers still use assembly language to write parts of video games and other applications for which speed and direct communication with hardware are critical. But most programmers today think and write on a higher level.

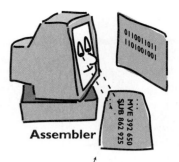

Assembler

Assembly-language program statements

Machine-language program statements

Assembler

An assembler translates each statement of assembly language into the corresponding machine-language statement.

High-Level Languages

Computer programming is an art form, like the creation of **poetry** or **music**.

—Donald E. Knuth, author of *The Art of Computer Programming*

High-level languages, which fall somewhere between natural human languages and precise machine languages, were developed during the early 1950s to simplify and streamline the programming process. Languages such as FORTRAN and COBOL made it possible for scientists, engineers, and business-people to write programs using familiar terminology and notation rather than cryptic machine instructions. Today programmers can choose from hundreds of other high-level languages.

Interpreters and compilers translate high-level programs into machine language. Whether interpreted or compiled, a single statement from a high-level program turns into several machine-language statements. A high-level language hides most of the nitty-gritty details of the machine operations from the programmer. As a result, it's easier for the programmer to think about the overall logic of the program—the big ideas.

Besides being easier to write and debug, high-level programs have the advantage of being transportable between machines. A program written in standard C can be compiled and run on any computer with a standard C compiler. The same applies for programs written in Java, Basic, FORTRAN, COBOL, and other standardized languages.

Transporting a program to a new machine isn't always that easy. Most high-level programs need to be partially rewritten to adjust to differences among hardware, compilers, operating systems, and user interfaces. For example, programmers might need to rewrite

Software development has become a global industry. These Romanian programmers write software for Motorola, an American corporation.

Programming in C++

SOFTWARE: *Visual C++ Compiler.*

THE GOAL: *To take the C++ number-guessing game program that started as an algorithm and turn it into a working piece of software*

1 You type the program into the text editor window.

2 The editor automatically indents statements as you type, so it's easy to see the logical structure of the program.

3 When you accidentally leave out a quotation mark, the editor points out the mistake with an arrow at the line where the error occurs and a message in the output window describing the problem. Like many editors this one marks **syntax errors**—violations of the grammar rules of the programming language.

4 After you correct the error and compile the program, you run the program to test for **logic errors**—errors in the logical structure that cause differences between what you want the program to do and what it actually does. In this case, when you test the program with a series of incorrect guesses, it fails to stop after seven guesses.

5 Likewise, when you correctly guess the answer, it fails to stop but asks you again for a guess.

6 The built-in andebugger enables you to run the program in slow motion so you can see how each statement affects the variables and the program output.

7 You see the logic error in the program where the statement "Counter++" (which increments the counter by one) was mistyped as "Counter—" (which decrements the counter by one), so the counter goes down instead of up. You correct the error and recompile the program.

8 When you test it, it ends the game when it should.

9 Like most programsan this one could go through several rounds of testing, debugging, and refining before the programmer is satisfied.

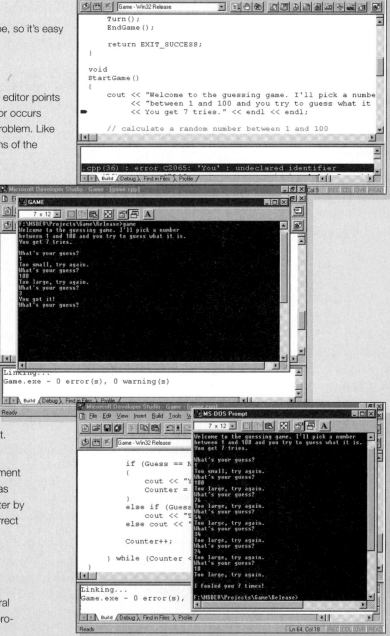

20 percent of the code when translating the Windows version of an application program into a Macintosh version, or vice versa. Still, high-level programs are far more portable than programs written in assembly and machine languages.

Of the hundreds of high-level languages that have been developed, a few have become well known because of their widespread use:

▶ FORTRAN (Formula Translation), the first commercial high-level programming language, was designed at IBM in the 1950s to solve scientific and engineering problems. Modern versions of FORTRAN are still used by many scientists and engineers today.

▶ COBOL (Common Business Oriented Language) was developed when the U.S. government in 1960 demanded a new language oriented toward business data processing problems. COBOL programmers still work in many data processing shops around the world.

▶ LISP (List Processing) was developed at MIT in the late 1950s to process nonnumeric data like characters, words, and other symbols. LISP is widely used in artificial intelligence research, in part because it's easy to write LISP programs that can write other programs.

▶ *Basic* (Beginner's All-purpose Symbolic Instruction Code; sometimes spelled with all caps: BASIC) was developed in the mid-1960s as an easy-to-learn, interactive alternative to FORTRAN for beginning programmers. Before Basic, a student typically had to submit a program, wait hours for output from a compiler, and repeat the process until every error was corrected. Because Basic was interpreted line by line rather than compiled as a whole, it could provide instant feedback as students typed statements and commands into their terminals. When personal computers appeared, Basic enjoyed unprecedented popularity among students, hobbyists, and programmers. Over the years Basic has evolved into a powerful, modern programming tool for amateur and professional programmers. True Basic is a modern version of Basic developed by the original inventors of Basic. The most popular Windows version of Basic today—in fact, the most popular programming language ever created—is Microsoft's *Visual Basic*. REALBasic is a Macintosh-based Basic similar to Visual Basic.

▶ Pascal (named for the seventeenth-century French mathematician, inventor, philosopher, and mystic) was developed in the early 1970s as an alternative to BASIC for beginning programmers. Pascal was designed to encourage structured programming, a technique described in the next

Pascal is popular as a student language because it's easy to learn and it encourages good programming style. This program listing shows the number-guessing game program in standard Pascal.

```
program Game (input, output);
(* Programmed by Clay Cowgill  and David Stuve *)

(*------------------------------------------------------------*)

var Number, Guess, Counter : integer
(*------------------------------------------------------------*)
begin
writeln('Welcome to the guessing game. I'll pick a number');
writeln('between 1 and 100, and you try to guess what it is.');
writeln('You get 7 tries.');
(* Calculate a random number between 1 and 100 *)
Number := abs (Random mod 100) + 1;
Counter := 0;
repeat (* turn *)
    writeln('What's your guess?');
    readln(Guess);
    if Guess = Number then
        writeln('You got it!')
    else
        if Guess < Number then
            writeln('Too small, try again.');
        else writeln('Too big, guess again.');
    Counter := Counter + 1;
until (Guess = Number) or (Counter = 7)
if Guess <> Number then
    begin
        writeln('I fooled you 7 times!');
    end
end.
```

section. Pascal is still popular as a student language, but it is seldom used by professional programmers.

▶ C was invented at Bell Labs in the early 1970s as a tool for programming operating systems such as UNIX. C is a complex language that's difficult to learn. But its power, flexibility, and efficiency have made it the language of choice for most professionals who program personal computers.

▶ C++ is the language we used in our User's View example. C++ is a variation of C that takes advantage of a modern programming methodology called object-oriented programming, described below.

▶ C+ is a Windows-only language from Microsoft that's similar to C++.

▶ Java is a modern programming language developed by Sun Microsystems. Java is similar to C++, but simpler to learn and to use. Java excels at producing Web-based applets that run on multiple platforms.

▶ J++ is a Java-like language from Microsoft for programming on the Windows platform.

▶ ActiveX is a Microsoft language designed specifically for creating Web components similar to Java applets.

▶ Python is a Java-like language popular with Linux open-source programmers.

▶ Ada (named for Ada King, the programming pioneer profiled in Chapter 1, "Computer Currents: From Calculation to Connection") is a massive language based on Pascal. It developed in the late 1970s for the U.S. Defense Department. Ada never caught on outside the walls of the military establishment.

▶ PROLOG (Programming Logic) is a popular language for artificial intelligence programming. As the name implies, PROLOG is designed for working with logical relationships between facts.

▶ LOGO is a dialect of LISP specially designed for children.

Computer software contains two kinds of information algorithms, which correspond to program code that performs some task, and data, upon which the algorithms operate. In a sense the algorithms are the gears and levers — the machinery that transforms the raw material of data. An unstructured program is like a huge, complicated machine that can't be easily broken down into sections. Any modification would require the entire machine to be disassembled. This difficulty is one reason why most programmers are afraid to modify unstructured code.

Unstructured programming

Structured programming breaks the big machine up into smaller machine modules, each of which has a clearly defined task in the overall processing of data. Structured programs are easier to understand and modify because problems can be isolated to individual modules and the input and output of each module in the assembly line are easier to understand.

Structured programming

Structured Programming

Programmers work the way medieval craftsmen built cathedrals—
one stone at a time.

—Mitch Kapor

A programming language can be a powerful tool in the hands of a skilled programmer. But tools alone don't guarantee quality; the best programmers have specific techniques for getting the most out of their software tools. In the short history of computer programming, computer scientists have developed several new methodologies that have made programmers more productive and programs more reliable.

For example, computer scientists in the late 1960s recognized that most FORTRAN and Basic programs were riddled with GoTo statements—statements used to transfer control to other parts of the program. (Remember "Go to Jail. Do not pass Go. Do not collect $200."?) The logical structure of a program with GoTo statements can resemble a tangled spider's web. The bigger the program, the bigger the logical maze and the more possibility for error. Every branch of a program represents a loose end that might be overlooked by the programmer.

In an attempt to overcome these problems, computer scientists developed **structured programming**—a technique to make the programming process easier and more productive. A structured program doesn't depend on the GoTo statement to control the logical flow. Instead it's built from smaller programs called **modules**, or *subprograms*, which are in turn made of even smaller modules. The programmer combines modules using the three basic control structures: sequence, repetition, and selection. A program is well structured if it meets the following requirements:

▶ It's made up of logically cohesive modules.
▶ The modules are arranged in a hierarchy.
▶ It's straightforward and readable.

The Pascal and Ada languages were designed to encourage structured programming and discourage "spaghetti code." The success of these languages prompted computer scientists to develop versions of BASIC and FORTRAN that were conducive to structured programming.

Object-Oriented Programming

Structured programming represented a big step forward for programmers; it enabled them to produce better, more reliable programs in less time. But structured programming wasn't the last word in programming; today **object-oriented programming** (OOP) has captured the attention of the software development community. Object-oriented programming was first used in the 1970s, most notably in a language called Smalltalk. In object-oriented programming a program is not just a collection of step-by-step instructions or procedures; it's a collection of objects. Objects contain both data and instructions and can send and receive messages. For example, an onscreen button in a multimedia program might be an object, containing both a physical description of the button's appearance and a script telling it what to do if it receives a mouse-click message from the operating system. This button object can be easily reused in different programs because it carries with it everything it needs to operate.

With OOP technology, programmers can build programs from prefabricated objects in the same way builders construct houses from prefabricated walls. OOP also makes it easy to use features from one program in other programs, so programmers don't have to start from scratch with every new program. The object that sorts addresses in alphabetical order in a mailing list database can also be used in a program that sorts hotel reservations alphabetically.

Smalltalk is still used for object-oriented programming, but today many other languages include object technology. C++, used in our example earlier, is a popular dialect of C that supports object-oriented programming. C++ doesn't contain *visual* objects like icons. On the surface it looks like just another language. But the object-oriented nature of the language enables programmers to write programs built around logical objects rather than procedures. Java has more of an object-oriented design than C++. There's even a version of Pascal, called Object Pascal, that supports object-oriented programming.

Object-oriented tools and techniques are becoming common in databases, multimedia authoring tools, and other software environments. Object-oriented programming is particularly

13.1
The Evolution of Basic

The Basic programming language has evolved through three major phases. These examples show how the programming process has changed during the last three decades. The first two Basic examples shown here are complete listings of programs to play the number-guessing game; the third example is a glimpse of a program to play a slot machine game.

1 **Early Basic.** The program with numbered lines is written in a simple version of Basic—the only kind that was available in the early days of the language. Statements are executed in numerical order unless control is transferred to another statement with a GoTo statement.

```
10 REM INITIALIZE
20 RANDOMIZE
30 PRINT "THE GUESSING GAME"
40 PRINT "I WILL THINK OF A NUMBER BETWEEN 1 AND 100."
50 PRINT "TRY TO GUESS WHAT IT IS"
60 LET C = 0
70 LET N = INT(RND(1) * 100)
80 INPUT "WHAT IS YOUR GUESS?";G
90 IF G = N THEN PRINT "THAT IS CORRECT!"
100 IF G < N THEN PRINT "TOO SMALL--TRY AGAIN"
110 IF G > N THEN PRINT "TOO BIG--TRY AGAIN"
120 LET C = C + 1
130 IF C = 7 THEN GOTO 180
140 IF G <> N THEN GOTO 80
150 IF G <> N THEN PRINT "I FOOLED YOU 7 TIMES! THE ANSWER WAS ";N
160 END
```

```
REM Guessing Game
REM written by Rajeev Pandey

DECLARE SUB StartGame (Counter!, Number!)
DECLARE SUB Turn (Counter!, Guess!, Number!)
DECLARE SUB EndGame (Number!)

CALL StartGame(Counter, Number)
DO
    CALL Turn(Counter, Guess, Number)
LOOP UNTIL (Guess = Number) OR (Counter = 7)
IF Guess <> Number THEN
    CALL EndGame(Number)
END IF

SUB EndGame (Number)
PRINT "I fooled you 7 times!"
PRINT "The answer was "; Number
END SUB

SUB StartGame (Counter, Number)
PRINT "Welcome to the guessing game. I'll think of a
number"
PRINT "between 1 and 100 and you will guess what it
is."
Counter = 0
RANDOMIZE TIMER
Number = INT(RND(1) * 100)
END SUB

SUB Turn (Counter, Guess, Number)
INPUT "What's your guess?"; Guess
IF Guess = Number THEN
    PRINT "You got it!"
ELSE
    IF Guess < Number THEN
        PRINT "Too small, try again."
    ELSE
        PRINT "Too big, try again."
    END IF
END IF
Counter = Counter + 1
END SUB
```

2 **Structured Basic.** The modular program on the bottom is written in QuickBASIC, a newer version of the language with many structured programming features. The main program has been reduced to a handful of statements at the top of the listing (after the DECLARE statement); these statements display the overall logic of the program. As it's running, the main program uses CALL statements to transfer control to each of the three subprograms, which take care of the game's beginning, each turn, and the game's end.

3 **Visual Basic.** The screen shows an example of Microsoft's popular Visual Basic, a modern programming environment that includes many of the ideas and tools of object-oriented programming and visual programming.

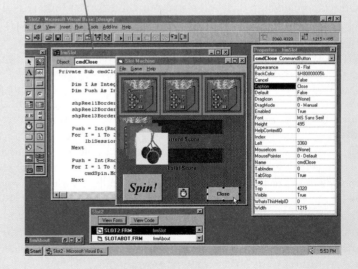

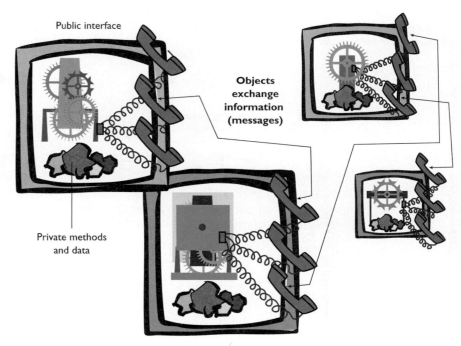

Public interface

Objects exchange information (messages)

Private methods and data

well suited for highly interactive programs (such as graphical operating systems, games, and customer transaction stations) and programs that imitate or reflect some dynamic part of the real world (such as simulations and air traffic control systems). Most experts believe that OOP is the wave of the future.

Data in OOP is more than raw material to be processed. In OOP, data is bound together with the methods and properties of an object. Each object can maintain its own store-house of data appropriate for that object.

Extreme Programming

The best part is to work **side by side** with someone else. It's a very **stimulating environment**, and you don't run into **roadblocks** or **mental blocks**

—Doug Watt, Senior Engineer

Extreme programming (XP) is a relatively new programming methodology that focuses more on the culture of programming than on technology. The traditional approach to programming is for a project to be divided among programmers, each of whom is responsible for particular programs or modules. Extreme takes a collaborative approach to application development. The entire programming team owns the code; each member of the team has a right to improve it and the responsibility for making it work properly. Extreme programmers work in pairs on projects rather than write code alone. Pair programming reduces the number of individual errors and ensures that more team members are familiar with all aspects of the code. Extreme programming involves close communication with customers and clients; they're considered part of the team. And in spite of its name, extreme programming doesn't involve marathon coding sessions to make deadlines for major releases. Instead, extreme programming emphasizes frequent releases of smaller updates and reasonable (40-hour) work weeks for programmers.

Smalltalk, the original object-oriented programming language, is so named because it was originally tested on children at the Xerox PARC laboratories.

Extreme programming is still outside the norm; its nonhierarchical approach runs counter to many corporate cultures, and it's still too new to have a long history of success stories. But the approach is growing in popularity—especially in organizations that embrace collaboration.

Visual Programming

Many people find it easier to work with pictures instead of words. **Visual programming** tools enable programmers to create large portions of their programs by drawing pictures and pointing to onscreen objects, eliminating much of the tedious coding of traditional programming. Apple's

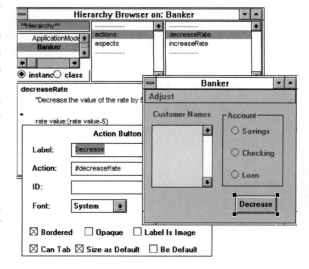

16.2
Object-Oriented Programming

The paradigm of structured programming follows the classic view of data as raw material being processed on an assembly line. At some level all computer programs process data in a mechanistic fashion. But at a higher level, object-oriented programming rejects the assembly line metaphor for another approach.

The fundamental tenet of OOP is that software should be designed using the same techniques that people use to understand and categorize the world around them.

In OOP a program is designed to consist of a group of objects—each with its own characteristics or attributes (called properties) and actions that it can do (called methods).

Every object has a public face: the properties and methods that other objects can see and interact with. Objects also have private methods for their internal use.

In OOP, data is bound together, or encapsulated, with the methods and properties of an object. Each object can maintain its own storehouse of data appropriate for that object.

OOP also relies on the idea of hierarchical categorization of objects to allow programmers to create new objects that are derived from objects that are already defined. The new object can inherit the properties and methods of the object it descends from and add new properties and methods as needed. Such hierarchies have been used by people for centuries in understanding the physical and biological world.

How might all of this work in practice, say, for a graphical operating system? For example, there could be a generic "window" object whose properties included its size, position, color, and so on and whose methods included things like closing and resizing. A more specialized window could be derived from this, for example, a window with scroll bars attached.

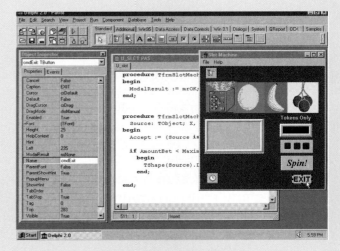

Delphi is a popular object-oriented development tool based on Pascal.

HyperCard was probably the first popular example of a visual programming environment. HyperCard includes a programming language called HyperTalk, but a HyperCard programmer doesn't need to speak HyperTalk to create working applications.

Today Microsoft's Visual Basic is widely used by professionals and hobbyists alike because of its visual approach to programming. Visual J++ applies a similar visual approach to Microsoft's Java-like language. Today's visual programming tools haven't completely transformed programming into a visual process; programmers must still understand how to read and write code to create complex programs. But visual programming can save hours of coding time, especially during the creation of user interfaces—the graphical shells that interact with users. Because they can simplify many of the most difficult parts of the programming process, visual languages make programming more accessible to nonprogrammers.

Languages for Users

Some computer languages are designed with nonprogrammers in mind. They aren't as powerful and versatile as professional programming languages, but they meet the modest needs of specific users.

Macro Languages

Many user-oriented languages are intended to enable users to create programs, called macros, that automate repetitive tasks. User-oriented macro languages (also called scripting languages) are built into many applications, utilities, and operating systems. Using a macro language, a spreadsheet user can build a program, or a macro, to automatically create end-of-month reports each month by locating data in other worksheets, inserting values into a new worksheet, and calculating results using formulas carried over from previous months. Using an operating system's scripting language, a user might automate the process of making backup copies of all documents created during the last seven days.

Some macro languages require you to design and type each macro by hand, just as you would if you were writing a Basic program. In fact, Microsoft Office includes a scripting variation of Visual Basic called Visual Basic for Applications (VBA). Another type of macro maker "watches" while the user performs a sequence of commands and actions; it then memorizes the sequence and turns it into a macro automatically. The user can then examine and edit the macro so that it performs the desired actions under any circumstances.

Fourth-Generation Languages

Many experts suggest that languages have evolved through four generations: machine language, assembly language, high-level languages, and fourth-generation languages, sometimes called 4GLs. Each generation of languages is easier to use and more like natural language than its predecessors. There's no consensus on exactly what constitutes a fourth-generation language, but these characteristics are most commonly mentioned:

▶ 4GLs use English-like phrases and sentences to issue instructions.
▶ 4GLs are nonprocedural. Pascal, C, and BASIC are procedural languages—tools for constructing procedures that tell the computer how to accomplish tasks. Nonprocedural languages enable users to focus on what needs to be done, not on how to do it.
▶ 4GLs increase productivity. Because a 4GL takes care of many of the how-to details, programmers can often get results by typing a few lines of code rather than a few pages.

One type of 4GL is the query language that enables a user to request information from a database with carefully worded English-like questions. A query language serves as a database user interface, hiding the intricacies of the database from the user. SQL (see Chapter 8, "Database Applications and Implications") is the standard query language for most database applications today. Like most query languages, SQL requires the user to master a few rules of syntax and logic. Still, a query language is easier to master than FORTRAN or COBOL.

Component Software

> When we make a **new tool**, we see a **new cosmos**
>
> —Freeman Dyson, physicist

Recent developments in the software industry may soon result in software that provides users with the kind of power formerly reserved for programmers—and at the same time reverse a long-standing trend toward bloated computer applications. Throughout most of the short history of the personal computer, applications have steadily grown in size as developers add more and more features to their products. Even though no single user needs all the features in a modern spreadsheet program, every user who buys that program must buy all the code that provides those features. Many modern applications are so bloated with features that they make huge demands on memory and hard disk space.

Component software tools may reverse the trend toward mega-applications by enabling users to construct small custom applications from software components. Component software isn't completely new; users have been able to add custom components to applications and operating systems for years. Many programs support skins—components designed to customize the way the program looks on the screen. But components aren't just for cosmetic purposes. Dozens of plug-in extensions add features and capabilities to Netscape Communicator, Microsoft Internet Explorer, Adobe Photoshop, Quark XPress, Macromedia Director, and other popular applications. This customizability is possible only if applications are programmed to allow it. More and more software programs, including operating systems, are designed with extensibility in mind.

Component software is the logical extension of object-oriented programming; it may soon reach a level where users and managers can build their own applications. Instead of buying an everything-but-the-kitchen-sink word processor, you might be able to buy word processor components—spelling checkers, outliners, formatters—based on your individual needs. Components can be distributed through the Internet as well as traditional software channels, so you can quickly download features when you need them. Web services (described in Chapter 11, "From Internet to Information Infrastructure,") are based on the idea of using components to create Web-centered systems and applications.

Programming for the Web

Many experts see a future in which PC applications will take a back seat to Web-based applications. Web-based personal information managers, reference tools, and games are steadily growing in popularity. Because of the distributed nature of the Web and the limited bandwidth of many Internet connections, Web-based applications present several challenges for users. Programmers can, and do, use a variety of languages, including C and C++, to write Web applications. But some programming tools are particularly useful for developing Web applications:

▶ *HTML* is, technically, a page-description language rather than a programming language. HTML commands tell Web browsers how to arrange text, graphics, and multimedia elements on Web pages, and how to link those pages. But there are many similarities between HTML coding and

This listing shows the guessing game program rewritten in Java, a C-like language that's ideal for cross-platform and Web programming.

```java
//guessing game program written by Keith Vertanen
import java.util.*;                    // needed for Random class
import java.io.*;                      // needed for BufferedReader class

class guessing_game {

    public static void main(String[] args) throws IOException {

        int number, guess, counter = 0;

        // we need a stdin object to receive input from the user
        BufferedReader stdin = new BufferedReader (new
            InputStreamReader(System.in));

        System.out.println("Welcome to the guessing game. I'll pick a number");
        System.out.println("between 1 and 100 and you try to guess what it is.");
        System.out.println("You get 7 tries.");
        System.out.println("");

        // create a new random number object
        Random rand = new Random();

        // calculate a random number between 1 and 100
        number = Math.abs(rand.nextInt() % 100) + 1;

        // do this loop for each guess. Leave the loop when the guess is
        // correct or when 7 incorrect guesses have been made
        do {
            System.out.println("What's your guess?");

            // allow the user to enter a line of text, convert to an integer
            guess = Integer.parseInt(stdin.readLine());

            if (guess == number)
                System.out.println("You guessed it!");
            else
                if (guess < number)
                else
                    System.out.println("Too small, try again.");
                else
                    System.out.println("Too big, guess again.");
            ++counter;
        } while ((counter < 7) && (guess!= number));
        if (guess !=number));
                    System.out.println("I fooled you 7 times - the number
                        was " + number + "!");

    } // method main
}
```

program writing, and many popular extensions to HTML take it far beyond the basics of page layout.

▶ *JavaScript* is an interpreted scripting language that enables Web page designers to add scripts to HTML code. Interpreted JavaScript scripts can add animation, interactivity, and other dynamic content to otherwise static Web pages. VBScript is Microsoft's answer to JavaScript based on Visual Basic.

▶ *Java* is a full-featured object-oriented language that's especially popular for creating Web **applets**—small compiled programs that run inside other applications—typically Web browsers. Java also excels at creating cross-platform applications that run on many different kinds of computers, regardless of operating systems. ActiveX is a Microsoft language similar in some ways to Java, but without support on all platforms and browsers.

▶ *Perl* (Practical Extraction and Reporting Language) is an interpreted scripting language that is particularly well-suited for writing scripts to process text—for example, complex Web forms. Perl runs on Web servers, not inside a Web browser.

▶ *XML* is a powerful markup language that overcomes many of the limitations of HTML. XML separates Web page content from layout, so Web pages can be designed to display different ways on different devices. XML is also particularly well suited for creating database-backed Web sites. Many experts expect a combination of XML and HTML to replace HTML as the dominant Web document development tool.

The Future of Programming?

Object-oriented programming. Visual programming. Component software. Distributed Web applications. With these trends gaining momentum, what can we say about the future of programming? It's not clear what programming languages will look like in the future, but three trends seem likely:

> It could well be that by the close of the twenty-first century, a new form of **truly accessible programming** will be the province of everyone, and will be viewed **like writing**, which was once the province of the ancient scribes but eventually became **universally accessible**.
>
> —Michael Dertouzos, in *What Will Be*

1. *Programming languages will continue to evolve in the direction of natural languages like English.* Today's programming languages, even the best of them, are far too limited and unintelligent. Tomorrow's programming tools should be able to understand what we want even if we don't specify every detail. When we consider artificial intelligence in the next chapter, we'll deal with the problems and promise of natural language computer communication.

2. *The line between programmer and user is likely to grow hazy.* As programming becomes easier, there's every reason to believe that computer users will have tools that allow them to construct applications without mastering the intricacies of a technical programming language.

3. *Computers will play an ever-increasing role in programming themselves.* Today's visual programming environments can create programs in response to user clicks and commands. Tomorrow's programming tools may be able to write entire programs with only a description of the problem supplied by users. The day after tomorrow we may see computers anticipating problems and programming solutions without human intervention!

Whatever happens, one thing seems likely: Future programming tools will have little in common with today's languages. When computer historians look back, they'll marvel at how difficult it was for us to instruct computers to perform even the simplest actions.

The State of Systems Development

In spite of advances in system sciences, the state of systems development, especially software, is less than ideal. Information system developers and end-users are confronted with two giant problems: cost and unreliability. When an engineer designs a bridge or a building, tried-and-true engineering principles and techniques ensure that the structure won't collapse unexpectedly.

> It's impossible to make anything foolproof, because **fools are so ingenious**.
>
> —Roger Berg, inventor

Unfortunately, we can't trust software the way we trust buildings; software designers simply don't have the time-honored techniques to ensure quality. **Software engineering** is a relatively new branch of the system sciences that attempts to apply engineering principles and techniques to the less-than-concrete world of computer software. We conclude this chapter with a brief look at the technical and ethical issues faced by system developers, software engineers, and managers—problems that affect all of us.

Software Problems

We build our computers the way we build our cities—
over time, without a plan, on top of ruins.
—Ellen Ullman, software engineer and author of *Close to the Machine*

As computers have evolved through the decades, the cost of computer hardware has steadily gone down. Every year brings more powerful, reliable machines and lower prices. At the same time the cost of developing computer software has gone up. The software industry abounds with stories of computer systems that cost millions of dollars more and took years longer to develop than expected. Many systems become so costly to develop that their developers are forced to abandon them before completion. According to one survey 75 percent of all system development undertaken in the United States is either never completed or, if it is completed, not used. Another recent study showed that 40 percent of IT application development projects are canceled before completion and 33 percent of the remaining projects have cost/time overruns or changes in scope, altogether costing U.S. companies and government agencies an estimated $145 billion per year.

But while prices rise, there's no corresponding increase in the reliability of software. Ever since Grace Hopper pulled a moth from the Mark II's relay, bugs have plagued computers, often with disastrous consequences, as you saw in the last chapter.

Software errors can take a variety of forms, including errors of omission, syntax errors, logic errors, clerical errors, capacity errors, and judgment errors. But whatever its form, a software error can be devilishly difficult to locate and even more difficult to remove. According to one study 15 to 20 percent of attempts to remove program errors actually introduce new errors!

Software Solutions

The major difference between a thing that might go wrong and a
thing that cannot possibly go wrong is that when a thing
that cannot possibly go wrong goes wrong it usually turns out to be
impossible to get at or repair.
—Douglas Adams, in *Mostly Harmless*

System developers and software engineers are responding to reliability and cost problems on five main fronts:

▶ *Programming techniques.* So far structured programming is the best known and most successful technique for increasing programmer productivity and program reliability. Programmers who use structured techniques can concentrate on the overall logic of their creations without getting distracted by minute details. The result is less expensive, more reliable software. But structured programming is no panacea; most experts consider it to be only a single step on a long road toward more dependable programming methodologies. It's too early to tell whether object-oriented programming and other more modern techniques will take us much farther down that road.

▶ *Programming environments.* Today's best programming tools include sophisticated text editors, debuggers, record-keeping programs, and translators, all interwoven into a seamless graphic work environment. A high-quality programming environment can help a programmer manage the complexities of a large project. As discussed earlier in this chapter, CASE (computer-aided system engineering) tools have emerged, enabling analysts and programmers to automate many of the tedious and error-prone steps involved in turning design specifications into programs. In spite of early promise, CASE tools haven't been widely adopted. Today the industry is more focused on environments built around component technology that makes it easier to reuse reliable code. Nevertheless, programming environments have a long way to go before they can guarantee reliable software, if that's even possible.

▶ *Program verification.* Software engineers would like to be able to prove the correctness of their programs in the same way mathematicians prove the correctness of theorems. Computer scientists have developed *program verification* techniques that work well for small programs. Unfortunately, these techniques have achieved only limited success with the complex commercial programs people depend on today. There's little hope for automated program verification either. Computer scientists have proven that some problems can't be solved with algorithms, and program verification is one such problem.

▶ *Clean-room programming.* One new experimental approach to software development is modeled after microchip manufacturing techniques. Clean-room programming combines formal notation, proofs of correctness, and statistical quality control with an evolutionary approach to programming. Programmers grow systems individually, certifying the quality of each before integrating it with the others. It's too early to tell whether this rigorous, engineering-like approach will achieve widespread quality gains, but early tests show some promise.

▶ *Human management.* Project management techniques from business and engineering have been applied successfully to many software engineering projects. These human management techniques have more to do with person-to-person communication than with programmer-to-machine communication. Because many information system failures result from human communication errors, successful human management can improve a system's overall reliability. But again the benefits of human management methodologies aren't great enough to offset the massive problems facing software engineers today.

Thousands of lives depend on reliable functioning of the computers and software used by air traffic controllers.

Software development is easier than it used to be, and computers today can accomplish far more than anyone dreamed a few decades ago. But system developers and software engineers can't always keep up with the fast-paced evolution in computer hardware, and it's still incredibly difficult to produce reliable, cost-effective software. But the reality of systems development in our fast-paced competitive business environment is many vendors like to bang out code and then fix it during the test cycle. Sooner or later, the tests must end and the product has to ship. The results can be expensive failures. For example, Nike blamed a sales shortfall of as much as $100 million for on a botched implementation of supply-chain management software that caused them to double-book orders, producing millions of unwanted shoes and not producing enough popular models. The software vendor claimed that Nike pushed the $400 million system into production too quickly and went live with too many suppliers and distributors at once. Another example—Hershey Food Corp. spent 2-1/2 years developing a $112 million order-taking and distribution system that combined software from three different software vendors and touched nearly every facet of its operations. When Hershey's system started delaying orders by as much as a week, the company missed crucial Halloween candy deliveries to retailers, forcing big chains such as Wal-Mart and Kmart to stock up on competitors' products. Hershey estimates the problems cost it $120 million in sales that year.

More than a decade ago, computer scientist Ted Lewis summed up the problem in one of his laws of computing. Today, when we're routinely asked to entrust our money, our health, our legal rights, and our lives to software, it's important for all of us to remember that law: Hardware is soft; software is hard.

Managerial and Ethical Issues

> The **problems** of the world cannot possibly be **solved by skeptics** or cynics whose horizons are limited by the obvious realities. We need [people] who can **dream of things that never were**.
> —John F. Kennedy, 35th president of the United States

Chief information officers and information systems managers must deal with many managerial and ethical ambiguities involved in information technology planning and systems development.

▶ *Management issues.* Managers face a myriad of questions and quandaries in IT planning and systems development. Some questions can be answered by describing what is already known about the company's strategy, information infrastructure, resources availability, and project plans. Many questions must be answered even though the manager may have incomplete

Avoiding Information Technology Project Failures

Less than a third of IT projects are completed on time, on budget and with the promised functionality. The major components of an IT failure are time wasted working on the wrong solution and the potential competitive advantage lost by not working on the right solution. Here are a few tips for information workers to avoid six ways IT projects can fail.

▶ ***IT projects need executive sponsorship.*** Many IT projects tend to cut acrossdepartments and force a lot of people to change the way they work every day. Such change, if not sold by senior management, can create fear, and every fearful middle manager in every department can create bureaucratic roadblocks that reduce the project's chance to succeed. Make sure the IT projects you are working on have an executive of the company supporting that project.

▶ ***IT projects need user input.*** Lack of user input is the most likely factor to characterize a bad IT project. It's important to discuss projects up front with everybody who has a stake in the outcome, including users and customers, business partners and internal departments on whose cooperation a project's success depends.

▶ ***IT projects need specifications.*** If the project requirements aren't well specified up front and the project begins anyway, you have no consensus among stakeholders. A series of meetings and discussions at the beginning of the project will help build consensus on what an IT project can and cannot do.

▶ ***IT projects need realistic expectations.*** Undefined expectations frequently lead to dreaded scope creep—in which an initially straightforward technology project is asked to solve more and more problems until it grows bloated and unmanageable. Scope creep, in turn, tends to destroy schedules and eat up resources. Make sure an project management process is in place that explicitly sets expectations and budgets resources.

▶ ***IT projects need cooperative business partners.*** Many IT projects involve a vendor of some sort—a software company, a system integrator, or a consultancy. When they're wooing you, those companies say they're your partners. But no matter how much they want your project to succeed or how honorable their intentions, they have pressures of their own that may lead to disagreements during the project. Make sure your company negotiates a reasonable and fair contract with the vendor.

▶ ***IT projects need open and honest communication.*** Workers don't want to be the bearers of bad news, and senior managers contrive not to hear that news if it is ever delivered. As a result, nobody sounds the alarm on IT projects that have disaster written all over them until it's too late. Make sure you participate in building a culture in your company that values open and honest communication.

information. Many questions require prescriptive answers: What should the information infrastructure look like? How should investments in information technology be justified? The answers to IT planning questions must be tailored to the particular situation of the information systems department and the company as a whole. How the IT planning questions are answered depends also on the individual decision style of the managers and the organizational decision style of the company. There are no easy answers in information systems work. Managers use the conceptual frameworks, presented in the previous three chapters, as guidelines for coping with the uncertainties of information systems. But no conceptual framework or technology yet devised can eliminate the uncertainty of managing an organization today.

▶ *Ethical issues.* An important aspect of information systems planning and development is from an ethical perspective. The almost unbelievable growth in the capacity, capability, and diversity of information technology has made it possible to develop some pretty amazing information systems. But frequently, persons form unrealistic expectations about what a system will and will not do because of misunderstanding, miscommunication, believing too much marketing hype, or other reasons. System analysts, programmers, and others involved in the development of a system have a professional duty to set realistic expectations by being honest in their representations about its capabilities.

Most professional organizations for information workers have included standards in their code of ethics that provide guidance on this issue. For example, The Association of Information

Technology Professionals (AITP) in its Code of Ethics and Standards of Conduct says that information workers have an obligation to advise their employers wisely, and to not misrepresent or withhold information concerning the capabilities of equipment, software or systems. The AITP code also warns against taking advantage of the lack of knowledge or inexperience on the part of others. Similarly, the Code of Good Practice of the Institute for Certification of Computer Professionals (ICCP) states that an information worker should not make false or exaggerated statements about any existing or expected situation regarding the use of computers. And the Association for Computing Machinery's (ACM) Code of Ethics and Professional Conduct requires information workers to not make deliberately false or deceptive claims about a system or system design, but rather offer full disclosure of all pertinent system limitations and problems. The guidelines are clear: there are no good excuses to use deceptive behavior in dealing with users, customers, or supervisors.

Ethics policies represent a double-edged sword for employers, especially companies that have many geographically dispersed locations. Ethics policies are difficult to enforce uniformly because their guidelines are broad concepts that are not always black-and-white and may vary by region, culture, and industry. If a corporation does, in fact, implement an ethical policy, it should be prepared to enforce it uniformly or risk losing its enforceability and, therefore, its benefits. On the other hand, at least in the United States, workers dislike an environment in which their every move, decision, phone call, email, and so on is scrutinized for ethical standards and acceptability.

But information system developers can err in the opposite direction when they try to avoid these ethical problems. To be on the safe side, they may deliberately underplay the capabilities of a new system. This can result in users forming an unrealistic expectation that the system will not meet their needs. So, there are dangers to both overselling and underselling technology:overselling has negative ethical implications, and underselling can lead to user rejection. The best approach is to strive for total honesty during every phase of systems development. Once expectations get out of hand, trust disappears between managers, systems developers, and users.

Site Posts Personal Info About Cops

By James Gordon Meek

It is becoming very easy to use information technology to development Web sites. This article raises some vexing issues regarding the ethical uses of information technology.

Imagine you're a cop. You deal with street scum every day in a risky profession. Then you find out someone just posted your name, occupation and home address on a well-publicized Web site.

For police officers in Kirkland, Wash., a Seattle suburb, it really happened.

Two local men . . . published a Web site..that listed by name thousands of police, corrections officers and court officials in 16 municipalities around metropolitan Seattle . . . [B]oth [are] convicted felons - say the disclosures are a public service intended to "level the field" in matters of justice.

Kirkland officials say it's an invasion of privacy. The city sued to shut down the site, www.justicefiles.org, after it published the home telephone numbers and Social Security numbers of about 70 Kirkland police officers. The lawsuit claimed the Web site put peace officers and their families at risk from violent criminals and identity thieves.

The legal fight over the site is being closely watched by Internet privacy advocates and First Amendment experts, who are conflicted over how much protection public servants should have under the law . . . A King County superior court judge gave the site a legal victory by ruling that its content is constitutionally protected political speech, denying Kirkland's request for an injunction.

In his decision, [the] Judge . . . wrote that the site could facilitate First Amendment speech directed at police, such as political protests. But he drew the line at posting their Social Security numbers, ordering them to be removed immediately.

A Washington, D.C., attorney well-versed in suing the government over public disclosure, says constitutional law holds little protection for the personal privacy of police officers. "[Police officers] are public officials," [he] says. "They have the right to compile information on us, and we should be able to compile information on them."

But for privacy advocates—who normally fight to increase privacy protections for individual citizens and favor less government secrecy - the case is vexing. Publishing such personal information might be going too far, says an analyst at the Electronic Privacy Information Center in Washington, D.C. "Even if you grant that public officials should have no privacy . . . you're also affecting the privacy interests of people who live in the same household, who are not public officials," [he] says.

[The] executive director at the National Fraternal Order of Police, hammers the court's ruling as a "perversion of the First Amendment." Worse, he says, it might encourage others to mimic the site elsewhere, exposing more cops to danger.

So why was Kirkland singled out? [One of the two men], a convicted marijuana grower, felt he was wrongly found guilty in a city court of making a false statement to police in an unrelated 1998 incident. His so-called "pissing match" with Kirkland officials escalated after he launched the site to retaliate.

Police investigated who was behind the online disclosures, and eventually contacted [hi]s employer, General Dynamics, about the site, according to Kirkland's assistant city attorney. The call got [the man] fired from his job as a network engineer though he denies using company computers to produce his site. When Kirkland subsequently filed suit last fall, [the man] posted maps to the residences of four cops who volunteered to put their names on the claim.

"Is there a little bit of vendetta there? Yes, probably, and it's not illegal either," [the man] says. He admits he'll feel remorse if a violent offender uses his site to locate and harm a police officer's family, but Kirkland officials "have gone out of their way to make my life a living hell," he says.

In a message posted online, [one of the two men] offered to pull the plug on his site if Kirkland creates a civilian police review board. The judge called that blackmail. [The man] denies that charge, and says he briefly considered shutting down his site.

But whether the site stays online or not, it has already been mirrored on overseas Web servers, which are untouchable by U.S. prosecutors. That renders Kirkland's injunction effort futile and it keeps the door open for more discomforting disclosures.

DISCUSSION QUESTIONS

1. Do the various points of view outlined in this article seem appropriate to you? How do feel about each of the points of view?
2. What types of controls, if any, should apply to the development of controversial Web sites?
3. Do you think information professionals have unique ethical responsibilities regarding the use of Web sites?

Summary

Information systems and software applications are developed using several planning and problem-solving processes. Organizations usually create an overall information technology plan before they develop a particular system. The information technology plan describes the intended overall use of information technology to meet the company's needs. The organization then follows the plan, using cost-benefit analysis to select specific information system projects to work on and project planning techniques to keep track of a specific system development project's schedule.

An information system has a life cycle that starts with the initial investigation of a problem; proceeds through analysis, design, development, and implementation phases. Then end-users use the system during an ongoing maintenance phase until the system is retired. Systems analysts, end-users, and programmers work together throughout the life cycle of a typical modern system. A variety of data collection techniques, systems modeling tools, and CASE (computer-aided systems engineering) tools have been developed to make their work easier and more effective.

Software applications, or programs, are critical parts of information systems. Computer programming is a specialized form of problem solving that involves developing an algorithm for solving a problem. Most programmers use stepwise refinement to repeatedly break a problem into smaller, more easily solvable problems. An algorithm typically is developed in pseudocode, which describes the logic of the program before being translated into a programming language. A translator program—either a compiler or an interpreter—checks for syntax errors (language errors) and, if it finds none, translates the program into machine language so the computer can execute the instructions. Logic errors might not surface until the translated program is run, and maybe not even then. The programming process isn't completed until the program is thoroughly tested for errors.

Computer languages have evolved through several generations, with each generation being easier to use and more powerful than the one that came before. Machine language—the original computer language of zeros and ones—is primitive and difficult to program. Assembly language uses a translator called an assembler to turn alphabetic codes into the binary numbers of machine language, but in every other way it is identical to machine language.

High-level languages, such as FORTRAN, COBOL, BASIC, Pascal, and C, are more like English and therefore easier to work with than either machine or assembly language. What's more, they generally can be transported between computers with a minimum of rewriting. Most modern languages encourage structured programming, a technique that involves combining subprograms using only the three fundamental control structures: sequence, selection, and repetition. Structured programming produces programs with fewer logic errors. Still, when program efficiency is critical, many programmers use languages such as C that enable them to work at a lower level of machine logic.

Many applications contain built-in macro languages, scripting languages, and query languages that put programming power in the hands of users. Query languages are representative of fourth-generation languages (4GLs) which are nonprocedural; that is, they enable the programmer to focus on defining the task rather than outlining the steps involved in accomplishing the task. Visual programming tools enable the programmer to use icons, drawing tools, menus, and dialog boxes to construct programs without writing code. Object-oriented programming (OOP) tools enable programmers to construct programs from objects with properties and provide the ability to send messages to each other; many believe that OOP represents the future of programming.

One of the most challenging problems facing system developers is the dual problem of system cost and reliability. Current system and software development techniques provide no assurance that an information system or software application will function without failure under all circumstances. As more and more human institutions rely on computer systems, it becomes increasingly important for system developers, software engineers, and managers to find ways to make systems that people can trust.

Chief information officers and information systems managers must deal with many managerial and ethical ambiguities involved in systems development. Managers must answer difficult questions about the company's strategy, information infrastructure, resources availability, and project plans. System developers, programmers, and other information workers have a professional duty to set realistic expectations for an information system by being honest in their representations to users about the system's capabilities. The best ethical approach is to strive for total honesty between information workers and information users during every phase of systems development.

Chapter Review

▼ Key Terms

algorithm (p. 440)
alpha testing (p. 434)
applet (p. 455)
assembler (p. 445)
assembly language (p. 445)
beta testing (p. 434)
C (p. 448)
C++ (p. 448)
CASE tools (p. 439)
coding (p. 442)
compiler (p. 444)
component software (p. 453)
control structure (p. 441)
cost-benefit analysis (p. 429)
critical path method (CPM) (p. 430)
critical success factors (CSF) (p. 429)
data dictionary (p. 438)
data flow diagram (DFD) (p. 438)
data structure (p. 438)
decision table (p. 438)

end-user (p. 431)
end-user development (p. 431)
extreme programming XP (p. 451)
fourth-generation language (4GL) (p. 453)
Gantt chart (p. 430)
high-level language (p. 445)
infrastructure (p. 429)
interpreter (p. 444)
Java (p. 448)
JavaScript (p. 455)
logic error (p. 446)
machine language (p. 445)
macro (p. 453)
macro (scripting) language (p. 453)
module (subprogram) (p. 449)
object-oriented programming (OOP) (p. 449)
organizational information requirements analysis (p. 429)

outsourcing (p. 431)
programming (p. 440)
programming environment (p. 444)
prototype (p. 433)
prototyping (p. 433)
pseudocode (p. 440)
software engineering (p. 456)
stepwise refinement (p. 440)
strategic planning (p. 428)
structured programming (p. 449)
syntax error (p. 446)
system flowchart (p. 438)
systems analyst (p. 431)
systems development (p. 431)
systems development life cycle (SDLC) (p. 431)
testing (p. 442)
top-down design (p. 440)
visual programming (p. 451)

▼ Interactive Quiz Questions

1. The *Computer Confluence* CD-ROM contains self-test quiz questions related to this chapter, including multiple choice, true or false, and matching questions.
2. The *Computer Confluence* Web site, **www.prenhall.com/beekman**, contains self-test exercises related to this chapter. Follow the instructions for taking a quiz. After you've completed your quiz, you can email the results to your instructor.

The Web site also contains open-ended discussion questions called Internet Explorations. Discuss one or more of the Internet Exploration questions at the section for this chapter.

▼ Review Questions

1. Define or describe each of the key terms in the "Key Terms" section. Check your answers using the glossary.
2. What are the major phases, or steps, in the information technology planning process of a business organization?
3. What is the critical success factors approach? Why is it useful in the information technology planning process?
4. What comprises the information infrastructure of a business organization?
5. What is the cost-benefit analysis approach? Why is it useful in the information technology planning process?
6. What is the purpose of project planning? How do managers use Gantt charts and the critical path method in project planning?
7. Outline and describe the major steps in the systems development life cycle.
8. Describe the data collection techniques used by systems analysts.

9. Describe the systems modeling tools used by systems analysts.
10. Here's an algorithm for directions to a university bookstore from a downtown location:
    Go south on 4th Street to Jefferson Street.
    Turn Left on Jefferson Street.
    Proceed on Jefferson past the stoplight to the booth at the campus entrance.
    If there's somebody in the booth, ask for a permit to park in the bookstore parking lot; otherwise, just keep going.
    When you reach the bookstore parking lot, keep circling the lot until you find an empty space.
    Park in the empty space.
    Find examples of sequence, selection, and repetition control structures in this algorithm.

11. Find examples of ambiguous statements that might keep the algorithm in question 10 from working properly.
12. Design an algorithm to play the part of the guesser in the number-guessing game featured in this chapter. If you base your algorithm on the right strategy, it will always be able to guess the correct number in seven or fewer tries. (Hint: Computer scientists call the right strategy binary search.)
13. When does it make sense to design a custom program rather than use off-the-shelf commercial software? Give some examples.

14. Why is structured programming so widely practiced today by software developers?
15. Why are so many computer languages in use today?
16. Assemblers, compilers, and interpreters are all language translators. How do they differ?
17. Give examples of several different kinds of computer errors, and describe how these errors affect people.
18. What techniques do software engineers use to improve software reliability?

▼ Discussion Questions

1. Why is planning for information technology in a business organization so important? Why do you think the information technology planning process might be difficult or confusing?
2. Read a newspaper or magazine article describing an information systems project. Identify the various systems development phases in the project. Discuss some of the problems and ethical dilemmas in the project.
3. Is programming a useful skill for a computer user? Why or why not?
4. Do you think computer professionals should have a code of ethics similar to those found in legal and medical professions? What should such a code cover?

5. Should programmers and systems analysts be licensed? Is programming and systems development a craft, a trade, or a profession?
6. Suppose you want to computerize a small business or nonprofit organization. What questions might a systems analyst ask when determining what kind of system you need?
7. Why do think it is important to have an end-user and a systems analyst on the project team in systems development?
8. What do you think programming and systems development will be like in 10 years? 20 years? 50 years?
9. Why is it so difficult to produce error-free software?

▼ Projects

1. The computer is often used as an excuse for human errors. Find some examples of "the computer did it" errors in newspapers, magazines, or conversations with others. For each example, try to determine whether the computer is, in fact, to blame.
2. Choose an information system you are familiar with, such as your school's class reservation system or the check-out system at a local retail store. Use data collection techniques to find out more about the system, and use systems modeling tools to document your findings.
3. Find several information system consulting businesses listed in the yellow pages of your phone book. Conduct a phone interview with a few systems analysts at the businesses to find out more about how they do systems development work. Use a word processor to compose a memo

summarizing your findings. Distribute the memo to your class.
4. Try to determine what safeguards are used to ensure that automated teller machines don't malfunction and that they can't be violated. You could do this by interviewing several bank or credit union employees, or by using a Web browser to find and read the Web sites of several ATM manufacturers.
5. Find out what safeguards are used to ensure the security of computer systems used in your local elections.
6. Interview several information system professionals in a large organization. Ask them to describe the information technology planning process in their organization. Present your findings to your class using presentation software such as Microsoft PowerPoint or Corel Presentations.

Case Studies

Becoming a Wireless Campus

Peter Chase, a student at Minnesota State University, sits in a group study area outside of the central computer lab and uses his laptop with a wireless PC card to connect to the campus LAN. Peter is with a group of students working on a project for class. When asked about his use of wireless technology, he replies, "I like the freedom to be connected to the Internet wherever and whenever I want. You can find a place on campus where you can be comfortable to do your work; you're not confined to one area, as you would be if you had a wired connection."

MSU is a beautiful campus on 277 acres of land, with many acres of open green space, sporting fields, ravines and parking lots. The core campus sits on 47 acres, containing 10 large academic buildings and three large dormitories.

In the previous year, the MSU Student Technology Committee (a subgroup of the Student Senate Association) recommended that funding be provided to move MSU towards the wireless revolution. With advice and encouragement from the university's Information Technology Services (ITS) staff, the students established a process model that resulting in a three-year plan being developed to cover the whole core campus. The students chose to cover "common student gathering points" first, leaving coverage of academic classrooms to the administration to fund.

The process model had seven steps. The Director of the Academic Computer Center, the university's ITS staff, and the Student Technology Committee comprised the development team.

▶ **Step 1.** The development team investigated the general area of wireless technology by attending technology conferences, contacting wireless and communications technology vendors and manufacturers, and inviting wireless vendors to campus for demonstrations

▶ **Step 2.** A prototype was developed to further enhance the development team's knowledge of wireless technology. They chose to use the library because it was a large space whose staff was requesting an upgrade from wired technology. This step also forced several questions. Where could we conveniently order wireless NICs at a low price? What are the technical differences between the various brands of access points? How does a university maintain network security in the wide-open wireless LAN?

▶ **Step 3. Site Survey/Planning.** The right locations for the wireless access points need to be determined. The development team used their common sense to locate an access point site. Then they walked around with their laptops,

checking how strong the signal was. By recording this information, they developed a site map, which indicated how many access points were needed for the desired coverage.

▶ **Step 4. Securing funding.** When the Student Senate stepped forward to fund this new technology, it provided seed money for the quick start that was key to the success of the project. Even if there had been funding from other sources, it would have slowed the process because of the time it would have taken to get funding.

▶ **Step 5. Implementation plan development plan.** The Student Senate funded coverage for "student areas" as the first year of the plan. This funding was based upon X-number access points covering X-general locations.

▶ **Step 6. Funding for administrative areas.** The College of Business provided funding for access points to be installed in their new laptop classrooms as part of Its Laptop Initiative. The administration assisted with providing access points for some colleges/departments.

▶ **Step 7. Assessment.** Wireless technology has added benefits that were not available before, and that would not be possible with wired Ethernet. For example, previously it was not possible for students to use their laptops while connected to the campus Ethernet out on the lawn. This is a new capability that would not have existed without the wireless initiative.

MSU found wireless a relatively easy technology to work with. There were significant cost savings with wireless technology when compared to wiring old buildings or getting Ethernet access to areas that could not be wired. Developing wireless technology at MSU has taken cooperative efforts, funding, and labor from many groups. The students in particular were commended for pushing forward into this technology. The students came up with the funds to get prototypes going, giving the university's networking staff successful experience to start the campus rolling towards becoming, arguably, "the most wireless campus."

Adapted from Wayne Sharp, "Becoming a Wireless Campus . . . A Student Initiative," *T.H.E. Journal*, Vol. 28, No. 10, pp. 60-66. Also on Web site http://www.thejournal.com/magazine/vault/A3482.cfm

Discussion Questions

1. Discuss the major steps in the development process for the MSU wireless system.
2. Discuss the pros and cons of the development team.
3. Discuss some of the problems in the wireless project you think occurred and how they may have been resolved. Do you think there were any ethical issues?
4. Discuss why you think the wireless project was a success or failure.

P.O.'d

John Sousa, owner of a Mail Boxes Etc. franchise, moves briskly to help his customers. His smile fades, however, when he attempts to price a customer's package using an Internet-based shipping, or manifest, system called iShip. "I have attempted to connect every hour on the hour, and it still hasn't worked," says Sousa. Gettting no joy from iShip, he turns to an archaic DOS-based system that dates back more than a decade. "It's not sophisticated, but it works great," he says with a shrug.

The iShip system is part of a massive technology overhaul MBE embarked on two years ago. The brainchild of MBE President and CEO Jim H. Amos Jr., the project was meant to position San Diego-based MBE as the premier shipping partner for e-tailers. "Because of our bricks-and-mortar on the ground, I thought we might have an opportunity that no one else had," says Amos.

By building a VSAT (very small aperture technology) satellite network to connect the 3,500 domestic franchises with corporate systems, an Internet-enabled point-of-sale (POS) system and the iShip manifest system, shipping at MBE would become enticingly simple. The idea was that a returning customer would need to give only his phone number to the MBE clerk for service. Up would pop his entire order history and recipient address information. Customers would no longer need to carry their address books into the store. They would feel instantly at home, as if they were part of a special group. At least, that was the plan. "It's a great idea, all right. It just doesn't work," says Sousa.

MBE started about two decades ago, when many of the outlets ran on little more than phones, fax machines, and simple Casio cash registers. Some owners added PCs throughout the 1990s, but there were no corporate technology standards. In fact, since MBE's franchise agreement didn't stipulate any particular technology requirements.

In mid-1999, an MBE executive team commenced a 30-city road show, dubbed Rolling Thunder, to paint the picture of Amos' technology vision for MBE and sketch out an implementation road map. Amos, along with CIO Ray Causey and several others, described the technology plan, its costs and time frame.

The executives emphasized a message of increasing revenue and protecting MBE's enviable number-one position in its market-sector. 80 percent of the franchisees agreed to install the new systems.

As the rollouts began during the next year and a half, it quickly became apparent that MBE was ill-prepared to handle the implementation and support issues of such a large project. "I bought the POS, iShip, and VSAT. I couldn't get any of it to work," says Cathy Thomas, owner of an MBE branch in Paoli, Pa. Desperate for technical support, Thomas repeatedly called her franchise area representative as well as the support number at headquarters. All she got was a recorded message. "I left voice mails that I was having major problems. They didn't call me back until four months later." Like Sousa, Thomas is using the old DOS system to keep her business running. "I was 100 percent for the systems, but this has been a total disaster," says Thomas. Franchise owners also say that they've had to pay more than the advertised $2,000. Boyd says that the system cost franchise owners upward of $4,500, depending on the configuration chosen.

MBE executives maintain there have been some challenges with the technology but say the implementation is proceeding as planned. Amos says, "We remain confident the technology platform is the best solution for our needs." MBE has spent in the neighborhood of $25 million on its technology program.

Adapted from Lauren Gibbons Paul, "P.O.'d", Darwin Magazine, May, 2001, pp. 50-58.

Discussion Questions

1. How do you think MBE should rethink its information technology strategy?
2. Do you think MBE's problems are primarily technical or human?
3. Do you think MBE should get rid of the system and start over?
4. How do you think MBE could have done a better job developing the system?

Sources and Resources

Books

As you might expect, there are hundreds of books on systems development and programming many of which are specifically written about particular systems analysis and design tools and programming languages and platforms. Most of the books listed here are more general.

Karel++: A Gentle Introduction to the Art of Object-Oriented Programming, by Joseph Bergin, Mark Stehlik, Jim Roberts, and Richard Pattis (New York: Wiley, 1997). This book provides a refreshingly different approach to learning how to program. Instead of immersing yourself in the many details of a full-blown programming language, you can guide Karel the robot through an object-filled robot world. Karel's language is similar to C++ and Java, but simpler and friendlier. The emphasis here is on logic and reasoning rather than calculation. A software simulator is available to accompany the book.

C by Dissection: The Essentials of C Programming, Third Edition, by Al Kelley and Ira Pohl (Reading, MA: Addison Wesley, 1995). This excellent text introduces beginners to the C language with lots of examples.

Learn C on the Macintosh, Second Edition, by Dave Mark (Reading, MA: Addison-Wesley, 1995), and **Learn Java on the Macintosh,** by Barry Boone and Dave Mark (Reading MA: Addison-Wesley Developers Press, 1996). Most programming books today assume you're working with Microsoft Windows. These two books offer Macintosh alternatives, providing excellent, accessible tutorials for beginning programmers. The accompanying CD-ROMs include special limited-functionality compilers for working through the tutorials.

Palm Programming: The Developer's Guide, by Neil Rhodes and Julie McKeehan (Sebastapol, CA: O'Reilly, 1999). Some of the most interesting opportunities for programmers today are in handheld devices like the Palm. If you know C, this book can show you what you need to know to develop applications for the Palm.

Understanding Object-Oriented Programming with Java, by Timothy Budd (Reading, MA: Addison-Wesley, 1998). There are dozens of how-to Java books on the market. This text explains the whys as well as the hows of this important new language. Budd uses Java examples to clearly illustrate the concepts of object-oriented programming.

The Analytical Engine: An Introduction to Computer Science Using the Internet, by Rick Decker and Stuart Hirshfield (Belmont, CA: ITP, 1998). This well-written, innovative text illustrates many of the concepts of computer science using a Web site to add interactivity.

Algorithmics: The Spirit of Computing, by David Harel (Reading, MA: Addison-Wesley, 1992). This book explores the central ideas of computer science from basic algorithms and data structures to more advanced concepts.

Dynamics of Software Development, by Jim McCarthy (Redmond, WA: Microsoft Press, 1995). A lifelong software developer offers advice in the form of rules (like "Don't flip the bozo bit") for shipping software on time. The book is filled with anecdotes and war stories from the front lines of software development.

The Mythical Man-Month: Essays on Software Engineering, Anniversary Edition, by Frederick P. Brooks, Jr. (Reading, MA: Addison-Wesley, 1995). This classic, often-quoted book clearly outlines the problems of managing large software projects. This twentieth-anniversary edition includes four new chapters that provide an up-to-date perspective.

Rescuing Prometheus: Four Monumental Projects That Changed Our World, By Thomas P. Hughes (New York: Vantage Books, 1999). This book profiles four of the biggest technological projects of the last century. These projects forced their developers to push the limits of systems design.

The Design of Inquiring Systems: Basic Concepts of Systems and Organization, by C. West Churchman (New York, NY: Basic Books, Inc., Publishers, 1971). This is one of the classic books in the systems field. Churchman uses the ideas from western philosophy of science to outline the possibilities of information system designs. You can understand these interesting ideas, because Churchman has a very readable writing style.

The Dream Machine: J.C.R. Licklider and the Revolution That Made Computing Personal, by M. Mitchell Waldrop (New York: Viking Press, 2001) "Lick," as his students and colleagues called him, was deeply involved in guiding the evolution of personal and networked computing from the 1950s through the 1980s, after leaving a career in cognitive psychology. Contrary to our stereotypical view of computer scientists, Licklider was profoundly interested in his fellow humans, and this interest helped him lead the design of technology adapted to human needs.

The Image, by K. E. Boulding (Ann Arbor, MI: University of Michigan Press, 1956). This book is a must read even today by students of systems development. In this classic book, Boulding provides a readable discussion of general systems theory and a description of the essential characteristics of all system.

Data Modeling, by G. Lawrence Sanders (Boyd & Fraser publishing company, 1995). This readable text is one of few short books about the structured methods used by system analysts to analyze existing organizational systems.

Why Information Systems Fail, by Henry C. Lucas (New York, NY: Columbia University Press, 1975). Lucas has published many information systems books since 1975, but this book is a classic in the information systems field. Lucas describes an understandable model of the major variables that contribute to the success or failure of an information system.

Process Innovation: Reengineering Work Through Information Technology, by Thomas H. Davenport (Boston, MA: Harvard Business School Press, 1993). This text discusses the necessity and the challenges of examining a business organization's day-to-day activities. Davenport discusses a model for systems development that an organization can use to take advantage of new information technologies.

Adaptive Software Development: A Collaborative Approach to Managing Complex Systems, by James A. Highsmith III (Dorset House, 1999). To survive in today's turbulent e-business world, software project teams must exhibit adaptability, speed, and collaboration. This innovative text, grounded in the science of complex adaptive systems theory, offers a practical, realistic approach to managing the high-speed, high-change projects characteristic of our highly uncertain economy.

Web Pages

Check the *Computer Confluence* Web site for links to the comp.risks forum, the Association for Computing Machinery (ACM), and other sites that cover material related to this chapter.

Part 5

Living with Computers

Information Age Implications

17 | Computers at Work, School, and Home

After you read this chapter you should be able to:

▼

Describe several ways in which computers have changed the quality of jobs, both positively and negatively

Anticipate how our society will adjust as more and more jobs are automated

Explain how the information age places new demands on our educational system

Describe several ways computers are used in classrooms today

Discuss the advantages and limitations of computers as instructional tools

Describe the role of computers in our homes and leisure activities in the next decade

▲

▼ In this chapter:

The future of jobs

How technology transforms cultures, economies, and jobs

The impact of information technology on workers

How information technology changes our educational needs, process, and outcomes

Computers at home—what's coming

. . . *and more.*

▼ On the CD-ROM:

Video clips of how computers are used in schools

Instant access to glossary and key word references

Interactive self-study quizzes

. . . *and more.*

▼ On the Web:

www.prenhall.com/beekman

Links to sites with tips for increasing productivity with computers

Statistics and analysis of the impact of technology on employment and education

Resources for developing your career

Discussions of the role and impact of technology in education

Tutorials, simulations, and other useful educational software

Entertaining and educational home computing resources

Resources for protecting our planet while using computers

Self-study exercises

. . . *and more.*

Steve Case Builds a Twenty-First Century Media Company

There's **too much focus on technology** in the industry, an obsession with bandwidth and the latest browsers. What's much more important is creating a **magical interactive experience**, for which the technology is certainly an enabler. **Human creativity** is really going to drive us

—Steve Case

When Steve Case saw Qube TV in the early 1980s, he was intrigued. Case was working at an entry-level job for Proctor and Gamble in Cincinnati, where the experimental interactive television network was being tested by Warner Bros. and American Express. He had no way of knowing that two decades later he would lead the biggest corporate merger in American history, a merger that would make Warner Bros., along with Time, CNN, Netscape, Compuserve, and America Online, into a media conglomerate unlike any the world had ever seen.

Steve Case

Case left Proctor and Gamble to work for Pizza Hut, where he dreamed up their pineapple topping, among other things. But when he went with his brother to the 1983 Consumer Electronics Show, he was interested in something bigger that pizza. He joined a struggling video game company and helped turn it into a new business to provide online service for Commodore 64 computer users. While Commodore faded, Case created similar services for Apple and Tandy computer users. By the end of the decade, the company had launched its own online service—America Online.

The reigning online services at the time, Compuserve, GEnie, and Prodigy, were text-based and difficult to use. AOL's user-friendly graphical interface, combined with aggressive marketing, soon made AOL into a major player. Even when cash was tight, Case refused buyout offers from Compuserve, Microsoft, and others. Instead, he scattered AOL disks like appleseeds—in the mail, in magazines, in airplanes, and elsewhere. And AOL continued to grow.

AOL's rapid growth wasn't trouble-free. In 1996, a service blackout left 6 million subscribers offline for 19 hours. High demand for services during the mid-1990s made it difficult for many users to connect, causing some to call the service "America on hold." In 1997, AOL responded by investing hundreds of millions of dollars to upgrading its network.

Case has been called "the statesman" because of his ability to negotiate even the most unlikely deals. In a two-week period in 1996, he brokered deals with four different competitors: Netscape, AT&T, Sun, and Microsoft. In 2000, he negotiated a merger in which AOL swallowed Time Warner, a much larger, older media corporation.

Today AOL isn't just the largest Internet service provider. It's the center of a new media constellation that may be the single most serious competitive threat to Microsoft's industry dominance. And as his company continues to penetrate new markets, Steve Case tirelessly evangalizes the Internet: "The impact of the Internet on the [21st] century will likely be similar to that of electricity on this past one." Steve Case may have a big impact on this century, too. ◗

Steve Case's successful media empire is built solidly on a new information infrastructure—a business built on a vision and creative use of information technology, providing new types of jobs and careers. As information technology reshapes our world, education plays an ever more important role in helping adults, as well as children, keep up with the changes going on around them. It's fitting, then, that computers are playing an ever-increasing role in the educational process in schools and homes. This chapter deals with the how computers are changing the ways people work, the growing role of computers in schools, and the changing role of education in a high-tech world. The chapter closes with a look at the growing impact of computers on our home life.

Computers and Jobs

> ### John Henry told his captain
> "A man ain't nothin' but a man
> But before I let your steam drill beat me down
> ### I'd die with a hammer in my hand . . ."
> —From the folk song "John Henry"

When we think about automated factories, computer-supported cooperative work, management information systems, and electronic commerce, it's easy to imagine utopian visions of computers in the workplace of tomorrow. But the real world isn't always picture perfect, and many workers today are experiencing computers in less positive ways. In this section, we look at some of the controversies and issues surrounding the automation of the workplace.

Computers and Job Quality

For many workers, computers have caused more problems than they have solved. Workers complain of stress, depersonalization, fatigue, boredom, and a variety of health problems attributed to computers. Some of these complaints are directly related to technology; others relate to human decisions about how technology is implemented.

De-Skilling and Up-Skilling

When a job is automated, it may be **de-skilled**; that is, it may be transformed so that it requires less skill. For example, computerized cash registers in many fast-food restaurants replace numbered buttons with buttons labeled "large fries" or "chocolate shake." Clerks who use these machines don't need to know math or think about prices. They simply push buttons for the food items ordered and take the money; computers do the rest.

Some of the most visible examples of de-skilling occur when offices automate clerical jobs. When word processors and databases replace typewriters and file cabinets, traditional typing-and-filing jobs disappear. Many secretaries are repositioned in data-entry jobs—mindless, repetitive jobs where the only measure of success is the number of keystrokes typed into a terminal each hour. When a clerical job—or any job—is de-skilled, the worker's control, responsibility, and job satisfaction are likely to go down. De-skilled jobs typically offer less status and less pay.

In sharp contrast to those whose jobs are de-skilled into electronic drudgery, many workers find their jobs **up-skilled** by automation. For example, many clerical jobs become more technical as offices adopt databases, spreadsheets, email systems, Internet connections, fax modems, and other information technology. In some cases, clerical workers use computer systems to do jobs high-paid professionals and technicians formerly did. While many clerical people enjoy the added challenge and responsibility, others are frustrated doing highly technical work with inadequate training. Clerical workers are seldom con-

Specialized terminals like this one make it easy to log restaurant orders. How is this person's job different as a result of this technology?

sulted before their jobs are computerized. And even though their work is more technically demanding than before, few clerical workers see this up-skilling reflected in their paychecks or level of responsibility.

Productivity and People

According to one study of 2,000 U.S. companies that implemented new office systems, at least 40 percent failed to achieve their intended results. Most of the failures were attributed to human or organizational factors rather than technical problems.

A computer system doesn't work in a vacuum. All too often computers are introduced into the workplace without any consideration of the way people work and interact. Workers are expected to adjust their work patterns to systems that are difficult and uncompromising. User training and support are often inadequate. It's hardly surprising that these computer-centered systems fail to spark productivity.

Many analysts argue that the most successful computer systems are **human-centered systems**. Such systems are designed to retain and enhance human skills rather than take them away. These analysts suggest that computer systems aren't likely to pay off unless they're accompanied by changes in the structure of work responsibilities, relationships with coworkers, and rewards for accomplishing job goals.

To create a human-centered system, systems analysts and designers must understand the work practices of the people who'll be using the system. It helps if users of the systems are involved in designing the system and the system-related jobs. In Norway, laws require that unionized workers be included in the planning and design of new computer systems. As a result, workers have greater control over their jobs and greater job satisfaction. Similar worker-centered approaches have been applied in Sweden, Britain, and, more recently, the United States.

Many experts believe that this human-centered approach is a key to increasing overall productivity. Productivity almost certainly increases as organizations adjust to information technology and information technology becomes more adaptable to the users' needs.

Monitoring and Surveillance

Another controversial aspect of office automation is **computer monitoring**—using computer technology to track, record, and evaluate worker performance, often without the knowledge of the worker. Monitoring systems can provide a manager with instant, onscreen reports showing the number of keystrokes for each clerk, the length of each phone call placed by an employee, details of Web wanderings, and the total amount of idle time for each computer. Some network software even enables a manager to view a copy of any worker's screen secretly at any time.

For a manager worried about worker productivity, computer monitoring can serve as a valuable source of information. But computer monitoring brings with it several problems:

▶ *Privacy*. In Chapters 8, "Database Applications and Implications,"10, "Inside the Internet and the Web," and 11, "From Internet to Information Infrastructure," we saw how the misuse of database and network technology can threaten personal privacy. Computer monitoring compounds that threat by providing employers with unprecedented data on workers. Some employers monitor personal email messages and punish or fire employees who send "unacceptable" messages.

▶ *Morale*. Privacy issues aside, computer monitoring can have a powerful negative impact on morale. Because employees can't tell when they're being monitored, many workers experience a great deal of stress and anxiety. The boss can be seen as an invisible eavesdropper rather than a team leader.

▶ *Devalued skills*. In the traditional office, workers were evaluated based on a variety of skills. A slow-typing secretary could be valued for her ability to anticipate when a job needed to be done or her willingness to help others with problems. Computer monitoring tends to reduce a worker's worth to simple quantities such as number of keystrokes per hour. In such systems, a worker might be penalized for repairing a sticky chair, showing a neighbor how to reboot a terminal, or helping a coworker overcome an emotional crisis.

▶ *Loss of quality*. Monitored workers tend to assume that if it's not being counted, it doesn't count. The result of this assumption is that quantity may become more important than quality.

Millions of workers are monitored by computer, including factory workers, telephone operators, truck drivers, and, in some cases, managers. Cyber-snooping goes far beyond counting keystrokes and idle time. According to a 2001 study by the American Management Association, three out of four U.S. companies engage in some kind of electronic surveillance of their employees, including reviewing email, monitoring phone use, videotaping, and checking computer files. In the words of the director of the study, "Workplace privacy is a contradiction in terms. It's an oxymoron. I know the illusion of privacy is there, but you are not using your own stuff. The phone, the keyboard, the connections, the job itself—they don't belong to you; they belong to the company, legally."

The Electronic Sweatshop

Computer monitoring is common practice in data-entry offices. A data-entry clerk has a single job: to read information from a printed source—a check, a hand-printed form, or something else—and type it into a computer's database. A typical data-entry shop might contain hundreds of clerks sitting at terminals in a massive, windowless room. Workers—often minorities and almost always female—are paid minimum wage to do mindless keyboarding. Many experience headaches, backaches, serious wrist injuries, stress, anxiety, and other health problems. And all the while, keystrokes and breaks are monitored electronically. Writer Barbara Garson calls these worker warehouses **electronic sweatshops** because working conditions bring to mind the oppressive factory sweatshops of the 19th century.

Many data entry workers spend their days in warehouse-sized buildings filled with computers.

A growing number of electronic sweatshops are located across national borders from corporate headquarters in countries with lax labor laws and low wage scales. The electronic immigrants in these offshore shops don't need green cards to telecommute across borders, and they work for a fraction of what workers in developed countries cost. A data-entry clerk in the Philippines, for example, earns about $6 per day. With wages that low many companies find it cost effective to have data entered twice and use software to compare both versions and correct errors.

The electronic sweatshop is the dark side of the electronic office. Ironically, information technology may soon make many electronic sweatshops irrelevant. Optical character recognition and voice recognition technologies (described in earlier chapters) are rapidly becoming practical for data-entry applications. OCR software is already used to read and recognize typed and hand-printed characters in many applications, and voice recognition systems are replacing directory assistance telephone operators. It's just a matter of time before machines replace most workers in electronic sweatshops.

Employment and Unemployment

My father had worked for the same firm for 12 years. **They fired him**.
They replaced him with a **tiny gadget** this big that does everything that my father does only it **does it much better.**
The **depressing thing** is my mother ran out and bought one.

—Woody Allen

When Woody Allen told this joke more than three decades ago, automation was generating a great deal of public controversy. Computers were new to the workplace, and people were reacting with both awe and fear. Many analysts predicted that automation would lead to massive unemployment and economic disaster. Others said that computers would generate countless new job opportunities. Today most people are used to seeing computers where they work, and the computers-versus-jobs debate has cooled down. Job automation may not be a hot topic in comedy clubs today, but it's still an important issue for millions of workers whose jobs are threatened by machines.

Workers Against Machines

Automation has threatened workers since the earliest days of the industrial revolution. In the early 19th century an English labor group called the *Luddites* smashed new textile machinery; they feared that the machines would take jobs away from skilled craftsmen. The Luddites and similar groups in other parts of Europe failed to stop the wheels of automation. Modern workers have been no more successful than their 19th-century counterparts in keeping computers and robots out of the workplace. Every year brings new technological breakthroughs that allow robots and computers to do jobs formerly reserved for humans.

Of course, information technology creates new jobs, too. Somebody has to design, build, program, sell, run, and repair the computers, robots, and networks. But many displaced workers don't have the education or skills to program computers, design robots, install networks, or even read printouts. Those workers are often forced to take low-tech, low-paying service jobs as cashiers or custodians, if they can find jobs at all. Because of automation the unskilled, uneducated worker may face a lifetime of minimum wage jobs or welfare. Technology may be helping to create an unbalanced society with two classes: a growing mass of poor uneducated people and a shrinking class of affluent educated people.

Robots do almost all of the assembly-line work in this factory.

Cautiously Optimistic Forecasts

Nobody knows for sure how information technology will affect employment in the coming decades; it's impossible to anticipate what might happen in 10 or 20 years. And experts are far from unanimous in their predictions—especially since the economic downturn of 2001.

Most experts agree that information technology will result in painful periods of adjustment for many factory workers, clerical workers, and other semiskilled and unskilled laborers whose jobs are automated or moved to Third World countries. But many also believe that the demand for professionals—especially engineers and teachers—is likely to rise as a result of shifts in the information economy.

Will we have enough skilled workers to fill those jobs? Economic growth may depend on whether we have a suitably trained workforce. The single most important key to a positive economic future may be education. But will we, as a society, be able to provide people with the kind of education they'll need? We'll deal with that question, and the critical issues surrounding education in the information age, in the next section of this chapter.

Will We Need a New Economy?

In the long run, education may not be enough. It seems likely that, at some time in the future, machines will be able to do most of the jobs people do today. We may face a future of *jobless growth*—a time when productivity increases not because of the work people do but because of the work of machines. If productivity isn't tied to employment, we'll have to ask some hard questions about our political, economic, and social system:

▌ Do governments have an obligation to provide permanent public assistance to the chronically unemployed?

▌ Should large companies be required to give several months' notice to workers whose jobs are being eliminated? Should they be required to retrain workers for other jobs?

▌ Should large companies be required to file employment impact statements before replacing people with machines in the same way they're required to file environmental impact statements before implementing policies that might harm the environment?

▌ If robots and computers are producing most of society's goods and services, should all the profits from those goods go to a few people who own the machines?

> If a worker is replaced by a robot, should the worker receive a share of the robot's "earnings" through stocks or profit sharing?

> The average workweek 150 years ago was 70 hours; for the last 50 years it has been steady at about 40. Should governments and businesses encourage job-sharing and other systems that allow for less-than-40-hour jobs?

> What will people do with their time if machines do most of the work? What new leisure activities should be made available?

> How will people define their identities if work becomes less central to their lives?

These questions force us to confront deep-seated cultural beliefs and economic traditions, and they don't come with easy answers. They suggest that we may be heading into a difficult period when many old rules don't apply anymore. But if we're successful at navigating the troubled waters of transition, we may find that automation fulfills the dream expressed by Aristotle more than 2,000 years ago:

If every instrument could accomplish its own work, obeying or anticipating the will of others . . . if the shuttle could weave, and the pick touch the lyre, without a hand to guide them, chief workmen would not need servants, nor masters slaves.

Education in the Information Age

The future is a race between **education** and **catastrophe**.
—H.G. Wells

As we've seen, the information age is changing the way we work. Some jobs are disappearing, others are emerging, and still others are being radically transformed by information technology. But the information age is not just affecting the workplace. Its influences are felt in our educational system, too. Before it's over, the information revolution will have a profound and permanent effect on the way we learn.

The Roots of Our Educational System

The American educational system was developed more than a century ago to teach students the basic facts and survival skills they would need for jobs in industry and agriculture—jobs they would probably hold for their entire adult lives. This industrial age system has been described as a factory model for three reasons:

1. It assumes that all students learn the same way and that all students should learn the same things.
2. The teacher's job is to "pour" facts into students, occasionally checking the level of knowledge in each student.
3. Students are expected to work individually, absorb facts, and spend most of their time sitting quietly in straight rows.

Despite its faults, the factory model of public education helped the United States dominate world markets for most of this century. But the world has changed drastically since the system was founded. Schools have changed, too, but not fast enough to keep pace with the information revolution. Most experts today agree that we need to rebuild our educational system to meet the demands of the information age.

Information Age Education

Education is the **kindling of a flame**, not the filling of a vessel.
—Socrates

What should education provide for students in the information age? Research and experience suggest several answers:

> *Technological familiarity.* Many of today's older workers are having trouble adjusting to the information age because of technophobia—the fear of technology. These people grew up in a world without computers, and they experience anxiety when they're forced to deal with them. To prepare for the future, students need to learn how to work comfortably with all kinds of knowledge tools, including pencils, books, calculators, computers, and the Internet.

But technological familiarity shouldn't stop with learning how to work with tools. Students need to have a clear understanding of the *limitations* of the technology and the ability to assess the benefits and risks of applying technology to a problem. They need to be able to *question* technology.

▶ *Literacy.* In the information age, it's more important than ever that students graduate with the ability to read and write. Many jobs that did not require reading or writing skills a generation ago now use high-tech equipment that demands literacy. A factory worker who can't read computer screens isn't likely to survive the transition to an automated factory.

▶ *Mathematics.* In the age of the five-dollar calculator many students think learning math is a waste of time. In fact, some educators argue that we spend too much time teaching students how to do things like long division and calculating square roots—functions that adults seldom, if ever, do by hand. These arithmetic skills have little to do with being able to think mathematically. To survive in a high-tech world, students need to be able to see the mathematical systems in the world around them and apply math concepts to solve problems. No calculator can do that.

▶ *Culture.* An education isn't complete without a strong cultural component. Liberal arts and social studies help us recognize the interconnections that turn information into knowledge. Culture gives us roots when the sands of time shift. It gives us historical perspective that allows us to see trends and prepare for the future. Culture provides a human framework with which to view the impact of technology. It also gives us the global perspective to live in a world where communication is determined more by technology than by geography.

▶ *Communication.* In the information age communication is a survival skill. Isolated factory workers and desk-bound pencil pushers are vanishing from the workplace. Modern jobs involve interactions—between people and machines and between people and people. The fast-paced, information-based society depends on our human ability to communicate, negotiate, cooperate, and collaborate, both locally and globally.

▶ *Learning how to learn.* Experts predict that most of the jobs that will exist in 10 years do not exist today and that most of those new jobs will require education past the high-school level. With this rapidly changing job market, it's unreasonable to assume that workers can be trained once for lifelong jobs. Instead of holding a single job for 40 years, today's high-school or college graduate is likely to change jobs several times. Those people who do keep the same jobs will have to deal with unprecedented change. The half-life of an engineer's specialized knowledge—the time it takes for half of that knowledge to be replaced by more current knowledge—is just over three years.

These facts suggest that we can no longer afford to think of education as a one-time vaccination against illiteracy. In the information age, learning must be a lifelong process. To prepare students for a lifetime of learning, schools must teach students more than facts; they must make sure students learn how to think and learn.

Computers Go to School

The only thing we know about the future is that **it will be inhabited by our children**. Its quality, in other words, is directly proportional to **world education**.

—Nicholas Negroponte, Director of the M.I.T. Media Lab

The information age is making new demands on our educational system, requiring radical changes in what and how people learn. Many educators believe that computers are essential parts of those changes. Ninety-nine percent of all elementary and secondary schools in the United States have installed computers. Students and teachers are using those computers in a variety of ways.

Computer-aided instruction (CAI) software typically combines tutorial material with drill-and-practice questions in an interactive format that provides instant feedback for each student. CAI is one of the most common types of courseware (educational software) for three reasons: It's relatively easy to produce, it can be easily combined with more traditional educational techniques, and it produces clear, demonstrable results.

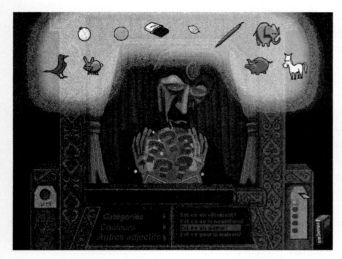

Students in this class build LEGO robots and write LOGO programs to control them.

CAI is useful for strengthening basic motor skills such as typing. In Typing Tutor 10, onscreen tutorials guide the student through a complete set of typing lessons, with the computer monitoring every keystroke for accuracy . Programs like French (above) for the Real World provide instruction and practice sessions for learning languages.

Programming tools—such as LOGO, Pascal, and Basic—enable young students to take a more active role programming the computer.

Simulations and games enable students to explore artificial environments, whether imaginary or based on reality. *Educational simulations* are metaphors designed to focus student attention on the most important concepts. While most educational simulations have the look and feel of a game, they challenge students to learn through exploration, experimentation, and interaction with other students. With a simulation students find and use information to draw conclusions and then experience the consequences of their actions without taking real-world risks.

Productivity tools such as word processors, spreadsheets, databases, graphics programs, desktop publishing software, Web browsers, and email programs—the software tools used by adults—are the tools students learn most often in schools. While only a few students take programming classes, classes in keyboarding, word processing, and Web research are often required for everybody. Once students learn to use these general-purpose tools, they can put them to work in and out of school.

Teachers are using computer-controlled media, including the Web, to convey information in a more dynamic form to their students. Depending on the way these media are used, the student's role might be to observe a presentation created by the teacher, to control or interact with a presentation on a CD-ROM or on the Web, or to use a multimedia authoring tool to create their own CD-ROM or Web presentation.

Star Wars Droid Works combines entertainment with education by simulating a robot factory. Given specifications and parts, players must apply principles of science and engineering to successfully construct a variety of robots.

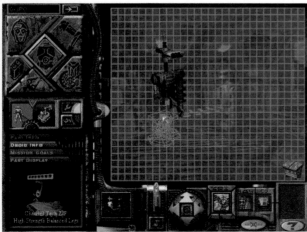

Distance education uses technology to extend the educational process beyond the walls of the school. Computers, modems, fax machines, satellite video transmissions, the Internet, and other communication technologies offer many promising possibilities. Students can network with others in any part of the world through the Internet. Students can use scientific equipment such as electron microscopes, telescopes, and other powerful tools around the world through real-time Internet connections. Two-way video links enable visiting experts to talk to students in outlying classrooms and answer their questions in real time. Networked school districts can offer multischool videoconference courses in Chinese, college-level calculus, and other subjects that might have tiny enrollments if offered only at a single school. Teachers can receive additional education without leaving their districts. The demand for distance education is growing rapidly. In some countries, distance education students compose 40 percent of the total undergraduate population. Some experts predict that the majority of college students will be off-campus students in a decade or two.

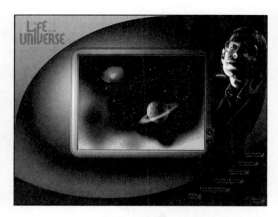

Professionally produced multimedia programs like Steven Hawkings's Life in the Universe *can make abstract concepts and facts more accessible and exciting.*

Computers at School: Midterm Grades

The business of education is to give the student both **useful information** and **life-enhancing experience**, one largely measurable, the other not. . . .

—John Gardner, in *The Art of Fiction*

Many schools have been using computers in classrooms for more than a decade. In these days of shrinking budgets, taxpayers are asking whether classroom information technology pays off. Has it lived up to its promise as an educational tool in the schools? According to most experts, the answer is mixed but optimistic.

High Marks

A number of independent studies in the 1990s confirm that information technology can improve education. Here are some findings:

▶ Students improve problem-solving skills, outscore classmates, and learn more rapidly in a variety of subject areas and situations when using technology as compared to conventional methods of study.

▶ Students find computer-based instruction more motivational, less intimidating, and easier to persist with than traditional instruction.

▶ In many cases students' self-esteem is increased when they use computers. This change is most dramatic in cases of at-risk youngsters and students with handicaps.

▶ Using technology encourages cooperative learning, turn taking among young children, peer tutoring, and other valuable social skills.

Classroom Connect is one organization that regularly offers interactive expeditions for students. For example, AmazonQuest allowed students to communicate with a team of explorers as they explored the Amazon rainforest.

▶ Information technology can make learning more student centered and stimulate increased teacher/student interaction.

▶ Well-designed interactive multimedia systems can encourage active processing and higher order thinking.

▶ Students who create interactive multimedia reports often learn better than those who learn with more traditional methods.

▶ Students can become more productive, more fluid writers with computers.

▶ Computers can help students master the basic skills needed to participate and succeed in the workforce.

▶ Positive changes occur gradually as teachers gain experience with the technology.

▶ Technology can facilitate educational reform.

Research shows that writing improves when students use word processors. Students in this Connecticut school are supplied with laptops for writing, research, and other assignments.

Room for Improvement

▌ This stuff is **so bad**, it must be **educational**.

—Aunt Selma on The Simpsons

Other findings temper—and sometimes contradict—these positive conclusions. Researchers have also found that the following:

▶ If the only thing that changes is the delivery medium (from traditional media to computer media), the advantages of technology are small or nonexistent.

▶ Kids and teachers forget advanced computer skills if they don't use them.

▶ Students have unequal access to technology; economically disadvantaged students have less computer access at school and at home. Sadly, these are the students who can benefit most when given access to technology.

▶ Technology doesn't reduce teacher workloads; if anything, it seems to make their jobs harder (of course, many teachers welcome the extra work because they believe it brings results).

▶ There's a gender gap that typically puts the computer room in the boys' domain; the gap can be reduced by stressing computer activities that involve collaboration.

▶ Many of the outcomes of technology-based education don't show up with traditional educational assessment methods.

▶ Sending students to a computer lab for 30 minutes a week has little or no value; computers are more effective when they're in classrooms where students can use them regularly.

Research suggests that technology can have a positive impact on education if it's part of a program that includes teacher training, ongoing support, and radical restructuring of the traditional "factory model" curriculum.

▶ Younger students may be better served by art, music, and shop classes than by computer classes; unfortunately, these important parts of the curriculum are often eliminated to make room for computers.

Stories abound of reduced dropout rates and attitudinal changes among at-risk students; improved math, reading, and language scores; and overall academic improvement among students in high-tech schools. But information technology doesn't always bring happy headlines. In some schools, computers are little more than expensive, time-consuming distractions. What makes technology work for some schools and not for others? Technology must be kept up to date, made accessible to all students, be backed by solid planning, and be supported with teacher training. Just as businesses need to rethink their organizational structures to automate successfully, schools need to be restructured to make effective use of information technology. To meet the educational challenges of the information age, we'll need to invest in research and planning involving teachers, students, administrators, parents, businesses, and community leaders.

The Classroom of Tomorrow

▌ The further one pursues knowledge, **the less one knows**.

—Lao Tse, 500 B.C.

To give us a head start in building the schools of the future, Apple, IBM, Microsoft, Toshiba, and other companies, along with some state and local governments, have helped create model technology classrooms and schools in communities around the United States and Canada. Most of these pilot projects suggest that technology can, in the proper context, have a dramatic effect on education. For example, here's a quote from Apple's Web site summarizing the results of the Apple Classroom of Tomorrow (ACOT) project:

After more than a decade of research, ACOT's research demonstrated that the introduction of technology into classrooms can significantly increase the potential for learning, especially when it is used to support collaboration, information access, and the expression and representation of students' thoughts and ideas. Realizing this opportunity for all students, however, required a broadly conceived approach to educational change that integrated new technologies and curricula with new ideas about learning and teaching, as well as with authentic forms of assessment.

Information technology, then, can be a powerful change agent, but not by itself. In an interview for the online magazine *ZineZone*, educational computing pioneer Seymour Papert was asked whether technology is a Trojan horse for systematic and lasting change. His reply: "I think the technology serves as a Trojan horse all right, but in the real story of the Trojan horse, it wasn't the horse that was effective, it was the soldiers inside the horse. And the technology is only going to be effective in changing education if you put an army inside it which is determined to make that change once it gets through the barrier."

Computers Come Home

The same year Ken Olson made this statement, Apple Computer introduced the Apple II computer.

> There is **no reason** for any individual to have a **computer** in their home.
> —Ken Olson, president of Digital Equipment Corporation, 1977\

In the years that followed, Apple, Commodore, Tandy, Atari, IBM, and dozens of other companies managed to sell computers to millions of individuals who had "no reason" to buy them.

Today there are more computers in homes than in schools. Most American homes contain at least one computer. The small office, home office market—dubbed *SOHO* by the industry—is one of the fastest growing computer markets today. While many home computers gather dust, others are being put to work, and play, in a variety of ways.

Household Business

Frank Gilbreth, a turn-of-the-century pioneer of motion study in industry, applied "scientific management" techniques to his home. He required his 12 children to keep records on bathroom "work-and-process charts" of each hair combing, tooth brushing, and bathing. He gave them demonstrations on efficient bathing techniques to minimize "unavoidable delays." While it may have worked for Gilbreth, this "scientific management" approach to home life is not likely to catch on today. Still, certain aspects of family life are unavoidably businesslike, and a growing number of people are turning to computers to help them take care of business.

Not everyone is convinced that computers are useful or practical at home. But those people who do use home computers generally find that they can put the same applications to work at home that they use in their offices: Web browsers for entertainment, research, shopping, and other applications; email programs for connecting with others; word processors for writing; personal information managers for tracking calendars and contacts; spreadsheets for answering what-if questions; and accounting programs for managing income and expenses.

Few home computer users type *every* financial transaction into the computer. Some people type in only "important" transactions. Others download transaction summary statements from their bank Web sites. But for most people computerized money management won't happen until there's an effortless way to record transactions—perhaps a device that, when inserted into the computer, can tell the software about each purchase and paid bill.

That device may turn out to be a smart card. A **smart card** looks like a standard credit card, but instead of a magnetic strip it contains an embedded

A home office like this one can be used for taking care of family business . . . or starting a family business.

A smart card contains a micro-processor and digital memory.

microprocessor and memory. (Memory cards, which contain memory but no microprocessors, are occasionally called smart cards even though they aren't really smart.) Some smart cards even contain touch-sensitive keypads for entering numbers. Whether it has a keypad or not, a smart card receives most of its input when it's slipped into a special slot on a computer. Data stored in smart cards can be password protected. There are hundreds of millions of smart cards in Europe, and they're rapidly infiltrating America.

Smart cards are obvious candidates to replace magnetic-strip credit cards. In addition to storing critical ID information, a smart card can automatically record each transaction for later retrieval. But smart cards have other applications, too. College students use smart cards as meal tickets. Office workers use smart cards as keys to access sensitive data on computers. Smart cards have replaced food stamps and drivers' licenses in some states. Many Europeans use smart cards to pay highway tolls and unscramble cable TV broadcasts. You might soon use one card to buy groceries, check out library books, and store personal medical information in case of an emergency. Future smart cards will use pattern recognition techniques to verify signatures on checks or credit slips and help prevent millions of dollars in fraud and forgery.

Education and Information

Newspapers as we know them won't exist. They will be printed for a **readership of one**. Television won't simply have sharper pictures. You'll have one button that says **tell me more**, and another button that says **tell me less**.

—Nicholas Negroponte, director of the MIT Media Lab

Millions of people use home computers for education and information. Many educational software programs described earlier in this chapter are used by children and adults in homes. **Edutainment** programs specifically geared toward home markets combine education with entertainment so they can compete with television and electronic games. Encyclopedias, dictionaries, atlases, almanacs, medical references, and other specialized references now come in low-cost CD-ROM or DVD-ROM versions—often with multimedia capability. Web references, which offer more up-to-the-minute information—often for free have eclipsed many CD-ROM references . Of course, Internet connections also provide email, discussion groups, and other communication options for home users.

As computer technology and communication technology converge on the home market, they're producing services that may soon threaten television and newspapers as our main sources of information. Television is a broadcast medium; it transmits news and information to broad audiences. Information technology enables **narrowcasting** services—custom newscasts and entertainment features aimed at narrow groups or individuals. (Individualized broadcasting is sometimes called pointcasting.) With a narrowcasting service, you might create a personalized news program that includes a piece on the latest Middle Eastern crisis, highlights of last night's Blazers vs. Lakers game, this weekend's weather forecast at the coast, announcements of upcoming local jazz concerts, and a reminder that there are only five more shopping days until your

CD-ROMs and Web sites can provide maps and navigation instructions for back-country trekkers and urban travelers alike. (Software: Yahoo! Maps, DeLorme Topo USA.)

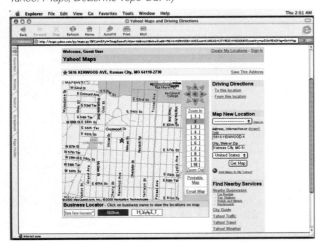

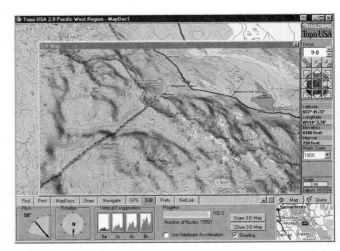

mother's birthday. Personalized news service can flag particular subjects ("I'm especially interested in articles on the Amazon rain forest") and ignore others ("No Hollywood gossip, please").

Several Web portals, including Excite and Yahoo! enable users to personalize their front pages with customized headlines, stock quotes, weather information, television and movie schedules, and other features. Avant Go and other wireless portals can automatically download customized content into PDAs and other handheld devices. These Web-based products hint at the kinds of customization we might see when television adds interactivity.

Personalized Web portals enable people to control what they see on their home pages, but not what they see on other sites. Some families depend on filtering software to block their browsers so children can't visit sites that contain pornography and other "inappropriate" content. Filtering programs can be customized, but they're not 100 percent accurate. They're also subject to the biases of their authors and corporate owners. In early 2000, extensive tests of American Online's filtering revealed that kids had free access to Web sites of conservative Republican and Libertarian parties but were blocked from viewing the Democratic and Green party sites. Young teens could access sites promoting gun use, including the National Rifle Association, but not the Coalition to Stop Gun Violence and other gun safety organizations. Both AOL and The Learning Company, who designed the filtering software, denied bias. But the findings show how censorship can squelch the free flow of ideas that's a critical part of the educational process.

Computer simulation games continually push the limits of PC graphics and animation toward the realism of film. (Software: Tony Hawk, Pro Skater 2.)

Home Entertainment Redefined

Television has a **"brightness"** knob, but it doesn't seem to work.
—Gallagher, stand-up comic

You don't want a television with knobs marked **"volume"** and **"brightness"** and **"contrast."** You want a television with knobs marked **"sex"** and **"violence"** and **"political bias."**
—Nicholas Negroponte, director of the MIT Media Lab

Regardless of how people say they use home computers, surveys suggest that many people use them mostly to play games. Computer games and video game machines (which are just special-purpose computers) represent a huge industry—one that is likely to evolve rapidly in the coming years.

Most computer games are simulations. Computer games can simulate board games, card games, sporting events, intergalactic battles, street fights, corporate takeovers, or something else, real or imaginary. Many require strategy and puzzle solving; others depend only on eye-hand coordination. Many of the most popular games require some of each. With dazzling graphics, digitized sound, and sophisticated effects, many of today's computer games represent state-of-the-art software. But in a few years these computer games are likely to look as primitive as early Pong games look today.

Enhanced realism of computer games may not be completely beneficial for society. In the years before the 1999 Columbine High School mass murder, the killers spent hundreds of hours blasting virtual people in graphic first-person games like Doom. In the aftermath of the tragedy many people suggested that the violent games were partially responsible for the horrific killings. A year later, published research confirmed a link between violent video games and real-world violence. Two studies suggested that even brief exposure to violent video games can temporarily increase aggressive behavior, and that children who play violent games tend to have lower grades and more aggressive tendencies in later years. Further research may confirm or clarify these results. In the meantime, pressure grows for game manufacturers to consider the impact of their products on young minds.

Sometimes the impact of video games on young minds is measurably positive. In a recent study, researchers at East Virginia Medical School in Norfolk, working with NASA scientists, used PlayStation games to successfully treat children diagnosed with attention deficit

Researchers are using video game technology in biofeedback experiments on children with attention deficit disorder.

disorder (ADD). Using basic biofeedback technology and off-the-shelf video games, children were able to quickly learn to control their brain waves so they could improve concentration. The fast-action games provided strong motivation for the young learners. A commercial product based on this project may soon be available to help the 5 to 7 percent of U.S. elementary-school students with ADD.

The entertainment industry is exploring a variety of ways of adding interactivity to entertainment products. A few years ago, one of the most popular types of games was **interactive fiction**—stories with primitive natural-language interfaces that gave players some control over plot. Today arcade-style games, puzzle-based adventure games, and other multimedia-rich genres capture most of the attention of computer gamers. But interactivity is finding its way into other entertainment technology—most notably on the Web and on DVDs.

Many DVD movies allow for customized movie viewing—language, subtitles, commentary soundtracks, and sometimes even camera angle are under viewer control. A few DVDs allow actual branching within a film. We may soont see truly **interactive movies**—features in which one or more of the characters or plot lines are controlled by the viewers.

We're also likely to see a growth in **interactive TV**—broadcast television with options for interactivity built in. In 1999 two popular game shows, *Wheel of Fortune* and *Jeopardy*, began broadcasting interactive versions that allowed viewers to play along with contestants. Some experts think this kind of programming is likely to increase sharply as more TV viewers buy set-top boxes with keyboards and other input devices. Interactive TV has been popular for years in Europe, where digital TV had an early audience.

Interactive TV and DVD are, for the most part, solitary activities. But the Internet opens up new possibilities for social entertainment, as well. We're already seeing multiplayer multimedia games on the Web. How long will it be until these games have the richness of plot and cinematography of today's films? When will today's chat rooms and virtual communities evolve into rich environments for interaction and exploration? As technology improves and the multimedia market grows, we can expect all kinds of hybrid forms of entertainment.

Creativity and Leisure

> If you can talk, **you can sing**.
> If you can walk, **you can dance**.
> —A saying from Zimbabwe

A 2000 report by the Childhood Alliance, a group of education experts, raises serious questions about computer use, especially in young children. "Intense use of computers can distract children and adults from ... essential experiences." Specifically, the time children spend in front of a computer screen is time they aren't involved in physical activities and self-generated, imaginative play. "A heavy diet of ready-made computer images and programmed toys appears to stunt imaginative thinking." The report also argues that computers expose kids to adult hazards, including repetitive-stress injury and social isolation.

Many people worry that television, computer games, and other media are replacing too many real-world activities. Instead of making up stories to share, we watch sitcoms on TV. Instead of playing music on guitars, we play music on boom boxes. Instead of playing one-on-one basketball, we play one-on-one video games.

Is electronic technology turning us into a mindless couch-potato culture? Perhaps. But there's another possibility. The same technology that mesmerizes us can also unlock our creativity. Word processors help many of us to become writers; graphics software brings out the artists among us; Web authoring tools provide us with worldwide publishing platforms; electronic music systems enable us to compose music even if we never mastered an instrument, and digital video and multimedia systems open doors to cable-access TV channels.

Will computers drain our creativity or amplify it? In the end it's up to us. . . .

Sarah McLachlan's Freedom Sessions was one of the first enhanced audio CDs that included video and animation along with standard audio tracks. Today many musicians use the Web and DVDs to deliver multimedia material to their fans.

CrossCurrentsCrossCurrentsCrossCurrents **CrossCurrents**

Cyber-Serfdom

Thomas L. Friedman

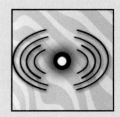

In the early days of the computer revolution, most managers didn't go near high-tech machinery. Today a PC is standard equipment on the desktop, and most executives carry several digital devices when they travel. In this article, reprinted from the January 30, 2001 issue of the New York Times, Thomas L. Friedman comments on the down side of this techno-trend.

AVOS, Switzerland—The Davos World Economic Forum is always useful for gauging global trends. In recent years much of the buzz at Davos was about what technology will do for us. This year, more and more, the buzz has been what technology is doing to us. If Davos is any indicator, there is a backlash brewing against the proliferation of technology in our lives.

When participants arrived at Davos this year they were given yet another gadget to communicate with other participants—a Compaq pocket PC. As I fumbled around trying to figure out how mine worked, and interfaced with the complex Davos e- mail system that you access with a badge, the Washington Post columnist Richard Cohen, who was trying to do the same, said to me: "I have so many devices now to make my life easier that I need someone just to carry them all around for me."

Then there was the panel about the 21st-century corporation, during which participants described this age of digital Darwinism in chilling terms: The key to winning in business today is adapt or die, get wired or get killed, work 24 hours a day from everywhere or be left behind. Finally, during the question time, Howard Stringer, chairman of Sony America, stood up and said: "Doesn't anyone here think this sounds like a vision of hell? While we are all competing or dying, when will there be time for sex or music or books? Stop the world, I want to get off."

To be sure, this is a developed- world problem. In much of Africa you don't see executives walking around, as you do in Europe, with so many beepers, phones and pagers clipped onto their belts that they look like telephone repairmen. But with the cost of this technology rapidly decreasing, it will spread faster than you think. And so will the social stresses associated with it. Apropos of such a future, I heard a lot of new phrases this week: "device creep," "Machines don't serve us, we serve them," and "My identity is now less important than the data that is stored about me." Have a nice day.

My favorite, though, was that we now live in an age of what a Microsoft researcher, Linda Stone, called continuous partial attention. I love that phrase. It means that while you are answering your email and talking to your kid, your cell phone rings and you have a conversation. You are now involved in a continuous flow of interactions in which you can only partially concentrate on each.

"If being fulfilled is about committing yourself to someone else, or some experience, that requires a level of sustained attention," said Ms. Stone. And that is what we are losing the skills for, because we are constantly scanning the world for opportunities and we are constantly in fear of missing something better. That has become incredibly spiritually depleting.

I am struck at how many people call my office, ask if I'm in, and, if I'm not, immediately ask to be connected to my cell phone or pager. (I carry neither.) You're never out anymore. The assumption now is that you're always in. Out is over. Now you are always in. And when you are always in you are always on. And when you are always on, what are you most like? A computer server.

They say these devices will eventually be invisible, but for now they feel in your face. And here's the scary part: It's just the beginning. By 2005 we will see a convergence of wireless technology, fiber optics, software applications and next-generation Internet switches, IP version 6, that will permit anything with electricity to have a Web address and run off the Internet—from your bedroom lights to your toaster to your pacemaker (which will report your heart rate directly to your doctor). This Evernet will allow us all to be online all the time from everywhere. People will boast: "I have 25 Web addresses in my house; how many do you have? My wired refrigerator automatically reorders milk. How about yours?"

The problem is that human beings simply are not designed to be like computer servers. For one thing, they are designed to sleep eight hours a night. So there is a big misfit brewing here. I still can't program my VCR; how am I going to program my toaster? As Jeff Garten, dean of the Yale School of Management and author of a smart new book that deals with some of these themes, "The Mind of the CEO," said: "Maybe it's not time for us to adapt or die, but for the technology to adapt or die."

DISCUSSION QUESTIONS

1. Can you identify with the author's description of "continuous partial attention? Give examples from your life of the concept.
2. Do you agree with the author's premise that there is a "big misfit brewing here?" Explain your answer.

Summary

As we enter the information age, our workplaces, schools, and homes are being transformed by information technology. This transformation has positive and negative repercussions for workers, students, teachers, and families.

Computers have enabled many organizations to provide services that wouldn't be possible otherwise, but so far they haven't produced the productivity gains that many experts expected. Experts speculate that productivity will rise as organizations adjust to the new technology and develop human-centered systems that are adapted to the needs and work habits of employees.

The impact of computers varies from job to job. Some jobs are de-skilled—transformed so they require less skill—while others are up-skilled into more technologically complex jobs. Computer monitoring is a controversial procedure that raises issues of privacy and in many cases lowers worker morale. De-skilling, monitoring, and health risks are particularly evident in electronic sweatshops—data-entry warehouses packed with low-paid keyboard operators.

The biggest problem of automation may be the elimination of jobs. So far most displaced workers have been able to find other jobs in our expanding economy. However, automation will almost certainly produce unemployment and pain for millions of people unless society is able to provide them with the education they'll need to take the new jobs created by technology. Automation may ultimately force us to make fundamental changes in our economic system. Only time will tell.

Our educational system was developed a century ago to train workers for lifelong jobs. In the information age, when students can expect to change jobs several times, we need schools that teach technological familiarity, literacy, mathematics, culture, communication, problem solving, and, most important, the ability to learn and adapt to an ever-changing world.

Students use a variety of instructional tools in schools today, including computer-aided instruction, programming tool, simulations and games, productivity tools, computer-controlled media, and distance education tools.

Clearly, information technology can have a positive educational impact, but computers alone can't guarantee improvement. Research, planning, teacher training, community involvement, and classroom restructuring should accompany new technology.

A small but growing number of families use home computers for basic business applications, education, information access, communication, entertainment, and creative pursuits. All these applications will radically change as the technology evolves over the next decade.

Chapter Review

▼ Key Terms

computer-aided instruction (CAI) (p. 477)
computer monitoring (p. 473)
courseware (p. 477)
de-skilling (p. 472)
distance education (p. 479)

edutainment (p. 482)
electronic sweatshop (p. 474)
filtering software (p. 483)
human-centered system (p. 473)
interactive fiction (p. 484)
interactive movies (p. 484)

interactive TV (p. 484)
narrowcasting (p. 482)
smart card (p. 481)
technophobia (p. 476)
up-skilling (p. 472)

▼ Interactive Quiz Questions

1. The *Computer Confluence* CD-ROM contains self-test quiz questions related to this chapter, including multiple choice, true or false, and matching questions.
2. The *Computer Confluence* Web site, **www.prenhall.com/beekman**, contains self-test exercises related to this chapter. Follow the instructions for taking a quiz. After you've completed your quiz, you can email the results to your instructor.

   The Web site also contains open-ended discussion questions called Internet Explorations. Discuss one or more of the Internet Exploration questions at the section for this chapter.

▼ Review Questions

1. Define or describe each of the key terms listed in the "Key Terms" section. Check your answers using the glossary.
2. What is de-skilling? What is up-skilling? Give examples of each.
3. What is the purpose of human-centered computer systems?
4. What are the main problems with computer monitoring of workers?
5. What are some of the controversies surrounding electronic sweatshops?
6. What were the goals of education in the industrial age? Which are still appropriate in the information age? Which are not?
7. What kind of an education does a student need to prepare for living and working in the information age?
8. How do educational simulation games differ from traditional computer-aided instruction? What are the advantages and disadvantages of each?
9. Describe how teachers and students can use multimedia in the classroom. Give several examples.
10. Give several examples of ways that distance learning can enhance education.
11. Technology alone is no guarantee that students will learn better or faster. What else is necessary to ensure success?
12. Describe several ways people use home computers.
13. What are smart cards, and how are they used?
14. How is home entertainment being changed by information technology and telecommunication?

▼ Discussion Questions

1. Why do you think it has been so difficult to demonstrate that computers increase productivity?
2. People who work in electronic sweatshops run the risk of being replaced by technology. Discuss the trade-offs of this dilemma from the point of view of the worker and society at large.
3. What do you think are the answers to the questions raised at the end of the section on automation and unemployment? How do you think most people would feel about these questions?
4. Socrates was illiterate and avoided the written word because he felt it weakened the mind. Similarly, many people today fear that we're weakening our children's minds by making them too dependent on computers and calculators. What do you think?
5. In many schools students spend two years of math education learning long division—a skill that's almost never used in the age of the five-dollar calculator. Some educators argue that students' time could be better spent learning other things. What do you think? What about calculating square roots by hand?
6. Do you think it's important for students to learn to program in LOGO, Pascal, Basic, or some other language? Why or why not?
7. Do you think educational games are good ways for students to learn in schools? Give examples that support your arguments.
8. What kind of productivity software tools should students learn how to use? Why?
9. Think about educational goals in relation to technology. What should people be able to do with no tools? What should people be able to do if they have access to pencils, papers, and books? What should people be able to do if they have access to information technology?
10. Describe your past school experience in terms of technology. How did it measure up? What has been missing from your education so far?
11. Do you think most families can benefit from a home computer today? Explain.
12. Do you think home computers strengthen families and communities? Explain.
13. Do you think home computers in the future will make people more or less creative? Why?

▼ Projects

1. Interview several people whose jobs have been changed by computers and the Internet. Use your word processor to describe your findings and then distribute the document to the other students in your class via email.
2. Think about how computers have affected the jobs you've held. Describe your experiences orally to your class.
3. Try several different types of educational software. If possible, observe students using the software. Prepare a report comparing the strengths and weaknesses of each.
4. Observe how computers are used in local schools or your campus. Report on your findings.
5. Survey the Web for educational resources on a particular subject. Report on your findings.
6. Using a multimedia authoring tool or HTML, design a simple courseware lesson. Make sure you set clear goals before you start. When your project is completed, try it with several students.
7. Plan a model technology school. Describe how it would differ from conventional schools and why.

Sources and Resources

Books

The Hacker Ethic and the Spirit of the Information Age, by Pekka Himanen (New York: Random House, 2001). This book argues that Linus Tovalds, Steve Wozniak, and other pioneers of the information revolution are defining a new work ethic based on curiosity, passion, and sharing rather than duty and guilt. Whether or not you agree with the arguments, you'll probably find the presentation worthwhile.

Holding on to Reality: The Nature or Information at the Turn of the Millennium, by Albert Borgmann (Chicago: The University of Chicago Press, 2000) The author is a philosopher and in this book he explores the idea of information that does justice both to its deep roots in human history and its broad implications for human culture at the edge of the 21st century.

The Social Life of Information, by J.S. Brown and P. Duguid (Cambridge, MA: Harvard Business School Press, 2000). This book is a pragmatic yet visionary perspective on the profound role that information technology will play in reshaping our society and its institutions. The authors argue that information technology does not work unless supported by viable communities and institutions, and that the preservation of social knowledge and the art of practice are key to unleashing the economic promise of the new technologies.

White Collar Sweatshop: The Deterioration of Work and Its Rewards in Corporate America, by Jill Andresky Fraser (New York: Norton, 2000). This book stretches the sweatshop metaphor beyond data entry warehouses, arguing that modern management techniques are oppressive to all but the top executives in many high-tech companies.

How People Learn: Brain, Mind, Experience, and School, by John D. Bransford, Editor, Ann L. Brown, Editor, Rodney R. Cocking, Editor, John B. Bransford, Editor (New York: National Academy Press, 1999). This book provides a summary of research in human learning and the implications of that research. It has relevance for educators, aspiring educators, and others interested in redesigning and reforming our schools.

High Tech, High Teach: Technology and Our Search for Meaning, John Naisbitt with Nana Naisbitt and Douglas Philips (New York: Broadway Books, 1999). In this book, the author of *Megatrends* examines a future in which technology saturates every aspect of American society. What impact will this "Technologically Intoxicated Zone" have on our lives and consciousness? How will our relationship with technology evolve? These are the kinds of questions *High Tech, High Teach* tackles.

Digital Illusion: Entertaining the Future with High Technology, edited by Clark Dodsworth, Jr. (Reading, MA: Addison-Wesley Publishing Company, 1998). The entertainment industry is the driving force behind many of the technological breakthroughs of the information age. This fascinating collection of papers explores the future of entertainment, including video games, digital video and film, virtual reality, networked games, and immersive amusement park rides. Big fun!

Adapting PCs for Disabilities, by Joseph J. Lazzaro (Reading, MA: Addison-Wesley, 1996). Many features of the modern personal computer are difficult for people with disabilities to use—unless the PC is designed or modified to make it more accessible for those special populations. On the other hand, PCs with the right software and peripherals can provide invaluable assistance for people with disabilities. This book/CD-ROM package is full of useful information and software for adapting an IBM-compatible PC for people with special needs.

Mindstorms: Children, Computers, and Powerful Ideas, Second Edition, by Seymour Papert (New York: Basic Books, 1999) and **The Children's Machine,** by Seymour Papert (New York: Basic Books, 1994). These two books outline the views of one widely respected theorist and researcher on technology in education: Seymour Papert, the inventor of LOGO. Mindstorms was written during the period when Papert was doing pioneering work with LOGO. In The Children's Machine, Papert discusses why the computer revolution failed to revolutionize education.

Amusing Ourselves to Death: Public Discourse in the Age of Show Business, by Neil Postman (New York: Viking Press, 1986), **Technopoly: The Surrender of Culture to Technology** (New York: Vintage Books, 1993), and **The End of Education: Redefining the Value of School,** by Neil Postman (New York, Knopf, 1995). In these books, noted social critic Neil Postman takes on schools and technology, two powerful forces that are shaping our lives. In *Amusing Ourselves to Death*, Postman argues that television has injured, and is injuring, our ability to think, by reducing every public discourse to just another form of entertainment. In *Technopoly* he argues that our tools, especially computers, no longer play supporting roles; instead, they radically shape our culture, our families, and our world views. In *The End of Education*, he presents a picture of modern education in which economic utility has become the defining principle. Postman presents compelling problems and suggests possible solutions in these important books.

Periodicals

Smart Business for the New Economy. This monthly used to be called *PC Computing*. In the 90s *PC Computing* focused on PC technology and business applications. But in the new decade, the PC is no longer the focal point of the "new" economy. In early 2000 *PC Computing* changed its name and broadened its focus to all kinds of information technology that have an impact on business and economy.

Information Week. This weekly news magazine focuses on business and the technology that drives it.

Upside. This monthly is aimed at managers, entrepreneurs, and others who want to track the business side rather than the technological side of the computer industry.

Forbes ASAP. This publication provides a thinking person's perspective on the high-tech workplace. Each year's "Big Issue" includes dozens of essays by famous and not-so-famous writers on a particular theme. (Some of those essays are reprinted in Crosscurrents in this text.)

Fast Company. This is another thought-provoking magazine that deals with the human issues of business in the digital age.

Small Business Computing. This magazine provides computer coverage for those businesses that aren't part of the Fortune 500.

mBusiness. This monthly covers the emerging mobile workforce and the technology that keeps them connected from the road.

Transform (**www.transformmag.com**). This magazine, formerly *Imaging and Document Solutions,* focuses on issues related to content and collaboration in the workplace.

Syllabus. This magazine focuses on higher education and technology. Themes of issues range from multimedia tools to distance education on the Web.

T.H.E. Journal (Technological Horizons in Education). This magazine covers both K–12 and higher education with a mixture of product announcements and articles.

Technos: Quarterly for Education and Technology. This publication by the Journal of the Agency for Instructional Technology bills itself as "a forum for the discussion of ideas about the use of technology in education, with a focus on reform." Most of the articles are clearly pro-technology, but many deal with controversial issues. Example: a roundtable discussion called "Violence, Games, and Art."

Technology & Learning. This magazine aimed at K-12 educators, focuses on uses of technology to enhance education.

Learning and Leading with Technology, from ISTE (480 Charnelton St., Eugene, OR 97401-2626, 800/336-5191). ISTE (International Society for Technology in Education) is an important and influential organization whose focus is the effective use of information technology in the classroom. *Learning and Leading with Technology* (formerly *The Computing Teacher*) is their most accessible and widely read publication.

Family PC. This magazine is aimed mostly at parents who want to help their kids put computers to good use.

Home Office Computing. This one is geared more toward people who use their computers to work at home.

Mac Home Journal. This monthly focuses on home applications for Macintosh users.

Popular Science. This tinkerer's magazine is a good source of information on the latest computerized gadgets for consumers.

Web Sites

The Web is bursting with exciting educational material, much of it created by students. Check the *Computer Confluence* Web site for links to many sites devoted to learning and teaching. You'll also find a sampling of Web links related to entertainment, family life, and home applications.

18 | Inventing the Future

Alan Kay Invents the Future

The best way to predict the future
is to **invent it.**

—Alan Kay

Alan Kay has been inventing the future for most of his life. Kay was a child prodigy who composed original music, built a harpsichord, and appeared on NBC as a "Quiz Kid." Kay's genius wasn't reflected in his grades; he had trouble conforming to the rigid structure of the schools he attended. After high school he worked as a jazz guitarist and an Air Force programmer before attending college.

His Ph.D. project was one of the first microcomputers, and one of several that Kay would eventually develop. In 1968 Kay was in the audience when Douglas Engelbart stunned the computer science world with a futuristic demonstration of interactive computing (see Chapter 7). Inspired by Engelbart's demonstration, Kay led a team of researchers at Xerox PARC (Palo Alto Research Center in California) in building the computer of the future—a computer that put the user in charge.

Working on a back-room computer called the Alto, Kay developed a bit-mapped screen display with icons and overlapping windows—the kind of display that became standard two decades later. Kay also championed the idea of a friendly user

Alan Kay

interface. To test user friendliness, Kay frequently brought children into the lab, "because they have no strong motivation for patience." With feedback from children, Kay developed the first painting program and Smalltalk, the groundbreaking object-oriented programming language.

In essence, Kay's team developed the first personal computer—a single-user desktop machine designed for interactive use. But Kay, who coined the term "personal computer," didn't see the Alto as one. In his mind a true personal computer could go everywhere with its owner, serving as a calculator, a calendar, a word processor, a graphics machine, a communication device, and a reference tool. Kay's vision of what he called the Dynabook is only now, three decades later, appearing on the horizon.

Xerox failed to turn the Alto into a commercial success. But when he visited PARC, Apple's Steve Jobs (see Chapter 3) was inspired by what he saw. Under Jobs a team of engineers and programmers built on the Xerox ideas, added many of their own, and developed the Macintosh—the first inexpensive computer to incorporate many of Kay's far-reaching ideas. Kay became a research fellow at Apple, where he called the Macintosh "the first personal computer good enough to criticize." Today virtually all PCs have user interfaces based on Kay's groundbreaking work.

Alan Kay's Dynabook was the early prototype for the modern personal computer.

Today Kay works as a research fellow for Disney, where he applies his vision to emerging technologies in communication, entertainment, and education. Kay continues his crusade for users, especially small users. He says, as with pencil and paper, "it's not a medium if children can't use it." In a recent collaborative research project, Kay and MIT researchers worked with school children to design artificial life forms in artificial environments inside the computer. Like many of Kay's research projects, the Vivarium project had little relationship to today's computer market. This kind of blue-sky research doesn't always lead to products or profits. But for Alan Kay it's the way to invent the future. ◗

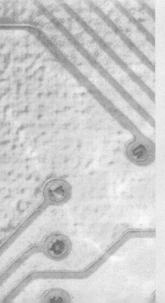

The future is being invented every day by people like Alan Kay—people who can see today the technology that will be central to tomorrow's society. We're racing into a future shaped by information technology. In this chapter we explore strategies for seeing into the future. We use those strategies to imagine how information technology might evolve and how that technology might affect our lives.

Tomorrow Never Knows

It is the **unexpected** that always happens.
—Old English proverb

There is no denying the importance of the future. In the words of scientist Charles F. Kettering, "We should be concerned about the future because we will have to spend the rest of our lives there." However, important or not, the future isn't easy to see.

The Hazards of Predicting the Future

Everything that can be invented has been invented.
—Charles H. Duell, director of the U.S. Patent Office, 1899

Who the hell wants to hear actors talk?
—Harry M. Warner, Warner Bros. Pictures, 1927

There is **no likelihood** man can ever tap the power of the atom.
—Robert Millikan, winner of the Nobel Prize in Physics, 1923

The 1930 movie Just Imagine *presented a bold, if not quite accurate, vision of the future; here Maureen O'Sullivan sits in her personal flying machine.*

In 1877, when Thomas Edison invented the phonograph, he thought of it as an office dictating machine and lost interest in it; recorded music did not become popular until 21 years later. When the Wright brothers offered their invention to the U.S. government and the British Royal Navy, they were told airplanes had no future in the military. A 1900 Mercedes-Benz study estimated that worldwide demand for cars would not exceed 1 million, primarily because of the limited number of available chauffeurs. History is full of stories of people who couldn't imagine the impact of new technology.

Technology is hard to foresee, and it is even harder to predict the impact that technology will have on society. Who could have predicted in 1950 the profound effects, both positive and negative, television would have on our world?

Four Ways to Predict the Future

The most profound technologies are those that **disappear**. They weave themselves into the fabric of **everyday life** until they are indistinguishable from it.
—Mark Weiser, head of the Xerox PARC Computer Science Laboratory

According to Alan Kay, there are four ways to predict the future. The best way is to invent the future, but it's not the only way.

Another way to predict the future is to take advantage of the fact that it generally takes 10 years to go from a new idea in the research laboratory to a commercial product. In today's highly competitive high-tech industry, many companies are able to shave some years off the research-to-product interval. In any case, today's research can give us an idea of the kinds of products we will be using in a few years. Of course, many researchers work behind carefully guarded doors, and research often takes surprising turns.

A third way is to look at products from the past and see what made them succeed. According to Kay, "There are certain things about human beings that if you remove, they wouldn't be human any more. For instance, we have to communicate with others or we're not humans. So every time someone has come up with a communications amplifier, it has succeeded the previous technology." The pen, the printing press, the telephone, the television, the personal computer, and the Internet are all successful communication amplifiers. What's next?

Finally, Kay says we can predict the future by recognizing the four phases of any technology or media business: hardware, software, service, and way of life. These phases apply to radio, television, video, audio, and all kinds of computers.

▶ *Hardware.* Inventors and engineers start the process by developing new hardware. But whether it's a television set, a personal computer, or a global communication network, the hardware is of little use without software.

▶ *Software.* The next step is software development. Television programs, sound recordings, video games, databases, and Web pages are examples of software that give value to hardware products.

▶ *Service.* Once the hardware and software exist, the focus turns to service. Innovative hardware and clever software aren't likely to take hold unless they serve human needs in some way. The personal computer industry is now in the service phase, and the companies that focus on serving their customers are generally the most successful.

▶ *Way of life.* The final phase happens when the technology becomes so entrenched that people don't think about it any more; they only notice if it isn't there. We seldom think of pencils as technological tools. They're part of our way of life, so much so that we'd have trouble getting along without them. Similarly, the electric motor, which was once a major technological breakthrough, is now all but invisible; we use dozens of motors every day without thinking about them. Computers are clearly headed in that direction.

Kay's four ways of predicting the future don't provide a foolproof crystal ball, but they can serve as a framework for thinking about tomorrow's technology. In the next section we turn our attention to research labs, where tomorrow's technology is being invented today. We examine trends and innovations that will shape future computer hardware and software. Then we look at how this technology will serve users as it eventually disappears into our way of life.

From Research to Reality: 21st-Century Information Technology

In laboratories scattered around the planet, ideas are sprouting from the minds of engineers and scientists that will collectively shape the future of information technology. While we can't be sure which of these ideas will bear fruit, we can speculate based on current trends.

> You can count **how many seeds** are in the apple, but not **how many apples** are in the seed.
> —Ken Kesey, author of *One Flew over the Cuckoo's Nest*

Tomorrow's Hardware: Trends and Innovations

The rapid evolution of computer hardware over the last few decades is nothing short of extraordinary. Computer hardware has relentlessly improved by several measures:

> The only thing that has consistently grown faster than hardware in the last 40 years is **human expectation**.
> —Bjarne Stroustrup, AT&T Bell Labs, designer of the C++ programming language

▶ *Speed.* The relay-based Mark I computer (discussed in Chapter 1) could only a few calculations each second. Today's personal computers are more than a million times faster! Computer speed today typically is measured in **MIPS (millions of instructions per second)**, where an instruction is the most primitive operation performed by the processor—moving a number to a memory location, comparing two numbers, and the like. The fastest machines can process more than *a billion* instructions per second!

▶ *Size*. Warehouse-sized computers are history. The central components of a modern computer are stored on a handful of tiny chips; the only parts of the system that occupy significant space on the desktop are peripherals.

▶ *Efficiency*. As the story goes, ENIAC, the first large-scale computer (see Chapter 1) dimmed the lights of Philadelphia when it was turned on. A modern desktop computer consumes about as much electricity as a television set. Portable computers consume even less.

▶ *Capacity*. Modern optical, magnetic, and semiconductor storage devices have all but eliminated storage as a constraint for most computing jobs.

▶ *Cost*. Industry watchers have pointed out that if the price of cars had dropped as fast as the price of computer chips, it would be cheaper to abandon a parked car than to put money in the meter!

Most experts believe these trends will continue, at least for a few years. If they do, we can expect the *price-to-performance ratio* (the level of performance per unit cost) to double every year or two for several more years. There are barriers on the horizon—engineers eventually will bump up against the physical limitations of silicon and other materials. But as Robert Noyce, co-inventor of the integrated circuit, pointed out, these barriers have seemed to be about 10 years away for many years. So far, engineers continue to find ways to push the barriers back.

The trends are undeniable, but it would be a mistake to assume that tomorrow's computer will simply be a smaller, more powerful version of today's PC. Technological advances emerging from laboratories will accelerate current trends and push computer technology in entirely new directions. In the following sections we'll look at just a few examples.

Alternative Chip Technologies

Many research labs are experimenting with alternatives to today's silicon chips. For example, IBM researchers have developed plastic chips that are more durable and energy efficient than silicon chips. Intel, Motorola, and AMD are working with the U.S. government to develop new laser etching technology called extreme ultraviolet lithography (EUVL) that could reduce chip size and increase performance radically. Motorola researchers have created chips that combine silicon with gallium arsenide, a semiconductor that conducts electricity faster than silicon and emits light that can be used for information applications; the research should soon produce chips that are much faster than any currently available. IBM and Motorola researchers are making progress producing chips based on carbon rather than silicon.

Other researchers are working on more radical research technologies. Superconductors that transmit electricity without heat could increase computer speed a hundredfold. Unfortunately, superconductor technology generally requires a super-cooled environment, which isn't practical for most applications. A more realistic alternative is the optical computer, which transmits information in light waves rather than electrical pulses. Optical computers outside research labs are currently limited to a few narrow applications such as robot vision. But when the technology is refined, general-purpose optical computers may process information hundreds of times faster than silicon computers.

Alternative Architectures

Some of the most revolutionary work in computer design involves not what's inside the processors, but how they're put together. One example is IBM's Blue Gene, a supercomputer being developed to help scientists crack the secrets of proteins in the human body. Blue Gene will have 1 million small, simple processors, each capable of handling eight threads of instructions simultaneously. The processors won't have power-hungry embedded caches, but they will have built-in memory to improve speed. The network of processors will be self-healing–it will detect failed components, seal them off, and direct work elsewhere. If it works as planned, Blue Gene will be the first *petaflop* computer, capable of handling 1 quadrillion (1,000,000,000,000,000) instructions per second—2 million times more than today's PC! (The fastest computers have reached *teraflop* speeds—trillions of operations per second.)

Alternative Storage Technologies

Smaller disks that hold more—the trend will continue, producing tiny hard disks that can store astronomical quantities of data. But solid state storage breakthroughs will threaten the dominance of disks in a few years. For example, Cambridge University researchers funded by Hitachi have developed a single-electron memory chip the size of a thumbnail that can store all the

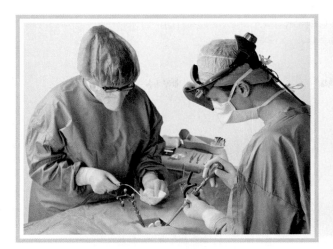

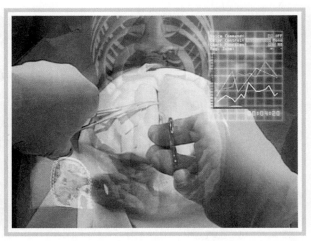

This surgeon's retinal scanner display makes video images and the patient's vital signs continually visible throughout the surgical procedure.

sounds and images of a full-length feature film. This experimental chip consumes very little power and retains memory for up to 10 years when the power is switched off.

Alternative Output Displays

Flat-panel screens are replacing desktop CRTs at an ever-increasing rate. Soon we'll be using ultra-high-resolution displays that are thin enough to hang on walls like pictures and efficient enough to run on batteries for days. LCD goggle displays—the visual equivalent to headphones—may soon be common for portable PC users who want to shut the rest of the world out. Those who need to see what's going on around them and inside their computer can wear eyeglasses with built-in transparent heads-up displays. Researchers at the University of Washington have developed a *retinal display* that works without a screen; it shines a focused beam of light through the wearer's pupil, moving across the field of vision to draw pixels directly on the retina. Fighter pilots, neurosurgeons, and people with limited vision are using these displays to see critical computer data without taking their eyes off of their work. We may eventually see these displays attached to PDAs and mobile phones.

This page of electronic paper is being reloaded with a fresh image.

On another front, researchers at MIT's Media Lab, Xerox PARC, Hewlett Packard, and elsewhere are working on pages made of *electronic paper*—a flexible, paper-like plastic substance filled with microscopic globules that appear either black or white depending on electrical charges. Electronic paper is currently used to make computer-controlled retail signs. In a few years it may be used to produce newspapers that automatically update, magazines that display animated images, and textbooks that can be revised rather than replaced.

Alternative Input Devices: Sensors

Technology forecaster Paul Saffo predicts that the next major breakthroughs will occur as researchers develop—and companies market—inexpensive **sensors** that enable digital devices to monitor the analog world. Temperature sensors, optical sensors, motion sensors, and other types of sensors already make it possible for computers to track a variety of real-world activities and conditions. But as these technologies mature, more sophisticated devices will serve as eyes, ears, and other types of sense organs for computer networks. Saffo wrote in a special anniversary issue of the *Communications of the ACM*:

> Two parallel universes currently exist—an everyday analog universe that we inhabit, and a newer digital universe created by humans, but inhabited by digital machines. We visit this digital world by peering through the portholes of our computer screens, and we manipulate with keyboard and mouse much as a nuclear technician works with radioactive material via glovebox and manipulator arms. . . . Now we are handing sensory organs and manipulators to the

Sensors in this LifeShirt (left) monitored life signs of Indy Racing League driver when he crashed in the 2001 Indy 500. "Smart dust" computers (right) at the University of California at Berkeley help monitor and control heating and cooling systems using environmental sensors and wireless communication links.

machines and inviting them to enter into analog reality. The scale of possible surprise this may generate over the next several decades as sensors, lasers, and microprocessors co-evolve is breathtakingly uncertain.

Tomorrow's Software: Evolving Applications and Interfaces

> Our goal was **bug-free**. The new goal is **resiliency**.
>
> It is much more important to recover from exceptions than to avoid them.
>
> —Bob Frankston, in *Beyond Calculation*

In any economy, infrastructures are the frameworks that are laid so future economic activity can take advantage of them. Just as the railroads provided the transportation network for the expanding 19th-century American economy, the airline and highway systems have served as the American economic infrastructure for much of this century. In the same way, tomorrow's economy is being shaped by an emerging **information infrastructure** of computers and networks. Computers and networks are essential parts of the information infrastructure, but they're of little value without software.

In computer research, software continues to be the hardest part. Chapter 13 discussed programming technologies, including object-oriented programming languages and visual programming environments. These technologies can help programmers produce more reliable software in less time. But computer scientists aren't even close to developing tools that will enable programmers to produce error-free software quickly.

Still, software technology is advancing rapidly, especially when viewed through the eyes of the user. Twenty years ago the typical computer could be operated only by a highly trained professional, and using a computer was pretty much synonymous with programming a computer; today computers are so easy to use that they're sold at shopping malls and operated by preschoolers. Fifteen years ago documents couldn't easily be transported between computers, or even between different applications on the same computer; today networks can provide seamless communication across platforms and applications, so hardware and software differences are no longer barriers.

The graphical user interface pioneered by Xerox and popularized by Apple and Microsoft has become an industry standard, making it possible for users to move back and forth between computer types almost as easily as drivers can adjust to different brands of cars. But experts expect user interfaces to continue to evolve for a while before they settle down into the kind of

Virtual reality user interfaces can enhance research and recreation. In Argonne's CAVE (left), a scientist can interactively study the relationships between the nucleic acids of the molecule. In a similar CAVE (right) at the Center for Supercomputer Applications at the University of Illinois, graduate student Paul Rajlich plays CAVE Quake II, a 3-D video game he created using VR technology.

long-lasting standard we're used to in automobiles. Today's WIMP (windows, icons, menus, and pointing devices) interface is easier to learn and use than earlier character-based interfaces, but it's not the end of the user interface evolution. Researcher Raj Reddy uses another acronym to describe emerging user interface technologies: SILK, for speech, image, language, and knowledge capabilities. SILK incorporates many important software technologies:

▶ *Speech and language.* While we still don't have a language-translating telephone or a foolproof dictation-taking "talkwriter," speech technology is maturing into a practical alternative to keyboard and mouse input. Voice recognition systems are used for security systems, automated voicemail systems, hands-free Web navigation, and other applications. New applications are being developed and marketed every day. With or without speech, *natural-language* processing of English-like commands will be part of future user interfaces. Researchers expect that we'll soon be using programs that read documents as we create them, edit them according to our instructions, and file them based on their content.

▶ *Image.* In the last decade computer graphics have become an integral part of the computing experience. Tomorrow's graphics won't just be still, flat images; they'll include three-dimensional models, animation, and video clips. Today's two-dimensional desktop interfaces will give way to three-dimensional workspace metaphors complete with 3-D animated objects—virtual workspaces unlike anything we use today. **Virtual reality** (VR) user interfaces will create the illusion that the user is immersed in a world inside the computer—an environment that contains both scenes and the controls to change those scenes.

▶ *Knowledge.* Many experts predict that knowledge will be the most important enhancement to the user interface of the future. Advances in the technology of knowledge—that elusive quality discussed in Chapter 14—will enable engineers to design **self-maintaining systems** that can diagnose and correct common problems without human intervention. Advances in knowledge will make user interfaces more friendly and forgiving. Intelligent applications will be able to decipher many ambiguous commands and correct common errors as they happen. But more importantly, knowledge will enable software agents to really be of service to users.

Tomorrow's Service: Truly Intelligent Agents

I don't want to sit and move stuff around on my screen all day and look at figures and have it recognize my **gestures** and listen to my **voice**.
I want to tell it what to do and then go away; I don't want to babysit this computer.
I want it to act **for me, not with me**.
—Esther Dyson, computer industry analyst and publisher

At Xerox PARC Alan Kay and his colleagues developed the first user interface based on icons— images that represent tools to be manipulated by users. Their pioneering work helped turn the computer into a productivity tool for millions of people. According to Kay, future user interfaces will be based on agents rather than tools.

Agents are software programs designed to be managed rather than manipulated. An intelligent software agent can ask questions as well as respond to commands, pay attention to its user's work patterns, serve as a guide and a coach, take on its owner's goals, and use reasoning to fabricate goals of its own.

Many PC applications include *wizards* and other agent-like software entities to guide users through complex tasks and answer questions when problems arise. The Internet is home to a rapidly growing population of **bots**—software robots that crawl around the Web collecting information, helping consumers make decisions, answering email, and even playing games. But today's wizards, bots, and agents aren't smart enough to manage the many details that a human assistant might juggle.

Tomorrow's agents will be better able to compete with human assistants, though. A well-trained software agent in the future might accomplish these tasks:

▶ Remind you that it's time to get the tires rotated on your car, and make an appointment for the rotation.
▶ Distribute notes to the other members of your study group or work group, and tell you which members opened those notes.
▶ Keep you posted on new articles on subjects that interest you, and know enough about those subjects to be selective without being rigid.
▶ Manage your appointments and keep track of your communications.
▶ Teach you new applications and answer reference questions.
▶ Defend your system and your home from viruses, intruders, and other security breaches.
▶ Help protect your privacy on and off the Net.

Agents are often portrayed with human characteristics; *2001's* Hal and the computers on TV's *Star Trek* are famous examples. Of course, agents don't need to look or sound human—they just need to possess considerable knowledge and intelligence.

Future agents may possess a degree of sensitivity, too. Researchers at MIT and IBM are developing *affective computers* that can detect the emotional states of their users and respond accordingly. Affective computers use sensors to determine a person's emotional state. Sensors range from simple audiovisual devices to mouse-embedded sensors that work like lie detectors, monitoring pulse or skin resistance. Early research has shown limited success at identifying emotions, but the machines still have much to learn. They can't for example, tell the difference between love and hate, because, from a physiological point of view, they look pretty much the same!

Tomorrow's Way of Life: Transparent Technology

In the first computing revolution, the ratio of people to computers was **N-to-1**.
In the second revolution, personal computers insisted the ratio be **1-to-1**—
one person, one computer. In the third revolution, we are exploring the impact of having **computers everywhere**, many per person, **1-to-N**.
—Bob Metcalfe, inventor of Ethernet and founder of 3Com

Since Alan Kay coined the term personal computer at Xerox PARC, hundreds of millions of personal computers have been sold. Today many researchers think that it's time to move beyond the PC because it commands too much of our attention. According to user interface expert Donald A. Norman, the PC has three main problems:

▶ A single device designed to perform many tasks can't do every task in a superior manner.
▶ A single machine can't suit every person in the world.
▶ The PC business model of yearly upgrades increases the level of complexity in the machines.

Norman, like other experts, believes we're entering a *post-PC era*. "This will be the generation where the technology disappears into the tool, serving valuable functions but keeping out of the way—the generation of the invisible computer."

Embedded Intelligence

Computers are disappearing into more of our tools all the time. Information appliances, including cell phones, fax machines, and GPS devices, perform their specialized functions while hiding the technological details from their users. Dozens of household appliances and tools have invisible computers. Even our cars are processing megabytes of information as we drive down the road.

Some car computers are invisible; others are more obvious. Several companies have introduced dashboard computers that can play CDs and DVDs, recognize spoken commands, alert the driver to incoming email messages, read those messages aloud, store and retrieve contacts and appointments, dial phone numbers, recite directions using GPS-based navigation systems, report mechanical problems, and even track stolen vehicles. IBM researchers are developing an indash "artificial passenger" to make commuting safer for drivers. This

Wearable computers can be practical tools for workers on the move, like those in the photo on the left. They can also be fashion statements as illustrated by the model in the photo above. The Charmed Communicator packs an Internet terminal, a phone, a TV, a radio, and a health monitoring device into a designer belt.

intelligent agent carries on conversations, watching for signs of fatigue in the driver. If it finds them, it might change the radio station, open a window, or even spray the driver with cold water. In 2001 Volkswagen AG became the first automobile company to mass-produce a car with an Internet connection. (Appropriately, the VW eGeneration was initially sold only on the Net.)

Computers may soon be part of our clothing, too. Most of today's *wearable computers* are strap-on units for active information gatherers. But researchers at MIT and elsewhere are stitching CPUs, keyboards, and touchpads right into the clothes, turning their wearers into wireless Internet nodes. These digital outfits aren't just high-tech fashion statements—when worn with the eyeglass monitors described earlier in the chapter, they might be invaluable for any number of jobs that require both activity and connectivity.

In Japan computer technology has even found its way into the bathroom. A number of Japanese fixture manufacturers sell computer-controlled smart toilets. Some models automatically collect and store information on blood pressure, pulse, temperature, urine, and weight. The information can be displayed on an LCD display, accumulated for months, and even transmitted by modem to a medical service. Users of these smart toilets get a mini-checkup whenever they visit the bathroom. Body-monitoring features give the toilet an entirely new function—a function that will undoubtedly save lives.

Ubiquitous Computers

When computers show up in our toilets, we're clearly entering an era of *ubiquitous computers*—computers everywhere. For several years researchers at Xerox PARC, Cambridge University, Olivetti, and elsewhere have been experimenting with technology that will make computers even more ubiquitous. PARC's Mark Weiser describes an experimental office equipped with intelligent devices, including smart badges described in Chapter 11: "Doors open only to the right badge wearer, rooms greet people by name, telephone calls can be automatically forwarded to wherever the recipient may be, receptionists actually know where people are, computer terminals retrieve the preferences of whoever is sitting at them, and appointment diaries write themselves."

From Internet to Omninet

Connectivity is a critical part of ubiquitous computing. When computers are embedded in everything, they need to be able to talk to each other—and to us. By connecting embedded computers to the Net, we give them voices and ears. All of these smart, connected devices will certainly change the Internet. As more machines become connected, the Net will evolve from today's loose digital fishnet into a tightly-woven, seamless fabric that surrounds us. In the words of Leonard Kleinrock, the UCLA computer scientist who set up the first ARPANET node three decades ago, "Tech will be everywhere, always there, always on, just the way electricity is there for

This thermostat, which can control such household items as air conditioning, heating, lights and appliances, can be monitored and controlled via the Internet

you." Human communication will be a tiny fraction of the traffic on the Net—the great majority will be machines communicating with other machines on behalf of humans. MIT AI lab director Rodney Brooks says "It won't be that you go onto the Internet—the network will come to you." Brooks is part of MIT's Oxygen, a research project that attempts to make computing as plentiful and ubiquitous as the air we breathe.

Ubiquitous computers offer convenience and efficiency beyond anything that's come before. They also raise serious questions about personal privacy, intimacy, and independence. But we'll face even more serious questions when the streams of information technology and biotechnology converge.

The Day after Tomorrow: Information Technology Meets Biology

> Our future is technological; but it will not be a world of **gray steel**.
> Rather our technological future is headed toward a **neo-biological civilization**.
> —Kevin Kelly, in *Out of Control*

The information age won't last forever. Analysts Stan Davis and Bill Davidson predict in their book *2020 Vision* that a bio-economy will replace the information economy sometime around the year 2020. Whether or not they're right, biotechnology and microtechnology will become more intertwined with information technology in the coming decades. There's no telling exactly what the results will be, but the possibilities are both intriguing and disturbing.

Borrowing from Biology

Ubiquitous computing will require new ways of thinking about, and developing, hardware and software. At the University of California, researchers on a project called Endeavor attempt to chart our course into the digital ocean of the future. According to Professor Randy Katz, lead investigator of Endeavor, "The supercomplex system of the future has to be able to organize itself so it can be more robust in its behavior, deal with failure, and then pick up the pieces and move on." In other words, the network of the future will be more like a biological system.

Neural nets, described in Chapter 14, enable individual computers to learn from experience because their design is inspired by biological nervous systems. Many researchers are experimenting with *genetic algorithms*—algorithms that evolve through many generations, creating survival-of-the-fittest programs. Paul Saffo, director of the Institute for the Future, suggests a biological imperative, too: "The network of today is engineered, and the network of 2050 is grown."

Future computers won't just draw inspiration from biological nervous systems—they'll connect to them. One example: Scientists at the Max Planck Institute for Biochemistry in Germany have electronically linked snail neurons onto chips and demonstrated that they could communicate with each other. This type of research could eventually lead to artificial retinas and prosthetic limbs that are extensions of the human nervous system.

These tiny mirrors can rotate up and down to switch data in an optical network. More than 500 mirrors are fabricated on less than a square inch of silicon.

Microtechnology

The incredible miniaturization achieved in the computer industry is enabling researchers to use microtechnology to develop micromachines—machines on the scale of a millionth of a meter. Microscopic moving parts are etched in silicon using a process similar to that of manufacturing computer chips. Major universities, corporations (including IBM, AT&T, and Lucent), government labs (including Sandia Labs), and small start-up companies are doing research in **micro-electro-mechanical systems (MEMS)**. For example, engineers at the University of California at Berkeley have built a motor twice as wide as a human hair that runs on static electricity. Japanese researchers have constructed a micro-car not much bigger than a grain of rice.

Many MEMS are built out of silicon—the same silicon used to produce computer chips. Silicon is stronger than steel, and silicon micromachines can be mass produced using the same kind of technology that's used to make microprocessors.

So far most applications of microtechnology have been microsensors—tiny devices that can detect pressure, temperature, and other environmental qualities. Microsensors are used in cars, planes, and spacecraft, but they show promise in medicine, too. BioMEMS—MEMS that apply chip technology to biological applications—may soon cure many forms of deafness, enable many blind people to see images and navigate, stimulate paralyzed limbs, diagnose bacterial agents, determine drug safety, and deliver drugs precisely where they're needed. Researchers at Johns Hopkins University have developed a smart pill that combines a thermometer with a transmitter so it can broadcast temperatures as it travels through a human digestive tract. This pill is a first step toward other pills that might play more active roles inside our bodies. Scientists speculate that tiny machines may someday be able to roam through the body, locating and destroying cancer cells and invading organisms!

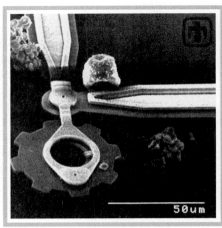

This micromachine isn't much larger than red blood cells (lower right and top left) or a grain of pollen (top right).

Nanotechnology

If microtechnology is carried to its extreme, it becomes **nanotechnology**—the manufacture of machines on a scale of a few billionths of a meter. Nanomachines would have to be constructed atom by atom using processes drawn from particle physics, biophysics, and molecular biology. Researchers at UCLA, Yale, Rice, and other facilities are working on molecular-scale electronics (moletronics) that could eventually produce a breed of computers that performs *billions* of times faster than today's fastest machines. Hewlett Packard's Stanley Williams and others are working on technology that may soon allow wires and switches to chemically assemble themselves at the molecular level, eliminating the need to etch circuits onto chips.

In 2001 IBM researchers built the first computer circuit contained within a single molecule. The circuit was created using carbon nanotubes—tiny cylindrical molecules with semiconductor properties similar to those found in silicon chips. That same year scientists at Bell Labs—the birthplace of the first transistor in 1947—created a transistor from a single molecule. These technological breakthroughs could carry the computing industry past the silicon dead end that's threatening to overturn Moore's Law within a few years. They may be stepping stones on the road to *quantum computers*—computers based on the properties of atoms and their nuclei and the laws of quantum mechanics.

Quantum computers are still decades away. But computers based on microtechnology and nanotechnology may be just a few years in the future. Many researchers think that molecular circuits could be produced at a fraction of the cost of today's complex microprocessors, because they're built through a purely chemical, or "self-assembly," process, similar to growing a crystal. "If we can truly make this kind of technology manufacturable . . . we'll have computing that's cheap enough to throw away," says Yale scientist Mark Reed.

Using another approach, biophysicists are studying natural molecular machines like the protein rotor that spins a bacterium's flagellum tail, hoping to use their findings to create molecular motors. Scientists at MIT are attempting to get E. coli bacteria to respond like circuits. At the same time, geneticists are gradually unlocking the secrets of DNA—biology's self-replicating molecular memory devices. These and other research threads may lead scientists to the breakthrough that will enable them to create atomic assembler devices that can construct nanomachines. Submicron computers, germ-sized robots, self-assembling machines, intelligent clothes, alchemy . . . the possibilities are staggering and the potential risks terrifying.

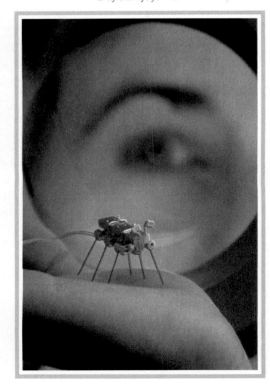

Tiny insect robots like these may be the forerunners of silicon-and-steel artificial life forms.

Artificial Life

For many researchers, the ultimate goal is to create **artificial life**—synthetic organisms that act like natural living systems. Some artificial life researchers create simple software organisms that exist only in computer memory; many of these organisms are similar to the computer viruses discussed in Chapter 12. Other researchers build colonies of tiny insect robots that communicate with each other and respond to changes in their environment. Artificial life researchers grapple with an array of problems, including the question of definition: Where exactly is the line between a clever machine and a living organism?

Advances in artificial intelligence, robotics, genetics, biotechnology, and microtechnology may someday make the line disappear altogether. Computers and robots will undoubtedly continue to take on more functions that have been traditionally reserved for humans. They may even grow and reproduce using carbon-based genetic technology borrowed from human biology. If they become smart enough to build intelligent machines themselves, almost anything is possible.

This speculation raises questions about the relationship between humans and the machines they create. It's important that we think about those questions while the technology is evolving, because our answers may help us to determine the course of that evolution.

Human Questions for a Computer Age

The **important thing** to forecast is not the automobile but the **parking problem**; not the television but the **soap opera**.

—Isaac Asimov

It's the **end of the world** as we know it and **I feel fine**.

—R.E.M.

In earlier chapters we examined many social and ethical issues related to information technology, including privacy, security, reliability, and intellectual property. These aren't the only critical issues before us. Before closing we'll briefly raise some other important, and as yet unanswered, questions of the information age.

Will Computers Be Democratic?

The higher the technology, the **higher the freedom**.
Technology enforces certain solutions: satellite dishes, computers, videos;
international telephone lines force pluralism and freedom onto a society.

—Lech Walesa

When machines and computers, profit motives, and property rights are considered **more important than people**, the giant triplets of **racism, materialism**, and **militarism** are incapable of being conquered.

—Martin Luther King, Jr.

In 1990, a spontaneous protest exploded across computer networks in reaction to the threat to privacy posed by Marketplace, a new CD-ROM product containing consumer information on millions of Americans. The firestorm of protest forced Lotus Development Corporation to cancel distribution of the product. In Santa Monica, California, homeless people used public access terminals in the library to lobby successfully for more access to public showers. In France, student organizations used computer networks to rapidly mobilize opposition to tuition increases. In 1999, environmentalists, labor organizations, human rights groups, and a handful of anarchists used the Internet to mobilize massive protests at the World Trade Organization's Seattle meeting. The protests brought many issues surrounding the secretive WTO into the global spotlight for the first time.

Computers are often used to promote the democratic ideals and causes of common people. Many analysts argue that modern information technology is, by its very nature, a force for equality and democracy. On the other hand, many powerful people and organizations use information technology to increase their wealth and influence.

Will personal computers and the Internet empower ordinary citizens to make better lives for themselves? Or will information technology produce a society of technocrats and technopeasants? Will computerized polls help elected officials better serve the needs of their constituents? Or will they just give the powerful another tool for staying in power? Will networks revitalize participatory democracy through electronic town meetings? Or will they give tyrants the tools to monitor and control citizens?

Will the Global Village Be a Community?

> Progress in commercial information technologies will improve productivity, bring the world closer together, and **enhance the quality of life**.
>
> —Stan Davis and Bill Davidson, in *2020 Vision*

> The **real question** before us lies here: do these instruments further **life and its values** or not?
>
> —Lewis Mumford, 1934

A typical computer today contains components from dozens of countries. The modern corporation uses computer networks for instant communication among offices scattered around the world. Information doesn't stop at international borders as it flows through networks that span the globe. Information technology enables organizations to overcome the age-old barriers of space and time, but questions remain.

In the post-Cold War era, will information technology be used to further peace, harmony, and understanding? Or will the intense competition of the global marketplace simply create new kinds of wars—information wars? Will electronic interconnections provide new opportunities for economically depressed countries? Or will they simply make it easier for information-rich countries to exploit developing nations from a distance? Will information technology be used to promote and preserve diverse communities, cultures, and ecosystems? Or will it undercut traditions, cultures, and roots?

Will We Become Information Slaves?

> Our inventions are wont to be **pretty toys** which distract our attention from serious things. They are but improved means to an **unimproved end**.
>
> —Henry David Thoreau

> **Computers are useless**. They can only give you answers.
>
> —Pablo Picasso

The information age has redefined our environment; it's almost as if the human species has been transplanted into a different world. Even though the change has happened almost overnight, most of us can't imagine going back to a world without computers. Still, the rapid changes raise questions.

Can human bodies and minds adapt to the higher stimulation, faster pace, and constant change of the information age? Will our information-heavy environment cause us to lose touch with the more fundamental human needs? Will we become so dependent on our "pretty toys" that we can't get by without them? Will we lose our sense of purpose and identity as our machines become more intelligent? Or will we learn to balance the demands of the technology with our biological and spiritual needs?

Prometheus brings fire from the heavens to humanity.

Standing on the Shoulders of Giants

> If I have seen farther than other men, it is because
> **I stood on the shoulders of giants**.
>
> —Isaac Newton

When we use computers, we're standing on the shoulders of Charles Babbage, Ada King, Alan Turing, Grace Hopper, Doug Engelbart, Alan Kay, and hundreds of others who invented the future for us. Because of their foresight and effort we can see farther than those who came before us.

In Greek mythology Prometheus (whose name means "forethought") stole fire from Zeus and gave it to humanity, along with all arts and civilization. Zeus was furious when he discovered what Prometheus had done. He feared that fire would make mortals think they were as great as the gods and that they would abuse its power. Like fire, the computer is a powerful and malleable tool. It can be used to empower or imprison, to explore or exploit, to create or destroy. We can choose. We've been given the tools. It's up to all of us to invent the future.

Borg in the Mirror

Peter Cochrane

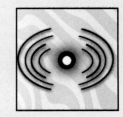

Throughout this book we've examined the convergence—the confluence—of technologies. In October, 1999, Forbes ASAP *published a special issue on The Great Convergence. In this article abridged from that issue, Peter Cochrane speculates about the next convergence—the coming together of human and machine. Cochrane is the head of research at British Telecommunications, a faculty member at the University of Bristol, and the author of Tips for Time Travelers.*

It's easy to imagine a future where information merges onto one global network. In one way or another, the Internet will absorb radio, television, personal computers, telephones, cameras, and so on.

But this is a baby step.

The next real technological advance is a radical symbiosis between humans and machines. The future will be about the creation of networked machinery and digital intelligence to help us deal with a world that's changing faster than our "wet ware" (brains) has evolved to accommodate. And that future demands a subsumption of technology itself into our carbon forms.

Just think of the millions of people with pacemakers, cochlear implants, pain relief modules, and other forms of electronics already embedded in their bodies. Their numbers remind us that we don't just use information technology to communicate, entertain, sell, and trade but to sustain life itself.

Right now, at the frontier of this research are paraplegics with chips implanted in their heads that interpret their brain signals, allowing them to control their computers by thinking—and, in the process, pioneering a new communications channel. Experiments with silicon retinal implants have also been encouraging. Early work on the use of silicon tracks to bypass spinal and other massive nervous system damage is also producing positive results. Waiting in the wings is the artificial pancreas. So is the internal pharmacy: Imagine confidently traveling the world knowing you carry a drugstore inside your own body that is ready to dispense, electronically, the right antibiotic on demand.

On the far horizon is the possibility of using silicon brain implants to enhance our memory and computational skills, and even to enable us to directly interface with machines. Impossible? On the contrary, the idea is about as wild as the crystal set radio of 1914 evolving to become the mobile phone of 1984. I remember suggesting in 1996 that chip implants would eradicate the need for keys, passports, drivers' licenses, identity cards, money, bank accounts, and central medical records. Two years later Professor Kevin Warwick at the University of Reading (in the U.K.) had a chip implanted in his arm to open doors automatically, allowing him access to secure buildings and to be tracked by his secretary. I now hear that diplomats are having similar electronic implants to counteract abduction. Obvious extensions would of course include the tagging of prisoners and criminals.

But medical and security purposes aside, the real reason we will invite computers into our brains is that we increasingly face problems far too complex for the human mind and intellect to solve—even to contemplate.

We need a third intelligence to help us cope with a world of growing complexity that has far outstripped our biological evolution. We need to assimilate more information and make decisions faster. A century ago a doctor could have read every published discourse on every aspect of medicine. The same was true for chemists, physicists, and engineers. Today a doctor could spend every waking hour reading the research papers on urology alone and still not be fully up-to-date. What chance for managers and politicians? Not a lot! We know less and less about more and more. Yet business, government, academia, and many other disciplines demand that we know ever more.

To cope and thrive in the future we will need to comprehend more but also see patterns between areas of knowledge—from understanding the ramifications of complex drug interactions to the dynamics of global pollution processes to thinking in 10 dimensions. The key to survival is not to understand certain things in minute detail but to comprehend everything well enough to make wise decisions. We need help.

Just contemplate the cost of some recent decisions that were made on the basis of a very poor understanding of the issues involved: mad cow disease, nuclear power, the contraceptive pill and thrombosis, genetically modified foods. In each case, what's been missing (and critical) has been our ability to understand what was happening and what was about to happen. The consequences of such ignorance are often tragic. If our brains are insufficient and not up to the task, then we have to create a third intelligence to help.

Before we can create this third intelligence, our machines must be given a range of sensory inputs from our world and the neural ability to create their own perceptions. Right now, a laptop has far more computational power than an ant but nothing of the intelligence. To overcome this obstacle, we will have to allow computer chips to become part of us, and allow ourselves to become part of machines.

All of this prompts people to ask: Will machines be able to read our minds? Will we ever tap into the vast resources of a giant machine's "mind"? Will we be able to communicate with machines just by thinking? The answer to all is a guarded yes. In each of these areas we already have evidence that some of this is possible.

But the question that interests me is: Will machines understand and think as we do? Personally, I hope not. We need to increase the diversity, as well as the depth, of thinking and not constrain it by imposing the limited domain of biology.

DISCUSSION QUESTIONS

1. What are your answers to the questions posed in the last two paragraphs of this article?
2. Should we "invite computers into our brain?"

Summary

Predicting the future isn't easy, but it's important. One of the best ways to predict the future of technology for the next decade or two is to examine the work being done in research labs today. Information and communication technology industries generally go through four phases: hardware, software, service, and way of life.

Tomorrow's computers will continue current trends toward smaller, more powerful, faster, more efficient, higher-capacity, cheaper machines. Some new technologies will enhance these trends; others may start new trends. We can expect significant advances in displays, storage devices, processors, and wireless networks. Tomorrow's economy will be shaped by the information infrastructure of computers and networks.

Software reliability will remain elusive, but user interfaces will continue the trend toward ease of use. Today's graphical user interfaces will gradually give way as speech, natural language, 3-D images, animation, video, artificial intelligence, and even virtual reality become more pervasive.

Perhaps the most important new user interface technology is the intelligent agent. Agents will be managed rather than manipulated by users. They'll carry out users' wishes and anticipate their needs. Most importantly, agents will serve as filters between users and the masses of information on networks.

We're heading into an era of ubiquitous computers—computers that are hardly noticeable because they're everywhere. Embedded computers will improve our everyday tools and, in some cases, give them entirely new functions.

Further into the future, information technology may become intertwined with microtechnology and bio-technology. The results may blur the line between living organisms and intelligent machines. We must be aware of the potential risks and benefits of future technology as we chart our course into the future.

Chapter Review

▼ Key Terms

agent (p. 444)
artificial life (p. 447)
bot (p. 444)
information infrastructure
　(p. 442)

micro-electro-mechanical systems
　(MEMS) (p. 446)
microtechnology (p. 000)
MIPS (millions of instructions per
　second) (p. 439)

nanotechnology (p. 447)
optical computer (p. 440)
self-maintaining system (p. 443)
sensor (p. 441)
virtual reality (p. 443)

▼ Interactive Quiz Questions

1. The *Computer Confluence* CD-ROM contains self-test quiz questions related to this chapter, including multiple choice, true or false, and matching questions.
2. The *Computer Confluence* Web site, **www.prenhall.com/beekman**, contains self-test exercises related to this chapter. Follow the instructions for taking a quiz. After you've completed your quiz, you can email the results to your instructor.

The Web site also contains open-ended discussion questions called Internet Explorations. Discuss one or more of the Internet Exploration questions at the section for this chapter.

▼ Review Questions

1. Define or describe each of the terms in the "Key Terms" section. Check your answers using the glossary.
2. What are the four phases of any technology or media business? Describe how each of these applies to two or more forms of modern electronic technology.
3. What trends in computer hardware evolution are likely to continue for the next few years?
4. Describe several new technologies that may produce significant performance improvements in future computers.
5. What did Raj Reddy mean when he said software will evolve from WIMP to SILK?
6. Why is the windows-and-icons GUI likely to be replaced by an agent-based user interface? What will this mean for computer users?
7. The information infrastructure will allow us to customize many of our transactions in an unprecedented way. Explain why, and give several examples.
8. Explain the concept of ubiquitous computers. Give examples of how it might apply in the office of the future and in the home of the future.
9. How might biology, microtechnology, and computer technology become intertwined in the future?

▼ Discussion Questions

1. Some of the most interesting technological ideas are emerging from interdisciplinary labs at MIT, Carnegie-Mellon University, Xerox, and elsewhere—labs where scientists, engineers, artists, and philosophers work together on projects that break down the traditional intellectual barriers. Why do you think this is so?
2. Millions of computers worldwide are already connected to networks. But unlike highways and railroads today's computer networks aren't widely available, easy to use, and obviously valuable to the general population. What will need to happen for the information infrastructure to transform our lives the way highways and railroads transformed our ancestors' lives?
3. Arthur C. Clarke and others have suggested that virtual reality will replace TV. Do you agree? If it does, is that a good thing?
4. What kinds of questions might be raised if humans develop biologically based computers? How might the computers change our society?
5. Discuss the questions raised in the section called "Human Questions for a Computer Age." Which of those questions are the most important? Which are hardest to answer?
6. Do you foresee a time when we will share the Earth with truly intelligent beings of our own creation? Why or why not?

▼ Projects

1. Imagine a future in which computers and information technology are forces of evil. Then imagine a future in which computers and information technology are used to further the common good. Write a paper describing both. Whether you use short-story style or essay style, include enough detail so that it's clear how the technology impacts human lives.
2. Write a letter to a long-lost classmate dated 50 years from today. In that letter describe your life during the past 50 years, including the ways information technology affected it.

Sources and Resources

Books

Most books about the future are extremely perishable because the future continuously turns into the past. Some of the best writing about the future can be found in science fiction, where speculating about the future is a way of life. The books listed here provide several nonfiction views of the future and techniques for exploring the world of tomorrow.

Dealers of Lightning: Xerox Parc and the Dawn of the Computer Age, by Michael Hiltzik (Harperbusiness, 2000). This book chronicles the story of a band of brilliant computer visionaries and their groundbreaking work at Xerox—work that defined much of what we take for granted when we use computers today.

Beyond Calculation: The Next Fifty Years of Computing, by Peter J. Denning and Robert M. Metcalfe (New York: Copernicus, 1997). 1997 marked the 50th anniversary of the transistor and of the Association for Computing Machinery, the premier organization for computer professionals. To mark the occasion, many of the pioneers who helped create the technology wrote articles predicting what the next 50 years might bring. This fascinating book is a collection of 20 speculative articles. Some deal exclusively with technology; others focus on social implications.

Digerati: Encounters with the Cyber Elite, by John Brockman (San Francisco: HardWired, 1996). The fast-paced world of computers and information technology is being shaped by hundreds of thousands of hard-working people, but some of those people have a disproportionate impact on the shaping of our future. This book profiles some of the key writers, academics, systems designers, entrepreneurs, and visionaries of the information age. It's especially interesting to see what these people say about each other.

The Media Lab: Inventing the Future at MIT, by Stewart Brand (New York: Viking, 1988). This is the book that brought the MIT Media Lab into the public eye. In spite of its age, the book does an admirable job of describing a future radically transformed by the interweaving of the computer, communication, and entertainment industries. It also provides an insightful look at technology researchers in action.

Being Digital, by Nicholas Negroponte (New York: Viking, 1996). The director of the MIT Media Lab wrote thought-provoking columns for *Wired* for many years. This collection of columns provides an optimistic, intelligent vision of a digital future.

When Things Start to Think, by Neil Gershenfeld (New York: Henry Holt and Company, 1999). Another researcher at MIT's Media Lab provides a peek at recent research projects and a glimpse of a future in which computers disappear into everyday objects. As you might expect, Gershenfeld doesn't dwell on the dark side of this emerging technology, but his future visions make for clear, interesting reading.

The Unfinished Revolution: Human-Centered Computers and What They Can Do for Us, by Michael L. Dertouzos (Harperbusiness, 2001). Dertouzos was the longtime head of the MIT Computer Science Department and a respected writer. This book, completed shortly before his death in 2001, argues that computers of the future will need to be better able to adapt to humans—not the other way around.

e-topia: "Urban life, Jim, but not as we know it," by William J. Mitchell (Cambridge, MA: MIT Press, 1999). Mitchell is an expert on architecture and information technology. In this book he outlines his vision of future cities that incorporate virtual as well as physical spaces to support a sustainable way of life.

Taming the Beast: Choice and Control in the Electronic Jungle, by Jason Ohler (Bloomington, IN: Technos Press, 1999). This book examines our relationship with technology with wit, intelligence, common sense, and sound advice. Ohler follows in the tradition of Marshall McLuhan, examining the unseen impact of our media creations on our lives.

Then What? A Funquiry Into the Nature of Technology, Human Transformation, and Marshall McLuhan, by Jason Ohler. Ohler, a former student of McLuhan, has 20 years experience as an educational technologist. His latest book is part fiction, part fact. It's both educational and entertaining.

The Art of the Long View, by Peter Schwartz (New York: Doubleday, 1996). Scenario planning is a particularly useful tool for highlighting the powerful forces that shape the future and choosing strategies that play out well in a variety of possible futures. Schwartz is a master of scenario planning, and this book describes his methodology and provides examples.

Out of Control: The New Biology of Machines, Social Systems, and the Economic World, by Kevin Kelly (Reading, MA: Addison-Wesley, 1996). Artificial life, artificial intelligence, genetic engineering, virtual reality, and nanotechnology blur the line between the "born" and the "made." Kevin Kelly's powerful, wonderfully readable book explores this line and provides fertile ground for speculation on all kinds of technological, social, and ethical questions.

Minds, Machines, and the Multiverse: The Quest for the Quantum Computer, by Julian Brown (Simon & Schuster, 2000). Quantum computers may someday make today's binary machines seem as obsolete as slide rules. This book explores the mind-boggling possibilities for this future technology.

The Age of Access: The New Culture of Hypercapitalism Where All of Life is a Paid-for Experience, by Jeremy Rifkin (New York: Penguin Books, 2000). In his latest book, Rifkin argues that we're shifting from an economy based on ownership of physical possessions to one based on paying for experiences. He warns of an approaching era in which giant companies charge us for almost every human experience.

Periodicals

Communications of the ACM. This technical journal is a good source for learning about research in computer science and related fields.

Scientific American. This venerable monthly is the most popular science magazine. It's well known for articles that present scientific and engineering research in ways that are accessible to non-scientists.

Technology Review: MIT's Magazine of Innovation (www.techreview.com). This magazine isn't just another collection of academic research briefs. It's a colorful, engaging periodical that illuminates current technological research and future trends.

Shift (www.shift.com). This relatively new Canadian magazine covers just about the same beat as *Wired*, listed in Chapter 1. But in recent years *Wired* has become more conservative, with articles about venture capital and stock options taking up more pages. So far, *Shift* seems to have a younger, sassier, more irreverent approach to covering the digital culture.

Web Pages

The World Wide Web is evolving rapidly in amazing ways, but there are still no direct links to the future. The Web links on the *Computer Confluence* page allow you to explore Xerox PARC, the MIT Media Lab, and other organizations dedicated to inventing the future. Other links transport you into speculative discussions about tomorrow's technology and its implications.

The Concise Computer Consumer's Guide

Buying a computer can be an intimidating process, but it doesn't need to be. With the right information, you should have no trouble finding the right system.

Chapter 3, "Hardware Basics: Peripherals," introduces several general principles that apply to just about any personal computer purchase (see Rules of Thumb box, "Computer Consumer Concepts"). But when you're actually ready to buy a system, you'll need more specific information to help you narrow down the myriad of options and choose the system that best meets your needs. The next few pages provide information on each component in a typical computer system; you can use this information to create a profile of an ideal computer system. The CD-ROM includes an interactive Consumer's Guide that can walk you through the process of creating this profile.

Because of the volatile nature of the computer marketplace, the consumer's guides in this book and CD-ROM can't tell you everything you need to know. You'll need more current information to help you turn your ideal system profile into a detailed brand-specific shopping list. The *Computer Confluence* Web site points you toward up-to-the-minute, consumer-oriented information. Use this Web data along with anything you can glean from magazines, knowledgeable friends, and other sources.

If money were no object, you could purchase a fully loaded, top-of-the-line system with every imaginable peripheral. If, like most of us, you're working with a limited budget, you'll need to be more discriminating. You'll need to figure out exactly which features and components you need, which ones you might want to add later, and which ones you won't need at all. If you have a clear idea of how you're going to use your system, you can assess the trade-offs involved in choosing features and options. For example, if you're a graphics artist, youprobably want to put more of your budget into a high-quality monitor if it means scrimping on audio speakers.

When shopping for a computer, you need to address several questions:

Is portability important? Portable computers are more expensive than desktop computers of equivalent capabilities. They also aren't as expandable as desktop boxes, so they aren't appropriate when specialized boards need to be installed. If you want to add peripherals to a

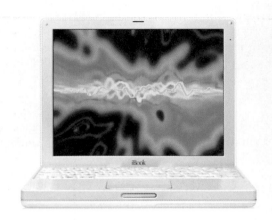

portable, they generally have to be external peripherals connected by USB or other cables. You have to decide whether the convenience of portability outweighs the additional expense and limited expandability.

Should you buy a Windows PC or a Macintosh? This is a highly personal decision; you'll probably meet partisans for both camps who argue with the passion of a religious zealot. The

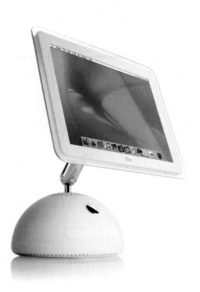

truth is that, while there are still critical differences between the two operating systems, both are capable of serving the needs of most users. If you don't already have a strong preference, check with others in your chosen field to see what they use and why. In general, Windows machines predominate in business, whereas Macs have loyal followings in publishing, graphics, and multimedia. Consider the kinds of software you want to use and find out what's available on each system. Spend some time getting to know both types of systems to see which you prefer.

What is your budget? If you have less than $800 to spend, you probably have to get a used computer or an extremely limited system. If you mostly need a word-processing and Web-surfing machine, an older system may be all you need. But most older systems can't run the latest software and have limited expansion options. If you have $800 to $1500 in your computer budget, you can buy a new system with standard capabilities that can handle today's most popular applications. If you can spend more than $1500, you can choose a high-performance system that can run many of the more demanding applications. In general, more expensive computer packages contain higher-quality peripherals as well.

Where do you buy a computer? Many people shop locally at computer specialty stores, superstores, and home electronic stores because of the local service, ease of repairs, and warranty replacements. Others choose mail-order companies for their competitive prices. Mail-order shopping can save money, but it can also mean additional hassles and risks if you don't do your homework or if you choose the wrong company. Leading computer magazines often rate mail-order companies for their service, prices, and reliability. Internet newsgroups can also help you find good deals and businesses with good reputations.

How do you plan to use your computer? Here's a list of computer applications. Which of these applications is most important to you? The applications you choose determine, to a large degree, what your ideal system looks like.

Desktop Productivity Applications
Word processing
Spreadsheet
Database
Publishing
Desktop publishing
Web publishing

Games
Simulations
Multiplayer gaming
Virtual reality

Communications
Online service access
Email
Internet/Web access
Voice mail/Fax

Technical Applications
CAD
Mathematical
Statistics
Programming languages

Financial Applications
Personal finance/Online banking
Accounting

Multimedia/Graphics
Graphic art
Animation
Video
Music
Presentation graphics
Multimedia authoring

CPU

Buy the fastest CPU you can afford. RAM also affects the overall performance of your computer, but it's generally easier to add RAM later than to upgrade a CPU. System speeds are meaured in megahertz, but megahertz don't tell the whole story. The architecture of the chip and the system board can have a profound effect on system speed. A late-model CPU such as a Pentium 4 or a Power PC G4 can easily outperform a CPU with an older design, even if the older CPU has a comparable clock speed. Computer magazines often run benchmark tests to compare CPU performance of common tasks. If you don't have access to their results, do some comparative testing yourself.

Disk Storage

Most new computers come with a single floppy disk drive, a 10- to 30-gigabyte hard drive, and a CD-ROM or DVD-ROM drive; unless your computing needs are minimal, you probably won't be satisfied with a system that doesn't include these basic components. If you're planning on doing graphic design, digital audio, multimedia authoring, or other storage-intensive jobs, you'll probably also want some kind of removable high-capacity disk drive for transporting and backing up large files, a CD-RW drive for creating CD-ROMs, and/or a DVD-R/CD-RW drive for reading and writing on high-capacity DVD disks.

RAM

Certain applications, especially those that manipulate digital images or audio, demand a great deal of RAM. In general, you should plan on getting a computer with at least 64 or 128 megabytes of RAM—more if you plan to use memory-intensive applications.

Video Monitor

The quality of the images you can display on your computer is a function not only of the monitor but also of the video adapter inside your system unit. If you plan to make extensive use of intricate color images, you will want a large-screen monitor (17" or greater) capable of supporting a resolution of at least 1024 3 768 pixels, a color depth of 16 million colors, and a noninterlaced refresh rate of at least 75 hertz. If you can afford it, you might consider a space-saving, energy-saving flat-screen monitor. Of course, the video card needs to support your chosen monitor's features and should contain at least 4MB of video RAM.

Input Devices

All computer systems have a keyboard and a pointing device, most commonly a mouse. Many keyboards are now ergonomically designed to reduce the risk of repetitive motion strain. Some users prefer a trackball to the mouse. If you plan to do much graphic design work, consider adding a pressure-sensitive graphics tablet to your system; it's far easier and more accurate to draw with a stylus than a mouse. For serious game playing, a joystick easily beats the mouse. Newer digital joysticks provide superior performance over their analog counterparts and offer more accurate control. If you plan to work with photographic images, you'll need a scanner, a digital camera, or both. A high quality scanner is less expensive and more versatile than a comparable digital camera, assuming you already have a non-digital camera.

Modem/Communications

Since much Web content is graphics intensive, you shouldn't consider anything less than a 56.6 Kbps modem for Web surfing. In many areas, cable modems and DSL connections can provide high-speed Internet access.

Ports and Slots

Until recently, virtually all PCs had standard serial and parallel ports for adding peripherals and several slots for adding internal devices and boards. Most newer PCs, following in the mouseprints of the Apple iMac, include high-speed, hot-swappable USB and FireWire (IEEE 1394) ports designed to work with the latest peripherals. (FireWire is ideal for, among other things, serious digital video editing, because it allows the computer to communicate directly with a digital video camera.)

Some new PCs include older slots and ports alongside the USB and FireWire ports; others are "legacy-free" models with only newer, faster ports. If you're buying all new peripherals, legacy-free machine makes sense; USB and FireWire peripherals are generally better than older models, and there's no reason to pay for ports you'll never use. But if you have a collection of aging peripherals, you'll probably want a machine that supports those peripherals.

Printer

Today's low-cost inkjet printers can produce excellent high-resolution printouts; many are capable of printing photo-quality color images. If your focus is digital photography, you may want to buy a printer that's optimized for photographs. If you'll be working exclusively with text and numbers, you might prefer a laser printer. Laser printers produce excellent printouts of text and black-and-white line art at a lower cost per page.

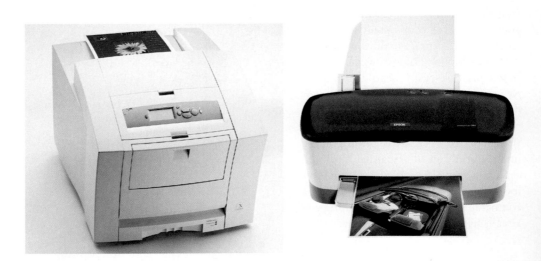

Sound Card/Speakers

All modern PCs and Macintoshes have built-in 16-bit sound cards capable of playing CD-quality audio and MIDI files. Advanced sound cards also supply wave table synthesis and the ability to create and play back studio-quality digital sound samples. These sound cards often contain extensive ROM with megabytes of prerecorded sound samples and expandable RAM banks. No sound system would be complete without a set of amplified, magnetically shielded speakers. The best systems include a separate bass subwoofer for more realistic nondirectional sound.

Software

Most systems come with systems software installed on the hard disk; some come with a number of preinstalled applications programs. Unless your system includes all the software you need, you have to spend part of your computer budget on software. If your software budget is modest, you may be able to meet most or all of your needs with an inexpensive integrated application such as Microsoft Works or AppleWorks. These all-purpose programs cost much less than more powerful office suites, and they demand much less disk space. Of course, integrated applications and software suites can't handle everybody's software needs. Multimedia work, engineering, and other specialized applications require specialized software. Don't overlook shareware and public domain software if your budget is tight.

Add-Ons

There are numerous hardware add-ons that appeal to different special interests. Depending on your needs, you may want to add a flatbed scanner for scanning text and graphics, a digital camera for digitizing real-world images, a MIDI keyboard for playing your own music, or a digital video camera for recording and manipulating full-motion digital video.

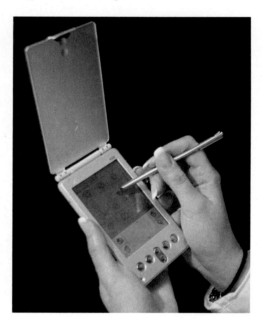

One popular type of peripheral is actually another computer—a handheld computer. Devices like the Palm, the Handspring Visor, and the Pocket PC enable you to carry critical information with you when you're away from your desk. You can use one of these handheld PCs to schedule appointments, track tasks, record short notes, do calculations, look up phone numbers, and read files while you're away from your PC. When you return it to its cradle, it can hot-synch with the desktop machine, making sure the most current information is on both computers. The stylus input of these devices is less than ideal for taking notes. But a folding keyboard can make a handheld computer into a supremely portable note-taking machine.

ACM Appendix

ACM Code of Ethics and Professional Conduct (Adopted by ACM Council October 16, 1992)

Commitment to ethical professional conduct is expected of every member (voting members, associate members, and student members) of the Association for Computing Machinery (ACM).

This Code, consisting of 24 imperatives formulated as statements of personal responsibility, identifies the elements of such a commitment. It contains many, but not all, issues professionals are likely to face. Section 1 outlines fundamental ethical considerations, while Section 2 addresses additional, more specific considerations of professional conduct. Statements in Section 3 pertain more specifically to individuals who have a leadership role, whether in the workplace or in a volunteer capacity such as with organizations like ACM. Principles involving compliance with this Code are given in Section 4.

The Code shall be supplemented by a set of Guidelines, which provide explanation to assist members in dealing with the various issues contained in the Code. It is expected that the Guidelines will be changed more frequently than the Code.

The Code and its supplemented Guidelines are intended to serve as a basis for ethical decision making in the conduct of professional work. Secondarily, they may serve as a basis for judging the merit of a formal complaint pertaining to violation of professional ethical standards.

It should be noted that although computing is not mentioned in the imperatives of Section 1, the Code is concerned with how these fundamental imperatives apply to one's conduct as a computing professional. These imperatives are expressed in a general form to emphasize that ethical principles which apply to computer ethics are derived from more general ethical principles.

It is understood that some words and phrases in a code of ethics are subject to varying interpretations, and that any ethical principle may conflict with other ethical principles in specific situations. Questions related to ethical conflicts can best be answered by thoughtful consideration of fundamental principles, rather than reliance on detailed regulations.

1. General moral imperatives

2. More specific professional responsibilities

3. Organizational leadership imperatives

4. Compliance with the code

1. General Moral Imperatives

As an ACM member I will . . .

1.1 Contribute to Society and Human Well-Being

This principle concerning the quality of life of all people affirms an obligation to protect fundamental human rights and to respect the diversity of all cultures. An essential aim of computing professionals is to minimize negative consequences of computing systems, including threats to health and safety. When designing or implementing systems, computing professionals must attempt to ensure that the products of their efforts will be used in socially responsible ways, will meet social needs, and will avoid harmful effects to health and welfare.

In addition to a safe social environment, human well-being includes a safe natural environment. Therefore, computing professionals who design and develop systems must be alert to, and make others aware of, any potential damage to the local or global environment.

1.2 Avoid Harm to Others

"Harm" means injury or negative consequences, such as undesirable loss of information, loss of property, property damage, or unwanted environmental impacts. This principle prohibits use of computing technology in ways that result in harm to any of the following: users, the general public, employees, and employers. Harmful actions include intentional destruction or modification of files and programs leading to serious loss of resources or unnecessary expenditure of human resources such as the time and effort required to purge systems of "computer viruses."

Well-intended actions, including those that accomplish assigned duties, may lead to harm unexpectedly. In such an event the responsible person or persons are obligated to undo or mitigate the negative consequences as much as possible. One way to avoid unintentional harm is to carefully consider potential impacts on all those affected by decisions made during design and implementation.

To minimize the possibility of indirectly harming others, computing professionals must minimize malfunctions by following generally accepted standards for system design and testing. Furthermore, it is often necessary to assess the social consequences of systems to project the likelihood of any serious harm to others. If system features are misrepresented to users, coworkers, or supervisors, the individual computing professional is responsible for any resulting injury.

In the work environment the computing professional has the additional obligation to report any signs of system dangers that might result in serious personal or social damage. If one's superiors do not act to curtail or mitigate such dangers, it may be necessary to "blow the whistle" to help correct the problem or reduce the risk. However, capricious or misguided reporting of violations can, itself, be harmful. Before reporting violations, all relevant aspects of the incident must be thoroughly assessed. In particular, the assessment of risk and responsibility must be credible. It is suggested that advice be sought from other computing professionals. See principle 2.5 regarding thorough evaluations.

1.3 Be Honest and Trustworthy

Honesty is an essential component of trust. Without trust an organization cannot function effectively. The honest computing professional will not make deliberately false or deceptive claims about a system or system design, but will instead provide full disclosure of all pertinent system limitations and problems.

A computer professional has a duty to be honest about his or her own qualifications, and about any circumstances that might lead to conflicts of interest.

Membership in volunteer organizations such as ACM may at times place individuals in situations where their statements or actions could be interpreted as carrying the "weight" of a larger group of professionals. An ACM member will exercise care to not misrepresent ACM or positions and policies of ACM or any ACM units.

1.4 Be Fair and Take Action Not to Discriminate

The values of equality, tolerance, respect for others, and the principles of equal justice govern this imperative. Discrimination on the basis of race, sex, religion, age, disability, national origin, or other such factors is an explicit violation of ACM policy and will not be tolerated.

Inequities between different groups of people may result from the use or misuse of information and technology. In a fair society, all individuals would have equal opportunity to participate in, or benefit from, the use of computer resources regardless of race, sex, religion, age, disability, national origin or other such similar factors. However, these ideals do not justify unauthorized use of computer resources nor do they provide an adequate basis for violation of any other ethical imperatives of this code.

1.5 Honor Property Rights Including Copyrights and Patents

Violation of copyrights, patents, trade secrets and the terms of license agreements is prohibited by law in most circumstances. Even when software is not so protected, such violations are contrary to professional behavior. Copies of software should be made only with proper authorization. Unauthorized duplication of materials must not be condoned.

1.6 Give Proper Credit for Intellectual Property

Computing professionals are obligated to protect the integrity of intellectual property. Specifically, one must not take credit for other's ideas or work, even in cases where the work has not been explicitly protected by copyright, patent, etc.

1.7 Respect the Privacy of Others

Computing and communication technology enables the collection and exchange of personal information on a scale unprecedented in the history of civilization. Thus there is increased potential for violating the privacy of individuals and groups. It is the responsibility of professionals to maintain the privacy and integrity of data describing individuals. This includes taking precautions to ensure the accuracy of data, as well as protecting it from unauthorized access or accidental disclosure to inappropriate individuals. Furthermore, procedures must be established to allow individuals to review their records and correct inaccuracies.

This imperative implies that only the necessary amount of personal information be collected in a system, that retention and disposal periods for that information be clearly defined and enforced, and that personal information gathered for a specific purpose not be used for other purposes without consent of the individual(s). These principles apply to electronic communications, including electronic mail, and prohibit procedures that capture or monitor electronic user data, including messages, without the permission of users or bona fide authorization related to system operation and maintenance. User data observed during the normal duties of system operation and maintenance must be treated with strictest confidentiality, except in cases where it is evidence for the violation of law, organizational regulations, or this Code. In these cases, the nature or contents of that information must be disclosed only to proper authorities.

1.8 Honor Confidentiality

The principle of honesty extends to issues of confidentiality of information whenever one has made an explicit promise to honor confidentiality or, implicitly, when private information not directly related to the performance of one's duties becomes available. The ethical concern is to respect all obligations of confidentiality to employers, clients, and users unless discharged from such obligations by requirements of the law or other principles of this Code.

2. More Specific Professional Responsibilities

As an ACM computing professional I will . . .

2.1 Strive to Achieve the Highest Quality, Effectiveness and Dignity in Both the Process and Products of Professional Work

Excellence is perhaps the most important obligation of a professional. The computing professional must strive to achieve quality and to be cognizant of the serious negative consequences that may result from poor quality in a system.

2.2 Acquire and Maintain Professional Competence

Excellence depends on individuals who take responsibility for acquiring and maintaining professional competence. A professional must participate in setting standards for appropriate levels of competence, and strive to achieve those standards. Upgrading technical knowledge and competence can be achieved in several ways: doing independent study; attending seminars, conferences, or courses; and being involved in professional organizations.

2.3 Know and Respect Existing Laws Pertaining to Professional Work

ACM members must obey existing local, state, province, national, and international laws unless there is a compelling ethical basis not to do so. Policies and procedures of the organizations in which one participates must also be obeyed. But compliance must be balanced with the recognition that sometimes existing laws and rules may be immoral or inappropriate and, therefore, must be challenged. Violation of a law or regulation may be ethical when that law or rule has inadequate moral basis or when it conflicts with another law judged to be more important. If one decides to violate a law or rule because it is viewed as unethical, or for any other reason, one must fully accept responsibility for one's actions and for the consequences.

2.4 Accept and Provide Appropriate Professional Review

Quality professional work, especially in the computing profession, depends on professional reviewing and critiquing. Whenever appropriate, individual members should seek and utilize peer review as well as provide critical review of the work of others.

2.5 Give Comprehensive and Thorough Evaluations of Computer Systems and Their Impacts, Including Analysis of Possible Risks

Computer professionals must strive to be perceptive, thorough, and objective when evaluating, recommending, and presenting system descriptions and alternatives. Computer professionals are in a position of special trust, and therefore have a special responsibility to provide objective, credible evaluations to employers, clients, users, and the public. When providing evaluations the professional must also identify any relevant conflicts of interest, as stated in imperative 1.3.

As noted in the discussion of principle 1.2 on avoiding harm, any signs of danger from systems must be reported to those who have opportunity and/or responsibility to resolve them. See the guidelines for imperative 1.2 for more details concerning harm, including the reporting of professional violations.

2.6 Honor Contracts, Agreements, and Assigned Responsibilities

Honoring one's commitments is a matter of integrity and honesty. For the computer professional this includes ensuring that system elements perform as intended. Also, when one contracts for work with another party, one has an obligation to keep that party properly informed about progress toward completing that work.

A computing professional has a responsibility to request a change in any assignment that he or she feels cannot be completed as defined. Only after serious consideration and with full disclosure of risks and concerns to the employer or client, should one accept the assignment. The major underlying principle here is the obligation to accept personal accountability for professional work. On some occasions other ethical principles may take greater priority.

A judgment that a specific assignment should not be performed may not be accepted. Having clearly identified one's concerns and reasons for that judgment, but failing to procure a change in that assignment, one may yet be obligated, by contract or by law, to proceed as directed. The computing professional's ethical judgment should be the final guide in deciding whether or not to proceed. Regardless of the decision, one must accept the responsibility for the consequences.

However, performing assignments "against one's own judgment" does not relieve the professional of responsibility for any negative consequences.

2.7 Improve Public Understanding of Computing and Its Consequences

Computing professionals have a responsibility to share technical knowledge with the public by encouraging understanding of computing, including the impacts of computer systems and their limitations. This imperative implies an obligation to counter any false views related to computing.

2.8 Access Computing and Communication Resources Only When Authorized To Do So

Theft or destruction of tangible and electronic property is prohibited by imperative 1.2—"Avoid harm to others." Trespassing and unauthorized use of a computer or communication system is addressed by this imperative. Trespassing includes accessing communication networks and computer systems, or accounts and/or files associated with those systems, without explicit authorization to do so. Individuals and organizations have the right to restrict access to their systems so long as they do not violate the discrimination principle (see 1.4). No one should enter or use another's computer system, software, or data files without permission. One must always have appropriate approval before using system resources, including communication ports, file space, other system peripherals, and computer time.

3. Organizational Leadership Imperatives

Background Note: This section draws extensively from the draft IFIP Code of Ethics, especially its sections on organizational ethics and international concerns. The ethical obligations of organizations tend to be neglected in most codes of professional conduct, perhaps because these codes are written from the perspective of the individual member. This dilemma is addressed by stating these imperatives from the perspective of the organizational leader. In this context "leader" is viewed as any organizational member who has leadership or educational responsibilities. These imperatives generally may apply to organizations as well as their leaders. In this context "organizations" are corporations, government agencies, and other "employers" as well as volunteer professional organizations.

As an ACM member and an organizational leader, I will . . .

3.1 Articulate Social Responsibilities of Members of an Organizational Unit and Encourage Full Acceptance of those Responsibilities

Because organizations of all kinds have impacts on the public, they must accept responsibilities to society. Organizational procedures and attitudes oriented toward quality and the welfare of society will reduce harm to members of the public, thereby serving public interest and fulfilling social responsibility. Therefore, organizational leaders must encourage full participation in meeting social responsibilities as well as quality performance.

3.2 Manage Personnel and Resources to Design and Build Information Systems that Enhance the Quality of Working Life

Organizational leaders are responsible for ensuring that computer systems enhance, not degrade, the quality of working life. When implementing a computer system, organizations must consider the personal and professional development, physical safety, and human dignity of all workers. Appropriate human-computer ergonomic standards should be considered in system design and in the workplace.

3.3 Acknowledge and Support Proper and Authorized Uses of an Organization's Computing and Communication Resources

Because computer systems can become tools to harm as well as to benefit an organization, the leadership has the responsibility to clearly define appropriate and inappropriate uses of organizational computing resources. While the number and scope of such rules should be minimal, they should be fully enforced when established.

3.4 Ensure that Users and those Who Will Be Affected by a System Have Their Needs Clearly Articulated During the Assessment and Design of Requirements; Later the System Must Be Validated to Meet Requirements

Current system users, potential users and other persons whose lives may be affected by a system must have their needs assessed and incorporated in the statement of requirements. System validation should ensure compliance with those requirements.

3.5 Articulate and Support Policies that Protect the Dignity of Users and Others Affected by a Computing System

Designing or implementing systems that deliberately or inadvertently demean individuals or groups is ethically unacceptable. Computer professionals who are in decision making positions should verify that systems are designed and implemented to protect personal privacy and enhance personal dignity.

3.6 Create Opportunities for Members of the Organization to Learn the Principles and Limitations of Computer Systems

This complements the imperative on public understanding (2.7). Educational opportunities are essential to facilitate optimal participation of all organizational members. Opportunities must be available to all members to help them improve their knowledge and skills in computing, including courses that familiarize them with the consequences and limitations of particular types of systems. In particular, professionals must be made aware of the dangers of building systems around oversimplified models, the improbability of anticipating and designing for every possible operating condition, and other issues related to the complexity of this profession.

4. Compliance with the Code

As an ACM member I will . . .

4.1 Uphold and Promote the Principles of this Code

The future of the computing profession depends on both technical and ethical excellence. Not only is it important for ACM computing professionals to adhere to the principles expressed in this Code, each member should encourage and support adherence by other members.

4.2 Treat Violations of this Code as Inconsistent with Membership in the ACM

Adherence of professionals to a code of ethics is largely a voluntary matter. However, if a member does not follow this code by engaging in gross misconduct, membership in ACM may be terminated.

This Code and the supplemental Guidelines were developed by the Task Force for the Revision of the ACM Code of Ethics and Professional Conduct: Ronald E. Anderson, Chair, Gerald Engel, Donald Gotterbarn, Grace C. Hertlein, Alex Hoffman, Bruce Jawer, Deborah G. Johnson, Doris K. Lidtke, Joyce Currie Little, Dianne Martin, Donn B. Parker, Judith A. Perrolle, and Richard S. Rosenberg. The Task Force was organized by ACM/SIGCAS and funding was provided by the ACM SIG Discretionary Fund. This Code and the supplemental Guidelines were adopted by the ACM Council on October 16, 1992.

Glossary

absolute reference   A reference in a spreadsheet to a specific cell address. *Chapter 6*

access-control software   Software that only allows user access according to the user's needs. Some users can only open files that are related to their work. Some users are allowed read-only access to files they can see but not change. *Chapter 12*

access time   The amount of time, measured in nanoseconds, it takes for a CPU to retrieve a unit of data from memory. Also the amount of time, measured in milliseconds, it takes for a CPU to retrieve a unit of data from a disk drive. *Chapter 2*

account   Monetary category that represents various types of income, expenses, and liabilities. *Chapter 6*

accounting and financial management software   Software especially designed for financial and accounting tasks. The software sets up accounts, keeps track of money flow between accounts, records transactions, adjusts balances in accounts, provides an audit trail, automates routine tasks such as check writing, and produces reports. *Chapter 6*

acquisition   An information activity that captures data about an event in the environment important to a person or an organization. *Chapter 13*

action document   Output from transaction processing to initiate an action by the recipient or to verify that a transaction has occurred, such as a billing statement, a receipt, or a payroll check. *Chapter 13*

active badge (smart badge)   A microprocessor-controlled ID badge that broadcasts infrared identification codes to a network receiver that updates a badge-location database. *Chapter 12, Chapter 18*

active cell   The cell containing the cursor in a spreadsheet. *Chapter 6*

ActiveX   A collection of programming technologies and tools that can be used to create programs that are similar in many ways to Java applets. *Chapter 10*

address   In a spreadsheet, the location of a cell, determined by row number and column number. *Chapter 6*

affective computers   Computers that use sensors to detect the emotional states of their users and respond accordingly. *Chapter 18*

agent   A software program that can ask questions, respond to commands, pay attention to its user's work patterns, serve as a guide and a coach, take on its owner's goals, and use reasoning to fabricate goals of its own. *Chapter 18*

AI   See artificial intelligence (AI).

algorithm   A set of step-by-step instructions that, when completed, solves a problem. *Chapter 4, Chapter 16*

All-in-one device   See multifunction peripheral

alpha testing   Initial testing of a system. Also called "pre-beta testing." *Chapter 16*

analog signal   A continuous wave. *Chapter 9*

analysis   The phase of the systems development life cycle in which the system's requirements are identified before design begins. *Chapter 16*

Analytical engine   The first computer, conceived by Charles Babbage. Programmed with punch cards, it included functions of input, output, processing, and storage. *Chapter 1*

animation   The process of simulating motion with a series of still pictures. *Chapter 7*

antivirus program   A program designed to search for viruses, notify users when they're found, and remove them from infected files. *Chapter 12*

applet   A small compiled program designed to run inside another application—typically a Web browser. *Chapter 4, Chapter 16*

application program (application)   Software tool that allows a computer to be used for specific purposes. *Chapter 0, Chapter 1*

application server   A specialized server that stores applications and makes them available to client programs that request them. *Chapter 10*

application service provider (ASP)   A company that manages and delivers application services on a contract basis. *Chapter 10*

application suite (office suite)   A collection of several related application programs that are also sold as separate programs. *Chapter 4*

architecture   Design that determines how individual components of the CPU are put together on the chip. More generally used to describe the way individual components are put together to create a complete computer system. *Chapter 2*

arithmetic logic unit (ALU)   The part of the CPU that performs data calculations and comparisons. *Chapter 2*

armature   The part of a disk drive that moves the read/write head across the disk surface. *Chapter 3*

artificial intelligence (AI)   The field of computer science devoted to making computers perceive, reason, and act in ways that have, until now, been reserved for human beings. *Chapter 14*

artificial life   Synthetic organisms that act like natural living systems. *Chapter 18*

ASCII (American Standard Code for Information Interchange)   A code that represents characters as 8-bit codes. Allows the binary computer to work with letters, digits, and special characters. *Chapter 2*

assembler   Translates assembly-language instructions into machine-language instructions. *Chapter 16*

assembly language   A language that is functionally equivalent to machine language but is easier to read, write, and understand. Programmers use alphabetic codes that correspond to the machine's numeric instructions. *Chapter 16*

asynchronous communication   Delayed communication, such as that used for newsgroups and mailing lists, where the sender and the recipients don't have to be logged in at the same time. *Chapter 9, Chapter 10*

asynchronous teleconference An online meeting between two or more people in which participants type, post, and read messages at their convenience. *Chapter 9*

attachment (email) A way to send formatted word processor documents, pictures, and other multimedia files via email. *Chapter 9, Chapter 11*

audio digitizer Hardware device or software program that captures a sound and stores it as a data file on a disk. *Chapter 7*

audit-control software Monitors and records computer transactions as they happen so auditors can trace and identify suspicious computer activity after the fact. *Chapter 12*

audit trail In accounting, a set of records enabling you to retrace the history of transactions. *Chapter 6*

automated office An office that uses computer systems and networks to streamline information flow and to automate many business processes. *Chapter 14*

automated teller machine (ATM) A device that enables users to remotely access and deposit money from their bank accounts through the use of a network. *Chapter 9*

automatic correction (autocorrect) Catches and corrects common typing errors. *Chapter 5*

automatic footnoting Word-processing feature that automatically places footnotes where they belong on the page. *Chapter 5*

automatic formatting (autoformat) Automatically applies formatting to the text. *Chapter 5*

automatic hyphenation Word-processing feature that automatically divides long words that fall at the ends of lines. *Chapter 5*

automatic link A link between worksheets in a spreadsheet that ensures that a change in one worksheet is reflected in the other. *Chapter 6*

automatic recalculation A spreadsheet capability that allows for easy correction of errors and makes it easy to try out different values while searching for solutions. *Chapter 6*

automatic speech recognition See speech recognition.

avatar A graphical body that is used to represent a person in a virtual meeting place; can range from a simple cartoon sketch to an elaborate 3-D figure or an exotic abstract icon. *Chapter 11*

B2B See business-to-business (B2B).

B2C See business-to-consumer (B2C).

backbone A collection of common pathways used to transmit large quantities of data between networks in a wide-area network (WAN). *Chapter 9*

backup The process of saving data—especially for data recovery. Many systems automatically back up data and software onto disks or tapes. *Chapter 12*

backward compatible Able to run software written for older CPUs. Also, when referring to a software program, able to read and write files compatible with older versions of the program. *Chapter 2*

bandwidth The quantity of information that can be transmitted through a communication medium in a given amount of time. *Chapter 9*

bar chart A chart that shows relative values with bars, appropriate when data fall into a few categories. *Chapter 6*

bar-code reader A reading tool that uses light to read universal product codes, inventory codes, and other codes created out of patterns of variable-width bars. *Chapter 3*

basic input/output system (BIOS) Firmware programs in ROM *Chapter 2*

batch processing A type of data processing in which transactions are accumulated and fed into computers in large batches. For most

applications today, interactive processing has replaced batch processing. *Chapter 8, Chapter 13*

batch spelling checker Checks all the words in your document in a batch when you issue the appropriate command. *Chapter 5.*

baud rate An older measurement of modem speed; today bits per second (bps) is a more accurate term. *Chapter 9*

bay An open area in the system box for disk drives and other peripheral devices. *Chapter 2*

beta testing Testing of almost-finished software by potential users. *Chapter 16*

binary A choice of two values, such as yes and no or zero and one. *Chapter 2*

binary number system A system that denotes all numbers with combinations of two digits. *Chapter 2*

biometrics Measurements of individual body characteristics, such as a voice print or fingerprint; sometimes used in computer security. *Chapter 12*

bit Binary digit. The smallest unit of information. A bit can have two values—0 or 1. *Chapter 2*

bit depth (color depth) The number of bits devoted to each pixel in a color display. *Chapter 7*

bit-mapped (raster) graphics Graphics in which images are stored and manipulated as organized collections of pixels rather than as shapes and lines. Contrast with object-oriented graphics. *Chapter 7*

bits per second (bps) The standard unit of measure for modem speed. *Chapter 9.*

bits per second (bps) A measurement to describe the transmission speed of a modem. *Chapter 9*

Bluetooth A type of wireless technology that enables mobile phones, handheld computers, and PCs to communicate with each other regardless of operating system. *Chapter 9*

Boolean logic A complex query structure supported by most search engines; one example is "American AND Indian BUT NOT Cleveland."

booting Loading the non-ROM part of the operating system into memory. *Chapter 4*

bot A software robot that crawls around the Web collecting information, helping consumers make decisions, answering email, and even playing games. *Chapter 18*

bounce The automatic return of an undeliverable email message to its sender. *Chapter 9*

bridge A hardware device connected that can pass messages between networks. *Chapter 9*

bps See bits per second.

broadband connection An Internet connection such as DSL or cable modem that offers higher bandwidth, and therefore faster transmission speed, than standard modem connections. *Chapter 10*

browse The process of finding information in a database or other data source, such as the World Wide Web. *Chapter 8*

bug An error in programming. *Chapter 4*

bullet charts Graphical elements, such as drawings and tables, integrated into a series of charts that list the main points of a presentation. *Chapter 7*

bulletin board system (BBS) An online version of the bulletin board. *Chapter 9*

burn To record data onto CD-R and CD-RW disks. *Chapter 3*

bus Group of wires on a circuit board. Information travels between components through a bus. *Chapter 2*

business alliance A cooperative arrangement between two or more business organizations with complementary capabilities. *Chapter 14*

business organization A system designed by people for the purpose of creating products and services for customers. *Chapter 13*

business process A related set of primary and support activities of an organization's value chain performed to achieve a particular business outcome. *Chapter 13*

business-to-business (B2B) A form of e-commerce in which a company handles transactions within its own value chain using an intranet, or with other businesses and organizations, such as its suppliers and bank, using an extranet. *Chapter 11, Chapter 15*

business-to-consumer (B2C) A form of e-commerce in which a company conducts transactions with individual customers using a Web site. *Chapter 11, Chapter 15*

button (command button) A hot spot on a screen that responds to mouse clicks. A button can be programmed to perform one of many tasks, such as opening a dialog box or launching an application. *Chapter 0, Chapter 7*

byte Grouping of 8 bits. *Chapter 2*

C One of the most widely-used programming languages today. *Chapter 16*

C++ A variant of the C programming language that supports object-oriented programming. *Chapter 16*

cable modem A type of broadband Internet connection that uses the same network of coaxial cables that delivers TV signals. *Chapter 10*

C# A programming language similar to Java in many ways, but without Java's cross-platform capabilities. *Chapter 10*

C2C See consumer-to-consumer (C2C).

CAD See computer-aided design.

CAI See computer-aided instruction.

CAM See computer-aided manufacturing.

camera-ready Typeset-quality pages, ready to be photographed and printed. *Chapter 5*

card See expansion slot.

carpal tunnel syndrome An affliction of the wrist and hand that results from repeating the same movements over long periods. *Chapter 3*

CASE tools Computer-assisted software engineering tools that enable analysts and programmers to automate many of the steps involved in turning design specifications into programs. *Chapter 16*

cathode ray tube (CRT) monitor A television-style monitor that is used as the output device for many desktop computers. *Chapter 3*

CD-R (compact disk–recordable) An optical disk you can write information on, but you cannot remove the information. *Chapter 3*

CD-ROM (compact disc–read-only memory) A type of optical disk that contains data that cannot be changed; CD-ROMs are commonly used to distribute commercial software programs. *Chapter 3.*

CD-ROM drive A common optical drive in computers that can read data from CD-ROM disks, *Chapter 3*

CD-RW (compact disk–rewritable) An optical disk that allows writing, erasing, and rewriting. *Chapter 3*

CD-RW drive A disk drive that can read and write on rewritable optical disks. *Chapter 3*

cell The intersection of a row and a column on the grid of a spreadsheet. *Chapter 6*

centralized database A database housed in a mainframe computer, accessible only to information-processing personnel. *Chapter 8*

central processing unit (CPU) Part of the computer that processes information, performs arithmetic calculations, and makes basic decisions based on information values. *Chapter 0, Chapter 2*

character-based interface A user interface based on text characters rather than graphics. *Chapter 4*

chat room Public real-time teleconference. *Chapter 9*

chief information officer (CIO) A top manager responsible for the information infrastructure and information systems in an organization. Sometimes referred to also as chief technology officer (CTO). *Chapter 14*

CIM See computer-integrated manufacturing.

circuit board Houses the CPU, along with other chips and electronic components in a computer. *Chapter 2*

click The action of pressing a button on a mouse. *Chapter 0, Chapter 1, Chapter 3*

client/server database Client programs in desktop computers send information requests through a network to server databases on mainframes, minicomputers, or desktop computers; the servers process queries and send the requested data back to the client. *Chapter 8*

client/server model For a local-area network, a hierarchical model in which one or more computers act as dedicated servers and all the remaining computers act as clients. The server fills requests from clients for data and other resources. *Chapter 9*

client/server model For Internet applications, a client program asks for information, and a server program fields the request and provides the requested information from databases and documents. The client might reside on a personal computer or the host computer, and the server might reside on the same host computer or another host computer elsewhere on the network. *Chapter 10*

clip art A collection of redrawn images that you can cut out and paste into your own documents. *Chapter 7*

Clipboard A special portion of memory for temporarily holding information for later use. *Chapter 5*

clock The timing device producing electrical pulses for synchronizing the computer's operations. *Chapter 2*

CMOS (complementary metal oxide semiconductor) A special low-energy kind of RAM that can store small amounts of data for long periods of time on batter power. CMOS RAM is used to store the date, time and calendar in a PC. CMOS RAM is called parameter RAM in Macintoshes. *Chapter 2.*

coaxial cable A type of cable used to connect nodes in computer networks. The same type of cable is also to transport television signals into homes. *Chapter 9*

code of ethics Code of conduct specifically for information professionals and developed by professional organizations such as AITP (Association for Information Technology Professionals) and ACM (Association for Computing Machinery). *Chapter 13*

coding Writing a program from an algorithm. *Chapter 16*

color depth (bit depth) The number of bits devoted to each pixel. *Chapter 3, Chapter 7*

color matching Technology enabling desktop publishers to match colors on the screen with printed colors

color monitor A monitor with the capability of displaying a wide range of colors, with greater depth than a gray-scale monitor. *Chapter 3, Chapter 5.*

columns Along with rows, comprise the grid of a spreadsheet. *Chapter 6*

command-line interface User interface that requires the user to type text commands on a command-line to communicate with the operating system. *Chapter 4*

communication A social process of people exchanging ideas or other messages through a physical medium. *Chapter 14*

communication software Software that enables computers to interact with each other over a phone line or other network. *Chapter 9*

communications satellite A satellite used to relay information between points on Earth. A typical communications satellite is geostationery; it matches the earth's rotation so it can hang in a stationary position relative to the spinning planet below. *Chapter 9*

compatibility The ability of a software program to run on a specific computer system. Also, the ability of a hardware device to function with a particular type of computer. *Chapter 2, Chapter 4*

competitive advantage The relative strength and ability of a business organization, compared to its competitors, to cope successfully with the threats and opportunities in the business environment. *Chapter 14*

competitive forces model An analytical tool used by managers to understand and evaluate the structure of an industry's business environment and the threats and opportunities of competition to a company. *Chapter 14*

compiler A translator program that translates an entire program from a high-level computer language before the program is run for the first time. *Chapter 4, Chapter 16*

complex instruction set computer processors (CISC) Instruction sets included in modern computers. Slower and less efficient than processors designed to execute fewer instructions. *Chapter 2*

component software Software designed in small, independent units (components) that can be plugged into applications and operating systems to add features as needed. *Chapter 16*

compression Making files smaller using special encoding schemes. File compression saves storage space on disk and saves transmission time when files are transferred through networks. *Chapter 7, Chapter 10, Chapter 11*

computed field In a database, a field containing formulas similar to spreadsheet formulas; they display values calculated from values in other numeric fields. *Chapter 8*

computer-aided design (CAD) The use of computers to design products. Often linked to computer-aided manufacturing (CAM). *Chapter 7, Chapter 13*

computer-aided instruction (CAI) Software programs for teaching that combine drill-and-practice software and tutorial software. *Chapter 17*

computer-aided manufacturing (CAM) The use of computers to control the manufacturing of parts. Often combined with computer-aided design (CAD) in computer-integrated manufacturing (CIM). *Chapter 7, Chapter 13*

computer crime Any crime accomplished through knowledge or use of computer technology. *Chapter 12*

computer-integrated manufacturing (CIM) The combination of computer-aided design (CAD) and computer-aided manufacturing (CAM); a major step toward a fully automated factory. *Chapter 7, Chapter 13*

computer monitoring Using computer technology to track, record, and evaluate worker performance, often without the knowledge of the worker. *Chapter 17*

computer security Protecting computer systems and the information they contain against unwanted access, damage, modification, or destruction. *Chapter 12*

computer telephony integration (CTI) The linking of computers and telephones to gain productivity; voicemail is one example.

concurrent processing A large computer working on several jobs at the same time. The computer uses multiple CPUs to process jobs simultaneously. *Chapter 4*

console (formula bar, edit line) In spreadsheet software, the long window above the worksheet where typing appears. *Chapter 6*

consumer-to-consumer (C2C) A form of e-commerce in which individuals sell and buy directly with each other using a Web site. *Chapter 15*

consumer portal A portal that includes search engines, email services, chat rooms, references, news and sports headlines, shopping malls, other services, and advertisements—many of the same things found in online services such as AOL. *Chapter 11*

context-sensitive menus Menus offering choices that depend on the context. *Chapter 4.*

contract (law) A type of law that covers trade secrets. *Chapter 12*

control structure Logical structures that control the order in which instructions are carried out. *Chapter 16*

cookies small files deposited on a user's hard disk by Web sites, enabling sites to remember what they know about their visitors between sessions. *Chapter 10, Chapter 11*

copying text Copying text from one part of a document and duplicating it in another section of the document or in a different document. *Chapter 5*

copy-protected software Software that prevents a disk from being copied. *Chapter 4*

copyright (law) A type of law that traditionally protects forms of literary expression. *Chapter 12*

copyrighted software Software that is legally protected against duplication. *Chapter 4*

corporate portal A specialized portal on an intranet that serves the employees of a particular corporation. *Chapter 11*

cost-benefit analysis A planning approach used by managers in business organizations to decide whether it is worthwhile to develop an information system. *Chapter 16*

cost leadership strategy The overall focus of a business organization to produce high-quality products and services at the lowest cost in an industry. *Chapter 14*

courseware Educational software. *Chapter 17*

CPU See central processing unit.

cracking Unauthorized access and/or vandalism of computer systems; short for criminal hacking. *Chapter 12*

cradle Device used in docking handheld computers that enables them to share information with desktop and laptop PC's. *Chapter 1*

critical path method (CPM) A planning tool used in business organizations to keep track of the schedule for an information system project. *Chapter 16*

critical success factor (CSF) An important aspect of a business organization, industry, or environment that top managers monitor to ensure the success of the organization. *Chapter 16*

CRT See cathode ray tube monitor.

current cell (active cell) The cell containing the cursor in a spreadsheet. *Chapter 6*

cursor A line or rectangle, sometimes flashing, that indicates your location on the screen or in a document. *Chapter 3, Chapter 5*

custom application An application programmed for a specific purpose, typically for a specific client. *Chapter 4*

customer relationship management systems (CRM) Software systems for organizing and tracking information on customers. *Chapter 8.*

cut-and-paste Copying or deleting text from one point and pasting it into another point in the document. *Chapter 5*

cyberspace A term used to describe the Internet and other on-line networks, especially the artificial realities and virtual communities that form on them. First coined by William Gibson in his novel, *Neuromancer. Chapter 11*

data Information in a form that can be read, used, and manipulated by a computer. *Chapter 1*

database-driven Web site A Web site that uses database technology to present information dynamically based on current conditions and client requests. *Chapter 10*

database A collection of information stored in an organized form in a computer. *Chapter 8*

database management system (DBMS)   A program or system of programs that can manipulate data in a large collection of files (the database), cross-referencing between files as needed. *Chapter 8*

database program   A software tool for organizing the storage and retrieval of the information in a database. *Chapter 8*

data compression   Reduces the size of a data file so it can be stored in a smaller space. *Chapter 7*

data dictionary   A catalog or directory of all the data stored in a database used in an information system. *Chapter 16*

date field   A field containing only dates. *Chapter 8*

data flow diagram (DFD)   A systems development modeling tool used to depict graphically the movement of data through a system. *Chapter 16*

data mining   The discovery and extraction of hidden predictive information from large databases. *Chapter 8*

data structure   Software construct that determines the logical structure of data. Data structures range from simple numeric lists and tables (arrays) to complex relations at the core of databases. *Chapter 16*

data transfer rate   The speed at which data is transferred, using a CD-RW drive. *Chapter 3*

data translation software   Software that enables users of different systems with incompatible file formats to read and modify each other's files. *Chapter 9*

data warehouse   An integrated collection of corporate data stored in one location. *Chapter 8*

data warehousing   Software to create and maintain large databases, or data warehouse, containing data on all aspects of the company. *Chapter 13*

DBMS   See database management system.

debugging   Finding and correcting errors—bugs—in computer software. *Chapter 4*

decision style   A manager's personal preferred approach for gathering information and making decisions. *Chapter 14*

decision support system (DSS)   An information system that supports managers in decision-making tasks. *Chapter 14*

decision table   A systems development used to show the conditions and actions for a set of decision rules in a tabular format. *Chapter 16*

decode unit   Takes the instruction read by the prefetcher an translates it into a form suitable for the the CPU's internal processing. *Chapter 2*

dedicated (special-purpose) computer   Computer that performs specific tasks, such as controlling temperature and humidity in an office building. *Chapter 1*

delayed teleconference   See asynchronous teleconference.

deleting text   Removing text from the document. *Chapter 5*

demo software   A program, usually available for free trial download, that is identical to a commercial program except that it has some key features disabled. *Chapter 4*

denial of service (DoS) attacks   A type of computer vandalism that bombards servers and Web sites with so much bogus traffic that they're effectively shut down, denying service to legitimate customers and clients. *Chapter 12*

design   The phase of the systems development life cycle that focuses on how the problem will be solved. *Chapter 16*

de-skilling   Transforming a job so that it requires less skill. *Chapter 17*

desktop   A visual representation of a desktop in a graphical user interface where the user performs tasks. *Chapter 4*

desktop publishing (DTP)   Software used mainly to produce print publications. Also, the process of using desktop publishing software to produce publications. *Chapter 0, Chapter 5*

development   The phase of the systems development life cycle in which the system is built and tested. *Chapter 16*

desktop system   A computer system designed to sit on a desktop. *Chapter 3*

device drivers: Small programs that allow input/output devices to communicate with the computer. *Chapter 4*

dialog box   In a graphical user interface, a box that enables the user to communicate with the computer. *Chapter 4*

dial-up connection   A temporary connection to an Internet host that uses a modem and standard telephone lines. *Chapter 10*

differentiation strategy   The overall focus of a business organization to produce high-quality products and services that are perceived by customers as particularly valuable and as uniquely different from the competition. *Chapter 14*

digital   Information made up of discrete units that can be counted. *Chapter 2*

digital camera   A camera that captures images and stores them as bit patterns on disks or other digital storage media instead of using film. *Chapter 3*

digital cash   A system for purchasing goods and services on the Internet without using credit cards. *Chapter 11*

digital divide   A term that describes the divide between the people who do and do not have access to the Internet. *Chapter 11*

digital image processing software   Enables the user to manipulate photographs and other high-resolution images. *Chapter 7*

digital signal   A stream of bits. *Chapter 9*

digital signature   A developing identity verification standard that uses encryption techniques to protect against email forgery. *Chapter 11*

digital video   Video reduced to a series of numbers and can be edited, stored, and played back without loss of quality. *Chapter 7*

digital video camera   A video camera that captures footage in digital form so that clips can be transferred to and from a computer for editing with no loss of quality. *Chapter 7*

digitize   Converting information into a digital form that can be stored in the computer's memory. *Chapter 3*

digitized sound   Sound recorded and stored in a computer or other electronic device as digital data. *Chapter 7*

direct (dedicated) connection   A dedicated, direct connection to the Internet through a LAN, with the computer having its own IP address. *Chapter 9, Chapter 10*

directory   A logical container used to group files and other directories. Also called a folder. *Chapter 4*

disinfectant program   See antivirus program

disk drive   Device used to retrieve information from a disk and, in some cases, to transfer data to it. *Chapter 3*

diskette (floppy disk)   A small, magnetically sensitive, flexible plastic wafer housed in a plastic case, used as a storage device. *Chapter 0, Chapter 3*

distance education   Using computers, networks, and other technology to extend the educational process beyond the walls of a school, connecting students and faculty at remote locations. *Chapter 17*

distributed computing   Integrating all kinds of computers, from mainframes to PCs, into a single, seamless system. *Chapter 11, Chapter 14*

distributed database   Data strewn out across networks on several different computers. *Chapter 8*

distributed denial of service (DDoS) attack   A denial of service attack in which the flood of messages comes from many compromised systems distributed across the Net. *Chapter 12*

DNS   See domain name system.

docking station   A device for expanding a laptop computer so that it has the power and flexibility of a desktop. *Chapter 1*

document   A computer file, such as a term paper or a chart created with a software application. *Chapter 4*

document imaging system Information technologies to scan, store, retrieve, and send bitmapped images of paper documents within an organization to reduce the flow of paper. *Chapter 14*

documentation Instructions for installing the software on a computer's hard disk. *Chapter 4*

domain A class of Internet addresses indicated by a suffix such as .com, .gov, or .net. *Chapter10*

domain name system (DNS) A system that translates a computer's numerical IP address into an easier-to-remember string of names separated by dots. *Chapter 10*

domain name registry A company that provides its customers with domain names that are easier to remember and use. *Chapter XXX*

dot com A company that uses the Internet exclusively to provide products and services to customers. *Chapter 15.*

dots per inch (dpi) A measurement of the density of pixels, defining the resolution of a graphic. *Chapter 7.*

dot-matrix printer An old-fashioned impact printer that uses pinpoint-size hammers to transfer ink to the page. The printed page is a matrix of tiny dots. *Chapter 3*

double-click To click a mouse button twice in rapid succession. *Chapter 0*

download To copy software from an online source to a local computer. *Chapter 9, Chapter 10, Chapter 11*

downloadable video Compressed video files that can be downloaded and viewed on a computer. *Chapter 10*

downstream traffic Information transmitted from the Internet to the subscriber. *Chapter 10*

drag To move the mouse while holding the mouse button down. Used for moving objects, selecting text, drawing, and other tasks. *Chapter 3*

drag-and-drop Editing feature that enables the user to move selected text or an object by dragging it (with the mouse) from one part of the screen to another. *Chapter 5*

drawing software Stores a picture as a collection of lines and shapes. Also stores shapes as shape formulas and text as text. *Chapter 7*

drum scanner A scanner used in publishing applications where image quality is critical. *Chapter 3*

DSL (digital subscriber line) A type of broadband connection to the Internet offered by phone companies. *Chapter 10*

DSS (decision support system) An information system that supports managers in decision-making tasks. *Chapter 14*

DTP (desktop publishing) See desktop publishing. *Chapter 5*

dual-boot PC A PC that can switch back and forth between two operating systems by rebooting. *Chapter 4*

DVD (digital video disk or digital versatile disk) Popular type of high-capacity optical disk used in both consumer video playback machines and computers. *Chapter 3*

DVD-R Recordable DVD disk. *Chapter 3*

DIMM Dual in-line memory module. *Chapter 2*

DVD-CD-RW drive A disk drive that combines the capabilities of a DVD-ROM drive and a CD-RW drive in a single unit. *Chapter 3*

DVD-RAM A type of optical disk with multigigabyte capacity that can be read, written, and erased. *Chapter 3*

DVD-ROM A type of optical disk with read-only capability that is the size of a CD-ROM but that holds much more information. *Chapter 3*

DVD-ROM drive An optical disk drive that can read high-capacity DVD disks. *Chapter 3*

dynamic HTML A relatively new version of HTML that supports formatting and layout features that aren't supported in standard HTML. *Chapter 10*

E

e-commerce See electronic commerce (e-commerce).

e-commerce software Software that provides the on-line transaction services provided on B2B, B2C, and C2C Web sites. *Chapter 15*

EDI See Electronic Data Interchange.

editing Inserting, deleting, copying, and moving text and other data within a document, and from one document to another. *Chapter 5*

educational simulation Software that enables students to explore artificial environments that are imaginary or based on reality. Most have the look and feel of a game, but they challenge students to learn through exploration, experimentation, and interaction with other students. *Chapter 17*

edutainment Programs geared toward home markets that combine education and entertainment. *Chapter 17*

effectiveness A measure of how well customers value the quality of a business organization's products and services. *Chapter 14*

efficiency A measure of how well a business organization produces desired products and services with less work or lower costs. *Chapter 14*

electronic book (ebook) A handheld device that displays digital representations of the contents of books. *Chapter 5*

electronic commerce (e-commerce) The sharing of business information, maintaining business relationships, and conducting business transactions through the use of telecommunications networks, especially the Internet. *Chapter 9, Chapter 11, Chapter 15*

electronic data interchange (EDI) A set of specifications for conducting basic business transactions over private networks. *Chapter 11, Chapter 13*

electronic funds transfer Automatic money transfers made inside computer networks, not through the use of cash or checks. *Chapter 9*

electronic mail (email) Allows Internet users to send mail messages, data files, and software programs to other Internet users and to users of most commercial networks and online services. *Chapter 0, Chapter 1, Chapter 9*

electronic meeting Communication among individuals in a meeting supported by a variety of information technologies including computer, voice, and video conferencing. *Chapter 14*

electronic organizer A specialized database program that automates an address/phone book, an appointment calendar, a to-do list, and miscellaneous notes. Also called a personal information manager (PIM). *Chapter 8*

electronic paper (e-paper) A flexible experimental output device that can be read like printed paper, erased, and reused. *Chapter 5, Chapter 18*

electronic sweatshop An office where each worker has a single job; computer monitoring is a common practice; wages are low; work conditions are poor; most of the work is mindless keyboarding; and repetitive stress injuries are common. *Chapter 17*

email See electronic mail.

email server A specialized server that acts like a local post office for a particular Internet host. *Chapter 11*

email virus A virus spread via email. *Chapter 12*

e-marketplace The business relationships conducted electronically via the Internet between a company and vendors, suppliers, and other organizations internationally. *Chapter 15.*

embedded computer Computer that is embedded into a consumer product, such as a wristwatch or game machine, to enhance those products. Also used to control hardware devices. *Chapter 1*

emulation A process that enables programs to run on a noncompatible operating system. *Chapter 4*

encryption Protects transmitted information by scrambling the transmissions. When a user encrypts a message by applying a secret numerical code (encryption key), the message can be transmitted or stored as an indecipherable garble of characters. The message can be read only after it's been reconstructed with a matching key. *Chapter 12*

end user An individual who uses an information system directly or uses the information produced by the system. *Chapter 16*

end-user development The development of an information system by end users without the direct involvement of a professional systems analyst. *Chapter 16*

enterprise network systems Large, complex networks with hundreds of computers that are tracked and maintained with network management system software. *Chapter 9*

enterprise resource planning (ERP) An approach of creating information systems to support business processes by simplifying and speeding up a company's entire transaction processing cycle. *Chapter 13*

entry barrier An innovative product or service, usually comprising new information technology, that is difficult for a competing company to emulate. *Chapter 14*

e-paper See electronic paper.

equation solver A feature of some spreadsheet programs that determines data values. *Chapter 6*

Ethernet A popular networking architecture developed in 1976 at Xerox. *Chapter 9*

ethics A moral philosophy of right and wrong. Computer ethics involve principles and guidelines to help users focus on the many technology-related dilemmas of our time. *Chapter 12*

equation solver A feature of some spreadsheet programs that determines data values. *Chapter 6*

ergonomics The science of designing work environments that enable people and things to interact efficiently and safely. *Chapter 3*

error message Message from the operating system or application that tells the user an error has occurred. *Chapter 4*

executive information system (EIS) An information system to support unstructured decision making by top managers. *Chapter 14*

expansion cards A special-purpose circuit board that can be inserted in one of a computer's expansion slots. *Chapter 2*

expansion slots An area inside the computer's housing that holds special-purpose circuit boards. *Chapter 2*

expert system (ES) An information system designed to replicate the decision-making process of a human expert. *Chapter 14*

expert system shell A generic expert system containing human interfaces and inference engines intended to simplify the process of designing an expert system. *Chapter 14*

export data Transmitting records and fields from a database program to another program. *Chapter 8*

exporting The process of transmitting records and fields from a program, such as a database program, into a form that can be read and processed by another program. *Chapter 5*

extranet A private TCP/IP network designed for outside use by customers, clients, and business partners of an organization. These networks are typically for electronic commerce. *Chapter 10, Chapter 11, Chapter 15*

extreme programming A relatively new programming methodology that focuses more on the culture of programming than on technology, in which the entire programming team "owns" the code; each member of the team has a right to improve it and the responsibility for making it work properly. *Chapter 16*

F

facsimile (fax) A technology that allows images of paper documents to be transmitted through telephone lines to a destination where they can be printed or displayed on a computer screen. *Chapter 9*

fair use The time-honored right to make copies of copyrighted material for personal and academic use and for other noncompetitive purposes. *Chapter 12*

FAQ (frequently asked questions) A list of frequently asked questions is posted for many newsgroups and mailing lists. The FAQs keep the groups from being cluttered with the same old questions and answers, if their members take advantage of them. *Chapter 11*

fax modem Hardware peripheral that enables a computer to send onscreen documents to a receiving fax machine by translating the document into signals that can be sent over phone wires and decoded by the receiving fax machine. *Chapter 9*

feedback loop In a computer simulation, the user and the computer responding to data from each other. *Chapter 6*

fiber optic cable High-capacity cable that uses light waves to carry information at blinding speeds. *Chapter 9*

field Each discrete chunk of information in a database record. *Chapter 8*

field type The characteristic of a field that determines the kind of information that can be stored in that field. *Chapter 8*. Also called data type. *Chapter 8*

file An organized collection of related information stored in a computer-readable form. *Chapter 2, Chapter 8*

file manager A program that enables users to manipulate files on their computers. *Chapter 8*

file server In a LAN, a computer used as a storehouse for software and data that are shared by several users. *Chapter 9*

file transfer protocol (FTP) A communications protocol that enables users to download files from remote servers to their computers and to upload files they want to share from their computers to these archives. *Chapter 10*

filtering software Software that, for the most part, keeps offensive and otherwise inappropriate Web content from being viewed by children, on-duty workers, and others. *Chapter 11, Chapter 18*

find and replace See search and replace.

Find command A command used to locate a particular word, string of characters, or formatting in a document. *Chapter 5*

firewall Software or hardware that guards against unauthorized access to an internal network; keeps internal networks secure while allowing communication with the rest of the Internet. *Chapter 12, Chapter 15*

firmware A program, usually for special-purpose computers, stored on a ROM chip so it cannot be altered. *Chapter 1*

FireWire See IEEE 1394.

flash memory A type of erasable memory chip used in cell phones, pagers, portable computers, and handheld computers, among other things. *Chapter 2, Chapter 3, Chapter 18*

flatbed scanner Scanner that looks and works like a photocopy machine, except that it creates computer files instead of paper copies. *Chapter 3*

floppy disk (diskette) A small, magnetically sensitive, flexible plastic wafer housed in a plastic case, used as a storage device. *Chapter 3*

folder A container for files and other folders. Also called a directory. *Chapter 4*

font A size and style of typeface. *Chapter 5*

footer Block of information that appears at the bottom of every page in a document, displaying repetitive information such as an automatically calculated page number. *Chapter 5*

form On the Web, a page (or part of a page) that enables visitors to enter information into fields; *Chapter 10*

form view A view of the database that shows one record at a time. *Chapter 8*

formatting The function of software, such as word processing software, that enables users to change the appearance of a document by specifying the font, point size, and style of any character in the document, as well as the overall layout of text and graphical elements in the document *Chapter 5*

formula Step-by-step procedure for calculating a number on a spreadsheet. *Chapter 6*

formula bar In spreadsheet software, the long window above the worksheet where typing appears. *Chapter 6*

fourth-generation language (4GL) Languages have evolved through machine language, assembly language, high-level languages, and into 4GLs. 4GLs use Englishlike phrases and sentences to issue instructions, are nonprocedural, and increase productivity. *Chapter 16*

frame In animation, one still picture in a video or animated sequence. *Chapter 7*

frame In Web design, subdivisions of a Web browser's viewing area that enable visitors to scroll and view different parts of a page—or even multiple pages—simultaneously. *Chapter 10*

FTP See file transfer protocol.

full-access dial-up connection Enables a computer connected via modem and phone line to temporarily have full Internet access and a temporary IP address. *Chapter 10*

full color A desktop published document that uses a wide range of color. Contrast with spot color. *Chapter 5*

function A predefined set of calculations, such as SUM and AVERAGE, in spreadsheet software. *Chapter 6*

Gantt chart A planning tool used in business organizations to show the schedule of an information system project visually. *Chapter 16*

gateway A computer connected to two networks that translates communication protocols and transfers information between the two. *Chapter 10*

geostationary Matching the Earth's rotation in a stationary position relative to the spinning planet below. *Chapter 9*

genetic algorithm An algorithm that automatically evolves through many generations. *Chapter 9, Chapter 18*

GB See gigabyte.

geographical information system (GIS) A specialized database that combines tables of data with demographic information and displays geographic and demographic data on maps. *Chapter 8, Chapter 14*

generation One cycle of backups; many data-processing shops keep several generations of backups so they can, if necessary, go back several days, weeks, or years to reconstruct data files. *Chapter 12*

generations of computers Designations for major changes in hardware. First-generation computers were built around vacuum tubes. Second-generation computers used transistors. Integrated circuits characterized third-generation computers. The invention of the microprocessor marked the beginning of fourth-generation computers. *Chapter 1*

gigabyte (GB) Approximately 1000MB. *Chapter 2*

GIGO Garbage in, garbage out. Valid output requires valid input. *Chapter 6*

GIS See geographical information system.

Global Positioning System (GPS) A defense department system with 24 satellites that can pinpoint any location on the Earth. *Chapter 9*

GPS See Global Positioning System.

GPS receiver A device that can use Global Positioning System signals to determine its location and communicate that information to a person or a computer. *Chapter 9*

grammar and style checker Component of word-processing software that analyzes each word in context, checking for content

errors, common grammatical errors, and stylistic problems. *Chapter 5*

graphical user interface (GUI) A user interface based on graphical displays. With a mouse, the user points to icons that represent files, folders, and disks. Documents are displayed in windows. The user selects commands from menus. *Chapter 4*

graphics tablet A pressure-sensitive touch tablet used as a pointing device. The user presses on the tablet with a stylus. *Chapter 3*

gray-scale graphics Graphics that allow each pixel to appear as black, white, or one of several shades of gray. *Chapter 7*

gray-scale monitor Monitor that displays black, white, and shades of gray but no other colors. *Chapter 3*

grid computing A form of distributed computing in which not files but processing power is shared between networked computers. *Chapter 11*

group decision support system (GDSS) An information system to support the semistructured decision making of managers working together as a group. *Chapter 14*

groupware Software designed to be used by work groups rather than individuals. *Chapter 5, Chapter 9, Chapter 14*

GUI See graphical user interface.

hacker Someone who uses computer skills to gain unauthorized access to computer systems. Also sometimes used to refer to particularly talented, dedicated programmer. *Chapter 12*

hacking Electronic trespassing and vandalism. *Chapter 12*

hand-held computer A portable computer small enough to be tucked into a jacket pocket. *Chapter 1*

handwriting recognition software Software that translates the user's handwritten forms into ASCII characters. *Chapter 3*

hard copy A paper copy, produced by a printer, of any information that can be displayed on the screen. *Chapter 3*

hard disk A rigid, magnetically sensitive disk that spins rapidly and continuously inside the computer chassis or in a separate box attached to the computer housing. Used as a storage device. *Chapter 0, Chapter 3*

hardware Physical parts of the computer system. *Chapter 0, Chapter 1*

hardware compression Compression using hardware rather than software. *Chapter 7*

header Block that appears at the top of every page in a document, displaying repetitive information such as a chapter title. *Chapter 5*

help file A documentation file that appears onscreen at the user's request. *Chapter 4*

helper application A program designed to help users view particular types of graphics, animation, audio, or video that can't be played by the browser. *Chapter 10*

hexadecimal Base 16 number system; often used to represent machine-language programs. *Chapter 16*

hierarchical menus Menus that organize commands into compact, efficient submenus. *Chapter 4*

high-level language A programming language that falls somewhere between natural human languages and precise machine languages, developed to streamline and simplify the programming process. *Chapter 4, Chapter 16*

high-performance computer See supercomputer.

home page The main entry page to a Web site. *Chapter 10*

host system A computer that provides services to multiple users. *Chapter 9*

hot swap To remove and replace peripheral devices without powering down the computer and peripherals. Some modern interface standards such as USB and FireWire, allow hot-swapping. *Chapter 3*

hot sync Synchronizing of data, typically between a handheld computer and a desktop PC. *Chapter 8*

HTML See Hypertext Markup Language.

human-centered system A system designed to retain and enhance human skills rather than take them away. *Chapter 17*

hyperlink A word, phrase, or picture that acts as a button, enabling the user to explore the Web or a multimedia document with mouse clicks. *Chapter 0, Chapter 10*

hypermedia The combination of text, numbers, graphics, animation, sound effects, music, and other media in hyperlinked documents. *Chapter 7, Chapter 10*

hypertext An interactive cross-referenced system that allows textual information to be linked in nonsequential ways. A hypertext document contains links that lead quickly to other parts of the document or to related documents. *Chapter 7, Chapter 10*

Hypertext Markup Language (HTML) An HTML document is a text file that includes codes that describe the format, layout, and logical structure of a hypermedia document. Most Web pages are created with HTML. *Chapter 10, Chapter 16*

HTTP (hypertext transfer protocol) The internet protocol used to transfer Web pages. *Chapter 10*

I

IEEE 1394 An industry standard for relatively new, extremely fast serial communications protocol, especially well suited for multimedia applications such as digital video. Apple computer, which developed the standard, refers to IEEE 1394 as FireWire. *Chapter 4*

icon In a graphical user interface, a picture that represents a file, folder, or disk. *Chapter 4*

idea processor A word-processing feature that enables the user to organize ideas, drawing them as nodes on a chart with arrows connecting related ideas. *Chapter 5*

identity theft Use of stolen information to assume the identity of another individual. *Chapter 8, Chapter 12*

imagesetters See phototypesetting machines

impact printer Printer that forms images by physically striking paper, ribbon, and print hammer together. *Chapter 3*

import data To move data into a program from another program or source. *Chapter 8*

image processing software Software that enables the user to manipulate photographs and other high-resolution images. *Chapter 7*

implementation The phase of the systems development life cycle in which the system is put into use. *Chapter 16*

industrial revolution The transition of society from an agricultural economy to an industrial economy. *Chapter 13*

inference engine The component of an expert system that applies user input to the knowledge base to produce the requested expert advice. *Chapter 14*

information Anything that can be communicated. *Chapter 2*

information appliance Network computer or other Internet-capable device used in offices and homes. *Chapter 1*

information economy An economy based on information-related work. *Chapter 13*

information infrastructure The framework, created by computers, networks, and software, upon which our information economy is built. *Chapter 18*

information overload The psychological state of coping with too much computer output; a hazard of the automated office. *Chapter 14*

information requirement The need of a manager to get the right information at the right time and in the right form for the situation at hand. *Chapter 14*

information system A collection of people, machines, data, and methods organized to accomplish specific functions and to solve specific problems. Programming is part of the larger process of designing, implementing, and managing an information system. *Chapter 13*

information systems manager A tactical-level manager responsible for the development and use of information systems in an organization. *Chapter 14*

information technology Technology component of an information system, including hardware, software, and communications, that performs the five information functions of acquisition, processing, storage and retrieval, presentation, and transmission. *Chapter 13*

information worker A person in the workforce who primarily creates, processes, uses, or distributes information. *Chapter 13*

Infrared technology A type of wireless networking that uses ports that can send and receive digital information short distances. Not widely used in networks because of distance and line-of-sight limitations, but practical for mobile users. *Chapter 9*

infrastructure An organization's information systems hardware, software, and telecommunications equipment, the information system department's staff, and the organizational procedures that affect accessing, processing, and using information in the company. *Chapter 16*

inkjet printer A nonimpact printer that sprays ink directly onto paper to produce printed text and graphic images. *Chapter 3*

innovation strategy The overall focus of a business organization to develop new ways to produce and distribute their products and services, or developing unique products and services that are perceived as valuable by customers. *Chapter 14*

input Information taken in by the computer. *Chapter 1*

input device Device for accepting input, such as a keyboard. *Chapter 2*

inserting text Adding text at any point in a document. *Chapter 5*

insertion bar Indicates your location in a document. *Chapter 5*

instant messaging A technology that enables users to create buddy lists, check for "buddies" who are logged in, and exchange typed messages and files with those who are. *Chapter 9, Chapter 11*

instruction Computer code telling the CPU to perform a specific action. *Chapter 2*

instruction set A vocabulary of instructions that can be executed by a specific processor. Generally newer processors can process instructions used by earlier models in the same CPU family. *Chapter 2*

integrated circuit A chip containing hundreds, thousands, or even millions of transistors. *Chapter 1*

integrated software Software packages that include several applications designed to work well together. *Chapter 4*

intellectual property The results of intellectual activities in the arts, science, and industry. *Chapter 12*

interactive fiction Stories with primitive natural-language interfaces that gave players some control over plot. *Chapter 17*

interactive movie Video-based or animated feature in which one or more characters are controlled by the viewers. *Chapter 17*

interactive multimedia Multimedia that enables the user to take an active part in the experience. *Chapter 7*

interactive processing Interacting with data through terminals, viewing and changing values online in real time. *Chapter 8*

interactive spelling checker A spelling checker that checks each word as it's typed, sometimes marking each mistyped word by underlining it. *Chapter 5*

interface standards Standards agreed upon by the computer industry to ensure that devices made by one manufacturer can be attached to systems made by other companies. *Chapter 3*

interactive TV Animated features in which one or more of the characters are controlled by the viewers. *Chapter 17*

internal modem A modem that is built into the system unit. *Chapter 3.*

international information system Any information system used to support an organization's international or global business activities. *Chapter 14*

Internet (Net) A global interconnected network of thousands of networks linking academic, research, government, and commercial institutions, and other organizations and individuals. *Chapter 0, Chapter 1, Chapter 10*

Internet appliances Non-PC devices such as set-top boxes that are connected to the Internet. *Chapter 10*

Internet service provider (ISP) A business that provides its customers with connections to the Internet along with other services. *Chapter 10*

Internet telephony (IP telephony) A combination of software and hardware technology that enables the Internet to, in effect, serve as a telephone network. Internet telephony systems can use standard telephones, computers, or both to send and receive voice messages. *Chapter 11*

Internet2 An alternative Internet-style network that provides faster network communications for universities and research institutions. *Chapter 11*

internetworking Connecting different types of networks and computer systems. *Chapter 10*

interorganizational information system (IOS) An information system designed to share data and conduct transactions electronically between companies using networking and telecommunication technologies. *Chapter 14*

interpreter A program that translates and transmits each programming statement individually. *Chapter 16*

intranet A self-contained intraorganizational network that is designed using Internet-based technology. *Chapter 1, Chapter 8, Chapter 11, Chapter 15*

investigation The first phase of the systems development life cycle; clearly defining the problem to be solved. *Chapter 16*

IP address A unique string of four numbers separated by periods that serves as a unique address for a computer on the Internet. The IP address of the host computer and sending computer is included with every packet of information that traverses the Internet, *Chapter 10*

ISDN A digital broadband service offered by phone companies. Because it is slower and more expensive than DSL and other broadband options, ISDN is not widely used today. *Chapter 9*

ISP See Internet service provider.

Java A platform-neutral, object-oriented programming language developed by Sun Microsystems for use on multiplatform networks. *Chapter 4, Chapter 10, Chapter 16*

JavaScript A Web scripting language similar to, but otherwise unrelated to, Java. *Chapter 10, Chapter 16*

Java virtual machine Software that gives a computer the capability to run Java programs. *Chapter 4*

jobless growth A period of time when productivity increases not because of the work people do but because of the work of machines. *Chapter 18*

joystick A gearshift-like device used as a controller for arcade-style computer games. *Chapter 3*

justification The alignment of text on a line: left justification (smooth left margin and ragged right margin), right justification, full justification (both margins are smooth), and center justification. *Chapter 5*

K See kilobyte

kerning The spacing between letter pairs in a document. *Chapter 5*

keyboard/mouse ports Ports for attaching keyboard and mouse to most older PCs. *Chapter 0, Chapter 1, Chapter 3*

keyboard Input device, similar to a typewriter keyboard, for entering data and commands into the computer. *Chapter 3*

key field A field that contains data that uniquely identifies the record. *Chapter 8*

kilobyte (K) About 1000 bytes of information. *Chapter 2*

knowledge base A database that contains both facts and a system of rules for determining and changing the relationship between those facts; the database component of an expert system. *Chapter 14*

label In a spreadsheet, a text entry that provides information on what a column or row represents. *Chapter 6*

LAN See local area network.

laptop computer A flat-screen, battery-powered portable computer that you can rest on your lap. *Chapter 1*

laser printer A nonimpact printer that uses a laser beam to create patterns of electrical charges on a rotating drum. The charged patterns attract black toner and transfer it to paper as the drum rotates. *Chapter 3*

LCD See liquid crystal display monitor.

Leading The spacing between lines of text. *Chapter 5*

Legacy-free PCs PCs using USB ports. *Chapter 3.*

line chart A chart that shows trends or relationships over time, or a relative distribution of one variable through another. *Chapter 6*

line printer An impact printer used by mainframes to produce massive printouts. They print characters only, not graphics. *Chapter 3*

links See hyperlinks. *Chapter 7.*

Linux An operating system based on UNIX, maintained by volunteers, and distributed for free. Linux is used mostly in servers and embedded computers, but is growing in popularity as a PC operating system. *Chapter 4*

liquid crystal display (LCD) monitor A flat-panel display monitor typically used for portable computers. *Chapter 3*

list view showing data by displaying several records in lists similar to a spreadsheet. *Chapter 8.*

local-area network (LAN) A network in which the computers are close to each other, usually in the same building. Typically includes a collection of computers and peripherals; each computer and shared peripheral is an individual node on the network. *Chapter 1, Chapter 9*

logic bomb A program designed to attack in response to a particular logical event or sequence of events. A type of software sabotage. *Chapter 12*

logic error An error in the logical structure of a computer program that causes differences between what you want the program to do and what it actually does. *Chapter 16*

LOGO A computer language developed in the 1960s for children. *Chapter 17*

login name A one-word name that you type to identify yourself when connecting—logging in—to a secure a computer system or network. Sometimes called user name. *Chapter 0, Chapter 9, Chapter10*

lossless compression Systems allowing files to be compressed and later decompressed without a loss of data. *Chapter 7*

lossy compression system A type of compression in which some quality is lost in the process of compression and decompression. *Chapter 7*

low-level languages Programming languages that require the programmer to think on the machine's level and to include an enormous amount of detail in every program, such as machine language and assembly language. *Chapter 16*

Luddites A group of 19th Century workers who smashed new textile machinery to protect their jobs; today the term is often used to describe someone who opposes new technology in general. *Chapter 17*

lurker   A person who silently monitors mailing lists and newsgroups without posting messages. *Chapter 11*

m-commerce   See mobile commerce (m-commerce)

machine language   The language that computers use to process instructions. Machine language uses numeric codes to represent basic computer operations. *Chapter 4, Chapter 16*

Mac OS   The operating system for the Apple Macintosh computer. *Chapter 4*

macro   Custom-designed embedded procedure program that automates tasks in application programs. *Chapter 6, Chapter 16*

macro (scripting) language   A user-oriented language that enables users to create programs (macros) that automate repetitive tasks. *Chapter 16*

macro virus   A virus that attaches itself to and is transmitted through macros embedded in documents; usually spread via email. *Chapter 12*

magnetic disk   Storage medium with random-access capability, accessed by the computer's disk drive. *Chapter 3*

magnetic-ink character reader   Reads numbers printed with magnetic ink on checks. *Chapter 3*

magnetic tape   A storage medium used with a tape drive to store large amounts of information in a small space at relatively low cost. *Chapter 3*

magneto-optical (MO) disks   A type of removable media that uses a combination of magnetic disk technology and optical disk technology. *Chapter 3*

mailing list   An email discussion group on special-interest topics. All subscribers receive messages sent to the group's mailing address. *Chapter 11*

mail merge   A feature of a word processors or other program that enables it to merge names and addresses from a database mailing list into personalized form letters and mailings. *Chapter 5, Chapter 8*

mainframe computer   Expensive, room-size computer, used mostly for large computing jobs. *Chapter 1*

maintenance   The phase of the systems development life cycle that involves evaluating, repairing, and enhancing the system. *Chapter 16*

management   The individuals in an organization responsible for using resources intelligently and ethically to accomplish the organization's goals. *Chapter 14*

management functions   The responsibilities of managers to plan, organize, direct, and control the various business processes in an organization. *Chapter 14*

management information system (MIS)   An information system that includes procedures for collecting data, a database for storing data, and software tools for analyzing data and producing a variety of reports for managers at different levels in the organization. *Chapter 14*

management levels   Three echelons of managers in an organization—operational, tactical, and strategic. *Chapter 14*

management reporting system   Synonym for management information system. *Chapter 14*

management roles   The interpersonal, informational, and decisional tasks managers perform interacting with other employees in the organization and in the organization's environment. *Chapter 14*

master pages   In desktop publishing, the pages that control the general layout of the document. *Chapter 5*

mathematics processing software   Software designed to deal with complex equations and calculations. A mathematics processor enables the user to create, manipulate, and solve equations easily. *Chapter 6*

megabit (Mb)   Approximately 1,000bits—one eighth the size of a megabyte. *Chapter 2*

MB   See megabyte.

megabyte (MB)   Approximately 1000K, or 1 million bytes. *Chapter 2*

megahertz (MHz)   A unit of measurement for a computer's clock speed; millions of clock cycles per second. *Chapter 2*

memory   Stores programs and the data they need to be instantly accessible to the CPU. *Chapter 0, Chapter 2*

memory-mapped I/O   Information for input and output stored in special areas of memory. *Chapter 2*

menu   An onscreen list of command choices. *Chapter 4*

menu bar   Part of the user interface. A bar that contains menus of choices. *Chapter 0, Chapter 4*

menu-driven interface   User interface that enables users to choose commands from onscreen lists called menus. *Chapter 4*

meta-search engine   A software tool that conducts parallel searches using several different search engines and directories. *Chapter 10*

metropolitan area network (MAN)   A service that links two or more LANs within a city. *Chapter 9*

MHz   See megahertz.

microcomputer   Small computer made possible by the microprocessor. Now known as a personal computer. *Chapter 1*

microcomputer revolution   Period that began in the mid-1970s when several companies introduced small microcomputers that were as powerful as their larger predecessors. *Chapter 1*

micro-electro-mechanical systems (MEMS)   Microscopic electricity-powered machines using a process similar to that of manufacturing computer chips. *Chapter 18*

microprocessor   Critical components of a complete computer, housed on a silicon chip. *Chapter 1, Chapter 2*

Microsoft Windows   The most popular and powerful PC operating system; uses a graphical user interface. *Chapter 4*

microtechnology   Technology that allows the development of micromachines, machines on the scale of a millionth of a meter. *Chapter 18*

middleware   Connectivity software linking the client and server machines in an intranet or other network. *Chapter 8, Chapter 15.*

MIDI (Musical Instrument Digital Interface)   A standard interface that allows electronic instruments and computers to communicate with each other and work together. *Chapter 7*

millisecond   A thousandth of a second. *Chapter 2*

MIPS (millions of instructions per second)   A measurement of computer speed, where an instruction is the most primitive operation performed by the processor—moving a number to a memory location, comparing two numbers, and the like. *Chapter 18*

mirror   To automatically duplicate copies of data to multiple disks, effectively creating instant backups. *Chapter 12*

MIS   See management information systems.

MO   See magneto-optical disks.

mobile commerce (m-commerce)   E-commerce conducted using wireless technologies such as handheld or laptop computers, cellular phones, and personal digital assistants. *Chapter 15*

model   A simplified representation of reality containing only the most relevant aspects of the real situation. *Chapter 14*

modeling   The use of computers to create abstract models of objects, organisms, organizations, and processes. *Chapter 6*

modem   Modulator/demodulator. A hardware device that connects a computer to a telephone line. *Chapter 9*

moderated (news group or mailing list)   Monitored by a moderator who filters out inappropriate or off-topic messages so subscribers don't need to receive or read them. *Chapter 11*

module (subprogram)   In structured programming, a computer program is built from smaller programs called modules. *Chapter 16*

monitor An output device that displays text and graphics onscreen. *Chapter 3*

monochrome monitor Monitor that displays two colors, usually black and white. *Chapter 3*

monospaced font A font in which all characters are equal width, like a typewriter's characters. *Chapter 5*

moral dilemma A predicament for which rules and ethics don't seem to apply, or to contradict one another. *Chapter 12*

morph Video clip in which one image metamorphoses into another. *Chapter 7*

Moore's Law The prediction made in 1965 by Gordon Moore that the power of a silicon chip of the same price would double about every 18 months for at least two decades. *Chapter 1*

mouse A handheld input device that, when moved around on a desktop or table, moves a pointer around the computer screen. *Chapter 0, Chapter 3*

motherboard The circuit board that contains a computer's CPU. Also called a system board. *Chapter 2*

moving text Transporting a block of text from one part of a document to another, or from one document to another. *Chapter 5*

MP3 A method of compression that can squeeze a music file to a fraction of its original CD file size with only slight loss of quality. *Chapter 7, Chapter 10*

MS-DOS (Microsoft Disk Operating System) An operating system with character-based user interface; it was widely used in the 1980s and early 1990s but has been superceded by Windows. *Chapter 4*

Multifunction peripheral (MFP) A device utilizing the fact that different tools can use similar technologies. For example, a multi-function device might combine a scanner, a printer, and a fax modem, to serve as a printer, a scanner, a color photocopy machine, and a fax machine. Also called an all-in-one-device. *Chapter 3*

multimedia Using some combination of text, graphics, animation, video, music, voice, and sound effects to communicate. *Chapter 7*

multimedia authoring software Enables the creation and editing of multimedia documents. *Chapter 7*

multiprocessing See parallel processing.

multitasking Concurrent processing for personal computers. The user can issue a command that initiates a process and continue working with other applications while the computer follows through on the command. *Chapter 4*

N

Nanosecond A billionth of a second; a common unit of measurement for read and write access time to RAM. *Chapter 2*

nanotechnology The manufacture of machines on a scale of a few billionths of a meter. *Chapter 18*

narrowband connection A dial-up Internet connection; named because it doesn't offer much bandwidth when compared to other types of connections. *Chapter 10*

narrowcasting Provides custom newscasts aimed at narrow groups or individuals. *Chapter 17*

National Infrastructure Protection Center A state-of-the-art command center created to fight the growing threat of system sabotage. The center includes representatives of various intelligence agencies (the departments of defense, transportation, energy, and treasury), and representatives of several major corporations. *Chapter 12*

natural-language Language that people speak and write every day. *Chapter 4, Chapter 8*

navigating Moving to different parts of a document. *Chapter 5*

Net (Internet) A global interconnected network of thousands of networks linking academic, research, government, and commercial institutions, and other organizations and individuals. *Chapter 1, Chapter 10*

netiquette Rules of etiquette that apply to Internet communication. *Chapter 11*

network A computer system that links two or more computers. *Chapter 9*

network card A network interface card that adds a LAN port to a PC. *Chapter 3*

network computer (NC) A computer designed to function as part of a network rather than as a PC. *Chapter 1*

network interface card (NIC) Card that adds an additional serial port to a computer. The port is especially designed for a direct network connection. *Chapter 9*

network license License for multiple copies or removing restrictions on software copying and use at a network site. *Chapter 9*

network operating system (NOS) Server operating system software for a local-area network. *Chapter 9*

network revolution The emergence of networks (clusters of computers linked together for communication and to share resources) and the beginning of the era of interpersonal computing. *Chapter 1*

newsgroup Ongoing public discussions on a particular subject consisting of notes written to a central Internet site and redistributed through a worldwide newsgroup network called. Usenet. You can check into and out of them whenever you want; all messages are posted on virtual bulletin boards for anyone to read anytime. *Chapter 11*

newsreader A client program that enables you to read newsgroups. Both text-based and graphical newsreaders are available. *Chapter 11*

Next Generation Internet (NGI) A future nationwide web of optical fiber integrated with intelligent management software to maintain high-speed connections. *Chapter 11*

NGI See Next Generation Internet (NGI).

NIC See network interface card.

node Each computer and shared peripheral on a local-area network. *Chapter 9*

nonlinear editing A type of video editing in which audio and video clips are stored in digital form on hard disks for immediate access via video editing software. *Chapter 7*

nonimpact printer A printer that produces characters without physically striking the page. *Chapter 3*

nonsequential software DEFINITION TK. *Chapter x*

nonvolatile memory Memory for permanent storage of information. *Chapter 2*

NOS See network operating system.

notebook computer Another term for laptop computer. *Chapter 1*

numeric field A field containing only numbers. *Chapter 8*

object-oriented database Instead of storing records in tables and hierarchies, stores software objects that contain procedures (or instructions) with data. *Chapter 8*

object-oriented (vector) graphics The storage of pictures as collections of lines, shapes, and other objects. *Chapter 7*

object-oriented programming (OOP) In OOP, a program is not a collection of step-by step instructions or procedures; it's a collection of objects. Objects contain both data and instructions and can send and receive messages. *Chapter 16*

OCR See optical character recognition.

office suite (application suite) Software bundle containing several application programs that are also sold as separate programs. *Chapter 4*

online Connected to the computer system and ready to communicate. *Chapter 9*

online banking use of the Internet to conduct basic banking transactions *Chapter 6*

online database   A commercial, public, or private database that can be accessed through telecommunication lines. *Chapter 9*

online help   Documentation and help available through a software company's Web site. *Chapter 4.*

online service   A service that enables hundreds of users at a time to send and receive information. America Online is an example. *Chapter 9*

OOP (object-oriented programming)   See object-oriented programming (OOP).

open   To load a file into an application program's workspace so it can be viewed and edited by the user. *Chapter 4*

open architecture   A design that allows expansion cards and peripherals to be added to a basic computer system. *Chapter 3*

open source software   Software that can be distributed and modified freely by users; Linux is the best-known example. *Chapter 4*

open standards   Standards not owned by any company. *Chapter 10*

opening a document   Copying a document file from disk into memory using an application program. *Chapter 5*

operating system (OS)   A system of programs that perform a variety of technical operations, providing an additional layer of insulation between the user and the bits-and-bytes world of computer hardware. *Chapter 0, Chapter 4*

optical character recognition (OCR)   Locating and identifying printed characters embedded in an image, allowing the text to be stored as an editable document. OCR can be performed by wand readers, pen scanners, and OCR software. *Chapter 3*

optical computer   A computer that transmits information in light waves rather than electrical pulses. *Chapter 18*

optical disk   A high-capacity, highly reliable storage medium. *Chapter 3*

optical disk drive   A disk drive that uses laser beams to read and write bits of information on the surface of an optical disk. *Chapter 3*

optical-mark reader   A reading device that uses reflected light to determine the location of pencil marks on standardized test answer sheets and similar forms. *Chapter 3*

organizational information requirements analysis   A planning approach used in business organizations to ensure that information technologies are integrated effectively to support business operations, managerial communications and decision making, and the organization's competitive strategy. *Chapter 16*

OS   See operating system.

outliner   Software that facilitates the arrangement of information into hierarchies or levels of ideas. Some word processors include outline views that serve the same function as separate outliners. *Chapter 5*

outlining   Arranging information into hierarchies or levels of ideas. *Chapter 5*

output   Information given out by the computer. *Chapter 1*

output device   Device for sending information from the computer, such as a monitor or printer. *Chapter 2*

outsourcing   The business practice of contracting systems development work to external consultants. *Chapter 16*

overhead projection panel   Equipment using lCD's to project computer screen images. *Chapter 3*

P2P   See peer to peer model

packet   A collection of information that travels as a unit through the Internet. Internet messages are broken into packets that travel independently to their destinations. *Chapter 10*

packet switching   The standard technique used to send information over the Internet. A message is broken into packets that travel independently from network to network toward their common destination, where they are reunited. *Chapter 10*

page-description language   A language used by many drawing programs that describes text fonts, illustrations, and other elements of the printed page. *Chapter 7*

page-layout software   In desktop publishing, used to combine various source documents into a coherent, visually appealing publication. *Chapter 5*

painting software   Enables you to paint pixels on the screen with a pointing device. *Chapter 7*

palette   A collection of colors available in drawing software. *Chapter 7*

palmtop computer   A handheld computer, sometimes called a personal digital assistant or PDA. *Chapter 1*

Palm OS   The operating system for palm and palm-compatible handheld computers. *Chapter 4*

paperless office   A vision of the office of the future in which magnetic and optical archives will replace reference books and file cabinets, electronic communication will replace letters and memos, and digital publications provided through the Internet and on-line services will replace newspapers and other periodicals. *Chapter 14*

paradigm shift   A change in thinking that results in a new way of seeing the world. *Chapter 13*

parallel port   A standard port on most PCs for attaching a printer or other device that communicates by sending or receiving bits in groups, rather than sequentially. *Chapter 3, Chapter 9*

parallel processing   Using multiple processors to divide jobs into pieces and work simultaneously on the pieces. *Chapter 2*

parameter Ram   CMOS RAM, a special low-energy kind of RAM used to store the date, time and calendar in Macintoshes. *Chapter 2*

password   A string of letters and numbers known only by you. A password is only effective as a security measure if it's chosen carefully. *Chapter 0, Chapter 9, Chapter 12*

patent (law)   A type of law that protects mechanical inventions. *Chapter 12*

PC   See personal computer.

PC card   A credit-card-size card that can be inserted into a slot to expand memory or add a peripheral to a computer; commonly used in portable computers. Sometimes called by its original name, PCM-CIA. *Chapter 2*

PDA   See personal digital assistant.

PDF (Portable Document Format)   Allows documents of all types to displayed on any computer screen, including the original formatting. *Chapter 5, Chapter 10*

peer-to-peer (P2P) computing   See peer-to-peer model.

peer-to-peer file sharing   Enabling networked users to make files on their hard drives available to others rather than posting them on central servers. *Chapter 11*

peer-to-peer model   A LAN model that allows every computer on the network to be both client and server. *Chapter 9*

peer-to-peer network   A network in which any computer can be both client and server, sharing information with other computers on the network. *Chapter 9*

pen-based computer   A keyboardless machine that accepts input from a stylus applied directly to a flat-panel screen. *Chapter 3*

pen scanner   Wireless pen-shaped scanners that can perform optical character recognition. *Chapter 3*

peripheral   Input, output, and secondary storage devices. *Chapter 2*

Perl (Practical Extraction and Reporting Language)   A Web scripting language that is particularly well-suited for writing scripts to process text—for example, complex Web forms.

personal communication   A handheld computer whose primary function is communication. *Chapter 9*

personal computer (PC)   A small, powerful, relatively low-cost microcomputer. *Chapter 0, Chapter 1*

personal digital assistant (PDA)   A pocket-sized computer used to organize appointments, tasks, notes, contacts, and other personal information. Sometimes called handheld computer or palmtop computer. Many PDAs include additional software and hardware for wireless communication. *Chapter 1, Chapter 8, Chapter 9*

personal information manager (PIM) A specialized database program that automates an address/phone book, an appointment calendar, a to-do list, and miscellaneous notes. Also called an electronic organizer. *Chapter 8*

phototypesetting machines Machines enabling desktop publications to be printed at 12000dpi or higher. *Chapter 5*

pie chart A round pie-shape chart with slices that show the relative proportions of the parts to a whole. *Chapter 6*

PIM See personal information manager.

pixel A picture element (dot) on a computer screen or printout. Groups of pixels compose the images on the monitor and the output of a printout. *Chapter 3, Chapter 7*

plagiarism The act of presenting someone else's work as one's own. *Chapter 8*

platform The combination of hardware and operating system software upon which application software is built. *Chapter 4*

platform independent The ability of a peripheral device to work on multiple platforms. For example, a USB disk drive could be used wit both Macintosh and Windows computers. *Chapter 3*

platter A flat disc that is the part of the hard disk that holds information. *Chapter 3*

plotter An automated drawing tool that produces finely scaled drawings by moving pen and/or paper in response to computer commands. *Chapter 3*

plug-in A software extension that adds new features. *Chapter 10*

point-of-sale (POS) terminal A terminal with a wand reader, barcode scanner, or other device that captures information at the checkout counter of a store. *Chapter 3*

point size Measurement of characters, with one point equal to 1/72 inch. *Chapter 5*

pointing stick A tiny joystick-like device embedded in the keyboard of a laptop computer. *Chapter 3*

pop-up menu A menu that can appear anywhere on the screen. *Chapter 3, Chapter 4*

port Socket that allows information to pass in and out. *Chapter 2, Chapter 9*

portable computer A small, battery-powered computer such as a laptop computer. *Chapter 1*

Portable Document Format (PDF) Allows documents of all types to be stored, viewed, or modified on any Windows or Macintosh computer, making it possible for many organizations to reduce paper flow. *Chapter 5*

portal A Web site designed as a Web entry station, offering quick and easy access to a variety of services. *Chapter 11.*

POS See point-of-sale terminal.

post-PC era An anticipated future generation where the technology disappears into the tool, serving valuable functions but keeping out of the way—the generation of the invisible computer. *Chapter 18*

PostScript A standard page-description language. *Chapter 5, Chapter 7*

Plain Old Telephone Service (POTS) Used with a modem for narrowband dial-up Internet connections. *Chapter 10*

PPP (point-to-point protocol) A protocol that enables a computer to connect to the Internet via modem and temporarily have full Internet access and IP address. *Chapter 10*

prefetch unit Part of the CPU that fetches the next several instructions from memory. *Chapter 2*

presentation An information activity that shows information to an end user in a useful format and medium. *Chapter 13*

presentation graphics software Automates the creation of visual aids for lectures, training sessions, and other presentations. Can include everything from spreadsheet charting programs to animation editing software, but most commonly used for creating and displaying a series of onscreen slides to serve as visual aids for presentations. *Chapter 7*

price-to-performance ratio The level of performance per unit cost. *Chapter 18*

print server A server that accepts, prioritizes prioritizes, and processes print jobs. *Chapter 9*

printer Output device that produces a paper copy of any information that can be displayed on the screen. *Chapter 0, Chapter 3*

processing An information activity that performs arithmetic or logical (decision-making) operations on information. *Chapter 13*

processor Part of the computer that processes information, performs arithmetic calculations, and makes basic decisions based on information values. *Chapter 2*

program Instructions that tell the hardware what to do to transform input into output. *Chapter 1, Chapter 4*

program verification The process of proving the correctness of a program. *Chapter 16*

programming A specialized form of problem solving. The process includes defining the problem; devising, refining, and testing the algorithm; writing the program; and testing and debugging the program. *Chapter 16*

programming environment An integrated compiler software package, including a text editor, a compiler, a debugger, and a variety of other programming utilities. *Chapter 16*

project management software Coordinates, schedules, and tracks complex work projects. *Chapter 16*

prompt Part of the user interface, characters (such as C:\) that prompt the user to enter information. *Chapter 4*

proportionally spaced font Fonts that allow more room for wide characters such as W than for narrow characters such as I. *Chapter 5*

protocol A set of rules for the exchange of data between a terminal and a computer or between two computers. *Chapter 9*

prototype A limited working system or subsystem that is created to give an idea of how the complete system will work. *Chapter 16*

prototyping A systems design methodology for building and evaluating an information system quickly. *Chapter 16*

pseudocode A cross between a computer language and plain English used for writing algorithms. *Chapter 16*

p-to-p See peer to peer model.

public domain software Free software that is not copyrighted, offered through World Wide Web sites, electronic bulletin boards, user groups, and other sources. *Chapter 4*

pull-down menu In a graphical user interface, a menu located at the top of the screen or window and accessed with a mouse or with keyboard shortcuts. Also called drop-down menu. *Chapter 4*

pull technology Technology in which browsers on client computers pull information from server machines. The browser needs to initiate a request before any information is delivered. *Chapter 11*

push technology Technology in which information is delivered automatically to a client computer. The user subscribes to a service and the server delivers that information periodically and unobtrusively. Contrast with pull technology. *Chapter 11*

quantum computer A computer based on the properties of atoms and their nuclei and the laws of quantum mechanics. *Chapter 18*

query An information request. *Chapter 8*

query language A special language for performing queries, more precise than the English language. *Chapter 8*

quick response strategy   A competitive strategy used by a business organization that focuses on reacting swiftly to a competitor's action or some change in the environment. *Chapter 14*

RAID (redundant array of independent disk)   A storage device that allows multiple hard disks to operate as a unit. *Chapter 8*

RAM   See random access memory.

random access   Storage method that allows information retrieval without regard to the order in which it was recorded. *Chapter 3*

random access memory (RAM)   Memory that stores program instructions and data temporarily. *Chapter 2*

range   A rectangular block of cells. *Chapter 6*

raster (bit-mapped) graphics   Painting programs create raster graphics that are, to the computer, simple maps showing how the pixels on the screen should be represented. *Chapter 7*

read-only memory (ROM)   Memory that includes permanent information only. The computer can only read information from it; it can never write any new information on it. *Chapter 2*

read/write head   The mechanism that reads information from, and writes information to, the spinning platter in a hard disk or disk drive. *Chapter 3*

real time   When a computer performs tasks immediately. *Chapter 8*

real-time communication   Internet communication that enables you to communicate with other users who are logged on at the same time. *Chapter 10, Chapter 11*

real-time processing   Processing the information about events as soon as they occur in the real world rather than saving them for later batch processing. *Chapter 13*

real-time streaming audio   Streaming transmission of radio broadcasts, concerts, news feeds, speeches, and other sound events as they happen. *Chapter 10*

real-time streaming video   Similar to streaming audio Webcasts, but with video. *Chapter 10*

real-time teleconference   An online meeting between two or more people in which participants sit at a computer or terminal, watching messages appear on the screen as they're typed by other participants, and typing comments for others to see immediately. *Chapter 9*

record   In a database, the information relating to one person, product, or event. *Chapter 8*

record matching   Compiling profiles by combining information from different database files by looking for a shared unique field. *Chapter 5*

reduced instruction set computer (RISC)   Processor designed to omit instructions that are seldom used, for the purpose of increasing speed. *Chapter 2*

register   Subdivision of the ALU in the CPU, usually 32 or 64 bits in size. *Chapter 2*

relational database   A program that allows files to be related to each other so that changes in one file are reflected in other files automatically. *Chapter 8*

relative reference   A reference to a spreadsheet cell in relation to the current cell. *Chapter 6*

remote access   Network access via phone line, TV cable system, or wireless link. *Chapter 9*

remote login   Enables users on one system to access other host systems across the network. *Chapter 10*

removable cartridge media   High-capacity transportable storage device. *Chapter 3*

repetitive-stress injuries   Injuries, such as carpal tunnel syndrome, caused by repeating the same movements over long periods of time. *Chapter 3*

replication   Automatic replication of values, labels, and formulas is a feature of spreadsheet software. *Chapter 6*

report   A database printout that is an ordered list of selected records and fields in an easy-to-read form. *Chapter 8*

resolution   Density of pixels, measured by the number of dots per inch. *Chapter 3, Chapter 7*

retinal display   A device that works without a screen by drawing pixels directly on the user's retina with a focused beam of light. *Chapter 18*

retirement   The final phase of the systems development life cycle, in which a system is phased out. *Chapter 16*

right to privacy   Freedom from interference into the private sphere of a person's affairs. *Chapter 8*

RISC   See reduced instruction set computer.

robot   A computer-controlled machine designed to perform specific manual tasks. *Chapter 13*

rollover   A common use of Web scripting, used to make onscreen buttons visibly change when the pointer rolls over them. *Chapter 10*

ROM   See read-only memory.

ROM cartridge   A removable permanent storage device used by some home video game machines. *Chapter 2*

router   A program or device that decides how to route Internet transmissions. *Chapter 6, Chapter 9*

rows   Along with columns, comprise the grid of a spreadsheet. *Chapter 6*

sabotage   A malicious attack on work, tools, or business. *Chapter 12*

sampler   An electronic musical instrument that can sample digital sounds, turn them into notes, and play them back at any pitch. *Chapter 7*

sampling rate   The rate that a sound wave is sampled; the more samples per second, the more closely the digitized sound approximates the original. *Chapter 7*

sans-serif font   Font without fine lines at the ends of the main strokes of each character. *Chapter 5*

satellite connection   H-speed Internet service via communication satellite. *Chapter 10*

saving a document   Making a disk file of your work for later retrieval. *Chapter 5*

scanner   An input device that makes a digital representation of any printed image. See flatbed scanner, slide scanner, drum scanner, and sheet-fed scanner. *Chapter 3.*

scatter chart   Discovers a relationship between two variables. *Chapter 6*

scientific visualization software   Uses shape, location in space, color, brightness, and motion to help us understand relationships that are invisible to us, providing graphical representation of numerical data. *Chapter 6*

scrolling   The movement of lines on and off the screen as you move through a document. *Chapter 5*

script   A short program that can add interactivity, animation, and other dynamic features to a Web page or multimedia document. *Chapter 10*

SCSI (Small Computer Systems Interface)   An interface design enabling several peripherals to by strung together and attached to a single port. *Chapter 3*

search   Looking for a specific record. *Chapter 8*

search and replace   Finding selected words or phrases throughout a document and replacing them with a different word or phrase. *Chapter 5*

search engine   A program for locating information on the Web. *Chapter 0, Chapter 1, Chapter 11*

search tool   See search engine.

select (records)   Looking for all records that match a set of criteria. *Chapter 8*

selecting text   Highlighting text, usually by dragging the cursor across it. *Chapter 5*

self-maintaining system   A system that can diagnose and correct common problems without human intervention. *Chapter 18*

semistructured decision   A set of conditions that for the most part is understood but because of a certain degree of uncertainty requires a decision maker to exercise judgment in selecting a course of action. *Chapter 14*

sensing device   Monitors temperature, humidity, pressure, and other physical quantities to provide data used in robotics, environmental climate control, and other applications. *Chapter 3*

sensor   A device that enables digital machines to monitor a physical quantity of the analog world—temperature, humidity, pressure, or some other quantities—to provide data used in robotics, environmental climate control, and other applications *Chapter 3, Chapter 18*

sequencing software   Software that enables a computer to be used as a tool for musical composition, recording, and editing. *Chapter 7*

sequential access   Storage method that requires the user to retrieve information by zipping through it in the order in which it was recorded. *Chapter 3*

serial port   A standard port on most PCs for attaching a modem or other device that can send and receive messages one bit at a time. *Chapter 3, Chapter 9*

serif font   Fonts embellished with fine lines at the ends of the main strokes of each character. *Chapter 5*

server   A computer especially designed to provide software and other resources to other computers over a network. *Chapter 1*

server   In a local-area network under the client/server model, a high-speed, high-capacity computer containing data and other resources to be shared with client computers. *Chapter 9*

service bureau   A business used by desktop publishers to provide camera-ready pages. *Chapter 5*

set-top box   A special-purpose computer designed to provide Internet access and other services using a standard television set and (usually) a cable TV connection. *Chapter 1, Chapter 7.*

shareware   Software that is free for the trying, with a send-payment-if-you-keep-it honor system. *Chapter 4*

sheet-fed scanner   Small scanner that accepts pages one at a time through a sheet feeder. *Chapter 3.*

shell   A program that puts a graphical face on top of a command line interface such as that of MS-DOS. *Chapter 4*

silicon chip   Hundreds of transistors packed into an integrated circuit on a piece of silicon. *Chapter 1*

simulation   A computer model of a real-life situation. *Chapter 6*

SIMMs   Single in-line memory module. *Chapter 2*

site license   License for multiple copies or removing restrictions on software copying and use at a network site. *Chapter 4, Chapter 9*

slide scanner   A scanner for slides and negatives only. *Chapter 3*

slot   Area in the computer's housing for inserting special-purpose circuit boards. *Chapter 2*

smart badge   See active badge (smart badge).

smart card   Looks like a standard credit card but uses an embedded microprocessor and memory instead of a magnetic strip. *Chapter 17*

smart weapon   A missile that uses computerized guidance systems to locate its target. *Chapter 12*

smart whiteboard   An input device that enters notes from a whiteboard to a PC . *Chapter 3*

SMIL (synchronized multimedia integration language)   An HTML-like markup language designed to make it possible to link time-based streaming media so, for example, sounds, video, and animation can be tightly integrated with each other.

social engineering   Slang for the use of deception to get individuals to reveal sensitive information. *Chapter 12*

social responsibility   Human behavior that balances both legal and ethical concerns. *Chapter 13*

software   Instructions that tell the hardware what to do to transform input into output. *Chapter 0, Chapter 1*

software components   Pieces of existing software that can be used to assemble Web services quickly. Component technology can, for example, make it easy to plug a shopping-cart component into an existing Web site. *Chapter 11*

software engineering   The application of engineering design principles and techniques to the development of computer software. *Chapter 16*

software license   An agreement allowing the use of a software program on a single machine. *Chapter 4*

software piracy   The illegal duplication of copyrighted software. *Chapter 12*

solid-state storage   Storage, such as flash memory, with no moving parts. Solid-state storage is likely to replace disk storage in the future. *Chapter 3*

sort   Arrange records in alphabetic or numeric order based on values in one or more fields. *Chapter 8*

sound card   A circuit board that allows the PC to accept microphone input, play music and other sound through speakers or headphone, and process sound in a variety of ways. *Chapter 3*

source document   In desktop publishing, the articles, chapters, drawings, maps, charts, and photographs that are to appear in the publication. Usually produced with standard word processors and graphics programs. *Chapter 5*

source document   In Web publishing, the original document containing the HTML code that produces a finished Web page. *Chapter 7, Chapter 10*

spam   Internet junk mail. *Chapter 9, Chapter 10*

speaker independence   Speech recognition technology that works without having to be trained to an individual voice. *Chapter 5*

special-purpose (dedicated) computer   A computer that performs a specific task, such as controlling temperature and humidity in an office building. *Chapter 1*

speech recognition   The identification of spoken words and sentences by a computer, making it possible for voice input to be converted into text files. *Chapter 5, Chapter 18*

spelling checker   A built-in component of a word processor or a separate program that compares words in a document with words in a disk-based dictionary and flags words not found in the dictionary. May operate in batch mode, checking all the words at once, or interactive mode, checking one word at a time. *Chapter 5*

spider   See Web crawler.

spoofing   A process used to steal passwords online. A spoofer launches a program that mimics a mainframe computer's login screen on an unattended terminal in a public lab. When an unsuspecting person types an ID and password, the program responds with an error message and remembers the secret codes. *Chapter 12*

speaker independence   The ability of automatic speech-recognition software to recognize speech without being trained to a speaker. *Chapter5*

spot color   The use of a single color or two to add interest to a page design *Chapter 5.*

spreadsheet software   Enables the user to control numbers, manipulating them in various ways. The software can manage budgeting, investment management, business projections, grade books, scientific simulations, checkbooks, financial planning and speculation, and other tasks involving numbers. *Chapter 6*

SQL A query language available for many different database management systems. More than a query language, SQL also accesses databases from a wide variety of vendors. *Chapter 8*

stack chart Stacked bars to show how proportions of a whole change over time. *Chapter 6*

statistical analysis software Specialized software that tests the strength of data relationships, produces graphs showing how two or more variables relate to each other, uncovers trends, and performs other statistical analyses. *Chapter 6*

statistics The science of analyzing and collecting data. *Chapter 6*

stepwise refinement Breaking programming problems into smaller problems, and breaking each smaller problem into a subproblem that can be subdivided in the same way. *Chapter 16*

storage and retrieval Information activities that systematically accumulate information for later use and locate the stored information when needed. *Chapter 13*

storage device Long-term repositories for data. Disks and tape drives are examples. *Chapter 2*

storyboard The first step in a video project, a guide for shooting and editing scenes. *Chapter 7*

strategic planning The process of a business organization identifying its goals and objectives, internal strengths and weaknesses, and competitive strategy. *Chapter 16*

strategic information system Any information system crucial to a company's competitive success. *Chapter 14*

strategy The intention of top managers of a business organization to pursue a set of activities to attain the organization's goals within the competitive business environment. *Chapter 14*

streaming audio and video Music, sounds, and moving pictures that are played while they're being downloaded, so they can are available to Web page visitors almost immediately after they're requested. *Chapter 7, Chapter 10*

structured decision A set of conditions that are understood well and procedures that are used to select a course of action. *Chapter 14*

structured programming A technique to make programming easier and more productive. Structured programs are built from smaller programs, called modules or subprograms, that are in turn made of even smaller modules. *Chapter 16*

style sheet Custom styles for each of the common elements in a document. *Chapter 5*

stylus A device used for pointing or writing with handheld computers and PDAs. *Chapter 3*

subnotebook computer A portable computer, smaller than a notebook or laptop, about the size of a hardbound book. *Chapter 1*

subprogram (module) In structured programming, a program is built from smaller programs called subprograms. *Chapter 16*

supercomputer A super-fast, super-powerful, and super-expensive computer used for applications that demand maximum power. *Chapter 1*

superscalar architecture definition TK. *Chapter XX*

surge protector A device that protects electronic equipment from sudden power surges. *Chapter 12*

switch Hardware that decides how to route Internet transmissions. Switches are similar to software routers, but faster and less flexible. *Chapter 10*

switching costs The time, money, and effort a customer or company expends when changing from one product, supplier, or system to a competing product, supplier, or system. *Chapter 14*

syntax error Violation of a programming language's grammar rules. *Chapter 16*

synthesizer A device that can produce—synthesize—music and other sounds electronically. A synthesizer might be a stand-alone

musical instrument or part of the circuitry on a computer's sound card. *Chapter 3, Chapter 7*

synthesized sound Synthetically generated computer sounds. *Chapter 7*

system A set of interrelated parts that work together to accomplish a goal or purpose. *Chapter 13*

system board The circuit board containing the computer's CPU. Often called motherboard. *Chapter 2.*

system flowchart A systems development modeling tool used to depict graphically the overall physical structure of an information system. *Chapter 16*

system software Software that handles the details of computing. Includes the operating system and utility programs. *Chapter 4*

system unit The box that contains a computer's main circuitry and storage devices. *Chapter 1*

systems analyst The computer professional primarily responsible for developing and managing an information system. *Chapter 16*

systems development A process of investigating a situation, designing a system solution, and acquiring the resources to implement the system. *Chapter 16*

systems development life cycle A sequence of steps or phases through which an information system passes between the time the system is conceived and the time it is phased out. *Chapter 16*

T

T1 A direct connect digital line that can transmit voice, data, and video at roughly 1.5Mbps. *Chapter 10*

T3 A direct connect digital line that transmits voice, data, and video even faster than a T1 connection. *Chapter 10*

table A grid of rows and columns; on many Web pages tables with hidden grids are used to align graphical images. *Chapter 10*

tape drive Storage device that uses magnetic tape to store information. *Chapter 3*

task bar A button bar that provides one-click access to open applications and tools, making it easy to switch back and forth between different tasks. *Chapter 4*

tax preparation software Provides a prefabricated worksheet where the user enters numbers into tax forms. Calculations are performed automatically, and the completed forms can be sent electronically to the IRS. *Chapter 6*

TB See terabyte.

TCP/IP (Transmission Control Protocol/Internet Protocol) Protocols developed as an experiment in internetworking, now the language of the Internet, allowing cross-network communication for almost every type of computer and network. *Chapter 10*

technophobia The fear of technology. *Chapter 17*

telecommunication Long-distance electronic communication in a variety of forms. *Chapter 9*

teleconference An online meeting between two or more people. *Chapter 9*

telemedicine The practice of doctors using the Web to work with patients who are outside the hospital walls in remote locations.

telephony Technology that enables computers to serve as speakerphones, answering machines, and complete voice mail systems. *Chapter 9*

Telnet The protocol that makes remote login through a command line interface possible. *Chapter 10*

template In desktop publishing, professionally designed empty documents that can be adapted to specific user needs. *Chapter 5*

template In spreadsheet software, a worksheet that contains labels and formulas but no data values. The template produces instant answers when you fill in the blanks. *Chapter 5, Chapter 6*

terabyte (TB) Approximately 1 million megabytes. *Chapter 2*

terminal Combination keyboard and screen that transfers information to and from a mainframe computer. *Chapter 1, Chapter 9*

terminal emulation Software that allows a PC to act as a dumb terminal—an input/output device that enables the user to send commands to and view information on the host computer. *Chapter 9, Chapter 10*

testing The process of checking the logic of an algorithm and the performance of a computer program. *Chapter 16*

text editing Refining text and correcting errors. *Chapter 5*

text editor An application that is similar to a word processor without the formatting features required by writers and publishers; some provide specialized features to aid in writing programs. *Chapter 16*

text formatting Controlling the format and style of a document. *Chapter 5*

thesaurus A synonym finder; often included with a word processor. *Chapter 5*

3-D modeling software Software that enables the user to create 3-D objects. The objects can be rotated, stretched, and combined with other model objects to create complex 3-D scenes. *Chapter 7, Chapter 9*

thin client A network computer, Internet appliance, or other device designed to connect to the Internet but not perform all the other tasks performed by a PC. *Chapter 10*

time bomb A logic bomb that is triggered by a time-related event. *Chapter 12*

timesharing Technique by which mainframe computers communicate with several users simultaneously. *Chapter 1*

top-down design A process for designing computer programs that starts at the top, with main ideas, and works down to the details. *Chapter 16*

touchpad (trackpad) A small flat-panel pointing device that is sensitive to light pressure. The user moves the pointer by dragging a finger across the pad. *Chapter 3*

touch screen Pointing device that responds when the user points to or touches different screen regions. *Chapter 3*

trackball Pointing device that remains stationary while the user moves a protruding ball to control the pointer on the screen. *Chapter 3*

track point A small handle that sits in the center of the keyboard, responding to finger pressure by moving the mouse in the direction it is pushed. *Chapter 3*

transaction An event that occurs in any of the primary activities of the organization's value chain. In accounting, an action that results in the movement of money from one account to another. *Chapter 6, Chapter 13*

transaction processing system An information system used to keep track of transactions and support the business operations of an organization. *Chapter 13*

transborder data flow The movement of information between individuals or organizations across international boundaries. *Chapter 14*

transistor Performs the same function as the vacuum tube by transferring electricity across a tiny resistor. *Chapter 1*

transmission An information activity that sends and distributes data and information to various locations. *Chapter 13*

Trojan horse A program that performs a useful task while at the same time carrying out some secret destructive act. A form of software sabotage. *Chapter 12*

True color Color that is 24-bit or greater, allowing more than 16 million color choices per pixel, creating photorealistic images. *Chapter 7*

tweening The automatic creation of in-between frames in an animation. *Chapter 7*

twisted pair A type of LAN cable that resembles the copper wires in standard telephone cables. *Chapter 9*

typeface A style of characters used for printing. *Chapter 5*

ubiquitous computers Computers everywhere. *Chapter 18*

Undo command The process of taking back the last operation performed. *Chapter 5*

Unicode A 65,000-character set for making letters, digits, and special characters fit into the computer's binary circuitry. *Chapter 2*

uninterruptible power supply (UPS) A hardware device that protects computers from data loss during power failures. *Chapter 12*

Universal serial bus (USB) A cross-platform interface that can transmit data faster than the traditional PC serial port. *Chapter 3, Chapter 9*

Universal product codes (UPC's) Codes created from patterns of variable-width bars that send scanned information to a mainframe computer. *Chapter 3.*

UNIX An operating system that allows a timesharing computer to communicate with several other computers or terminals at once. UNIX is the most widely available multi-user operating system in use. It is also widely used on Internet hosts. *Chapter 4, Chapter 10*

unstructured decision Fuzzy, complex situations that require a decision maker to exercise judgment to select a course of action. *Chapter 14*

upgrade A new and improved version of a software program. *Chapter 4*

upload To post software or documents to an online source so they're available for others. *Chapter 9, Chapter 10, Chapter 11*

up-skilling Transforming a job so it requires more skill. *Chapter 17*

upstream traffic Information transmitted from the subscriber to the Internet. *Chapter 10*

URL (uniform resource locator) The address of a Web site. *Chapter 0, Chapter 1, Chapter 10*

user interface The look and feel of the computing experience from a human point of view. Also, the component of an information system that helps a user interact with the system. *Chapter 4, Chapter 14*

user name See login name.

utility program Tools for doing system maintenance and some repairs that are not automatically handled by the operating system. *Chapter 4*

vaccine program See antivirus program.

validator A spreadsheet feature for checking the validity of logic and calculations. *Chapter 6*

value chain model A conceptual framework for understanding a business organization. An organization is a sequence of activities, each of which adds something valuable to the production of a product or service. *Chapter 13*

values The numbers that are the raw material used by spreadsheet software to perform calculations. *Chapter 6*

VBScript A Web scripting language. *Chapter 10*

VDT See video display terminal.

vector (object-oriented) graphics The storage of pictures as collections of lines, shapes, and other objects. *Chapter 7*

vertical-market application A computer application designed specifically for a particular business or industry. *Chapter 4*

vertical portal (vortal) A specialized portal that, like vertical market software, is targeted at members of a particular industry or economic sector. *Chapter 11*

video adapter A circuit board installed inside the main system unit connecting the monitor to the computer. *Chapter 3*

video digitizer Converts analog video signals into digital data. *Chapter 7*

video display terminal (VDT) Output device that displays text and graphics and receives messages from the computer. *Chapter 3*

video editing software Software for editing digital video, including titles, sound, and special effect. *Chapter 7*

video memory (VRAM) A special portion of RAM dedicated to holding video images. *Chapter 3*

video port A port for plugging a color monitor into a computer's video board. *Chapter 3*

video projector A projector that can project computer screen images for meetings and classes. *Chapter 3*

video teleconference Face-to-face communication over long distances using video and computer technology. *Chapter 3, Chapter 9, Chapter 11*

virtual memory Use of part of a computer hard disk as a substitute for RAM. *Chapter 4*

virtual private network (VPN) A network that uses encryption software to create private "tunnels" through the public Internet. *Chapter 15*

virtual reality Technology that creates the illusion that the user is immersed in a world that exists only inside the computer, an environment that contains both scenes and the controls to change those scenes. *Chapter 4, Chapter 18*

virus Software that spreads from program to program, or from disk to disk and uses each infected program or disk to make more copies of itself. A form of software sabotage. *Chapter 12*

visual programming Allows programmers to create large portions of their programs by drawing pictures and pointing to onscreen objects, eliminating much of the coding of traditional programming. *Chapter 16*

voice input Use of a microphone to speak commands and text data to a computer, which uses speech recognition software to interpret the input. *Chapter 3*

voice mail A telephone-based messaging system with many of the features of an email system. *Chapter 9*

volatile memory Memory, such as RAM, that loses its contents when it loses electrical power. *Chapter 2*

VRAM See video memory.

WAN See wide area network.

wand reader A reading device that uses light to read alphabetic and numeric characters written in a specially designed typeface found on sales tags and credit card slips. *Chapter 3*

wave form audio Sound-editing software in which a visual image is manipulated using the sound's wave form. *Chapter 7.*

wearable computer A strap-on computer unit for active information gatherers. *Chapter 18*

Web authoring software Software that facilitates creating of Web pages, typically by making the process similar to desktop publishing. *Chapter 10*

Web browser An application program that enables you to explore the Web by clicking hyperlinks in Web pages stored on Web sites. *Chapter 1, Chapter 10*

Web bug An invisible piece of code embedded in HTML-formatted email that is programmed to send information about its receiver's Web use back to its creator. *Chapter 11, Chapter 12*

Web casting Delivering of streaming audio or video via the Web. Sometimes refers to push technology. *Chapter 11*

Web crawler A software robot that systematically explores the Web, retrieves information about pages, and indexes the retrieved information in a database. *Chapter 11*

Web hosting service A company that provides B2B and B2C e-commerce software and expertise to run small and midsized businesses on line. *Chapter 15*

Webjacker Someone who hijacks legitimate Web sites, redirecting unsuspecting visitors to bogus or offensive alternate sites. *Chapter 8*

Web page A single document on the World Wide Web (WWW), made up of text and images and interlinked with other documents. *Chapter 1, Chapter 10*

Web server A server that stores Web pages and sends them to client programs—Web browsers—that request them. *Chapter 10*

Web services New kinds of Web-based applications that can be assembled quickly using existing software components, *Chapter 11*

Web site A collection of related Web pages stored on the same server. *Chapter 1, Chapter 10*

what if question A feature of spreadsheet software that allows speculation by providing instant answers to hypothetical questions. *Chapter 6*

WI-FI A popular wireless LAN technology that allows multiple computers to connect to a LAN through a base station up to 150 feet away. Often referred to as 802.11b. *Chapter 9, Chapter 11*

wide-area network (WAN) A network that extends over a long distance. Each network site is a node on the network. *Chapter 1, Chapter 9*

Windows Aee Microsoft Windows.

window In a graphical user interface, a framed area that can be opened, closed, and rearranged with the mouse. Documents are displayed in windows. *Chapter 4*

wireless broadband connection See WI-FI.

wireless keyboard A keyboard that uses infrared signals rather than wires to communicate with a computer. *Chapter 3*

wireless network A network in which a node has a tiny radio or infrared transmitter connected to its network port so it can send and receive data through the air rather than through cables. *Chapter 9*

wizard A software help agent that walks the user through a complex process. *Chapter 5, Chapter 18*

word size The number of bits a CPU can process at one time, typically 8,16,32, or 64. *Chapter 2*

word wrap The process of automatically moving words that do not fit on the current line to the next line in a document. *Chapter 5*

workgroup A committee, a product design team, an executive board, or any other group of people in an organization who act as a single social unit to perform some task. *Chapter 14*

workflow The path of information as it flows through a workgroup. *Chapter 14*

worksheet A spreadsheet document that appears on the screen as a grid of numbered rows and columns. *Chapter 6*

workstation A high-end desktop computer with massive computing power but is less expensive than a minicomputer. Workstations are the most powerful of the desktop computers. *Chapter 1*

World Wide Web (WWW, Web) Part of the Internet, a collection of multimedia documents created by organizations and users worldwide. Documents are linked in a hypertext Web that allows users to explore them with simple mouse clicks. *Chapter 1, Chapter 10*

worm A program that uses computer hosts to reproduce itself. Worm programs travel independently over computer networks, seeking out uninfected workstations to occupy. A form of software sabotage. *Chapter 12*

writeback The final phase of execution, in which the bus unit writes the results of the instruction back into memory or some other device. *Chapter 2*

WYSIWYG (**What you see is what you get**)   With a word processor, the arrangement of the words on the screen represents a close approximation to the arrangement of words on the printed page. *Chapter 5, Chapter 7*

XHTML   Markup language that combines features of HTML and XML; its advantage is its backward compatibility with HTML. *Chapter 10*

XML (**extensible markup language**)   A language that enables Web developers to control and display data the way they control text and graphics. Forms, database queries, and other data-intensive operations that can't be completely constructed with standard HTML are much easier with XML. *Chapter 10, Chapter 16*

Y2K bug (**millennium bug**)   The international sensation about the two-digit date problem when the year changed from 1999 to 2000. *Chapter 12*

Credits

Index